Praise for *Waging War*

"WAYNE E. LEE's *Waging War* weaves a vast, global tapestry depicting how wars have been conducted from prehistory to the modern age. Drawing on an impressively wide range of disciplines and scholarship, *Waging War* traces the origins and dynamics of military innovations throughout history and how their influence shaped the past and present conduct of war around the world. With *Waging War*, Lee takes his place among the leading practitioners of global military history."

—Roger Spiller, *U.S. Army Command
and General Staff College, Emeritus*

"WAYNE E. LEE presents war in all its messy, bloody complexity from Neolithic societies to today's struggle with ISIS in the Middle East. Through a selection of well-chosen examples, he offers an exceptionally clear and incisive analysis of how war has been waged on land, sea, and in the air. This is an important book for those seeking to understand humanity's capacity for self-destruction."

—Peter H. Wilson, *University of Hull*

"WAYNE E. LEE's *Waging War* is truly a world historical account of how humans have waged war on each other from early human history to the present. It is particularly refreshing that Lee recognizes the waging of war as a human problem that has affected all peoples around the world, but that he does not argue for a universal lesson explaining why this is so. Rather, he focuses on the consequences of innovation in warfare, and how these innovations were communicated, adapted, and adopted across very different cultures and societies over time. This text will be invaluable for world historians seeking a cogent and nuanced narrative about the intersections between culture and the diffusion of military innovation on local, regional, and global scales."

—Heather Streets-Salter, *Northeastern University*

Waging War

Waging War

Conflict, Culture, and Innovation in World History

Wayne E. Lee

Oxford   New York
OXFORD UNIVERSITY PRESS

Oxford University Press is a department of the University of Oxford.
It furthers the University's objective of excellence in research,
scholarship, and education by publishing worldwide.

Oxford   New York
Auckland   Cape Town   Dar es Salaam   Hong Kong   Karachi
Kuala Lumpur   Madrid   Melbourne   Mexico City   Nairobi
New Delhi   Shanghai   Taipei   Toronto

With offices in
Argentina   Austria   Brazil   Chile   Czech Republic   France   Greece
Guatemala   Hungary   Italy   Japan   Poland   Portugal   Singapore
South Korea   Switzerland   Thailand   Turkey   Ukraine   Vietnam

For titles covered by Section 112 of the US Higher Education
Opportunity Act, please visit www.oup.com/us/he for the
latest information about pricing and alternate formats.

Published by Oxford University Press
198 Madison Avenue, New York, New York 10016
http://www.oup.com

Library of Congress Cataloging-in-Publication Data
Lee, Wayne E., 1965-
Waging war : conflict, culture, and innovation in world history / Wayne E. Lee,
University of North Carolina at Chapel Hill. -- 1st edition.
    pages cm
    Includes index.
    ISBN 978-0-19-979745-5 (pbk. : alk. paper) 1. Military art and science--History.
2. History, Military. I. Title.
    U27.L44 2015
    355.02--dc23
                                                                    2015008401

Printing number: 9 8 7 6 5 4 3 2 1

Printed in the United States of America
on acid-free paper

A book about humans at war,

dedicated to peace,

and in memory of all those who have worked,

and sometimes died,

to achieve that peace.

Contents

List of Figures

List of Maps

List of Tables

Preface

THIS BOOK WAS WRITTEN for all those interested in or concerned with the history of war. It is not a comprehensive summary, nor does it advance a single explanatory thesis about the nature, history, or future of war. It instead presents selected examples, drawn from around the world and across many millennia, of how humans have warred with each other. More specifically, it examines how humans have innovated at conflict and how they have dealt with each others' innovations. War is a lethal competition, but it is also a complex activity at which humans have competed at doing "better" than their enemies. Presented with the task of examining war on a global scale over millennia one must pick and choose what to write about. I have chosen to examine the process and consequences of innovation. Where does innovation come from? Do innovations represent conscious calculations of likely advantage? What roles do precedents, beliefs, ideologies, or unspoken assumptions play in shaping the creation and movement of innovation? How do innovative ideas and technologies interact? One point that emerges from answering these questions in the following pages is that there is no one answer to any of these questions. War among humans has been nothing if not variable. Theorists have repeatedly sought universal truths within the clash of arms. We will encounter many such possible truths within the pages of this book, but one of the clearest "lessons" of history is that there are few universal lessons. Variety is the watchword. Understanding that variety, however, can bring wisdom—wisdom in the recognition of complexity. Neither history nor life is amenable to black-and-white solutions or single-variable explanations. I hope this book has at least that little bit of wisdom to offer.

The extent to which it succeeds owes much to the many people who have watched me struggle through this process and who have tried to lift me from the mire and provide clarity. History truly is a collaborative discipline, especially when done on this scale. My friends and colleagues listed here have done their very best to prevent me from making foolish mistakes. They deserve no blame, however, for whatever foolishness remains. Alex Roland has read every chapter and provided consistently cogent and sometimes pungent advice. Toward the end of the process I also turned to some nonacademic friends to be my "lay readers." Brad Luebbert and my father, Dwayne Lee, all read the entire manuscript, even as I badgered them to meet *my* deadline. I also sought a variety of specialists' opinions for each of the chapters. Everett Wheeler was a particular stalwart, providing his usual incisive critique on chapters 1 through 7 (although I'm sure he'll be disappointed with the ways I continue to disagree with him about some things). Chapter 1 was a particular challenge, and I benefited from commentary, discussions, and sources from Kathryn Barbier, John Mitani, Michael Galaty, Bill Parkinson, Jonathan Haws, and Stephen LeBlanc. I won't drag this on endlessly by listing all those who helped chapter by chapter, and several people helped with or read more than one. Let it suffice to say that I could not have done it without the help of Joe Bongiovi, Sarah Melville, Sara Bush, Ralph Sawyer, Peter Lorge, Cliff Rogers, Timothy May, Joe Caddell, Kenneth Swope, Kahraman Şakul, Virginia Aksan, Jamel Ostwald, John Lynn, Morgan Pitelka, Stanley Carpenter, Randy Papadopoulos, David Silbey, Rick Herrera, Roger Spiller, Robert Citino, Richard Kohn, Bob Wetteman, Paul Springer, Mike Pavelec, Greg Daddis, and Lien-Hang Nguyen. I'm also indebted to the comments provided by the reviewers commissioned by Oxford, including Eugenia C. Kiesling, Brian E. Crim, Charles Lipson, Steven Sodergren, Mark Grimsley, Reina Pennington, and the others who remained anonymous, although insightful. Several students in my spring 2015 "Global History of Warfare" class provided helpful critiques, and I remain grateful for the way all my students at the University of North Carolina have kept me on my toes. In writing this list of thanks, I can only hope I have not left anyone out. Oxford's illustration researcher, Francelle Carapetyan, and the cartographer, George Chakvetadze, have been marvels of efficiency and creativity. Almost last, I must thank my editor, Charles Cavaliere, who first had the temerity to think such a book could be written, and then the guts to trust me to do it. He's been very patient. Lastly, and truly most importantly, is my wife, Rhonda Mawhood Lee. Not only has she been a consistent, patient, and forgiving supporter, she also has been a superlative editor. She too has gone over every chapter with a fine-toothed comb. I could not be more grateful.

A NOTE ON THE ARCHITECTURE

Waging War was originally conceived for use by students and the general reader. And although it is now much more than that, I have nevertheless limited the number of citations, and almost entirely have avoided diving into scholarly debates in the text or even in the notes. I readily acknowledge where debate exists, but in no sense have I tried to provide a comprehensive approach to the literature. Chapter 1 is a bit of an exception, in part because the debates are so polarized, in part because there have been so many very recent discoveries, and in part because it strays so far from traditional history. In the remaining chapters I have tended to restrict citations to obscure facts, specific interpretations, and direct quotes. No citations are provided for encyclopedia-type facts or relatively settled narratives. For convenience, excepting quotes, the citations are collected at the end of the paragraph.

I assume some general knowledge on the part of the reader. This book is not a narrative of assorted "key" or "decisive" wars or battles. Some more obscure combats are narrated here to serve as examples or as threads to structure the argument. But I assume the reader knows something about World War II, has heard of the Cold War, and may even know a little something about feudalism or Alexander the Great. For the convenience of readers, however, each chapter has a short timeline of relevant events and a very brief listing of key works on the subject. I also should note that small parts of chapter 1 have been published in the Winter 2015 edition of *Military History Quarterly* (*MHQ*). Finally, although this is very much a world history, the military rise of the West and my own academic background undeniably tip the balance of coverage in that direction. Industrialization further narrows the focus in the later chapters, but only to a point. Much of the final chapter is about the response to Western military methods.

About the Author

WAYNE E. LEE is a professor of history at the University of North Carolina, and currently the chair of the Curriculum in Peace, War, and Defense. He is the author of *Barbarians and Brothers: Anglo-American Warfare, 1500–1865* (Oxford University Press, 2011) and *Crowds and Soldiers in Revolutionary North Carolina: The Culture of Violence in Riot and War* (University Press of Florida, 2001). He has edited two other volumes on world military history and written numerous articles or chapters on various aspects of early modern warfare. Lee has also worked as an archaeologist on numerous projects in Greece, Albania, Croatia, and Virginia. He has published extensively in that field, most recently as a primary author and coeditor of an interdisciplinary volume titled *Light and Shadow: Isolation and Interaction in the Shala Valley of Northern Albania* (Cotsen Institute of Archaeology Press, 2013), winner of the Society for American Archaeology's 2014 Book Award. Dr. Lee served in the US Army from 1987 to 1992.

Introduction:
Capacity, Calculation, and Culture

PUT BLUNTLY, this book is about the long and unfortunate history of humans seeking ever more effective ways to kill each other. It is written in the belief that understanding how we wage war not only tells us something about war itself but also teaches us something important about human history in general. As chapter 1 will explore, some form of lethal conflict that we might call war has been a part of human existence from our earliest days as a species. *Waging War* is therefore not primarily about the causes of war in general or of any particular war. Nor is it an attempt to create a theory about the nature of war or to speculate about its future—although these issues will come up. It is about *warfare*; it is about how humans have sought to impose their will on each other over time and around the world. *Waging War* takes a global and long-term perspective because that quest for military success has produced an enormous variety of forms and methods, and is best understood as a reciprocal process of the exchange of ideas and technologies between cultures. This is a world history because war is a global phenomenon, and innovations in one culture or one region have nearly always had some impact in others.

Innovation, its roots and its reception, is the organizing theme of the book. Saying something comprehensible about conflict around the world over many millennia presents a substantial organizational challenge. Examining innovation provides a consistent set of questions to use in each case while also corresponding to critical issues in military history. What is the role of conflict in the origins of the state? Did Roman systems of discipline really change Renaissance European military practice? Did European adaptation to gunpowder drive its countries' rise to world power? Did Japanese enthusiasm for muskets lead to the political unification of Japan? Did the ideas of the French Revolution create mass conscript armies? Did interwar German tank enthusiasts create a new form of maneuver warfare? To even the casual student of history these are readily recognizable and significant questions in both military history and the history of the world in general. We will find that the answers to all of these questions, and more, are complicated—usually more complicated than one expects.

Innovation is hardly a new theme in military history. As the preceding list of rhetorical questions suggests, military historians have long looked for the roots and consequences of changes in military practice. One oft-used explanatory system is that of the "challenge-and-response" dynamic. A society confronted by defeat or some new, looming threat will actively struggle to find a counter. Historian Geoffrey Parker, for example, in explaining the rise of the relative military power of the West, notes that "in areas [like western Europe] contested by multiple polities the need for military innovation could become extremely strong."[1] The implicit dynamic in this statement is one of direct, conscious response: historical actors determined the need for a new system or a new technology and therefore developed one. As we will see, this was surely the case in many instances.

Often presented hand in hand with the challenge-and-response dynamic is the idea that successful military innovation produces a new paradigm, quickly copied by nearby competitors in order to survive. Historian John Lynn, analyzing military developments in the West, suggests that success could lead a particular system to become "paradigmatic." In his words, "From time to time, a particular army became a model for its age; it provided the paradigm for other armies and thus defined the core characteristics for a stage of military evolution. Until the mid-twentieth century, an army won the role of paradigm on the battlefield; in other words, victory chose the paradigm."[2] There is real power to this argument, especially considered over a longer sweep of history than Lynn examines. Other analysts have even suggested that failure to adopt paradigmatic armies or practices leads to societal extinction. War was an existential affair, and those military systems that failed to adapt dropped out. Even without existential pressure, writers from Thucydides to modern sociologists have argued for something social scientists now call "institutional isomorphism." Thucydides' version is a bit more poetic than the sociologists': "It is just as true in politics as it is in any art or craft: new methods must drive out old ones."[3]

Waging War acknowledges this competitive dynamic and tries to push it beyond its usual regional confines. Too often the unit of analysis is a single nation, or a single region, or "the West." As historian Patrick Porter points out, the new syntheses created by "reciprocity and strategic interaction" occur at a world level. The unit of analysis in world history, he notes, "is not the walled-off tribe or nation, but the nexus of contact between peoples, such as trade routes, oceans, the trail of beliefs and faiths."[4] Much of this book explores that process of contact, studying not just the innovation itself but the reaction it produces among other societies encountering it in its fully developed form.

In addition to the competitive dynamic at regional or world levels, many key innovations relevant to the conduct of war appeared through cultural flows, subsistence pattern shifts, or profit-oriented nonmilitary invention with unanticipated military-spinoff effects. The chariot likely began as a wagon for carrying goods; riding a horse began as a better way to hunt horses; the internal combustion engine was not invented to power tanks. All of these, however, dramatically changed the nature of warfare.

Thus far we have used the word "innovation" rather loosely, but it is important to emphasize that the word is used here in its broadest possible sense. No one can deny the importance of technology to military affairs. Indeed, some have posited technology as the single most important variable in the history of warfare (if not in the history of war). Military or military-related innovations are not just technological, however; they are also ideas—ideas, for example, about institutions, organizations, or methods of combat. *Waging War* often treats technologies and ideas together, especially since new technologies typically required ideas about how to use them. Not even a spear, as we will see in chapter 3, has only one way to use it. The relationship between a technology and ideas about its use is particularly crucial in intercultural contact. Arnold Pacey noted that inventions are rarely just "received" by a different society. Instead, "recipients of a new body of knowledge and technique 'interrogate' it on the basis of their own experience and knowledge of local conditions. . . . The initial 'transfer of technology' itself is only the first stage in a larger process."[5] To mention just one example from chapter 8, Native Americans had their own needs for and responses to gunpowder weapons that had little to do with how such weapons were used by Europeans. Beyond this notion of a culturally conditioned reception of technology, however, there are some ideas of crucial importance to history and to military history that emerged more or less independent of any specific technology. Examples include the state, the concept of "doctrine," centralized state taxation systems, conscription, and collective synchronized discipline. I make no attempt to rank significance, or even to claim that the innovations covered here are the most significant ones. I do not, for example, explore the emergence of iron in any detail—surely a monumental innovation in military affairs. The innovations covered in *Waging War*, however, will take us around the world and through many centuries of change.

As we make that journey, examining the creation, diffusion, response, or adaptation to military technologies and ideas, we must look deeply at the societies involved. The Greek phalanx, for example, makes no sense outside the Greek social, political, and cultural world. It was not *just* a military innovation; it was a manifestation of the Greek world. *Waging War*'s greatest value lies in this reality: that properly examining world military history opens up world history more generally. The approach here is not, and cannot be, narrowly military. It must be holistic.

CAPACITY, CALCULATION, AND CULTURE

To manage the complexity of a holistic approach, *Waging War* uses three guiding and deliberately memorable concepts: capacity, calculation, and culture. Asking about the influence of each of these terms on a military innovation or, conversely, asking about that innovation's influence on these three concepts generates a more complex understanding of the interrelatedness of all human activity and warfare.[6]

Capacity

In *Waging War*, capacity refers to the ability of any given social organization to raise or commit resources, including people, to a conflict or to a military establishment. To mention a simple example, wealthy, industrialized states like nineteenth-century Britain, France, or Germany, with sophisticated taxation systems that accumulated capital for state use, could invest in building steel and steam navies. Japan, emerging from two centuries of isolation in the late nineteenth century, lacked both the financial and the industrial "capacity" to do so. Eventually, however, Japan built that capacity and became a modern naval power.

For most of human history, capacity was determined by the relationship of a society to its organic energy sources. Human activity depended on tapping the products of fields and forests, whether crops, grasses for animals, or wood for fuel. "Wealth" was measured by the areal extent of the organic resources one controlled. From the Bronze Age forward, that kind of wealth was supplemented by the ability to control trade networks accessing mineral resources that were usually only available in a few locations. As we will see in the following chapters, the social processes for exploiting the organic economy changed over time, and also differed by ecological zone. Some early states, for example, imposed social differentiation on the larger part of the population and thereby generated a surplus of resources, which could be used to sustain a standing army. Doing so required the administrative ability to extract that surplus on an expansive territorial basis—every field claimed by the state, even ones far away, had to give up a portion of its produce to the state administration. Managing such an extractive system typically required tiered regional authorities who were responsive to central control. Relatively egalitarian "tribal" peoples generally remained demographically small-scale societies because they lacked such tiered systems of governance that could project authority expansively. The ecology of subsistence mattered as well. Steppe-dwellers' dependence on grasslands to sustain their flocks and herds created very different systems of distributing authority and accumulating surplus—with military effects explored in chapter 5.[7]

Many of the chapters in *Waging War* describe societies still fundamentally bound by their organic economy. But some innovations made different demands on the organic economy than others, and so the relationship of capacity to military innovation was far from static. As one example, typically the building of warships demanded state-level systems of capital accumulation, and the greater the accumulative powers of the state (that is, the greater its capacity), the more effective it was at naval war.

A crucial shift occurred in the nineteenth century as humans learned to exploit the energy potential of mineral sources—first coal and then oil. The organic economy and the need to feed soldiers and subjects never went away, but in a mineral economy strategic priorities shifted away from the quest for expansive areal control of organic energy sources. As we will discuss in chapters 10 and 11, controlling *points* on the landscape became more important than controlling expansive *spaces*. What mattered in this punctuated strategic geography were those points where mineral energy sources were either found or burned—mines and factories—and the lines of connection between the two. In parallel and contemporaneously, military power increasingly depended on spending capital on the materials of war, rather than just on manpower. Swords, spears, and shields had always been important, but such materials were cheap relative to manpower costs. And, to be clear, "capacity" in those simpler technological eras was not even always about "money," or wealth, as such. It was about influence systems: How many men could a ruler reliably expect to show up when he called for his army? The answer depended on state or tribal systems of distributing power and authority, and those systems are part of the definition of capacity. To a certain extent with gunpowder weapons, and then especially with industrialization, a key, if not *the* key, measure of capacity became the availability of capital to invest in the purchase of weapons. In this respect we will review, for example, the impact of global trade after 1500, reformed taxation systems in Europe and Qing China, and the relationship between industrial production and European imperialism.[8]

Calculation

Calculation is simpler. As implied by the challenge-and-response dynamic just discussed, some military innovations emerged from the conscious seeking of advantage. Maurice of Nassau, for example, looking in the 1590s for a better way to deliver firepower on the battlefield within the limits of matchlock muskets, coinvented a form of volley fire using the countermarch (see chapter 7). This was a "calculated" innovation designed to solve a specific problem. As we will see, however, even this calculation occurred in a specific cultural context. Maurice was being advised by someone who in turn was drawing on a garbled literary transmission of certain Roman and Greek practices. Those practices had a particular resonance within Europe because of a wider contemporary cultural fascination with the ancients. Furthermore, calculations are made by individuals within their specific vision of what "winning" was, or what "victory" meant. Because calculation is an act based on perception, it is deeply influenced by culture. Nevertheless, calculation occurs though a select leadership's conscious balancing of a specific vision of victory against their understanding of the limits of material reality. In short, we must give credence to the real role of human calculated inventiveness in seeking advantage in war's deadly competition. We will see this calculation repeatedly in *Waging War*.

Culture

It should be clear already that there are strong overlaps between calculation and culture. In fact, the former can become the latter. A specific calculation, like Maurice of Nassau's, once adopted, can grow to be seen as the "right way" of doing things, and may then persist for reasons that have nothing to do with its efficiency. It continues instead for reasons that we would read as cultural. As a trivial example, consider the hand salute used in many militaries. Originally a calculated action made to initiate peaceful face-to-face dialogue (conjecturally, either a knight raising his helmet visor, or a more universal "see, my hand is empty of weapons" gesture), it continues as a way of acknowledging hierarchy and communicating respect because it has acquired that cultural meaning.

Introducing a slippery concept like culture opens up a host of complexities, but that is really the point. Our effort to be holistic in examining warfare and innovation demands that we treat warring societies in their full complexity. In its briefest essence, "culture" represents a broadly shared set of ideas about how the world functions and how one can survive and succeed within it. Very often those ideas are not even consciously expressed. Indeed, the more important they are, and the more widely shared they are, the less those ideas are openly referred to. The task of the historian is to detect and elaborate what we might call "embedded assumptions" about the way the world works. Returning to the salute, consider how its present meaning and function persist unquestioned. It is rooted in the culture so deeply as not to need explication or discussion.

The salute, however, also provides the opportunity to note that there are different "levels" of culture. The salute is not used among civilians in Western (or other) societies; it is a component of a subculture, the "military culture." Any large society can have a host of subcultures. In *Waging War* we will generally deal only with three or four. One of those might be called "societal culture," which is the broadest possible category, referring to those sets of ideas shared by all or most members of a society, and therefore impinging on military behavior through the individuals who participate in fighting. As just suggested, however, militaries can have their own culture, especially as they become institutionalized (indeed, there is such a thing as institutional or organizational culture, of which military culture can be considered an example). There are sets of behaviors deemed appropriate for those within an institutional military. Yet another cultural subset is that of "strategic culture." Here we refer to how a set of senior political and military leaders possess a long-developed sense of what victory means and how one normally achieves it. That sense is conditioned by the strategic challenges faced by their state or community, by the leadership's desire to remain in power, their own institutional investment, and more. Each state experiences security challenges in a different way and in a different context, and so strategic cultures vary by community. A number of analysts of the modern American military, for example, have suggested that American strategic culture prefers to substitute firepower and technological investment in weaponry for manpower. The current popular shorthand for that strategic culture is the fear of putting "boots on the ground." As a "cultural" phenomenon, however, strategic culture is a particularly conscious and nominally rational set of beliefs—it usually has a consistent internal and overt logic, although it may not be recognizable as such to others outside the culture.

Finally, we must emphasize that no culture, at any level, acts as a straitjacket on choice or calculation. Culture provides a repertoire of choices from which to select. It influences perception and limits the horizon of possibilities perceived by individual actors, but it does not *determine* action. To return to our trivial example of salutes, any given individual can render a sarcastic salute, a lazy one, a crisp one, or a salute followed by a handshake, or can refuse to salute at all. Those are all choices that manipulate the meaning of the gesture. It is worth pointing out, however, that they are all choices made within the unspoken framework of what a salute is supposed to mean. Furthermore, cultures also change. Virtually every military, for example, has its own unique version of a salute. In the pages that follow we will see more consequential examples of how a set of practices—perhaps calculated practices—in one society can evolve over time as cultural phenomena.[9]

To simplify and compress, *Waging War* examines the roots of and responses to innovations in the conduct of war, and it does so through these three variables of capacity (the ability to commit resources to conflict), calculation (the conscious attempt to improve fighting methods or equipment), and culture (the evolving societal or organizational frames of reference that set the limits of the imagination). I have been brief in providing these definitions, and sparing in the use of examples, because all of these arguments and concepts are built into the chapters that follow. Those examples will speak more clearly than any further effort at definition. So let us begin with the very origins of war. Or, to frame it as a question, how did humans first begin to use coordinated and collective lethal or potentially lethal violence to solve social problems?

Notes

1. Geoffrey Parker, ed. *The Cambridge Illustrated History of Warfare: The Triumph of the West* (Cambridge, UK: Cambridge University Press, 1995), 5–6 (quote).

2. John A. Lynn, "The Evolution of Army Style in the Modern West, 800–2000," *International History Review* 18 (1996): 510 (quote).

3. Jack S. Levy and William R. Thompson, *The Arc of War: Origins, Escalation, and Transformation* (Chicago: University of Chicago Press, 2011), 59; Peter Turchin, "Warfare and the Evolution of Social Complexity: A Multilevel-Selection Approach," *Structure and Dynamics* 4.3 (2010): 1–37, available at http://www.escholarship.org/uc/item/7j11945r (accessed December 12, 2014); Paul J. DiMaggio and Walter W. Powell, "The Iron Cage Revisited: Institutional Isomorphism and Collective Rationality in Organizational Fields," *American Sociological Review* 48.2 (1983): 147–60; Thucydides 1.71 in *History of the Peloponnesian War*, trans. Rex Warner (New York: Penguin Books, 1954), 77 (quote).

4. Patrick Porter, *Military Orientalism: Eastern War through Western Eyes* (New York: Columbia University Press, 2009), 191 (quote).

5. Arnold Pacey, *Technology in World Civilization: A Thousand-Year History* (Cambridge, MA: MIT Press, 1900), vii–viii.

6. I first introduced these three concepts for a slightly different purpose in Wayne E. Lee, *Barbarians and Brothers: Anglo-American Warfare, 1500–1865* (New York: Oxford University Press, 2011), 5–8.

7. I borrow this conceptual framework from John Landers, *The Field and the Forge: Population, Production, and Power in the Pre-Industrial West* (New York: Oxford University Press, 2003).

8. This is a key argument in Azar Gat, *War in Human Civilization* (Oxford: Oxford University Press, 2006).

9. I define these terms in greater detail in Wayne E. Lee, "Warfare and Culture," in *Warfare and Culture in World History*, ed. Wayne E. Lee (New York: New York University Press, 2011), 1–11. See also Jeremy Black, *War and the Cultural Turn* (Malden, MA: Polity, 2011).

1

The Origins of War and of the State

to 2500 BCE

Is War Innate? • War among Animals: Chimpanzees • The Evidence for Early Human Warfare • Biology and Selection • Sedentism, Agriculture, and War • A Lord among Lords and the Rise of the State • Warring Complex Societies outside the State

HISTORIANS HAVE A TENDENCY to treat war as something waged solely by states. The origins of lethal human conflict, however, not only long predated the state but likely played a role in its origins. A real understanding of the nature of human conflict must begin with the long prehistory of deadly conflict between bands of humans living in small groups as foragers or hunter-gatherers, and eventually in farming communities before the dawn of the state. That long era of prestate war shaped human social organization, and with it the nature of warfare in the historic era. Humans evolved, biologically and culturally, in an environment of competition with other humans. Sometimes that competition included direct violent conflict between social groups. One critical adaptation to the presence or threat of conflict was to expand the size and cohesion of the social group. An enlarged social group strained food resources, but also better prepared the group for direct conflict. Adapting for larger group sizes, while simultaneously coping with the consequent strain on local resources, produced both new subsistence strategies and ever more complex social organizations—eventually including the state. Competition and conflict also drove early technological innovations: tools, new weapons, and fortifications not least among them. Historic human societies have a "dual inheritance" derived from a long process of biological adaptation, supplemented, but not entirely replaced, by a still ongoing process of sociocultural evolution. We are a product of our past. Violence has deeply shaped that past, although this by no means binds us irrevocably to it.

IS WAR INNATE?

Scholars in various fields continue to debate the nature and extent of human conflict before the emergence of the state. Most writers during much of the twentieth century tended to follow the philosophical principle associated with the eighteenth-century philosopher Jean Jacques Rousseau, in which "primitive" humans, in an egalitarian, prestate "state of nature," were naturally and fundamentally peaceful. They presumably lived in an environment of abundant shared resources free from violent territoriality or any other form of conflict. In some ways Rousseau's construction was merely a philosophical starting point for arguments about social organization, reflecting no real understanding of human prehistory. Similarly, Thomas Hobbes's seventeenth-century opposite formulation of a state of nature in which each warred against all, famously leading to lives that were "solitary, poor, nasty, brutish, and short," was also a philosophical first principle, constructed to explain the origins of government. These extremes have set the two poles of the debate over early human violence ever since. That debate has been and continues to be highly polarized, with perhaps an unnecessary fixation on whether conflict is innate to humans. Perhaps the most notorious moment in this ongoing discussion occurred in 1986 when a UNESCO meeting in Seville, Spain, attended by a host of eminent scientists of human behavior, issued a statement, later adopted by the American Anthropological Association, the American Psychological Association, and the American Sociological Association, asserting bluntly that "it is scientifically incorrect to say that we have inherited a tendency to make war from our animal ancestors. . . . [And] it is scientifically incorrect to say that war or any other violent behaviour is genetically programmed into our human nature. . . . [And] it is scientifically incorrect to say that in the course of human evolution there has been a selection for aggressive behaviour more than for other kinds of behaviour."[1] In fairness, the delegates were reacting to a fear that modern political actors might attempt to explain away violence by flip references to innate characteristics. As a society, we can surely neither allow nor accept that, but this sort of categorical language does a disservice to honest investigation of the human condition and its origins.[2] Despite such moments, the debate began to shift dramatically when in 1996 Lawrence Keeley published *War Before Civilization*. Keeley made an impassioned plea for reimagining the role of violence in human experience, and he made the striking claim that prestate societies experienced extreme male fatality rates. Keeley's work and additional studies have settled on "the somewhat shocking estimates . . . [that] between 15 and 25% of males and about 5% of females" in human forager societies died from warfare. This per capita rate far exceeds those of later state-based societies.[3] Since Keeley's work, archaeologists and anthropologists have renewed the debate begun by Hobbes and Rousseau. To use the simplest terms, as suggested in a recent review, there are the "deep rooters," who believe in the long evolutionary history of intergroup violence, and the "inventors," who argue that human conflict emerged more recently because of changes in human social organization.[4] The debate between the two schools continues, and new evidence continues to accumulate. I take a "deep rooter" position, but I also emphasize that conflict and cooperation are inextricably linked. The best and the worst of humanity evolved hand in hand.

This chapter reviews three categories of evidence or theories. The first is the now increasingly well-known issue of chimpanzee "war." The second is archaeological evidence from the whole course of human prehistory that speaks to the existence of lethal human violence—including some particularly recent and significant discoveries. Finally, it reviews some key shifts over the last two decades, and even in the last five years, in theories on biological selection and the role of conflict. For the most part I avoid a potential fourth category of evidence, that of ethnographic analogy, or the use of evidence from historically recorded nonstate societies. Such analogies are ignored here in part because all modern observations of less complex human societies have occurred in a context in which those societies have been affected by the existence of more complex societies in some way. For 99 percent of their evolutionary history members of the genus *Homo* lived as foragers in very small groups or bands, constantly on the move within bounded regions, and interacting only with like bands. (Although "hunter-gatherer" is sometimes used synonymously with forager, it can include somewhat more complex, even sedentary societies.) Ethnographic analogy certainly has a place in analyzing prehistoric foragers, and the implications of such work undergird many of the conclusions here, but its complexities and endless caveats preclude a full discussion.[5]

WAR AMONG ANIMALS: CHIMPANZEES

Among other things, the signers of the UNESCO declaration claimed that "only a few cases of destructive intra-species fighting between organized groups have ever been reported among naturally living species, and none of these involve the use of tools designed to be weapons." Setting aside the rather limiting condition requiring tools, this statement has proven increasingly untenable. Where animal behaviorists once saw intraspecies conflict as generally resolved by flight or nonlethal fights ending in submission, there is more and more evidence for lethal intraspecies violence especially among social animals: ants, meerkats, banded mongooses, gerbils, lions, prairie dogs, wolves, spotted hyenas, and especially chimpanzees. To be sure, many of these examples are of infanticide, rather than "organized war" as we traditionally think about it. Nevertheless, the killings serve the genetic function of prioritizing the killer's genes, thus selecting for individuals most capable of dominating the social environment, including through the use of lethal violence. Furthermore, among chimpanzees we find something very much like war—including what biologists call "coalitionary killing," strategy, and aggressive territorial intrusion (not merely defensive territoriality).[6]

The revelation of chimpanzee violence came as something of a surprise. Jane Goodall began her famous study of chimpanzees in the wild by acclimating them to humans through feeding them some six hundred bananas a day over eight years. The widely disseminated images of her interacting with them, her understandable advocacy in the face of the threat to their habitat, and the long history of chimpanzees as "performers" had generated a public perception of a friendly, peaceful, intelligent ape. In the early 1970s, however, when she cut off the banana supply, her study group of about fifty chimps split into two competing factions, one of thirty-five and one of fifteen. The larger band persistently raided the smaller one, and within a couple of years had killed most of the males in the smaller group (and probably two of the females). It is worth noting that the first killing included the use of a rock (i.e., a tool). Goodall's observations ignited a storm of discussion about whether her hand-fed community had been "unnaturally" altered by her intervention. Even subsequent studies were at times accused of being "tainted" by the pressure of surrounding human (nonscientist) activity, which also presumably "unnaturally" stressed the chimpanzee populations.

In one sense, this objection misses the point entirely. Populations in nature tend to grow until they strain locally available resources. They then either move, force a part of their own population to move (fission), or compete with other users of those resources. This tendency for a population to grow beyond local carrying capacity is even more marked among humans, who have long lacked a predator. Even when human adaptation increases local subsistence carrying capacity, human population then rapidly swells to that new level.[7] Goodall's intervention may merely have accelerated the process for this one population group; she essentially sustained an overly large community in a too-small area. Sometimes a natural disaster (or, in this case, a scientist withdrawing food) may reduce the ratio of resources to population. At other times the population may grow in response to moving into a resource-rich zone, but eventually the ratio of resources to population will become unsustainable. When either of these things happens, other members of the same species who occupy the same ecological niche become the most likely competitor for those resources. "Resources" in a subsistence system are frequently tied to territory, and so territoriality and at least defensive aggression to secure it can be one trait selected for in the evolutionary process. Among the more sophisticated social animals, group cooperation in territorial defense proves more effective than not. This results for chimpanzees in what Michael Ghiglieri calls a "natural strategy . . . to establish, maintain, defend, or expand a kin group territory via lethal warfare . . . [something] most likely when one community outnumbers a neighboring one." In essence, he argues, "These killer apes simply acted out the logic of reproductive advantage. They gained more of the two resources that limited their reproduction most: females and the territory needed to raise more offspring."[8] These findings have recently been substantiated by a collaborative study of chimpanzee killings in eighteen different communities under study.[9]

Some key traits in chimpanzee group conflicts seem to recur in prestate human conflict. First, conflict is not endemic but episodic. Being a neighbor does not guarantee conflict, but territories are clearly marked, patrolled, and defended, and usually a dangerous buffer zone develops between those territories. Chimpanzees in one community avoided the border area of their territory, spending 75 percent of their time in the central 35 percent of their range, suggesting an awareness of the threat of conflict even when conflict was not constant. Second, casualty rates can be very high (in Goodall's Gombe community, 30 percent of the original male population was killed by other chimps after the group fissioned) but are accrued over time, not in single attacks. Third, conflict begins not through simple "aggression" but rather in response to ecological pressures and perceptions of advantage. Specifically, conflicts begin when one group enjoys an overall numerical advantage. Attacks are launched only when a local numerical edge exists (averaging 8 to 1 in observed killings), and usually with the benefit of surprise. Fourth, raids are conducted by groups of males and are shot through with male sociality and even training activity (adult chimpanzees have been observed to correct the patrolling behaviors of adolescent members). Finally, females are only rarely killed. Instead, they are usually either ignored or socially absorbed by the winner (infants are killed and usually cannibalized).[10]

Figure 1.1 Chimpanzee boundary patrol. Chimpanzees moving single file on the boundary of their territory.

This collection of behaviors can only be called "war." It is organized group activity, conducted with lethal effects, that diminishes one group for the benefit of another. Its existence among chimpanzees, who are our fellow hominids and our closest living genetic relatives, suggests that even where the archaeological evidence falters, human evolution likely has long taken place in the context of such violence. On the other hand, an equally close genetic relative, the bonobo, or "pygmy chimpanzee," famously seems to live almost violence-free. Their social behaviors are highly sexualized. Hierarchies are established through the females, and coalitions of females control aggressive actions by the physically larger males. Rather than using aggression to establish or control social relations, the bonobos prefer sex, of almost any variety. Humans are clearly more aggressive than the bonobo and more socially bonded and cooperative than the chimpanzee. If the evidence from our genetic cousins is somewhat mixed, what is the archaeological evidence for human conflict?

THE EVIDENCE FOR EARLY HUMAN WARFARE

Recognizable states at war with each other and with surrounding nonstate peoples had clearly emerged in the Middle East by 3500 BCE (Uruk) or 3100 BCE (predynastic Egypt), in north China (Xia or the Erlitou culture) arguably by 1800 BCE, and in India (Harappan) by 2500–2000 BCE (although the evidence for war in the Indus Valley Harappan civilization is not as marked as elsewhere). Sedentism, agriculture, and state formation occurred much later in the Western Hemisphere, but existed in central Mexico by 100 BCE and in the highlands of Peru by around 500 CE. We will return to the emergence of states later in this chapter, but for now these dates mark a kind of end point; a point at which state-based war incontrovertibly existed. From this point we will flip the chronology and survey the evidence for human conflict proceeding backwards through time. Because that evidence becomes murkier the deeper we proceed into the human past, it makes sense to begin with what is clearest, and progress in reverse, farther and farther into the human prehistoric and evolutionary past.

The Neolithic

Considerable continuity existed between later states and the complex social organizations that immediately preceded them. We will deal with the nature of that cultural evolution later in this chapter. It suffices at this point to note

---

A Note on Chronology

Talking about the deep human past has long required an assortment of chronological terms in order to deal with the problem of human social development occurring at different rates in different places on the planet. For example, "Neolithic" generally refers to an Old World human society engaged in some form of agriculture, but not yet capable of working tool-quality metals (copper, bronze, and later iron). Both the starting condition (farming) and the end condition (metalworking) occurred at different absolute dates in different places (the term is not used at all in the Americas). Much of northwest Europe, for example, remained "Neolithic" long after the Middle East had entered the "Bronze Age." This chapter blends evidence that might otherwise seem to come from very different times, but *does* come from similar levels of development. For example, the nature of warfare in preagricultural society in Spain can be considered roughly equivalent to that in preagricultural society in Egypt, although the former lasted much longer in absolute terms than the latter. Also note that traditionally dates older than about 10,000 BCE are referred to in terms of "before present," usually presented here as "years ago." Thus 10,000 BCE becomes twelve thousand years ago, or 12,000 BP.

Figure 1.2 Tower at Jericho.

that the archaeological evidence for prestate warfare in the agricultural Neolithic (fortification, settlement destruction, paintings, and weapons development) seems at least as undeniable as that for the era of states. Indeed, we can jump backwards right to the very beginning of the Neolithic to two of the earliest agricultural communities, one at Jericho, founded about 9000 BCE near the Jordan River in the modern West Bank (see Figure 1.2), and the other at Çatalhöyük, occupied roughly from 7500 BCE to 5700 BCE in what is now southern Turkey (see Figure 1.3). Both sites are critical to our understanding of human development since both were among the first "towns" in human history, and both were associated with the earliest phases in the invention of agriculture. Jericho seems to have been a nucleated town first, fortified later, with agriculture arriving somewhat before the wall, but this sequence is still unclear. What is undeniable, however, is that by around 8000 BCE Jericho's inhabitants had surrounded themselves with an extensive elliptical wall, nearly four meters tall, two meters thick at the base, and incorporating a massive circular tower eight and half meters tall, with an interior circular staircase. As can be seen in Figure 1.3, Çatalhöyük is not precisely "walled," but was built much like the cliff dwellings of the American southwest, in which many individual dwellings are conjoined, lack ground-level exterior

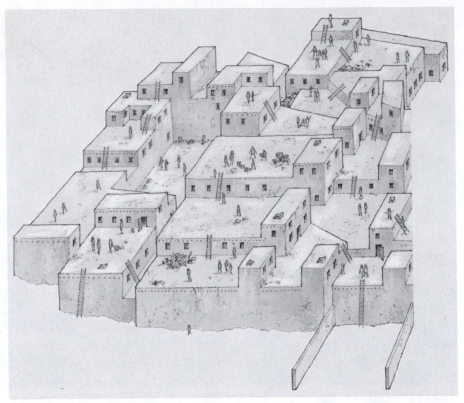

Figure 1.3 Çatalhöyük. One of the earliest agricultural villages in human history, located in southern Anatolia. Note the lack of exterior doors or ground floor windows.

windows or doors, and thus presented a uniform blank wall to the outside world (access was through the roofs).[11]

Given how central these sites are for our understanding of human civilization and its origins, the argument about the role of war in their development has been contentious. Some archaeologists assert that Jericho's wall was intended for flood control, but that assertion fails to explain the tower. Other arguments that the tower was poorly designed for defense (it did not project beyond the wall to provide lines of fire down the wall) simply support the idea that it was among the first of its kind, if not *the* first. In a similar instance of seemingly wishful interpretation, a wall painting at Çatalhöyük arguably shows a warrior, armed with a sling and mace, standing over a headless body and flanked by two vultures (vultures are a frequent theme in paintings from the site). The excavator, however, described the scene in this way: "A headless body lies between the two birds of prey, a man armed with a sling is actually warding off their attacks" (see Figure 1.4).[12]

One can dispute the function of the walls at Jericho, or the issue of Çatalhöyük's being fortified, or the meaning of the wall painting there, but the early Neolithic village at Tell Maghzaliyah (ca. 7000 BCE), along the Tigris River,

Figure 1.4 A warrior standing over a headless man, flanked by vultures. From a fresco at Çatalhöyük, Shrine VIII.8.

was clearly fortified, as was the contemporary site at Ba'ja (ca. 8500–7000 BCE) with its four-meter-high walls. Finally, the somewhat later site at Hacilar near Çatalhöyük, shows a clear archaeological sequence of an unwalled village destroyed around 5500 BCE, rebuilt with a wall 1.5–3 meters thick, destroyed again in 5250 BCE, rebuilt with even stronger walls, and then finally destroyed and abandoned around 4800 BCE.[13]

There is certainly no doubt about conflict in the later Neolithic, especially after the introduction of copper working (technically the Chalcolithic Age). A good example is the clearly documented massive siege and destruction of Hamoukar near the Iraq-Syria border, on a tributary of the Euphrates River, around 3500 BCE. Recent excavations at the site have found that the city was encircled by a thick mud-brick wall over three meters high, that the city was substantially if not completely destroyed by fire, and, most tellingly, that several thousand sling bullets lie among the wreckage. The excavators have even suggested that the attackers came from the emerging and apparently competing urban civilization farther south at Uruk in Sumer. The destruction of Hamoukar may have been part of the process that led Uruk to emerge as the first state (again, reflecting the contentiousness of this subject, it is worth noting that some critics have suggested that these findings at Hamoukar simply cannot be, since it was "too early for organized warfare").[14]

The relative rarity of very early fortified sites like Jericho, and their later proliferation by 3500 BCE, may suggest that the most common form of warfare in the early Neolithic was between newly sedentary (and increasingly agricultural) people and the still wandering foragers around them, and not between competing sedentary towns. This makes sense from a variety of perspectives. Sedentism and agriculture represented an increase in subsistence carrying capacity, initially *reducing* the impulse for conflict between similar peoples. But sedentism, and especially agriculture and the domestication of animals, *increased* the reward for foragers of raiding sedentary villages. There was now "stuff" to be taken, and mobile domesticated animals, present in the Middle East after about 8500 BCE, were the easiest thing to steal. Such raids by small foraging bands against larger nucleated towns would have been risky, however, and so fortification remained only a rare necessity at truly exceptional sites (like Jericho and Çatalhöyük) until sedentary villages themselves began to compete with each other. The destruction of Hamoukar seems to represent an example of this transition to war between sedentary agriculturalists. Their competition in turn fostered greater social complexity and urbanism—a subject we will reexamine later in this chapter. For now we return to the problem of recounting the evidence for early human warfare. Since all of the sites discussed in this section, even if "prestate," were certainly agricultural and sedentary, and some scholars have argued that it was this very condition that led to the development of warfare, we must look farther back. Another argument for turning our attention to such an early period is that the introduction of new weapons in this period (really straddling the divide between the Mesolithic and the Early Neolithic), including the bow, sling, dagger, and mace, tell us relatively little about "warfare," since, with the probable exception of the mace, all of these weapons had uses in hunting.

Epipaleolithic/Mesolithic

The best evidence for warfare prior to the development of settled agricultural communities comes from the skeletal evidence of massacres. Sedentism based on intensive local foraging emerged in the Near East approximately 13,000 BCE, with agriculture following at around 9000 BCE.[15] In Central Europe sedentism emerged around 10,500 BCE, with agriculture arriving from the Near East by around 5500 BCE. Right on the cusp of the emergence of agriculture in Europe, and thus undermining the contention that early farmers enjoyed a period of peace as a result of their relative prosperity, is the massacre site at Talheim, near Heilbronn in Germany, dating from 5000 BCE (see Figure 1.5). The site is a mass burial of thirty-four individuals (eighteen adults and sixteen children). The bodies were piled indiscriminately on top of each other, apparently simply dumped, all the victims having died violently. Careful study of the injuries has determined that "the majority of the victims were attacked from behind as they were standing, presumably as they tried to protect themselves or flee. Having already been struck, many individuals were then hit again as they knelt or even lay on the ground. . . . In addition to the majority of the skulls being smashed, serious injuries were also inflicted upon other parts of the body—the arms, legs, and pelvis."[16] Recent studies have gone further and suggest that the massacre was committed by outside aggressors seeking to completely destroy the settlement and take over their territory and resources. Also from this transitional period from the Mesolithic to the Neolithic in Spain is a series of rock art paintings that clearly portray battles between large groups of archers, as many as twenty to thirty on a side, and that some would say even show formations with visibly ranked leaders (see Figure 1.6).[17]

The Talheim victims were almost certainly transitional farmers and thus properly belong to the early Neolithic. Immediately preceding this period,

Figure 1.5 Talheim massacre. A detail of the Neolithic burial pit at Talheim, ca. 5000 BCE, near Heilbronn, Germany.

and in the same region, however, at the Ofnet cave in Bavaria, there are two burial pits containing the skulls and vertebrae of thirty-three to thirty-eight individuals, mostly children and adult females (only four adult males), dating from about 6500 BCE—clearly preceding the arrival of agriculture in the region. Half of the skulls show clear evidence of head trauma from blunt weapons, and some show cut marks. The absence of other bones suggests head taking and curation (they were all stained with red ochre). It is far from clear that all these skulls were from the same community, but they are certainly evidence for substantial conflict of a lethal variety.[18]

Not only are Talheim and Ofnet dramatic, but their geographic proximity and their existence on either side of the generally accepted moment for the regional introduction of agriculture suggest a continuity of conflict, if not a *constancy* of conflict. A variety of other sites from Mesolithic postglacial Europe suggest lethal human conflict, but even taken together they do not yet tell us much about its frequency.[19]

A similar problem exists with the even earlier and more dramatic site at Jebel Sahaba in Sudan. The cemetery contains fifty-nine burials dating from between 12,000 and 10,000 BCE—at or even before the origins of sedentism

Figure 1.6 A rock art depiction of battle from transitional Mesolithic/Neolithic Spain.

in the region and well preceding agriculture. A few of the bodies were buried at the same time, but it is otherwise difficult to pin down how many separate incidents the burials represent. Of the fifty-nine bodies, some twenty-four, including children, and almost as many females as males, had stone projectile points either embedded in bone or positioned in such a way that suggested they had penetrated the body (see Figure 1.7). It is likely that at least some of the others also died by violence, and very recent research seems to indicate that there were even more wounds on the bodies than first reported. Unlike at Talheim, these bodies apparently were recovered by survivors and carefully interred, perhaps even in family groups. The number of bodies, the injuries, the violent deaths of women and children, and the careful interment of the bodies all suggest repeated attacks on a substantial sedentary community by an enemy or group of enemies.[20]

To this evidence from the Mesolithic, some critics have responded by saying that Talheim, Ofnet, and Jebel Sahaba all represent conflict from a period during which humans, at least in these places, were settling into sedentary patterns of life, thereby emphasizing and hardening territoriality and intensifying competition for local resources. The site at Jebel Sahaba, for example, overlooks the Nile and was close to its second cataract, an area then rich in a variety of food sources. This kind of early sedentism occurred in such pockets of resource-rich zones around the world, and likely turned into competitive territoriality as local populations expanded and too-large communities split, or fissioned. Those newly sedentary communities also likely continued to compete with still-extant mobile forager communities moving through or around the area. The very size of the Jebel Sahaba cemetery (fifty-nine bodies) suggests *either* a community much larger than a typical forager group or multigenerational use of the same location, which itself implies a strong sense of territoriality. To respond to this charge that organized human conflict emerged only with sedentism and territoriality, we must continue our plunge deeper into the human past.[21]

Figure 1.7 Jebel Sahaba burials. Two of the fifty-nine burials at Jebel Sahaba, ca. 12,000 to 10,000 BCE. The pencils indicate projectile angle and location.

Middle and Upper Paleolithic

At this point, it may be helpful to recall why we are pursuing the archaeological evidence for violent human conflict deeper and deeper into the past. The question at stake is whether or not biological selection processes operated on human evolution to favor traits, especially group size and self-sacrificing cooperation (usually called altruism), that provided a competitive advantage in intergroup conflict. As we move backwards into the Paleolithic era proper we are now firmly in the long *evolutionary* history of humans, and indeed of humans of more than one species, focusing here primarily on *Homo erectus*, *Homo neanderthalensis*, and, finally, the earliest *Homo sapiens*. The dominant model for the hominin and then human populating of the planet is now the "two wave" model. The first wave of *Homo* migrated out of Africa around 1.5 to 1.8 million years ago. Those migrants established populations in Europe and southwest Asia who eventually evolved into *Homo neanderthalensis*. Meanwhile in East and South Asia the emigrants from Africa followed separate evolutionary tracks whose exact outlines are less well documented, but did eventually genetically intermingle with both Neandertals and modern *Homo sapiens*. Meanwhile, the *Homo* population back in Africa also continued to evolve, eventually producing the "Anatomically Modern Human" (AMH), *Homo sapiens*, between 400,000 and 200,000 years ago. At that point, say 150,000 years ago, roughly three types of humans existed in Europe, Africa, and Asia. Although they were anatomically distinct species, they nevertheless exhibited no substantial behavioral difference that is reflected in the archaeological record. They produced similar suites of stone tools, they still lacked the ability to fish, and they depended on gathering and some large game hunting. They relied on local stone for their tools (suggesting a lack of distant trade systems or complex social networks), they did not build structures, and they rarely used bone, ivory, or shell. They could build fires, they had spears (there are surviving wooden spear shafts dated to 400,000 years ago), they made pigments from natural iron or manganese ores, and they at least sometimes buried their dead. Then, two crucial things happened.

First, from about 125,000 to 70,000 years ago, modern humans in Africa began to display more creative behaviors, including some indicating consciousness, complex problem solving, early language formation, and ritual. Almost simultaneously, and almost certainly related, about 125,000 years ago *H. sapiens* began to migrate out of Africa, into the Middle East, and, as recently discovered at Jebel Faya, across the Arabian Peninsula to the Persian Gulf. A recent find in Israel confirms the simultaneous existence there of both Neandertals and modern humans at least 55,000 years ago, but *H. sapiens'* migrations further north stalled, perhaps due to competition with resident *Homo* populations there, as well as continued glacial conditions. Genetic studies, however, suggest that modern humans continued to move east into South Asia and beyond. The recent discovery of the oldest examples of human art in Indonesia (roughly forty thousand years old) probably reflects this migration.[22]

Second, around 70,000 to 40,000 years ago, human cognitive development accelerated further, marked by a diversification of tool types and of materials used, distant sourcing for materials, art and ornamentation, and likely a new stage in language development. There is certainly no doubt that one consequence was a rapid population expansion that saw *H. sapiens* spread across Eurasia with startling speed (see Map 1.1). The social brain hypothesis (which among other things correlates the size of the neocortex to the size of the sustainable social network) suggests that, in addition to new tools, the new human cognitive and linguistic capability contributed to the establishment and maintenance of larger social groups that could sustain multiple tiers of social organization. Chimpanzees can sustain nontiered communities of maybe fifty individuals, based on constant face-to-face interaction. Neandertals had moved to a tiered social organization of multiple camps of twelve to fifteen individuals each, composing macrobands of two hundred or so. The evidence from modern humans living in forager societies, however, suggests camps or "bands" ranging from fifteen to fifty individuals, with an average of seventeen such bands combining into a macro band, forming a coherent

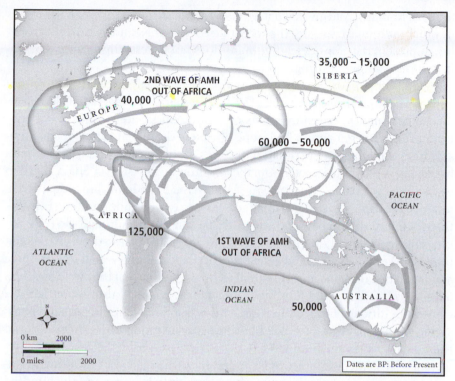

Map 1.1 Anatomically modern humans' (AMH) migration out of Africa. Map shows the general chronology and direction of migration, which appears to have occurred in two waves, the first directed primarily to the east, with a later wave moving into Europe.

community ranging from 250 to 800. Some theorists posit the emergence already in the Upper Paleolithic of an even higher tier of "global networks" of 2,000–2,500 people. These connections were sustained through language and other forms of symbolic activity. Language and symbols of identity released modern humans, and possibly Neandertals, from dependence on proximity. They could now sustain relationships beyond the face-to-face encounter, but modern humans took that advantage further than had Neandertals.[23]

H. sapiens's enhanced social capability and new technologies (notably the atlatl spear thrower developed at least 30,000 to 40,000 years ago) gave them a competitive advantage as they expanded into territories inhabited by other archaic humans. In some theories, the larger group size may itself have promoted technological experimentation and knowledge retention. It has long been theorized or suggested that the in-migration of modern humans pressured, isolated, and eventually eliminated the Neandertal population, if not through actual genocide, then by pushing them into more and more marginal zones where their reproduction rates suffered. There is little physical evidence that suggests that this competition was violent, but some evidence does exist both of intra-Neandertal violence and violence between Neandertals and modern humans. And given what we know about the role of women as victims in much of human warfare, the recent discovery of Neandertal DNA surviving in present day non-African humans does not necessarily suggest a peaceful process of interbreeding.[24]

As in later periods, the evidence for violence is artistic, skeletal, and technological. There are several examples of early cave art (ca. 20,000–12,000 BP) depicting human figures pierced by spears or arrows. And there is skeletal evidence from the Neandertal period in Europe of violent death and cannibalism, arguably for dietary (rather than ritual) purposes. One of the most dramatic examples has emerged relatively recently from the El Sidrón site in Asturias, Spain, dated to approximately 50,000 years ago. At least twelve Neandertal individuals were found in the deposit (six adults, three adolescents, two juveniles, and one infant—three of the adults can be identified as female and three adults and the three adolescents as male). Many (if not all) of the remains possessed cut marks and other signs of butchering, and recent genetic analysis has revealed that all three adult men had the same mitochondrial DNA, suggesting that they were brothers, cousins, or uncles, as did four other individuals, while all three adult females came from different lineages. In short, this was a family group, probably massacred in one incident, by a neighboring separate group of Neandertals, and then butchered by them for food.[25]

There are other examples of Neandertal cannibalism, but thinking in statistical terms here is challenging. There have only been some four hundred Neandertal individuals ever discovered, and not often their whole skeleton. Currently there are roughly twenty-seven Neandertals and nineteen *H. sapiens* from the Paleolithic whose skeletons show evidence of violent death. But many fatal injuries would leave no mark on the skeleton. Furthermore, victims of massacres in the prehistoric past were as likely to be left unburied as not, and their remains thus scattered. Such numbers and conditions make it difficult to sustain statistical claims for the omnipresence of violence (or its lack), but the massacre and eating of a family as represented at the El Sidrón site certainly suggests the possibility, like Jebel Sahaba much later, of at least intermittent extreme, indiscriminate, and presumably terrifying violence. We also know from a variety of European *H. sapiens* sites (the Magdalenian culture) that cannibalism was practiced by modern humans in the upper Paleolithic. In a dramatic example from Gough's Cave in England, about 14,700 years ago five bodies were processed, including cracking the long bones to extract marrow and shaping a skull cap into a cup for drinking (Figure 1.8).

Both Neandertals and early *H. sapiens* therefore provide at least some evidence for cannibalism and violence. So what about *H. sapiens* violence *against* Neandertals? Here the evidence is scant, and there is an emerging possibility that at least in parts of Europe the chronological overlap of Neandertal and *H. sapiens* may have been shorter than once believed, or even regionally nonexistent. There is some evidence of such violence, however, such as in the Les Rois cave in France, in which the bones of a modern human were found

Figure 1.8 Skull modified into a drinking cup. From Gough's Cave, ca. 14,700 BP.

alongside the skull of a Neandertal child, and the child's jawbone bears the marks of having been processed for food. Furthermore, a recent reanalysis of a wound inflicted on a Neandertal skeleton known as Shanidar 3 (found in Iraq's Zagros Mountains in the 1950s) suggests that it was inflicted by a thrown spear, possibly using an atlatl, and therefore almost certainly by a modern human.[26]

Some scholars have argued for a long history of human warfare, others for a very short history, others that it existed only under certain social conditions (that is, that conflict might disappear for centuries at a time under certain conditions). The basic contention here is that coordinated lethal conflict between groups of humans intent on increasing their access to resources of various types has existed *at all times* and *in all places*, but *not all the time*. Even when it was not actively occurring, however, its threat affected social development and organization. Conflict or war does not dominate the archaeological record of prestate societies surveyed here, but it does suffuse it, deep into the Paleolithic, and it remains today visibly evident among our close genetic kin the chimpanzees. One scholar, Samuel Bowles, agreeing with the chronology and pervasiveness of lethal human conflict suggested by the evidence given here, and working from estimates of the lethality of forager warfare, has developed a mathematical model to argue for the biological evolution of cooperative altruism within human groups, suggesting that "for many groups and for substantial periods of human prehistory, lethal group conflict may have been frequent enough to support the proliferation of quite costly forms of altruism."[27] In this way, as much of the rest of this chapter will show, cooperation and conflict proved to be two sides of the same coin, each reinforcing the other, as one group enhanced cooperation to succeed at conflict, and the persistence of conflict necessitated ever more complex forms of cooperation.[28]

BIOLOGY AND SELECTION

Bowles makes two key points. First, there have been sufficient generations of sufficiently lethal human conflict to have generated selective pressure on human evolution. If we accept this evolutionary time depth for human conflict, and with it the *possibility* of genetic selection to cope with it, Bowles then asks: What kinds of traits might it have favored? His answer is altruistic cooperation. This claim is of particular importance for military historians. Genetically speaking, the willingness of an individual to take risks, even self-sacrificial risks, on behalf of another seems to violate the primary genetic imperative to survive and reproduce. If altruism had biological origins (and it *is* visible in certain nonhuman cooperating species), what selection processes created it?

The current orthodoxy on this subject argues that evolutionary selection works at an individual level, favoring traits that promote individual survival and reproduction. In this view, "species" do not evolve as a group. Individuals within a species evolve, and the most reproductively successful then outcompete the other individuals and pass on their genes more prolifically until their traits come to (re)define the species. What would promote risky altruism within this individually competitive dynamic? Beginning in the mid-1960s biologists argued for the principle of "inclusive fitness," in which individuals within a group cooperate in order to promote the survival of their own genes via their survival in close relatives. The more closely related the group, the greater the incentive to cooperate: a brother who acts to promote multiple siblings' reproductive success insures the propagation of 50 percent (on average) of his own genetic code in each sibling, and so on (self = 2 brothers = 4 nephews = 8 cousins).[29]

Recently, one of the original innovators of inclusive fitness, E. O. Wilson, along with Martin Nowak and others working in evolutionary game theory, have argued that there is in fact such a thing as selection that operates at a group level and not just on individuals. Without completely dismissing inclusive fitness, they argue for multilevel selection. Individual selection continues, including for group behaviors via inclusive fitness, but group selection also operates. Furthermore—and why it matters here—the key selection pressure encouraging group behaviors is the existence of competition from other members of the same species living in different groups. For Wilson, the key criteria initiating group selection favoring cooperation was the creation of a "protected nest," a form of living that promotes sociality, without necessarily eliminating continued intragroup competition and selection. From that initial stage, Nowak argues that populations of cooperators will outcompete selfish populations, although they may have to survive through several disadvantageous generations until selfish actors' reputations gather sufficient weight to create cooperative actions against them, favoring cooperators in the long run over selfish "defectors." In short, hereditary altruists form groups that cooperate and organize to outcompete nonaltruist groups, "through both direct conflict and differential competence in exploiting the environment."[30]

Therefore, competition and its most dramatic form, violent conflict, acted as a selection pressure on human biological evolution, favoring the selection of group behaviors like male solidarity, a "shoot on sight" attitude toward intrusive strangers, the ability to incorporate the defeated remnants of other groups, risk calculation in assessing the threat of other groups, and, most importantly, greater social complexity to sustain larger group sizes which provided an important advantage in violent conflict.

It is this last characteristic that points us to the other side of the conflict coin: cooperation. For humans, being "good" at conflict depends on more than physical size, keen eyesight, or other physical attributes. It also means being good at cooperating. Recent studies of infants suggest that the ability and desire to reward cooperators exists at the genetic level, and ethnographic work among bands of foragers frequently shows that not only do they depend on cooperation within the group, but the group actively controls aggressive, dominance-seeking individuals—although they never fully eliminate dominant males nor their quest for dominance.[31] Summarized another way by anthropologist Bruce Knauft, "Collective socialization in gregarious groups . . . provided a distinctive evolutionary niche for the genus *Homo*," but it did so alongside, and even complementing, human "biogenetically self-interested behavior."[32] The evolution of cooperation thus can be linked to the existence of lethal conflict, which promoted, in Bowles and Gintis's words, "a particular form of [cooperative] altruism, often hostile toward outsiders and punishing toward insiders who violate norms, [and it] coevolved with a set of institutions—sharing food and making war are examples—that at once protected a group's altruistic members and made group-level cooperation the *sine qua non* of survival."[33] Modern humans are thus products of a grand dialectic tension between developing internal cooperation to be more successfully aggressive against outsiders within the same species, in the quest for resources. Success in conflict prioritized ever better cooperation to enlarge group size, but, once enlarged, they needed more resources to sustain themselves, and so on.

Group identity formation and hostile stranger reaction, which, taken together, we might call ethnocentrism, did not guarantee conflict. Indeed, the additional evolved characteristic of risk assessment probably meant that conflict was not *constant*. Its risk, however, was ever-present, and therefore social behaviors evolved to be prepared for and good at conflict—much like the boundary avoidance and patrolling behaviors of chimpanzees. Furthermore, when conflict did emerge, it could take a wide variety of forms as the group balanced perceived need versus potential risk. Conflict could include displays of strength (what the ethnographic record calls "ritual" battle), threats of aggression, watchfulness, and careful scouting, while lethal violence probably took place under conditions of reduced risk: either strategically ("there are more of us than them overall") or tactically (reliance on ambush or pounce-and-flee tactics that create a local mismatch in numbers).

The selective pressure to avoid risks associated with conflict no doubt escalated with the invention of weapons, especially the spear (which is at least four hundred thousand years old, but probably closer to one million years old). Weapons made conflict potentially more lethal, and they have existed long enough to have had an evolutionary effect on behavior. Given the coevolution of risk assessment and resource conflict, it seems likely that few social groups *preferred* conflict. Conflict may even have remained rare for long periods when group fission and migration remained an option.

Flipping the coin back to conflict, however, humans have tended to fill up the landscape quickly. From at least the rapid human migrations around Eurasia from about 40,000 to 60,000 years ago they have spread rapidly across the entire globe, moving as foragers and presumably impelled by more than simple curiosity. The most reasonable model for most of human biological history is one of small kin groups existing in a universe of similarly equipped and similarly subsisting kin groups, bouncing off each other, fissioning as they grew too large, probably mostly in a watchful kind of "peace," since rarely would any single group possess a sustained advantage over another. But compete they did, and that competition would continuously refine the intragroup dynamics discussed above. Furthermore, given the small size of the group during the evolutionary period of human prehistory, accident or chance encounters that killed one or more males would render that group vulnerable to a nearby group that had not been reduced in that way. The size of the group was critical, and it is in this context that we must understand the huge selective advantage conveyed by the ability, perhaps first biological, and then cultural, to enlarge the group size. It is also important to emphasize that the advantage of a larger group was not just about winning a "battle." Group size enhanced group survival because it represented their ability to retaliate against any other group that attacked it.

Informed readers will note that I have made almost no mention of the selective pressures exerted by either humans hunting or humans being preyed upon by other top predators—the so-called "man the hunter" or "man the hunted" hypotheses. These pressures certainly had evolutionary consequences, possibly related to war, certainly related to tool and weapon development, and almost equally certainly to human cooperative and mating behaviors. But what I argue for here is a "man the competitor" hypothesis, one that smoothly links biological evolution in a continuum with cultural evolution— what Wilson calls "gene-culture coevolution." It is this dynamic of humans *in competition with each other* and therefore seeking ever more organizational capacity that was the real shaper of war as a social phenomenon, first biologically and then culturally. As conflict continued in "cultural time" (as opposed to "evolutionary time"), it continued to promote greater cooperation within the group, with solutions now achieved through cultural adaptation and transmission more rapidly than had occurred genetically. Solutions to selective pressures could now be reached through learning and problem solving, and then taught to succeeding generations.[34]

This sort of "sociocultural evolution," however, did not take place on a clean slate. It is part of a continuum of selection processes that continued where biology left off. In historian Azar Gat's formulation, "Cultural evolution has then continued biological evolution in creating greater complexity, simply by force of the competition that takes place among reproducing, propagating replicators of any sort," whether biological organisms or social units.[35] For most of the existence of the genus *Homo* we have been foragers, and biological evolution in the context of intraspecies resource competition and conflict has produced key characteristics of our species. In the last forty to seventy thousand years we embarked on a separate, parallel, and *much faster* process of sociocultural evolution, in response to a similar set of pressures, but now acting primarily on the interaction of larger and larger groups made possible by the cognitive revolution of the Upper Paleolithic.

In short, modern humans are the products of a "dual inheritance," and we must acknowledge the conditions, mechanisms, and legacies of both. Consider, for example, that for two million years humans evolved in conditions in which intragroup solidarity at the microband level was continuously selected for and reinforced through biological mechanisms. The capacity for solidarity beyond the microband size, however, has only existed for *perhaps* fifty thousand years, and has been partially biologically, but mostly culturally, selected for. Is it here that we find the roots of the powerful bonds between small groups of men engaged in conflict? And is it also here that we find the powerful and persistent ethnocentrism that enables one group to label members of another as "Others" and thereby to treat them with more extreme violence?

But let us return to the progressive enlargement of the social group. Biological changes in the brain had allowed for the formation of groups beyond nuclear kin and the face-to-face encounter. Microbands became bands as language, consciousness, ritual, art, and other behaviors expanded altruistic cooperation. To be sure, *H. sapiens* remained in their forager bands for thousands of years more, but not only were their larger bands now more competitive than those of other archaic humans, they also proved more adaptive to new climates and new ecologies. The subsistence limits inherent to foraging, however, impose a maximum group size on forager bands, and so group fissioning continued to occur as population rose within a group. Fissioning in turn generated neighboring groups competing for the same set of resources.

Consider what happened as a naturally bounded resource zone, for example a river valley or a coastal delta, filled with competing bands. Resource competition put a premium on those cultural traits that allowed a group to succeed at conflict. Much like the original success of the cognitive revolution, a key trait in any such competition would be group size, solidarity, and access to a greater genetic diversity of mates, all achievable through defeating and incorporating parts of another band, and then using that still greater size to drive out other competitors. Success would initially create a surplus of resources, but that surplus would in turn generate further population expansion, and a return to the original problem, only now operating within a larger region with a larger group. The larger the group, however, the more complex the necessary social dynamics to preserve it, and the more complex the required resource exploitation. It should be obvious where this argument is heading, but it is worth reiterating that this process occurred slowly, in fits and starts, and generated endless variation in part because of the great variety of the planet's ecologies, and in part because of the inventive capacities of the human brain.[36]

Some caveats are necessary to all this. To claim a role for biological evolution in producing potentially violent ethnocentrism is not to claim that we are trapped in these behaviors. Culture can overrule biology, especially in group behaviors, but this argument does suggest the power behind such behavior. And asserting that this process of cultural evolution has occurred does not entail that there was only one track of human experience, or that one track was "better" than another, or more progressive, or even inevitable. Nevertheless, I argue, as anthropologist Bruce Trigger has written, that there has been "a strong tendency" for sociocultural evolution "to move in the general direction of greater complexity." Put simply, as described above, more complex societies compete more successfully with less complex ones for control of territory and other resources. "As a result of such competition, in all but the poorest and most marginal environments (and increasingly even in these) smaller-scale societies must either acquire the key attributes of more complex societies or be displaced or absorbed by them."[37] Human cooperation and social complexity evolved both biologically and culturally in the face of human conflict. They were and remain two sides of the same coin.

SEDENTISM, AGRICULTURE, AND WAR

At the forager level social complexity remained very low. In part this resulted from the ability of our forager ancestors to respond to competitive pressure by simply moving elsewhere. Conflict arguably played a role in those decisions, but as our forager ancestors filled up the landscape, and especially as they identified specific resource-rich zones, they had an incentive to settle in those zones and defend them. Furthermore, their increasing skill as hunters may have led to an overkill of large game (although that game population may have died out for reasons unrelated to human hunting). Whatever the cause, the archaeological record is clear that in the late Paleolithic, beginning perhaps as early as 20,000 years ago in the eastern Mediterranean and slowly spreading into Europe and elsewhere, humans greatly diversified their diet into smaller game, aquatic resources (fish and shellfish), and, especially, more and more wild plants. This "broad spectrum revolution" in diet contributed not only to filling up the planet, but also to wider social variation, since large game hunting represented a relatively unitary ecological niche in much of the world. This dietary expansion also encouraged the identification of varied ecological zones as being "resource rich," and those forager bands that encountered them and learned to exploit them more intensively began to become more sedentary. This kind of intensively exploited, broad-spectrum diet increased the carrying capacity of a given region, but it also thereby led to further regional population growth, eventually requiring even more effective resource exploitation. Thus some sedentary foragers in resource-rich zones developed into what we call "complex hunter-gatherers." The process got nudged along as the last ice age ended. The period of warming that followed encouraged the growth of wild cereals in various parts of the Middle East, and human exploitation of those and other seed- and nut-producing plants repeatedly in the same location may more or less accidentally have led to agriculture.[38] People gathering wild seed plants naturally focused on the largest and easiest seeds to process. They carried them back to their campsite, where, mixed with waste, the seeds repropagated, with each generation selecting for those plants most suitable for human consumption. Meanwhile, humans "prepared themselves" for agriculture by learning how to process gathered seeds and nuts with millstones and other tools. Eventually the process could be artificially directed and controlled, becoming true agriculture. In a similar way, animal domestication may have proceeded as humans struggled to cope with the disappearance of game species in their natural state, through overhunting, climate change, or a combination of both.[39]

War may also have played a role in these transitions, but the arguments are speculative, or inferred by ethnographic analogy from a much later period. But one suggestion is that a group, having successfully settled in a desirable resource zone, would then have had to defend it from surrounding groups of mobile foragers. Investment in heavy tools (especially millstones) used to process seeds would also have encouraged efforts at defense. Territoriality and boundary marking in these circumstances became even more intense. Arguably, this need for defense is why sedentary and then agricultural settlements tended to nucleate, and perhaps even to fortify: once again there was strength in numbers, and the process of fortification may have intensified sedentism in turn, perhaps even contributing thereby to the development of agriculture. Meanwhile, once sedentism became associated with true agriculture, its initial superiority in carrying capacity allowed for social stratification. Those males able to dominate local social relations through personal influence and manipulation of their cooperating kin were able to translate their power into control of the agricultural surplus, which they could in turn use to recruit others to elite roles, craft specialization, and all the diversification in labor that eventually would become "civilization."

Pastoral peoples who relied more heavily on domesticated animals had a similar problem. Although not sedentary, they nevertheless became dependent on specific pastures, usually seasonally available, and they also had to defend their animals from other humans while moving them from pasture to pasture. Their mobile lifestyle encouraged a different style of warfare, typically based on a tribal system of social stratification that was less steep than agricultural villages, and that discouraged labor diversification. Nevertheless, pastoral peoples' relationship to land and competition with others for it drove their system of war, a system much aided by their ability to swoop into agricultural zones to plunder and then depart (using their stock to carry away their plunder). Thus began the long adversarial relationship between sedentary agricultural peoples and the still very large population of *mobile* foragers and, later, pastoral nomads. In particularly dense zones, this may have led to fortification in the manner of Jericho. Its early simple walls would have been a poor defense against the organized state-level warfare of a later era, but those walls, like the simple wooden palisades regularly found in the ethnographic record, solved the "pounce and flee" threat posed by a demographically smaller but highly mobile enemy.

Thus we find ourselves back at the archaeological evidence from the birth of agriculture. These early agricultural societies were still *relatively* egalitarian. They certainly were not states—neither Jericho nor Çatalhöyük, for example, had a "palace"—but there is evidence for some social differentiation. Of course, even bands were never fully egalitarian. Hierarchical power has always existed in human societies, in part because of the biological drives to reproduce already discussed. In-group cooperative altruism moderated single-male dominance but did not eliminate it. The cultural evolution of social complexity allowed for drastically more unequal hierarchies. Indeed, the very definition of "civilization" can be tied to the redefining of social relations beyond kinship. In anthropologist Bruce Trigger's formulation, instead of kinship, social relations became defined by

> a hierarchy of social divisions that cut horizontally across societies and were unequal in power, wealth, and social prestige. In these societies a tiny ruling group that used coercive powers to augment its authority was sustained by agricultural surpluses and labour systematically appropriated from a much larger number of agricultural producers. Full-time specialists (artisans, bureaucrats,

soldiers, retainers) also supported and served the ruling group and the government apparatus it controlled.[40]

It is critical to note that these processes did not take place all at once, or even quickly, but they were deeply interrelated and mutually reinforcing. They did not even necessarily have to happen in the same order: in the Americas, the different biology of agricultural domesticates meant that people began to cultivate them *before* becoming sedentary. They moved from resource zone to resource zone, and one component of their seasonal movement was to return to where they had deliberately planted the year before. In the Near East, however, it is clear that sedentism preceded and probably encouraged agriculture. These developments, especially where agriculture proved a demanding process requiring irrigation, combined with building walls (admittedly not a universal phenomenon) and the need to defend against outside mobile raiders, all contributed to social stratification and the diversification of labor. Those characteristics turned out to convey a competitive advantage in most temperate ecological zones, leading to the spread of a Neolithic "package" which included more than just farming; it also brought social complexity, at least minimally diversified labor, hierarchical social systems, and very often a warrior elite.

Imagine the rest of the world (outside of new agricultural communities like Jericho or Çatalhöyük) filled with mobile foragers, living in independent bands of fifty to one hundred people. The domestication of plants and animals dramatically accelerated population growth among the new farmers; according to one estimate the birth rate compared to foragers or hunter-gatherers may have doubled.[41] Farming allowed for much larger populations to live in the confined spaces of agricultural villages (both Çatalhöyük and Jericho supported populations in the thousands), giving those villages greater access to male military labor, especially outside of the harvest or planting seasons. These farmer-villagers did not necessarily go out on conquest campaigns, although they may have. All they had to do was move from one valley into the next, colonizing new ground. Their population advantage allowed them to defend it against foragers, whose risk assessment suggested that it was probably better to move elsewhere. Population density may have pressed the farmers to move, but they also may have fissioned under cultural pressure, as the men in a new generation felt the urge to make their own name and become a big man within their own circle (a pattern not unlike that attributed to, for example, the Vikings of a later era). Moving to the next valley gave them the space to do so. As these farmers pushed into new territory, they clashed with the remaining mobile peoples, with complex hunter-gatherers, and with other expanding farmers.

This narrative of expansion from the origin point of agriculture in the Middle East northwestward into Europe has been supported by genetic studies of early farmers in Europe as well as by other forms of archaeological

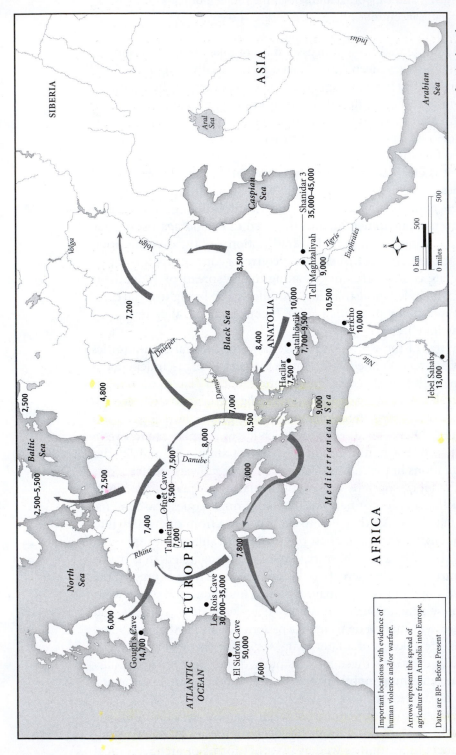

Map 1.2 Sites of evidence for human violence and the spread of agriculture into Europe. The arrows indicate the movement of agricultural practices from the origin point in the Near East and Anatolia. Much of this movement was by the farmers themselves, with some imitation and sometimes alongside surviving hunter-gatherer societies. Agricultural data derived from Bellwood, *First Farmers*, Fig. 4.1.

analysis. Farming peoples, not just the idea of farming, migrated into Europe from the Near East—although some hunter-gatherer populations in Europe successfully retreated and survived and/or adopted farming and greater social complexity (see Map 1.2). Furthermore, the archaeological evidence regarding the expansion of these farmers, some of it reviewed above with respect to Talheim and Ofnet, clearly indicates that not only was the expansion not always peaceful, but, after pushing back the Mesolithic hunter-gatherers, the new farming arrivals turned on each other in increasingly lethal competition.[42]

A LORD AMONG LORDS AND THE RISE OF THE STATE

This process of socially stratified societies expanding and competing for territory in turn created more complex societies, as each sought competitive advantage. These evolved through subtly differentiated stages including petty chiefdoms, chiefdoms, inchoate states, petty states, and eventually states. This process was not unilinear. Imagine, for example, a regional cluster of linguistically related agricultural villages, politically autonomous, each partially socially stratified, and each more or less controlled by a single kin network, with a "head-of-kin" figure. A talented (or lucky) kin leader, seeking to cement his local control, perhaps especially in the face of declining local resources relative to population growth, might successfully mobilize his village to attack a neighboring village, subordinating the defeated population, further stratifying this now expanded and more complex society, with himself more firmly ensconced at the top—now someone we might call a "petty chief." Further luck and further success in using his now-expanded manpower against the other remaining single villages might elevate him (and his original village) further, the village becoming the capital of a chiefdom and he a "paramount chief." Bad luck, or an alliance by individual villages against him, however, might destroy or devastate his original village after his first successful attack, and that incipient chiefdom would "cycle" back down to a simple village.

In essence this same process, operating at more and more complex levels, eventually generated the state, as, for example, a petty chief competed not with an individual village but with *another* petty chief, and a chiefdom competed with other chiefdoms, and so on. At each stage the quest for competitive advantage generated mechanisms for further social complexity, with much of that complexity designed to efficiently mobilize military capability. Indeed, as social complexity increased, the "resources" that communities were competing for became not just food but those things useful in a future conflict: initially manpower, but eventually metals, horses, and the other important ingredients of ancient armies. Even the first so-called pristine states, a term meaning a state formed in the absence of other states and usually referring to Egypt, Sumer, northern China, the Indus valley, central Mexico, and the Andean highlands, developed through a feedback process of the interaction of smaller petty states eventually swallowed up by one successful one. The conquered societies were then welded together through authoritarian rule combining force and an ideology, usually rooted in presumed spiritual power and access, that legitimated the rule of someone we would now call a "king." In this sense, the state itself is the innovation providing a competitive advantage. "Secondary" states then arose in response to the first "pristine" states through competitive necessity: they had to develop similar resource mobilization capacities in order to survive. The arguments among archaeologists about when a "state" first emerged in a given region are, in some ways, simply a function of the many shades of gray between one level of complexity and the next.

But what did it mean to be a "state," and what were its competitive advantages? There are two issues here: What competitive advantage did states provide, and how did they provide it? Frequently "state" is defined by its capacities: What could it *do?* But given the argument here for cultural evolution driven by an environment of conflict, we should turn the question on its head and ask what local rulers *needed* in order to outcompete their neighbors, and what they created to meet those needs. To explore this question, we return to some of the fundamental concepts provided by John Landers as discussed in the introduction. Mobilizing military labor from an agricultural society requires the accumulation, storage, and transport of agricultural goods to support a body of men organized for war. Raising those men in the first place can be done by maintaining them as permanent professionals on the surplus generated by others, or by demanding men from the entire population (typically outside the sowing or harvest season). More commonly, societies have used some combination of both. Furthermore, equipping a military force from the Bronze Age forward required controlling, or at least tapping, long-distance trade networks that accessed mines and other resources (for example, horse-breeding areas) and then supporting a class of craft specialists with the same agricultural surplus required for the army. Generating agricultural stockpiles requires *expansive* control of a farming region, something difficult to achieve from a single center. Controlling distant trade creates a similar imperative. Resource mobilization therefore requires regional centers, whose loyalty and reliability the central government wants to be assured of. Finally, the agricultural surplus can be enlarged by enforcing steeper social divisions: conquered or enslaved labor receives less of the annual produce, but that sort of labor force requires coercive management wielded out beyond even the regional centers, down into the individual villages.

If these are the requirements of war making, consider how they correspond to a commonly accepted definition of a state: a society with marked social stratification, with a centralized and internally specialized government capable of extending bureaucratic control out into a settlement hierarchy consisting of at least three and usually four tiers (meaning there is a center, dispersed regional centers, and then tiered subordinate communities extending out yet further to generate expansive territorial exploitation). The bureaucracy manages the coercive mechanisms necessary for conscripting the male population and distributes the agricultural surplus required to sustain them. Membership (and thus loyalty) in the system is promoted through unequal reward distribution (favoring armed elites), backed by a more generalized normative system of metaphysical beliefs emanating from a ritual center under centralized control. Some city-states were somewhat exceptional in that they lacked a full four-tiered hierarchy of settlements, but they were otherwise fully centralized and socially differentiated, and had at least two and usually three tiers of settlements.

In other words, we can tie virtually every one of the so-called definitional characteristics of the state to the ways they provided a competitive advantage in conflicts with other states or nascent states. Furthermore, those characteristics also reflect the role of warfare and conquest in the state formation process. An incipient state needed first the military capacity to conquer other similar social entities and then the bureaucratic capacity to extend and retain control over those populations. (Note that this refers to war between similar societies, not between nomadic and settled peoples. The latter conflicts were a kind of wild card in this relationship, one that contributed to the variety of solutions that emerged within this competitive cultural evolution.) In terms of techniques, this meant sending expeditionary campaigns equipped with agricultural-surplus to either destroy, drive out, or force the surrender and subordination of another sedentary population. This is no longer the "pounce and flee" technique of forager warfare. Pounce-and-flee raids could in the long run drive out or even effectively annihilate an enemy population; they might even incorporate remnant bits of that enemy population; but they could not *subordinate* an intact enemy population. State, or nascent state–based campaigns represented a new kind of "take and hold" warfare, a style that encouraged fortification. That in turn encouraged the ability to besiege, which encouraged the enlargement of armies and a deeper reliance on agricultural surplus, all activities that then favored even greater centralization and stratification.

Once the enemy's village, town, or city had been taken and held, since the enemy sedentary population was already stratified, "subordination" actually meant the replacement or co-option of the local elite, who would then continue to exercise their control over the local laboring (or enslaved) population, now at the behest of a more distant center. In this way the successful ruler of the emergent state was actually a lord among lords. Every regional center had its own "lord" and its own regional elite. The regions were nominally obedient to the state center, but, as any historian can tell you, the relationship actually was riddled by power games and strategies ranging from self-interested cooperation (perhaps the norm), to truculence, to tax skimming, to collusion with other state rulers, to outright rebellion. Such competition among elites is the usual stuff of history.

(a)

(b)

Figure 1.9 *a & b* The "Towns" Palette from protodynastic Egypt, ca. 3100 BCE. Depicts fortified cities being taken. Animals on the reverse may represent plunder.

I have thus far spoken in generalities, and have ignored other processes that no doubt contributed to the development of social complexity. Nevertheless, these general outlines of state formation through progressive centralization of power and greater complexity are widely attested in the archaeological, ethnographic, and even historical record of state formation.[43] An example from one of the pristine states will suffice for specifics, although we will see more aspects of this general process in the next chapter. Early Dynastic and Old Kingdom Egypt (3100–2100 BCE) is generally accepted as one of first emergent states. Once fully formed, Egypt remained generally peaceful for quite a long time, isolated in the Nile valley from potential enemies by the surrounding deserts. As historian Azar Gat describes it, however, "The Egypt that comes under literate, historical light did not emerge full blown. It had to be created, 'unified,' from a multiplicity of petty polities, in a protohistorical process that is only vaguely recorded in tradition and by archaeology, and in which warfare played a central role."[44] This combined process of conquest and unification may be preserved visually in the so-called Towns Palette, dating from ca. 3100 BCE (see Figure 1.9 a & b), which depicts a series of uniquely identified fortified settlements, apparently being besieged. The other side shows rows of domesticated animals and crops, possibly representing the resultant plunder, or profits of conquest.

The previous two thousand years had seen the forager population pressured by climatic change to converge on the Nile valley, becoming sedentary and agricultural, with rising populations and increasingly complex trade networks, especially after the discovery of copperworking as early as 4000 BCE. Population had concentrated in stratified protocity-states by 3500 BCE, while regional trade within an isolated and fairly unitary ecological niche created a shared regional "Egyptian" culture. The appearance of monumental tombs and rich grave goods (including weapons) suggests the emergence of a powerful military elite. For example, a painting on the Abydos Vase from roughly 3800 BCE shows a plumed royal figure brandishing a mace and about to execute bound captives, while a contemporary work of rock art shows a similar figure standing in a boat wielding a mace in what would become the classic pharaonic pose of smiting an enemy. And there are clear depictions of combat and execution in the so-called Painted Tomb from about 3300 BCE (note that a mace is a weapon difficult to associate with any activity other than warfare). By 3150 BCE southern Egypt consisted of four independent petty states, apparently in more or less constant military and economic competition. The Towns Palette may reflect a stage in the consolidation of those states, in which first southern (or "Upper") Egypt unified under the center at Hierakonpolis, which later conquered northern ("Lower") Egypt over a period of several generations (see Map 1.3). We are again archaeologically blessed by striking visual evidence for this process in the famous Narmer Palette (see Figure 1.10). It shows the first ruler of a united Egypt, King Narmer (referred to in later records as Menes), defeating his enemies, on one side wearing the white crown of Upper Egypt,

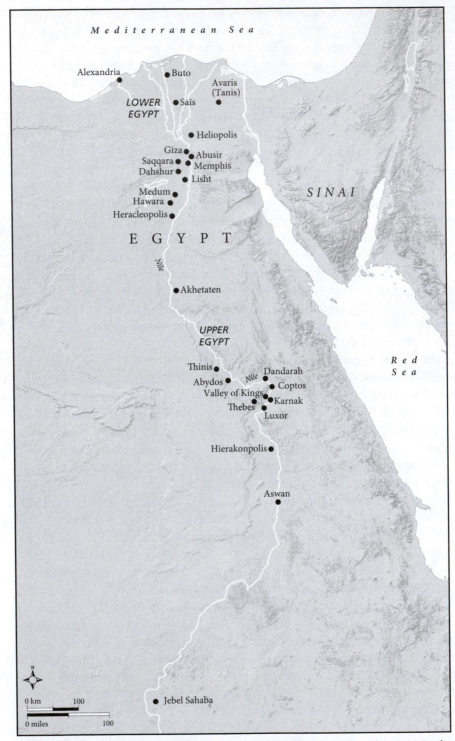

Map 1.3 Predynastic Upper and Lower Egypt. Jebel Sahaba was not a dynastic site, but is included here for reference.

Figure 1.10 *a & b* **The Narmer Palette, First Dynasty Egypt, ca. 3100–2890** BCE. Commemorates the victories of King Narmer identified as King Menes, the unifier of Upper and Lower Egypt. King Menes is shown on both sides, dispatching enemies. He wears the crown of Upper Egypt on one side, and Lower Egypt's crown on the other.

and on the other the red crown of Lower Egypt, "ritually smiting a prisoner with his mace, marching in triumph among the corpses of his enemies whose decapitated heads [on the reverse] are placed between their legs, and capturing rival cities."[45] With the Nile valley unified under a single center, and given the extraordinary productivity of the valley under such a steeply stratified society, it was centuries before Egypt found itself in competition with outside powers or was seriously threatened by internal upheaval.[46]

WARRING COMPLEX SOCIETIES OUTSIDE THE STATE

Our discussion thus far has been almost entirely about state formation among agricultural people. Nonstate peoples obviously continued to war, with each other and with neighboring or intrusive states. Indeed, the existence and spread of the state played a significant role in shaping nonstate peoples' warfare practices and social organization. State pressure encouraged a separate evolution of social complexity. One crucial version was the one found among nomadic pastoral peoples, who long resisted either becoming a state or being conquered by one. The difference in their cultural evolution is rooted in subsistence systems. Those peoples who moved out (or who were pushed out) into zones that could not sustain agriculture developed methods of subsistence based on domesticated animals. Doing so, especially in marginal zones, required remaining mobile to move the flocks from pasture to pasture, especially seasonally. It further demanded that the usual face-to-face group size be relatively small: each human required multiple animals to sustain him or her for the year; and each animal required a certain minimum daily acreage of pasture, quickly consumed, thus discouraging any great gathering of people in one place for very long. As discussed previously, however, these conditions did not necessarily mean that nomadic pastoralists were not territorial. The quality of pastures differed; ancestors were buried in specific places; waterholes could be scarce, and so on. Territoriality and continued competition with each other, as well as the desire to prey on settled peoples with more dense populations and stockpiles of craft-made goods, encouraged social formations that transcended the small daily face-to-face group. Kinship bound together bands of relatives by blood and marriage into clans, who might even move across the pasture zones in coordinated but distinct paths. Multiple clans formed into tribes, based on notions of kinship rooted in a distant ancestor, bound together strongly enough to provide for defense (usually through reactive revenge raids affirming the strength of the group, rather than through territorial defense) and occasionally offensive raiding of sedentary peoples.

Nomadic pastoral tribes' ability to move deep into areas where sedentary armies had trouble following provided protection, and so social formations larger than the tribe were unusual—the competitive dynamic did not require them. Within tribes, status differentiation is low; leadership depends on personal reputation and consensus; cooperation between clans is not unusual, but neither is it the norm. Even so, climatic shifts or energetic invasive states could create more competitive conditions that forced or encouraged tribes to "confederate," occasionally becoming powerful enough, given the other demanding aspects of their lifestyle, to destroy states and perhaps even to conquer them. When they conquered, they then absorbed aspects of the state system, especially surplus accumulation and bureaucratic rule. This punctuated dynamic of so-called barbarian tribal confederations emerging from their pastoral lands to interrupt the pattern of sedentary competition has played an enormous role in human history. Often those tribal confederations could sustain state-like imperial rule only relatively briefly, although the more thoroughly they shed tribal systems and values, essentially becoming a new elite at the top of a sedentary agricultural state, the longer they were likely to rule. Examples of both recur frequently in this book.

CONCLUSION

In many ways this chapter is simply arguing for continuity between the long experience of prehistoric human conflict and more "modern" warfare between states. The common but artificial attempt to limit the definition of "war" to something that is organized, or centrally directed, or has open "battles," or has crossed some "military horizon" or "threshold," misses something about the fundamental nature of war. War was (and is) the use of potentially lethal force by cooperating groups in order to solve some perceived problem or achieve some desired end—say stealing the women and goods of a neighbor. To say that a revenge killing by a tribe or small community was merely a "feud," rather than an act of war, is to miss the potential role of a revenge killing in solving a problem experienced by that society. As just discussed with regard to tribal societies, one of the functions of the group was to provide a credible threat of retaliation in the event of an attack on one of its members, thereby forestalling attacks, or at least limiting them. There *is* a difference between individual murder and war, but it is also possible for an individual killing to be a part of a larger conflict between separate human societies. That continuum of conflict, more or less continuously throughout human prehistory, generated first human biological and then sociocultural *innovation*. Social differentiation and complexity aimed at increasing the group size proved the most effective innovation in that competition, at least within those ecological zones suited to agriculture. The rise of the state was merely one outcome in a continuous but erratic line of development, at the end of which human societies were competing at *raising* resources in order to compete *for* resources. In our terms, the state emerged to raise capacity, but also depended heavily on preserving capacity. The state was in some ways more brittle than a nonstate society; it could be conquered more easily or fall apart through a system failure. In states "resources" increasingly meant more than food or women. It meant those things necessary to continue the violent competition: manpower, technology, infrastructure, key geographic locations, minerals, prestige goods to sustain social differentiation, and so on.

This last characteristic of social differentiation and stratification is key. As a society became more complex, access

TIMELINE

1.5–1.8 million BP	First migration of *Homo* out of Africa into Eurasia
125,000 BP	First migration of modern humans from Africa into Eurasia
60,000 BP	Renewed or resurgent migration of modern humans from Africa
60k–40k BP	Accelerating cognitive development in modern humans
14k–12k BP	Jebel Sahaba cemetery
11,000 BP	Agriculture appearing in the Near East and Anatolia
5500 BCE	Agriculture arriving in central Europe
3100 BCE	Unification of Upper and Lower Egypt

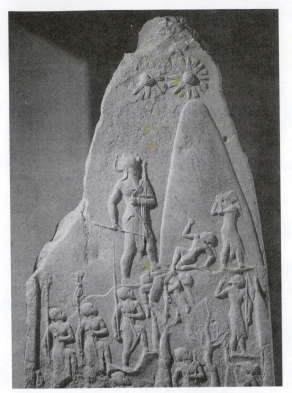

Figure 1.11 The victory stele of Naram-Sin, ca. 2240 BCE.

to power within it narrowed. Small independent communities partially stratified into having "big men," and then, if they subordinated another community, the conqueror's closest associates, or "retinue," also became "big men" relative to the newly conquered. Big men, or (perhaps a better word at this stage) "lords," did not wield power as individuals; they wielded it through their influence over other lords. And every lord in a system of lords retained his personal retinue of armed followers, who were rewarded through the unequal distribution of surplus and spoils, and were used to wield power over the rest of the social pyramid—even as some of those members actively sought entry into the retinue as a form of social mobility. That mass of the population was also increasingly subjected to a program of ritual and cult that directed normative values toward obedience to the lord among lords. Kings were kings because they manipulated both force *and* belief—something spectacularly captured in the victory stele of Naram-Sin, king of the enlarging Akkadian Empire in Mesopotamia from 2254 to 2218 BCE (see Figure 1.11). Here is the king, enlarged beyond life-size, armed and ascending above his defeated enemies, seemingly in communication with his patron god shining at the top of the stele, and himself wearing the horns indicating a divinity bestowed on him at the insistence of his subjects. It was men like this who could proclaim, in this case through a hymn, things like:

> I [King Shulgi of Ur, ca. 2000 BCE] am a king, offspring begotten by a king and borne by a queen . . . . When I sprang up, muscular as a cheetah, galloping like a thoroughbred ass at full gallop, the favor of the god An brought me joy; to my delight the god Enlil spoke favorably about me, and they gave me the sceptre because of my righteousness. I place my foot on the neck of the foreign lands; the fame of my weapons is established as far as the south, and my victory is established in the highlands. . . . I go ahead of the main body of my troops and I clear the terrain for my scouts. I have a positive passion for weapons. Not only do I carry lance and spear, I also know how to handle sling-stones with a sling. The clay bullets, the treacherous pellets that I shoot, fly around like a violent rainstorm. In my rage I do not let them miss.[47]

An emergent state, or, more accurately, the top elites of an emergent state, emphasized the confluence of their coercive power with ritual or sacred power; they constructed an artistic and literary discourse to highlight their successful military activity and to tighten their connection to the divine. Ironically, however, in state warfare the actual physical role of the lords as warriors was losing importance. After all, numbers mattered: enemy cities were fortified, and the role of the aristocratic warrior was shifting from fighting to mobilizing and leading masses of men. In that new role it became all the more important for them to maintain control of the discourse and ensure that they received the credit for victory. The next chapter looks specifically at a variety of ancient states, and at the innovation that prolonged the warrior role of aristocrats while camouflaging the centrality of mobilizing masses of men to serve in countless sieges: the chariot.

Further Reading

Dawson, Doyne. "The Origins of War: Biological and Anthropological Theories." *History and Theory* 35.1 (February 1996): 1–28.

Ferrill, Arther. *The Origins of War: From the Stone Age to Alexander the Great.* Rev. ed. Boulder, CO: Westview, 1997.

Fry, Douglas P., ed. *War, Peace, and Human Nature: The Convergence of Evolutionary and Cultural Views.* New York: Oxford University Press, 2013.

Gat, Azar. *War in Human Civilization.* Oxford: Oxford University Press, 2006.

Ghiglieri, Michael Patrick. *The Dark Side of Man: Tracing the Origins of Male Violence.* Reading, MA: Perseus, 1999.

Guilaine, Jean, and Jean Zammit. *The Origins of War: Violence in Prehistory.* Malden, MA: Blackwell, 2005.

Hamblin, William J. *Warfare in the Ancient Near East to 1600 B.C.: Holy Warriors at the Dawn of History.* New York: Routledge, 2006.

Johnson, Allen W., and Timothy K. Earle. *The Evolution of Human Societies from Foraging Group to Agrarian State.* 2nd ed. Stanford, CA: Stanford University Press, 2000.

Keeley, Lawrence H. *War Before Civilization.* New York: Oxford University Press, 1996.

Kelly, Raymond C. *Warless Societies and the Origins of War.* Ann Arbor: University of Michigan Press, 2000.

Klein, Richard G. "Anatomy, Behavior, and Modern Human Origins." *Journal of World Prehistory* 9.2 (1995): 167–98.

LeBlanc, Steven A., and Katherine E. Register. *Constant Battles: The Myth of the Peaceful, Noble Savage.* New York: St. Martin's, 2003.

Otterbein, Keith F. *How War Began.* College Station: Texas A&M University Press, 2004.

Smith, David Livingstone. *The Most Dangerous Animal: Human Nature and the Origins of War.* New York: St. Martin's, 2007.

Thorpe, I. J. N. "Anthropology, Archaeology, and the Origin of Warfare." *World Archaeology* 35 (2003): 145–65.

Trigger, Bruce G. *Understanding Early Civilizations.* New York: Cambridge University Press, 2007.

Van de Mieroop, Marc. *A History of the Ancient Near East, ca. 3000–323 BC.* 2nd ed. Malden, MA: Blackwell, 2007.

Van der Dennen, J., and V. Falger, eds. *Sociobiology and Conflict: Evolutionary Perspectives on Competition, Cooperation, Violence and Warfare.* London: Chapman & Hall, 1990.

Wrangham, Richard W., and Dale Peterson. *Demonic Males: Apes and the Origins of Human Violence.* Boston: Houghton Mifflin, 1996.

Notes

1. Seville Statement on Violence, Spain, 1986, available at http://www.unesco.org/cpp/uk/declarations/seville.pdf, accessed March 27, 2015.

2. Fear of this political use of "innateness" persists. Jonathan Haas and Matthew Piscitelli, "The Prehistory of Warfare: Misled by Ethnography," in *War, Peace, and Human Nature: The Convergence of Evolutionary and Cultural Views*, ed. Douglas P. Fry (New York: Oxford University Press, 2013), 168–90, esp. pp. 168–69.

3. Lawrence H. Keeley, *War Before Civilization* (New York: Oxford University Press, 1996); Steven A. LeBlanc, "Warfare and Human Nature," in *The Evolution of Violence*, ed. T. K. Shackelford and R. D. Hansen (New York: Springer, 2014), 73–97 (quote 80); Steven A. LeBlanc, "Forager Warfare and Our Evolutionary Past," in *Re-examining a Pacified Past: Violence and Warfare among Hunter-Gatherers*, ed. M. W. Allen and T. L. Jones (Walnut Creek, CA: Left Coast, 2014), 26–46. My thanks to Steven LeBlanc for providing me with an advance copy of his paper and discussing these issues with me.

4. John Horgan, "New Study of Prehistoric Skeletons Undermines Claim That War Has Deep Evolutionary Roots," *Cross-check*, *Scientific American* blog, July 24, 2013, available at http://blogs.scientificamerican.com/cross-check/2013/07/24/new-study-of-prehistoric-skeletons-undermines-claim-that-war-has-deep-evolutionary-roots/, accessed June 4, 2014. For a caustic view of inventors and a useful summary of the issues, see LeBlanc, "Warfare and Human Nature."

5. LeBlanc, "Warfare and Human Nature," 74–75. See also the recent syntheses in Mark W. Allen and Terry L. Jones, eds., *Violence and Warfare among Hunter-Gatherers* (Walnut Creek, CA: Left Coast, 2014), that generally support a long chronology for human conflict.

6. Jason S. Gilchrist, "Female Eviction, Abortion, and Infanticide in Banded Mongooses (*Mungos mungo*): Implications for Social Control of Reproduction and Synchronized Parturition," *Behavioral Ecology* 17.4 (2006): 664–69; T. H. Clutton-Brock et al., "Infanticide and Expulsion of Females in a Cooperative Mammal," *Proceedings: Biological Sciences* 265 (1998): 2291–95; G. Hausfater, "Infanticide: Comparative and Evolutionary Perspectives," *Current Anthropology* 25 (1984): 500–502; Anne E. Pusey and Craig Packer, "Infanticide in Lions," in *Infanticide and Parental Care*, ed. S. Parmigiani, and F. S. vom Saal (Chur, Switzerland: Harwood Academic Press, 1994), 277–300; J. L. Hoogland, "Infanticide in Prairie Dogs: Lactating Females Kill Offspring of Close Kin," *Science* 230.4729 (November 1985): 1037–40.

7. Steven A. LeBlanc and Katherine E. Register, *Constant Battles: The Myth of the Peaceful, Noble Savage* (New York: St. Martin's, 2003), 45.

8. Michael Patrick Ghiglieri, *The Dark Side of Man: Tracing the Origins of Male Violence* (Reading, MA: Perseus, 1999), 174. Recent ethnographic work has also suggested the increased reproductive advantage of warfare among human foraging societies. Luke Glowacki and Richard Wrangham, "Warfare and Reproductive Success in a Tribal Population," *PNAS* 112.2 (2015): 348–53.

9. Michael L. Wilson et al., "Lethal Aggression in *Pan* is Better Explained by Adaptive Strategies than Human Impacts," *Nature* 513 (September 2014): 414–17. Wilson's findings specifically exclude human interference in generating conflict; they find it instead an adaptive strategy "such that

killers ultimately gain fitness benefits by increasing their access to resources such as food or mates." Also John C. Mitani, "Co-operation and Competition in Chimpanzees: Current Understanding and Future Challenges," *Evolutionary Anthropology* 18 (2009): 215–27, esp. p. 220.

10. Richard Wrangham, "Evolution of Coalitionary Killing," *Yearbook of Physical Anthropology* 42 (1999): 1–30, 11; Ghiglieri, *Dark Side of Man*, 171; T. Nishida, et al., "Group Extinction and Female Transfer in Wild Chimpanzees in the Mahale National Park, Tanzania," *Zeitschrift für Tierpsychologie* 67 (1985): 284–301.

11. Simcha Lev-Yadun, Avi Gopher, and Shahal Abbo, "The Cradle of Agriculture," *Science* 288.5471 (June 2000): 1602–3.

12. James Mellaart, *Çatal Hüyük: A Neolithic Town in Anatolia* (New York: McGraw-Hill, 1967), plate 46 (p. 94).

13. Peter Bellwood, *First Farmers: The Origins of Agricultural Societies* (Malden, MA: Blackwell, 2005), 61; Hans Georg K. Gebel, "The Significance of Ba'ja for Early Near Eastern Neolithic Research," *Orient and Occident* 8.1 (2003): 17–19, available online at http://www.exoriente.org/baja/, accessed October 13, 2014; William J. Hamblin, *Warfare in the Ancient Near East to 1600 B.C.: Holy Warriors at the Dawn of History* (New York: Routledge, 2006), 25–27.

14. Clemens Reichel, "Hamoukar," *Oriental Institute 2008–2009 Annual Report*, 77–87, available online at http://oi.uchicago.edu/pdf/08-09_Hamoukar.pdf, accessed June 13, 2011 (quote 80).

15. There is emerging evidence in Jordan and Turkey, however (Wadi Faynan and Göbekli Tepe, respectively), that communal formation centered on ritual sites may have *preceded* true sedentism, and may even have helped cause it.

16. Jean Guilaine and Jean Zammit, *The Origins of War: Violence in Prehistory*, trans. Melanie Hersey (Malden, MA: Blackwell, 2005), 89.

17. Joachim Wahl and Iris Trautmann, "The Neolithic Massacre at Talheim: A Pivotal Find in Conflict Archaeology," in *Sticks, Stones, and Broken Bones: Neolithic Violence in a European Perspective*, ed. Rick Schulting and Linda Fibiger (Oxford: Oxford University Press, 2012), 77–100. This conclusion is supported by a nearly contemporaneous site at Asparn-Schletz in Austria in which the remains of sixty-seven individuals were found in the ditch enclosing the settlement site. The bones show many lethal injuries, and there is a dearth of young women in the assemblage. Maria Teschler-Nicola, "The Early Neolithic site Asparn/Schletz (Lower Austria): Anthropological Evidence of Interpersonal Violence," in Schulting and Fibiger, *Sticks, Stones*, 101–120; Guilaine and Zammit, *Origins of War*, 103–11; George Nash, "Assessing Rank and Warfare-Strategy in Prehistoric Hunter-Gatherer Society: A Study of Representational Warrior Figures in Rock-Art from the Spanish Levant, Southeastern Spain," in *Warfare, Violence and Slavery in Prehistory*, ed. Mike Parker Pearson and I. J. N. Thorpe (Oxford: Archaeopress, 2005), 75–86.

18. Guilaine and Zammit, *Origins of War* 80–81; I. J. N. Thorpe, "Anthropology, Archaeology, and the Origin of Warfare," *World Archaeology* 35 (2003): 157; Jörg Orschiedt, "The Head Burials from Ofnet Cave: An Example of Warlike Conflict in the Mesolithic," in Pearson and Thorpe, *Warfare, Violence and Slavery*, 67–73.

19. Guilaine and Zammit, *Origins of War*, 75–81; Virginia Hutton Estabrook, "Violence and Warfare in the European Mesolithic and Paleolithic," in *Violence and Warfare among Hunter-Gatherers*, ed. Mark W. Allen and Terry L. Jones (Walnut Creek, CA: Left Coast, 2014), 49–69.

20. This work is still unpublished, but is previewed briefly at "The Skeletons of Jebel Sahaba," July 14, 2014, at the *Archaeology*

magazine website, http://www.archaeology
.org/news/2305–140714–egypt-conflict-
cemetery, accessed October 8, 2014. Fred
Wendorf, "A Nubian Final Paleolithic
Graveyard near Jebel Sahaba, Sudan," in
The Prehistory of Nubia, ed. Fred Wendorf
(Dallas, TX: Southern Methodist Univer-
sity Press, 1968), 2:954–995.

21. Virginia Estabrook's work provides a good
summary of how the Mesolithic (in
Europe) is now more accepted as a period
of lethal human conflict, but she and
others argue that it represented a transition from a less conflictual Paleolithic.
Estabrook, "Violence and Warfare."

22. S. Armitage et al., "The Southern Route
'Out of Africa': Evidence for an Early Ex-
pansion of Modern Humans into Arabia,"
Science 331.6016 (January 2011): 453–56;
Chris Stringer, *The Origin of Our Species*
(New York: Penguin Group, 2011), 123,
215, 226, 229–233; Hugo Reyes-Centeno
et al., "Genomic and Cranial Phenotype
Data Support Multiple Modern Human
Dispersals from African and a Southern
Route into Asia," *PNAS* 111.20 (May 20,
2014), 7248–7253, doi:10.1073/pnas
.1323666111. Adam Powell et al., "Late
Pleistocene Demography and the Appearance of Modern Human Behavior," *Science*
324.5932 (June 2009): 1298–1301; Leslie C.
Aiello and R. I. M. Dunbar, "Neocortex
Size, Group Size, and the Evolution of
Language," *Current Anthropology* 34.2
(1993): 184–193. Evidence for even earlier
complex technologies, included hafted
tools made by Neandertals, remains controversial. Paul Peter Anthony Mazza
et al., "A New Paleolithic Discovery:
Tar-Hafted Stone Tools in a European
Mid-Pleistocene Bone-Bearing Bed," *Journal of Archaeological Science* 33 (2006):
1310–1318; Israel Hershkovitz, et al.,
"Levantine Cranium from Manot Cave
(Israel) Foreshadows the First European
Modern Humans," *Nature* (28 January
2015); Tom Higham et al., "The Earliest

Evidence for Anatomically Modern
Humans in Northwestern Europe," *Nature*
479 (24 November 2011): 521–24.

23. Stringer, *Origin*, 115, 219–221; Powell
et al., "Late Pleistocene Demography."
Contrarily, studies focusing entirely on
correlating the size of the neocortex to
the ability to sustain larger social groups
suggest that Neandertals and *H. sapiens*
should have been able to sustain similar
group sizes of around 150, but the archaeological evidence for Neandertals suggests
smaller group sizes in practice. That may
have been a result of resource scarcity in
late Ice Age Europe, requiring smaller
groups for a given subsistence zone.
Aiello and Dunbar, "Neocortex Size";
Matt Grove, Eiluned Pearce, and
R. I. M. Dunbar, "Fission-Fusion and the
Evolution of Hominin Social Systems,"
Journal of Human Evolution 62.2 (2012):
191–200; Chip Walter, *Last Ape Standing*
(New York: Walker, 2013), 107 (for
Neandertal group size of 12–25); Robert
Layton and Sean O'Hara, "Human Social
Evolution: A Comparison of Hunter-
Gatherer and Chimpanzee Social Organi-
zation" (83–114), Sam G. Roberts "Con-
straints on Social Networks" (115–34),
and Matt Grove, "The Archaeology of
Group Size," (391–412), all in *Social Brain,
Distributed Mind*, ed. Robin Dunbar, Clive
Gamble, and John Gowlett (Oxford:
Oxford University Press for the British
Academy, 2010); Brian Hayden,
"Neandertal Social Structure," *Oxford
Journal of Archaeology* 31.1 (2012): 1–26;
Stringer, *Origin*, 116.

24. Recent work in Africa may have pushed the
invention of the atlatl to 70,000 years ago.
Kyle S. Brown et al., "An Early and Enduring Advanced Technology Originating
71,000 Years Ago in South Africa," *Nature*
491 (November 2012): 590–93; Stringer,
Origin, 219; Powell et al., "Late Pleistocene
Demography"; Vania Yotova et al., "An
X-Linked Haplotype of Neandertal Origin

Is Present Among All Non-African Populations," *Molecular Biology and Evolution* 28.7 (2011): 1957–62; Sriram Sankararaman et al., "The Date of Interbreeding between Neandertals and Modern Humans," *PLoS Genetics* 8.10 (October 4, 2012): e1002947, doi:10.1371/journal.pgen .1002947.

25. Guilaine and Zammit, *Origins of War*, 52–60 (the characterization of some of this early rock art as showing human-on-human violence remains contested); Carles Lalueza-Fox et al., "Genetic Evidence for Patrilocal Mating Behavior Among Neandertal Groups," *PNAS* 108.1 (2011): 250–53. The "neighboring group" hypothesis has not been fully published, but was presented by Carles Lalueza-Fox, "Neandertal Paleogenomics and the El Sidrón cave," at the Royal Society conference, Ancient DNA: The First Three Decades, November 18–19, 2013, audio available at https://royalsociety.org/ events/2013/ancient-dna/, accessed October 9, 2014. Note, however, a recent study suggests that immediately prior to the arrival of *H. sapiens*, the *H. neanderthalensis* population underwent a demographic crisis that substantially shrank their population (evidenced by a sharply lowered genetic diversity in the population after 48,000 years ago). Love Dalén et al., "Partial Genetic Turnover in Neandertals: Continuity in the East and Population Replacement in the West," *Molecular Biology and Evolution* 29.8 (2012): 1893–97.

26. LeBlanc, "Warfare and Human Nature," 78; Haas and Piscitelli, "The Prehistory of Warfare," 182–83, surveys the published results of 2,930 *H. sapiens* skeletal remains from some four hundred sites dating prior to 10,000 BP and finds only a small number with trauma. This includes, however, many remains that are only very partially preserved, and obviously misses any nonskeletal trauma. It is also true, however, that skeletal trauma can often be interpreted as violence short of war, or even as mortuary ritual. See, for example, S. Prat et al. "The Oldest Anatomically Modern Humans from Far Southeast Europe: Direct Dating, Culture and Behavior," *PLoS ONE* 6.6 (2011): e20834. For early cannibalism: Elizabeth Culotta, "Neanderthals Were Cannibals, Bones Show," *Science* 286.5437 (October 1999): 18–19; Yolanda Fernández-Jalvo, J. Carlos Diez, Isabel Cáceres, and Jordi Rosell, "Human Cannibalism in the early Pleistocene of Europe (Gran Dolina, Sierra de Atapuerca, Burgos, Spain)," *Journal of Human Evolution* 37 (1999): 591–622; Eudald Carbonell et al., "Cultural Cannibalism as a Paleoeconomic System in the European Lower Pleistocene," *Current Anthropology* 51 (2010): 539–50; Silvia M. Bello, Simon A. Parfitt, and Chris B. Stringer, "Earliest Directly-Dated Human Skull Cups," *PLoS ONE* 6.2 (2011): e17026. For Neandertal-Human coexistence: R. E. Wood et al., "The Chronology of the Earliest Upper Palaeolithic in Northern Iberia: New Insights from L'Arbreda, Labeko Koba and La Viña," *Journal of Human Evolution* 69 (April 2014): 91–109; University of the Basque Country, "Neanderthals and Cro-magnons Did Not Coexist on the Iberian Peninsula, Suggests Re-analysis of Dating," *ScienceDaily*, April 14, 2014, http://www.sciencedaily .com/releases/2014/04/140414092000.htm, accessed June 4, 2014. For Neandertal-AMH violence: Walter, *Last Ape Standing*, 117; Fernando V. Ramirez Rozzi et al., "Cutmarked Human Remains Bearing Neandertal Features and Modern Human Remains Associated with the Aurignacian at Les Rois," *Journal of Anthropological Sciences* 87 (2009): 153–85; Steven E. Churchill et al., "Shanidar 3 Neandertal Rib Puncture Wound and Paleolithic Weaponry," *Journal of Human Evolution* 57.2 (2009): 163–78; Stringer, *Origin*, 147–48, 155.

27. Samuel Bowles, "Did Warfare Among Ancestral Hunter-Gatherers Affect the Evolution of Human Social Behaviors?" *Science* 324.5932 (June 2009): 1297, elaborated in Samuel Bowles and Herbert Gintis, *A Cooperative Species: Human Reciprocity and its Evolution* (Princeton, NJ: Princeton University Press, 2011). Also: Jung-Kyoo Choi and Samuel Bowles, "The Coevolution of Parochial Altruism and War," *Science* 318.5850 (October 2007): 636–40.

28. Even Kelly's argument downplaying the selective effect of violent competition among foragers acknowledges its presence as a possibility: "The potential for lethal intergroup violence is an ambient condition of existence in both cases [chimpanzees and human unsegmented foragers], and we can conclude that this potentiality has been an integral contextual feature of human (hominid) evolution from the beginning of the Paleolithic period to the ethnographic present. Three responses to this condition are noted in both cases: (i) avoidance, (ii) positive engagement in friendly relations with neighboring local groups, and (iii) aggression that may result in territorial gain or loss." Raymond C. Kelly, "The Evolution of Lethal Intergroup Violence," *PNAS* 102.43 (2005): 15294–98 (quote 15296).

29. A good summary for nonbiologists is Azar Gat, *War in Human Civilization* (Oxford: Oxford University Press, 2006).

30. Martin A. Nowak, *Super Cooperators: Altruism, Evolution, and Why We Need Each Other to Succeed* (New York: Free Press, 2011), especially 83, 110–12; Edward O. Wilson, *The Social Conquest of Earth* (New York: Liveright, 2012), 41–43, 51–58, 140–42, 148–57, 166 and 224, 241 (quotes); Stringer, *Origins*, 154–55; Peter Turchin, *War and Peace and War: The Life Cycles of Imperial Nations* (New York: Pi, 2005), 7, 132–34; Steven Pinker, *The Better Angels of Our Nature: Why Violence Has*

Declined (New York: Viking, 2011); Anthony C. Lopez, Rose McDermott, and Michael Bang Petersen, "States in Mind: Evolution, Coalitional Psychology, and International Politics," *International Security* 36.2 (2011): 48–83.

31. J. Kiley Hamlin, Karen Wynn, and Paul Bloom, "Social Evaluation by Preverbal Infants," *Nature* 450 (November 2007): 557–60.

32. Bruce M. Knauft, "The Human Evolution of Cooperative Interest," in *A Natural History of Peace*, ed. Thomas Gregor (Nashville, TN: Vanderbilt University Press, 1996), 71–94 (quote 77). There has been a surge of work on the evolution of human cooperation, much of which, however, downplays the role of conflict. Fry, *War, Peace, and Human Nature*; John Edward Terrell, *A Talent for Friendship: Rediscovery of a Remarkable Trait* (New York: Oxford University Press, 2015) (thanks to John Terrell for sharing an early proof with me); Douglas P. Fry, "The Evolution of Cooperation: What's War Got to Do With It?" *Reviews in Anthropology* 42.2 (2013): 102–21.

33. Bowles and Gintis, *A Cooperative Species*, 110.

34. Wilson, *Social Conquest*, 195 (on gene-culture coevolution); Gat, *War in Human Civilization*, outlines a slightly different version of "man the competitor" and inspired my thinking here.

35. Gat, *War in Human Civilization*, 153.

36. Steven A. LeBlanc, "Warfare and the Development of Social Complexity: Some Demographic and Environmental Factors," in *The Archaeology of Warfare: Prehistories of Raiding and Conquest*, ed. Elizabeth N. Arkush and Mark W. Allen (Gainesville: University Press of Florida, 2006), 437–68 (esp. 438–45).

37. Bruce G. Trigger, *Understanding Early Civilizations* (New York: Cambridge University Press, 2007), 42.

38. Especially when nudged along by the brief return of glacial conditions known as the

"Younger Dryas," roughly 11,000 to 9,500 BCE.

39. Mary C. Stiner, "Thirty Years on the 'Broad Spectrum Revolution' and Paleolithic Demography," *PNAS* 98 (June 2001): 6993–96.

40. Trigger, *Understanding Early Civilizations*, 44.

41. LeBlanc and Register, *Constant Battles*, 111–13, 131–33.

42. Bellwood, *First Farmers*; Ron Pinhasi, Joaquim Fort, and Albert J. Ammerman, "Tracing the Origin and Spread of Agriculture in Europe," *PLOS Biology* 3.12 (2005): e410; W. Haak et al., "Ancient DNA from European Early Neolithic Farmers Reveals Their Near Eastern Affinities," PLoS Biology 8.11 (2010): e1000536; Mark Golitko and Lawrence H. Keeley, "Beating Ploughshares Back into Swords: Warfare in the *Linearbandkeramik*," *Antiquity* 81 (2007): 332–42.

43. Joyce Marcus, "The Archaeological Evidence for Social Evolution," *Annual Review of Anthropology* 37 (2008): 251–66; Charles S. Spencer and Elsa M. Redmond, "Primary State Formation in Mesoamerica," *Annual Review of Anthropology* 33 (2004): 173–99; Charles Stanish, "The Origin of State Societies in South America," *Annual Review of Anthropology* 30 (2001): 41–64.

44. Gat, *War in Human Civilization*, 251 (quote). Much of the theory of social complexity summarized here is derived from Gat, as well as Trigger, *Understanding Early Civilizations*. This emphasis on the role of conflict has been supported by mathematical models proposed in Peter Turchin et al., "War, Space, and the Evolution of Old World Complex Societies," *PNAS* 110.41 (2014): 16384–89; Peter Turchin, "Warfare and the Evolution of Social Complexity: A Multilevel-Selection Approach," *Structure and Dynamics* 4.3 (2011): http://www.escholarship.org/uc/item/7j11945r.

45. Hamblin, *Warfare in the Ancient Near East*, 318–19; Donald B. Redford, ed., *The Oxford Encyclopedia of Ancient Egypt* (Oxford: Oxford University Press, 2001), 2:494 (s.v. "Narmer"); text description of both sides in the latter.

46. Toby Wilkinson, *Genesis of the Pharaohs* (London: Thames & Hudson, 2003), 69, 79.

47. "A Praise Poem of Culgi (Culgi B)," Document 2.4.2.02 in J. A. Black, G. Cunningham, E. Fluckiger-Hawker, E. Robson, and G. Zólyomi, *The Electronic Text Corpus of Sumerian Literature*, http://www-etcsl.orient.ox.ac.uk/cgi-bin/etcsl.cgi?text=t.2.4.2.02&charenc=j#), accessed June 23, 2011.

2

Carts, Chariots,
Catastrophe, and Cavalry

3500–700 BCE

Kings and Carts • Inventing the Chariot: Tribes, Horses, and Bronze on the Steppe, 6000–1600 BCE • Chariots and the Urban Politics of the Near East and Egypt, 1500–1200 BCE • Chariots under Heaven: China, 1200–400 BCE • Gods and Heroes: The Chariot in India and Europe • Catastrophe, Cavalry, and the Decline of the Chariot in the Near East

CHAPTER 1 PRESENTED a somewhat pessimistic image of the history of human interaction. It argued for a perhaps surprising ubiquity and long history of significant lethal human conflict. That seeming pessimism, however, was required by the very long time frame of the argument. Conflict was *not* constant throughout the whole of human evolutionary history, but it *was* threatening enough and endemic enough to play a significant role in both biological and cultural evolution, fostering the increasing complexity of human social organization, up to and including the state itself. As also suggested in the last chapter, however, cooperation was a key component in the evolved response to conflict. Cooperation is more than social complexity, however. It also includes exchange between groups that otherwise considered each other "strangers"—not necessarily enemies, but certainly "not us." As we will see in this chapter, military innovations do not move only through conflict or conquest. They also move as ideas or objects through trade, imitation, and other forms of exchange. The chariot, once conceived by historians as a literal vehicle of conquest, one that moved *by* conquest, when examined more carefully can be seen as a combination of techniques, technologies, and ideas that moved around Eurasia through a variety of means and with surprising twists. Wherever it went, however, the chariot reinforced social differentiation. Furthermore, although invented on the steppe among tribal peoples, it eventually proved of greater military benefit to states, a social organization better adapted to mobilize the resources necessary to build large numbers of chariots.

To explain innovation is never easy. Where do ideas come from? Is it simply that necessity really is the mother of invention? In this chapter, as elsewhere, we will explore the context in which particular innovations emerged, but it often proves easier to explain why other societies, encountering the new idea or new technology, then adopted (or adapted) it. This chapter will use the best available archaeological and linguistic evidence to explain the domestication of the horse, the earliest riding of horses, and ultimately the origins of the chariot (really the chariot *system*) in the Pontic-Caspian and Central Asian steppe. That invention occurred in the context of steppe tribes' interaction with the emergent states of Mesopotamia, which quickly adopted the chariot to replace their own war carts—sometimes by simply hiring both the chariot and the charioteer from off the steppe. We then examine the Near East and Egypt to explore in some detail how the chariot functioned culturally and militarily, followed by a shorter look at the parallels and differences in the rest of Eurasia. As is often the case in this book, we will find that people filtered their response to the chariot and the assorted technologies that it required through a cultural lens, but they also reacted with conscious calculations regarding its military potential, and were ultimately limited by the material capacity of their society to sustain the new technology.

It must be emphasized that this chapter is *not* a summary of Bronze Age warfare in all its complexity in all of these places. The chariot is a revealing window, but it was not the be-all and end-all of war in that era, a truth to which we will return at various points. Finally, it must be said that there is significant scholarly disagreement on a number of the subjects covered here. The first part of this chapter is based on archaeological work in the steppes of the former Soviet Union. That work is only now becoming widely known, and in some cases it contradicts the conventional wisdom on matters such as Greek origins, the Mitanni, the first *riding* of horses, and more. There remains room for debate, but this chapter represents what can be known from the available evidence.

KINGS AND CARTS

A puzzling object appears in bright colors on several surviving artifacts from the dawn of the Near Eastern state, specifically the competing city-states of Sumer in Mesopotamia around 2500 BCE. For someone familiar with the chariots of a later era, the object may not seem so puzzling, until one looks closer. The carts (not true chariots) shown in Figures 2.1 and 2.2 appear on two famous artifacts, each intended to celebrate the sovereignty and power of a Sumerian king. These carts are clearly part of an army, and although shown operating in conjunction with infantry, they are intended to convey a superiority of power and resources. In the case of the Stele of Vultures, for example, only the king is shown riding in the cart. What makes these images puzzling is the unclear utility of these vehicles. What might they have been good for?

Figure 2.1 The Stele of Vultures, ca. 2440 BCE. A monument celebrating the victory of the city of Lagash over Umma in Mesopotamia.

Drawn by donkeys or donkey-onager hybrids, they would have been slow and uncomfortable, bouncing over even the smoothest terrain on unsprung solid wooden wheels. Modern tests have suggested a top speed of 10–12 miles per hour, equivalent to a man's running pace, although slower than human sprinting speed. Furthermore, the four-wheeled carts lacked pivoting front wheels, making sharp turns all but impossible. Finally, lacking missile weapons, the soldiers mounted on these vehicles seemed to have had no other function than to protect the other passengers.[1]

This often-cited "precursor" to the chariot, for all its apparent frailties and weaknesses, was nevertheless important to the history of the true chariot because of the way it embedded prestige in the act of riding in a cart. The animal/vehicle/harness combination was expensive, so that few could afford it, and it

Figure 2.2 Sumerian War Cart depicted on the Standard of Ur (detail), ca. 2600 BCE.

lifted its rider above the battlefield. We also know that such carts were used in ritual processions of both kings and the statues of gods. The vehicles themselves shared in the glory of their passengers and cargo. Historian William Hamblin has suggested that the military effectiveness of the war cart may even have resided in this cultural perception of the cart as the conveyor of divine power. One's arrival on the battlefield literally meant the approach of a godlike enemy.[2]

There is little doubt that war carts mattered on the battlefield to the Sumerians and their successors in Mesopotamia and westward into Syria. We have textual evidence for as many as sixty in an army from around 2400 BCE, and the carts and their teams were kept in special stables. An enemy familiar with them, however, would have had little trouble either resisting them, killing the slow-moving team, or dodging their slow charge and even slower turn. The truly significant military innovations in domesticating the horse (rather than donkeys), riding on horseback, and even chariot design occurred out on the steppe, not in the states of the Near East. So let us turn back the page and examine the archaeological and linguistic evidence for developments on the steppe, supplemented toward the end of this story with textual evidence from the emergent states.

INVENTING THE CHARIOT: TRIBES, HORSES, AND BRONZE ON THE STEPPE, 6000–1600 BCE

Chapter 1 described how Neolithic farmers from Anatolia migrated west into the Balkans, from which they and/or their "Neolithic package" continued to spread out across Europe. Farming and domesticated cattle also diffused east from the Balkans, north of the Black Sea, crossing the Dniester and then the Dnieper Rivers from 5800 to 5000 BCE (Map 1.2). As it spread farther east, however, especially as it edged into the grasslands of the Pontic-Caspian steppe, cattle keeping and herding replaced farming. To the foragers who already lived on the edges of the steppe, the arrival of sheep, goats, and cattle meant a tremendous increase in "storable" wealth. The archaeological record shows a clear increase in social differentiation and complexity at that time—not into states, but certainly into "tribes" led by distinctive chiefs. This tribal-herding subsistence system spread further east to the Ural River basin, where, for a time, it stopped. Crucially, this zone was already home to the largest concentration of wild horses in the world. The indigenous peoples had hunted these horses for centuries, but the newly arriving pastoralists quickly understood the advantages of herding horses for subsistence. Horses, unlike cattle, could forage for themselves in the winter, using their hooves to dig through the snow to find grass (a trait we will return to in chapter 5). This domestication of horses for meat would have bred them simultaneously for tameness and size, and within a few hundred years the horses were being ridden.[3]

Close examination of the teeth of horse skeletons has demonstrated conclusively that they were being fitted with a bridle and bit and ridden by eastern steppe dwellers, probably to hunt other horses, no later than 3700 to 3500 BCE (evidence is from a site at Botai in northern Kazakhstan). Genetic studies of horse domestication suggest that this first direct evidence likely reflects several hundred years of development that had begun further west on the steppe in what is now Ukraine, southwest Russia and west Kazakhstan. Riding horses had several effects. It immediately increased the herd size that could be managed by one person. Increasing the herd size, however, demanded more pasture, possibly increasing regional conflict over land. It also dramatically increased the returns from predatory raids. Riding raiders could now appear with less warning, attack and retreat more rapidly, and use their horses to carry or herd the spoils of their success. Note that this is not necessarily an argument for "cavalry"—these early raiders did not have to, and probably did not, fight on horseback. Merely being carried there and away was sufficient. These steppe riders, raiders, and warriors were in continuous interaction with the agricultural world to their west, which they raided for glory, plunder, and women. When pressed by climatic oscillations on the steppe, they also settled in new territories.[4]

Chariots on the Grass

The steppe dwellers' interaction with farmers took on a new importance when the farmers of Mesopotamia began making bronze tools and weapons sometime early in the fourth millennium BCE and simultaneously took the first steps toward true state formation. Objects of early arsenical bronze (copper alloyed with arsenic rather than tin) from Uruk in Mesopotamia appear in a chief's grave of the Maikop culture on the northern edge of the Caucasus mountains sometime between 3700 and 3200 BCE. The Maikop people were farmers, living between the emerging states to their south and tribal herdsmen to the north. They took advantage of their position to become middlemen in long-distance trade, something for which they may have invented the wheeled cart. A Maikop grave from this era preserves evidence of cart wheels, probably the first such evidence in Europe. Even if the Maikop traders did not invent the wagon, it seems clear that they introduced it to the steppe horse riders. Evidence of wheeled carts or wagons mushrooms across Europe and the upper Near East after about 3400 BCE. The wagon was immediately useful on the steppe, and a climate shift toward aridity at that time may also have encouraged the herders to pursue more consistent, longer-range seasonal movement as a way to feed their herds. This wagon-dwelling, horse-riding, long-distance nomadic lifestyle quickly spread around the western steppe and penetrated into eastern Europe from 3300 to 2500 BCE.

This new population of mobile pastoral nomads, riding bitted horses, who were adopting metal goods and metalworking technologies from the cities of Mesopotamia, Iran, and the Indus, while simultaneously increasingly serving as the *source* for those metals (note the copper and tin sources identified in Map 2.1), generated friction, conflict, and advantage-seeking. At some point in this environment of intensified competition among steppe residents, some of those peoples just southeast of the Urals began to fortify their settlements (probably seasonal winter sites). Soon thereafter, not later than about 2100 BCE, some among them, perhaps having seen a Mesopotamian war cart, grasped the advantages of being elevated above the battlefield, standing to fight, and using their horses to draw the vehicle quickly, while using only two wheels, a design that allowed the vehicle to turn much more quickly. In short, they developed a true chariot.

The evidence for these surmises comes from the Sintashta site (see Map 2.1), on the eastern edge of the Central Asian steppe. This fortified village not only provides the first evidence of a true chariot, but also evidence of intensive bronze working in every single residence within its walls. The Sintashta people had trade networks with the regional urban centers of Bactria and Margiana (BMAC on Map 2.1), and through them with the more distant Bronze Age states of Elam, Ur, and Harappa. Stimulated by the trade possibilities and the continued climatic drying out of the steppe, regional warfare escalated. Weapon types proliferated (including, perhaps for the first time in the steppe, the javelin), and the spoked, two-wheeled chariot appeared (see Figure 2.3), ridden by warriors using javelins, and controlling their horses with bits and cheek pieces designed to elicit tight turns. The earliest Near Eastern depictions of this combination (bitted horses pulling lightweight, spoked, two-wheeled chariots) date to around 1900 BCE—two hundred years later. Near Eastern carts, even two-wheeled carts, were much older, but

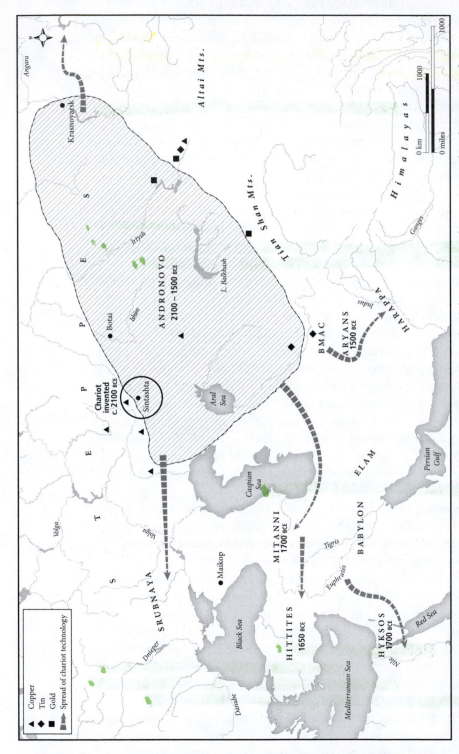

Map 2.1 The emergence and initial spread of the chariot, ca. 2100-1500 BCE. The chariot seems to have originated in the steppe in the Andronovo culture area, possibly at Sintashta. The map shows other key sites at Maikop and Botai, as well as the peoples and states through which it passed and was adopted. Key copper and tin sources are also marked. Much of the data here is based on Anthony, *The Horse*, Fig. 16.1.

58

SINTASHTA GRAVE 30

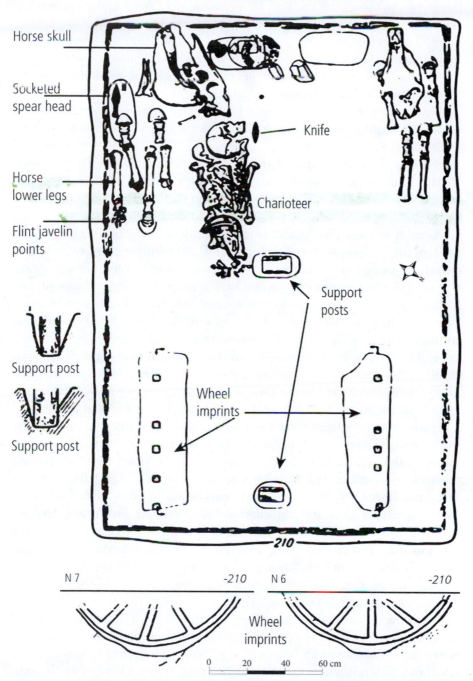

Horse skull

Socketed spear head

Horse lower legs

Flint javelin points

Support post

Support post

Knife

Charioteer

Support posts

Wheel imprints

N 7   −210   N 6   −210

Wheel imprints

0   20   40   60 cm

Figure 2.3 Excavation of the chariot grave at Sintashta, ca. 2000 BCE (in modern Russia). Among the earliest evidence for a two-wheeled, spoked chariot.

this particular combination of technologies greatly increased the cost and therefore the associated prestige. In archaeologist David Anthony's estimation, even for the steppe inventors,

> chariots were supreme advertisements of wealth; difficult to make and requiring great athletic skill *and* a team of specially trained horses to drive, they were available only to those who could delegate much of their daily labor to hired herders. A chariot was material proof that the driver was able to fund a substantial alliance or was supported by someone who had the means.[5]

Analysis of the grave goods of the Sintashta people affirms an increasing identification of the horse with war, men, and, above all, *privilege*. This close cultural identification between the chariot and aristocratic prestige followed the technology into the agricultural world and there sank deep roots.

As with wagons, chariot technology rapidly diffused around the region, perhaps urged along by its military impact. Unlike with wagons, some of that movement occurred by conquest, although copying had a more significant effect, as the technology was carried by the migration of small groups, not conquering hordes. Different groups around the Sintashta site copied many aspects of their material culture, and over time developed into two different cultural "packages," known as the Srubnaya and Andronovo (the term package is used here to imply that although there was a shared regional material culture, they were not necessarily a single ethnically related people). The former spread westward to the Dnieper. The latter rapidly moved across the eastern steppe to the Altai Mountains and south to the edges of Bactria and Margiana, intensifying material exchanges and cultural interchange with the settled peoples there. They also asserted control over the rich copper and tin mines in the Zeravshan valley (see Map 2.1). By 1600 BCE, peoples carrying the Andronovo cultural package had displaced, if not destroyed, the Bactrian/Margiana towns. Within a hundred years some of these Indo-European-speaking, expert metalworking, chariot-riding warriors with a now deep experience of urban civilization appeared as the Mitanni dynasty, controlling the non-Indo-European-speaking Hurrians of northern Syria and southern Armenia. Another branch, known to us from the Indic Rig Veda texts as Aryans, moved east into Punjab to displace the remnants of the Harappan civilization (see Map 2.3 on page 75).

An important caveat is required here. Myths and racist narratives of Aryan invasions have a violent history that continues to resonate among fringe believers in white European "natural" superiority. Understandable academic reluctance to lend credence to those myths has created a kind of Aryan antimyth, resistant to the recent archaeological work briefly surveyed here. That work suggests that there was indeed a kind of explosion of Indo-European chariot riders from the steppe. Note, however, that their "wave" of "conquests" was of relatively short range, extending from the Pontic-Caspian steppe to the Indus and eastern Anatolia. In the latter case they merely replaced one dynasty with their own, quickly blending with the local population. Other movements of the chariot represent the transmission of an idea rather than the movement of a single people.

In fact, although the artistic and literary evidence in Anatolia and Syria suggests that the chariot had a dramatic impact as a technological system, it actually argues *against* the disruptive arrival of conquerors. What is more likely is that the idea, probably accompanied by a limited number of mercenary experts, trickled through the Armenian mountains and was adopted more or less simultaneously throughout the region, initially on a small scale. The horse itself had already arrived in the urban Near East by 2100 BCE: tellingly, in Uruk texts the first word for horse was "ass from the mountains."[6] From just after 2000 BCE, a few artistic representations of spoked, two-wheeled chariots materialize around the Near East. Only after about 1850 BCE do there appear a wider assortment of images from Syria and Anatolia of such chariots carrying warriors armed with bows, and even firing those bows from inside the chariot (Figure 2.4).[7]

Figure 2.4 Cylinder seal, Syria, ca. 1750-1600 BCE, showing a two-wheeled, spoked chariot and archer.

Although the Sintashta chariot riders had relied on javelins, as had the Sumerian war-cart riders, this new combination of the chariot with the composite recurve bow, itself apparently long available in the Near East as a prestige weapon, was the weapon system that would spread through the Near East and somewhat later to Egypt. We will return to this bow technology in Chapter 5, but a brief word is required here. The earliest and simplest bows, called "self bows," were constructed from a single homogenous stave of wood. Incremental improvements in power were made by wood selection and seasoning, but serious increases in power came mostly from thickening and/or lengthening the stave (and thus the length of the draw—thus the "longbow"). Bows the height of a standing man would be awkward at best in a chariot. A "recurve" bow used geometry to compress the length of the stave into a series of curves opposed to the draw, increasing its power relative to its length. A "composite" bow combined materials with different compressive or recoiling strengths, usually in a recurved shape, dramatically increasing the power of the bow and reducing the energy lost to stave vibration. In the ancient and medieval worlds, a composite bow was made from sinew glued to a wood core, which was in turn glued to an inner layer of horn. This produced a bow of remarkable power, one that easily matched the range of the longer (and cheaper) self bows used by infantry. The main disadvantages of the composite bow were its vulnerability to moisture and its labor cost, which tended to limit its numbers (relative to a force of infantry). A small force of chariots, however, with charioteers firing a composite bow, could be a formidable combination of firepower, speed, and intimidation.[8]

Exactly how this new combination came about and how it spread into the Near East are unclear. We know that it occurred in the Middle Bronze Age, roughly 1900–1600 BCE, and the Mitanni/Hurrians and the Hittites were key players. The earliest images we have of spoked, two-wheeled chariots in the Near East come almost exclusively from contexts closely or directly associated with these two groups. The Hurrians were an assortment of peoples emerging as a series of smaller states in the upper reaches of the Tigris and Euphrates Rivers around 1800 BCE, but who eventually were ruled by an intrusive aristocracy known as the Mitanni. The Hittites of central Anatolia coalesced into a powerful state by around 1650 BCE. In neither case does there seem to have been an "invasion" or conquest of chariot riders from the steppe. The technology seems to have filtered in, accompanied by a few experts, and to have found ready acceptance among societies long familiar with war carts. One theory is that both the Hittites and the Mitanni were hired in as mercenaries from off the steppe, very likely because of their skill with chariots. The Hurrians, for example, originally from the hills and mountains separating Mesopotamia from the steppe, and thus in touch with both the steppe and urban Mesopotamia, may have brought in their future rulers initially as mercenaries. The Mitanni spoke an Indo-European language, probably arrived from the Andronovo cultural zone, and referred to their warrior elites as the *maryannu*, meaning "chariot warrior" (see Map 2.1). These early developments are shrouded by an absence of documents from the "dark age" surrounding 1600 BCE, but by 1550 BCE the Mitanni had asserted dynastic control over a Hurrian state and expanded it.

The Mitanni-ruled Hurrians and the Hittites competed with each other both before and after the end of the Middle Bronze Age around 1600. Both pushed south and east, generating conflict and further population movements. The Hittites, among their activities, sacked Babylon itself in 1595, and thus helped create a brief dark age ("dark" because of the cessation of Babylonian record-keeping). Furthermore, the process of Hittite and Hurrian/Mitanni state formation and conflict may have pushed other peoples southward into Palestine, possibly carrying chariot technology with them. We know that they in turn displaced the so-called Hyksos peoples from Palestine into Egypt, and the Hyksos arrived in Egypt with the bow-chariot combination (and perhaps even the improved composite recurve bow, as well as more substantial armor and helmets). The Hyksos established their own dynasty controlling the north of Egypt beginning around 1670 BCE. Like the debate over the Aryan movement into India (discussed below), the nature of the Hyksos movement is disputed: Was it conquest based on the possession of new weapons or was it simply a migration into a weakened state? The records here, as for India, are inadequate, but it is at the very least a remarkable coincidence that a new ruler arrived at the same time as a new military system in both Egypt and India. What is clear, when textual sources resumed around 1500, is that true chariots had by then become a sine qua non for warfare throughout the Near East, Egypt, and beyond.[9]

Why that should be the case is an interesting question. The usefulness of even this new form of chariot remains something of a mystery and demands further explanation.

CHARIOTS AND THE URBAN POLITICS OF THE NEAR EAST AND EGYPT, 1500–1200 BCE

Context—social, cultural, political, and more—is essential to understanding the reception of a new military idea or technology. To understand the appeal of the chariot in the middle of the second millennium BCE, we need to examine the region as a whole. The Mesopotamian basin, Anatolia, Syria-Palestine, and Egypt had been divided into competing states and even imperial systems for over 1,500 years. The elites of these urban agricultural societies legitimated their rule by claiming divine power and authority. Good agricultural land was at a premium throughout the region; in many places substantial amounts of labor had been invested in irrigation. Rulers used war to control territory and the labor on it, but success in war also conveyed the impression of divine favor. We have seen how Near Eastern rulers had used war carts over the preceding thousand years, but the prevalence of walled cities (outside of Egypt) in this contest for territory and labor demanded large numbers of infantry and a concomitant expertise in sieges. Centralized authority fragmented badly in the brief dark age after 1600 BCE, but from 1500 BCE larger and more coherent regional states re-emerged, coalescing into a system of great powers (especially Egypt, Babylonia, Assyria, Elam, the Hittites, and the Mittani), who communicated with each other in a shared diplomatic language, married into each other's families, traded extensively by sea and land for ores and other prestige goods, warred over boundary zones between them, and based their military superiority—at least in their discourse—on the possession and use of armies of chariots.

But what did chariots really do within this military system? Territorial conquest had long required sieges, and sieges required infantry to surround the cities and assault the walls. Charioteers, even armed with a bow, contributed little to a siege. Furthermore, despite the remarkable sophistication and complexity of the bentwood construction used in the most advanced chariots, it remained an extremely difficult proposition to maintain one's balance in a moving, springless, open-backed vehicle, moving at the gallop across unpaved ground, while using both hands to fire a bow (although in those chariots with the axle at the rear of the car the draft pole may have provided some shock absorption). As with war carts, the initial impulse to adopt the true chariot probably was cultural: chariots reinforced the elite status of the aristocratic warriors granted the privilege to ride in them. This tentative conclusion is suggested by the small size of Middle Bronze Age Anatolian chariot forces (forty chariots here, eighty there, perhaps as many as one or two hundred). These numbers are not that different from the number of war carts in earlier Sumerian armies. But this new speedier chariot may have been a good deal more frightening when encountered on the battlefield, especially equipped with the bow, rather than the old carts' javelins. When powerful states reemerged in the Late Bronze Age around 1500 BCE we begin to see much larger chariot forces in all of the Near Eastern states and in Egypt.[10]

So what did a Late Bronze Age (roughly 1500–1200 BCE) chariot battle look like? Two scenarios can be considered: chariot versus infantry, and chariot versus chariot. In the former, even a small number of the new chariots would present a truly frightening spectacle when bearing down at the gallop on infantry, especially if, as some historians argue, the infantry of the time tended to be mostly untrained conscripts grouped around a small core of more professional palace guards. More likely, however, chariots would drive to within bowshot of infantry, pause, launch a flight of arrows, and then reposition for another flight, and so on, with relative impunity. Some modern reconstructions have suggested that an archer could indeed fire a bow while moving, even at speeds up to 28 km per hour. If the infantry countercharged, the chariots could simply drive away. If the infantry wavered and appeared about to break, however, then the chariots could charge and enact the oft-depicted scenes of running over dead and dying enemies (see Figure 2.5). The major exception here would be if those infantry were armed with bows, which could wreak havoc among charging horses, while also probably forcing standing chariots to remain at the edge of their range. But in general the best counter to the chariot seemed to be other chariots—especially since that placed the elite riders in a direct contest with their elite counterparts. Chariots encountering each other likely avoided closing,

Figure 2.5 An Egyptian chariot, ca. 1340 BCE. A wooden chest depicting Tutankhamun in his chariot, riding over his enemies and firing a bow. From the tomb of Tutankhamun, Valley of the Kings, Thebes, Egypt.

choosing instead to circle in place, loosing arrows at enemy chariots, in a generally indecisive way. In this scenario chariots were like the cavalry of later eras: their effectiveness derived from good timing and using them in appropriate combinations with infantry.[11]

Much has been made of the supposed differences between Late Bronze Age Hittite and Egyptian chariots. Egyptian reliefs of the Battle of Kadesh (1274 BCE) show Hittite chariots structurally similar to the Egyptian ones, but carrying three rather than two men, a driver, a shield bearer, and a third warrior sometimes shown with a lance perhaps seven feet long. Contemporary and later representations of Hittite chariots, however, show two men, one with a bow. Furthermore, the uniformity of the Egyptian portrayal of Hittites at Kadesh may have been an artistic way to differentiate Hittite from Egyptian. An army of lance-armed chariots fighting bow-armed chariots would have had a very different dynamic than that described here, but there is good reason to doubt the usefulness or even physical possibility of using a spear or lance from within the cart of a moving chariot (except in self-defense against enemy infantrymen).[12]

The discussion thus far has avoided the question of why a battle would be fought in the first place, given the prevalence of sieges. The answer for this era, like other periods similarly dominated by fortresses and sieges, is that an army en route to lay siege is often most vulnerable while still en route—provided the defender has the forces to meet the attacker in the field. Since infantry were the key to the eventual siege, having chariots to defeat the enemy's infantry, or to defeat the chariots that were protecting that infantry, made good sense. Chariots were *not* the sole determinant of victory, but an army without them would have had a severe disadvantage in open battle.

War carts could have done none of the things that made chariots so useful. But war carts had prepared the cultural ground for accepting chariots as a new platform for elite display. The chariots' increasingly apparent usefulness, possibly even decisiveness, however, meant that elites began to calculate the value of increasing their numbers. New Kingdom Egypt (1550–1069 BCE), established after the ouster of the Hyksos rulers in the north, rapidly incorporated chariots into the army in just this way. Chariots first fit perfectly into an increasingly martial ethos for Egypt's rulers, for whom, in one historian's estimation, "the mastery of the art of warfare [now] was considered a paradigm of kingship and essential criterion for royal succession."[13] The chariot proved a natural platform for royal display (see Figure 2.5):

"Then his Majesty appeared on the chariot like Mont [the god of war] in his might. He drew his bow while holding four arrows together in his fist. Thus he rode northward shooting at [the copper targets] . . . each arrow coming out at the back of its target while he attacked the next."[14]

The rulers' need for military glory led to a greater centralization of the Egyptian forces. The usefulness of the new chariots in Egypt's expansionist wars into Palestine and Syria led to a massive expansion of their numbers, so that the numbers of chariot crew involved far exceeded the ranks of the available aristocrats. More professional, lower-status soldiers became charioteers, and by doing so they achieved a new prestige and status.

The increase of numbers was significant. Allied Syrians and Palestinians fighting the Egyptians at the Battle of Megiddo in 1457 BCE seem to have had two very finely decorated chariots for the prince of Megiddo, thirty more finely worked chariots for the allied princes, and then 892 more regular chariots for what the Egyptian source calls "his wretched army."[15] This ranked pyramid of chariot quality and cost, compared to the *total* chariot count for Middle Bronze Age forces recounted above, seems to reflect the addition of a whole new social layer of chariot riders, designed to bulk up the numbers. At Kadesh, each side may have had as many as 3,500 chariots. These specific numbers remain debatable, but the magnitude of expansion in the size of chariot forces seems clear; and both Megiddo and Kadesh suggest 5 to 1 ratios of infantry to chariotry. At this scale the question of state capacity becomes critical, because chariots were *expensive*.[16]

Just how expensive? Costs escalated for a variety of reasons. First, every chariot probably "required half a dozen men—carpenter, bowyer, groom, metal-worker, and a servant or two—to maintain [it] in combat readiness," and for every "pair of horses pulling a chariot, another half a dozen horses would be needed in reserve for breeding, training, and replacement for horses that were injured, captured or killed."[17] These two requirements of skilled labor and horses present an interesting contrast in terms of state capacity. For the human labor, states represented the type of society most conducive to solving this problem. States could use their hierarchical coercive structure to mobilize and direct varied types of labor and craftsmen and then sustain them on an agricultural surplus reaped through centralized taxation. For a state, such labor was expensive but accessible. In contrast, the requirement for additional horses in a sedentary agricultural society was an extremely expensive one, and difficult for a state to sustain. In steppe societies, herded animals converted grass to energy usable by humans, as people ate the meat and dairy products or traded them. Agricultural societies invested labor to produce grains, which, if turned over to animals, represented a net loss of energy. One estimate suggests that each team of horses required eight to ten acres of grain. Although Egypt appears to have successfully bred its own horses, probably because of the legendary fertility (and navigability) of the Nile, other state-based societies in China and India depended on trading with steppe dwellers to sustain their herds. Furthermore, the materials required to build chariots were themselves expensive. An individual chariot did not require a large amount of bronze, but multiplied by hundreds or thousands, the total demand became substantial. Copper was relatively accessible for Egypt, but the nearest tin mines were likely in the Zeravshan valley in modern Uzbekistan. Wherever the tin came from, bronze production in Egypt required maintaining a far-flung and active trade network. Even the elm and birch wood used in Egyptian chariots came from northern Syria and Anatolia. A chariot cart may have cost the financial equivalent of thirty slaves. Even the new composite bows were expensive compared to the old self bows, requiring the gathering and preparation of three to five different kinds of material (not counting the arrows), and generally a minimum of one year's preparation (including seasoning, drying, and the actual crafting) for each bow.[18]

The irony here is that the chariot system was invented in a tribal context on the nomadic steppe, but, with the exception of the horses themselves, the system most benefited those states with the capacity to harness the resources necessary to produce hundreds or thousands of chariots. The process of inventing the chariot came more naturally to one type of society, but proved more to the advantage of a completely different type. The wealthier the state, the more chariots they could afford, and this differential may have contributed to the empire-building capabilities of the "club" of great powers in the Late Bronze Age Near East, which progressively subordinated other, smaller, autonomous city-states. The introduction of the chariot into other state societies had some striking similarities, but also surprising variations.

CHARIOTS UNDER HEAVEN: CHINA, 1200–400 BCE

For many centuries, Chinese culture has been portrayed by both Eastern and Western scholars as dominated by a desire for peace and order. In Chinese legend, the earliest founding dynasties of China bred golden ages of peace and virtue, to which later dynasties aspired. These eras supposedly were dominated by a Confucian ideology that emphasized the civilian over the martial, the *wen* over the *wu*. The debate over the reality of this divide, or at least over later eras' supposed indifference to martial skills, continues to exercise historians, but it is increasingly clear that the prehistoric and semilegendary periods of Chinese history were anything but peaceful and stable. In ways much like the generalized pattern of state formation described in chapter 1, sedentary agricultural communities in northern China, especially along the Yellow River, competed with, warred with, and conquered each other, in a halting, cyclical process, perhaps stimulated by hostile relations with the nonagricultural peoples on the nearby steppe, until a fully formed bureaucratic, militarized, and conquering Xia dynasty emerged around 2200 BCE.

It is difficult to say much with precision about the nature of war in the period of gradual accumulation and centralization of power that preceded the Xia state (the Neolithic Lungshan culture). The view that it was a relatively peaceful period, marked by only limited violence, depends on an interpretation of Neolithic Chinese wall building as almost exclusively for flood control. There is a reasonable case to make that the carefully elevated and walled cities along the Yellow River were built in that way to counter the river's notorious unpredictability. The earliest settlements were protected by a ditch, and the spoil was used to elevate the building site of the city, creating a "platform city." Progressively, however, over several thousand years, cities were not only elevated but walled, using a method that has a clear methodological and technological continuity from roughly 4000 BCE well into the historic period. Those later walled cities were undeniably designed for defense. The basic technique was to dig a ditch or moat, and then pile up the spoil into a mounded wall. In China, however, the "piling" was done systematically in thin layers (generally around 10 cm each, but with some variability), shaped by forms on the sides, and then laboriously compacted to provide resilience. The resulting "rammed earth walls" were extraordinarily thick and durable, reaching, even in the Neolithic, twenty-five meters thick at the base. Various refinements were added over millennia, but the basic technique remained the same. Further cultural continuity in warfare is suggested by the similarity of some distinctive hand weapons from the Neolithic Lungshan into the Han dynasty, notably the dagger-ax, or *ge* (see Figure 2.8).

The apparent extinction of some communities for the benefit of others and the archaeological discovery of ritual sacrificial victims both argue for the rise of centralized militant power. The Xia state itself appears to have begun its climb by virtually extinguishing the San Miao people. Much as described in chapter 1, Xia rulers built up personal retinues of followers based on "charisma, personal prowess, clan connections, and martial skill," then using their success to build around that core a force of more or less submissive martial aristocrats.[19] Xia warriors fought in loosely organized bodies of infantry, with bows, axes, clubs, dagger-axes, and some spears, generally tipped with stone rather than metal.[20]

The Shang dynasty emerged initially as rebels who defeated and scattered the Xia around 1600 BCE. Shang social order was based on a "hierarchically organized, bronze-manufacturing aristocratic patrilineage, led by a king" who claimed religious power and thereby authority, and who buttressed that claim through widespread human sacrifice (for theocratic power) and aggressive efforts to control metalworking and mines (for more material power).[21] The ruling elite had a "strong martial orientation" reflected in "elaborately decorated bronze and highly polished jade weapons, stylized metallic human and animal face masks, and other symbols of authority and achievement, including great axes."[22] The Shang also continued the tradition of fortified cities, often with a separately fortified palatial quarter within the city. The Shang were territorially expansive, but it is important to recognize that their rule did not extend over all of what is now China (see Map 2.2).

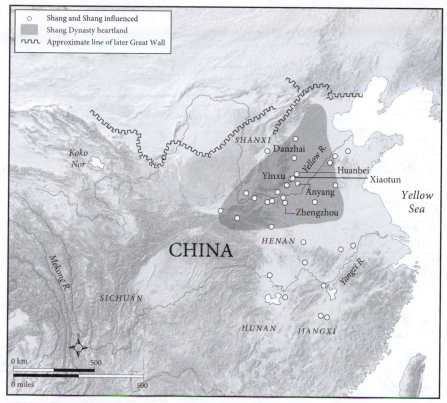

Map 2.2 Shang Dynasty China, ca. 1600–1045 BCE. The line of the later Great Wall is shown here marking the approximate boundary between the steppe and the agricultural zone of north China.

Shang control ebbed and flowed over time, depending in large part on their relative military capability, wielded in a region filled with impressive rammed-earth fortresses. Furthermore, it is probably a mistake to think of their wars as "ritualized" low-casualty affairs, as they have sometimes been described. Shang warriors initially fought much like their Xia predecessors, lacking swords, revering skill at archery, but also fighting in close combat with spears and dagger axes, with only leather armor and small shields. It was "an intensely violent clash primarily wrought with shock weapons intended to destroy the enemy as quickly and thoroughly as possible" resulting in heavy casualties and enslavement or even sacrifice of prisoners.[23] To their Qiang enemies, a tribal people west and northwest of the Shang who practiced a mix of pastoralism, agriculture, and hunting, the Shang rulers were particularly harsh. Qiang captives were "enslaved or sacrificed . . . in large numbers ranging from one through several tens to even three or four hundred."[24] For their part, the Qiang regularly (if not constantly) raided into Shang territory, and, like later steppe peoples, tended to raid more frequently when the ruling dynasty showed weakness—demonstrating an early version

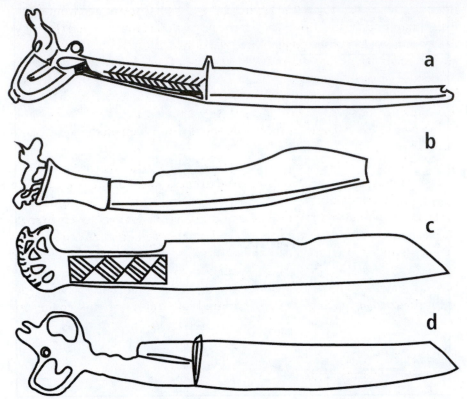

Figure 2.6 The influence of the steppe horse culture around Eurasia. (a) is a bronze dagger from Shang China (1600–1045 BCE). (b) and (c) are from the Rostovka cemetery of the Seima-Turbino culture in the Ural Mountains, ca. 1800 BCE. (d) is an unprovenienced "Persian" bronze dagger for sale on the art market.

of the later antagonistic relationship between the steppe and "civilized" China. The influence of the steppe on the Shang was pervasive, extending even to the design of bronze daggers (see Figure 2.6a–c), but most dramatically through the chariot and the horse.[25]

The chariot arrived in Shang China from the steppe around 1200 BCE in its more or less fully matured form and carrying bow-armed warriors in the chariot car. There is no evidence for earlier precursor forms with solid wheels (or four wheels) as seen in the Near East. Throughout the Shang and the following Zhou dynasties, chariot design remained very similar to advanced Near Eastern models, and it was almost identical to the steppe precursors found across Central Asia, stretching all the way to Lchashen in Armenia. The Chinese version follows later steppe design in having more spokes per wheel (16–20) than the Near Eastern design, perhaps because it had wheels with a wider diameter (120–45 cm vs. 75–90 cm), and also because of the rougher terrain prevalent in China. The Chinese also retained the axle centered on the chariot body (placing less weight on the horses, but making the ride considerably rougher) (see Figures 2.7 and 2.8). Constructed from wood, rattan, bamboo, bronze, and leather, the box was rectangular, and the larger ones would easily accommodate three warriors, with strikingly low walls on all four sides. The Zhou may have briefly used four-horse chariots, but the two-horse version dominated at least until the Spring and Autumn period (ca. 771–400 BCE). The elites who fought from the chariots, probably two-man crews in the Shang period and three in later eras, relied primarily on the bow and arrow—perhaps fired from the cart and even on the move—and the dagger-ax.[26]

As in the Near East, the chariot's military advantage was not as initially clear to Shang rulers as its cultural attractiveness was. For the two hundred years after their introduction little evidence attests any serious Shang effort to expand the number of chariots. The few found have been exclusively in royal burials. Furthermore, archaeological evidence suggests that Shang chariots were surrounded by large contingents of infantry, emphasizing their probable use more as "visibility platforms," if not command vehicles, rather than as large separate "units" of chariots. Textual sources indicate battle contingents of chariots *perhaps* as large as three hundred, in armies rarely exceeding ten

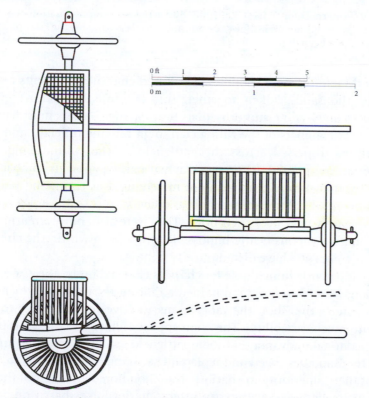

Figure 2.7 A chariot excavated at Lchashen, Armenia, dated to ca. 1250 BCE. This design represents a "later" steppe design that appeared in China in almost exactly this form.

Figure 2.8 Western Zhou chariot, ca. 1000–800 BCE. Artist's representation of a Zhou-era chariot. Although it shows the box and wheels accurately, the chariot was unlikely to have been drawn by four horses, or to have held three men in the cart.

thousand men (or, more commonly, hundred-chariot contingents in a force of three thousand). Taken together, this (admittedly unclear) evidence suggests to one leading authority that "most Shang chariots must have been reserved for members of the ruling clan, high-ranking officials, and important officers dispersed across the battlefield."[27] The cultural importance, however, of the martial aristocracy's actual participation in combat probably meant that the chariots were not merely used as command platforms. Chinese martial culture valued skill at archery, and so these leading men would certainly have used their bows. They were also, however, armed with close-combat weapons nearly impossible to use from within the chariot, so they may frequently have dismounted to fight.[28]

This apparently limited role for chariots changed under the Zhou. Where the Shang seemed to have maintained a ratio of thirty infantrymen to one chariot, under the Zhou the ratio seems to have moved closer to ten to one (with much variability). The Zhou appear to have used chariots in a way calculated to take advantage of their battlefield utility. In fact, one argument is that the Zhou destroyed and replaced the Shang (ca. 1045 BCE) in part *because* of their superiority in chariots. The Zhou homeland west of the Shang may have made it easier to expand their chariot forces based on access to steppe-supplied horses. King Wu of Zhou famously used three hundred chariots at the climactic Battle of Mu-yeh to defeat the Shang, and he supposedly had one thousand available at the time of his ascension. Archaeologically recovered chariots, much more common from the Zhou period, are not exclusively in royal graves (in one graveyard of 367 graves virtually every one had a chariot!), and they were less ornate than those of the Shang dynasty. For the Zhou the chariot seems to have been a crucial, calculated, military implement, but it also remained a relatively limited part of their overall force, at least compared to the five to one ratio suggested by Egyptian evidence. That may reflect the limited capacity of the Zhou state or a continued aristocratic vision of the chariots' role. As evidence supporting the limited-capacity argument, it is during the Zhou dynasty that we get the first hints of what would become a long Chinese pattern of acquiring horses from the northern nomadic peoples.[29]

By the so-called Spring and Autumn period of Chinese history (ca. 700 to 400 BCE), chariots had clearly become a crucial part of a Chinese army. In fact, the relative strength of a given state was measured by the number of chariots that they could put into the field—with some Spring and Autumn rulers of states much smaller than the Zhou supposedly fielding one thousand chariots. As their relative numbers increased, chariots were increasingly seen as capable of penetrating enemy formations and operating as pursuit vehicles. The *Liu-t'ao*, written in the Warring States period (475–221 BCE), called them "the feathers and wings of the army, the means to penetrate solid formations, press strong enemies, and cut off their flight."[30] There also had likely been a shift from the targeted archery of the Shang and Zhou to the massed volleys of the Spring and Autumn and Warring States periods.[31]

In sum, the chariot arrived in northern China as a new tool in the hands of an old enemy—the seminomadic pastoralists already accustomed to raiding their agricultural neighbors. Ironically, the Shang adoption of the chariot increased interaction between settled and steppe societies, as the Chinese depended on the steppe for horses. For virtually the rest of premodern Chinese history, rulers had to learn to deal with the steppe both as an incipient threat and as an indispensable source of horses. The initial limit on equine availability restricted their early use to the elite, perhaps even to royalty. But their apparent utility in battle suggested expanding their numbers (a process that occurred more slowly than in Egypt), and in greater numbers they became more and more militarily significant.

GODS AND HEROES: THE CHARIOT IN INDIA AND EUROPE

As we follow the chariot around Eurasia, it is appropriate to again emphasize that these descriptions of war and military systems in the Near East, China, and now India and Europe are only snippets of a larger whole. By examining the adoption and impact of this single technology we learn something fundamental about the nature of those societies. The chariot was not necessarily the most important or decisive element in these respective systems of warfare, although some have argued that it was. Compared to Egypt and China we know a good deal less about the movement of the chariot into India and Europe, but some basic outlines are clear, and they confirm the role of prestige and social status in the process.

India

The Indus River valley was home to one of the first state systems. The Harappan civilization flourished from about 2600 to 1900 BCE and was marked by an impressive network of sophisticated cities. A relative dearth of narrative art and its still undeciphered script, however, have limited our knowledge of Harappan history and warfare. Excavations at the first two major sites (Harappa and Mohenjo-Daro) did not initially uncover city walls, leading many to conclude that Harappan society had emerged relatively peacefully. Both cities, however, had fortified citadels within the city and were guarded by regional fortification systems. Furthermore, other contemporary cities (notably at Dholavira, Kalibangan, and Balu) not only had a citadel but also had impressive circuit walls and gate systems. The weapons recovered from all these sites are relatively unimpressive (spearheads, for example, were thin and flat) and not particularly numerous, nor has any body armor been found.[32]

The Harappans' contact with the urban civilizations of Mesopotamia and the Bactria-Margiana area to the north may have provided the lure for the Aryans' move into the region. As discussed previously, steppe peoples sharing the Andronovo cultural package advanced into the Bactria-Margiana region and replaced or destroyed the urban culture there by 1600 BCE. One branch of those people appears to have continued across the mountain passes into northern India. Despite substantial controversy over this "Aryan invasion," the literary and archaeological evidence increasingly supports the picture of a large-scale movement of Indo-European speakers, who called themselves Aryans, into the Indus and Ganges valleys starting around 1600–1500 BCE. The question remains, however: Did they "conquer" or merely "migrate"? Some evidence suggests that the Harappan civilization had already broken down by that time, and there is substantial evidence that refugees from the river valley cities fled into the interior forests of the subcontinent. The "invaders" may have encountered only limited resistance by scattered inhabitants. There is scattered evidence for human-induced destruction (some ash layers, and a few bodies found on Harappan sites of people who had been violently killed). The invaders, of course, built expansive legends about their arrival. Most famously, a single line from the Rig Veda, one of a series of texts composed shortly after the Aryan arrival in India, declares that Indra (an Aryan god) "smote the vanguard of the Vrichivans" at "Hariyupiya"—which some have reasonably equated with Harappa.[33]

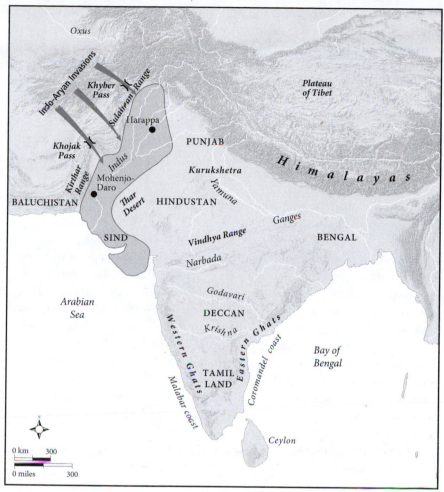

Map 2.3 Indo-Aryan invasions of Indus valley, ca. 1600 BCE.

What matters here is that the Aryan god Indra was a charioteer. The Rig Veda describes the Aryan gods as warriors, who destroyed forts and defeated the native Dasyus, routing them with their chariots. From the Vedic texts and some limited archaeological evidence, we know that these "invincible" "charioteers," "foremost in the fights" and "seeking spoils," drove carts strongly resembling the Sintashta model: two-wheeled, with four to eight spokes to a wheel, pulled by two horses, and generally carrying two men, a driver and an archer.[34] Despite detailed scholarly exegesis of the Vedic texts and the later epic poem the Mahabharata, it is difficult to reach many conclusions about how the Aryans fought and how they used their chariots. Clearly, however, the ancestors of the authors of the Vedic texts, regardless of whether they arrived as conquerors of the Harappans, certainly moved into northern India, brought with them the chariot, and portrayed their gods and heroes as chariot-fighters. Those chariots remained war vehicles of prestige and power in India for much longer than in China or the Near East. Even the emergence of elephants as a new conveyance for kings at war and as key components of an Indian army did not displace the chariot either on the battlefield or in terms of prestige. The chariot remained one of the four key elements (infantry, chariotry, cavalry, and elephants) even well after Alexander the Great's arrival in 326 BCE.[35]

Europe

In Western literature there are few scenes as familiar as the bloody combats of *The Iliad*'s Greek chariot warriors:

> Hector leapt to ground from his chariot fully armed and brandishing two sharp spears went striding down his lines, ranging flank to flank, driving his fighters to battle, rousing grisly war—and around the Trojans whirled, bracing to meet the Argives [Greeks] face-to-face: but against their mass the Argives closed ranks, the fighting about to break, the troops squaring off and Atrides [Agamemnon], tense to outfight them all, charged first.
>
> In from the blind side he [Coon] came—Agamemnon never saw him—tensed with a spear and slashed him under the elbow, down the forearm—a glint of metal—the point ripped through his flesh and the lord of fighting men Atrides shuddered.
>
> . . .
>
> And back he sprang in the car and told his driver to make for the hollow ships, racked with pain.[36]

Although there is no doubt of the importance of the chariot in the matured Mycenaean state system of Bronze Age Greece, the style of chariot fighting in *The Iliad* (essentially battle taxis, carrying heavily armed elites who fought with thrusting spears) represented the imagination of the much later era when Homer was composing a half-remembered story. The origins of the chariot in Greece are obscure, but, like its movement into Anatolia, it seems likely to have moved as an *idea* rather than as a tool employed by migrating or conquering people. Chariots first appear in Greek art around 1600 BCE, contemporaneous with the expansion of chariot use around the Near East. Components of the Mycenaean horse harness are now recognized as closely derived from an older steppe version. It nevertheless seems clear that the Mycenaean states evolved from the indigenous Greek population, not as an intrusive arrival. As those states matured they progressively adopted many of the cultural forms of the Minoans on Crete, whom they later conquered, while also establishing themselves as a peripheral player in the great-power system then present in the Near East. It is likely that the Mycenaeans adopted the chariot as part of their emulation of the great powers of the Near East. We even have a letter from the mid-1200s BCE referring to a Mycenaean royal who had once ridden with the personal charioteer of the Hittite king. There is no question that the Mycenaean rulers valued the chariot as a weapon of war and as a symbol of prestige, and they invested much labor and wealth in building large numbers of them, arguably against all military logic. Greece's topography seemingly provides almost no battlefields where chariots could have deployed in large numbers, unlike the Gangetic plain of India, the steppe, or the plains of Syria, Palestine, and Mesopotamia (although the latter was dramatically cut up by irrigation canals). They were probably only useable on the relatively small and still quite rough plains in the immediate vicinity of the main palaces.[37]

The significance of the chariot to the Mycenaean states of Greece is undeniable even if its exact battlefield use remains elusive. The Linear B "archives" of the palaces at Pylos and Knossos record substantial accumulations of chariots and chariot equipment. Knossos recorded 1,000 pairs of wheels and 340 chariot cars of two types, and the Pylos tablets show at least 200 pairs of wheels and other equipment. Some scholars assert that Greek charioteers used a lance from within the moving chariot, generally following the claim about some contemporary Hittite chariot warriors (discussed earlier). Others support the battle-taxi thesis, based not just on Homer but on some of the very few artistic portrayals of chariots from the Mycenaean period. It seems more likely, however, partly based on a number of Greek mainland and Cypriot images from the Bronze Age, that the Greeks, following Near Eastern practice, used bows from within the chariot. In support of this argument we have the remarkable suit of armor from Dendra (see Figure 2.9), weighing thirty to forty pounds and encasing the body in a tubular sheath of bronze nearly to the knees. The weight and especially the length of this armor strongly suggest that its wearer avoided dismounting from his chariot. (Similar armor corselets for chariot crewmen are attested from the Near East, some estimated to weigh between thirty-seven and fifty-eight pounds.) Suggestions that this armored warrior used a lance or spear from within the chariot have been demolished by studies of the physics and geometry of that combination. Perhaps clearest of all, at Pylos the chariot "manufactory" also contained some five hundred bronze arrowheads, while the Knossos tablets recorded 6,010 and 2,630 arrows in various batches. It seems probable that the Greeks used a bow from their chariot, following the dominant practice of the Near East—although in Greece, they probably did so from a stationary chariot, and there is little evidence for massed chariot charges. The rough Greek topography, however, restricted the chariot's speed, perhaps

Figure 2.9 Mycenaean bronze armor from Dendra, late fifteenth century BCE.

Figure 2.10 Gold signet ring showing a Mycenaean chariot, late sixteenth century BCE. From Shaft Grave IV of Grave Circle A at Mycenae.

encouraging more armor, and even the retention of a spear for defense against infantry.[38]

Another understanding of the Mycenaean chariot, however, deemphasizes, without eliminating, its military role, especially given the topography of Greece. It argues instead for the chariot's continued primary role as an instrument of social power. Robert Schon argues that it was unlikely for chariots to be used in conflict *between* Mycenaean-ruled regions inside Greece (much less outside Greece, given the difficulties of sea transport) because of the dividing mountains (or seas). Its probable military role was against non-chariot-equipped peoples *within* a region. The chariot's greatest military advantage was against those who lacked them and were unused to them, and they may have functioned well in expanding and consolidating regional control. He argues further that the Mycenaean road network was designed to support the mobility of chariots on a regional basis, allowing for their rapid movement to various points of the realm, where their visibility and presence would reinforce the message of the center's power. And finally, their use in key elite activities such as hunting and racing contributed to bonding the aristocratic elite to their group identity as players in the central state (see Figure 2.10).[39]

Certainly the cost of building and then maintaining a force of chariots was substantial and required a sophisticated administrative apparatus. Indeed, the Linear B archives related to chariots are almost entirely a record of parts and repairmen managed by the central state. When the Mycenaean states collapsed (or were destroyed) around 1100 BCE, the ability to maintain large chariot forces disappeared as well. They essentially do not reappear in the Greek dark ages or later except as an idealized memory—where they continued to be deployed in art, literature, and even ritual as emblems of heroic status.

CATASTROPHE, CAVALRY, AND THE DECLINE
OF THE CHARIOT IN THE NEAR EAST

The chariot had barely arrived in China by 1200 BCE. In India it had been present for three hundred years or so, and would continue to be a substantial part of Indian armies for centuries to come. In the eastern Mediterranean, however, the period around 1200 BCE marked the beginning of a dramatic decline in chariot use, and, indeed, a decline of many of the state-based civilizations in the region. Between 1225 and 1175 BCE some kind of "catastrophe," or combination of catastrophes, destroyed kingdom after kingdom in Greece, Anatolia, and across the Levant, and seriously threatened the Egyptian state, which survived but emerged initially diminished. Much of the region plunged into a "dark age" lasting some three hundred years or more. Intriguingly, the states that reemerged or survived increasingly deemphasized or entirely lacked chariots, instead favoring infantry and, for perhaps the first time among sedentary agricultural peoples, cavalry.[40]

As previously discussed, steppe herders may have been riding horses as early as 3700–4000 BCE, and men riding horses appeared in Near Eastern art as early as the second millennium. Even during the peak of the Bronze Age "chariot era" there are signs of armed men on horseback, perhaps most notably in an Egyptian relief of Hittite cavalry from the late fourteenth century BCE (see Figure 2.11). This is not at all to suggest that the arrival of cavalry *displaced* chariots in some violent fashion, although a strong if controversial case has been made for the arrival of people fighting in a new infantry style, with iron weapons, who overwhelmed the chariots. Whatever the source of the catastrophe, it seems to have had two significant effects on the continuing use of chariots. First, the destruction or diminution of the states that built them meant that they were not being built during the dark ages, and not all of the reemergent states

Figure 2.11 Egyptian Pharaoh Sethi I chasing Hittite forces, including cavalry, late fourteenth century BCE. In the mass of the pursuit are two soldiers riding horses. Relief from Thebes.

chose to reinvest in that expensive technology. Those that did so combined it with cavalry forces, relegating the chariots to more specialized roles in smaller numbers (although it sometimes retained its prestige function as a vehicle for the king himself). One major state that survived the catastrophe—Assyria—retained its chariotry into the Iron Age, but the Assyrians also progressively shifted the balance of their forces toward cavalry. Second, the catastrophe may have undermined the cultural prestige associated with chariots—not destroying it, but opening up alternative forms of martial prestige.[41]

Consider the relative prestige of riding versus being pulled. It had long been *possible* to ride horses (earlier theories about horse breeds during the chariot age being too small for riding have been discarded). A horse of thirteen to fourteen hands (132–43 cm) in height is sufficiently large for riding, and Egyptians and Hittites had horses of that height. But Robin Archer argues that these smaller breeds, although rideable, were mounted well back on the horse's rump, with the rider's knees raised, much as one would ride a donkey. Such a posture did not suit royal dignity, and indeed there is some illuminating advice to King Zimri-Lin from the 1760s BCE:

> My lord should preserve his royal dignity. Even though you are the king of the [nomad] Haneans, you are also the king of the Akkadians. Thus my lord should not ride horses, but a chariot [cart?] with mules, and maintain the prestige of his sovereignty.[42]

Later generations of domesticated horses were larger and could be ridden with no loss of dignity.

The shift to cavalry, therefore, like the adoption of the chariot, reflected calculation, culture, and capacity. States lost the capacity to maintain chariots while the cultural role formerly associated with them diminished over time. Both the prestige needs and the expense of the chariot were obviated by the calculation that cheaper cavalry, previously looked down upon, could fulfill virtually the same battlefield roles of flanking and pursuit, and could do so over a much wider variety of terrain. For cavalry to emerge to fill these roles, however, required the cultural disruption of the catastrophe, perhaps combined with continued improvement in the size of the horse.

CONCLUSION

The most obvious implication of the chariot is the startling connectedness of the ancient world. Technologies and ideas moved freely and sometimes rapidly around Eurasia. But they also shifted as they moved, sometimes subtly, sometimes significantly. A simplistic interpretation might suggest that the chariot emerged as a technology in one place and then spread outward, more or less evenly across space, apparently due to its inherent military value. But as we have seen, such a view does not tell the whole story. The component parts of the chariot emerged in response to the necessities and logic of life on the steppe. When transplanted to regions ruled by states, the chariot advantaged those state-based civilizations that could martial the necessary resources and labor to make large forces of this new vehicle. Those states, however, adopted it initially not because of their sense of its military value but rather because of its ability to convey power and prestige—something that Stuart Piggott has called a technological "package-deal" that moved from society to society *because* of its social meaning.[43] The chariot was fast, expensive, new, and exotic, and it lifted the warrior above the masses. It reinforced privilege, but simultaneously bound the aristocratic elite to the ruler of the state, who alone had the necessary resources to supply the chariots in which they rode to battle to protect his rule. And note again that the chariot did not necessarily spread by *conquest*. In Anatolia and the Near East the matured chariot fulfilled a cultural role already established by war carts, and so the movement of the idea (not necessarily the people initially using it) was relatively rapid. Similarly, although more slowly, the chariot moved into Shang China as an idea, and its real military value was only exploited after a couple of centuries of limited use—use, it is important to emphasize, that did not lead to any major changes in chariot design. In Egypt and the Near East, the military advantage of the new chariot over the cart was more immediately clear, and centralized states quickly moved to make chariots the premier arms of their military system. A similar dynamic may have occurred in Greece, in which the chariot suggested itself to a newly emerging set of states as a key symbol of state power, valued by the elite leadership who retained it and invested in it despite all apparent geographic logic.

All the while, however, in China, India, the Near East, and Greece, the proliferation of fortifications and the requirements of territorial warfare demanded the deployment of large forces of infantry. Infantry had always been there, and in some ways the safe delivery of infantrymen to a siege was the sine qua non of state-based conquest warfare. In the Mediterranean and Near East, in the wake of the catastrophe, there seems to have been a gradual shift in thinking about how best to recruit, train, and deploy infantrymen. But that is the subject of the next chapter.

TIMELINE

(all dates are BCE; some Egyptian dates are precise; the rest are approximate)

3700	Horses being ridden on Central Asian Steppe; wagons in use
2500	War carts in use in Mesopotamian cities
2000	Spoked, two-wheeled chariot grave at Sintashta
1850–1750	First images of spoked, two-wheeled chariots appear in Syria and Anatolia
1670–1600	Hyksos movement into Lower Egypt
1600	Beginning of Shang Dynasty in China; Aryans move into northern India
1274	Battle of Kadesh
1200	Chariot arrives in China; beginning of widespread collapse of states in the Near East
1045	Beginning of Zhou Dynasty in China

Further Reading

Anthony, David W. *The Horse, The Wheel, and Language: How Bronze-Age Riders from the Eurasian Steppes Shaped the Modern World.* Princeton, NJ: Princeton University Press, 2007.

Azzaroli, A. *An Early History of Horsemanship.* Leiden: Brill, 1985.

Barua, Pradeep P. *The State at War in South Asia.* Lincoln: University of Nebraska Press, 2005.

Beal, Richard H. *The Organisation of the Hittite Military.* Heidelberg, Germany: Carl Winter, 1992.

Cotterell, Arthur. *Chariot: The Astounding Rise and Fall of the World's First War Machine.* London: Pimlico, 2004.

Cunliffe, Barry. *Europe between the Oceans: Themes and Variations, 9000 BC–AD 1000.* New Haven, CT: Yale University Press, 2008.

Drews, Robert. *The End of the Bronze Age: Changes in Warfare and the Catastrophe ca. 1200 B.C.* Princeton, NJ: Princeton University Press, 1993.

Drews, Robert. *Early Riders: The Beginnings of Mounted Warfare in Asia and Europe.* New York: Routledge, 2004.

Fagan, Garrett G., and Matthew Trundle, eds. *New Perspectives on Ancient Warfare.* Leiden: Brill, 2010.

Greenhalgh, P. A. L. *Early Greek Warfare: Horsemen and Chariots in the Homeric and Archaic Ages.* Cambridge, UK: Cambridge University Press, 1973.

Hamblin, William J. *Warfare in the Ancient Near East to 1600 B.C.: Holy Warriors at the Dawn of History.* New York: Routledge, 2006.

Littauer, Mary A., and Joost H. Crouwel. *Wheeled Vehicles and Ridden Animals in the Ancient Near East.* Leiden: Brill, 1979.

Littauer, Mary A., and Joost H. Crouwel. *Selected Writings on Chariots and Other Early Vehicles, Riding and Harness.* Edited by Peter Raulwing. Leiden: Brill, 2002.

Macqueen, J. G. *The Hittites and Their Contemporaries in Asia Minor.* Rev. ed. London: Thames & Hudson, 1986.

Piggott, Stuart. *Wagon, Chariot and Carriage: Symbol and Status in the History of Transport.* New York: Thames & Hudson, 1992.

Raaflaub, Kurt, and Nathan Rosenstein, eds. *War and Society in the Ancient and Medieval Worlds.* Washington, DC: Center For Hellenic Studies, 1999.

Sandor, Bela I. "The Rise and Decline of the Tutankhamun-Class Chariot." *Oxford Journal of Archaeology* 23.2 (2004): 153–75.

Sawyer, Ralph D. *Ancient Chinese Warfare.* New York: Basic Books, 2011.

Shaughnessy, Edward H. "Historical Perspectives on the Introduction of the Chariot into China." *Harvard Journal of Asiatic Studies* 48.1 (1988): 189–237.

Singh, Sarva Daman. *Ancient Indian Warfare, with Special Reference to the Vedic Period.* Leiden: Brill, 1965.

Spalinger, Anthony J. *War in Ancient Egypt: The New Kingdom.* Malden, MA: Blackwell, 2005.

Van de Mieroop, Marc. *A History of the Ancient Near East, ca. 3000–323 BC.* 2nd ed. Malden, MA: Blackwell, 2007.

Veldmeijer, André, and Salima Ikram, eds. *Chasing Chariots.* Leiden: Sidestone, 2013.

Notes

1. Tests discussed in William J. Hamblin, *Warfare in the Ancient Near East to 1600 B.C.: Holy Warriors at the Dawn of History* (New York: Routledge, 2006), 136.

2. Hamblin, *Warfare*, 91.

3. Much of the following on steppe developments is derived from David W. Anthony, *The Horse, The Wheel, and Language: How*

Bronze-Age Riders from the Eurasian Steppes Shaped the Modern World (Princeton, NJ: Princeton University Press, 2007).

4. For recent studies pushing back horse domestication and riding to this early date, see Alan K. Outram et al., "The Earliest Horse Harnessing and Milking," *Science* 323.5919 (March 2009): 1332–35 doi:10.1126/science.1168594; Vera Warmuth et al., "Reconstructing the Origin and Spread of Horse Domestication in the Eurasian Steppe," *PNAS* 109.21 (2012): 8202–6, doi:10.1073/pnas.1111122109; Anthony, *The Horse*, 216–22, 460.

5. Anthony, *The Horse*, 405.

6. Anthony, *The Horse*, 416.

7. Images cataloged by Hamblin, *Warfare*, 147–49; also P. R. S. Moorey, "The Emergence of the Light, Horse-Drawn Chariot in the Near-East c. 2000–1500 B.C.," *World Archaeology* 18.2 (1986): 196–215.

8. D. Miller, E. McEwen, and C. Bergman, "Experimental Approaches to Near Eastern Archery," *World Archaeology* 18 (1986): 178–95. The composite recurve bow, although present in the Near East well before the spoked-wheel chariot, did not arrive in Egypt until the Hyksos period.

9. Anthony, *The Horse*, 43–52; Eric H. Cline, *1177 B.C.: The Year Civilization Collapsed* (Princeton, NJ: Princeton University Press, 2014), 15, 30–31; Christopher I. Beckwith, *Empires of the Silk Road: A History of Central Eurasia from the Bronze Age to the Present* (Princeton, NJ: Princeton University Press, 2009), 29–57.

10. Richard H. Beal, *The Organisation of the Hittite Military* (Heidelberg, Germany: Carl Winter, 1992), 144–46, 282–87; Moorey, "Emergence," 204; Robert Drews, *The End of the Bronze Age: Changes in Warfare and the Catastrophe ca. 1200 B.C.* (Princeton, NJ: Princeton University Press, 1993), 106.

11. For a recent discussion of chariot battle tactics, see Joost Crouwel, "Studying the Six Chariots from the Tomb of Tutankhamun— An Update," in *Chasing Chariots*, ed. André Veldmeijer and Salima Ikram (Leiden: Sidestone, 2013), 87–88. The version here does not follow his precisely.

12. Beal, *Organisation*, 148; later neo-Hittite image in Kurt Bittel, *Les Hittites* (Paris: Gallimard, 1976), 257. Drews, *End of the Bronze Age*, 121–22, assumes that Hittite chariots were also bow-armed, arguing that the Kadesh portrayal avoids showing bows for artistic and ideological reasons. Mary Littauer and J. H. Crouwel, "Chariots in Late Bronze Age Greece," *Antiquity* 57 (1983): 187–92.

13. Andrea M. Gnirs, "Ancient Egypt," in *War and Society in the Ancient and Medieval Worlds*, ed. Kurt Raaflaub and Nathan Rosenstein (Washington, DC: Center for Hellenic Studies, 1999), 84.

14. Great Sphinx Stela of Amenhotep II, quoted in Gnirs, "Ancient Egypt," 84.

15. Plunder list, Annals of Thutmose III (ca. 1450 BC), in James Henry Breasted, *Ancient Records of Egypt: The Eighteenth Dynasty* (Chicago: University of Chicago Press, 1906; reprint, Champaign: University of Illinois Press, 2001), 187.

16. Anthony J. Spalinger, *War in Ancient Egypt: The New Kingdom* (Malden, MA: Blackwell, 2005), discusses the debate over numbers.

17. Hamblin, *Warfare*, 146.

18. Drews, *End of the Bronze Age*, 110–11; Stuart Piggott, *Wagon, Chariot and Carriage: Symbol and Status in the History of Transport* (New York: Thames & Hudson, 1992), 45.

19. Ralph D. Sawyer, *Ancient Chinese Warfare* (New York: Basic Books, 2011) (quote p. 96; also 16–17.

20. Sawyer, *Ancient Chinese Warfare*, 83.

21. Quoted in Robin D. S. Yates, "Early China," in Raaflaub and Rosenstein, *War and Society*, 11. Further support in Sawyer, *Ancient Chinese Warfare*, 100, 206.

22. Sawyer, *Ancient Chinese Warfare*, 206.

23. Sawyer, *Ancient Chinese Warfare*, 153.

24. Sawyer, *Ancient Chinese Warfare*, 167.

25. The daggers shown in Figure 2.6 can be found in Chris Peers, *Soldiers of the Dragon:*

Chinese Armies, 1500 BC–AD 1840 (Oxford: Osprey, 2006), 20; Anthony, *The Horse*, 446; and http://www.sephari.com/p-6901-bronze-horse-head-sword.aspx accessed 8/6/2011.

26. Edward H. Shaughnessy, "Historical Perspectives on the Introduction of The Chariot into China," *Harvard Journal of Asiatic Studies* 48.1 (1988): passim; Sawyer, *Ancient Chinese Warfare*, 334.

27. Sawyer, *Ancient Chinese Warfare*, 365.

28. Shaughnessy, "Historical Perspectives," 195–98. There is controversy here, further elaborated in Sawyer, but I prefer Shaughnessy's explanation. Sawyer, *Ancient Chinese Warfare*, 223, 367. (Sawyer thinks they served together in a body; Shaughnessy thinks they served among infantry).

29. Sawyer, *Ancient Chinese Warfare*, 360; Shaughnessy, "Historical Perspectives," 198.

30. Quoted in Sawyer, *Ancient Chinese Warfare*, 362.

31. Sawyer, *Ancient Chinese Warfare*, 332.

32. Excavations of Harappan sites are reported by the Archaeological Survey of India, available at http://asi.nic.in/asi_excavations.asp; Pradeep P. Barua, *The State at War in South Asia* (Lincoln: University of Nebraska Press, 2005), 4.

33. Rigveda 6.XXVII.5 in *The Hymns of the Rigveda*, trans. Ralph T. H. Griffith, 2nd ed. (Benares: Lazarus and Co., 1890), 2:352 available online at https://archive.org/details/hymnsrigveda00grifgoog, accessed April 5, 2015. For the end of the Harappan civilization see Gwen Robbins Schug et al., "Infection, Disease, and Biosocial Processes at the End of the Indus Civilization," *PLoS ONE* 8.12 (2013): e84814, doi:10.1371/journal.pone.0084814.

34. Sarva Daman Singh, *Ancient Indian Warfare with Special Reference to the Vedic Period* (Leiden: Brill, 1965), 27–33; quotes from Rigveda 5.XXXV.7 in *Hymns of the Rigveda*, 2:230.

35. Beckwith, *Empires*, 42, 50–57.

36. *Iliad* 11.245–320, trans. Robert Fagles (New York: Viking Penguin, 1990), 303–305.

37. Scholarly opinion currently rejects the idea of the Mycenaeans as invaders from either Anatolia or the steppe (made most prominently by Drews, *The Coming of the Greeks*). Compare Piggott, *Wagon*, 60–63; Walter Gauss, "Aegina Kolonna," in *The Oxford Handbook of the Bronze Age Aegean*, ed. Eric. H. Cline (Oxford: Oxford University Press, 2010), 737–51. There are undeniable links, however, between Mycenaean chariot technology and its steppe predecessor. Barry Cunliffe, *Europe between the Oceans: Themes and Variations, 9000 BC–AD 1000* (New Haven, CT: Yale University Press, 2008), 224–26; Anthony, *Horse*, 369, 401, 502–35; Cline, *1177*, 84–85.

38. P. A. L. Greenhalgh, *Early Greek Warfare: Horsemen and Chariots in the Homeric and Archaic Ages* (Cambridge, UK: Cambridge University Press, 1973), 10–11; Littauer and Crouwel, "Chariots in Late Bronze Age Greece"; Robert Schon, "Chariots, Industry, and Elite Power at Pylos," in *Rethinking Mycenaean Palaces II*, rev. ed., ed. Michael L. Galaty and William A. Parkinson (Los Angeles: Cotsen Institute of Archaeology, 2008), 138; Drews, *End of the Bronze Age*, 111, 119–25.

39. Schon, "Chariots, Industry, and Elite Power," 133–45.

40. Cline, *1177*.

41. Drews, *End of the Bronze Age*. The Assyrian army of the Iron Age is discussed in the next chapter.

42. A. Azzaroli, *An Early History of Horsemanship* (Leiden: Brill, 1985), 42; Robin Archer, "Chariotry to Cavalry: Developments in the Early First Millennium," in *New Perspectives on Ancient Warfare*, eds. Garrett Fagan and Matthew Trundle (Leiden: Brill, 2010), 57–80, esp. 69–70; quote from Hamblin, *Warfare*, 141.

43. Piggott, *Wagon*, 45.

3

Men in Lines with Spears

900–300 BCE

Masses of Men in the Background • *Assyria Reborn* • *Communal Solidarity and the Greek Hoplite Phalanx* • *The Macedonian Sarissa Phalanx*

THE SPEAR IS the oldest attestable crafted weapon. Untipped wood spears survive from 400,000 years ago. Over millennia they became progressively more sophisticated. A separate point was added, first stone, then bronze or iron. Some were designed and balanced to be thrown, while others were held in the hand(s) and are called "thrusting" spears. Spears have always been potentially useful for either hunting or war, and so their existence in limited numbers, without other sources to shed light on their use, tells us very little about them as weapons of war. The point here, however, is that the use of a spear in human conflict is a very old practice indeed. Therefore, the central innovation of this chapter is decidedly not technological. Spears improved over time, to be sure, but the real innovation was how men were organized to use them. As men learned to ride horses and cavalry assumed an ever more important battlefield role, the spear emerged as an infantryman's best recourse: horses were generally unwilling to impale themselves on a sharp point. So the focus of this chapter is the calculated arraying of men into linear formations and training them to act in concert, a process most closely associated with the use of thrusting spears or pikes, held in one or two hands, often accompanied by a shield.

There are a surprisingly large number of ways to do this. The emergence of men in lines with spears might even seem an exceedingly obvious development, something explicable simply because spears were relatively cheap, as they required little metal, and by the view that "any idiot can hold a spear." In its barest essence the latter statement is true. Many militias and scratch forces throughout history, even as late as the mid-nineteenth century CE, were handed a spear and told to get in line. In fact, however, a spear point held some three to fifteen feet from the body is awkward to control, and if it is pushed aside, its holder becomes defenseless. Its real efficacy, especially against horsemen, comes when large blocks of men use them together, presenting a hedge of sharp points capable of either stopping their enemy or pressing them backward on the battlefield. Building that capability was more complex than it might seem. Understanding its emergence is variously a tale about state and empire formation, professionalism, bureaucratically supplied standing armies, and, finally, varying cultural sources of corporate cohesion. It is about capacity, calculation, and culture.[1]

Like the weapon itself, the story began very early. So this chapter begins with the "masses of men in the background" of the ancient Bronze Age kingdoms, some of whom held spears and marched in formation. It then turns to the more complex evidence for the Neo-Assyrian Empire of the early Iron Age. We then focus on two of the most well-studied but still ultimately puzzling versions: the Greek hoplite phalanx and the Macedonian pike-armed variant. Those stories, although often told, are critical to the development of Western warfare. They did not establish some consistent Western style of fighting, as has been argued by Victor Davis Hanson, but they did contribute to a model for formal, linear, uniform, synchronized cohesion among infantrymen. That model put down deep roots in the Western literary canon and proved amenable to imitation later in Western history. It is also critical to note, however, that a key part of the story was the *difficulty* of imitating the specifics of either the Greek or the Macedonian version of men in lines with spears. Theirs was a unique creation.[2]

MASSES OF MEN IN THE BACKGROUND

Uniformly armed infantry arrayed in regular formations and acting in concert are often argued to be a creation of the state, the idea being that state capacity, in the form of coercive hierarchy, social differentiation, and food surplus management is required to force men to fight in a communal role in a line of battle. Although it is not clear why that would be, the empirical historical evidence seems to bear it out. There are few if any examples of nonstate peoples fighting in such a style without external pressure from state-level societies. In the early nineteenth century the Zulus adopted a thrusting spear and close-combat tactical style, but may have done so under the regional pressure created by the movement of the Dutch Afrikaners into the interior of Africa. Under Spanish pressure, the Araucanian Indians of sixteenth-century Chile restructured their society to adopt pike and shot formations. Other nonstate spear users tended to throw them, and they did so as individual warriors acting within a crowd of like-armed men. They did not generally adopt tactics that required them to act in concert with each other, at the command of a central figure. The Iron Age "barbarian" chiefdoms of northwest Europe also sometimes used spear- and shield-carrying infantry, but their mass formations lacked the same level of cooperative coherence found in contemporary states.[3]

We find a linear, uniform formation of spearmen, however, in the earliest of all states at Sumer. Two famous images from the middle of the third millennium BCE, both discussed briefly in the previous chapter (see Figure 2.1, and also Figure 3.1), depict formed spear-armed infantry. In the Stele of Vultures (ca. 2450 BCE) helmeted men are lined up with rectangular, seemingly overlapping shields, carrying their spears with two hands, and also apparently arrayed in depth, perhaps six deep. The Standard of Ur, from the same region and basically the same period, seems to show something similar, although here the men lack shields, and the nature of the formation is less clear. Neither group is particularly well armored, but they do share a uniformity of equipment and posture that at least *suggests* the possibility of a formation that fought in concert and relied on projecting spear points from a solid line. Unfortunately, we cannot know from these two unique pieces of evidence whether this uniformity extended to all the infantry raised in ancient Sumer. Worse, the contemporary textual records allow us to say almost nothing about the invention of this formation in the first place. Was it a deliberate calculation of advantage? Was their depiction merely artistic convention? Was it simply a way to make them look more impressive through uniformity, much like the four-wheeled war cart was designed to enhance status through imagery rather than function? Were such uniformly armed

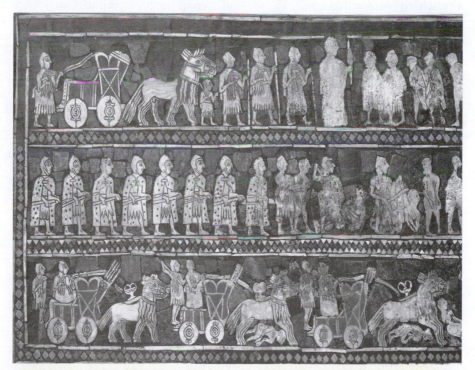

Figure 3.1 The Standard of Ur, ca. 2600 BCE. Note the spear-carrying infantry in the central register.

men made possible by the expansion of capacity represented by the state's division of labor and (re)distribution of food? There are really more questions here than answers, and unfortunately we cannot say much more about other early states.

The Middle Bronze Age kingdoms of the Levant and Anatolia had infantrymen with spears (although with very little body armor), but how they were used is not clear. We can say a bit more about Egypt. There, in the Middle Kingdom period prior to the introduction of the chariot (ca. 2000–1700 BCE), substantial evidence exists for spearmen in seemingly regular formations. Most famously, a wooden model from around 2000 BCE depicts a formation of forty spear- and shield-equipped Egyptian infantry in company with forty Nubian archers, although they are shown marching rather than fighting. Literary sources also suggest that Middle Kingdom Egyptian armies opened the battle with an exchange of arrows, followed by the advance of ax- or spear-armed infantry into hand-to-hand combat. On the other hand, neither these men nor any other early Egyptian infantry wore armor or even helmets. Egyptians clearly had spearmen from an early date, but during the period of the New Kingdom (ca. 1550–1077 BCE), Egyptian iconography increasingly focused on the chariot, secondarily on foot archers, with spearmen a rare and distant third (more common are infantrymen with sickle sword and ax). But this may be a problem derived from our sources' emphasis on the role of royalty, which preferred to ignore the mass of men in the background. One group of such men, with spears, recedes into the corner of one depiction of the great battle at Kadesh.[4]

The evidence is even more scant elsewhere in the Bronze Age world. We know very little about warfare among the Harappans in India, although spearheads have been found in their cities. The Aryans who replaced them, and their successors down to the Mauryan state that confronted Alexander the Great in 326 BCE, emphasized the mounted arms and the bow in their portrayals of war. As a result we have only a hazy understanding of their infantry formations, although it is clear that they were more central to the battle than their written epics suggest. We do know, however, that they fought with swords and bows. Infantry in Shang and Zhou China carried a roughly rectangular single-handed shield about twenty-eight by thirty-two inches, the dagger-ax (discussed in chapter 2), sometimes a short spear (about five feet), and bows. Some scholars have suggested, based on minimal archaeological data, a greater emphasis on spears over the dagger-ax in the late Shang, but there is no evidence for formation or usage. One document from the Zhou era suggests peasant infantry being trained to advance in ranks and keep their order. During the Warring States era, hundreds of years later, infantry seem to have shifted to using swords (and bows). Bronze Age Greece presents a different problem, to which we will return later in this chapter.[5]

All of these Bronze Age state-based societies fought for the control of territory and the capture of cities. Controlling territory and labor meant increasing wealth and power, and thus competing more effectively with dangerous neighbors. Taking and garrisoning towns required masses of men, generally men on foot. But were such men used offensively on the battlefield? Historians Doyne Dawson and Robert Drews have separately argued that the answer is no, at least not until the very end of the Bronze Age. In their view, Bronze Age infantry fought simply as unformed skirmishers. Such troops did the dirty work of laying siege or chasing enemies into the hills where chariots could not follow, but battles, they argue, were decided by the clash of chariots. Drews argues further that it was the introduction of a new form of infantry by outside migrating peoples that brought about the downfall of the chariot and the catastrophe at the end of the Bronze Age (discussed in chapter 2). In his view this wave of invaders was distinguished by being primarily foot soldiers who came equipped with iron weapons of new types, emphasizing javelins over bows, and using newly invented iron swords. These men moved quickly around the battlefield and learned to swarm and overwhelm chariots. Those states that survived the invaders, or rebuilt themselves afterward, found that they now needed to create an infantry force capable of confronting this new challenge. Such a force required a different organizational emphasis designed to deal with these fast moving "swarmers." The new state-based infantry of the Iron Age would fight in close order, use thrusting spears, and wear more personal armor than infantry ever had before. This can at best remain an unproven hypothesis. It is certainly true, however, that as our sources improve with the opening of the Iron Age, the role of infantry emerges more clearly, and it is undeniable that Assyria, the first great imperial state, *did* employ a large permanent force of professional infantrymen, including spearmen. The mass of men in the background had begun to move to the front of the stage.[6]

ASSYRIA REBORN

Bronze Age Assyria had been a prominent member of the "club" of great powers, and the catastrophe surrounding the transition to the Iron Age diminished but did not destroy the kingdom. Assyria emerged from the dark ages more or less intact (now referred to as the "Neo-Assyrian" empire) and in the middle of the ninth century began to expand into what would become a substantial territorial empire, interrupted by a contraction from 810 to 746 BCE, until its ultimate destruction in 627 BCE. The Assyrian homeland centered on the cities of Nineveh and Assur on the upper reaches of the Tigris River. By the seventh century BCE the Assyrians had incorporated all of the Tigris and Euphrates basin, swept through the Levant (Lebanon and Palestine), and even forced Egypt into submission (see Map 3.1).

The Assyrian kings ruled a state often characterized as highly militaristic. It may not have been that different from its neighbors, but there is little doubt that war seemed to be the chief business of the Assyrian state. As in the early

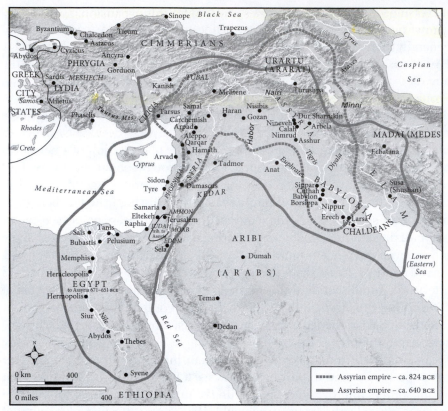

Map 3.1 The Expansion of the Neo-Assyrian Empire, 824–640 BCE.

states explored in chapter 1, war was the semi-sacred activity of Assyria's kings, who justified their claims to power based on their success in war, which allegedly demonstrated the favor of their gods. To be fair, the Assyrians believed themselves surrounded by a host of enemies of varying types: the mountain kingdoms to the north (notably Urartu), the Elamites to the southeast, the Babylonian Empire to the south, and the Anatolian powers to the northwest (the Neo-Hittites and Phrygians), not to mention whoever had caused the catastrophe. Assyrian expansion resembled that of later empires in that it proceeded in stages and typically without a preconceived plan. Efforts to control trade routes led to conflict—especially for metals, which Assyria generally lacked. Defeated regions were then made tributary but were allowed to retain substantial autonomy—in essence becoming client states. "Rebellion" or simple truculence spurred Assyrian "reconquest," often followed by full incorporation and provincialization within the empire. Some further territory, beyond the new province, then became perceived as a potential new source of trouble, creating a new security concern, and so on. In this the Assyrians were hardly unique; such has often been the path of imperial expansion.

As in other contemporary states, the tool for this expansion, the Assyrian army, was seen as a personal extension of the king's will. The prestigious center of that army remained the riders—those men who rode alongside the king, especially in chariots. The Neo-Assyrian army retained chariotry as a key part of the army, although it evolved over time from the light driver-and-archer-style chariot reminiscent of the Bronze Age to a heavier version carrying as many as four warriors (compare Figures 3.2 and 3.3). Contrary to some recent popular studies, however, the chariotry probably was not the most significant or decisive component of their army. Part of the reason for the evolutionary changes in the chariot's construction and tactical significance was that the Assyrians were the first sedentary people to develop true mounted cavalry. That development too was evolutionary, and may have resulted from campaigning in territory too rough for chariots. Early Assyrian horsemen fought as two riders in parallel, one holding the reins for the other while he fired his bow (a kind of "cabless chariot"). In time the Assyrians developed their cavalry into a potent force of mounted archers (and possibly lancers), thereby diminishing and changing the role of the chariots. Even late in the empire, however, mounted combat, and especially in chariots, remained at the center of Assyrian martial culture, if for no other reason than that the king himself rode to war in his chariot. Sargon II (r. 722–705 BCE) gives a sense of this combined personal and mounted

Figure 3.2 Neo-Assyrian chariot, ninth century BCE. This image shows King Ashurnasirpal II (883–859 BCE) hunting lions in a "light" chariot. Compare to the heavier chariot in Fig. 3.3. From the palace of Ashurnasirpal II in Nimrud, Mesopotamia.

Figure 3.3 Neo-Assyrian chariot and horse archer, seventh century BCE. This image shows a "heavy" war chariot and a mounted horse archer during the campaigns of Ashurbanipal (668–627 BCE) against the kingdom of Elam. From Ashurbanipal's palace in Nineveh.

prestige in part of his famous account of his eighth campaign. In 714 BCE Sargon advanced against the king of Urartu, and at the end of an exhausting mountain march faced an entrenched enemy. Sargon claimed that he ignored his own tired infantry, disdained his well-arrayed and prepared foe, and even left behind much of his own army. Instead, he wrote, "With only my single chariot and the horsemen who ride with me, who never leave me in hostile or friendly territory, the elite squadron of Sin-ah-usur [Sargon's brother], I fell upon him like a furious arrow, I defeated him and forced him into retreat. I made a huge carnage of him, spreading out the corpses of his warriors like malt."[7]

Setting aside the likely royal exaggeration in this passage, it is evident from other parts of this same narrative, and from abundant surviving Assyrian narrative art, that the kings of Assyria took great pride in their role as takers and destroyers of cities. Common sense suggests, and Assyrian depictions of sieges make clear, that taking the great walled cities of the ancient Near East was an intensive and laborious task, requiring large numbers of infantry. In this, the Assyrians became experts. They deployed specialized pioneers to undermine walls, covered assaults with bowmen, and attacked the walls with scaling ladders, siege towers, and various types of wheeled battering rams (see Figure 3.4). Within artistic portrayals we find a number of different types of infantry with varying arms and armor, some seemingly Assyrian and others supposedly allied "auxiliaries." Within this variety, spearmen played a central role. Unfortunately, these surviving records do not tell us much about these infantry in *battle*. We see them in the more or less chaotic stages of a siege, but few accounts or depictions clarify the role of infantry in the Assyrian army beyond their indispensable use as labor and as assault troops in sieges.

Figure 3.4 An Assyrian siege, eighth century BCE. Stone relief carving of an attack on a city by King Ashurbanipal, found in Nimrud. Note the undermining of the walls, covering fire from archers, and the wheeled battering ram/siege tower.

In one sense the royal emphasis in the surviving records continues to push this mass of men into the background, but it is still possible to look through and beyond this discourse to understand something of the role of men in lines with spears within the Assyrian army.

Doing so, however, requires some care. The evidence comes primarily from royal propaganda, some royal and provincial bureaucratic accounts, letters, archaeological remains of weapons, and, above all, the fantastically detailed sculptures commemorating Assyrian victories. These latter sources (used several times in this chapter already) especially convey a distinctive impression of professionalism, complexity, and skill. Of course, that is what they were *designed* to convey: an impression of the awesome might of Assyria. It may be that earlier Bronze Age kingdoms had similar capabilities and specialization (save the mounted cavalry), but simply did not deign to portray it. As discussed earlier, formations of spearmen certainly existed in early Bronze Age armies. Furthermore, none of these sources provide the kind of narrative description or detail that we have for the Greeks and Romans. Nevertheless, checking the sources against the archaeological evidence and carefully comparing the Assyrian Empire to later periods, it is possible to make some reasonable conclusions about its infantry.[8]

What strikes the modern analyst most forcibly about the Assyrian army is its sophistication, the specialization of troops, and the balance of arms, even, in modern terms, the use of "combined arms." In addition to combining chariotry, cavalry, archers, slingers, spearmen, and assorted other ethnic troop types, Assyrian armies, at least during the last two centuries of the empire, were sustained by a massive, centralized logistical system that prepared depots around the empire and tasked provincial administrators to provide for the army. Records suggest that the army campaigned in all seasons of the year, and its core elements could march at almost a moment's notice. Both of these facts suggest a standing force with continuously renewed stockpiles of provisions. The Assyrians maintained centralized armories and built an extensive road and postal network to communicate to the corners of the empire. One room in a workshop at Fort Shalmaneser, excavated in 1989, contained a corroded mass of armor and weapons as much as four feet deep. The bureaucracy managed a system of taking in horses that could handle as many as one hundred animals a day, while the single garrison of Kar-Assur consumed a daily quantity of 70,500 liters of barley (for the men) and 57,800 liters of fodder (for the horses), most of which came from royal granaries. When on the move the army built fortified camps; they managed extensive river crossings, including floating chariots across rivers or even building pontoon bridges; and they shifted from one logistical system to another as they moved from provincial territory into enemy territory, all while maintaining at least a minimum of centralized distribution of rations to supplement on-the-march foraging.[9]

Within this system infantry was a key component of the Assyrian army. Later records suggest that the Assyrians fielded as many as eight infantrymen for every cavalryman. As suggested in the previous chapter, the delivery of infantry to a siege was a key function of the field army as a whole. The Assyrian army appears also to have won its battles at least partly because of its infantry's skill, and portrayals of campaigns in wooded or marshy areas focus heavily on the actions of men on foot. The question remains, however: Were these "men in lines with spears"? Were these men who stood side by side in linear formations who won battles through the cohesion and irresistibility of their formation, a formation that was also proof against the new possibility of charges by horsemen?[10]

Many of the spearmen found on Assyrian reliefs wore little armor (primarily a disk-shaped breastplate), carried a long (6–7 foot) iron-bladed thrusting spear, and protected themselves either with a substantial round shield (apparently made of wicker, 3–3.5 feet in diameter), or later with an even larger "tower" shield (also wicker, 4–4.5 feet tall; in some siege contexts even taller). Some scholars have identified these lightly armored men as a kind of regular auxiliary (as opposed to a temporary tribal levy or allied contingent), sometimes called the Qurreans, possibly recruited from a particular ethnicity or based on that ethnicity's style of fighting. Whatever their origin, they seem to have been burdened with much of the army's dirty work, especially leading the assault in sieges.[11]

A second type of spearman has been identified as the "regular" Assyrian infantry. Interestingly, they could be referred to interchangeably as *sāb arīti*, shield bearer, or *nāš asmarē*, spearman. Their equipment (and the auxiliaries') evolved over this period, but to greatly generalize, over time they acquired more armor, made of lamellar bronze scales. They usually used round shields (although they also employed tower shields), probably made of leather and wood or wicker, with a bronze boss in the center. They wore a conical iron helmet and carried the same six- to seven-foot-long thrusting spear. They are most often seen paired with an archer, literally one beside the other, the spearman providing protection for the archer. From its earliest incarnation in the ninth century, the Assyrian army had paired an archer and a shield bearer, at least in siege contexts, and the combination of the archer with a spearman may be a continuation of that tradition. There is also clear textual evidence for them operating together in either exact or roughly comparable numbers. One document detailing a provincial governor's force shows 10 chariots, 97 cavalrymen, 440 archers, 80 Assyrian spearmen, and 360 Qurrean spearmen. Combining the spearmen, there were 440 to match the 440 archers. Another text documented the use of prisoners in a similar way: "I incorporated 30,500 bowmen and 30,500 shield-carriers (from the prisoners) into my standing army."[12]

Most Assyrian military art focuses on sieges, and there the pairing of an archer and an assaulting or covering spear/shield man is common. Such pairing may not have been as direct in an open field battle, but there are few portrayals of such contests to work with. The images of the battle at the Ulai River (ca. 653 BCE) do show the spearmen and archers working side by side (see Figure 3.5). On the other hand, another image depicts spearmen apparently operating in a linear formation without archer support, although in this image (see Figure 3.6) they are pursuing fugitives from an already broken army. Images from the Balawat gates (ca. 860 BCE) show archers, spearmen, and swordsmen all involved in dispatching the enemy infantry in close combat. At least one image from those gates shows a field battle in which archers are covered by shield men. Tactically it seems likely, given the predominance of the paired imagery and the documents of parallel numbers, that an Assyrian infantry force in the field lined up a linear formation of spear- and shield-bearing infantrymen to cover a line of archers directly behind them, firing over the infantry's heads. Meanwhile the Assyrian chariotry and cavalry opened the fight with archery and attempts to flank the enemy formation. Eventually the infantry would close to some form of hand-to-hand combat. When an enemy formation broke, the lighter spearmen led the pursuit, along with the mounted troops, followed up by the remainder.[13]

Figure 3.5 Assyrian spearman/archer teams, mid-seventh century BCE. Carving of the Battle of Ulai River, ca. 653 BCE. From Ashurbanipal's palace in Nineveh.

If the evidence for Assyrian tactics remains vague, it is much clearer that these men—archers, auxiliaries, and "regular" Assyrians—were part of a standing professional force. Much like armies in the emergence of other states, the core of the Assyrian army probably began life as the royal bodyguard, emulated on a smaller scale in the retinues of other high Assyrian officials (provincial governors and the like). Their equipment evolved over time, although probably not as systematically or as consistently as is sometimes argued, and they provided a model for expanding the army around them with other recruits. In smaller states, the expansion of the army around the bodyguard/retinue usually relied on temporary levies from the population. As Assyria grew, however, the problem of distance suggested the need for a standing force of professionals. Marching from the Assyrian heartland into the Levant or Egypt required a significant amount of time, time that local levies from a farming population found difficult to spare—the more so since, as discussed previously, the Assyrians at times campaigned throughout the year. The Assyrians conducted five campaigns into Egypt over eleven years, an effort across a distance that would have put enormous burdens on militia-style levies. This enforced professionalization of a large army beyond the

Figure 3.6 Assyrian spearmen in mountainous country, ca. 700 BCE.

small royal core is a common phenomenon among empires or large states trying to cope with the problem of campaigning at a distance, especially when that campaigning became constant. A state can potentially turn to mercenaries, finding professional soldiers for hire simply because an environment of constant conflict has created such men. Greece experienced this after its own period of extended, repeated conflicts in the fifth century BCE: veteran Greek soldiers literally camped in caves on the tip of the Mani Peninsula of southern Greece, waiting for potential employers to sail by. Assyria, however, chose to maintain and equip regular standing forces, refilled and expanded by men taken in the conquest of other territories, and further fleshed out by allied contingents. Esarhaddon (r. 680–669 BCE), for example, recorded how he took prisoners from a conquered city and "examined them," selecting those "soldiers, skilled in battle and combat" and attaching them to his royal guard, including "a group of charioteers, a group of cavalry, . . . officials, [engin]eers, troops, light troops, shield bearers, scouts, farmers, shepherds, (and) orchard keepers." Making the martial implications explicit, Esarhaddon noted that adding these men to his guard "filled Assyria in its entirety like a quiver."[14] The Assyrians did not invent this process, but as the first truly imperial-sized state, they were the first to have *as many* professional soldiers as they did, especially professional infantry. That breadth and depth of skill and experience may have been their key advantage in the field.[15]

Assyrian success had other foundations as well. Clearly their army was tactically more flexible than its opponents. The combination of different troop types, not least their first use of cavalry, allowed them to pursue their enemies across all terrains, fight different sorts of battles, and conduct the countless sieges. The sophistication of their logistics was also central to their success. Finally, the Assyrians notoriously were masters of psychological warfare. There is some debate here, but when the Assyrians described their victories, they were careful to do so in a way designed to use terror to discourage further resistance. An early (ninth century) trope of Assyrian victory was "I burnt their adolescent boys and girls." A more extended example makes the point even more emphatically. When Assurnasirpal II (r. 883–859 BCE) marched his army against the rebellious city of Suru, he so frightened the inhabitants that they rushed out to surrender immediately, pleading for their lives. Nevertheless, he wreaked a terrible vengeance, which he then recorded on the temple walls, where future visitors would be sure to see it:

> With my staunch heart and fierce weapons I besieged the [already surrendered] city. . . . I erected a pile in front of his gate; I flayed as many nobles as had rebelled against me (and) draped their skins over the pile. . . . I flayed many right through my land (and) some I draped their skins over the walls. I slashed the flesh of the eunuchs (and) of the royal eunuchs who were guilty. I brought [the chief rebel] to Nineveh, flayed him, (and) draped his skin over the wall of Nineveh.[16]

This form of highly violent propaganda declined as the empire matured. Emperors in the eighth century continued to celebrate their strength and their humiliation of their enemies, but wholesale slaughter and torture outside the battlefield or the actual process of storming a city seems to have subsided. Furthermore, some scholars maintain that the Assyrians did not differ substantially from their neighbors and predecessors in their treatment of defeated enemies. The ancient Near Eastern powers shared a level of ruthlessness that now appalls us but that was hardly abnormal in the long history of human conflict. The Assyrians may simply have been more prolific or adept at putting such tactics to work in propaganda.[17]

Assyrian success no doubt arose from a combination of all these factors: a professional, experienced, and balanced army, supported by a competent imperial bureaucracy, and led by politically astute kings who, when deemed necessary, cultivated a reputation for ruthlessness. Tactically, however, as much as they depended on infantry, even professional infantry carrying spears who were capable of fighting in close combat, it does not appear that Assyrian success was based on the solidity and irresistibility of infantry on the open battlefield, nor was the success of the Persians who followed them—despite their innovative combination of the archer with the spearman in the same person. Putting men in lines with spears at the cultural and physical center of the battlefield was an invention of the Greeks.[18]

COMMUNAL SOLIDARITY AND THE GREEK HOPLITE PHALANX

The basic image of the Greek hoplite and the phalanx is well known, if only through popular movies, graphic novels, and their ubiquitous presence in textbooks of military history and Western civilization. Nevertheless, the story of the hoplite phalanx remains worth telling, although the extraordinarily technical debates that continue to rage over its origins and even some of its basic characteristics make it hard to do it justice in a short space. Ironically, as much as classical scholars complain of gaps in the records, compared to what has come before in this chapter, the sources for the hoplite phalanx are voluminous indeed, particularly from the period of its maturity, if not from the era of its origins. We begin with the mature phalanx and its individual hoplites of the Classical period, roughly 500 BCE to 323 BCE, before returning to the question of origins.

First there is a question of terms. A hoplite was a Greek infantryman, named after the assemblage of weapons and armor that he carried (*hopla*). "Phalanx" is the term applied retrospectively to the formation in which these men fought: a long rectangle of closely packed files of men, generally eight deep, all armed with shield and spear. In its original meaning in Homer's epics the term referred merely to groups of warriors, subsequently acquiring the connotation of a densely packed body of men, and only much later being applied to the specific battle formation of the classical Greek hoplite. The nature of the formation was closely tied to the men's equipment, and so, without suggesting that one automatically followed from the other, let us begin with the equipment.[19]

A classical hoplite wore a heavy bronze helmet, perhaps four or five pounds. In its most famous "Corinthian" shape it completely enclosed the head and face, including the ears (see Figure 3.7). In the fifth and fourth centuries hoplites increasingly used more open-faced helmets with additional openings for the ears; sometimes they wore just felt or leather caps. A similar process of lightening the load affected the design of the breastplate, which in its earliest incarnations was solid bronze, covering chest and back. Later versions (after the mid-sixth century BCE) shifted to a stiffened linen and leather combination

Figure 3.7 Classical Greek hoplite. A Greek bronze from Dodona, ca. 510–500 BCE.

that was both lighter and cooler. Bronze greaves protected the shins, apparently also flexibly gripping the wearer's legs, but no doubt irritating them over any long period. They too became less common over time, as did the even rarer examples of thigh or arm guards. The most important item of defensive equipment was undoubtedly the shield (*aspis*). This shield seems to have been a purely Greek invention, made of wood, sometimes covered with a thin bronze sheet. It was about three feet across with a dramatically concave, or bowl, shape, finished by a straight rim, and made with two handles, one in the center for the forearm, the other near the rim for the hand to grasp. Held this way on the left arm, the shield in rest position (it may have weighed thirteen to sixteen pounds) was held with the rim on the bearer's shoulder. Extended outward from the body in a defensive posture, much of its diameter projected to the left of the soldier, providing protection for his neighbor to the left, who therefore famously pressed to his right seeking its cover during a battlefield advance. The key offensive weapon for the hoplite was his eight-foot thrusting spear, iron-tipped on one end and with a bronze butt spike on the other, a backup if the spear broke and also suitable for stabbing downward into prone enemies. Like the spear of the Assyrians shown in Figure 3.5, it was primarily wielded overhand, although some have suggested that it may have been carried underhand during the initial charge. Finally, the hoplite carried a sword as a last resort.[20]

Except for the relatively heavy body armor, this assemblage of equipment, or "panoply," is not that different from what we have seen among the Assyrians. What made the hoplite phalanx unique was the system in which it was used. There were two key differences. First, with the infamous exception of Sparta, the Greek hoplites were not professionals. They were citizens of the individual Greek city-states, who provided their own equipment, considered fighting a civic duty, and normally expected to fight relatively brief campaigns in the summer not far from their home city. Second, there was no direct blending of spearman and archer within the formation (at least not in its mature classical form—more on that in a moment). Instead, and this is the key point, the battle turned on the solidity and irresistibility of the formation itself, not on firepower or on the individual skill of each warrior in close combat.

In the field, at least when Greek faced Greek, and often beyond, a phalanx battle had a highly ritualistic quality that both sides understood. By "ritual" I do not mean restrained or limited. Rather, the battle was an act surrounded by predictable phases of preparation and completion which served to solemnize, motivate, and commemorate all at once. At the center of all this symbolic rhetoric was the commitment of the individual to the success of the group. Battle was preceded by religious sacrifices, the taking of omens, and speeches from the generals to their men. Each side generally allowed the other the time to draw up in the long linear formation typical to the phalanx, filling some open agricultural plain in the otherwise rough, rocky, and ravine-riddled Greek landscape. They marched into the line in files of eight (usually), with a veteran file leader and file closer. The files closed up tightly side by side, encouraged to do so by the protection offered by their neighbor's shield. That tendency went to work as the two lines advanced toward each other (rarely did one side remain stationary to receive the other's advance). The whole vast line tended to drift to the right, occasionally leading each army's right flank at the moment of contact to extend beyond and overlap the enemy's left flank. The advance was slow; the armor was too heavy and the summer too hot for it to be anything else. To run any distance was most unusual. After the Athenian defeat of the Persians at Marathon in 490 BCE, the Athenian dramatist Aristophanes made a point of reminding his Athenian audience of the distinctive glory of that moment, having his veterans exclaim: "To the battle-shock we ran."[21] It is unclear exactly what happened at the moment of contact. In one possible sequence of events, each phalanx increased its speed to a trot over the last twenty yards or so, crashing spears and shields into the enemy, hoping to bowl them over with the momentum of the initial onset. In another sequence, the hoplites slowed at the last moment and reset their battle line as they stepped forward into the fray. Either way, the first two or three ranks of each side closed up their files and presented their shields while stabbing overhand with their spear, seeking an opening in their enemy's defenses. Meanwhile the next five or six ranks held their spears upright and pressed forward against the men in front. That pressure could end up with the two opposing front ranks' shields pressing literally against each other, with the back ranks leaning their shoulders into the concave bowl of their shield and pressing into the backs of their file leaders, a phase the Greeks

Figure 3.8 The Chigi vase, ca. 650 BCE. One of the few representations of a phalanx in combat, painted very early in its development. It continues to generate much discussion.

called the *othismos*, the push. Each side thus hoped to force the other back, creating confusion, tripping, or falling, while the advancing troops trampled over and stabbed downward at the fallen. In the end, one side gave way and fled. The battle itself and the killing within it was no ritual—it was a bloody and destructive fight—but as soon as the battle was completed, ritual reasserted itself. Pursuit of the defeated was generally prohibited. The victor stripped the enemy dead of their equipment; the loser requested a truce to recover the bodies, thereby admitting defeat; and the victors erected a trophy to commemorate their collective success.

This system used by two armies against each other produced a vicious, usually short, close-quarter battle, but also (despite the viciousness) relatively few casualties. In most battles in history, the vast majority of casualties came from the losing side as they fled. Turning to flee generated a moment of vulnerability. Some were killed immediately. Others discarded their weapons as they fled, and so were killed as they ran, vulnerable to swifter pursuers. Greek hoplite clashes, however, generated fewer casualties because the "swifter pursuers" simply did not exist. The hoplite army in its classical form had few light troops and little cavalry, who could have done real damage to a fleeing army. Victorious hoplites were probably just as exhausted as their opponents and not given to pursuit. Contemporary Persians, encountering this kind of battle, were both appalled and impressed. The Greek historian Herodotus, admittedly a biased source, has the Persian general Mardonius in 490 BCE describe the manner of Greek warfare: "When they declare war on each other, they go off together to the smoothest and levellest bit of ground they can find, and have their battle on it—with the result that even the victors never get off without heavy losses, and as for the losers—well, they're wiped out."[22] Mardonius exaggerated the system's lethality, but the Persians and others also quickly moved to hire Greek hoplites as mercenaries. The phalanx, for all its idiosyncrasies, proved that it could be the irresistible force and an immovable wall at one and the same time.

Origins

Where did this formation, this "system," come from? Its exact origins lie in the poorly recorded Archaic period of Greece, evolving into its mature form over the period from 700 BCE to 500 BCE. We must rely on archaeological evidence, extremely limited texts, and a certain inescapable amount of speculation, but the phalanx seems to represent a peculiar combination of Greek culture, the city-states' demographic growth (and thus capacity), and a calculation about the efficacy of the formation itself.

As we saw in chapter 2, the Mycenaeans of Bronze Age Greece built their martial rhetoric and imagery around the chariot, but they too had "masses of men in the background." There are a number of contemporary portrayals from Mycenae and Knossos of organized groups of uniformly equipped spearmen. Beyond that it is difficult to say much about Bronze Age Greek infantrymen.

During the long, undocumented centuries that followed the twelfth-century catastrophe, the Greeks ceased using the chariot in significant numbers. It continued to be a prestige and ceremonial vehicle, hence its prominence in the much later *Iliad* and its frequent depiction on the funerary vases of Dark Age Greece. What we see instead, both archaeologically and in the battle descriptions of Homer (whose work is best avoided as a historical portrait of *any* single period, but if pressed into service is most reliable for the ninth and eighth centuries), are loose groups of individual warriors, probably nobles and their retinues, using bows, javelins (often identifiable in vase paintings by the throwing loop attached to the shaft), and a long thrusting spear. They wore more armor than one would find in the contemporary state armies of the Iron Age Near East, but these Greeks were aristocratic warriors providing their own equipment and were more interested in self-preservation than cost. There is also a fascinating possibility of influence from Assyria. The helmets of the Assyrian Qurrean auxiliaries are almost identical to that of a bronze helmet found at Argos, Greece, both dating from the eighth century BCE. The Argos

(a)   (b)

Figure 3.9 *a & b* Assyrian influence in Greece? 3.9a shows Qurrean auxiliaries of the Assyrian army at the siege of Lachish, ca. 700 BCE. 3.9b is the helmet and armor found in a grave at Argos, Greece, from about 750 BCE. Note the distinctly similar helmets.

helmet, however, was accompanied by a bronze cuirass much heavier than anything worn in the Near East at the time (see Figure 3.9a and b).

The individual components of the hoplite panoply, including even the large, round, two-handled shield, crept into art and artifacts over the course of the eighth century, and especially in the early seventh century. The battle portrayals from that period, however, show missile throwers and heavily armored infantry all mixed up together, perhaps not unlike the Assyrian system, or even less linear than theirs (see Figures 3.10, 3.11, and 3.12). It seems clear that the individual elements of the hoplite panoply were adopted, including even the two-handed circular shield, well before the tightly formed phalanx had been

Figure 3.10 A Greek vase, ca. 730 BCE, with warriors carrying a variety of shield types. A round shield was one among many types, even for otherwise uniformly armed infantrymen, here also carrying two javelins.

Figure 3.11 A Greek vase from Paros, ca. 700 BCE, showing an assortment of warrior types. Some figures appear to be wearing components of the hoplite panoply, but unlike later hoplites, relying on bows and javelins.

Figure 3.12 A Greek vase, ca. 670 BCE, **mixed hoplites and missile troops?** More and more armed like later hoplites, the warriors here seem to be fighting with missile troops mixed in.

created. Recently, historian Hans van Wees has claimed that this form of mixed combat persisted well into the sixth and even the early fifth century BCE, arguing for a truly slow evolutionary development of the matured spearman-only phalanx. He supports his case in part by citing the Chigi vase (see Figure 3.8) from about 650 BCE, which still shows some men in the phalanx carrying javelins as well as spears. Van Wees goes further, arguing that even the classical phalanx (after 500 BCE) continued to fight in a relatively open formation, unlike what was described earlier in this chapter. I disagree both with this later dating and with the idea of an "open formation" classical phalanx and continue to hold to the traditional view that something like the mature phalanx was in place by the time of the Chigi vase, filled by hoplites more heavily armored than contemporary infantry in the Near East and than the classical hoplites of the fifth century. But why did it appear at all, whether in the seventh century or the fifth? Or, more importantly, why did it function as it did?[23]

The answer lies in the history of the Greek city-state itself, the polis. As Greece's population recovered during the Archaic period, beginning sometime after 800 BCE many Greek communities coalesced around central towns. A town, or *asty*, typically had two centers: a market area and public gathering place (the *agora*), and a fortified and elevated place of refuge called the *acropolis*, often also associated with temples or ritual spaces—of which Athens' is now the most famous. Surrounding this urban center was the agrarian hinterland (*chora*) where many of the people who identified with the *asty* lived and farmed, traveling to the center for business, marketing, protection, and ritual. Such an arrangement of space and function is not unusual; indeed, it corresponds rather well to city-state development both earlier and later elsewhere in the world. But for reasons that are not fully clear, the farmers of that community managed to rein in their aristocratic leaders, while simultaneously creating a tightly bound self-identified community that united the residents of *chora* and *asty* into a single community, something the Greeks called the polis. That word had a meaning beyond simply city or even city-state. It was not merely a tangible place, but rather a collection of ideas and loyalties. Although we now generally refer to the various poleis by their place names, such as Athens, Corinth, or Sparta, the ancient Greeks thought of the polis as the community of people. Thus, inscriptions refer not to a place, but rather to a people: "The council and assembly of the Athenians decree . . ." or the "constitution of the Spartans says . . ." The idea of the polis became so important to the Greeks that it became part and parcel of what it meant to be Greek. Exile from one's polis was the worst of punishments. Some scholars have suggested that this relative political egalitarianism actually resulted from the creation of the egalitarian phalanx: distributed military service led to distributed political power (although not all citizens could afford to fight in the phalanx, it still represented a wider cross section of society than older aristocratic systems of fighting). The evidence does not really support such direct cause-and-effect clarity, but something happened during the Archaic age to invigorate a unique degree of communal cohesion and participatory government in a city-state level society.[24]

What we *can* say is that this coherent community, composed of citizens with political rights in the state, developed in parallel with the phalanx. Each reinforced the other over time: neighbors became filemates and filemates became neighbors (broadly speaking; there is no evidence of actual neighbors serving next to each other). This expansion of *committed* military service beyond the narrow pool of aristocrats, as opposed to the Near Eastern style of *conscripted* military service, represented a significant expansion of a community's military capacity—at least in self-defense. Indeed, its origins may lie partly in a calculation of military necessity in which communities struggled for control of Greece's relatively scarce farmland, and competitive pressures led them to enlarge their armies. In this case they broadened the pool of soldiers by turning to a broader social spectrum (beyond the aristocrats) and incorporating them into a relatively simple system that had the virtue of being temporary—it was a militia, not a standing force. Furthermore, this emerging culture of committed corporatism lent the phalanx cohesion. It was not the spears and shields that made the formation strong. As on all battlefields, the efficacy of the army lay in the willingness of its members to continue to fight. The values associated with fighting in the phalanx reflected the corporate quality of life in the polis. The most potent symbol of that corporatism proved to be the shield: an object that protected one's neighbor as well as one's self, leading to the Greek expression "Men wear their helmets and breastplates for their own needs, but they carry shields for the men of the entire line." It was a crime under Athenian law to throw away one's shield, as doing so suggested that one had fled the field.[25]

Consider the rhetorical focus in the following two contrasting passages. The first is from *The Iliad*, probably composed in the eighth century. Although it is true that *The Iliad* frequently acknowledged the presence of "masses of men in the background," it was a poem that above all celebrated the exploits of individual warriors.

> *And right in the midst sprang Agamemnon first*
> *and killed a fighter, Bienor, veteran captain,*
> *then his aide Oileus lashing on their team.*
> *Down from the car he'd leapt, squaring off,*

charging in full fury, full face, straight
into Agamemnon's spearhead ramming sharp— . . .
He battered Oileus down despite the Trojan's rage
and the lord of fighters left them lying there, both dead
and their chests gleamed like bronze as he stripped them bare.[26]

In contrast, compare the emphasis of the late seventh-century Greek poet Tyrtaios.[27]

And it is a good thing for his city and all the people share with him
when a man plants his feet and stands in the foremost spears
relentlessly, all thought of foul flight completely forgotten,
and has well trained his heart to be steadfast and to endure,
and with words encourages the man who is stationed beside him.

or

Those who, standing their ground and closing their ranks together,
endure the onset at close quarters and fight in the front,
they lose fewer men. They also protect the army behind them.
Once they flinch, the spirit of the whole army falls apart.

This is an entirely different style and emphasis within the discourse on war, distinguished both from what had preceded it in Greece and from what we have seen in Assyria and elsewhere in the Bronze and Iron Ages. Although it has been suggested that neither Tyrtaios nor the Chigi vase prove a *deep* phalanx, or even a heavy infantry-only phalanx (his poems seem to include missile throwers in and among the hoplites), both suggest the development of the organizational and ideological core of the phalanx, to which additional ranks could be added as the city-state's population expanded. Within this new formation (deep or not) something dramatic had happened not only to the warriors' sense of social equality but also to their rhetorical emphasis on *what mattered* in combat. The prowess of the individual warrior of *The Iliad* (often delivered to battle by his chariot) had yielded to the efficacy of men in lines with spears, reliant on each other, and holding fast for the sake of the community. The phalanx was an innovation if for no other reason than that. This shift in discourse made the actions of the group the thing that mattered in battle. Social and psychic investment was increasingly channeled to those men who fought in that way.[28]

The bottom line is that the phalanx's exact origins and even chronology must remain unclear, but its development was clearly an evolutionary process interacting with the values of the polis. Once in place, however, the virtue of steadfast courage in the collective fight, not the aristocratic display of individual skill, became the core value that made the phalanx so cohesive and effective.

The clash of hoplite phalanxes was not the sum total of Greek warfare. Among the citizens of most mainland Greek poleis, the phalanx occupied the center of their cultural vision and practice of war, at least until the fourth century. But there were other forms of war within Greece or fought by Greeks, less ritualized, less honored, but hardly unimportant. Everett Wheeler, for example, points out that the Greeks could fight a much more unrestrained form of war, the *polemos akeryktos/aspondos*, "war without heralds/truce." Furthermore, not all Greeks lived in poleis. Some retained more tribal and distributed forms of residence and subsistence, forming an *ethnos*. Such communities tended to fight more as individual skirmishers, throwing javelins and wearing little armor. In time such men, called peltasts, formed increasingly important parts of Greek armies fighting around and with the phalanx, or operating independently at the behest and in the hire of a polis. Indeed, hiring mercenaries in general, hoplites or peltasts, became much more common as the wars of the late fifth century and the fourth became longer and more geographically distant. Amateur citizens, supposed to be only briefly in arms, became de facto professional soldiers after extended campaigns abroad. Gone too long from their farms, they instead sold their skills to whoever would hire them. The immutable requirements of distance and time thus created professionals, not, in this case, by state command, but simply by the circumstances of continuous warfare. The competitive demands of warfare in the late Classical period also produced a proliferation of tactical adjustments, troop types—including the aforementioned peltasts—and combinations thereof, something that further encouraged the emergence of mercenaries and professional soldiers. Finally, the Spartans departed from this whole paradigm, while simultaneously constituting its most efficient practitioners, because they had deliberately cultivated a role for themselves as professional hoplites from a very early date, sustained on the backs of the conquered surrounding peoples of Laconia and Messenia in southern Greece.[29]

The phalanx was not the sum of Greek warfare, but it made Greeks famous. It was the ideological and material center of their way of war from at least 600 BCE down to their defeat by Philip of Macedon in 338 BCE, and it was demonstrably effective. Mardonius's ridicule of its foolishness notwithstanding, after the Persians experienced it, they rapidly moved to hire Greeks into their own forces, although they proved uninterested in or incapable of copying it themselves. This raises two questions: What made the Greek phalanx so effective—effective in this case against a Persian Empire that by 490 BCE had conquered much of the world from India to Egypt to Anatolia? And, secondly, why was it so hard to copy? The answers are multiple, interestingly related, and overlapping. No single explanation will do.

One easy explanation for the phalanx's success was the sheer weight of the formation, meaning its human density as well as the armor its individual soldiers carried. Near Eastern formations of "men in lines with spears," the Persian version included, do not appear to have fought in such close formation, and its members certainly did not wear as much armor. Another suggestion has been that this way of fighting was seen by others as particularly vicious at the cutting edge of combat. The close-quarters, face-to-face battle simply overwhelmed those not accustomed to it. I argue that the "closeness" of the fight did not present a problem. It would not have surprised an Assyrian spearman accustomed to storming the walls of a city; there is little fighting in history more "vicious" and personal than that fought on the walls during an assault. The apparent "heaviness" and "viciousness," in reality are merely *symptoms* of the formation's fundamental cohesion. Heavy can be brittle and easily broken. Vicious can be passing, followed by flight. What made the phalanx dauntingly effective to those not accustomed to it was its combination of corporate persistence, behind relatively heavy protective armor, and its fundamentally *collective tactical action*: the hedge of spears, tightly formed, well protected by armor and shield, and imbued with a deeply evolved set of cultural ideals of mutual support. This was not the comradeship of a "band of brothers," but rather a profoundly individualistic competitive desire that paradoxically sought to display prowess by *persisting* in place, by not running, by fighting and enduring for the whole, and thereby proving individual worth.[30]

Furthermore, in an odd and perhaps unexpected way, the Greeks' equipment encouraged this cohesive persistence. The effect of the shield within this cultural system is obvious. But consider the helmet. It is an oft-neglected truth that battles are not won simply through killing the enemy. Battles are won (at least prior to the era of truly remote-controlled warfare) by inspiring sufficient fear in the enemy that they flee or become passive. Killing is one way to do that, but a more efficient way is to create conditions in which much larger numbers of the enemy begin to *anticipate* death and react based on that fear. It is for this reason that an elephant could have an outsized effect on those inexperienced with their limitations, or that a cavalry charge very often never had to contact an enemy formation: undisciplined or inexperienced infantrymen simply lost faith that they could resist. Most famous of all is the flank or rear attack. The advantage of a flank attack is usually explained in geometric terms: a linear formation is weaker on its narrow end, or, it cannot turn to meet the attack and is thus hit in its unshielded side, and so on. Instead, consider that flanking attacks, or any other similar form of bad news, such as the death of a general, is often perceived first by the men in the rear, who are not actively fighting and thus are free to survey the battlefield. Infected with fear, they might take one step backward to consider what is happening. In any sort of close formation, let alone a Greek phalanx, that backward step would immediately be noticed by the man to his front, creating a sense of moral (or even physical) pressure lifted. Thus panic can cascade from the rear forward. The Greeks were aware of the problem and placed veteran soldiers in the rear rank for just this reason. Furthermore, note how the Corinthian-style closed helmet makes it more difficult for a Greek soldier to be aware of his surroundings. Their equipment, helmet and shield (if pressed into the backs of their fellows in front of them), rendered them more single-minded and forward-oriented. It was not at all uncommon for a Greek army to succeed on one wing, without ever realizing that its other wing had been defeated. Whichever army was able to figure that out and take advantage first was often the ultimate victor.[31]

All of these realities taken together explain why the phalanx proved difficult for the Persians, and many other peoples, to copy. Its effectiveness *did* derive partly from its equipment, and that could be copied. But the paradoxically individualistic corporate cohesion that held the phalanx together on the battlefield was a deeply evolved and unique product rooted in the Greek culture of the polis. That said, however, it was not hard to look at the phalanx and see the material advantages of deep blocks of men presenting a hedge of spears, especially as cavalry gained importance. An adjusted version of the Greek phalanx, clearly copying its basic concepts, emerged just to the north of Greece proper, in Macedon.

THE MACEDONIAN SARISSA PHALANX

We can deal with the Macedonian version of the phalanx much more briefly because in many ways it resulted from a calculated copying and tinkering with the *material* aspects of the Greek version while building it on completely different *moral* and cultural foundations. In essence, Philip II, who ruled Macedon from 359 BCE to 336 BCE, mastered the tricky task of expanding a king's personal retinue into something both larger and more professional while retaining the retinue's powerful sense of personal loyalty. Macedon had long had kings—contemporary Greeks considered it backward in that way—but the Macedonian kingship was far from autocratic. Philip ruled a basically rural people, who lived scattered around the countryside in subordination to an aristocratic class who retained substantial autonomy for themselves. Prior to his reforms, a Macedonian army in the field was composed of an aristocratic cavalry, who claimed special status as "companions" of the king, and a poorly armed peasant militia. Macedon had neither an urban center nor a farming middle class capable of affording the hoplite panoply. Although no autocrat, the Macedonian king was traditionally the supreme commander of the army, and that authority seems to have given him some freedom to impose change. He certainly seems to have had more flexibility to innovate and restructure the state's military system than a typically fractious Greek city-state would have. Even so, even Philip's reforms may not have come all at once. King Archelaus, one of his predecessors who ruled from 413 BCE to 399 BCE, had improved the Macedonian infantry, increasing the weight of their armor, if not entirely converting them to hoplites, and there is some evidence of hoplite-style infantry in Macedonia by the 370s. By the beginning of Philip's reign in 359 the military value of a solid block of phalanx infantry, operating in combination with light-armed skirmishers and cavalry—a combination increasingly common in Greece proper by the fourth century—had become clear. But copying the organic corporate cohesion of the polis-based phalanx was difficult. Greek hoplite mercenaries no longer relied on polis-based cohesion, but they were both veteran professionals and men born into the value system from which it derived. Philip wanted that same solidity and irresistibility, but he needed some other foundation for it. Furthermore, Philip's ambitions demanded an army that could stay in arms for longer than a single season—one that could march the distances required for conquest and control without needing to return home for the harvest.[32]

His solution was to take that rude peasant militia, supply them with their equipment from the state's coffers, and then pay them regularly from state revenues—a process initiated in part because of Philip's taking of the gold and silver mines at Crenides (renamed Philippi) in 356 BCE. He then sustained the process by expanding the state through conquest. As part of that reorganization he also strengthened and elaborated the relationship between himself and those men, calling them his *pezhetairoi*, or "foot companions." His military successes, and especially those of his son Alexander, further welded his men to him—in part because of the material rewards that success provided. Furthermore, as much as this book may at times emphasize deep cultural and material forces, personality can leave an indelible imprint on an army, shaping its culture and redefining its future. There can be little doubt of the impact of Philip and Alexander on creating the culture of a professional, cohesive, long-serving, and loyal force of infantrymen.[33]

Philip also shifted the material foundation of the phalanx, perhaps out of an initial concern over the improbability of turning his peasants into soldiers. Instead of the eight-foot thrusting spear and broad shield, he armed his men with the sarissa, a sixteen- to eighteen-foot pike, held with two hands, with a heavy counterbalance on the butt end (see Figure 3.13). With both hands busy, the shield was reduced in size and held in position by a loop over the shoulder and neck. He deepened the formation to ten and later sixteen men, and with sixteen men across, the 256-man *syntagma* became the basic unit of the Macedonian phalanx. At this depth and with such a long pike, the first four or five ranks would advance with their pikes lowered, leaving their opponents to cope with a veritable thicket of points projecting at varying distances

Figure 3.13 Modern reenactors comparing the reach of the sarissa to that of the hoplite spear.

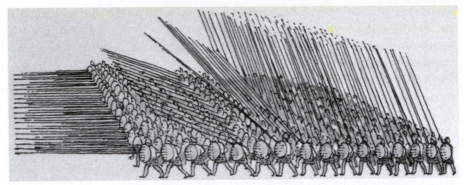

Figure 3.14 The Macedonian phalanx. An artist's reconstruction of one *syntagma* (256 men: 16 wide and 16 deep) of a Macedonian phalanx.

from the front (see Figure 3.14). Individuals within this formation simply did not need as much armor as did traditional hoplites, and so in some ways they became more mobile—especially when tasked with nonphalangial duties like storming a city or pursuing skirmishers into rough terrain (when they used neither the sarissa nor the phalanx formation). The phalangites' success in a wide variety of situations derived from yet another reform: unlike the Greeks' amateur ideal for their hoplites, Philip instituted training for his new peasant troops. According to later classical sources, Philip "held unremitting exercises in full kit as well as competitive exercises."[34]

In open battle the sarissa phalanx served as the anvil of Philip and Alexander's army. Around it and to screen it, he deployed contingents of mercenary skirmishers of various types, and he greatly strengthened the traditional Macedonian cavalry to act as hammer to the anvil. Philip's army was not initially very large. Its success in conquering Greece allowed for some expansion, but the force that Alexander took into Persia probably numbered only some forty thousand men, of which twenty thousand were actually from Macedon. Literally at the center of this army was Philip's new form of men in lines with spears, described by one ancient source as a battle line that was

> indeed wild and rough, yet it protects behind its spears wedges of tough, densely packed soldiers who cannot be budged. They themselves call it a phalanx, an infantry column that holds its ground. Man is locked to man, arms to arms. Attention fixed on their commander's signal, they have been trained to follow the standards and hold formation. Whatever is commanded, they obey.[35]

Enemy troops probably rarely actually tried to push themselves into the pikes. Instead, the phalanx's motion, or its immovability, created gaps in enemy lines as they tried to maneuver around it, creating opportunities for the Macedonian cavalry. As is well known, Alexander was wildly, improbably successful with this army. He rapidly overran and destroyed the Persian Empire, extending the Macedonians' reach over the course of eleven years of continuous campaigning from Greece, to Egypt, through Persia, and on into India. When Alexander died the new Macedonian empire quickly dissolved into squabbling components ruled by Macedonian dynasts, the "successors." They continued to rely on the phalanx at the center of armies now much augmented and complicated by the many different peoples of the eastern Mediterranean and southwest Asia. The Macedonian kingdoms would famously go down in defeat before the Romans.

CONCLUSION

There have been many versions of "men in lines with spears" in the history of human conflict. We could have explored similar developments in China, or Japan, or the Zulus of southern Africa in a much later era; the late medieval Swiss pike formations will appear in chapters 7 and 9. It is, after all, a simple idea, and the capacity requirement is generally very low—spears are simple and cheap. But as the examples in this chapter attest, the potential variations on the basic idea are many, and both culture and calculation shaped the end result. A cohesive mass of spear- or pikemen was a powerful formation, even when facing cavalry. Achieving that cohesion, however, was the trick. As we will see in the next chapter, Rome and Han China found other paths to cohesion, with and without spears, in the form of synchronized discipline.

TIMELINE

ca. 1200 BCE	End of the Bronze Age
ca. 911 BCE	Neo-Assyrian Empire reemerges from the catastrophe
	The Archaic Period of Greek History (ca. 800–510 BCE)
ca. 650 BCE	Chigi vase showing emerging Greek phalanx
627 BCE	End of Neo-Assyrian Empire
	The Classical Period of Greek History (ca. 510–323 BCE)
490–479 BCE	Greek-Persian Wars
431–404 BCE	Peloponnesian War between Athens and Sparta
359–336 BCE	Reign of Philip II of Macedon

Further Reading

Connolly, Peter. *Greece and Rome at War.* Englewood Cliffs, NJ: Prentice Hall, 1981.

Dawson, Doyne. *The First Armies.* London: Cassell, 2001.

Deszö, Thomas. "The Reconstruction of the Neo-Assyrian Army as Depicted on the Assyrian Palace Reliefs, 745–612 BC." *Acta Archaeologica Academiae Scientiarium Hungaricae* 57 (2006): 87–130.

Hanson, Victor Davis. *The Western Way of War: Infantry Battle in Classical Greece.* 2nd ed. Berkeley: University of California Press, 1998.

Kagan, Donald, and Gregory F. Viggiano, eds. *Men of Bronze: Hoplite Warfare in Modern Greece.* Princeton, NJ: Princeton University Press, 2013.

Lendon, J. E. *Soldiers and Ghosts: A History of Battle in Classical Antiquity.* New Haven, CT: Yale University Press, 2005.

Partridge, Robert B. *Fighting Pharaohs: Weapons and Warfare in Ancient Egypt.* Manchester, UK: Peartree, 2002.

Raaflaub, Kurt, and Nathan Rosenstein, eds. *War and Society in the Ancient and Medieval Worlds: Asia, the Mediterranean, Europe, and*

Mesoamerica. Washington, DC: Center for Hellenic Studies, 1999.

Sabin, Philip, Hans van Wees, and Michael Whitby, eds. *The Cambridge History of Greek and Roman Warfare*. Cambridge, UK: Cambridge University Press, 2007.

Snodgrass, A. M. *Arms and Armor of the Greeks*. Baltimore, MD: Johns Hopkins University Press, 1967, 1999.

Van Wees, Hans. *Greek Warfare: Myth and Realities*. London: Duckworth, 2004.

Notes

1. Hartmut Thieme, "Lower Palaeolithic Hunting Spears From Germany," *Nature* 385 (February 1997): 807–10, doi:10.1038/385807a0.

2. In several of his books; first argued in Victor Davis Hanson, *The Western Way of War: Infantry Battle in Classical Greece*, 3rd ed. (New York: Alfred A. Knopf, 2009).

3. Robert Charles Padden, "Cultural Change and Military Resistance in Araucanian Chile, 1550–1730," *Southwestern Journal of Anthropology* 13 (1957): 103–21.

4. William J. Hamblin, *Warfare in the Ancient Near East to 1600 B.C.: Holy Warriors at the Dawn of History* (New York: Routledge, 2006), 252–54, 423, 430; Doyne Dawson, *The First Armies* (London: Cassell, 2001), 112, 137; Anthony J. Spalinger, *War in Ancient Egypt: The New Kingdom* (Malden, MA: Blackwell, 2005), 16–17; fig 13.6b.

5. Pradeep P. Barua, *The State at War in South Asia* (Lincoln: University of Nebraska Press, 2005), 1–12; C. J. Peers, *Soldiers of the Dragon: Chinese Armies, 1500 BC–AD 1840* (New York: Osprey, 2006), 25; Ralph D. Sawyer, *Ancient Chinese Warfare* (New York: Basic Books, 2011).

6. Dawson, *First Armies*, 133, 139, 149–50; Robert Drews, *The End of the Bronze Age: Changes in Warfare and the Catastrophe ca. 1200 B.C.* (Princeton, NJ: Princeton University Press, 1993). Drews's conclusions are generally held to be too specific about tactics and the role of iron. The idea, however, that a succession of invaders fighting in a new way catalyzed a broader set of events that constituted the catastrophe of ca. 1200 BCE continues to have merit. See Eric H. Cline, *1177 B.C.: The Year Civilization Collapsed* (Princeton, NJ: Princeton University Press, 2014), esp. 164–65.

7. For a discussion of the origin of cavalry and its appearance in Assyria see Robert Drews, *Early Riders: The Beginnings of Mounted Warfare in Asia and Europe* (New York: Routledge, 2004), 65–66; Robin Archer, "Chariotry to Cavalry: Developments in the Early First Millennium," in *New Perspectives on Ancient Warfare*, eds. Garrett M. Fagan and Matthew Trundle (Leiden: Brill, 2010), 57–80. Benjamin R. Foster, ed., *Before the Muses: An Anthology of Akkadian Literature*, 3rd ed. (Bethesda, MD: CDL, 2005), 798 (quote).

8. Amy E. Barron criticizes unthinking use of the sculptures, but her comparison of the art to the artifacts supports the overall realism of the former. "Late Assyrian Arms and Armour: Art versus Artifact" (PhD diss., University of Toronto, 2010).

9. H. W. F. Saggs, "Assyrian Warfare in the Sargonid Period," *Iraq* 25.2 (1963): 145–54 (esp. 146–47); Barron, "Late Assyrian Arms," 25 and passim; Richard A. Gabriel, *The Great Armies of Antiquity* (Westport, CT: Praeger, 2002), 130; for horses: Arther Ferrill, *The Origins of War* (London: Thames & Hudson, 1985), 72, citing J. N. Postgate, *Taxation and Conscription in the Assyrian Empire* (Rome: Biblical Institute Press, 1974), 17; for Kar-Assur: Marc Van de Mieroop, *A History of the Ancient Near East, ca. 3000–323 BC*, 2nd ed. (Malden, MA: Blackwell, 2007), 231; for camps and

river crossing: Yigael Yadin, *The Art of Warfare in Biblical Lands in the Light of Archaeological Study*, vol. 2 (New York: McGraw-Hill, 1963), 292, 304; for logistics on the march: F. M. Fales, "Grain Reserves, Daily Rations, and the Size of the Assyrian Army," *State Archives of Assyria Bulletin* 3 (1989): 23–34.

10. Dawson, *First Armies*, 190.

11. This summary condenses much debate (and also change over time), but generally follows Barron, "Assyrian Arms," 97–100.

12. Dawson, *First Armies*, 187; Barron, "Assyrian Arms," 135 (quote).

13. Davide Nadali, "Assyrian Open Field Battles: An Attempt at Reconstruction and Analysis," in *Studies on War in the Ancient Near East*, ed. J. Vidal (Münster, Germany: Ugarit Verlag, 2010), 117–52; Garrett G. Fagan, "'I Fell upon Him Like a Furious Arrow': Toward a Reconstruction of the Assyrian Tactical System," in Fagan and Trundle, *New Perspectives on Ancient Warfare*, 81–100; JoAnn Scurlock, "Neo-Assyrian Battle Tactics," in *Crossing Boundaries and Linking Horizons*, ed. Gordon D. Young, Mark W. Chavalas, and Richard E. Averbeck (Bethesda, MD: CDL, 1997), 491–517.

14. Esarhaddon 033.r.iii.14–22, Royal Inscriptions of the Neo-Assyrian Period, available at http://oracc.museum.upenn .edu/rinap/rinap4/Q003262/html, accessed October 29, 2011.

15. Saggs, "Assyrian Warfare," 145–47.

16. A. Kirk Grayson, *Assyrian Rulers of the Early First Millennium BC* (Toronto: University of Toronto Press, 1991), 1:201, 199. Saggs, "Assyrian Warfare," makes the point that this sort of thing was not "sadism," but calculated terror, designed to forestall re-bellion and undermine the confidence of enemies.

17. Sarah C. Melville, "The Last Campaign: the Assyrian Way of War and the Collapse of the Empire," in *Warfare and Culture in World History*, ed. Wayne E. Lee (New York: New York University Press, 2011), 21–22;

Frederick Mario Fales, "On *Pax Assyriaca* in the Eighth-Seventh Centuries BCE and Its Implications," in *Isaiah's Vision of Peace in Biblical and Modern International Relations: Swords into Plowshares*, ed. Raymond Cohen and Raymond Westbrook (New York: Palgrave Macmillan, 2008): 17–35.

18. Dawson, *First Armies*, 193.

19. Terminology is discussed in E. Wheeler, "Land Battle," in *The Cambridge History of Greek and Roman Warfare*, ed. Philip Sabin, Hans van Wees, and Michael Whitby (Cambridge, UK: Cambridge University Press, 2007), 1:192; and Wheeler, "Intro-duction," in *The Armies of Classical Greece*, ed. Everett Wheeler (Burlington, VT: Ashgate, 2007), xxvii. I am much indebted to both of these sources, and for additional personal discussions with Wheeler for much of what follows (although we con-tinue to disagree on some points).

20. Gregory S. Aldrete has conducted useful experiments on the strength and weight of the linen cuirass. See his personal website, http://www.uwgb.edu/aldreteg/Linothorax .html, accessed October 14, 2014; Thucy-dides 5.71 in *The Landmark Thucydides*, ed. Robert B. Strassler (New York: Free Press, 1996), 343; Peter Hunt, "Military Forces," in Sabin, van Wees, and Whitby, *Cambridge History*, 1:111–17, is a good summary. Hanson, *Western Way of War*, Parts 2 and 4, remains a standard reference. All of these issues are repeated and debated in the essays in Donald Kagan and Gregory F. Viggiano, eds., *Men of Bronze: Hoplite Warfare in Modern Greece* (Princeton, NJ: Princeton University Press, 2013).

21. Aristophanes, *The Acharnians*, trans. Benjamin B. Rogers (Cambridge, MA: Harvard University Press, 1967), 69 (700).

22. Herodotus 7.9.2 in *The Histories*, trans. Aubrey de Sélincourt (New York: Penguin, 1954), 445. Wheeler notes that this is satirical, but also that it represents an accurate reflection of the ritual quality of hoplite battle (if not an accurate reflection

of casualties). Wheeler, "Land Battle," 190–91.

23. Hans van Wees, *Greek Warfare: Myths and Realities* (London: Duckworth, 2004), 166–83. Anthony Snodgrass, "Setting the Frame Chronologically," in Kagan and Viggiano, *Men in Bronze*, 85–94, handles these issues even-handedly.

24. Kurt A. Raaflaub, "Soldiers, Citizens, and the Evolution of the Early Greek *Poleis*," in *The Development of the Polis in Archaic Greece*, ed. Lynette Gail Mitchell and Peter John Rhodes (London: Routledge, 1997), 26–32; A. M. Snodgrass, "Hoplite Reform and History," *Journal of Hellenic Studies* 85 (1965): 110–22; Snodgrass, "The 'Hoplite Reform' Revisited," *Dialogues d'histoire Ancienne* 19 (1993): 47–61. See the introduction to Kagan and Viggiano, *Men in Bronze*, for more on this debate.

25. Plutarch, *Moralia* 241 f.16, trans. Frank Cole Babbitt (Cambridge, MA: Harvard University Press, 1968) 3:465.

26. Homer, *The Iliad* 11.106–119, trans. Robert Fagles (New York: Viking Penguin, 1990), 299.

27. Richmond Lattimore, trans., *Greek Lyrics*, 2nd ed. (Chicago: University of Chicago Press, 1960), 13–15.

28. On "discourse," see John A. Lynn, *Battle: A Cultural History of Combat and Culture* (Boulder, CO: Westview, 2003), xix–xxii; Kurt Raaflaub, "Archaic and Classical Greece," in *War and Society in the Ancient and Medieval Worlds: Asia, the Mediterranean, Europe, and Mesoamerica*, ed. Kurt Raaflaub and Nathan Rosenstein (Washington, DC: Center for Hellenic Studies, 1999), 137; J. E. Lendon, *Soldiers and Ghosts: A History of Battle in Classical Antiquity* (New Haven, CT: Yale University Press, 2005), chs. 2 and 3; van Wees, *Greek Warfare*, 240.

29. Wheeler, "Land Battles," 190.

30. Lendon, *Soldiers and Ghosts*.

31. John Keegan, *The Face of Battle* (New York: Viking, 1976), 173, suggests that falling apart from the rear was a common phenomenon, based on contemporary observations of the retreat of the French formations at Waterloo. Thucydides 1.62 and 5.72–73, and cf. 4.126.

32. Joseph Roisman and Ian Worthington, eds., *A Companion to Ancient Macedonia* (Malden, MA: Wiley-Blackwell, 2010), 379, 448–50, 492–93; Alan B. Lloyd, "Philip II and Alexander the Great: The Moulding of Macedon's Army," in *Battle in Antiquity*, ed. Alan B. Lloyd (London: Duckworth, 1996), 169–98.

33. Lloyd, "Philip II and Alexander," 172, 177–78, 188. On the role of personalities within organizational culture see Mark Grimsley, "Success and Failure in Civil War Armies: Clues from Organizational Culture," in Lee, *Warfare and Culture in World History*, 115–42.

34. For technical discussion of the sarissa phalanx formation, see Everett L. Wheeler, "The Legion as Phalanx in the Late Empire, Part I," in *L'armée romaine de Dioclétien à Valentinien I*, ed. Yann Le Bohec and Catherine Wolff (Lyon: De Boccard, 2004): 309–58, esp. 327–31. Diodorus XVI.3, quoted in Lloyd, "Philip II and Alexander," 169–98, quote 171.

35. Quintus Curtius 3.2.13–14, quoted in Lloyd, "Philip II and Alexander," 190.

4

Discipline and Frontiers in the Agricultural Empires: Rome and China

300 BCE–400 CE

Rome: Disciplina and Limes • Infantrymen and Walls in Han China

LARGE, BUREAUCRATIC AGRICULTURAL empires face some basic and seemingly intractable security issues. The ruler at the center wants reliable troops, responsive to his (or her) command, but also must disperse them widely to control the interior and to defend (or expand) the perimeter. By definition, empires contain an assortment of ethnicities and conquered peoples who lack a "natural" loyalty to the center, and whose populace often makes up a substantial portion of the imperial military. Ethnically heterogeneous and widely dispersed forces are prone to develop local loyalties or, perhaps worse, loyalties to regional commanders who then constitute a threat to the center. The problem becomes clear when contrasted to the Greek military system just examined in chapter 3. The men of the Greek phalanx were ethnically, linguistically, geographically, and culturally homogenous; their loyalty to their polis was beyond question. Macedonian troops, at least prior to Alexander's successful expansion, held a traditional personal loyalty to their monarch reinforced by the rewards that came with Philip's and Alexander's successes. In contrast, the long-lived empires of Rome and Han China repeatedly struggled to balance external security and internal loyalty.

This chapter advances the sweeping generalization, designed to cover developments over centuries of change, that both Rome and Han China sought to resolve these problems through systems of bureaucratic military professionalism and normative discipline designed to create loyalty to the metropolitan center while enhancing tactical efficiency. In the early stages of empire, each society could impose discipline through the lure of rewards paid for by expansion. Obedience brought rewards in the form of reliable pay and plunder. As expansion slowed or ceased, however, both empires enhanced their systems of bureaucratized internal taxation to pay for an army that no longer paid for itself, built systems of frontier fortifications designed to reduce the number of men in the military (and to keep them occupied), and emphasized routinized normative discipline in standing armies of long service. Although they are crucial capacity issues, taxation and bureaucracy are a problem beyond the scope of this chapter. We focus instead on the two military innovations: an ideology of discipline and an infrastructure of frontier fortifications. Although neither was totally successful, they left profound legacies for the future of both Europe and China.

This chapter differs somewhat from its predecessors. Like the others, it focuses on key innovations (discipline and fortified frontiers) and examines their evolution, nature, and impact. But these innovations are unlike, for example, the chariot, in that they did not move around from a single originating point. This chapter is more of a comparative history, examining two societies' approaches to a similar set of problems. Comparison is both fruitful and fraught, not least because the nature of the surviving sources from the two societies can differ enormously. This is particularly problematic when seeking the underlying ideology for something as amorphous as "discipline." On that subject for Rome our best descriptive sources are from outsiders like Polybius (a Greek) or Josephus (a Jew) who felt compelled to describe things potentially unfamiliar to their prospective audience, but who might exaggerate for political purposes. Our other good source on discipline is a late would-be reformer, Vegetius, writing in the late fourth or early fifth century CE, who was trying to recall and recommend a golden era of disciplined infantry to his own supposedly corrupt age—using earlier sources that are now lost. For China's first unified empire, the short-lived Qin, or its successor dynasty, the Han, we simply do not have the same kind of outsider accounts. The best sources are three in number: the advice manuals of the earlier Warring States era, which were incorporated into martial training for much of the rest of Chinese history; Han period bureaucratic records; and the work of chroniclers, most famously Sima Qian and his father, Sima Tan, who wrote a massive history of China in the decades before and after the turn of the first century BCE. For the frontier systems, the differences between Roman and Chinese sources are even more profound. Rome's imperial frontier fortifications have been extensively surveyed, studied, excavated, and published. China's famous Great Wall dates from a much later era, and its predecessor wall systems from the Qin, Han, and other periods have simply not been as extensively studied. We will begin with the better-known Roman example, and the ensuing discussion of Han China will occasionally make explicit comparative references to the Roman experience.

ROME: *DISCIPLINA* AND *LIMES*

Much of Rome's early history is a mystery, shot through with later myth making. It began as one city-state among many on the Italian peninsula. After some very serious early struggles, Rome achieved dominance within

Italy. Several key characteristics of the Romans' approach to war and their later successes developed during this early period, including expansionism, inclusiveness, and the tactical system known as the legion.

As Nathan Rosenstein has pointed out, war and expansion helped early Rome solve domestic problems. Like most ancient societies, Rome possessed an aristocracy, the so-called patricians, whose lineage defined their status. Those aristocrats dominated the original Roman state. Early in Rome's history, however, the patricians and the plebeians, who were generally poorer but also included a substantial number of wealthy men, engaged in a long struggle over sharing political power, ending with essentially legal equality by 287 BCE. Over time wealthy plebeians moved into patrician circles, creating a kind of combined nobility of the wealthy, but the lineage division remained wide, if not unbridgeable. This struggle of the orders coincided and interacted with Rome's early wars in Italy, in that war and conquest eased social conflict by generating pride and personal wealth (through booty) for both patrician and pleb alike. Conquest may even have increased the pool of land available for distribution to Roman citizens. In one historian's interpretation, the struggle of the orders converted Rome from an "exclusive aristocratic society" to "a unified and cohesive citizen body."[1]

With respect to citizenship, Rome's early wars in Italy also demonstrated its distinctively inclusive way of dealing with former enemies. Rome established a pattern of allowing its conquered enemies to retain substantial political autonomy at the cost of formally becoming allies (*socii* or *foederati*) and having to provide troops for Rome's wars. During and especially after the Second Punic War (218–201 BCE), Rome tightened its military obligation for Italians, and also began imposing tribute on those communities conquered outside Italy (*tributum* was first imposed in Sicily in the 220s BCE). Nevertheless, the Romans not only included their allies in the distribution of the spoils of victory, they also started, beginning no later than the fourth century BCE, to extend Roman citizenship to some of their now-conquered former enemies. Citizenship carried rights and privileges within the Roman system, as well as the obligation to serve in the military. Although not all forms of citizenship were equal (early non-Roman citizens, for example, could not participate in the voting process in Rome), having citizenship nevertheless proved increasingly desirable as Rome's expansion continued. This process gradually endowed Rome with a massive manpower pool from which to draw. The existence of that pool did not enlarge any given field army. Generally speaking, field armies could only be as large as logistics would allow. In the wake of a battlefield defeat, however, of which Republican Rome suffered many, Rome was repeatedly able to raise yet another army, on the backs of peoples apparently persuaded by their inclusion that revolt was not in their interest. This system was not without friction. Under the pressure of constant Roman demands for military service, and *desiring* full Roman citizenship, many of the Italian allies revolted in the Social War (91–88 BCE). After bitter fighting, the

Roman response was to grant full citizenship in 90 BCE to all those Italians who had not revolted, and then to *all* Italians soon thereafter. This expansive vision of citizenship differed radically from the closed polis of the Greeks or the imperial logic of the Assyrians, for whom conquered peoples were subjects at best, not citizens. And although the Romans often displayed a prejudice against "legislated Romans," they nevertheless admitted them, even if it sometimes took a revolt to persuade the Roman leadership to do so. This "subtle flexibility of Roman identity" with its pattern of inclusion continued under the empire in various stages of increasing incorporation, until finally citizenship was extended to the entire empire in 212 CE.[2]

Expansion fed expansion, while Roman political inclusion swelled the pool of politically committed military labor and fed Rome's overall military capacity. But Roman enthusiasm for war arose from more than its economic benefits; it was also fed by Roman culture. The Roman aristocracy, patrician or wealthy plebeian, saw war as an opportunity to shine: an arena in which to display the aggressive courage, or *virtus*, and earn the glory, or *fama*, so essential to political success and stature in Rome. That desire to display *virtus* also played a role in the nature and success of the legion.

The Legion

Sometime early in the Republic, the Romans evolved their tactical organization from a variant of the Greek phalanx into the legion. The exact intermediate stages are much debated, but we have a clearer picture of what the legion looked like and how it operated by the third century BCE. The first key change was the provision of a subsistence allowance at the end of the fifth century, as Romans fought longer campaigns farther from home and soldiers could no longer afford to provide for themselves. At this early stage, and in a state still lacking coinage in any quantity, this did not yet qualify as "pay" in a traditional sense, but it created a precedent of state support to allow its citizens to campaign for extended times. Eventually it would become true pay supporting a career in the army. In the matured legion of the middle Republic there were four types of infantry, all citizens who met minimum property requirements, and who until the mid-second century BCE provided their own equipment (in addition, a small number of wealthier citizens formed a detachment of three hundred cavalry attached to each legion). The poorest and youngest men served as *velites*, unarmored but for a shield, who carried several javelins and fought in loose formations as skirmishers. The next two categories, the *hastati* and *principes*, resembled each other closely, separated only by their age (hastati were younger) and perhaps a certain richness of equipment. Both types, organized in maniples ("handfuls") of 120 men divided into two centuries of 60 men each, carried a large oval shield weighing twenty to twenty-two pounds, two heavy javelins (*pila*) of perhaps five pounds each, and a short stabbing sword, and were armored with a helmet and either a small breastplate or a mail shirt (see Figure 4.1). From some point in the third century, the second *pilum* was abandoned. Finally, the oldest, and presumably steadiest, men, the *triarii*, organized in half-sized maniples (still of two centuries each), fought in the manner of the old phalanx, carrying a shield and long thrusting spear. Each legion consisted of ten maniples of each type, adding up to four to five thousand men.[3]

The legion proved to be a highly flexible tactical system. The first key to that flexibility was its multilayered articulation: armies divided into legions, which subdivided into maniples, which subdivided into centuries, each with its own officer or subofficer. These divisions were not just artifacts of how the men were recruited; they corresponded to tactical roles. The maniples of hastati and principes lay at the core. All the hastati maniples, for example, lined up side by side in blocks, leaving a gap wide enough between each maniple for the principes maniples behind them to move into the gaps between the hastati maniples. Modern scholars refer to this as the *quincunx*, or checkerboard,

Figure 4.1 Relief showing Roman hastati/principes, end of second century BCE. From the monument of Domitius Ahenobarbus.

formation. There is a good deal of debate about how this worked in practice. Although Polybius says that the centuries lined up side by side, some have suggested (primarily from the meaning of their names, one "prior" and one "posterior") that one century lined up behind the other, and then just before the line moved into contact, the posterior century moved forward to fill in the gaps between the maniples. Others have argued that the legion never filled the gaps, simply fighting as they were (see Figures 4.2 and 4.3). I argue that in some fashion the maniples must have deployed into a continuous line,

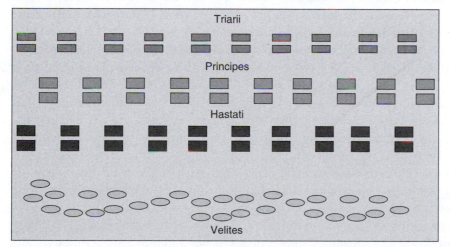

Figure 4.2 The manipular legion in the *quincunx*. There are ten maniples in each line. Each maniple is made up of two centuries, here shown with the centuries drawn up one behind the other. During the middle Republic each century had sixty men, save the *triarii*, who had thirty men each.

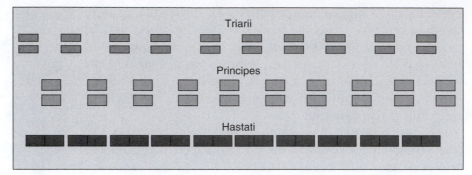

Figure 4.3 The manipular legion in an early stage of the battle. The *velites* (skirmishers) have withdrawn and the *hastati* centuries are now deployed side by side filling the gaps. If pressed they withdrew through the gaps in the *principes*.

probably with troops from the rear of the maniple flowing into the gaps (whether or not it was done by century).[4]

When attacking, which was much the Roman preference, the hastati advanced first (after an initial exchange of missiles between the velites and enemy skirmishers), throwing their pila on the run from about thirty meters, and then drawing their swords and charging. The combination of the shower of heavy javelins, often dragging down their enemies' shields, followed up so quickly by charging swordsmen, could prove overwhelming. Some enemies apparently found the Roman sword, borrowed from the Spanish, terrifying. Livy reported that "for men who had seen the wounds dealt by javelins and arrows and occasionally by lances, since they were used to fighting with the Greeks and Illyrians, when they had seen bodies chopped to pieces by the Spanish sword, arms torn away, shoulders and all, or heads separated from bodies, with the necks completely severed, or vitals laid open, and the other fearful wounds, realized in a general panic with what weapons and what men they had to fight."[5] If the hastati charge failed to break the enemy, they could retreat through the gaps in the principes and allow the principes their turn. If the battle went against them as well, both could retreat behind the triarii, who would then close ranks and fight in the more static defensive style of the phalanx. Such a moment represented a battle on the edge of defeat, generating the Roman proverb for a desperate situation: "Matters have come to the triarii."[6]

Despite disputes about the details, the basic outlines of this system are relatively well known, as are its tactical virtues. But where did it come from, and what does it have to do with the theme of discipline? Historian John Lendon has suggested a cultural explanation, to which I add the Romans' calculated awareness of its battlefield efficacy. Lendon argues that the early Roman phalanx proved poorly adapted to the extreme aggressiveness expected by the Roman ethic of *virtus*. *Fama* proved difficult to earn in the stolid immovability of that formation. As we saw in chapter 3, however, the phalanx required restraining individuals' preference for showy aggression, and so the Romans nurtured a counterpoise ethic of *disciplina*, originally meaning simply a brake on excessive aggression. For the phalanx to succeed required balancing the *virtus* and *disciplina*. Furthermore, the Greek phalanx had built its cohesive strength upon a communal sense of commitment. Rome, however, possessed of a historically ingrained cultural fear of military coups, mobilized its men in a way that at least seemed to deliberately split up neighbors into different legions. Some other form of cohesion was required to keep the men in their ranks, and the cultivated virtue of *disciplina* filled that role. The Romans also soon found that many of their early enemies fought in fast-moving formations of lightly armed troops, moving into and out of the hills of the central spine of Italy. Fighting them encouraged the Romans to develop a system that could be *both* speedy and stolid, immovable *and* ferocious. As Lendon points out, the manipular legion gave scope to aggression, especially for the younger men at the front of the legion, while also retaining a version of the old phalanx in the form of the triarii, manned by older, steadier, veterans. Thus, he argues, the "true secret of the manipular legion was that it made the soldiers in it braver."[7] To this individualistic effect we can add that the multi-echeloned legion also encouraged aggressive risk taking by its leadership. The built-in system of reserves allowed Roman generals to roll the dice and make large gambles, because their tactical system provided a backup in case the gamble failed. A few other ancient armies may have used a reserve in battle, but for the Romans such a reserve was built into their system.

The manipular legion of the middle Republic, recruited from propertied citizens generally obliged to serve six-year terms, and balancing *virtus* and *disciplina* in a manner rooted in Roman culture, was not yet the separate military culture of the professional, long-serving, frontier-defending, corporally disciplined legions of legend. Of course those legions of legend never existed on exactly those terms, but substantial changes did occur as Rome expanded beyond the Italian peninsula and became a truly imperial power. In the course of that expansion a combination of crises during the late Republic led to a series of reforms (ca. 100 BCE), often attributed to the plebeian consul Gaius Marius, although the changes were probably more evolutionary than singular. One reform was tactical: the manipular legion became instead the cohort legion (often called the Marian legion). Instead of thirty maniples, the legion now consisted of ten cohorts of three maniples each, and the cohort became the real tactical unit. This change reduced the legionary commander's work: he now had ten subordinate tactical units rather than thirty (we do not know enough about command arrangements within the legion to be sure of the exact flow of orders, but the change in the number of tactical units is clear). This reduced number accords well with modern business principles of how many direct subordinates one leader can effectively supervise. Furthermore, those ten cohorts were now standardized into a single type of infantry, based on the old hastati/principes model. The citizens who formerly had served as cavalry or velites now became legionary heavy infantry, while the role of cavalry and skirmishers was increasingly filled by men from allied states.

The full details of these changes are not important to us here. More important than this tactical tinkering was Marius casting the final straw in an ongoing shift in the Roman recruitment system. Through various previous emergencies, Rome had progressively lowered the property requirement for military service, and had even occasionally allowed landless citizens to join the legions. Marius, pressed by German tribes invading Italy at the end of the second century BCE and by a roughly concurrent series of wars in Africa, outmaneuvered his political opponents and recruited volunteers from the landless citizens, the *capite censi*, or head count. As this kind of recruitment grew more common, it had the concomitant effects of requiring the state to equip those soldiers, and also, portentously, of generating veterans who demanded land upon their release from service. Often, the "state," represented by the conservative Senate, declined to do so. Politically minded generals took the task upon themselves, thereby fostering a personal loyalty between the general and his soldiers that contributed substantially to the outbreak of the civil wars that finally ended the Republic.[8]

Marius neither foresaw nor intended that this would become the norm, but so it did, although slowly, and at first only in emergencies. The landless recruits' lack of economic options, however, probably saw such men remaining in the ranks longer, or returning more readily. Growing reliance on the head count for military service had implications far beyond the civil wars. In conjunction with continued territorial expansion, especially in conjunction with the later imperial establishment of stable frontiers, the shift in recruitment also affected the nature and quality of military service, now increasingly professional and "disciplined" in a more modern sense of the word. Poor recruits became dependent on the army, and although Marius's reforms did not immediately destroy the old Roman value of leaving the army to return to civilian life, poorer recruits all too often did not have that option. They stayed in the ranks longer and longer, drawing their salary, hoping for the opportunity for plunder, and also hoping eventually to be provided with land in some new territory as a retirement package. When Octavian, now Augustus, finally ended the period of civil war and established the Empire in 27 BCE, he also set about regularizing the military establishment. Service became increasingly professional because it became increasingly long. Citizens in the Republic had been obligated for six years; Augustus dictated sixteen years and four in the reserves. The service obligation would later jump to twenty-five years. Noncitizens served in *auxilia*, originally as specialist troops like skirmishers and cavalry, but from the second century CE *auxilia* increasingly included heavy infantry. They served for twenty-five years with the promise of citizenship for them and their children upon retirement. Central encampments also became more permanent, both for legions and for smaller detachments nearer the frontier. Many retired soldiers took their land in *colonia* in conquered provinces, where they served as a potent agency of Romanization. Furthermore, although not all *colonia* were on the frontier, in Cicero's words from an earlier era, these *colonia* were more than towns; they were "the ramparts of empire."[9]

Normative Discipline and Collective Training

All this history is intended to explain the subtitles of this section and their relationship to each other: *disciplina* and *limes*. For the Romans, "discipline" began in the Republic as a restraint on the aggressive inclinations of individual soldier-citizens for whom military service was temporary, considered a privilege, and served as an opportunity for self-display and social advancement. Over the long history of the Republic this ethic of obedience to command over self-serving aggression was reinforced by embedding it in Roman culture. Soldiers swore an oath (the *sacramentum*) binding them to obey their officers; in the Empire the oath would be to the emperor. The oath, and thus their service, had a religious quality, providing a divine spur to their obedience. In addition, the Romans deployed other incentives in the form of rewards and punishments. Individual rewards tended to encourage *virtus*, recognizing the first man over an enemy wall, for example, while punishments emphasized the sacrilege of disobedience and divested individuals (and units) of social status through "dishonorable discharge, disbandment, demotions, temporary expulsion, flogging, various types of humiliation, and fines."[10] Some crimes merited death. This long-developed matrix of discipline was originally designed simply to restrain tactically questionable battlefield enthusiasm and to encourage obedience to command. Under the Empire, it was turned more and more toward creating a comprehensive controlling institution, designed for the less enthusiastic, poorer, professional soldiers of the Empire, and especially for maintaining the routine of frontier service. Immediately upon his accession to the principate, Augustus "sought to routinize the [now] professional army and to legitimate it through *disciplina militaris*."[11] This shift gained further impetus when the frontier stabilized, and it may have been this that inspired Hadrian in the early second century CE to deify *disciplina* as a cult within the army (see Figure 4.4). The imperial army's more professional discipline instilled a comprehensive and *normative* ethic of response to command, in which soldiers obeyed because it was normal to do so. To use an old joke of a modern drill sergeant: "When I say jump, you say 'How high?'— on the way up." The soldier of the middle Republic (like the

Figure 4.4 A Roman bronze sesterce showing the emperor Hadrian, ca. 134–138 CE. Hadrian is shown marching in front of legionary standard bearers; at their feet is the word *disciplina*.

amateur militia of almost any era), rather than jumping, might instead have asked "Why?" Crucially, the Roman army's centurions meant that it was comparatively well equipped to supply the supervision needed to instill normative discipline. Although often rather casually translated to a modern audience as "sergeants," centurions were much more than that. They were simultaneously inspirational leaders and agents of the Roman army's legal and sacred power to punish and control its soldiers. There were six of them per cohort, each with an assistant (an *optio*), creating a ratio of authority figure to soldier of 1 to 40, a ratio for small units better than that found in most European armies until the sixteenth century.[12]

This matrix of inducement, punishment, and reward, which produced a normative ethic of obedience, was increasingly used to enforce an understanding of discipline that included training, especially training in collective forms of fighting. This aspect of discipline is strikingly visible in the account of Josephus, a participant in, and chronicler of, the Roman-Jewish war of 66 to 73 CE. Josephus fought and lost against the Romans, joined the winners, and wrote sycophantically, his critics say, in praise of his new patrons' military skill. His audience, however, would have known something about his subject matter, and his details of training and punishment cannot be too far off. Josephus stressed the way Roman drills and practices replicated the reality of battle, famously calling "their drills bloodless battles, their battles bloody drills." Roman soldiers trained daily, preparing physically and mentally for the battlefield. Equally important, Josephus emphasized how their daily routine was structured and disciplined for the better security of the army. Activities in the camp and on the march were carefully articulated through each level of command, creating a unity of action and motion that extended to the battlefield: "Whether attacking or retreating [they] move as one man." Josephus saw this unity of action arising partly from fear, "for military law demands the death penalty not only for leaving a post but even for trivial misdemeanours." From his perspective, this form of discipline, even when coupled with reward, produced "submission to their superiors." Although many of these punishments had existed in the Republican army, and while there would always be examples of Roman soldiers and units resisting discipline or falling into sloth and indolence, this overall conception of discipline seems to differ from the old ethic of restraint balancing aggression. What it produced, said Josephus, was an army that fought "as a single body; so knit together [were] their ranks, so flexible their manoeuvres."[13]

Vegetius, a Roman writer from a much later era (late fourth or early fifth century CE) who sought to reform the army of his day, idealized the early imperial army and made explicit this connection between discipline and training to produce collective action. Alongside training recruits in individual skills, he recommended group exercises to practice moving into and out of precise linear formations, maintaining strict intervals, and even a "military step," "for nothing should be maintained more on the march or in battle, than that all soldiers should keep ranks as they move. The only way that this can be done is by learning through constant training to manoeuvre quickly and evenly." In Vegetius's view, this kind of "drill-at-arms . . . and military expertise" had been the source of all the Roman victories of old.[14] In making this plea for a collective form of discipline, achieved through training, in which men moved and fought in synchronization with each other, Vegetius provided a vision that would help crystallize European thinking in a much later era—a process we will return to in chapter 7.

This evolved Roman system combining cultural inducements to obedience, economic investment in the survival of the state, a system of authority articulated down to the lowest subunit, systems for reward and punishment, and a rigorous program of training in fighting as part of a unit all solved critical problems of an expansive agricultural empire. At stake was a great deal more than simple obedience on the battlefield. The system generated loyalties to the center by filtering all military glory through the person of the emperor. And as the incorporation of the auxilia into the imperial army became more formal, including the incentive to participate through the promise of citizenship (from at least 54 CE, but with earlier precedents), it helped Romanize that population by disciplining them in Roman values. Some auxilia even had Roman officers; all were subject to Roman military law. Furthermore, the peasants of agrarian states very often lacked the individual fighting skills that were developed in tribal or pastoral peoples. Roman training to fight as a group gave them the tools to overcome the individualistic skills common to many of their enemies. Ironically, Roman collective training was applied to weapons often thought of as individualistic: the sword and javelin. The hoplite phalanx depended on truly mutual effort for its effect. That mutuality, however, was achieved not by professionals but by amateurs in a kind of "undisciplined corporatism." In contrast, the Roman system took men armed with individualistic weapons and multiplied their effect through training in collective action; in another shorthand, they were "disciplined individualists." In a similar vein, Roman training provided soldiers with the confidence to face enemy cavalry. Charging cavalry usually defeated infantry by scaring them into flight, not by crashing into them (horse archers firing from a distance are another matter). This was not just about the nature of the formation; we know the Romans continued to use the phalanx when necessary, even during the Empire. What mattered was that men who stood together and *believed* that doing so would stop a horseman usually did stop him. Finally, this comprehensive and normative form of discipline kept the soldiers on task during the long, boring routine of manning the increasingly stable and often fortified frontiers of the Empire.[15]

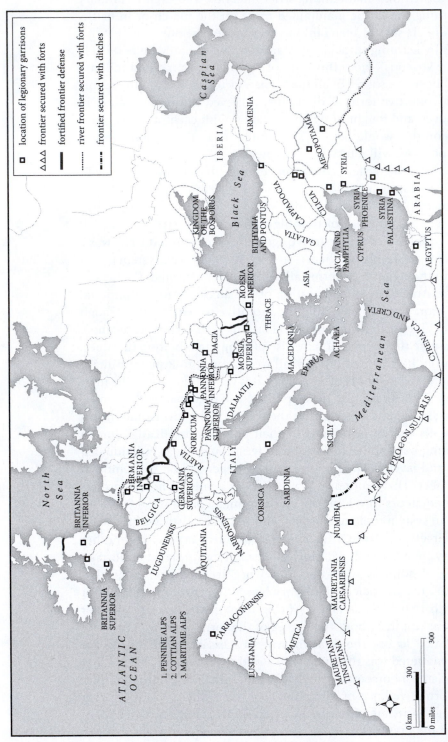

Map 4.1 The Roman frontier, early third century CE. The map shows the distribution of legionary garrisons and the different types of fortified frontiers.

Fortifying the Frontier

Rome's manpower reserves, its tactical system, and a peculiar relentlessness, even in the face of defeat, powered its successful expansion. Eventually, however, for reasons that need not detain us here, Roman expansion more or less ceased in the early second century CE. Rome made sporadic efforts to continue the process (for example, in Scotland, Armenia, and the Euphrates valley), and tinkered extensively with the precise location of the Empire's boundary. The determination that the Empire had a boundary, however, meant that it had to be defended. Rome's strategic problem, however unwillingly, and however counter to their tradition of aggressive war, became one of defense and the maintenance of internal order—both of which protected Roman military capacity by preserving the tax income generated by a prosperous commercial and agrarian population.

The shift to defense was neither conscious nor deliberate, nor was it immediate. But as it became increasingly undeniable, the frontier gradually hardened, becoming the *limes*—patrolled, demarcated, and often fortified. In an odd way the frontier was defined by where the roads ended. The Romans had a long tradition of building impressively durable roads to facilitate the movement of infantrymen around their territory, so the roads followed and marked the progress of their expansion. Wherever Roman soldiers operated, they built roads (through the combined labor of soldiers and slaves). Where Roman soldiers camped, they built modest and orderly forts of palisaded ditches. On "active" frontiers, beyond which lay the "enemy," the network of forts and roads gradually grew denser, and as the Romans remained in one

Figure 4.5 A reconstruction of the Roman *limes* in upper Germany.

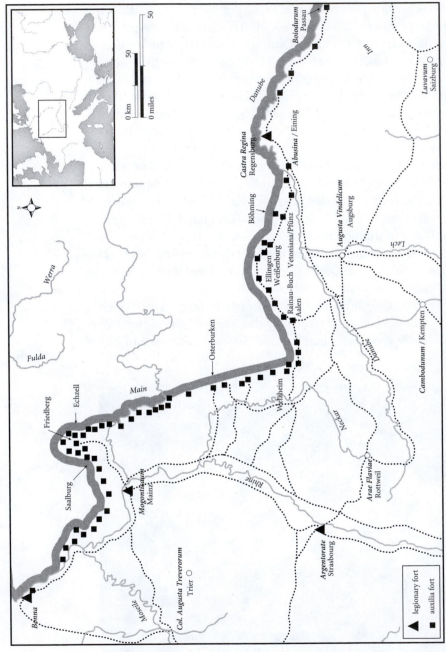

Map 4.2 The Roman frontier system or limes in Upper Germany and Raetia, ca. mid-second century CE. In addition to the small forts indicated on the map, much of this line was palisaded, and dotted by small watchtowers of varying design, usually about 500 meters apart. The *limes* differed around the Empire, varying in design according to topography and the likely threat. (Castra Regina became a legionary fort only late in the century.) Map based on the one in David J. Breeze, *The Frontiers of Imperial Rome* (Barnsley, UK: Pen & Sword, 2011), 57.

region longer and longer, the forts became more and more permanent. Linking them together, first with roads and then in some places with linear ditches and palisades, punctuated by watchtowers, became a natural part of the army's activity. It kept soldiers busy and it served a security function. The *limes* did not look the same in all parts of the Empire, nor did it remain static in any one place. The stone walls and towers of Hadrian's Wall in the north of England provide its most famous image, one replicated on a less impressive scale across much of Germany. In the east and in North Africa, however, linear obstacles proved less useful, and the *limes* depended more on natural obstacles, control of major routes of potential invasion, occasional outpost garrisons, and even more strongly on roads, both to aid patrolling the frontier and to connect distant garrisons to that frontier.

In some ways it is misleading to refer to this frontier as being "fortified." These walls and forts, even as late as the fourth century CE, were not designed to be besieged. They served several military functions, but they were not intended to be impenetrable. They provided bases from which Roman units could patrol beyond the wall and send early warning of major military movements. They offered some security against small-scale banditry and raids. And they provided a logistical infrastructure upon which major Roman forces could concentrate.[16]

Some historians protest that Roman frontier fortifications did not represent a consistent strategy for defending the frontier, and it is true that the strategic rationale for some aspects of their construction, or even of their locations, sometimes defies easy explanation. There is, for example, a sixty kilometer stretch in western Germany that runs almost entirely straight, slicing like a ruler across the countryside, without regard for the rolling, even occasionally precipitous, terrain over which it runs. Nevertheless, the *limes* undeniably enabled an "economy of force"; they allowed a smaller number of troops to manage more territory, especially when the walls are understood primarily as a more or less natural outgrowth of the road network. The consciousness of such military calculations in the creation, evolution, and management of the *limes* becomes all the more apparent when compared to similar efforts in Han China, another expansive agricultural empire that also relied on infantry, discipline, roads, and walls.[17]

INFANTRYMEN AND WALLS IN HAN CHINA

There are remarkable parallels between the military systems of Republican and then Imperial Rome and those of Qin (221–207 BCE) and then Han China (202 BCE–220 CE). Those parallels reflect the similar security requirements of an expansive, centralized, agricultural empire. But those similarities must not be overplayed—the differences were at times extreme. Perhaps most crucially, once unified into a single dynastic empire, China's primary enemy was a steppe-based, nomadic, and *mounted* enemy on its northern and northwestern frontiers. Such an enemy presented problems of a different order than those faced by Rome on the Rhine and in Britain. Although Rome did face mounted enemies in the east and on the Danube, those enemies, many of them states, could not disappear into the terrain as nomads did into the steppe. Furthermore, China's empire encompassed a more extensive continental territory lacking the relative ease of transport and communication that the Mediterranean Sea provided Rome (although it must be noted that the Yellow and Yangzi Rivers were central to military movement in China, and riverine navies proved essential in consolidating dynastic power). Older interpretations of Chinese military history suggested that this landlocked continental orientation and China's isolation from other major centralizing powers produced its particular "defensiveness [and] her primary concern for social order at home instead of expansion abroad."[18] This supposed internal and continental orientation was accentuated after the fourth century BCE by the emergence of the constant threat of the mounted steppe nomad, first exemplified by the Xiongnu. The steppe threat was real, but we must be careful not to suggest or reinforce an old argument about a "Chinese way of war" that interprets Chinese culture as exclusively favoring civilian values, or even as eschewing aggressive war (something obviously nonsensical in the face of the empire's size and its repeated efforts to expand or restore its frontiers).

Indeed, one way to read the famous "military classics," the deeply influential works on war produced in the Warring States era that preceded the Han (discussed below), reveals not one but two intertwined and sometimes alternating strategic cultures. One assumed the omnipresence of war, the need for preparedness, preferred offensive strategies, and acknowledged that wars of conquest could be righteous, provided the population was incorporated, settled, and returned to being productive. The other, a more Confucian version, saw "warfare as aberrant and usually avoidable through good government, and prefer[red], when conflict [was] unavoidable, accommodationist and defensive strategies."[19] Read in this way, the principle of *wu* (the martial or military) existed alongside, and not just in opposition to, the principle of *wen* (the literate or civil). Their interaction strongly influenced Chinese military institutions, but there was no single Chinese style of war or military. As we will see, however, perhaps a better explanation for this difference is that the military classics were composed during a period of state-on-state warfare within the Chinese heartland, and were revitalized during the eleventh century when China again faced neighboring competing states. Much of the rest of China's imperial military history, however, was of a unified state facing either the occasional internal rebellion or a steppe enemy that was generally not vulnerable to offensive war. In this sense Chinese strategic *culture* did not oscillate so much as its strategic *situation* did. Built on a tradition of state-on-state wars, but now facing a steppe enemy and trying to maintain a stable frontier, Han China, like the Roman Empire, came to value a standing professional military and a concomitant imposed discipline that was applied to levies of the general population.[20]

Precedents

The Han empire emerged from a cycle of state formation, disintegration, and re-formation. The Zhou dynasty (discussed briefly in chapter 2) collapsed into a welter of competing states, at first slowly during the so-called Spring and Autumn period (771 BCE to 476 BCE), as increasingly autonomous regions nonetheless continued to profess a lingering nominal allegiance to the fading power of the Zhou emperor. During this period, warfare was seen as the "ultimate trial of honor" fought primarily by aristocrats with additional manpower from the urban populace. War was a struggle for preeminence within a culturally homogenous system, and the rules of combat were designed to showcase aristocratic honor, even to the point of "prohibit[ing] taking advantage of an adversary's difficulties."[21] Somewhat paradoxically, however, this war for "honor" was also existential. The Spring and Autumn period saw at least 110 states extinguished or absorbed by others, leaving twenty-two larger ones to survive into the truly anarchic and deeply competitive Warring States era (475 BCE to 221 BCE).[22]

The length and intensity of the Warring States era created critical precedents for the succeeding Qin and Han dynasties, and indeed for much of the rest of Chinese history. Most notably, there was a new emphasis on large numbers of infantry, conscripted from the countryside (not just the urban followers of the aristocracy), who served in increasingly professional and centrally disciplined forces, and who were led by men trained in a school of thought about how to succeed in war. Where the armies of earlier eras were tactically dominated by aristocrats and their chariots, those warring states on the northern and southern frontiers, finding the terrain awkward for employing chariots, increasingly turned to infantry. Those infantrymen gained effectiveness with the diffusion of iron weapons (common by the middle of the fourth century BCE), swords, lamellar armor, and especially the crossbow, introduced sometime around 500 BCE. The competing states then began to seek ways to raise more and more men to serve as infantry. This move toward mass infantry levies was exemplified by the reforms of Shang Yang of Qin, who after 359 BCE imposed a rectangular grid on the countryside, divided the population into units, conducted administration via military districts, and subjected the entire male population to military conscription. Tactically, infantrymen were organized into units and subunits, extending down to a squad of five men.[23]

The Warring States era also put a new emphasis on the role and skill of a professional military commander. He became "a specialist who held office through mastery of military techniques."[24] Tied to this professional class of generals was the emergence of a literature on the conduct of war, exemplified by Wu Qi, Sun Bin, and, most famously, Sunzi (commonly romanized as Sun Tzu).[25] Unlike the early Roman ideological focus on *virtus* and *fama*, central to this Chinese martial literature was a cynical rationalist attitude that "scorned war for personal glory and acts of individual bravery." The authors' vision of war emphasized the "hierarchy and discipline" central to Chinese culture.[26] For them combat was "an intellectual discipline in which the powers of mind and textual mastery of the commander, along with the unthinking obedience and uniform actions of the troops, guaranteed victory."[27]

This environment of existential competition produced powerful states, fielding predominantly infantry armies of as many as one hundred thousand men, composed of disciplined conscripts, "coordinated in action by signals and commanded by professional military men with more concern for winning and less for ritual."[28] The final victor proved to be the state of Qin, ruled by Qin Shihuangdi, who destroyed or subsumed the other warring states and established the first, albeit short-lived, dynasty to unify northern and southern China (the Shang and Zhou had controlled only the north). Qin Shihuangdi has become famous in the present day due to the vast, larger-than-life-size terracotta army uncovered near his tomb (see Figure 4.6). The arrangement and armament of the infantrymen, although modeled with individual faces and hands, strongly suggest a disciplined, centrally equipped force, arrayed in linear, mutually supporting formations, and accustomed to deploying units armed with different weapon combinations (among the infantry alone the figures are variously armed with swords, halberds, spears, axes, bows, and crossbows, with the latter perhaps dominating). Less famous, but more critical, the Qin "Legalist" view of rule, originating with earlier Qin rulers like Shang Yang and culminating with the Qin emperor, demanded a thorough program of standardization and control. Newly unified China encompassed a host of different dialects, systems of weights and measures, and regional bureaucracies, with powerful local aristocrats still resistant to centralized rule. The Qin created systems and standards to smooth over those differences and to contain aristocratic autonomy, including everything from a common writing system to the width of a wagon's axles. Many of the Legalist ideas were rejected by Confucianists, but the standardization of communication networks, measures, and language contributed greatly to later dynasties' ability to mobilize military resources and to the creation of a common Chinese identity. As for

Figure 4.6 Terracotta warriors in the army of Emperor Qin Shi Huangdi ca. 259–210 BCE.

the Qin themselves, however, the emperor's harshness and the ineffectiveness of his successor generated rebellion after only fourteen years. With rebellion came a fresh competition for power.[29]

The winner of that competition was the state of Han, led by Liu Bang, who in 202 BCE founded a dynasty that would last until 221 CE, although it suffered through a civil war and interregnum (ca. 9–25 CE) that divided the dynasty into two halves: the "Former," or "Western," Han and the "Later," or "Eastern," Han. In its early years the Han military was structured to deal with enemies like itself. The long wars of the Warring States period had only briefly been interrupted by Qin unification. And the chaos surrounding the fall of the Qin dynasty again entailed wars of "like against like." Furthermore, the Han dynasty did not make itself the supreme ruler of the former Qin territory all at once. Its initial victories established firm control over the western territories, which were directly subordinated to the center in thirteen military commanderies (akin to Roman provinces). The eastern territories, however, initially were allowed to continue as independent clients, ruled by kings—often relatives of the emperor. These internal challenges kept the early Western Han military focused on combating regional rebellion, a threat that subsided only after the Han crushed a final rebellion of the eastern client kings in 154 BCE (although reformed and centralized, not all of those "kingdoms" were ever fully abolished). In this context of "internal" war, the Former Han continued the Warring States and Qin tradition of universal conscription designed to produce large infantry armies. The Later Han, however, in the wake of the civil war and interregnum, and the associated severe population loss and contraction of the tax base, abolished conscription around 30–31 CE in favor of a more professional, standing force. This final shift to a professional force continued a trend begun late in the Former Han, and matched the shift in the threat environment. As the likelihood of internal war subsided, the threat from the steppe increased, and that threat seemed to demand a more professional army.[30]

The Steppe Problem

Qin and then Han centralization and increasing power had an ironic effect on surrounding peoples. The presence of a state, and the associated challenges and opportunities it presented to nomadic tribal peoples, tended to encourage those peoples to confederate into more coherent and powerful groups, often under a single ruler. The Xiongnu, for example, were a nomadic people living on the steppe to the north and west of central China, who appear to have become mounted cavalry by the fifth century BCE. Their confederation around the same time as the Qin unification of China transformed them into an ongoing and serious military threat to agricultural China.[31]

The problem posed by a mounted, steppe-based enemy, explored in more detail in chapter 5, boils down to logistics and mobility. Horse nomads lived and fought on horseback; their entire force was more mobile than an agricultural state's army of mixed infantry and cavalry. Furthermore, the nomads' mobile lifestyle meant that their logistics were as portable as they themselves were, if not quite as speedy. Accustomed to constant movement, they did not have to make special arrangements to transport food—their supplies, meaning their flocks, were never far away, their horses provided milk, and, in emergencies, blood and meat. The nomads could concentrate and appear without warning, and then retreat deep into the steppe if threatened, easily exhausting the logistical capacity of a sedentary society's army to follow them. In addition, in an open-field battle the nomads usually possessed the tactical advantage of being lifelong archers, firing from horseback. They could deliver vast amounts of firepower and then retreat if pressed, often turning tactical retreats into traps when they turned on their pursuers. The Qin and the Han, despite these challenges, at times felt compelled to take the offensive against the Xiongnu, and although they might temporarily force them from a region, they could rarely defeat them. At least one Han emperor nearly lost his life venturing out onto the steppe.[32]

Early military failures against the Xiongnu led the first Former Han emperors to adopt a policy of diplomatic gifts and marriages to keep them at bay. In time, the expense and perceived humiliation of that process led Emperor Wudi (r. 140–87 BCE) to mount more aggressive campaigns. He and his generals successfully ousted the Xiongnu from the Ordos (the region within the "loop" of the Yellow River, held by the Qin but lost during the early Han period), and began the process of extending Han control into the far northwest. His campaigns vastly extended Han territory, fully incorporating Hexi into the empire and establishing protectorates and clients in the "Western Regions" (Xiyou, see Map 4.3), but they also drained the Han treasury. Furthermore, all that expense bought only some twenty years of peace on the northern frontier, and for prestige reasons his successors found themselves committed to maintaining control of the region and paying the necessary costs to do so.[33]

Forswearing aggressive campaigns into the steppe, Wudi's successors found it cheaper and easier to combine diplomacy with frontier fortifications, partially sustained by agricultural military colonists. That shift in turn encouraged the development of a longer-service professional army rather than short-term conscripts. To be sure, the Xiongnu threat also led the Chinese to develop their own cavalry, and the Han relied extensively on recruiting allies from among other nomadic peoples. Rome also had emphasized cavalry on a new scale as Rome's frontier stopped expanding, and especially as more mounted enemies appeared from the east. But our concern here is with how and why the Han army developed a disciplined, professional infantry force reliant on synchronized tactical action. Unfortunately, as this brief overview suggests, there was extensive variation in the Han military over the course of the dynasty, and our historical sources are actually fairly obscure about

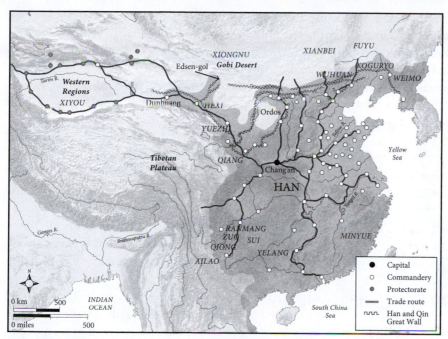

Map 4.3 The Han empire ca. 87 BCE. Map indicates the general extent of Han control, including its western conquests. Much of the Han wall used sections of the earlier Qin wall. The newer Han sections were built after this date. Wall locations are approximate.

tactical details, recruitment, and training, and even the nature of discipline. So we will first describe the military system of the Han (focusing on the infantry), then examine their attitude toward discipline and training, and finally relate both to the use of frontier fortifications.

The Han Military

Under the conscription system of the Former Han, men aged from twenty-three to fifty-six were obliged to serve for two years in the Han army. They spent the first year training in their home commandery and their second on active service. After returning home they constituted a trained emergency constabulary in their home districts. This conscription system initially produced the bulk of the army, especially the infantry. In time, however, the political threat of commandery forces overly loyal to their commander, combined with the rising Xiongnu threat, led the Han to turn to increasingly professional, longer-service soldiers, recruited with wages, often predominantly from among criminals. This trend began during the Former Han, with professional soldiers accounting for over half the Han army during the reign of emperor Wudi (r. 140–87 BCE), but became more pronounced in the Later Han, culminating in the eventual abolition of conscription in 30–31 CE. In addition, responding to the Xiongnu threat, the Chinese had also developed their own cavalry (as well as allying with steppe peoples), and they had their own mounted archers by the fourth century BCE. By the end of the Former Han period such cavalry were central to the army, but they never matched the Xiongnu's native skill. Recruiting directly from steppe peoples therefore remained central to Han diplomacy—a process greatly simplified when the Xiongnu confederation broke apart into northern and southern components, with the latter acting as a tributary of the Later Han by 50 CE.[34]

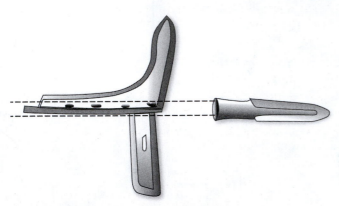

Figure 4.7 The Qin and Han ji or "halberd." This drawing shows the metal components as surviving from the tomb of Emperor Qin Shihuangdi. The dotted lines indicate where the wooden pole would have joined them together. The design is clearly an elaboration of the earlier dagger-ax.

Whether conscripted or professional, as during the Warring States and the Qin, Han-era infantrymen served in a variety of tactical roles. Crossbowmen were crucial, and were considered elite (as were cavalry recruits and the men who served in the riverine navy). There is contradictory evidence, but the crossbowmen seem to have commonly fought in close association with halberdiers (men with a weapon evolved from the dagger-ax described in chapter 2, now wielded more like a spear, with a point and a hook, much like the medieval European halberd), spearmen, and swordsmen (see Figure 4.7).

Compared to contemporary armies in Europe or elsewhere, the Han military operated on an enormous scale. Historian Michael Loewe calculates that in 141 BCE there were nearly fifty-four million people in the Han empire, generating a theoretical conscript pool ranging from approximately 270,000 to 1,000,000 men per year, and there is substantial evidence that the Han emperor Wudi at times maintained over 300,000 cavalry and 400,000 infantry in the field. To manage and supply such a host required a sophisticated bureaucracy and a simply staggering logistical service. Estimates prepared by a Han official in 60 BCE showed that even a force of 60,000 men would need 250,000 *shi* (19.97 liters per *shi*) of animal fodder monthly, plus 216,000 *shi* of grain for the men. The latter alone would require 1,440 wagons for transport. Other documents show that one month's ration of grain for 10,000 men added up to 33,000 *shi* requiring 1,320 wagons. Just the salt for this force would require an additional 360 wagons. On occasion, rather than move grain to the army, Han rulers simply dispatched the army to the frontier and set them to growing the grain they would need. Surviving records document the issue of clothing to the soldiers, as well as tools, signaling gear, and weapons. From around 119 BCE, weapons were manufactured according to carefully defined standards by government agencies as a state monopoly. We know, for example, that crossbows were made according to several standard specifications of draw weight. This bureaucratization of war reflected the demands of a large territorial empire managed from a single center. In one sense there is no surprise here; as argued in chapter 1, a key aspect of the state was its capacity to manage the materials of war. The Han were simply operating on a vastly larger scale. But efficient empire management required more than just bureaucracy—it also demanded a disciplined army.[35]

An argument made here for the Roman army was that increasing bureaucratization, professionalization, and length of service, while accepting recruits of a lower social status, tended to produce increasingly modern-looking forms of legalistic, corporal discipline, imposed by a hierarchical state and designed to produce normative obedience over a period of long service. The routine of frontier management stimulated this kind of disciplinary structure, since other rewards were lacking: no great hauls of plunder could be expected from manning the frontier. Normative discipline and its repetitive routine also allowed for complex training, which in turn enabled collective, synchronized, tactical movements, conducted more or less automatically on the battlefield. This synchronization could be effective in a variety of circumstances, but was especially useful for infantry facing a mounted enemy. There is also evidence for all these processes in the Chinese tradition, growing out of the Warring States era, and then fully bureaucratized during the Han period, especially in association with the problem of the Xiongnu frontier.

Like much else about Chinese military practice, the origins of collective, synchronized, tactics imposed through normative discipline lie in the Warring States period. The declining importance of aristocratic peer competition on the battlefield and the expansion of military participation through conscripting the rural peasantry suggested the need for judicial and state-based systems of discipline. Furthermore, obedience as a *normative* value was greatly strengthened during the Han era (and thereafter) by the deep cultural imprint of Confucian ideals of filial piety. The Warring States treatise *Methods of the Sima Fa* (*Ssu-Ma Fa*) advocated combining corporal and normative discipline: punishments could be severe but should also be limited, while soldiers' doubts should be assuaged and the general should be magnanimous.[36] In some ways, the famous Sunzi moved closer to the heart of the issue in his advice to the prospective general to consistently instruct the army. Consistency of instruction would produce obedience, and in time that obedience would become normative, or, in Sunzi's words, "One whose orders are consistently carried out has established a mutual relationship with the people."[37] And in the *Methods of the Sima Fa*, we see the problem of heterogeneity dealt with through discipline: "It is not forming a battle array that is difficult; it is reaching the point that the men can be ordered into formation that is hard. . . . Men from each [of the four quarters] have their own nature. Character differs from region to region. Through teaching they come to have regional habits, the customs of each state [thus] being different. [Only] through the Tao [the way of warfare] are their customs transformed."[38] Historian Mark Lewis finds this philosophy of pervasive obedience to be a consistent theme in the martial literature of the Warring States period. In his words, Chinese leaders sought an army "unified as a single body" in which training was used "to turn previously autonomous fighting men into standardized, predictable, functionally differentiated members of a co-ordinate whole in which the integrated squad [of five men] and not the individual soldier was the lowest independent tactical unit, and each unit gained meaning solely through its place in the larger formation."[39]

These squads were designed to operate in specific formations that combined their different weapons in a variety of ways. Lances and bows were used in combination with swords and halberds, in unison, moving into different formations in accord with changes in the enemy's proximity while, above all, holding a solid line.[40] In the Tai Gong's "secret teachings" we see this system clearly: "The long weapons and strong crossbows should occupy the fore; the short weapons and weak crossbows should occupy the rear, firing and resting in turn. Even if large numbers of the enemy's chariots and cavalry should arrive, they must maintain a solid formation."[41] And the *Methods of Sima Fa*" emphasized the need to "order the rows and files" and to "set the correct [spacing between] the horizontal and vertical."[42] Similarly, Wei Liaozi pointed out that "deploying the army [has] standard orders; the dispersal and density of the lines and squads have standard methods; and arraying the rows from front to rear has its appropriateness and suitability."[43]

These famous *bingfa*, or "art of war," texts, often referred to as the "Seven Military Classics," were composed during the earlier era of Warring States, and they remained relatively obscure during the Han era. They were only compiled and assigned classic status by later Chinese scholars in the Song dynasty around the eleventh century CE. There are problems, therefore, with using them as evidence for the Han period, especially with respect to strategic thought, since the Warring States period was one of state against state within China's agricultural heartland. On the other hand, there is some evidence of continuous reference to the *bingfa* in the Han and afterwards, especially to Sunzi, and the limited textual, archaeological, and narrative records that we have from the Han era duplicate the martial classics' sense of discipline and synchronized tactics. Administrative documents found in the frontier garrisons in the far northwest of the Han empire (in the Edsen-gol region, marked on Map 4.3) document the functioning of a professional military bureaucracy that sent soldiers to distant lands for long service, and there kept them supplied and controlled under a detailed disciplinary routine designed to protect Han lands and trade routes against a hostile, mobile, and unpredictable steppe-based enemy.[44]

Han tactics also suggest the continued role of training in synchronized tactics. Evidence from the Qin terracotta warriors suggests that the crossbowmen in that era were already working in unison, with ranks alternating as one fired and the other reloaded. Chao Cuo, writing in the early second century BCE, pointed out that Han infantry employed in complementary formations, combining swords, crossbows, and halberds, all protected by armor, could be irresistible to the Xiongnu. One Han campaign against the Xiongnu in 93 BCE succeeded when the Han infantry preserved their formation and delivered concentrated, disciplined crossbow fire in unified volleys. Another campaign in 99 BCE, however, showed both the strengths and weaknesses of the Han infantry against the Xiongnu. The Han general Li Ling deliberately set out into Xiongnu territory with only five thousand infantrymen, without cavalry support. There were political and personal reasons for his rashness, but his decision also reflected Han confidence in their martial superiority. Li soon found himself surrounded by some thirty thousand Xiongnu horsemen. He retreated to a strong position, and, in the words of a near-contemporary chronicle, he "ordered his men to use the baggage trains improvising as a circular laager-rampart. He personally led his elite fighters holding halberds and shields to take up battle formation outside the encirclement, while the archers and crossbowmen with their bows fully drawn took up the rear making preparations for the Xiongnu assaults." The Xiongnu charged and were repulsed by the halberdiers, who then withdrew into the laager. When the Xiongnu rallied to pursue the apparently fleeing halberdiers, the Han archers behind the wagons devastated them. This static tactical superiority, however, could not overcome the problem of Xiongnu mobility. They called in reinforcements and Li Ling began a long fighting retreat. Although he repeatedly damaged his pursuers, in the end his force was almost wiped out.[45]

Li Ling's initial successes and ultimate failure against the Xiongnu suggest the problems the Han faced. The mass infantry armies of the Warring States era, so useful for internal competition and even for suppressing rebellion, lost effectiveness once the Han had established control over central China and found themselves instead facing a mounted steppe enemy. As these accounts and the Edsen-gol documents suggest, however, infantry could continue to play key roles in frontier management, and on the right terrain could even defeat the Xiongnu, but the pressures for change were clear. On one hand, the Han needed a cavalry force equipped to deal with the Xiongnu on more or less equal terms. On the other hand, the Han needed long-service infantry, not short-term conscripts. They needed men who could remain on the frontier for years.[46]

The Han Frontier

After the aggressive campaigns of Emperor Wudi, the economy of force provided by a frontier fortification system backed by military-agricultural colonies became ever more central to the Han approach to their steppe enemy. The building of walls and their accompanying forts was only one choice among many in dealing with the Xiongnu, and different rulers tried different combinations of solutions. The earliest Han rulers, as mentioned previously, had maintained a long period of relatively peaceful accommodation through diplomacy and gifts (essentially bribes). When Wudi abandoned bribes for an offensive campaign, he demonstrated the enormous costs of offensive war against the steppe warriors, but his successes also ruled out a return to the peaceful preceding strategy. His successors fell back on a fortified and managed frontier, combined with military-agricultural colonies, whose mission at times might be described as agricultural aggression. By planting crops and building irrigation networks using a centralized labor force, the Han could make the frontier regions easier for them to operate within, and more difficult for the nomads.[47]

Much about the Han frontier system remains obscure, in part because detailed archaeological surveys of surviving Han-era walls have only recently begun, and in part because of the more famous "Great Wall" built centuries later. Some of the northern states during the Warring States era had built and maintained "long walls" on their northern frontiers. After the Qin unification, the Qin emperor expanded his control in the northwest, cleared out the nomads from the loop of the Yellow River and the Ordos Desert, and then enclosed that territory within a new line of fortifications and walls connected to the older systems. This was probably not a continuous wall as popularly understood, but rather a series of walls integrated into the natural topography, stronger at critical passes and backed or supplemented by stand-alone forts. It was substantial enough to merit reference as a boundary in later centuries, but the Qin walls themselves, built rapidly and primarily from soil and wood and abandoned during the early Han period, deteriorated. A prolonged period of Xiongnu raids after 200 BCE led to substantial repairing of the old Qin walls, although the Han had abandoned much of the old Qin territory to the far north and west and many early Han walls were built well south of the old Qin walls, indicating their retreat from Xiongnu. Eventually, however, as the Han expanded into new territory to the northwest around 115 BCE, they returned to the line of the Qin wall and then actively built new walls. Those walls, in a more arid and less populous region, survive to a greater extent, and their outline suggests the ways in which the Han used them to economize on managing a militarized frontier.[48]

As can be seen in Map 4.3, the Han expansion achieved under Wudi included a long corridor to the northwest (the Hexi region), designed to control access to the trade routes into and out of central Asia—a set of routes later known collectively as the "silk road." Controlling this region weakened the Xiongnu and also allowed the Han to trade for the horses of the Ferghana region in central Asia. In addition to establishing formal commanderies as far west as Dunhuang, the Han also established a protectorate over the "western regions" (Xiyou) by about 60 BCE, with powerful military-agricultural colonies scattered in key zones through that region by 33 BCE. Gaining and then administering that protectorate required first consolidating and protecting the Hexi corridor east of Dunhuang. To do so, the Han progressively extended the Qin fortification lines, established agricultural garrisons, and even imported civilian populations to sustain the troops. Each commandery had a commandant, in charge of perhaps three companies each, divided into four to six platoons, and those into as many as ten sections of three to five men. In Hexi these soldiers manned a raised causeway, with a protective ditch, punctuated by square or rectangular watch towers. Some of the towers were as tall as forty to fifty feet, and they were carefully situated within sight of each other, using the topography where possible to expand the distance between them (often three to five kilometers, see Figure 4.8). There is some evidence of connecting walls on top of the causeway between the towers, but it is unclear how extensive those walls were. Instead, a smoothed covering of sand was spread over the embankments, designed to reveal nocturnal intruders, and patrols were regularly dispatched to detect such incursions. Surviving equipment lists suggest that the towers mounted heavy crossbows on swivels, as well as storing more mundane maintenance equipment and signaling gear. Behind the line of watchtowers were occasional larger fortresses, designed to house full companies, made of thickly built walls of rammed earth like those described in chapter 2.[49]

One calculation, based on the number of towers in one well-preserved region, suggests that only eight hundred men were needed *on the line itself* for one 250 kilometer stretch. Broader regional calculations suggest that the

(a)　　　　　　　　　　　　　　　　　　(b)

Figure 4.8 *a* & *b* Han watchtowers. (a) is one example of a genre of Eastern Han-period (25–220 CE) architectural models of watchtowers. (b) is the ruin of an actual Han tower from the Dunhuang frontier region.

shockingly small total of 3,250 men were used for the entire thousand-kilometer line from Dunhuang to Shuofang. To this total, of course, we must add those in the company forts to the rear and in headquarters, and so on. An even more generic estimate by another Han general referred to the full length of the northern frontier, running from the Liaodong Peninsula (near what is now North Korea) all the way into Hexi, roughly 5,750 kilometers, which, he says, was manned by only "several thousand officers and soldiers" on "the walls and beacon towers," where apparently they could not be harmed "even if large enemy hordes assault them."[50]

The ability to use so few troops over such a long frontier strongly suggests an economy-of-force approach to guarding the frontiers. Like the Roman *limes*, these lines served as tripwire, intelligence system, and local defense. The forces directly on the causeway or at the major passes could defend against small threats; for larger enemy movements they could rapidly transmit signals down the line to alert regional Han forces, especially cavalry. One document from the region describes a raid by ninety enemy horsemen, who attacked a watchtower and took some weapons and a prisoner. The local cavalry response force of 182 horsemen gave chase.[51] More generally, another Han source noted that the governors of the commanderies maintained ten thousand cavalry "with which they tour the walls and beacon stations of the defenses and give chase to the enemy."[52]

Again, there is no doubt that the Han saw cavalry, usually recruited from allied nomads, as the decisive element in defending themselves from the Xiongnu. But cavalry could not be everywhere at once. Protecting a sedentary agricultural society from a mobile and unpredictable enemy demanded a system that provided warning of large enemy movements and perhaps contained the smaller ones, and could do so with a relatively small force-to-space ratio. That meant infantry, individually cheaper than cavalrymen, deployed on a long frontier, operating from walls, towers, and forts, and disciplined to maintain the necessary endless routine. Furthermore, if those infantry confronted nomadic horse archers in the open—admittedly not a situation they would normally seek out—their only hope lay in a synchronized use of combined arms. For the Han, much as Rome had discovered, the answers to these challenges lay in normative discipline, collective training, frontier fortifications allowing for an economy of force, and the way each of those factors reinforced the others.

CONCLUSION

In the long term, the Han dynasty could not survive its own internal weaknesses and its many enemies. But its longevity and expansiveness left critical cultural and military legacies for the rest of Chinese history, much like Rome did for Europe. Mass disciplined armies, first born in the Warring States era, but now increasingly centralized, bureaucratized, and subject to a routinized military discipline, became a standard component of the Chinese vision of the military. The infantry of those armies, confronting a mounted enemy, relied on closely ranked formations using collective synchronized tactics, combining polearms and firepower.[53] Both Rome and Qin/Han China worked within a legalistic and bureaucratic structure that granted the state the power and the administrative skill to extract financial and human resources from their population. The Roman bureaucracy mostly disappeared with the collapse of the empire in the fifth century CE, although its legal forms remained and rebounded centuries later. Officials of successor Chinese dynasties, in contrast, retained and honed their bureaucratic skills during dynastic changes and were able to mobilize resources to an extraordinary extent.[54] Moreover, "building . . . a unified empire with a territory no smaller than the Han empire at its peak of glory became the 'Manifest Destiny' of China in the minds of the imperial leadership and the political consciousness of every great ruler."[55] The Han achievement imposed a cultural uniformity on its territory in much the way that the Romans had, and future dynasties were more successful than the politically fragmented European states at holding or reunifying that territory. As for universal military service, that ideal persisted among the

TIMELINE

	Rome
343–290 BCE	The Three Samnite Wars, the most difficult of Rome's expansion within Italy
3rd century BCE	Evolutionary emergence of manipular legion in Rome
108 BCE	Marius's fighting in Africa; recruits from landless citizens
27 BCE	Traditional date for the end of Roman Republic and elevation of Augustus to the principate (emperor); military service extended to twenty years
117–138 CE	Reign of Hadrian; attempt to stabilize the frontier
212 CE	Roman citizenship expanded to the entire empire
476 CE	Traditional date for the fall of Rome in the west

	China
475–221 BCE	Warring States era
221–207 BCE	Qin dynasty
202 BCE–220 CE	Han dynasty (202 BCE–9 CE "Former" or Western Han; 25–220 CE "Later" or Eastern Han)
141–87 BCE	Reign of Emperor Wudi, and aggressive campaigns into the steppe
30–31 CE	Han abolish conscription

European heirs of Rome, and although it was attenuated somewhat in the Middle Ages, it never disappeared. In contrast, the Later Han abandoned the principle of universal service, thereby contributing to a "civilization" at the center of the Han cultural zone and the restriction of a military career to distinct groups. Later Han armies "relied largely on professional soldiers paid for by scutage from the *gengfu* tax [paid to avoid conscription as labor], and aided by troops from the [allied] southern Xiongnu, the Wuhuan, and Qiang."[56] This administrative shift to professional forces divorced from an increasingly nonmartial population was matched by an ideological change. The official rise of Confucianism and the creation of a civil bureaucracy that spanned dynasties generated an abiding, if frequently frustrated, effort to contain military men and to emphasize civilian virtues over martial ones. The extent of this "civilianization," however, continues to be debated. It is true, for example, that the Han preserved and transmitted the *bingfa* literature from the Warring States period, which continued to shape Chinese military thought for centuries. Furthermore, the steppe threat remained, and repeatedly intruded violently on Chinese affairs. The Han also bequeathed a legacy of various frontier management strategies: the diplomatic, the offensive, and the fortified. Their heirs would try all of them, more or less successfully. As the threat to Rome's frontiers intensified in the second century CE, they too invested more heavily in cavalry forces. In the next chapter we will examine that evolution, as well as the details of the steppe nomadic horse-archer system that caused the Han so much trouble, and which would dominate much of Eurasia until well into the modern era.[57]

Further Reading

Chang, Chun-Shu. *The Rise of the Chinese Empire.* 2 vols. Ann Arbor: University of Michigan Press, 2007.

Di Cosmo, Nicola, ed. *Military Culture in Imperial China.* Cambridge, MA: Harvard University Press, 2009.

Goldsworthy, Adrian Keith. *The Roman Army at War, 100 BC–AD 200.* Oxford: Oxford University Press, 1996.

Kierman, Frank A., Jr., and John K. Fairbank, eds. *Chinese Ways in Warfare.* Cambridge, MA: Harvard University Press, 1974.

Lendon, J. E. *Soldiers and Ghosts: A History of Battle in Classical Antiquity.* New Haven, CT: Yale University Press, 2005.

Lewis, Mark Edward. *Sanctioned Violence in Early China.* Albany: State University of New York Press, 1990.

Luttwak, Edward N. *The Grand Strategy of the Roman Empire.* Baltimore: Johns Hopkins University Press, 1976.

Raaflaub, Kurt, and Nathan Rosenstein, eds. *War and Society in the Ancient and Medieval Worlds: Asia, the Mediterranean, Europe, and Mesoamerica.* Washington, DC: Center for Hellenic Studies, 1999.

Roth, Jonathan P. *Roman Warfare.* Cambridge, UK: Cambridge University Press, 2009.

Sage, Michael M. *The Republican Roman Army: A Sourcebook.* New York: Routledge, 2008.

Sawyer, Ralph D., ed. and trans. *The Seven Military Classics of Ancient China.* Boulder, CO: Westview, 1993.

Southern, Pat. *The Roman Army: A Social and Institutional History.* New York: Oxford University Press, 2007.

Sun Tzu. *The Art of War.* Translated by Ralph D. Sawyer. New York: Basic Books, 1994.

Van de Ven, Hans, ed. *Warfare in Chinese History.* Leiden: Brill, 2000.

Waldron, Arthur. *The Great Wall of China: From History to Myth.* Cambridge, UK: Cambridge University Press, 1990.

Notes

1. Nat... ...ican Rome," in War ... ...e Ancient and Medieval Worlds: Asia, the Mediterranean, Europe, und Mesoamerica, eds. Kurt Raaflaub and Nathan Rosenstein (Washington, DC: Center for Hellenic Studies, 1999), 196–99; Kurt A. Raaflaub, ed., Social Struggles in Archaic Rome: New Perspectives on the Conflict of the Orders (Berkeley: University of California Press, 1986), 7 (quote).

2. Rosenstein, "Republican Rome," 199; Arthur M. Eckstein, Mediterranean Anarchy, Interstate War, and the Rise of Rome (Berkeley: University of California Press, 2009), 312 (quote); Patrick Kent, "The Roman Army's Emergence from its Italian Origins," (PhD diss., University of North Carolina, 2012); Seth Kendall, The Struggle for Roman Citizenship: Romans, Allies, and the Wars of 91–77 BCE (Piscataway, NJ: Gorgias, 2013).

3. The details of the manipular legion are described in countless publications, as are the debates over those details. The general works listed under "Further Reading" are good places to begin. For pay: Pat Southern, The Roman Army: A Social and Institutional History (New York: Oxford University Press, 2007), 105–6; Livy 4.59–60, quoted in Michael M. Sage, The Republican Roman Army: A Sourcebook (New York: Routledge, 2008), 140–1.

4. Polybius 6.23–24, quoted in The Rise of the Roman Empire, trans. Ian Scott-Kilvert (New York: Penguin, 1979). The quincunx is clearly described in Polybius's account of Zama (where the Romans altered the usual pattern) at 15.9. "Flowing" is a key word. Scholars have gotten hung up on the idea that centuries or maniples must have moved as blocks. The large-scale reenactment in the movie Spartacus (dir. Stanley Kubrick, 1960) or videos of the training regimen of South Korean riot police both show how blocks of foot ... can flow into various form... Korean Riot Police Trainin... video, posted by "infinityc... April 23, 2011, http://www... ...om/ watch?v=sbFSVh1mmiw, accessed October 18, 2014.

5. Livy 31.34.4, in History of Rome, vol. 9, Books 31–34, trans. Evan T. Sage (Cambridge, MA: Loeb Classical Library, 1935).

6. Livy 8.8.5–8, discussed by Sage, Republican Roman Army, 73 (quote).

7. J. E. Lendon, Soldiers and Ghosts: A History of Battle in Classical Antiquity (New Haven, CT: Yale University Press, 2005), 191 (quote).

8. Sage, Republican Roman Army, 238–39; Arthur Keaveney, The Army in the Roman Revolution (New York: Routledge, 2007), 25–28, 58–69.

9. Southern, Roman Army, 99; Lawrence Keppie, The Making of the Roman Army: From Republic to Empire (Norman: University of Oklahoma Press, 1984, 1999), 146–47, 191–97; Cicero, On the Agrarian Law, 2.73, quoted in Sage, Republican Roman Army, 36.

10. Lee L. Brice, "Disciplining Octavian: A Case Study of Roman Military Culture, 44–30 BCE," in Warfare and Culture in World History, ed. Wayne E. Lee (New York: NYU Press, 2011), 40.

11. Sara Elise Phang, Roman Military Service: Ideologies of Discipline in the Late Republic and Early Principate (Cambridge, UK: Cambridge University Press, 2008), 3 (quote).

12. Phang correctly observes that the Romans also saw disciplina in the context of behavior off the battlefield that needed to be controlled; effeminacy, sloth, and degeneration, for example, had to be avoided in order to perform better on the battlefield. While not denying this meaning, I focus here on the more direct battlefield

implications. Phang, *Roman Military Service*. See the critical review of Phang by Jonathan Roth, *Journal of Roman Archaeology* 25 (2012): 750–58; Keppie, *Making of the Roman Army*, 145–52; Sage, *Republican Roman Army*, 123–24; Harold Lucius Axtell, *The Deification of Abstract Ideas in Roman Literature and Inscriptions* (Chicago: University of Chicago Press, 1907), 35; Ian Haynes, *Blood of the Provinces: The Roman Auxilia and the Making of Provincial Society from Augustus to the Severans* (Oxford: Oxford University Press, 2013), 205; Stefan G. Chrissanthos "Keeping Military Discipline," in *The Oxford Handbook of Warfare in the Classical World*, ed. Brian Campbell and Lawrence A. Tritle (New York: Oxford University Press, 2013), 320–28; Graeme A. Ward, "Centurions: The Practice of Roman Officership," (PhD diss., University of North Carolina, 2012). In the late Republic centuries grew to eighty men instead of sixty. In the Marian legion one cohort would have had six centuries of eighty men, with a centurion and an optio for each century—thus twelve leaders for 480 men.

13. Josephus, *The Jewish War* 3.86–109, trans. G. A. Williamson, rev. ed. (New York: Dorset, 1970), 195–97.

14. Vegetius, *Epitome of Military Science* 1.9, 1.1, trans. N. P. Milner (Liverpool, UK: Liverpool University Press, 1993), 10–11, 2–3.

15. Denis B. Saddington, *The Development of the Roman Auxiliary Forces from Caesar to Vespasian, 49 BC–AD 79* (Harare: University of Zimbabwe, 1982), 187–92; Everett L. Wheeler, "The Legion as Phalanx in the Late Empire, Part I," in *L'armée romaine de Dioclétien à Valentinien I*, ed., Yann Le Bohec and Catherine Wolff (Lyon, France: De Boccard, 2004), 309–58, and "Part II," *Revue des Études Militaires Anciennes* 1 (2004): 147–75.

16. Edward N. Luttwak, *The Grand Strategy of the Roman Empire* (Baltimore: Johns Hopkins University Press, 1976); Everett L.

Wheeler, "Methodological Limits and the Mirage of Roman Strategy," *Journal of Military History* 57 (1993), 7–42, 215–240; James Lacey, "The Grand Strategy of the Roman Empire," in *Successful Strategies: Triumphing in War and Peace from Antiquity to the Present*, ed. Williamson Murray and Richard Hart Sinnreich (Cambridge, UK: Cambridge University Press, 2014), 38–64.

17. Derek Williams, *The Reach of Rome* (New York: St. Martin's, 1996), 165–66; personal survey by author. Following Wheeler and Lacey, I find many of the objections by modern historians to the notion of Roman strategic planning to be ludicrous. Luttwak was surely overly systematic, but his critics are far too dismissive of the military function(s) of the *limes*.

18. John K. Fairbank, "Varieties of the Chinese Military Experience," in *Chinese Ways in Warfare*, ed. Frank A. Kierman, Jr., and John K. Fairbank (Cambridge, MA: Harvard University Press, 1974), 3 (quote). (I use Pinyin transliterations of Chinese, except where I quote a source that uses a different system of transliteration, usually Wade-Giles.)

19. Hans Van de Ven, ed. *Warfare in Chinese History* (Leiden: Brill, 2000), 4 (quote).

20. Alastair Iain Johnston, *Cultural Realism: Strategic Culture and Grant Strategy in Chinese History* (Princeton, NJ: Princeton University Press, 1995); Nicola Di Cosmo, "Introduction," in *Military Culture in Imperial China*, ed. Nicola Di Cosmo (Cambridge, MA: Harvard University Press, 2009), 1–22; Robin McNeal, *Conquer and Govern: Early Chinese Military Texts from the Yizhou Shu* (Honolulu: University of Hawai'i Press, 2012), 1–2, 73–4, 128–9; Peter Lorge, "The Missing Frontier in Chinese Military Thought," paper presented at the Society for Military History Conference, Ogden, Utah, April 17, 2008; Peter Lorge, "Grand Strategy and *The Discourses on Salt and Iron*," unpublished paper provided to the author. I am grateful

for extensive discussions with Peter Lorge on this issue.

21. Mark Edward Lewis, *Sanctioned Violence in Early China* (Albany: State University of New York Press, 1990), 37–38 (quotes), 55.

22. Fairbank, "Varieties," 5.

23. Lewis, *Sanctioned Violence*, 9, 60, 94, 54–65.

24. Lewis, *Sanctioned Violence*, 11 (quote).

25. A short summary of these writers and their works can be found in Ralph D. Sawyer, "Military Writings," in *A Military History of China*, ed., David A. Graff and Robin Higham (Boulder, CO: Westview, 2002), 97–114.

26. Van de Ven, *Warfare*, 9, 3 (quotes).

27. Lewis, *Sanctioned Violence*, 11.

28. Fairbank, "Varieties," 5 (quote).

29. Edward L. Dreyer, "Continuity and Change," in Graff and Higham, *Military History of China*, 21; Yang Hong, ed., *Weapons in Ancient China* (New York: Science Press, 1992); Chun-shu Chang, *The Rise of the Chinese Empire*, vol. 1, *Nation, State, and Imperialism in Early China, ca. 1600 B.C.–A.D. 8* (Ann Arbor: University of Michigan Press, 2006), 45–64.

30. Mark Edward Lewis, "The Han Abolition of Universal Military Service," in Van de Ven, *Warfare*, 36, 40, 43; Michael Loewe, "The Western Han Army: Organization, Leadership, and Operation," in Di Cosmo, *Military Culture in Imperial China*, 68, 80.

31. Thomas J. Barfield, *The Perilous Frontier: Nomadic Empires and China* (New York: Blackwell, 1989); Arthur Waldron, *The Great Wall of China: From History to Myth* (Cambridge, UK: Cambridge University Press, 1990), 36. This has been documented elsewhere as a "tribal zone" effect, and similar consequences are suggested for the tribal neighbors of imperial Rome.

32. Kenneth Warren Chase, *Firearms: A Global History to 1700* (Cambridge, UK: Cambridge University Press, 2003), 8–23; Waldron, *Great Wall*, 32–33, 39; Michael Loewe, "The Campaigns of Han Wu-ti," in Kierman and Fairbank, *Chinese Ways in Warfare*, 76.

33. Chang, *Rise of the Chinese Empire*, 218–26.

34. Loewe, "Campaigns," 90, 100; Lewis, "Han Abolition," 35; Van de Ven, *Warfare*, 12; for earlier moves to longer service on frontier garrisons, see Michael Loewe, *Records of Han Administration* (Cambridge, UK: Cambridge University Press, 1967), 1:82; Rafe de Crespigny, "The Military Culture of Later Han," in Di Cosmo, *Military Culture in Imperial China*, 91–93; Chang, *Rise of the Chinese Empire*, 178–79.

35. Most of statistical data in this paragraph derives from Loewe, "Campaigns," 80–98. Wudi's forces are from Chang, *Rise of the Chinese Empire*, 178.

36. Ralph D. Sawyer, ed. and trans., *The Seven Military Classics of Ancient China* (Boulder, CO: Westview, 1993), 138.

37. Sun Tzu, *Art of War*, trans. Ralph D. Sawyer (New York: Basic Books, 1994), 210 (quote).

38. Sawyer, *Seven Military Classics*, 140–41 (quote).

39. Lewis, *Sanctioned Violence*, 104 (quote).

40. Lewis, *Sanctioned Violence*, 104–9.

41. Sawyer, *Seven Military Classics*, 104 (quote).

42. Sawyer, *Seven Military Classics*, 138 (quote).

43. Sawyer, *Seven Military Classics*, 274 (quote).

44. The Tang writer Li Jing in the 630s CE quoted extensively from Sunzi and Wei Liaozi, *bingfa* authors of the Warring States era. David A. Graff, "China, Byzantium, and the Shadow of the Steppe," *Dumbarton Oaks Papers* 65 (2011): 157–68. Crucial to this discussion is Loewe, *Records*, which reproduces and discusses the Han military and administrative documents, printed on wooden strips, dated primarily to the period between 102 BCE and 98 CE and recovered archaeologically at various sites in the Edsen-gol region in the 1920s and 1930s. Denis Twitchett and Michael Loewe, eds. *The Cambridge History of China*, vol. 1, *The Ch'in and Han Empires, 221 BC–AD 220* (Cambridge, UK: Cambridge

University Press, 1987), 405–12; Loewe, *Records*, 1:100–102 (and passim).

45. Robin D. S. Yates, "The Rise of Qin and the Military Conquest of the Warring States," in *The First Emperor: China's Terracotta Army*, ed. Jane Portal (Cambridge, MA: Harvard University Press, 2007), 31–57, here p. 43; Marcos Martinón-Torres et al., "Making Weapons for the Terracotta Army," *Archaeology International* 13/14 (2009–2011): 65–75, doi:10.5334/ai.1316; Loewe, "Campaigns," 101; Lewis, "Han Abolition," 45–47; Joseph P. Yap, trans., *Wars with the Xiongnu: A Translation from the Zizhi Tongjian* (Bloomington, IN: Authorhouse, 2009), 237 (quote).

46. This is the point of Lewis, "Han Abolition." Also summarized by Nathan Rosenstein, "War, State Formation, and the Evolution of Military Institutions in Ancient China and Rome," in *Rome and China: Comparative Perspectives on Ancient World Empires*, ed. Walter Scheidel (New York: Oxford University Press, 2009), 44–45.

47. Waldron, *Great Wall*, 8, 40–42; Loewe, "Campaigns," 74; Edward L. Dreyer, "Zhao Chongguo: A Professional Soldier of the Former Han Dynasty." *Journal of Military History* 72.3 (2008): 665–725. Chang elaborates on this process in great detail in both volumes of *Rise of the Chinese Empire*.

48. Waldron, *Great Wall*, 15–29, and Xu Pingfang, "Archaeology of the Great Wall of the Qin and Han," *Journal of East Asian Archaeology* 3.1–2 (2001): 259–81; Loewe,

"Western Han Army," in Di Cosmo, *Military Culture in Imperial China*, 70–71.

49. Chang, *Rise of the Chinese Empire*, 230–31, elaborated in much greater detail in vol. 2; much of this material comes from Loewe, *Records*, vol. 1, and Loewe, "Western Han Army," 80–83.

50. Loewe, *Records*, 1:83–91; Loewe, "Western Han Army," 81; Dreyer, "Zhao Chongguo," 700.

51. Loewe, *Records*, 1:99 (cf. 1:101–4).

52. Quoted in Loewe, "Campaigns," 92.

53. See, for example, the Tang dynasty (ca. 630–49 CE) advice of Li Jing, discussed by David A. Graff, "China, Byzantium," 160.

54. Dreyer, "Continuity and Change," in Di Cosmo, *Military Culture in Imperial China*, 23.

55. Chang, *Rise of the Chinese Empire*, 266 (quote).

56. Rafe de Crespigny, "Military Culture of Later Han," in Di Cosmo, *Military Culture in Imperial China*, 93 (quote); Dreyer, "Continuity and Change," 25 (quote).

57. Fairbank, "Varieties," 4–11; Loewe, "Western Han Army," 87; Dreyer, "Continuity and Change," 22–23; Robin Higham and David A. Graff, "Introduction," in Graff and Higham, *Military History of China*, 14; Kenneth Swope, "Of Bureaucrats and Bandits: Confucianism and Antirebel Strategy at the End of the Ming Dynasty," in *Warfare and Culture in World History*, ed. Wayne Lee (New York: New York University Press, 2011), 61–88; Waldron, *Great Wall*, 43ff.

5

The Horsemen of Europe
and the Steppe

400–1450 CE

European Heavy Horsemen • The Steppe Warrior System • The Mongols

IN THE LONG written history of human conflict, few innovations have been as important as fighting from horseback. A mounted warrior gains height, speed, weight, tactical and strategic mobility, and, above all, a distinct psychological advantage over a man on foot. We have already seen how this innovation likely emerged among western steppe peoples during the Bronze Age, and first appeared among sedentary societies with the Iron Age Assyrians. In that sense this chapter is not about the process of first invention. Instead, it recognizes that there is enormous variety in how societies have dealt with the tactical and logistical possibilities and challenges associated with combining a man, a horse, and an assortment of different weapons. Man and horse had to be fed, and the horses themselves varied dramatically, providing different capabilities while changing over time and with deliberate breeding. Crucially, as with the chariot, riding often implied an elevated social status—at least in sedentary hierarchical societies—and the cultural consequences of drawing such distinctions could have significant military implications. This chapter explores and contrasts two critical variants of the warrior on horseback before the invention of gunpowder: the European "heavy horseman," more popularly thought of as the "knight," and the steppe horse archer, here exemplified by its most successful and best-documented exemplars, the Mongols united under Chinggis Khan.

Many other stories of mounted warriors could be told, even for this specific period: the Byzantines, the various dynastic empires of the Turks, the imperial cavalry of China, or even the steppe predecessors to the Mongols. All developed different and variously successful systems. Furthermore, it cannot be stated strongly enough that the pages which follow do *not* explain the totality of the western European medieval system of war, nor even that of the Mongols. We will analyze and contextualize one aspect of their military system, the horsemen, and by placing them side by side we will see more clearly the role of culture and capacity in shaping their respective and very different methods of war.

EUROPEAN HEAVY HORSEMEN

The Legacy of Rome, 300–700 CE

The history of western Europe, military or otherwise, makes sense only when understood as an amalgam of a Roman and a Germanic past. The Roman construction of a fortified frontier in northern Europe and in Britain (described in chapter 4) and the Roman extension of bureaucratic administration and taxation into those regions fostered urbanization and the spread of Roman ideas and practices. Military garrisons and provincial administrative centers attracted traders, women, and non-Romans from beyond the frontier. Communities sprang up around the soldiers, nominally separated from the local population by the army's prohibition against their marrying while in the ranks. Some things are hard to legislate, however, and the soldiers increasingly integrated themselves—a process poignantly attested by the appearance of so many children's leather shoes inside the bounds of Roman frontier forts. The forts in turn were connected to the imperial heartland via the dense network of Roman military roads, roads built to last, many carrying traffic to this day. This was the Roman infrastructure of empire: forts-cum-communities, roads, and administrative systems that taxed the countryside to pay for it all. This infrastructure recovered from the crisis of the third century (ca. 235–284 CE) and resisted the waves of invasion that began in the fourth century, at times fighting and at times adapting to the Germanic invaders, eventually succumbing and transforming politically. But the resilience of the old Roman systems profoundly shaped the resulting social and political systems of northwest Europe. Meanwhile, in southeastern Europe and the Near East, the Romans survived. They morphed into what we call the Byzantines and spoke Greek rather than Latin, but never ceased to think of themselves as *hoi Romaioi*—the Romans. Theirs, however, is a different story.[1]

As the Roman legions of the fourth century progressively lost the capacity to keep enemies out of the empire's territory, three things happened. First, the army essentially divided into two parts: the frontier troops (*limitanei*) and central field armies (*comitatenses*) positioned deeper within the empire. The field armies were increasingly composed of "barbarians," Germanic or steppe peoples hired into Roman service, and now invested in protecting what they, in effect, controlled. Though the empire initially had hired these soldiers into the army as individuals, eventually the Roman political elite, growing ever more desperate, began to hire whole peoples en masse, who served under their own leaders, while nominally under Roman pay and authority. Emperor Julian, for example, defeated the Salian Franks in 358 CE, but then allowed them to settle within the empire as allies, fighting as a group within the imperial army. This process was a far cry from the older system of *auxilia* recruited from noncitizens, lured by the promise of citizenship, and progressively Romanized through long service under Roman disciplinary systems and leadership. Second, and more to the point of this chapter, the Roman field armies, whether "Roman" or hired Germans or steppe peoples, depended more and more heavily on mounted troops, allowing them to respond to the proliferation of threats emerging all around the boundaries of the empire. Some of these men were "mounted infantry" who would dismount to fight, but the Romans had also developed (or copied) a four-crowned saddle that allowed for the vigorous use of weapons from horseback even in the absence of stirrups (stirrups had appeared in Mongolia during the Xiongnu period, and were brought to Europe by the Avars, but not until the eighth century CE). Third, threatened local communities, often joined by small units of *limitanei*, fortified themselves, building on or transforming the old garrison forts into walled cities, or simply walling in the separate civilian community (see Figure 5.1).[2]

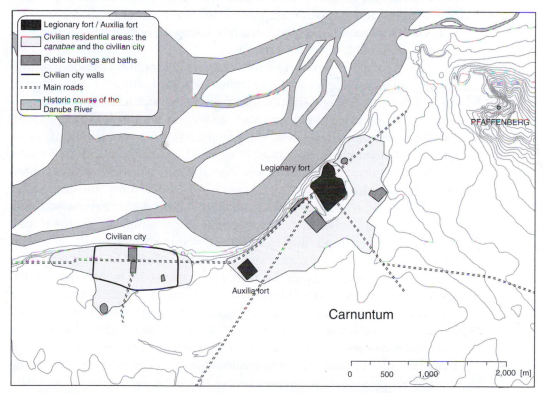

Figure 5.1 Roman Carnuntum. On the Danube, southeast of modern Vienna, Carnuntum began as a legionary fort sometime before 6 CE. It gradually added a military community of family members and contractors that grew up immediately around the fort (the *canabae*). In the second century, as provincial capital of Pannonia Superior, it attracted other civilians who built a separate town nearby but outside direct military control. After a German attack ca. 168 CE, that town gained walls.

As the provinces experienced greater turmoil, tax revenue diminished, limiting the ability of the emperor to solve problems, or even to pay his hired allies. Those "allies," along with fresh invaders, set themselves up as semi- or fully independent kingdoms, seemingly moving around freely within the borders of the old empire, further reducing imperial tax revenue (see Map 5.1). Nevertheless, Rome and its infrastructure left a deep imprint. The new Germanic kings were wise to the legitimacy conferred by nominal ties to the declining imperial center, and even wiser to the benefits of tapping Roman administrative expertise. Some of these "Romano-German" kings continued to issue coins in the imperial Roman style; the Visigothic ruler Athaulf publically swore to sustain Roman civilization, while Lombard kings in Italy and Visigothic rulers in Spain adopted the dynastic name "Flavius."[3] At the same time, identity as "German," or, more specifically, as Frankish, or Visigothic, or Lombard, proved to be highly malleable. Successful Germanic leaders rewarded their warrior followers; to be a warrior was to have a claim on status, reward, and exemption from taxes. "Romans" could "become" Frankish (or Gothic or whatever), and thus gain political privilege through military service, while simultaneously retaining their former Roman connections and networks of patronage. Roman Europe thus became Romano-German Europe, never entirely losing its connection to the past, but also irrevocably altered.

Both Roman and German societies had a long tradition of nominal universal military service, something that now persisted primarily in the form of the fortification militia. Nevertheless, the dominant process within military systems during this era was *decentralization*. The frontier had disappeared, and local defenses emerged, now pointed in virtually all directions, often with old Roman cities, now heavily fortified, as regional centers. Smaller villa-forts provided refuge, delay, warning, and rally points, while local elites, whether old imperial servitors or new Germanic nobility, mustered their more professional cadre of "armed followers"—much like the retinues of "big men" discussed in chapter 1. Those retinues increasingly fought (or at least traveled) mounted, and although their service was theoretically legally required, they expected the rewards of military success. In the fragmented economy, the primary reward was land, and as successful leaders doled it out, they thereby furthered the process of decentralization. Each member of a royal retinue expected to acquire enough land to support and reward his followers, and so on. The process of mobilization, therefore, looked something like this: A king going to war first called on those men currently living in his household—typically relatives of great lords now scattered around the kingdom, who themselves had formerly been in the king's household, and who now sent their sons, nephews, or even their clients' sons to attend the king directly. The king would then send for those more distant lords to come themselves, still his "retinue" in name, but now in practice semi-independent local masters, who had their own retinues they were expected to bring, and who

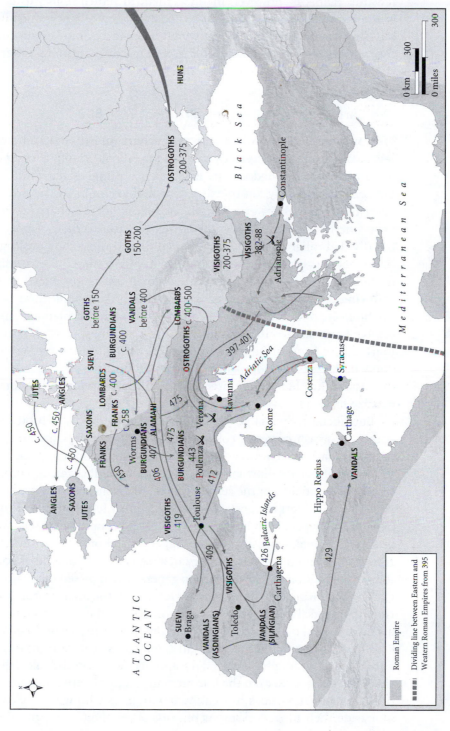

Map 5.1 Incursions into the Roman Empire by Germanic and other peoples, ca. 200–475.

would eagerly seek such service for as long as it brought success and further rewards. Setbacks, however, inclined them to return home, to defend and hold their own land, and possibly to construct new alliances and allegiances, building on the independence provided by a secure home estate. Meanwhile the military service of nonlandholders was increasingly marginalized, except in the emergency defense of the walls.[4]

The Carolingians and Recentralization, 700–850

This process of decentralization was crucially interrupted and temporarily reversed by the Carolingian dynasty of the Franks, and to a lesser extent by the Anglo-Saxon kingdoms in England. Carolingian recentralization depended, quite simply, on their success, and exemplified the processes just described, but with fewer setbacks. The Merovingian dynasty of Franks had been one of the most important of the Romano-German successor states, but divided inheritance had fragmented their power. The Carolingians, initially servitors to the Merovingians, eventually assumed the kingship in the middle of the eighth century. They fortuitously produced a string of able kings who lacked the divisive competition of royal brothers (aside from the brief life of Charlemagne's brother Carloman). Charlemagne more than doubled the size of the Frankish realm, and his spectacular success was marked and legitimized by the pope's crowning him as a new Roman emperor in 800 CE. The pope's imprimatur and his own successes allowed him to reassert the old legal requirement of military service and to formally categorize its types.

Bureaucratically unable to use the old Roman model of funding an army based on a cash currency collected through taxation, Charlemagne established gradations of service based on land ownership and even tailored, at the lower levels, to allow groups of five small landholders to combine their resources to provide for the service of one. In essence, there were four categories. The wealthiest category, generally the great lords of the kingdom, were expected to appear with horse, lance, shield, and sword. The second category was roughly analogous, obligated to appear with horse, shield, and lance. The third group would serve as infantry in a "select levy" capable of going on offensive expeditions. This third group generally comprised the majority of any Carolingian army. The final category reasserted the ancient Roman expectation of universal military service and constituted the "general levy" in which all men could be expected to serve in defense of the walls (see Figure 5.2). This system nominally obligated all freemen to service in one category or another, and although Charlemagne and his successors did take advantage of this legal obligation, even the Carolingian recentralization depended heavily on the personal retinues of wealthy landholders who willingly went to war alongside their king, seeking its rewards. Thus the Carolingians' success at offensive war bred further success and sustained their dynasty.

Figure 5.2 Variously equipped cavalry and "select-levy" infantry. This thirteenth-cenutury manuscript illustration shows cavalry equipped in different ways, roughly corresponding to their personal wealth, fighting alongside expeditionary infantry in the vein of the Carolingian select levy. (Note, however, the infantry's lack of armor.)

Much historical ink has been spilled to discredit an old image of a Carolingian army composed of mounted knights winning battles by charging with the lance into direct shock combat with their overwhelmed foes. And it is indeed true that Carolingian success depended on much more than simply heavy cavalry. They won their wars by overwhelming their enemies with superior numbers (at the strategic level) raised through the select levy, and through infantry-dominated sieges and engineering campaigns. Like the late Roman field armies, however, the mounted component of the army could move quickly over long distances and respond to emergent threats. Furthermore, there remains compelling evidence for the centrality of the cavalry charge, especially against poorly prepared men on foot. And there is no question that those men who were mounted and armored were also the wealthy and powerful, meaning, in this case, great landowners. Although perfectly willing to fight on foot, and they frequently did so, they mentally defined their service as *mounted* service, legally, culturally, and economically. Finally, as already discussed, the law notwithstanding, they saw their service as contingent upon the rewards of the king's success. As the Carolingians were forced onto the defensive, and as their power fragmented after 850, the land-owners looked to defend their own local interests, the select levy of infantry became smaller, and the intertwined cultural and military significance of the "knight" on horseback began to grow—even as siege warfare remained centrally important.[5]

Invaders, Aristocratic Entrenchment, and Private Expansion, 850–1300

Partly based on Roman roots, Carolingian success imposed a certain degree of legal and cultural uniformity across much of north-central Europe. It reasserted legal expectations of universal military service, but it simultaneously tied that service to the amount of land one owned. The Carolingian expansion thus reinforced and expanded the landed class, and the landed class was a warrior class. Unfortunately, Europe in the ninth century faced fresh waves of invaders at the same time that the Carolingian dynasty fragmented. Charlemagne's son Louis proved a weaker ruler, and he confronted a wave of Viking raids around much of the kingdom, while almost simultaneously the "Saracens," Muslim sea-borne invaders, established bases in the western Mediterranean and raided southern France and Italy. Worse, Louis had three sons. A series of internal wars among them in the 830s and 840s finally produced the treaty of Verdun (843), which divided the Frankish empire into three separate kingdoms, beginning a process of political decentralization that reinforced the increasing need for local defense against raiders coming from all directions. The Vikings attacked the north, the Saracens the south, and beginning in 890 the steppe horse archer forces of the Magyars migrated into the Danube valley and raided central Europe from the east. Under these conditions of political fragmentation and constant and unpredictable threat (the Vikings and Saracens could appear from the sea without warning, while the Magyars possessed the swift movement associated with the steppe life-style), local forces increasingly focused on defending themselves, and relied more and more on local fortifications and mounted, rapid response forces. Together these processes entrenched the power of the landowning aristocracy at the expense of the central state, while reinforcing the role of the martial household, trained to horseback, readily available, and protected within one of the now-proliferating castles, designed primarily to protect the household of the lord.

This system of the landed lord, served by a personal retinue of mounted warriors, supplemented by kin and vassalage obligations to similar lords, and protected by a personal fortress that guaranteed his relative political autonomy, survived the invasions of the ninth and tenth centuries and came to define the Latin West—admittedly with endless variations on this theme. Once the threats of the ninth century had passed, that system turned outward (again), but not in the centralized, empire-building manner of the Carolingians. Individual lords sought wealth, sometimes literally the gold and coin not often found within

Europe, but even more they fought to expand their patrimony at the expense of others and thereby provide for multiple sons in an increasingly primogeniture-based world. Some "expansion" was internal: the endless wars between aristocrats whose ups and downs are nearly impossible to track. Perhaps the most significant instance of such internal movements was William of Normandy's successful invasion and conquest of England in 1066. But such ambitions also drove wars of expansion on the periphery of the Latin West, from southern Spain to Ireland, from Scotland to Poland, and eventually even the Crusades into the Holy Land.[6]

The well-documented career of William Marshal of Normandy, England, and Ireland provides examples of all these processes, and also illuminates the ongoing cultural dominance of the "knight on horseback." A third son from a powerful but declining family, as a young man he was able to gain placement as a squire in the household of a substantial lord, William de Tancarville. Trained to arms there, and ultimately knighted by de Tancarville in 1166, Marshal sought to join the retinue—the military household, or *mesnie*—of some other great lord. He found initial success in the tournament circuit, the dangerous mock battles that provided an outlet for the finely honed skills of the martial aristocracy as well as an opportunity for profit and advancement. That venue provided a bare minimum of financial security, but, even better, his successes in it may have contributed to a notoriety that landed him a position as a household knight of Eleanor of Aquitaine. Now positioned in a royal household, Marshal successfully navigated the complex political contests between King Henry II and his presumed successors, sometimes falling from favor, but somehow always rebounding. When Richard I became king of England upon Henry II's death, he turned to Marshal for help securing England while he himself went on crusade (Marshal had already been to the east). As part of their arrangement, Marshal received lands sufficient to make him a great lord himself. Richard died shortly after his return from crusade, and in the ensuing turmoil, his successor, King John, lost his lands in Normandy. Marshal's failed efforts to retain his own lands in Normandy by swearing homage to the king of France blackened his reputation with King John. In recompense, Marshal tightened control over his lands in Ireland, heretofore only loosely under his control. In doing so he not only rewarded the loyal members of his own *mesnie*, but he also seems to have engaged in some "private," albeit carefully legitimized, expansion in Ireland.[7]

Battle, Cavalry, and Infantry: The Tugs of Calculation and Culture

William Marshal's career also reflects the military system represented by the knight and his followers, both the calculation that made them effective fighters and the increasing weight of culture that emphasized and ultimately ossified the aristocrat on horseback. The traditional, persistent, and still popular image of medieval warfare represents the knightly army as a colorful band of amateurish, aggressive, honor-seeking, dueling individualists. In this view battle (and war) was dominated by the charge of heavily armed and armored cavalrymen, wielding couched lances. After the initial crash the battle devolved into a series of individual duels until one side or the other fled (in the movie versions one side is usually annihilated). Virtually everything about this image is simply wrong. First, as for the Carolingians, war in William Marshal's time was much more a matter of raids, devastation, and above all sieges than an affair of battles. For all of those purposes infantry was much more valuable, and nearly always outnumbered the knightly cavalry, who frequently fought on foot anyway. Furthermore, in an argument first consistently laid out by J. F. Verbruggen, and now generally accepted, even the knights tended to fight in tightly ranked formations, relying primarily on the organic small-group cohesion of military households who had lived and fought together, and secondarily on the collective cohesion inherent in dense formations. Verbruggen also noted the extent to which medieval armies formed tactical units, maintained reserves, and fought in tactically articulated ways. For example, the poem written to celebrate William Marshal's life recounts a tournament in which Philip of Alsace combined infantry units with his knights. Philip carefully maintained his own knights in their tightly "serried ranks," while positioning his common foot-soldiers to act as a reserve, who would suddenly appear on the flanks of his enemy once their own ranks were disordered.[8]

In his later life, William Marshal was a deeply experienced warrior, and in many ways a consummate professional. He knew the business of war, and he chose methods that would achieve his ends—including "chevauchee" raids of burning and devastation. On the other hand, his early career, and even the poem written to celebrate his life, speaks to the increasing cultural emphasis on the martial role of the aristocratic knight, whose culturally normative position was on horseback. In one thirteenth-century commentator's words, "No animal is more noble than the horse, since it is by horses that princes, magnates and knights are separated from lesser people."[9] That does not mean a knight always rode into combat, but he was inextricably associated with his horse, and it was his deeds that were perceived to matter on the battlefield. This cultural focus progressively demanded more and more social resources for equipping the knight, both to protect him from improving crossbows (an ancient weapon reentering common use in Europe in the last decades of the eleventh century) and also to make him more effective combating other knights. The knight's armor became heavier and heavier, as plate progressively supplemented and then substituted for chain mail, both on the knight himself and on his horse. And as the knight grew heavier, he became less and less tactically flexible—in part because of a general unwillingness to dismount (in some ways not unreasonable given the increasing weight of his gear, see Figure 5.3). The horse itself contributed to the cost of this investment. One historian has shown that the cost of a horse can be correlated to a

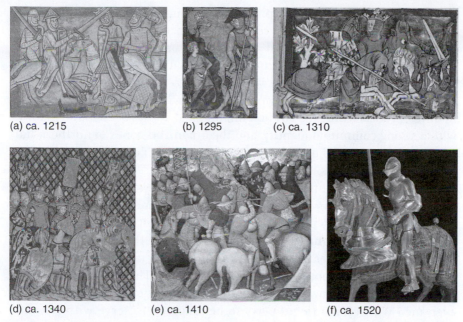

(a) ca. 1215   (b) 1295   (c) ca. 1310

(d) ca. 1340   (e) ca. 1410   (f) ca. 1520

Figure 5.3 *a–f* **The increasing weight of armor, 1200–1550.** Note the addition of plate over chainmail, the closing in of the helmets, and the addition of more and more armor to the horse.

knight's social status: as he moved up the ladder of prominence he traded up for a better warhorse. Worse, a knight required multiple horses on campaign—at least one to ride while on the march, a packhorse, and then the actual warhorse on which to fight. The last, increasingly bred for size to carry the weight of its own armor as well as the armored warrior, represented a significant initial investment—costing many times the price of a normal horse—as well as an ongoing logistical burden. One calculation suggests that an army with ten thousand European horses required two hundred acres of green fodder every day.[10]

Ironically, even as the desire for "great horses" peaked, they were becoming obsolete, along with the knight himself, partly because of fourteenth-century improvements in various types of infantry. Nonknightly infantry had always been there, firing crossbows and otherwise fighting in battle, devastating villages, and doing the dirty work of a siege, but within those parts of the Latin West where the cultural focus remained on the knight, their role had been culturally minimized. The very unexpectedness of the infantry employed by Philip of Alsace in the tournament discussed earlier reflected that minimization. In its most drastic form, that cultural disregard led the French knights at Crecy in 1346 to ride down their own mercenary crossbowmen as they retreated and were unable to get out of the way. As discussed in the previous chapter, the critical requirement for infantry to resist cavalry is the discipline and training that allows them to *believe* they can do so. Without a social investment in training and disciplining them, much of the infantry of western Europe, for most of the period covered here, lacked that belief. As Stephen Morillo has argued, it was not that cavalry got better after the fifth century, even with the arrival of the stirrup; rather, infantry got worse. The social investment in the mounted aristocrat over the succeeding centuries did little to change that. In the fourteenth century, however, exceptions began to emerge in different social contexts. The best infantry had always been found in towns with a strong communal identity, and the urbanized zones of northern Italy and Flanders produced notable infantry forces, which often fought as mercenaries for other powers.[11]

In addition to the urban communal militias, there had been a long tradition of archers in Europe and in England (they are prominent figures in the Bayeux Tapestry depicting the Norman conquest of England in 1066), but their importance and role began to transform in the thirteenth century. The English encounter with the Welsh longbow induced them to hire Welshmen and to adopt the longbow themselves. The 1252 update to the Assize of Arms, the law regulating military service expectations, required even men with very little property to be prepared to serve with bow and arrows. Over the course of the next 150 years, not only did the longbow become a weapon of the "militia," but England developed a corps of professional archers, often mounted in order to travel at the speed of the knights, and increasingly supplied with bows and arrows from the royal government. The hunting bow of the thirteenth century evolved into the much heavier-draw war bows of the fourteenth century and beyond. With a draw weight ranging from 90 to 140 pounds, with extreme examples at 180 pounds, the longbow required tremendous strength and training. In the fifteenth and sixteenth centuries, if not before, English militia bowmen were expected to shoot at targets ranged at 160 to 240 yards, and to do so with considerable accuracy—targets in some instances were a mere eighteen inches wide.

These are daunting numbers, suggesting constant training for both strength and accuracy, and the archers bore the imprint of that training on their bodies. The skeletons of professional English bowmen, recovered from the wreck of the *Mary Rose* (sunk in 1545), reveal deformed shoulders and twisted spines corresponding to repeated extreme exertion drawing a heavy bow. Similar bone deformations appear to identify the archers' bodies excavated from the battlefield at Towton (1461).

Despite its demonstrated ability to pierce chainmail, or even some plate armor at close range, and despite the famous English successes against the French between 1346 and 1415, societies outside England proved reluctant or unable to adopt the longbow, both because of the required training and because of the social prejudice that favored the knight and feared arming the peasantry. Instead, as will be explored in greater detail in chapter 7, the Swiss pike phalanx, developed in yet another society that lacked a social investment in the mounted knight, provided a different model for a truly flexible infantry. Theirs proved to be a system that could be widely imitated.[12]

The European heavy horseman was a great deal more than a military tactical system. Its development reflected a particular historical trajectory strongly shaped at its outset by political decentralization. That process entrenched an aristocracy invested in its martial role in society, and who persistently identified that role as one performed on horseback. These men were not blundering amateurs, but profoundly skilled warriors, whose skills and experience allowed them to accomplish sometimes extraordinary feats. Over time, however, their cultural investment in their role and in their traditional means of fulfilling it blinded them to other possibilities. In essence they became more and more dedicated to improving their ability to fight each other. Simultaneously, their entrenched political power resisted the ongoing efforts of kings to create more centralized states. In these circumstances kings actually *relied* on the martial inclinations of their more powerful subjects. Far from decrying their power and autonomy, as historian Maurice Keen has neatly observed, "it was positively in a ruler's interest to cultivate rather than to castigate their traditional outlook, to present himself as the companion and generous patron of his martial, aristocratic subjects, to heed their sensibilities and maintain their privileges. Otherwise he risked losing control of his war machine." In this view, knights turned out to fight for kings not because of a feudal obligation, or even because they were being paid, but rather because it fit "their traditional sense of their standing in society and its functional obligations."[13]

A series of changes beginning in the fourteenth century coincided to break down this system. We have already mentioned the emergence of several types of infantry that proved capable of defeating cavalry—a capability that had long been scarce in Latin Europe. Furthermore, despite the turbulence of the Hundred Years War between France and England, concurrent climate changes, and the population losses from the Black Death in 1348 and 1349, some monarchs were laying key foundations between 1350 and 1450 to build stronger centralized states that could tap the wealth of their populace and gain a more controlling centralized role over military activity—if not yet a monopoly of armed force. The arrival of gunpowder would build on, stimulate, and redirect those processes, all of which would change the military role of the European aristocrat on horseback.

THE STEPPE WARRIOR SYSTEM

The European heavy horseman, epitomized by the aristocratic knight perched atop a socially stratified society, is only one of many ways to incorporate the power and mobility of the horse into a military system. Using the horse to enhance fighting power reflected calculation—the conscious awareness of the added potency of the horse's weight, speed, and psychological impact on the battlefield—but the particular European version also reflected the influences of culture and capacity. As we have seen, we cannot understand the European knight purely as a combat system. Their behavior, their tactics, and even their arms and armor reflected their sense of themselves and their place in society. In terms of capacity, their numbers were constrained by the cost of horses in a sedentary agricultural society. All of these relationships and interactions look very different when one turns to an alternative system for incorporating the horse—that of the nomads of the Eurasian steppe. It may seem a bit tardy only now to pick up the issue of the steppe nomads and their horses. Indeed, one of their key characteristics is the relative constancy of their lifestyle and their military methods from a very early date until well into the nineteenth century. Even within this book we have already encountered the Xiongnu on the edges of the Han empire. Nomadic societies, however, if not necessarily illiterate, were not given to record-keeping, and our best sources for life on the steppe were created during those moments when they emerged from the grasslands and carved out empires within the sedentary world. Of those, the most dramatically successful in many ways were the Mongols under the leadership of Chinggis Khan (whose name is often romanized as Genghis) and his immediate successors. Much of the rest of this chapter will therefore construct a portrait of a generic "steppe warrior system." We will then use the Mongols of the thirteenth century as a well-documented example of that long-established system, modified in some significant ways by Chinggis Khan, and then taken on an extraordinary path of conquest. The steppe warrior system was perhaps the most effective military system in the world at that time, although it was difficult to project overseas or into forests and jungle. One of the key reasons for its success was the tight relationship between the way the nomads lived and the way they fought. We must, therefore, begin with the nature of the steppe and life upon it.

The steppe is a geographical term for a semiarid grassy zone, generally lacking sufficient rain for reliable cultivation, which in Eurasia exists in a long continuous belt, stretching from the edges of northern Korea, through Mongolia, central Asia and Ukraine, before narrowing down and ending on the Great Hungarian Plain (see Map 5.2). Bounded to the north by the forested and frigid taiga, at times the belt is pinched by mountains and deserts to the south. It makes sense to divide the belt into two large zones: the Mongolian/Manchurian steppe and the central Asian/Russian steppe, with the two connected by a narrow series of routes that squeeze between encroaching mountains and deserts. In this way the steppe was both an obstacle and highway between the great sedentary civilizations in China and those in Europe and the Middle East. Under the right political conditions, the entire steppe could be traversed. The famous Silk Road, for example, ran across its southeastern quadrant, connecting China to central Asia. The armies of sedentary societies bordering the steppe, however, found it more of an obstacle than a throughway. Movement on the steppe required adaptation to its demands.

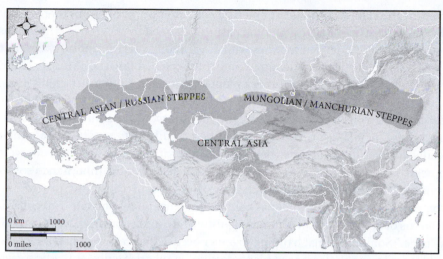

Map 5.2 The Eurasian steppe.

The people who lived on the steppe were nomads of necessity. Deep in pre-history they may have been foragers and hunters (as discussed in chapters 1 and 2). With the domestication of animals it became possible to derive most of their subsistence from herds of sheep, goats, yaks, and horses, sustained on the endless grasslands of the steppe, and providing milk, meat, and trade goods to their owners. Endless though the steppe might seem, aridity and the severity of the winter meant that the grasses had limits. A given region could sustain only so many animals for so long. People tended to live in small famil-ial camps of eight to fifty individuals accompanied by their herds and moving about within a more or less defined region during each season. When summer turned to winter, they migrated south or to a different set of pastures at a lower elevation, and then moved about within that new region until the season changed again. They did not "wander." Families or groups of families had customary pastures, and changes were usually the cause or consequence of war. Even so, the steppe nomads did not necessarily think in terms of the con-trol of land—they calculated power in terms of the control of animals and of people. When a family patriarch within a steppe society divided his holdings, his "appanages," evenly among his sons, he was dividing flocks and/or his rule over people. Such rule might roughly correspond to territory, but was not de-fined by a precise boundary. Dividing the patriarchal holdings into equivalent appanages meant that each generation perceived itself as having less than the previous one. Furthermore, as any given encampment grew too big, it would spin off another. If one multiplies across many encampments this process of growth and fission combined with the system of divided inheritance, the in-tense competition for pasture becomes easy to imagine.

At one level this competition was regulated or contained by familial ties be-tween neighboring camps, which would occasionally come together in a larger gathering to renew friendships and exchange brides. Those large gatherings defined the clan, whose leaders emerged via merit, primarily from their skill at defending or expanding the regional pastures claimed by the clan at large. Clans were nominally extended families with a common ancestor, but on the steppe there were other ways to acquire companions and followers, through blood brothership or simply by acquiring a reputation for success that attracted a *nöker*, a kind of comrade-follower (here and elsewhere I use the Mongol terms, but the concept was widely shared on the steppe, and the words were often very similar in other steppe languages). Well-established clan leaders sought to pass their leadership on to their sons, but incompetent or juvenile descendants were quickly removed or isolated—a form of mediated political inheritance sometimes called tanistry. Neighboring clans on the steppe constantly jostled and competed with others, sometimes banding together under pressure into confederations or alliances, usually along linguistic lines, into something we might call a "tribe." Sometimes that banding together occurred forcefully, when a successful leader of one clan imposed his leadership on others. Steppe nomadic societies were not necessarily egalitarian, but the equal division of land among sons and tanistry meant that accumulated political power could quickly dissipate from one generation to the next. Furthermore, their shared lifestyle as herders strongly ingrained a certain kind of rough-and-ready equality. Chinggis Khan would assume godlike status, but unlike an Egyptian pharaoh or a Roman emperor he would continue to provide hospitality to and feast with his fellow warriors. He did not live in royal isolation; his society provided no mechanism for a leader to do so.[14]

The social and ecological structure of nomads' lives meant that they *usually* arrived in the sedentary world as raiders rather than conquerors. Small independent clans living on the edge of the steppe raided across the climatic boundary, or even maintained an ongoing semiextortionate relationship with neighboring farmers, demanding food or goods in exchange for not attacking. It is important not to overplay their predatory role, however. Recent research has emphasized the importance of trade between nomadic and sedentary societies, as well as, in some cases, the nomads' own craftwork and even limited agricultural capabilities. Most of the time the nomadic clans' political fragility prevented them from doing too much damage to the non-steppe world. They were always a threat to be managed, however. Sometimes, because of demographic pressure, or climatic change and a reduction of available pasture, or the emergence of a particularly successful leader, or perhaps even because a neighboring sedentary state had grown powerful and therefore capable of sustaining the needs of a strong nomadic state, a politically united confederation of steppe clans could emerge from the steppe in the role of conquerors rather than raiders. When they did, the close relationship between their lifestyle and their mode of fighting, now magnified by greater numbers, made them terrifying military opponents.[15]

To greatly simplify, there were three key components to the steppe nomads' military potency. The first was simply the similarity of their lifestyle to the nature of a campaign. The implications of this are many and sometimes un-expected. Unlike most state-based societies, in which soldiers either served part time or were a select group sustained by the labor of others, among the nomads virtually all men were considered to be warriors. Their equipment (about which more in a moment) was for the most part the same gear they needed to survive on the steppe: primarily their horses and a bow. With some notable exceptions, whatever armor and steel they possessed came through trade or plunder of the sedentary world. Furthermore, the mobility sought by every army came to them naturally. Moving all their possessions with them was integral to their lifestyle. It is difficult to overstate the importance of this single truth. The nineteenth-century theorist of war Carl von Clausewitz (dis-cussed in chapter 11) famously remarked, "Everything in war is very simple, but the simplest thing is difficult. The difficulties accumulate and end by producing a kind of friction that is inconceivable unless one has experienced war."[16] Sedentary armies have sought to lessen friction through training, dis-cipline, and the articulation of authority through numerous levels of com-mand. For the nomads, purposeful, directed movement across long distances came naturally. Even better, a nomad society on the move on the steppe car-ried its logistics, its "baggage," with it as a matter of course. Their armies could do much the same. In addition to this general superiority in long-distance movement, the nomads' normal hunting technique directly paral-leled their military tactics in the open field. Called the *nerge*, men on horseback formed long lines, moving forward side by side, sometimes ex-tending over the horizon, but still managing to sweep forward and curl inward, with the extreme ends eventually meeting to form a circle and thereby enclose the stampeded game. Finally, the men who were expected to do all these things needed little formal "training" in basic combat skills (although some recent research has suggested that the Mongols did supplement life skills with formal training). The 2nd-century BCE Chinese historian Sima Qian may have exaggerated in describing the childhood of Xiongnu boys, but his point is generally supported by observers from other times: "The little boys start out by learning to ride sheep and shoot birds and rats with a bow and arrow, and when they get a little older they shoot foxes and hares, which are used for food. Thus all of the young men are able to use a bow and act as armed cavalry in time of war."[17]

Sima Qian's observation points out both of the other key components of the steppe nomads' success: their use of the steppe horse and their mastery of the composite, recurve horse bow. The steppe horse, especially the breed used by the Mongols, was (and is) notably shorter than the domesticated working horses of sedentary societies, had greater stamina at speed and harder hooves that rarely needed shoeing, and, crucially, could subsist entirely on grass, and was even capable of kicking its way through ice and snow to the grass below. In theory, a sedentary working horse can also exist on fresh or stored grass, but most sedentary societies cannot afford to dedicate the necessary acreage to feed their horses on grass alone, and they therefore rely on some form of grain (which concentrates caloric production per acre). A horse's digestive system, however, requires the roughage of grass or hay in addition to grain. On the march, sedentary-bred horses would either have to spread out each day, or they would need that mix of grass and grain brought to them by wagons. In winter, the entire feed requirement would have to be transported to the horses. In contrast, the smaller steppe horses could live entirely on grass and needed much less of it (almost half that of a full-size European horse). For the nomads, spreading out their herds while on the steppe was a relatively easy operation. Perhaps most intriguingly, the nomads *preferred* to campaign beginning in the autumn, with their horses fattened from the summer's pasturage, capable of eating winter grass, and now able to ride over frozen rivers. Winter campaigns were the bane of sedentary armies. Contemporary sources also agree that each nomad rode to war with a string of at least three horses, and perhaps as many as ten, never riding the same horse for more than a day, allowing the others to rest. Modern accounts of Mongolian horses suggest that they can sustain a galloping pace for thirty-five kilometers (such long races are a common pastime in modern Mongolia). The nomads also milked their mares (mares and some geldings were the preferred mount) to produce yogurt and a fermented beverage called *qumis*, sustaining them when operating away from their other livestock. In extremis they were known to briefly open a vein in a horse's neck and drink the blood. More colorfully, the Mongols salted strips of meat by placing them under the saddle blanket against the horse's skin, where the friction would rub the horse's salty sweat into the meat to preserve it (this also apparently served as a treatment for saddle sores). Early Western observers, seeing a Mongol reach under the saddle and peel out a strip of meat, sometimes thought they were literally eating their horses alive.[18]

It is not that steppe armies did not have "baggage." Their slower carts, accompanied by their families, tents, and herds of sheep, followed behind them. But a nomadic army could operate for longer, and at a much greater distance, away from their baggage train than any sedentary society's army. A Mongol army could cover as much as sixty miles a day. They could not sustain that pace for long, but that speed, and their relative independence from their baggage, gave steppe peoples extraordinary strategic mobility, at least while they were on the steppe. If threatened by a superior sedentary army, they could withdraw into the grasslands, where their opponents could follow only briefly before running out of provisions. The ancient Greek historian Herodotus noted this characteristic of the nomadic Scythians, saying:

> I do not praise the Scythians in all respects, but in this, the most important: that they have contrived that no one who attacks them can escape, and no one can catch them if they do not want to be found. For when men have no established cities or forts, but are all nomads and mounted archers, not living by

tilling the soil but by raising cattle and carrying their dwellings on wagons, how can they not be invincible and unapproachable?[19]

One modern estimate is that a sedentary army moving into the steppe could last only five days before having to turn back. It would begin starving within ten days (five days in, and five days out).[20]

In battle, the nomads also retained the usual advantages of tactical mobility; they could shift positions rapidly in response to opportunity or danger. One of their most commonly used tactics was that of feigned flight. Pretending to be routed by an enemy charge, they would flee, and as the enemy pursued and their formation lost cohesion, the nomads would unexpectedly halt, turn, and charge their surprised foes. This may seem a fairly simple trick, and it was so often repeated as to be predictable. But most ancient authors acknowledge its effectiveness, pointing out that there are few things more difficult for a sedentary society's army than to halt in the midst of a full-speed retreat and return to the fight, or to resist the temptation of pursuing an enemy who is showing his back.

Once in the fight, the nomads' primary weapon was the composite recurve bow, sometimes simply called a horse bow—the final key to their military success (see Figure 5.4). Chapter 2 outlined the basic characteristics of

Figure 5.4 Mongolian mounted archer. Although taken in 1895, this photograph accurately represents the horse, bow, and posture of a Mongolian steppe warrior.

the composite recurve bow, which seems to have first appeared in the sedentary Middle East in the seventeenth century BCE. Its origins, however, were clearly associated with pastoral, and probably nomadic, peoples, and it was they who continued to tinker with and refine the basic technology. To restate the basics from chapter 2, a composite recurve bow combined geometry and different materials to produce a powerful bow short enough to be used from horseback. A nomad's bow was made from animal sinew glued to a wood core, in turn glued to an inner layer of horn. The main disadvantages of this construction were a vulnerability to moisture and the time required for its manufacture (the seasoning and glue-drying time could last from one to five years). Some key improvements occurred in fourth to sixth centuries CE, at precisely the same time as iron stirrups appeared. Although the significance of the stirrup to couching a lance can be debated, there is little doubt about the advantages conferred to a rider able to rise up from his seat when firing a bow. Using the legs as a shock absorber greatly enhances the accuracy of a shot from a moving horse. In fact, some texts suggest that an expert rider would release his arrow at the precise moment that all four legs of his horse were in the air, fully isolating his aim from the effects of the ground.[21]

Debate persists on exactly how steppe cavalry forces used their bows. Did they caracole—that is, charge to within direct fire range, fire, and then retire, only to circle back to fire again? Did they remain at extreme range (perhaps four hundred yards) and fire light and possibly even unfletched arrows at 45-degree angles, relying on the "shower effect" of clouds of descending arrows at terminal velocity? Did they, as was hypothesized for chariots, ride toward, through, and beyond enemy formations, firing the whole time? We know that some training exercises seemed designed for this purpose: firing at target to the front, to the side, and to the rear in succession. The reality is probably some combination of all these techniques and more. The key here is the combination of the bow with the mobility of the steppe horse (whose rider might even switch in midbattle to a second horse from his string if he felt his mount tire) and a lifetime's experience of hunting with that bow from horseback. In the terse summary composed by contemporary Chinese historians explaining Mongol rule over China (called the Yuan dynasty), "Yuan arose in the northern areas. By nature they are good at riding and archery. Therefore they took possession of the world through this advantage of bows and horses."[22]

The Mongols were neither the first nor the last of the steppe-based conquerors. There had been a long history of steppe-sedentary interaction, peaceful and otherwise, with enormous consequences for both: the Scythians and the Greco-Persian world; the Xiongnu and the Han Chinese; the Huns, Sarmatians, and others moving westward into European Rome; and various Persian dynasties whose rulers had originated in the steppe. The Muslim Arab conquests of the seventh to ninth centuries CE had the interesting and complex side effect of attracting or dragging various Turkic peoples from central Asia into the sedentary Middle East, some of whom there became founders of new dynastic empires. The empires they founded became fundamentally sedentary and bureaucratic. They maintained aspects of the steppe military system, however, primarily the emphasis on the horse archer, although now typically based on grain- and fodder-fed, stable-kept, full-size horses. Key examples included the Seljuk Turks, who ruled over the Anatolian peninsula and its periphery from roughly 1000 CE to 1200 CE, until they were finally fully destroyed by the invading Mongols in the 1260s. The Mamluks began as Turkish slave soldiers belonging to the Arab Muslim dynasty ruling Egypt in the thirteenth century. They gradually usurped more and more power, eventually becoming the de facto rulers. They played a key role in limiting Mongol conquests, defeating a tentative Mongol invasion of the Levant at Ayn Jalut (in what is now northern Israel) in 1260. Perhaps most importantly, another Turkish dynasty emerged as the Ottomans in the fourteenth century in the wake of the Mongol conquest. They would challenge the Europeans and rule over much of the Middle East and southeastern Europe into the twentieth century. We will return to their history in chapter 7.

THE MONGOLS

It is the Mongols and their remarkable ascension to dominance over most of Eurasia that concern us here. To repeat, they are in one sense merely an example of the steppe warrior system at its most powerful, selected and discussed here partly because their success generated more records than we have for most other steppe peoples. In addition, however, Chinggis Khan himself has been credited with several specific innovations within the steppe system that built on and multiplied its strengths. Examining them will further clarify the unique qualities and limitations of steppe-based power. In the end, a key component of the scale of the Mongols' success was the extent to which Chinggis Khan and his heirs rose above the traditional political dynamics of the steppe, as well as their flexible incorporation of the peoples and skills of other communities. On the other hand, their ultimate collapse resulted from the extent to which they were unable to leave behind the steppe and its traditions.

In the late twelfth century the Mongols were an assortment of competing tribes that also engaged in more or less constant competition with other neighboring steppe peoples. By no means a dominant or united people, they also had the usual contentious trade and raiding relationship with the sedentary Chinese to their south. At that time "China" was divided into three dynastic empires: the northern Jurchen Jin (themselves formerly nomads from the northeast), the Xi Xia (or Tanguts) in the northwestern corridor that the Han had wrested from the Xiongnu (discussed in the previous chapter), and finally the agricultural heartland of China in the south, ruled by the Song dynasty (see Map 5.3). Although the Mongols under Chinggis Khan and his successors would conquer far beyond the boundaries of China, sedentary China's seemingly endless wealth repeatedly lured them back.[23]

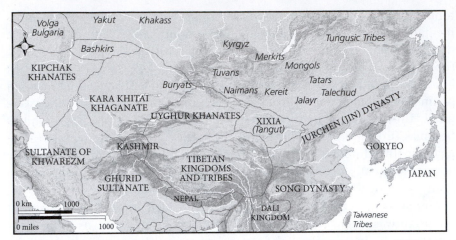

Map 5.3 China and Central Asia on the eve of the Mongol conquests, ca. 1200.

The early life of Chinggis Khan, then known as Temujin, began within this politically fractured competitive arena. The details of his rise to power within the steppe were recorded after his death in the so-called *Secret History*. Although it includes substantial mythologizing, it is clear that he began life as a virtual exile, a member of a nearly destroyed patriline. Only slowly did he cobble together a network of friends and patrons, creating his own following, as he himself remained a part of another's following (to use the European terms, he acquired a retinue, while also making himself a retainer). In time, aided by good luck, great personal charisma, and political savvy, he enlarged his following through military success, encompassing and, crucially, *incorporating* several defeated peoples, until he emerged as the ruler of all eastern Mongolia. At this point, his patron Wang Khan Toghrul, ruler of the Kereits, finally perceived him as a threat and the two clashed. Temujin emerged victorious in 1203, leaving only the Naimans unsubdued within greater Mongolia. He soon defeated them as well, and the gathered tribes of the Mongolian steppe proclaimed Temujin the "great khan," Chinggis Khan, in 1206.

It is important to note that it took most of his life for Chinggis Khan to become the ruler of the united steppe peoples of Mongolia. His exact birth year is disputed, but by 1206 he was between thirty-nine and forty-four years old, and he would die in 1227. In over twenty years of struggle he became the ruler of the united Mongols. In twenty more years he would conquer two of the three Chinese empires, the Khwarezm Empire of central Asia, Transoxiana, and Persia. He would also send a great raiding army to circle the Caspian Sea and lay the groundwork for further conquests by his successors.

It was during the early struggles within Mongolia that Chinggis Khan forged the tools that differentiated his steppe army from those that preceded it. His innovations, building on the natural strengths of the steppe warrior system, were fundamentally political and institutional. Each mitigated the fractious nature of steppe politics and bound the army to him and to his successors. First, Chinggis Khan seems to have further systematized a widespread steppe practice of dividing and subdividing an army into decimal-based units, from the *tümen* of 10,000 to the *minqan* of 1,000, the *jaghun* of 100, and finally the *arban* of 10. This sort of rationalized subdivision may seem obvious now, but one must recall that in much of the medieval world, "units" of soldiers were simply the contingents of various leaders, their size more or less dependent on each leader's personal resources. Some mercenary units of specialists (Genoese crossbowmen for example) might create semistandard unit sizes, but that was hardly the norm. The Mongols' decimal subdivisions allowed the commander to oversee and give orders to a predictable and limited number of subordinates. As in the Roman military system, discussed in the previous chapter, the Mongol system limited the number of direct subordinates to ten, who in turn had ten subordinates, and so on.[24]

Second, Chinggis deliberately broke up the traditional tribal structure of the army. On one hand, he created a system of promotion by merit, to which any man could aspire, no matter their background, as long as they proved their skill and loyalty. Chinggis then cemented that loyalty through a generous system of rewards, funded by his continued success. Those men thus promoted owed their position to him, not to the strength of their tribal contingent or to their family connections. In addition, Chinggis allowed and encouraged those military leaders to recruit from across tribal lines, a practice that became easier as the expanding Mongol empire incorporated more and more steppe peoples. In combination these two practices undermined the tribe as a source of competing centers of authority. Chinggis's royal bodyguard, the *keshik*, also undermined rival tribal authority. It became not just a pool of accomplished warriors but also a repository for the sons of great tribal leaders. Serving in the keshik, never far from Chinggis himself, made the latter vulnerable as hostages, but it also trained and indoctrinated them as loyal members of his military household. Many later rose to command positions.[25]

One last key component of the Mongol conquests, although not rooted in the years before 1206, was their army's incorporation of the skills of the conquered. Folding in conquered Turkish-speaking steppe peoples was relatively straightforward (indeed, the expanding empire after Chinggis's death is probably best called a Turco-Mongol empire). But the Mongols were eclectic, if forceful, gatherers of talent. Technicians and artisans from conquered cities were literally herded back to the Mongol homeland. On the military side, perhaps the most famous example of this process was the use of Arab siege engineers to run the growing Mongol siege train (see Figure 5.5). Such men introduced the counterweight trebuchet to China. In turn, it is very likely that Chinese manufacturers of gunpowder introduced their product (then used primarily as an incendiary) to the rest of Eurasia.[26]

Figure 5.5 Illustration of a Mongol siege. From the chronicles of Rashid al-Din, ca. 1310. Note the Arab siege engineer operating a trebuchet.

Success proved the key ingredient in implementing all these changes. With military success and the resulting captured resources, Chinggis could reward those loyal to him and push through remarkable changes to the usual steppe customs. "Mongol" success attracted non-Mongols to their banner, in much the same way that "Franks" or "Lombards" filled their ranks with a variety of ethnicities based on the attractions of success and the prestige associated with belonging to the ruling group. And Chinggis Khan and his immediate successors had no lack of success. His own conquests included most of Jin China, Manchuria, and the central Asian steppe as far as the Caspian Sea. He died in 1227 at the close of his successful campaign against the Xi Xia, and his forces had already raided deep into Afghanistan and eastern Russia. His son Ogodei oversaw the final conquest of the Jin, of the Kipchak Turks on the Russian steppe, and of European Russia. The massive campaign directed into Poland and Hungary was interrupted by Ogodei's death. Afterward the Mongols' energy was redirected into conquering Afghanistan, Persia, Iraq, and Anatolia, checked only by the Mamluks of Egypt. The final jewel in the crown was Song China, conquered in 1271 after some forty years of struggle. It is essential to emphasize that many of these conquests, especially in China, depended heavily on the massive mobilization of the infantry and the technical resources of other conquered sedentary societies. Mongol success bred further success. The steppe horseman remained at the core of Mongol power, however, and required constant refreshing of men and horses from the steppe population.

Equally critical to point out here, however, is that Mongol success was based *both* on the strength of the steppe warrior system *and* on Chinggis's partial suppression of the steppe's usually fractious politics. Only by suppressing

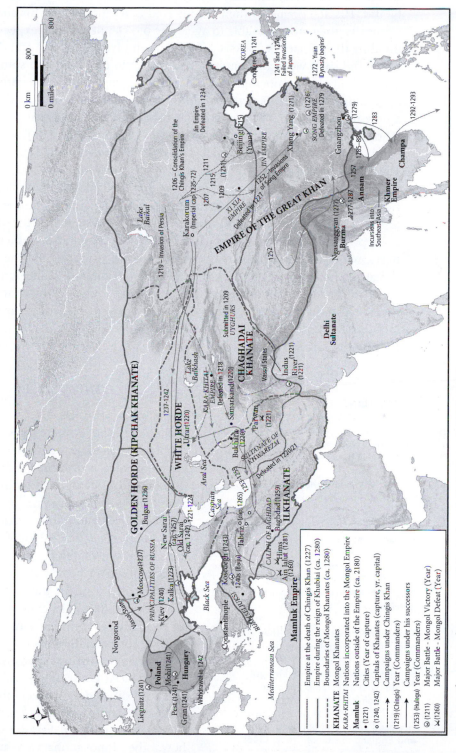

Map 5.4 The Mongol Empire and its early subdivisions, ca. 1206–1280.

The map includes the following labels:

800

0 km 800
0 miles

KOREA — Conquered in 1241

1241 and 1274:
Failed invasions
of Japan

1272 – Yuan
Dynasty begins

Jin Empire
Defeated in 1234

1206 – Consolidation of the
Chingis Khan's Empire

Beijing (1215)
1211

Xiang Yang (1271)

(1276)
SONG EMPIRE
Defeated in 1279

Guangzhou
(1279)

1285–88

1283

1292–1293

Champa

Lake
Baikal

1219 – Invasion of Persia

1215
1209 (1211)
1207

Karakorum
o (Imperial cap.) 1235–72

XI XIA
EMPIRE
Defeated in 1227

JIN EMPIRE

1252 Invasions
of Song Empire

EMPIRE OF THE GREAT KHAN

Khmer
Empire

Ngasaunggyan (1270)
4277–1287
Annam
Burma
1257

Incursions into
Southeast Asia

1252

GOLDEN HORDE (KIPCHAK KHANATE)

1237–1242

WHITE HORDE

Submitted in 1209
UYGHURS

CHAGHADAI
KHANATE

Delhi
Sultanate

Lake
Balkhash

KARA-KHITAI
EMPIRE
Defeated in 1218

Samarkand (1220)
Bukhara (1220)

Vassal States

Indus
River (1221)

(1221)

Bulgar (1236)

New Sarai
(cap.) 1257
Old Sarai
(cap. 1242) 1221–1224

Aral Sea

Ufrat (1220)

SULTANATE OF
KHWAREZM
Defeated in 1220/21

Ta'yan
(1221)

Caspian
Sea

Moscow (1237)

Kiev (1240)
Kalka (1223)

Vassal

1253–1259

Tabriz o (cap. 1265)

1246 (Batu)
Kosedegh (1243)

CALIPH OF BAGHDAD

o Baghdad (1259)

Hims
Ain Jalut (1281)
(1260)

ILKHANATE

Black Sea

Constantinople

BULGARS (DS)

Novgorod

Vassal

Liegnitz (1241)
Poland
Pest (1241)
Gran (1241)
Mohi (1241)
Hungary
Withdrawal in 1242

Mediterranean Sea

Mamluk Empire

Legend:

Empire at the death of Chingis Khan (1227)
Empire during the reign of Khubiai (ca. 1280)
Boundaries of Mongol Khanates (ca. 1280)
KHANATE Mongol Khanates
KARA-KHITAI Nations incorporated into the Mongol Empire
Mamluk Nations outside of the Empire (ca. 2180)
o (1221) Cities (Year of capture)
o (1240, 1242) Capitals of Khanates (capture, yr. capital)
(1219) (Chingis) Year (Commanders)
Campaigns under Chingis Khan
Campaigns under his successors
(1253) (Hulegu) Year (Commanders)
⊕ (1211) Major Battle - Mongol Victory (Year)
✕ (1260) Major Battle - Mongol Defeat (Year)

175

steppe society's usual tendency to break apart was he able to accomplish what he did. His achievements then empowered and emboldened his successors. Ironically, they proved unable to avoid the old steppe cultural expectation of dividing the patriarch's flocks. Chinggis's multiplying sons and grandsons divided and subdivided the empire, sending it into civil war, and spinning off smaller and smaller subempires, or "hordes," on the steppe or separate Mongol kingdoms in the sedentary zones—most notably the Mongol Yuan dynasty in a now-unified China and the Ilkhanate of Persia, Iraq, and eastern Anatolia ("horde" derives from the Mongol word *ordu*, "military camp"). The Yuan succumbed in 1368 to a succession of poor rulers followed by internal rebellion. The other Mongol subempires continued to subdivide into smaller and smaller powers, until they were overwhelmed by other rising peoples. The steppe warrior system, however, retained enormous potency. It reemerged repeatedly to reshape the history of surrounding sedentary societies, not least the Manchus, a steppe people who conquered China in 1644 and established the Qing dynasty, which lasted into the twentieth century (see chapter 9). The military threat of the steppe horseman, who uniquely combined strategic mobility, logistical freedom, tactical speed, firepower, and even a limited capacity for the direct cavalry charge, forced all the surrounding military systems to adapt. Only when those states developed more modern gunpowder weapons did they finally discover a permanent defense against the steppe warrior system.

TIMELINE

358	Romans defeat Salian Franks and name them *foederati*—"allies"; they settle inside the empire
476	Traditional date for the end of the Western Roman Empire
800	Crowning of Charlemagne as Holy Roman emperor
843	Division of Frankish kingdom into three parts; onset of attacks by Vikings, Saracens, and Magyars (the last from 890)
1206	Temujin becomes Chinggis Khan, ruler of the Mongolian people
1271	Song dynasty conquered; Mongol (Yuan) dynasty established over united China
1337–1453	Hundred Years War between France and England (Battle of Crecy, 1346)

CONCLUSION

At this point in *Waging War* we have described all the key elements of war on land during the pre-gunpowder age in Eurasia: the hierarchical state, iron, horsemen, fortifications, and disciplined infantry. Each appeared in different ways in different places, according to idiosyncratic cultural and ecological conditions. All of these systems, however, shared the critical limitations imposed by the nature of the organic economy described in the Introduction. Energy expenditure depended ultimately on vegetative growth. Force mobilization and logistics literally depended on controlling and harvesting expansive territory that produced crops, trees, and/or grass. The vast difference between the steppe grasslands and agricultural Europe or China then produced key differences in how other innovations were used. The

European knight and the steppe warrior were both empowered by their horses, but in very different ways. That difference was mostly ecological, but there were also critical cultural differences rooted in social organization and previous history.

Missing from the story thus far is war at sea. Naval warfare throughout this period was also heavily dependent on muscle power sustained by the organic economy, critically supplemented by wind power. The next chapter reviews the nature of war under oars, and in the following chapters we will examine how the intervention of chemical energy in the form of gunpowder began to change the nature of war. We will also find, however, that many things remained the same.

Further Reading

Bachrach, Bernard S. *Early Carolingian Warfare: Prelude to Empire*. Philadelphia: University of Pennsylvania Press, 2001.

Barfield, Thomas J. *The Perilous Frontier: Nomadic Empires and China*. New York: Blackwell, 1989.

Contamine, Philippe. *War in the Middle Ages*. Translated by Michael Jones. Oxford: Basil Blackwell, 1984.

Crouch, David. *William Marshal: Knighthood, War and Chivalry, 1147–1219*. 2nd ed. London: Longman, 2002.

Halsall, Guy. *Warfare and Society in the Barbarian West, 450–900*. New York: Routledge, 2003.

Keen, Maurice H., ed. *Medieval Warfare: A History*. New York: Oxford University Press, 1999.

May, Timothy. *The Mongol Art of War*. Yardley, PA: Westholme, 2007.

Morgan, David. *The Mongols*. 2nd ed. Malden, MA: Blackwell, 2007.

Ratchnevsky, Paul. *Genghis Khan: His Life and Legacy*. Translated by Thomas Nivison Haining. Oxford: Blackwell, 1991.

Verbruggen, J. F. *The Art of Warfare in Western Europe during the Middle Ages*. 2nd ed. Woodbridge, UK: Boydell, 1997.

Notes

1. Elizabeth M. Greene, "Women and Families in the Auxiliary Military Communities of the Roman West in the First and Second Centuries AD" (PhD diss., University of North Carolina at Chapel Hill, 2011).

2. Peter Connolly and Carol van Driel-Murray, "The Roman Cavalry Saddle," *Britannia* 22 (1991): 33–50. Roman imperial decline and the role of "barbarians" in the Roman army is a complex issue. A good summary is Peter J. Heather, "Holding the Line: Frontier Defense and the Later Roman Empire," in *Makers of Ancient Strategy: From the Persian Wars to the Fall of Rome*, ed. Victor Davis Hanson (Princeton, NJ: Princeton University Press, 2010), 227–46.

3. All examples from Bernard S. Bachrach, "Early Medieval Europe," in *War and Society in the Ancient and Medieval Worlds: Asia, the Mediterranean, Europe, and Mesoamerica*, ed. Kurt Raaflaub and Nathan Rosenstein (Washington, DC: Center for Hellenic Studies, 1999), 273.

4. Guy Halsall, *Warfare and Society in the Barbarian West, 450–900* (New York: Routledge, 2003), 46–48.

5. Bernard Bachrach, "Charles Martel, Mounted Shock Combat, the Stirrup, and Feudalism," *Studies in Medieval and Renaissance History* 7 (1970): 49–75. The textual evidence for tactical details in the eighth and ninth centuries is very thin. But despite some claims to the contrary, Clifford Rogers ably demonstrates that the Franks regularly used cavalry-only forces, conducted charges with those forces, and expected such charges to defeat infantry forces. Clifford J. Rogers, "Carolingian Cavalry in Battle: The Evidence Reconsidered," in *Crusading and Warfare in the Middle Ages: Realities and Representations. Essays in Honour of John France*, ed. Simon John and Nicolas Morton (Farnham, UK: Ashgate, 2014), 1–11; John France, *Perilous Glory: The Rise of Western Military Power* (New Haven, CT: Yale University Press, 2011), 108 (for an earlier example).

6. John Gillingham, "An Age of Expansion, c. 1020–1204," in *Medieval Warfare: A History*, ed. Maurice H. Keen (New York: Oxford University Press, 1999), 59–88; Robert Bartlett, *The Making of Europe: Conquest, Colonization, and Cultural Change, 950–1350* (Princeton, NJ: Princeton University Press, 1993).

7. Here I follow David Crouch, *William Marshal: Knighthood, War and Chivalry, 1147–1219*, 2nd ed. (London: Pearson, 1990).

8. Many examples in J. F. Verbruggen, *The Art of Warfare in Western Europe during the Middle Ages*, 2nd ed. (Woodbridge, UK: Boydell, 1997), see especially 73–77, 83–89, 98. For the infantry in the tournament see ibid., 36 (citing *Histoire de Guillaume le Maréchal* 1, vv. 2715–40).

9. R. H. C. Davis, *The Medieval Warhorse: Origin, Development and Redevelopment* (London: Thames & Hudson, 1989), 107–8 (quote).

10. Andrew Ayton, *Knights and Warhorses: Military Service and the English Aristocracy under Edward III* (Woodbridge, UK: Boydell, 1994), 252, 255. Recent studies demonstrate that well-made plate armor still allowed for a wide freedom of movement; fallen knights were not like turtles on their backs, unable to rise. The weight and vision restrictions, however, are undeniable. Armor progression in Kelly DeVries and Robert Douglas Smith, *Medieval Military Technology*, 2nd ed. (Toronto: University of Toronto Press, 2012), 63–93.

11. Kelly DeVries, *Infantry Warfare in the Early Fourteenth Century: Discipline, Tactics, and Technology* (Woodbridge, UK: Boydell, 1996); Stephen Morillo, Jeremy Black, and Paul Lococo, *War in World History* (New York: McGraw-Hill, 2009), 1:74, 122–23; Verbruggen, *Art of Warfare*, 172.

12. Robert Hardy, *Longbow: A Social and Military History* (Sparkford, UK: Patrick Stephens, 1992), 32–38, 41–56; Michael Prestwich, *Armies and Warfare in the Middle Ages: The English Experience* (New Haven, CT: Yale University Press, 1996), 131–45; Hugh D. H. Soar, *Secrets of the English War Bow* (Yardley, PA: Westholme, 2006), 191–95; Ann Stirland, *The Men of the Mary Rose: Raising the Dead* (Phoenix Mill, UK: Sutton, 2005), 89–156; Christopher Knüsel, "Activity-Related Skeletal Change," in *Blood Red Roses: The Archaeology of a Mass Grave from the Battle of Towton, AD 1461*, ed. Veronica Fiorato, Anthea Boylston, and Christopher Knüsel, (Oxford: Oxbow, 2000), 103–18.

13. Keen, "Introduction," in Keen, *Medieval Warfare*, 7 (quote).

14. David Morgan, *The Mongols*, 2nd ed. (Malden, MA: Blackwell, 2007), 30–37. Thanks to Timothy May for conversations on the issue of pasture and appanages.

15. Thomas Barfield argues that strong state dynasties in China led to strong tribal states on the neighboring steppe, since the former could afford the tribute and trade

demanded by their threatening neighbor. The tribute and expanded trade (usually in horses) funded steppe centralization. The Mongols broke this pattern by engaging in actual conquest of China. Thomas J. Barfield, *The Perilous Frontier: Nomadic Empires and China* (New York: Blackwell, 1989). The Mongols broke this pattern by engaging in actual conquest of China.

16. Carl von Clausewitz, *On War*, trans. Michael Howard and Peter Paret (Princeton, NJ: Princeton University Press, 1976), 119 (quote).

17. Timothy May, "The Training of an Inner Asian Nomad Army in the Pre-Modern Period," *Journal of Military History* 70.3 (2006): 617–35; Edward L. Shaughnessy, "Historical Perspectives on the Introduction of the Chariot into China," *Harvard Journal of Asiatic Studies* 48.1 (1988): 200 (quote).

18. The average height of a Mongolian horse is 12–14 hands (48–56 inches); the Arabian breed is 14.1–15.1 hands (57–61 inches); the American Saddlebred is 15–16 (60–64 inches); and the Hanoverian warmblood (bred for farm and cavalry use in the eighteenth century) is 16–16.2 hands on average. Modern guidelines for feeding domestic working horses recommend twenty-five pounds of feed daily for a thousand-pound horse, combining long-stemmed forage (hay) with the more concentrated nourishment found in grain. Although it is possible to feed such a horse entirely from pasture grass, that requires tough grasses and lots of acreage. Instead, premodern farmers divided the feeding load between grain and grass/hay (hay is cut and stored grass). For the Mongol horse's independence from grain or stored hay, see D. Sinor, "Horse and Pasture in Inner Asian History," *Oriens Extremus* 19 (1972): 171–83, esp. 177, 173; Charles R. Bowlus, *The Battle of Lechfeld and Its Aftermath, August 955: The End of the Age of Migrations in the Latin West* (Aldershot, UK: Ashgate, 2006), 24–26.

19. Herodotus 4.46, in *Herodotus*, trans. A. D. Godley (Cambridge, MA: Harvard University Press, 1920).

20. Kenneth Warren Chase, *Firearms: A Global History to 1700* (Cambridge, UK: Cambridge University Press, 2003), 17.

21. Bowlus, *Lechfeld*, 27–28, on construction time.

22. May, "Training of an Inner Asian Nomad Army"; John Masson Smith, Jr., "Ayn Jalut: Mamluk Success or Mongol Failure?," *Harvard Journal of Asiatic Studies* 44.2 (1984): 307–45; Sinor, "Horse and Pasture," 171 (quote).

23. Morgan, *Mongols*, 41–45.

24. Timothy May, *The Mongol Art of War* (Yardley, PA: Westholme, 2007), 31.

25. Paul Ratchnevsky, *Genghis Khan: His Life and Legacy* (Oxford: Blackwell, 1991), 90–93.

26. Thomas T. Allsen, "The Circulation of Military Technology in the Mongolian Empire," in *Warfare in Inner Asian History, 500–1800*, ed. Nicola Di Cosmo (Leiden: Brill, 2002), 265–93; Thomas T. Allsen, "Ever Closer Encounters: The Appropriation of Culture and the Apportionment of Peoples in the Mongol Empire," *Journal of Early Modern History* 1 (1997): 2–23.

6

War under Oars

700 BCE–1600 CE

The Earliest Shipping • The Trireme and the Mediterranean • Variations on a Theme: Hellenistic Invention and Gigantism, Rome, Greek Fire, and the Gunpowder Galley

THE MOVEMENT OF GOODS AND PEOPLE by wind and water represents the most important exception to the normal limitations of the organic economy. Even in the absence of sails to harness the wind, oar-, paddle-, or pole-driven shipping is vastly more energy efficient than land transport, especially over long distances. Humans therefore rapidly turned to the water to move themselves and their goods. The advantages of that system led to the extension of armed conflict onto water as peoples competed to control or safeguard their access to it. Ironically, the extension of conflict onto the waters to preserve access to water transport led to a ship design that forfeited carrying capacity in pursuit of tactical advantage: the oared-galley warship, designed for speed, armed with a ram for much of its history, and requiring an enormous crew relative to its overall displacement. In short, the galley sacrificed carrying capacity for speed and maneuverability. It was therefore expensive to build, maintain, and man, but within the Mediterranean's favorable environment, and within some other confined waters, it proved extremely effective. Once invented, the purpose-built warship proved impossible to ignore, and those who wanted to compete at sea were forced to imitate it and to bear its expense. In some ways not unlike the chariot, the war galley benefited most those states with greater resources.

State capacity is therefore a crucial variable in understanding the purpose-built warship, oared or otherwise. But warship design was also driven by cultural conservatism and conscious calculation. The uncompromising need to stay afloat, and the lethal consequences of failed experimentation, tended to make shipbuilding a conservative craft, one that changed in an evolutionary rather than revolutionary fashion. Those changes, however, usually derived from tactical or economic calculation rather than from broader changes in cultural preference. That said, we will also note some interesting ways that culture influenced even something as seemingly practical as ship design.

This chapter covers an enormous chronological range. For all of it, at least in the Mediterranean, the galley reigned supreme as a vessel of war. Despite some substantial variation in design, the nature of oared-galley technology combined with the nature of the Mediterranean Sea to create certain basic constants or structures in the nature of war under oars. Technology and geography thus provide the unity for this chapter, although, as always, politics, culture, and economics effected major changes in the basic system. It is true that oared warships appeared outside the Mediterranean, and rowed galleys and gunboats continued to be used into the nineteenth century in lakes, rivers, and harbors, and even on the open sea. The most famous to Western readers were those of the Vikings, but the navies of Korea, Japan, and China also depended heavily on different forms of oared warships. This chapter, however, leans on the unity of the Mediterranean experience, and we begin there with the first evidence of human movement across the sea.

THE EARLIEST SHIPPING

Recent archaeological work has provided stunning evidence of the human ability to move by sea. It has been known for some time that *Homo sapiens*, migrating east from Africa, rapidly moved by water into Oceania, arriving in Australia 40,000 to 60,000 years ago. In 2008, however, researchers on the island of Crete discovered tools dating to 130,000 years ago, dramatically changing our understanding of the human use of the sea. Virtually nothing is known of how such early voyagers moved at sea, or how frequently they did so. It is clear, however, that the Mediterranean offered an environment conducive to the regular movement of people and goods on the open sea as early as the Mesolithic. From around 11,000 BCE hunter-gatherers living in the Franchthi cave in southern Greece regularly traveled to the volcanic island of Melos for its valuable obsidian. Melian obsidian became a common trade good across the eastern Mediterranean, and archaeologists cite its wide distribution as evidence for just how early and extensive seaborne trade must have been. By the Neolithic, the evidence for movement by sea is common, and furthermore the colonization of islands by new farmers, apparently carrying seed and domesticated animals, must have required substantial vessels. In the Aegean and eastern Mediterranean these early craft were large canoes or longboats. Images surviving from the early Bronze Age (around 2600 BCE) show vessels some fifty to sixty-five feet long, holding perhaps twenty-five rowers.[1]

Meanwhile another boatbuilding tradition emerged on the Nile River in Egypt. The course of the Nile, flowing south to north, and its prevailing winds, blowing north to south, encouraged navigation on the river. Beginning with bundles of reeds tied together at the ends that more or less naturally formed a boat-shaped raft, Egyptian builders added a third dimension by stacking the bundles, and then added a single square sail to enable sailing upstream using the north-to-south winds. The Egyptians then replicated that form using planks, probably to solve the problem of moving heavy loads. By not later than about 2400 BCE they had replaced paddles with oars, added a steering oar or oars hung over the rear quarter, and reinforced the structure with a stem to stern tensioning rope carried above the deck on crutches (which we will see again later, repositioned, in Greek galleys). This riverboat-building tradition soon extended to seagoing craft. Some evidence suggests that it was the Egyptian and contemporary Mesopotamian use of the sail on riverboats that spread into the Levant and Aegean boatbuilding tradition.[2]

As discussed in chapter 2, the Eastern Mediterranean Bronze Age saw the rise of substantial states, intimately tied to and even dependent on long-distance trade networks (most notably for tin, and in Egypt also for timber). Those wealthy states may have begun the process of distinguishing between merchant ships and warships. The famous Minoan naval frescos from the seventeenth century BCE at Akrotiri on the island of Thera are inconclusive regarding that distinction. Although they may show a military expedition at sea, a religious procession is equally likely, and no evidence suggests that the ships had features making them into weapons or weapon platforms, although they may have had racks for storing spears. Any fighting at sea must have involved boarding and some limited exchange of missile weapons. Analysis of the Mycenaean successors to the Minoans suggests the same, but the presence of warriors aboard ship and their use of elevated firing platforms or castles are more distinct. In other words, there *was* a distinction between warships and other ships, but the distinction may have been very limited, and therefore relatively cheap to implement. These were not yet purpose-built warships. Agreeing with the Mycenaean evidence is the Egyptian portrayal of the attack of the Sea Peoples around 1200 BCE. Egyptian galleys are shown with platforms for archers and lookouts, although as yet the only specifically naval "weapon" clearly shown was the grappling hook. Normally the grappling hook is presumed to simplify boarding and capturing an opponent's ship, but one scholar theorizes that the Egyptians actually used their grapnels to capsize their enemies after sweeping the decks clear with arrow fire.[3]

The collapse of many states at the end of the Bronze Age casts a veil of uncertainty over what happened next in ship design, but the late Bronze evidence suggests a strong continuity in the basic design of the oared galley through the dark ages and into the historic period. During the dark ages galleys probably served as both merchant ships and warships. In the ninth century BCE, however, as more evidence becomes available, we also begin to detect the emergence of a critical new feature: the ram. The appearance of the ram is a fascinating example of the domino-like effects of some innovations, which themselves may have emerged in an ad hoc fashion, but which stimulate calculated responses once they arrived.

Late Bronze Age Mycenaean ships possessed a projecting forefoot as a more or less natural result of their construction: in essence the keel projected slightly forward of where it joined the vertically rising stem (bow), and it was then shaped into a point to move smoothly through the water. It was not yet a ram—it did not project far forward enough; indeed, in surviving artwork, it did not project beyond the decorated stempost (see Figure 6.1a)—but the potential was clearly there. At some point before about 800 BCE that natural extension was lengthened, perhaps at first merely to simplify beaching. Between 750 to 650 BCE it evolved into a true waterline ram designed to burst the planking of an enemy ship. This sort of modification was initially almost without cost: it arose from the very nature of the ship. It quickly became clear, however, that reinforcement and redesign were required to save the ship from the impact on itself when ramming another, and the eventual sheathing of the forefoot in a heavy bronze cap greatly increased the cost of the whole design (see Figure 6.1f). The ram, therefore, initially ad hoc and inexpensive, became deliberate, expensive, and specific to purpose-built warships. Furthermore, it may have helped create a whole new trajectory in galley design.[4]

Wielding a ram put a premium on speed and maneuverability, as well as requiring a stiffer design in order to withstand the shock of delivering that

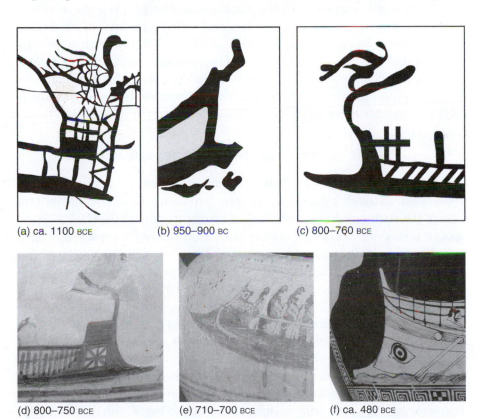

(a) ca. 1100 BCE   (b) 950–900 BC   (c) 800–760 BCE

(d) 800–750 BCE   (e) 710–700 BCE   (f) ca. 480 BCE

Figure 6.1 *a–f* **The evolution of the galley's forefoot into a ram.** As these early Greek representations of galleys suggest, the construction of galleys naturally included a "forefoot" where the keel joined the stempost. In time, that forefoot was lengthened and the join of the stempost to the keel became more curved, until finally the keel projection was deliberately squared off into an offensive ram and then capped with bronze (as seen in 6.1f).

blow. Building a deck over the heads of the rowers stiffened the ship longitudinally and provided a fighting platform higher above the waterline. Initially the deck rested on a picket-fence-like series of supports, between which sat the rowers. In time the rowers were more thoroughly enclosed and protected, a style of ship later called the cataphract. The next stage, probably in response to the increasing weight of these first changes was to "stack" rowers, adding deck-level rowers to those now below deck. Stacking the rowers also allowed the ship designer to pack more muscle power into a shorter vessel, making it more maneuverable. In historian Lionel Casson's words, "The introduction of the ram thus triggered the development of a powerful type of war galley with raised deck and screened sides. And the raised deck, in its turn, made possible a rearrangement of the oars that was to determine the entire future course of the ancient warship." Most if not all of these early innovations were likely made by the Phoenicians, producing what was later called a bireme: an oared ship with two banks of oars, one below the deck and one at the deck level, with one rower per oar. Evidence from Greece suggests that this design converted a single-banked vessel of some 125 feet in length, twenty-five oars to a side (fifty total oarsmen, thus the Greek *pentekonter*), into a much stiffer, shorter, and more maneuverable vessel, still called a *pentekonter* for its fifty total oarsmen, but with its rowers now stacked on top of each other in a vessel probably only sixty-five feet long. This combination of features, known in Phoenicia not later than 700 BCE, was copied by the neighboring maritime Greeks within a century. The fifty-oared bireme became the standard warship of the eastern Mediterranean for nearly two hundred years.[5]

THE TRIREME AND THE MEDITERRANEAN

The Greeks in turn produced their own innovation, sometime in the seventh century BCE, although it did not become the dominant class of warship until the end of the sixth century. In essence they sought to expand the total available muscle power while keeping it compressed within almost the same total length, thereby maximizing speed and maneuverability while limiting "hogging" (the bending that occurs when the center of the vessel experiences upward wave pressure while the two ends sag downward). They created a complex arrangement of oarsmen in a ship of war known to posterity in its Latin form of trireme. In Greek it was the *trieres*—the "three-fitted." Its design served as the core concept for the galley for the rest of antiquity, and the trireme itself would remain in service in various ancient navies until the late Roman Empire. The precise story of its invention remains unknown, and even the exact arrangement of the oars and oarsmen is controversial (no wreck of a trireme has ever been found), but a great deal is known or has been reasonably estimated. It is best to begin with its basic design and performance characteristics and then discuss how it was used.[6]

Although it carried 170 rowers in three superimposed banks (85 per side), the trireme was only 115–120 feet long at the waterline, still shorter than the old single-banked *pentekonter*. Furthermore, it was still only some twelve feet wide (yielding a length-to-beam ratio of about ten to one; in contrast, seventeenth- and eighteenth-century sailing warships had ratios generally between 3.7 to 1 and 4.3 to 1; see Table 6.1).[7] Following long-established shipbuilding techniques in the eastern Mediterranean, the

	Length (feet)	Beam or deck width	Height waterline to deck (boarding obstacle height)	Ratio length to beam	Oarsmen	Deck crew	Marines	Displacement (metric tons)	Men/ton of displacement
Single-banked pentekonter	125	12		10.4	50	2+			
Bireme pentekonter	65	12		5.4	50	2+			
Greek trireme	118	12	8.5	9.8	170	16	14	50	4
Quinquereme (the "five")	135	17.5	12.5	7.7	282	20	75	100	3.77
Quinquereme (the "five") (alternate) (ca. 264 BCE)	142	20		7.1	328	28	40	100	3.96
Roman Liburnian	59	9.9	6.9	6.0	50	5	5		
Venetian 17th-cent. war galley	160	23		7.0					
Venetian *gallia sotil* (standard galley) of 16th cent.	137	17		8.1	144		125	200	1.345
Byzantine 10th-cent. bireme dromon	103	12.5	5.6	8.2	100				
Korean panoksŏn	52–76	28		1.8–2.7		125			
Korean turtle ship	110	28	10	3.9	40		50		
HMS *Victory* (1765)	186	52.1	25	3.6		850		3080	0.28

Table 6.1: **Dimensions of selected galley types**. These dimensions (in feet) are representative and some are quite speculative. Also, any given ship could vary. The intention is to compare ratios of length to beam, crew size, and the number of men per ton of displacement. The HMS *Victory* is included for comparison.

Figure 6.2 The arrangement of the rowers in a trireme. Here as reconstructed in the *Olympias*.

trireme was built up from the keel as a shell, with the planks joined edge to edge with tenons (peg-like extensions that fit into holes in the edge of the adjacent plank)—and possibly further reinforced by internal sewing. This differed from the techniques of northern and western European boatbuilders, who began with a skeleton frame and then attached planks to it. Shell construction created a sleek hull profile and a relatively lightweight vessel relative to its volume. It was blessedly free of corrosive iron, but its rigidity depended on the connective tissue of decks and benches that stretched from one side of the ship to the other. To further reinforce the vessel and to prevent hogging, the Greeks stretched two cables (*hypozomata*) around the outside of the hull from bow to stern, one on each side, well above the waterline. The ends passed inside the vessel to some form of tensioning mechanism. The most critical and long-debated aspect of the design, however, was the arrangement of the rowers. Much research and experimentation has led to a general agreement on the basics (see Figure 6.2). Each oar was worked by one man, and the design allowed all the oars to be the same length and thus interchangeable.

The lowest bank of rowers, the fifty-four *thalamites*, worked their oar through the hull near the waterline, with the oarport partially sealed with a leather bag. Just above them, and slightly outboard, and also working their oars blindly through an oarport, were fifty-four *zygites*. Finally, the highest and most prestigious tier, the sixty-two *thranites*, sat at the top of the hull, beneath the deck raised above their heads, and rowed their oars via an outrigger or rowing frame that projected slightly from the hull, providing them with a mechanical advantage to compensate for their height above the water. Only they could actually see their oars in the water. The rowing frame also supported the deck above the rowers and provided the structure for screens that could be placed to protect the thranites when going into combat.[8]

No ancient author recorded the speed of the trireme, but calculations based on recorded voyages and experimental data have suggested that a trireme could cruise for some days at seven to eight knots, resting ashore at night and often at midday. In combat conditions, it could sprint at almost ten knots. These are extraordinary speeds for a human-powered vessel of that size (ten knots for an oared vessel has been exceeded only by modern racing shells), which caused some doubt, especially as the data for later sixteenth-century galleys suggested a sprint speed of eight knots, and something closer to 4.8 knots for cruising—numbers roughly equivalent to those achieved by the experimental trireme *Olympias* reconstructed in the mid-1980s. The trireme, like earlier galleys, could also use simple square sails for long-distance travel. By almost any measure, the design of the trireme achieved remarkable results in terms of speed, but at the cost of operating at the very limit of its materials, and of almost swamping the vessel with men,

Figure 6.3 The *Olympias*, a reconstruction of an Athenian trireme. Note the edge-joined construction, the double steering oars, and the three superimposed banks of rowers, with an outrigger for the top bank.

with logistical implications that will be discussed shortly.[9] But first, how was the trireme used in battle?

Any ram-equipped galley (see Figure 6.3) had the choice of two basic tactics, used separately or in combination: ramming or boarding. The trireme's speed and maneuverability encouraged using the ram, punching the bronze tip of the vessel into the vulnerable side or stern of an enemy galley and functionally wrecking it—typically, triremes did not fully sink; they simply settled and filled with water. Alternatively, if the necessary angle could not be achieved, a skillful steersman and crew could slice their ship down the side of a slower-reacting enemy vessel and snap off its oars, crippling it at least temporarily. Ramming or raking tactics, however, required gaining an angle on the enemy—ram-on-ram contact was a toss of the dice. Fleets therefore tended to approach each other with the ships in line abreast, their rams facing each other. Finessing one's enemy into a vulnerable position required skilled oarsmen and steersmen. The Greeks had terms for the two maneuvers involved: the *diekplous* and the *periplous*, the pass-through and the encirclement. The pass-through allowed more skillful crews to rake an enemy's oars and then turn quickly and ram them in the stern, or in their broadside if they were attempting to turn and face their enemy. The periplous allowed swifter ships to gain the flanks of the enemy fleet and charge in for a broadside strike.[10]

The first reasonably clear extant narrative of war at sea provides an example of how this process might work. When the Persians invaded Greece in 480 BCE, they marched their massive land army along the Aegean coast, shadowed and supplied by an equally large Persian fleet. Because of the size of their crews and the fragility of their design, galley fleets tended to beach at the end of each day (about which more below). In this case, the Persian fleet, oared-galleys and sailing vessels both, accompanied the army to provide logistics, but they in turn depended on the army to provide a secure shoreline. A small Greek force of infantry prepared to block the coastal pass at Thermopylae, while the combined Greek fleet of some 271 triremes based itself nearby at Artemisium on the northern shore of Euboea (see Map 6.1). The Persian fleet arrived in advance of its army and set up on the shore opposite the Greeks. Knowing that the Persian fleet had recently suffered from a storm, and fearing that a Persian detachment was circling Euboea to trap the Greek fleet, the Greeks attacked. Their fleet advanced in line abreast, and the Persians rushed from the beaches to meet them. The Persians' greater numbers encouraged them to attempt

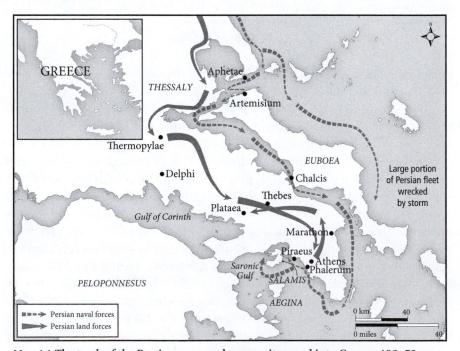

Map 6.1 The track of the Persian army and navy as it moved into Greece, 480–79 BCE.

the periplous. Anticipating such a move, the Greek triremes on each flank backed water (rowed backwards), retreating slowly and bowing the line into a deeper and deeper curve until the Greek flanks finally met each other, closing the formation into a giant circle, with all their rams pointing outward. Persian ships outside the circle, confounded by this formation, and themselves now out of formation, were suddenly vulnerable. The Greeks sounded the attack and launched themselves into their enemy, ramming and raking the confused Persians, many of whom proved unable to turn to meet the threat.[11]

This sort of finesse was difficult to accomplish. Although there would be other famous examples of superior seamanship practiced by the Athenians against less skillful Greek fleets during the Peloponnesian War, the older and more common tactic was to board. All naval combat prior to the ram, and much of it afterward, depended on boarding, of which the main variations were to employ greater or lesser amounts of missile fire before and during the act of boarding and/or to use additional implements to make boarding easier (such as the Egyptian grappling hooks already mentioned). Triremes carried an abundance of rowers, as well as twenty to thirty marines and sailors. All of them could fight in a boarding battle, especially in a great fleet action, in which many ships clustered among each other and the ability to maneuver or even row disappeared. Something quite like that happened at the Battle of Salamis, just weeks after Artemisium.

Despite the Greek fleet's success at Artemisium, once the Persian army pushed through the Spartan land force at Thermopylae, the Greek fleet lost its own secure shoreline, and it retreated south to the waters off Athens. There the fleet evacuated the residents of Athens to the island of Salamis. As the Persian army and navy resumed their progress south into the heart of Greece, the Greeks lined up their triremes on the shores of Salamis to await the Persian fleet. The other Greek cities preferred to retreat to the Isthmus of Corinth, but Athens had provided much the largest contingent of ships, and the Athenians insisted on fighting near their now-abandoned homes to protect their families on the island. The contending fleets that met in the waters between Salamis and the Athenian port at Piraeus were enormous, but the Persian fleet was much larger, perhaps six hundred to eight hundred Persian ships versus three hundred Greek. The Greek fleet beached on the island of Salamis was secure from the Persian army, provided they could defeat the Persian fleet. The trick would be to convince the Persians to enter the narrow waters between Salamis and Piraeus and accept battle. The exact details of what followed are much disputed; our ancient sources are hard to reconcile with each other and with the geography. What is abundantly clear, however, is that the Persian fleet did enter the narrow waters, where the Greek fleet was protected from envelopment (periplous), and was able to use the shoreline of Salamis behind them to prevent a diekplous. The Persian fleet entered the straits at night and formed three lines along the Attic coast, with their rams pointed west toward Salamis. In the morning the Greeks launched from the Salamis shore and used their superior maneuverability initially to disrupt the ordered Persian line. The great depth of the Persian fleet and the purported eagerness of their ships' captains to come to grips with the Greeks quickly produced a confused mass of tangled ships. In those conditions the battle was dominated by boarding, and the Greeks proved superior in that fight as well. Individual Persian ships began to flee south and east, aiming for the beaches at Phaleron (south of Piraeus). Soon the whole fleet was retreating.[12]

These two stories, Artemisium and Salamis, focusing on the tactical choices of ramming versus boarding, conceal perhaps even more important issues: financing and manning. Skill could clearly be a decisive factor, and this was more than merely the skill of a captain or a steersman. Synchronized rowing was one thing, but spinning a trireme in place when the steering oar had lost purchase, shifting oars inboard on command while raking an enemy's oars, or, perhaps most importantly, rising from the benches to fight in the boarding battle, all put a premium on dedicated and experienced men. The general rule in the ancient world was that oarsmen were not slaves. In Greece they were usually free citizens, although naval mercenaries were not uncommon. There were some intriguing exceptions, but the general rule held. As for financing, ships of war, lacking any other purpose, were expensive to build and maintain. The earliest trireme-fielding powers in the eastern Mediterranean were the wealthiest: Persian Phoenicia, Egypt, Carthage, Samos, Miletus, Corinth, and Corcyra. The Athenians were able to build their fleet, which was significantly larger than that of any other Greek state, only because of the recent discovery of silver in the mines at Laurium. Furthermore, after the initial repulse of the Persian invasion, the Greeks chose to continue the fight against Persia, pursuing its fleets across the Aegean. Athens led the alliance while members contributed ships, or funds in lieu of ships. Over time Athenian control of those funds allowed them to convert the voluntary league into an empire, ruled by their naval dominance. That dominance, in turn, was challenged only during the Peloponnesian War against Sparta, when the Persians began to fund the building and manning of a Spartan navy. In short, the trireme, and galley warfare in general, was as much about capacity as it was about calculated ship design. Money and men mattered as much as tactics.[13]

Having said that, and having described the galley through its most famous exemplar, the trireme, let us now turn to the implications of the galley more generally, and especially its relationship to state capacity and Mediterranean geography. Many if not all of these considerations applied not only to the Greeks or their predecessors but also to the Romans, the Byzantines, and the states that followed them through the sixteenth century. All were in some ways consequences of the nature of the galley.

The first and most obvious point is that during periods when multiple powerful states were competing for control of the sea, fleets got bigger. The enormously wealthy Persian Empire, preparing to invade the maritime Aegean, had gathered in contingents from its coastal provinces, primarily Egyptians, Phoenicians, and the Ionian Greeks of Anatolia, eventually amassing fleets totaling in the hundreds. As already discussed, the Athenians, embroiled in a naval race with the Greek island state of Aegina and newly enriched by the silver mines at Laurium, built some two hundred triremes. When the Greeks turned on each other during the Peloponnesian War (431–404 BCE), they regularly confronted each other with fleets numbering well over a hundred triremes on each side. Athenian records from the fourth century BCE suggest that Athens continued to maintain between 200 and 380 triremes. When the great successor states of Alexander's empire competed with each other, their fleets often numbered well over one hundred ships to a side, even though, as we will see, those fleets included many new types of larger and more expensive ships. During the First Punic War, the Romans and Carthaginians each repeatedly launched fleets of two hundred or more warships, as did the competing sides during the Roman civil wars that ended the Republic.[14]

The point of dwelling on fleet size is to emphasize the problem of expense. Purpose-built warships were expensive to construct, and all of the states just mentioned were forced to spend centralized state funds on their navies. Athens had traditionally relied on the resources of wealthy citizens to fund triremes, but the massive expansion of its fleet had required the state use of the new silver mines, and later the resources of its new empire. Their Peloponnesian opponents turned to the Persians to raise adequate funds. Maintaining these fleets represented a further expense. A galley could have a relatively long life of twenty years or more, but only if regularly removed from the water to dry out the hull. Athens built a large complex of ship sheds for that purpose in the port at Piraeus. Ship sheds are known from other ancient ports (notably Kition in Cyprus), and the Carthaginians famously built a "roundhouse" in their port to receive and maintain their fleet. On a small scale, a warship can be used as a predatory, private enterprise vessel, whose essentially piratical activities could pay for its own construction and maintenance. But when wealthy states competed with each other, and depended on purpose-built warships to do so, fleets grew larger, and only the state could bear the costs.

Furthermore, a fleet of oared galleys required an enormous number of men relative to the cargo capacity of the vessel. Some rough comparisons suggest the scale of the problem: a trireme displaced about fifty metric tons while carrying a two-hundred-man crew (including marines); that works out to a ratio of four men per ton. The *Mary Rose*, an English warship in 1536, displaced about 700 tons with a crew of 415, for a ratio of 0.6 men per ton, while Admiral Lord Nelson's flagship, the *Victory*, launched in 1765, displaced about 3,080 tons with a crew of 850, for a ratio of 0.28 men per ton (see Table 6.1). No galley could carry more than the absolute bare minimum of food and water for its crew. One estimate suggests that a galley could carry at most two weeks' worth of water, and that estimate seems generous. At a thirsty minimum of two liters per man per day, two weeks of water for a trireme would weigh seven tons, a substantial fraction of the normal total displacement of the ship.

Water was a particular problem for *fleets*. Individual galleys could find any number of places to beach for the night and rewater. But the large fleets of the classical period would have needed very large amounts of water, and suitable locations were relatively few and well known to both sides. Thucydides' account of the Athenian fleet of 134 galleys sent to Sicily in 415 BCE illustrates the problems. He noted that they divided the fleet into three squadrons, "to avoid sailing all together and thus lacking sufficient water, or provisions at the stations where they might land." They meanwhile sent an advance party of three ships to determine which ports in Italy would be willing to receive them. Furthermore, the galleys were supported by thirty cargo ships carrying food, "bakers, stone-masons and carpenters, and the tools for raising fortifications," and many more cargo ships sailing as private traders to support the expedition. After crossing from Corcyra to Italy, they were disappointed to find the southern Italian ports closed to them, some even refusing them the privilege of anchoring and gathering water.[15]

Reinforcing all of these logistical challenges, especially prior to the arrival of the compass in the West in the late twelfth century CE, was the general inability of any ancient or medieval sailor to navigate out of sight of land. The story of Odysseus, blown out to sea and then lost for ten years, though mythical, feelingly conveys the problem. Very little is known about ancient maps, but contemporary directions on land tended to be lists of places with approximate travel times between them. A sailor out of sight of shore had no way to determine his relative position, and only a rudimentary ability to determine his direction—although the Phoenicians reportedly could navigate somewhat by the stars, and open-water sailing was known between Egypt and Phoenicia, Greece, and Anatolia. This navigational uncertainty alone tended to keep fleets close to shore, and greatly encouraged beaching each night. Even sixteenth-century galleys, their sailing masters equipped with a compass and maps that provided directional guidance between key points on the Mediterranean coast, continued to prefer coastal routes, or relatively short open-water hops between known points.[16]

These logistical and navigational factors dramatically affected the operating range of ships and fleets. The galley design was fundamentally unsuited to use in the Atlantic, except within protected waters. They could operate in the Red Sea, the Persian Gulf, and to a lesser extent in the Indian Ocean, but logistics and ship design usually confined the galley to coastal waters or contained seas. The Mediterranean's virtual lack of tides also made nightly beaching a simple proposition; the Atlantic and Indian Oceans are not nearly so forgiving. Galleys could not stay away from shore for long. They preferred not to do so at all, and if they traveled long distances, which they generally did by following the coast, they needed a secure base or shoreline at the other end. At a strategic level this created the option of defeating an enemy's naval power by attacking its bases. Alexander the Great took this course against the Persians, reasoning after Miletus's capture that he could disband his fleet. Arrian reported, "As he now held Asia with his land troops, he no longer needed a navy, and that by capturing the Persian coast bases he would break up their fleet, since they would have nowhere to make up their crews from, and, in fact, no seaport in Asia."[17] This strategic necessity was clear to the Athenians, who fortified the Piraeus to protect that facility and its communication to Athens proper from the superior land power of the Spartans. Furthermore, the larger the fleet, the shorter its radius of action.

All these realities meant that galley fleets, more so than later sailing fleets, fought amphibiously. They operated in constant interaction with the land: they needed bases or friendly beachable coasts, both at the strategic level of power projection and tactically in their daily movements.[18]

Strategically, these logistical and navigational limits on galley fleets in the Mediterranean created several key locations in that sea, as well as concentrating conflict on the coasts, and very often near those key locations (see Map 6.2). Ships following the Mediterranean coast confronted several locations where a short open-water stretch would greatly shorten their trip: from Corcyra to the heel of Italy (modern Brindisi), various island hops across the Aegean between Anatolia and mainland Greece, and from southwest Sicily to Carthage. For different reasons the Isthmus of Corinth was almost as important, since there galleys could be shipped overland into and out of the Gulf of Corinth, avoiding the long and potentially dangerous trip around the Peloponnese. This in turn made the western entrance to the gulf another key location, as were, for related reasons, the southern tips of the Peloponnese, around which all other east-west traffic had to pass.

VARIATIONS ON A THEME

These conditions and restrictions applied to virtually all oared warfare in Europe until the introduction of gunpowder, and even thereafter. But within these strictures we can identify variations in tactical technique and ship design, based on the competing powers' evolving calculations of conditions and strategic need, and in some cases even based on cultural preference. Given the unity of conditions, however, it remains fair to describe these later incarnations of war under oars as variations on a theme. As such, we will deal with each of them much more briefly.

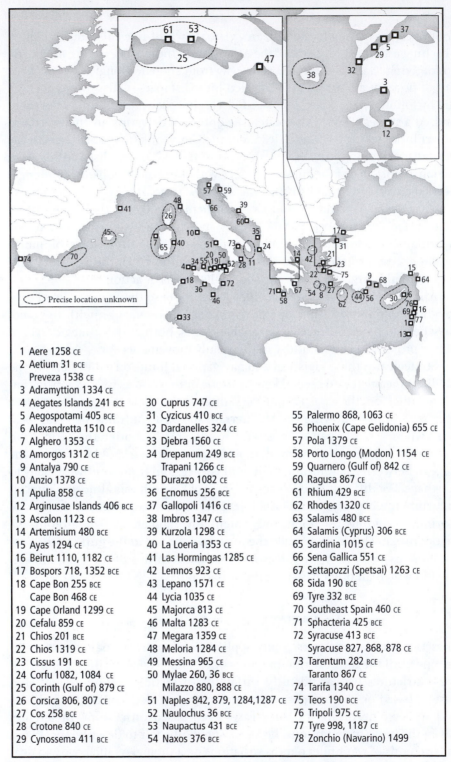

1 Aere 1258 CE
2 Aetium 31 BCE
  Preveza 1538 CE
3 Adramyttion 1334 CE
4 Aegates Islands 241 BCE
5 Aegospotami 405 BCE
6 Alexandretta 1510 CE
7 Alghero 1353 CE
8 Amorgos 1312 CE
9 Antalya 790 CE
10 Anzio 1378 CE
11 Apulia 858 CE
12 Arginusae Islands 406 BCE
13 Ascalon 1123 CE
14 Artemisium 480 BCE
15 Ayas 1294 CE
16 Beirut 1110, 1182 CE
17 Bospors 718, 1352 BCE
18 Cape Bon 255 BCE
   Cape Bon 468 CE
19 Cape Orland 1299 CE
20 Cefalu 859 CE
21 Chios 201 BCE
22 Chios 1319 CE
23 Cissus 191 BCE
24 Corfu 1082, 1084 CE
25 Corinth (Gulf of) 879 CE
26 Corsica 806, 807 CE
27 Cos 258 BCE
28 Crotone 840 CE
29 Cynossema 411 BCE

30 Cuprus 747 CE
31 Cyzicus 410 BCE
32 Dardanelles 324 CE
33 Djebra 1560 CE
34 Drepanum 249 BCE
   Trapani 1266 CE
35 Durazzo 1082 CE
36 Ecnomus 256 BCE
37 Gallopoli 1416 CE
38 Imbros 1347 CE
39 Kurzola 1298 CE
40 La Loeria 1353 CE
41 Las Hormingas 1285 CE
42 Lemnos 923 CE
43 Lepano 1571 CE
44 Lycia 1035 CE
45 Majorca 813 CE
46 Malta 1283 CE
47 Megara 1359 CE
48 Meloria 1284 CE
49 Messina 965 CE
50 Mylae 260, 36 BCE
   Milazzo 880, 888 CE
51 Naples 842, 879, 1284,1287 CE
52 Naulochus 36 BCE
53 Naupactus 431 BCE
54 Naxos 376 BCE

55 Palermo 868, 1063 CE
56 Phoenix (Cape Gelidonia) 655 CE
57 Pola 1379 CE
58 Porto Longo (Modon) 1154 CE
59 Quarnero (Gulf of) 842 CE
60 Ragusa 867 CE
61 Rhium 429 BCE
62 Rhodes 1320 CE
63 Salamis 480 BCE
64 Salamis (Cyprus) 306 BCE
65 Sardinia 1015 CE
66 Sena Gallica 551 CE
67 Settapozzi (Spetsai) 1263 CE
68 Sida 190 BCE
69 Tyre 332 BCE
70 Southeast Spain 460 CE
71 Sphacteria 425 BCE
72 Syracuse 413 BCE
   Syracuse 827, 868, 878 CE
73 Tarentum 282 BCE
   Taranto 867 CE
74 Tarifa 1340 CE
75 Teos 190 BCE
76 Tripoli 975 CE
77 Tyre 998, 1187 CE
78 Zonchio (Navarino) 1499

Map 6.2 Galley fleet battles in the Mediterranean, 500 BCE–1600 CE. Note persistent proximity to coast as well as the concentration of battles in certain key locations.

Hellenistic Invention and Gigantism

The bireme pentekonter ruled the seas for perhaps two hundred years (700 BCE to 500 BCE); the trireme for another hundred (500 BCE to 400 BCE, and persisting as a warship long after). In the 150 years from 400 BCE to 250 BCE a veritable host of new types of galleys emerged. The speed and variety of invention seem to have been greatly stimulated by the competitive presence at sea of many more wealthy centralized states. After defeating the Athenian expedition to Sicily in 413 BCE, Syracuse began to aspire to regional power in competition with the Carthaginians, generating the first new round of naval innovation. More importantly, after Alexander's death in 323 BCE, the fragmentation of his empire into a variety of competing successor states generated a kind of naval arms race. Later, a new round of Sicilian entanglements brought Rome and Carthage into conflict, spurring yet another round of innovation at sea. The exact nature of the changes, however, reflected a variety of pressures: a calculated quest for tactical advantage, a reaction to the problems of manning ships, an attempt to solve the problem of inexperience at sea, and cultural inclination. Historian Lionel Casson has divided this arms race into three stages, reflecting the different pressures in play, and we will follow his division here.

But first, a note on terminology. The trireme, or *trieres*, was so named because of its three superimposed banks of oars, each oar of which was rowed by one man. The ships of the fourth and third centuries BCE had etymologically similar names: *tetrereis* ("fours"), *pentereis* ("fives"), and so on up to a "forty." I follow most modern practice in referring to them by their English equivalents. In no case did any of these ships have more than three superimposed banks of oars, which seems to be the limit of feasibility. The number instead reflects the number of files of rowers on each side. Changes involved various combinations of multiple rowers on one or more banks of oars.

In the first stage, lasting roughly from 400 BCE to 350 BCE, Dionysius of Syracuse deliberately invented the "five" as part of his confrontation with Carthage. The latter power, it appears, had invented the "four," perhaps having copied it from an earlier version introduced by their parent state in Phoenicia. These changes were simple evolutions from the bireme and the trireme design: the four had two banks of oars with two oarsmen on each oar, while the five added a rower to two of the three banks of the trireme. Both modifications were made without any significant change to the overall length of the ship. Dionysius does not seem to have had many fives, but this new design entered service as his flagship, packing more men and more mass into a space much like a trireme's without sacrificing much speed. Over the course of his rule he built a few more, and his son apparently had sixes (presumably simply doubling up on the third tier of oars). The majority of the Syracusan fleet continued to be triremes, however, in which company the fives and sixes continued to fight in basically the same way, choosing between the ramming and boarding option as conditions and skills suited. The greater mass of the fours and fives may have given them an advantage in ramming, especially head-on, even as their height gave them an advantage in boarding. Initially few in number, Dionysius's ships attracted notice. Soon they were being not only copied but expanded upon.[19]

In Casson's second phase (roughly 315–288 BCE), the cutthroat competition following Alexander's death hastened the pace of innovation. By 289 BCE a full suite of ships of various sizes had entered service, up to and including a sixteen. One ancient source, for example, listed a fleet of 90 fours, 10 fives, 3 nines, 10 tens, and 30 smaller vessels. The details of these larger ships elude us, although it is likely that a sixteen had two banks of sweep oars, wielded by eight men each. All of these larger and slower "polyremes" reflected two key changes. First, they could carry many more marines, as well as catapults and towers, all useful to the increasing tactical emphasis on the boarding battle. Second, that emphasis on the boarding battle reflected the difficulty of finding skilled oarsmen. On any multiman oar, only the rower at the end of the oar had to be skilled. In this sense design followed tactical practice, which in turn was driven by issues of social organization and mobilization. William Murray has recently argued that these large polyremes' initial and perhaps prime function was to aid in besieging and assaulting harbor fortifications. They also had value in fleet actions, however, as they were capable of wading into the fight as a massive weapons platform that could also run down inattentive smaller galleys. Because they could be overwhelmed and outmaneuvered by a horde of smaller galleys, the polyremes traveled with an escort of the other vessels.[20]

It also seems that the successor kings were already competing with each other in showmanship. That tendency accelerated further in Casson's third phase after 288 BCE as we find evidence for truly massive ships denominated as fourteens, fifteens, sixteens, twenties, thirties and even the remarkable forty (built near the end of the third century BCE). Casson has hypothesized, generally without objection from other scholars, that these vessels were vast catamarans—two connected hulls. The forty, for example, consisted of two twenties connected by an enormous deck supporting 2,850 marines and four hundred crewmen, in addition to the staggering four thousand oarsmen. Although this last ship was only intended as a parade vessel, it attests to the cultural tendency of the Hellenistic kings to use gigantism as a form of competitive display, whether it was the Colossus of Rhodes, the Lighthouse of Alexandria, or the forty of Ptolemy Philopater. This cultural reason for these larger ships seems further supported by the lack of evidence for any ship larger than a ten having ever participated in battle.[21]

Rome

Polybius famously claimed that Rome had no navy prior to the First Punic War with Carthage (264–241 BCE). That war, fought for the control of the island of Sicily, demanded a navy, and in Polybius's narrative the Roman senate ordered the construction of 100 fives and 20 threes. Lacking experienced ship-wrights, the Romans turned to a fortuitously wrecked Carthaginian five and copied it. Polybius thus constructed a remarkably tenacious myth, in spite of clear evidence that Rome had substantial maritime and naval experience from its early years. To be sure, most Roman military activity to that point had been on land, and their naval activities were little remarked on by the ancient sources. Careful reading, however, shows several likely Roman naval raids or even battles in the fifth and fourth centuries, and a special Roman magistracy for naval matters was created in 311 BCE. Truly large fleets comprised of cutting-edge ships as had been developed among the Hellenistic powers, how-ever, probably represented a new challenge for Rome. Once engaged in large-scale naval war, the Romans proved adept sailors, but during the Empire their control of the entire circumference of the Mediterranean slowed the pace of naval innovation. Competition was scarce for over two centuries, and given the cost of warships it proved an easy choice to economize on naval forces—although Rome's wealth delayed that process for many years. There are thus two stories from Rome's naval history to tell here. One is their introduction to large-scale fleet action during the First Punic War, and the other is the tale of capacity and calculation during the imperial Pax Romana at sea.[22]

The war with Carthage began over exactly the issues mentioned in the introduction to this chapter: the need to protect, if not control, the movement of goods at sea. In 264 BCE Carthage, long the recognized naval master of the western Mediterranean, intervened in a conflict in Messana, Sicily. Messana lay at a key point in the Mediterranean: the strait between Sicily and the toe of Italy. Ships sailing west from the Aegean could either pass through the straits or endure a long and dangerous detour around the south coast of Sicily. Rome feared Carthaginian control of such a key location, and they inter-vened to block it. A twenty-three-year war ensued, with many of the decisive engagements fought at sea. Although the Romans were not the naval neo-phytes often portrayed, Polybius's story may indicate that when the war began they as yet lacked fives (sometimes called "quinqueremes"), or at least had very few of them. Knowing they would be fighting such ships in the Car-thaginian fleet, they set to building equivalents in large numbers.

There are enormous differences of opinion about the exact characteristics of the Carthaginian and the Roman five. Recent work suggests that although it differed somewhat from that invented by Dionysius of Syracuse (being based on a different Phoenician shipbuilding tradition), it too had three tiers of oars, the top two managed by two rowers, the bottom by one. Necessarily heavier and wider than a trireme, the five carried more troops, and was often depicted with at least one tower to give an advantage in missile fire (see Figure 6.4). Polybius claims that Roman inexperience led them to favor boarding over ramming, desiring to convert the war at sea into something more like a land battle. The reality is probably simpler. The Carthaginians *were* more experienced, much like the Athenians had been more experienced

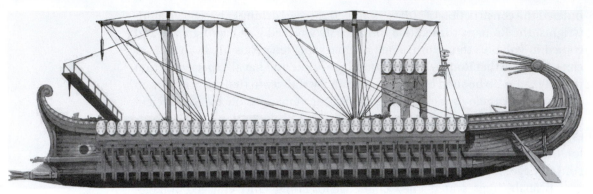

Figure 6.4 A Roman five, or quinquereme. Note the castle for missile fire and the forward mounted *corvus*.

than the other Greeks during the early stages of the Peloponnesian War. Facing a veteran galley fleet, fearing being outmaneuvered, and sailing in many hurriedly constructed ships that were potentially still green in timber, the Romans may have sought the security of boarding tactics.

To this end, at the Battle of Mylae (260 BCE) the Romans adapted an older Hellenistic notion of a boarding bridge into something they called the *corvus* (Latin for raven). Under normal conditions boarding occurred in the confusion of massed ships or after a successful ramming attack had temporarily joined two ships, allowing the marines of one to leap to the deck of another. The corvus was a swinging boarding bridge, mounted to the front of a Roman five, that could be dropped onto an enemy deck, where its beak-like spike (thus the name) would secure the vessels together. The bridge allowed two files of men to run abreast onto the enemy ship, greatly increasing their chances. The Carthaginians, supposedly surprised by the corvus at Mylae, were decisively beaten, despite outnumbering the Romans (the Romans had 83 fives and 20 threes; the Carthaginians 129 fives and one seven). The Romans reprised the corvus in 256 BCE at the battle of Ecnomus, but it does not appear in the sources again. It was no doubt an awkward, top-heavy contraption, especially in any sort of wind, and it would seem that as the Romans continued to fight at sea against the Carthaginians, and later against other Mediterranean sea powers, their increased skill rendered that tool less necessary. Alternatively, they may have redesigned it to be less obvious, even collapsible, and its use may have become a matter of course—unmentioned the same way that the archers' castles went unmentioned but are clearly visible in various contemporary representations. They were standard. Rome did not win every battle in the war, and lost several fleets to storms, but in the end they regularly defeated the Carthaginians at sea.[23]

Rome's ultimate victory in the First Punic War left it the master of the western Mediterranean. At the start of the Second Punic War (218–201 BCE) Rome had some 220 fives available to counter Carthage's 50. Over the next hundred years Rome extended its control over the rest of the Mediterranean littoral, primarily through its armies, but often operating in conjunction with fleets. From the 160s BCE the Romans let their indigenous sea power lapse and were relying more on their Greek allies. Even during the Mithridatic War (88–84 BCE) and the subsequent piracy problem (70–67 BCE), the Romans relied heavily on allied fleets, a situation that continued during the Roman civil wars. Octavian won his final and decisive victory in those wars in the naval battle at Actium (31 BCE). As the Emperor Augustus he recognized the need for some form of standing navy, but he reorganized it in much the way he had the army. He streamlined its organization, standardized its components, and tied its leadership to himself. Although Augustus established two great war-fleet bases at Misenum (north of Naples) and Ravenna (on the northern Adriatic), later supplemented by additional fleets in the east, he also started the trend of reducing the size of individual ships within the navy, thereby drastically reducing the manning requirement. The new standard warship for the Roman imperial period (with a somewhat smaller variant used on the Rhine and Danube Rivers) was the Liburnian galley, a two-banked ship adapted from the pirate galleys used on the Dalmatian coast.

Over the long years of the Empire the Romans initially sustained their investment in a standing navy, and the riverine component proved an essential adjunct to the land forces guarding the European frontier. The seagoing fleet, however, suffered as Rome's finances faced serious challenges from the third century CE onward. The emergent threats at that time seemed confined to the land, and the navy increasingly was deemed of secondary importance, although it had long been a crucial component of the Roman communication network linking the empire together. As a result, when real seaborne threats appeared in the middle of the third century CE, the remnants of the standing Roman fleets were quickly swept away, to be replaced by emergency mobilizations. The restoration of imperial stability under Diocletian and Constantine did not extend to fully rebuilding the devastated navy. The division of the empire into eastern and western halves provided a seedbed for a future Byzantine navy based around the maritime communities of the Aegean, but the Western Empire in the fifth century found itself incapable of stopping the Vandals' naval forces based in North Africa. The naval weakness of late imperial Rome reflected no lack of tactical or technological ability. The multiplication of threats at land and sea combined with internal instability had ruined Roman finances, and, as we have often observed in this chapter, navies were expensive. In the crises of the late Empire they proved beyond the capacity of a struggling Rome.[24]

The Byzantines and Greek Fire

The Eastern Empire and its capital at Constantinople, however, survived. Not only did it survive, but by the middle of the sixth century it had resurged dramatically, reencompassing much of the old empire, and Constantinople's position astride the key trade routes of the eastern Mediterranean and the entrance into the Black Sea brought renewed wealth. With wealth came naval power, and with naval power came further expansion and further wealth generation. Wealth and naval power reinforced each other. But neither expansion nor naval power was endless. The fleet restored in the seventh century declined in the eighth, revived in the ninth, and peaked in the tenth century, to suffer almost permanent decline thereafter. Unfortunately it is impossible here to do justice to the roughly 1,200 years of Byzantine imperial and naval history. Byzantine galleys underwent a slow process of evolution, but also maintained a certain stability, based again on the fundamental conditions inherent to the galley and to the Mediterranean. We cannot skip over the Byzantines entirely, however, in part because this evolutionary progression reveals something about the nature of innovation at sea, and partly because of the Byzantines' fascinating and creative use of Greek fire.

Before discussing that mysterious substance, we must deal with the development of the Byzantine galley, or *dromon*. One reason it is difficult to do justice to Byzantine naval history is the startling lack of images or archaeological sources. There are, for example, no detailed descriptions or pictures of dromons from the writings of Procopius in the mid-sixth century CE until the late ninth century. There are some reasonably detailed textual descriptions, the best coming from the tenth-century naval revival. We know that the later Roman emphasis on generally smaller ships continued into the Eastern Empire and the Byzantine period. Constantine's fleet in battle in 324 CE had only thirty-oared and fifty-oared-galleys. But as John Pryor and Elizabeth Jeffreys have argued, there is an extraordinary lack of clarity in the sources' use of terms in the ensuing centuries. We can be certain that there was no one type of dromon that persisted unchanged for generations. In Pryor and Jeffreys's analysis the dromon evolved from the Liburnian galley, following three key lines of change, each evolutionary. Early versions of the dromon followed the Liburnian in having fifty rowers (twenty-five per side), in a fully decked monoreme, where the Liburnian had been only partially decked over the rowers (biremes were known as well, and gradually became the dominant type). This change probably reflected the tendency in ship construction over this period to move away from shell construction to frame construction. Frame construction encouraged the building of cross-members between gunwales, which in turn could support a full deck even on a small ship.

Furthermore, since the classical waterline ram was specifically shaped to damage shell-constructed vessels, the shift to frame construction rendered it obsolete (as did the longer-term shift to preferring boarding over ramming). Images from the late Roman period through the Byzantine show the waterline ram evolving in stages from the classical three-finned, bronze-sheathed keel extension into a single-pointed ram that curved upward more and more, eventually rising above the waterline, and even ceasing to be an extension of the keel. The waterline ram seems to have disappeared by the sixth century CE,

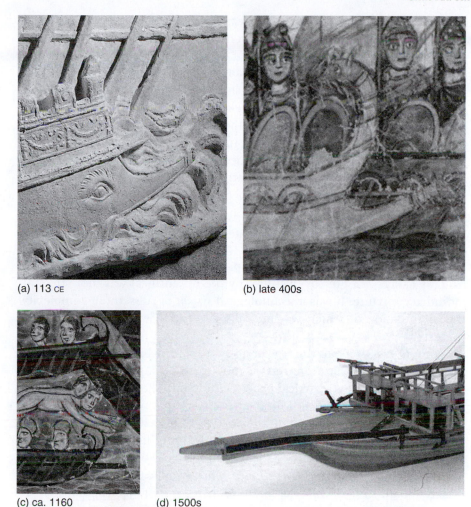

(a) 113 CE

(b) late 400s

(c) ca. 1160

(d) 1500s

Figure 6.5 *a-d* **Evolution of the ram in the Roman empire through the Byzantine and Venetian periods.** (a) shows a Roman Liburnian from 113 CE; (b) is a Byzantine dromon from a fifth-century manuscript; (c) is a dromon as drawn in an twelfth-century manuscript, while (d) is a model of sixteenth-century Venetian galley. Note how the "ram" first lifts above the waterline, and then seems to be deliberately structured to "ride over" enemy ships. By the Venetian period it is a spur designed to aid in boarding.

replaced by a spur that could "ride up and over the oars of an enemy ship, smashing them" preparatory to boarding. The spur further served as a boarding bridge, as it would continue to do on the galleys of the sixteenth century (see Figure 6.5).

Simultaneously the sail plan evolved from the old single- or double-masted square sail to a triangular lateen rig, probably progressively adapted from smaller Mediterranean fishing vessels that used such a sail. By the tenth century this basic configuration had further evolved back into a hundred-oared bireme. By then, however, the key weapon of the Byzantine dromon had become Greek fire, and therein lie several intriguing mysteries.[25]

Ancient sources report that in 678 CE, with Constantinople threatened by an Arab siege, a Greek engineer named Kallinikos brought the empire a decisive weapon mounted in the bow of a ship and capable of projecting a liquid fire from a bronze tube (a *siphon* in Greek) some distance in front of the ship. The fire would burn on the surface of the water and purportedly could only be extinguished by sand, urine, vinegar, or vinegar-soaked hides. Directed downwind against wooden vessels, especially those not expecting it, the results would be devastating. This story might seem to have been an invention appearing in the nick of time as a deus ex machina. In fact, however, it was likely based on a long chemical tradition of experimentation combined with the also long-extant technology of the piston-driven force pump used in fire engines and to empty water from mine shafts. What Kallinikos provided was a new combination of materials, and especially the projecting tube. Greek fire (usually called "sea fire" or "wet fire" by the Byzantines) was more than an incendiary mixture. It was a technological *system* of substantial complexity, the combination of which was radically successful within certain tactical contexts.

Without entering into the long and voluminous debate over the secrets of the mixture or its projection, certain things can be supposed from the evidence and from recent practical experimentation by John Haldon. The mix was no doubt primarily based on the petroleum that naturally seeped to or near the surface of the ground in the northern Caucasus oil fields, centered around modern Maikop and Krasnodar, and Byzantine documents tracked the location and productivity of such locations. Possibly refined, and likely mixed with pine resin and other ingredients, it appears to have been preheated aboard ship to thin the mixture, increase its range (perhaps ten to fifteen meters), and make it more flammable. It was then sprayed through the siphon by a force pump and ignited by a torch mounted at the mouth of the siphon. The Byzantines also invented a hand version of the projector, although Haldon suspects that this probably sprayed only the incendiary fuel, and neither ignited it nor relied on preheating.[26]

Critical to our theme of innovation and its spread, Greek fire was a carefully maintained secret of the Byzantine state. Parts of the secret, based as it was on a longer chemical tradition, leaked out, and there seems to have been an increase in incendiary use by various Islamic and Western powers in subsequent centuries—primarily pots of a flaming incendiary flung by catapult. Keeping the secret, however, depended not just on the formula. Supposedly none of the makers of the various components knew the secrets of the others, and only a handful of people, including the emperor himself, knew the full secret. After 678 CE, its use in sometimes large amounts was attested frequently through the eighth and ninth centuries, and then again in 949, 1043, 1147, 1162, 1171, and 1187. The secret thus survived for five hundred years, until it was finally lost. There is no evidence that it was used in the failed defense of Constantinople against the Fourth Crusade in 1204, and it was never mentioned again thereafter. One explanation for its disappearance was the Byzantines' loss of access to the petroleum fields, but Alex Roland has argued that the turbulent and lethal world of Byzantine imperial politics did not lend itself to successfully passing on such a complex secret, and that it may have been lost long before 1204. It also has generally been believed that the full secret of Greek fire did not spread beyond the Byzantines. The well-documented capture of thirty-six siphons and a substantial amount of fuel by the Bulgars in 814 did not apparently enable them to use it. There is, however, limited but real evidence that some Muslim engineers did acquire and use aspects of the system, and there is even a mention of the Venetians employing it in 1081. If this is correct, it is odd and unusual that such a potent weapon should disappear so completely. Unlike Greek fire, the formula for gunpowder and the mechanisms for its use spread widely, with significant ramifications for the design and use of galleys.[27]

The Gunpowder Galley

For centuries after the fall of the Western Roman Empire Byzantium was the only power wealthy enough to sustain a fleet of purpose-built warships in the Mediterranean. Smaller states had proliferated, but few could afford the substantial cost of maintaining a "navy" in the strictest sense of that term. After the Crusaders sacked Constantinople in 1204, even the Byzantines found it a challenge to maintain a substantial navy. The wealthy empires generated by the Arab explosion of the seventh and eighth centuries mustered navies to attack Byzantium, but afterward focused their energies elsewhere. In part stimulated by the Crusades, the Italian city-states emerged in the eleventh and twelfth centuries as maritime trading powers and invested in maintaining their profitable links to the east. Venice was only one of those cities, and although it would eventually compete with the maritime power of the Spanish, the Genoese, the Byzantines, and the Ottomans, all of whom ended up building similar ships and for similar reasons, Venice can serve as an example of the overall processes and ships involved. As we will see, gunpowder and cannon changed some of the dynamics, but the fundamental nature of the oared galley continued to shape war at sea.

Venice grew out of a refugee population on an assortment of islands just off the northeastern Italian coast, gradually emerging as a trading and sea power around 1000 CE. As the Venetians began to dominate the northern Adriatic, they increasingly provided their own maritime security as the Byzantine Empire lost the power to do so. They may have built some early warships designed for the specific task of defending their harbors, but it was only after Venice played a major role in transporting the Crusaders that it acquired the wealth to become a Mediterranean naval power. Venice's origins as a trading state had long-term implications for its view of empire and naval power. Venice generally avoided competing for large territorial spaces, seeking rather to control key ports and hinterlands that would secure their trading routes. In the early stages of this process (roughly 1000–1280) they fought their naval battles with a combination of galleys and heavier sailing "round ships." The former were used to initiate battle; the latter were slower and taller, difficult to board, and effective platforms for missile fire, and thus often relatively invulnerable to galley attacks. One authority suggests that throughout this early period the Venetians made no distinction between galleys designed for trade and those designed for war.[28]

The evidence is clearer for the late thirteenth and fourteenth century, showing that the Venetians began to build light galleys intended entirely for military purposes. Nevertheless, the majority of their shipbuilding continued to focus on dual-purpose vessels. The real difference now was the expansion of the Venetian state's role in shipbuilding and trade. Beginning in the 1290s the Venetians began building "great galleys." Built at the state-run Venice Arsenal, and then usually leased to private merchants, these galleys sought to combine the best of all possible worlds, and were for a time wildly successful. Relatively large and broad for a galley (generally a 6:1 ratio of length to width, compared to a Greek trireme's 10:1), their cargo capacity was nevertheless limited. As carriers of small-bulk, high-value goods from the east, designed to defend themselves and capable of maneuvering under oars when in and around ports, they were eminently cost effective. Furthermore, their design, licensing, manning, and routing were defined by the state itself. Usually dispatched in groups for further security, these vessels dominated Mediterranean trading routes for two centuries, until they proved vulnerable to galleys armed with cannon in the early sixteenth century. The great galleys then lost their role as trading vessels (supplanted by heavier and more capacious sailing round ships), but retained, along with their lighter companions, a key role in warfare for another century.[29]

The introduction of gunpowder brought a series of changes, but the key point is how those changes emerged and evolved *with* gunpowder weapons' evolution. As the design, cost, and effectiveness of cannon and firearms evolved, so did the impact of gunpowder on war at sea. The story here is of two different systems coevolving with each other. From our perspective it might seem that the pace of change was rapid, as most of it occurred within the sixteenth century. But from the point of view of individuals at the time, the future of the galley and its use of cannon must have been uncertain.

Traditionally historians have pointed to gunpowder and cannon as the beginning of the demise of the galley. They have argued that the large round sailing ship, built broader of beam and of a stouter design to survive oceanic waves and weather, was capable of carrying many more cannon, and thus rapidly overwhelmed the fleets of galleys. As John Guilmartin has pointed out, although this would eventually prove true, it dramatically oversimplifies a complex process. The cannon of the fifteenth and sixteenth centuries were themselves evolving in effectiveness. The first of those deployed on ships tended to be antipersonnel weapons used in a manner not that different from the long-standard catapults and archers. In that sense, cannon at first merely reinforced the defensive advantage round ships already had over galleys because of their greater height. As larger cannon became available in the early sixteenth century, however, galleys gained a substantial offensive advantage, even against round ships. The long centerline of the galley provided the recoil room for a very large cannon mounted in the bow, the fire of which could be aimed without regard to the wind. In short, there was an oscillation of advantage: the long dominance of the war galley was first challenged by the enlarging round ships of the fifteenth century, whose height and weight, with small cannon mounted in their high castles, made them invulnerable to attack by a galley. The placement of a large cannon firing thirty- to fifty-pound balls in a galley's centerline (common by the 1510s), however, returned the galley to a dominant position in battle. Galleys mounting cannon retained that advantage for as long as guns continued to be expensive. The large guns of the sixteenth century were generally made of bronze, and both the metal and the labor involved were expensive. The massive assortment of cannon on later sailing ships of the line became possible only after a dramatic reduction in the cost of cannon. A galley carrying one to seven guns (usually one large centerline gun and up to four smaller guns on either side, in an expanded bow section) was a formidable weapon (see Figures 6.5d and 6.6). Adding guns to galleys in this way, however, again reemphasized purpose-built warships. Venice's multipurpose great galley or round ships could not compete. The return of purpose-built warship fleets meant that once again only the great powers could afford to compete.[30]

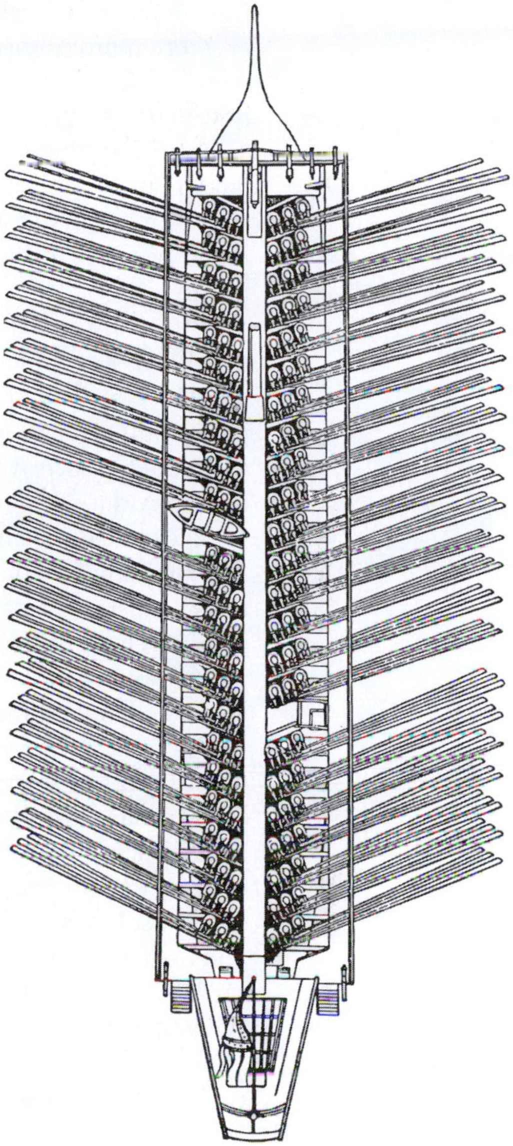

Figure 6.6 A Venetian Galley. An "ordinary" galley, here with 23 banks of oars per side, arranged with three rowers per bench, angled so they can all sit at the same level. Guns are positioned in the bow.

This new capability also changed the calculus behind galley tactics. The galley's ability to do damage at a distance, and the probability that a large cannon firing into a closely packed deck of rowers would devastate the crew, provided a significant tactical advantage to the larger of two forces in any confrontation of a relatively small group of galleys. Large fleet actions, however, often proved indecisive, since a long line of galleys abreast presented a daunting force to attack head-on, much like their ancient counterparts, but now made even more so by cannon.

Ironically, therefore, despite the introduction of cannon, some of the fundamentals of galley warfare set by the nature of the vessel persisted into the sixteenth century or were even reinforced. The trend in antiquity had been to prefer boarding over ramming, and that proved even more true in the sixteenth century. The waterline ram had disappeared sometime between 500 CE and 1000 CE, and the private-enterprise quality of war at sea in the early Middle Ages and into the sixteenth century had prioritized capture over sinking. The projecting spur of Byzantine vessels persisted in early modern European and Ottoman galleys, serving as a boarding bridge of sorts, although potential boarders would now await the final blast of their guns before rushing forward (see Figure 6.5d).

The oarage system had changed slightly, but here too the trends are oddly similar. Early Venetian triremes renewed the classical system of one man per oar, but instead of stacking the men, they placed them side by side on a single angled bench, each rowing an oar of slightly different length (see Figure 6.6). This arrangement of one man per oar seems to be the most energy-efficient arrangement, but, like the ancients, the combatants in the sixteenth-century Mediterranean moved over time toward multiple rowers per oar. Like their predecessors, it seems likely that this drift reflected a problem in acquiring quality manpower. With multiple men per oar, only one needed skill. Where ancient fleets were manned almost entirely by free citizens, the galley crews of the fifteenth and sixteenth centuries were a mix of professional sailors, pressed soldiers, slaves, and convicts, depending on the level of emergency and the state in question. More than most of its contemporaries, Venice relied on free men recruited from several key hinterlands, especially Dalmatia and the Venetian possessions in Greece. As the Ottomans progressively reduced Venetian territorial control, their navy struggled accordingly (thus, perhaps, the shift to multiple men per oar).[31]

The massive crews (relative to the ship's capacity) presented the same logistical challenges as they had a thousand years previously, keeping voyages short and close to land and watering locations. These provisioning and routing issues meant that galley fleets of the era, like their ancient counterparts, could not blockade ports. They needed their own port or landing place; simply floating offshore to stop sorties by a blockaded fleet was not an option.

This combination of technological continuity and change did produce one key and revealing change in the strategic environment. With the advent of cannon and the fortresses that supported them on land (the bastioned artillery fortress described in the next chapter), fortified port facilities enhanced the already substantial defensive strength of a galley fleet. Recall that even ancient galley fleets, armed with a ram in the bow and with the ability to back water, could beach themselves with the rams pointing out. Doing so made them fairly secure. Adding a cannon to the bow of a galley enhanced that defensive capability and extended its range. Adding a substantial artillery fortress with cannon capable of reaching out even further made defeating a fleet backing water under its protection a very difficult nut to crack. In these circumstances strategy focused more than ever on taking and holding key fortified ports to protect and provision fleets. Expeditionary offensive fleets operating against such ports were at a substantial disadvantage. As a result, "fleet actions" were rare. War at sea, in John Guilmartin's term, was more "amphibious" than naval, and could be characterized by long periods of what was essentially piracy punctuated by occasional expeditions. Those expeditions depended on seizing some land base, from which sailors could launch an attack on a major port facility. The multistage complexity of that strategic environment fostered indecisiveness. Cannon aboard larger ships of the line did eventually change this situation, generally overwhelming galleys with the weight of their fire, but that is a story for another chapter.[32]

CONCLUSION

In some ways this chapter is mistitled as "War under Oars." It has focused on the Mediterranean galley, whose design and operating environment determined much about war at sea for almost two millennia. Oared warships have existed in other contexts, however, with differing qualities. The Viking longships are often folded into this broad category, but in many ways they were primarily sailing ships with galley-like length-to-breadth ratios. It was their shallow draft and their ability to row upriver that made them such notorious raiders. They were not "warships" in the sense of being designed to fight another ship at sea, and thus are not considered in detail here.

More interesting perhaps were the rowed warships of the Korean navy. Some eleventh-century Korean ships may have relied on rams, but by the fourteenth century they had already begun using cannon. Unlike Mediterranean galleys, however, Korean ships were flat-bottomed, and were built heavily enough to cope with the tides and weather of the northwest Pacific. From the late fourteenth century the Korean Chosŏn dynasty began to invest in a state navy designed to deal with the persistent problem of assorted, mostly Japanese, pirates. That navy, although allowed to deteriorate after successfully dispersing the pirates, provided the essential foundations of seamanship and shipbuilding for the Korean navy that fought off a major Japanese invasion from 1592 to 1598. At the beginning of that war the standard Korean warship was the *panoksŏn*, a sail-and-oar combination warship, fully decked over to protect the oarsmen (its name translates as "superstructured ship"), with a high castle amidships for command purposes, and mounting cannon on the deck but also capable of ramming. Its high sides resisted the preferred Japanese tactic of boarding. Further distinguishing it from Mediterranean galleys, the *panokšŏn* was built at a 2.5:1 ratio of length to breadth (there were various sizes, one standard being seventy feet long and twenty-eight feet wide).

In addition to the *panokšŏn*, under the pressure of the Japanese invasion, the Korean admiral Yi Sun-sin resurrected and improved an older design for a "turtle ship," or *kŏbukšŏn*. These now-famous vessels were like the *panokšŏn* in their overall design, probably 100 to 120 feet long, with 30 to 40 feet of beam (a 3:1 ratio). They differed in completely enclosing *both* the rowers and the crew under a spiked dome. Designed to resist Japanese boarding tactics (not cannon fire), the ship fired various cannon and other missiles from underneath the dome through loopholes in the sides. The spiked roof plates were hexagonal, resembling the scutes of a turtle shell, but it is unclear if they were actually made of iron as is usually claimed. Most authorities argue that the Korean use of ship-killing cannon devastated Japanese fleets which preferred to board. The turtle ships amplified that difference in design, combining protection from boarding with the ranged fire of cannon. Only a few turtle ships were launched, but they proved key to disrupting Japanese fleets and to the eventual Korean defeat of the Japanese invasion.[33]

These more extreme variations within the broad category of "war under oars" reinforce the sense of the powerful role played by environment and by cultural traditions of shipbuilding within the narrower category of the Mediterranean war galley. Furthermore, the long history covered in this chapter has provided several examples of the different ways that a specific core innovation evolves in response to changing political, economic, and cultural conditions. First, even given the Mediterranean's favorable climate, the fundamental nature of the oared galley, that is, a long, narrow vessel propelled by numerous oarsmen, remained stable over a very long period. This stability is striking because of the very substantial logistical challenges and manning requirements of such vessels. It would seem that the tactical advantages of having a large crew in a highly maneuverable ship simply were too significant to be ignored. Design fluctuated somewhat to accommodate the cost of manning and the relative availability of skilled oarsmen, but the fundamental design, statistically attested by the stable length-to-breadth ratio, as well as the ratio of crew to carrying capacity (measured by displacement), remained nearly constant (see Table 6.1).

Second, although the propulsion system (oars) and associated design remained stable, the ram experienced significant evolutionary change interrupted by a noticeable period of stability from roughly 700 BCE to 100 CE. The ram emerged from the ancient techniques used by eastern Mediterranean shipbuilders to join the keel to the stem, achieving its classical form and function around 700 BCE. It retained that basic design through the beginning of the Roman imperial period, but then it again experienced an era of design drift. The ram slowly curved up out of the water, eventually morphing into a "spur" well above the water, which allowed it to ride up and over its enemies' sides, serving as a kind of boarding bridge. The periods of change in ram design (1300–700 BCE and 100–1500 CE) are not well documented, so we cannot detect the efforts of single shipbuilders or designers. Instead we see evolution.

Third, and in contrast, some design changes were clearly calculated. Dionysus of Syracuse seems to have deliberately invented—or at least paid for the invention of—the "five." Its appearance almost immediately stimulated a whole era of similar inventions, each intended, it would seem, to outdo the previous one. Calculation and culture blend and intermingle almost inextricably in this story, with culture perhaps responsible for the most extreme changes.

Fourth, there is an obvious and unsurprising relationship between the level of competition and the rate of design innovation. The Hellenistic period saw rapid changes in design because numerous wealthy states were competing at sea. Once the Romans had pacified the sea, however, they returned to older and cheaper designs, which persisted even when seaborne threats began to reemerge, because cost was now a major concern within a declining Roman economy.

Fifth, there was no apparent direct relationship between naval power and democracy, despite the common argument that the expansion of the fleets in classical Greece led to an expansion of democracy. In the Greek system only citizens served as soldiers, but there was a minimum level of wealth required to purchase a hoplite's gear. To be a rower, however, was virtually cost-free. Therefore it is argued that the rise in the strategic significance of the fleet within the Athenian empire gave those poorer citizens a louder voice in the Athenian democracy. This may be true for Athens, but the same manning requirement existed in other societies without the corresponding democratic effect. Even in Venice, possibly the closest parallel to Athens in its reliance on free rowers (if not citizens), there is no indication of democracy expanding, especially in its far-flung naval recruiting grounds. As it turns out, even the Greek example is contentious, since, unlike the hoplite, the rowers rarely appeared in Greek literature as individuals or as collective agents shown in a positive light.[34]

TIMELINE

	Rome
750–650 BCE	Emergence of ram
ca. 600 BCE	Appearance of trireme
399 BCE	Appearance of the first "five"
264–241 BCE	First Punic War
31 BCE	Roman dominance of the full Mediterranean coastline complete
320s	Constantine reestablishes fleet in the Eastern Roman Empire
678	First use of Greek fire
ca. 1180s	Secret of Greek fire lost?
1400s	Venetians begin building purpose-built war galleys
1510s	Centerline gun galleys in use
1592–98	Japanese invasion of Korea; turtle ships in use.

Sixth, the addition of cannon to war at sea did not immediately signal the end of the galley. The combined systems interacted in unexpected and complex ways: early cannon at first seemed to dethrone the galley, but then actually reinforced its superiority during the sixteenth century—for as long as guns remained expensive. Its ability to maneuver independent of the wind and its tight turning radius gave a galley with a heavy centerline gun a pronounced advantage over sailing round ships. Eventually, as gun and gunpowder production cheapened, the heavier sailing vessels could mount extensive broadsides of cannon. Although they still lacked maneuverability, their firepower became overwhelming—a development discussed in chapter 8. Gunpowder's addition of chemical energy to battlefields on land and sea created many such complex interactions with preexisting technologies and military systems. For that story, we move to the next chapter.

Further Reading

Casson, Lionel. *Ships and Seamanship in the Ancient World.* Princeton, NJ: Princeton University Press, 1971.

Guilmartin, John F., Jr. *Gunpowder and Galleys: Changing Technology and Mediterranean Warfare at Sea in the Sixteenth Century.* Rev. ed. Annapolis, MD: Naval Institute Press, 2000.

Guilmartin, John F., Jr. *Galleons and Galleys.* London: Cassell, 2002.

Hale, John R. *Lords of the Sea: The Epic Story of the Athenian Navy and the Birth of Democracy.* New York: Penguin, 2010.

Lane, Frederic Chapin. *Venetian Ships and Shipbuilders of the Renaissance.* Baltimore: Johns Hopkins Press, 1934.

Morrison, J. S., and J. F. Coates. *Greek and Roman Oared Warships.* Oxford: Oxbow, 1996.

Morrison, J. S., J. F. Coates, and N. B. Rankov. *The Athenian Trireme: The History and Reconstruction of an Ancient Greek Warship.* 2nd ed. Cambridge, UK: Cambridge University Press, 2000.

Murray, William M. *The Age of Titans: The Rise and Fall of the Great Hellenistic Navies.* Oxford: Oxford University Press, 2012.

Pitassi, Michael. *Roman Warships.* Woodbridge, UK: Boydell, 2011.

Pryor, John H., and Elizabeth M. Jeffreys. *The Age of the Dromon: The Byzantine Navy ca 500–1204.* Leiden: Brill, 2006.

Starr, Chester G. *The Influence of Sea Power on Ancient History.* Oxford: Oxford University Press, 1989.

Starr, Chester G. *The Roman Imperial Navy, 31 B.C.–A.D. 324.* 3rd ed. Chicago: Ares, 1941.

Wachsmann, Shelley. *Seagoing Ships and Seamanship in the Bronze Age Levant.* College Station: Texas A&M University Press, 1998.

Notes

1. Thomas F. Strasser et al., "Stone Age Seafaring in the Mediterranean: Evidence from the Plakias Region for Lower Palaeolithic and Mesolithic Habitation of Crete," *Hesperia* 79 (2010): 145–90; Barry Cunliffe, *Europe Between the Oceans: Themes and Variations, 9000 BC–AD 1000* (New Haven, CT: Yale University Press, 2008), 71, 95, 175–76.

2. On Egyptian boats: Lionel Casson, *Ships and Seamanship in the Ancient World* (Princeton, NJ: Princeton University Press, 1971), 11–22; Shelley Wachsmann, *Seagoing Ships and Seamanship in the Bronze Age Levant* (College Station: Texas A&M University Press, 1998), 9–38; for the appearance of the sail in the Levant around 2000 BCE, see Cunliffe, *Europe Between the Oceans*, 187–88.

3. M. George Prytulak, "Weapons on the Thera Ships?" *International Journal of Nautical Archaeology and Underwater Exploration* 11 (1982): 3–6; Wachsmann, *Seagoing Ships*, 31, 83–122, 133–35, 143, 155–57, 317–19; Casson, *Ships and Seamanship*, 35–38.

4. The join of the keel and the upright stem is a complex carpentry problem. The role of that problem in producing a forefoot, then a proto-ram, and finally a true ram is discussed in Wachsmann, *Seagoing Ships*, 157–58; Frederick H. van Doorninck, Jr., "Protogeometric Longships and the Introduction of the Ram," *International Journal of Nautical Archaeology and Underwater Exploration* 11 (1982): 277–86; Michael Wedde, *Towards a Hermeneutics of Aegean Bronze Age Ship Imagery* (Mannheim, Germany: Bibliopolis, 2000), 170–72. Thomas F. Tartaron, *Maritime Networks in the Mycenaean World* (Cambridge, UK: Cambridge University Press, 2013), 58–62; Casson, *Ships and Seamanship*, 49; J. S. Morrison and J. F. Coates, *Greek and Roman Oared Warships* (Oxford: Oxbow Books, 1996), 178, argues for a reverse causal connection—that the stronger two-level ship allowed for the installation of a ram on the already extant forefoot.

5. Casson, *Ships and Seamanship*, 52–56, quote 53.

6. Casson, *Ships and Seamanship*, 81. This dating remains controversial. An alternate hypothesis identifies a Phoenician trireme as early as the late eighth century BCE, lacking the outrigger, and strikingly tall. In this theory the Greek modification was the outrigger and thus the ability to pack more oarsmen into a shorter vertical space. See Morrison and Coates, *Greek and Roman Oared Warships*, 180–81. Although they argue for a somewhat earlier date (late eighth or early seventh century), they acknowledge that the trireme did not enter into common use until the late sixth century (178). Wallinga, offering a different chronology and process of invention, reasonably asks why the smallish Greek states would invest so much in a purpose-built warship. H. T. Wallinga, *Ships and Sea-Power before the Great Persian War: The Ancestry of the Ancient Trireme* (Leiden: Brill, 1993). On the trireme, key works are Casson, *Ships and Seamanship*, 77–96; J. S. Morrison and J. F. Coates. *The Athenian Trireme: The History and Reconstruction of an Ancient Greek Warship*, 2nd ed. (Cambridge, UK: Cambridge University Press, 2000); and J. S. Morrison and R. T. Williams, *Greek Oared Ships, 900–323 B.C.* (Cambridge, UK: Cambridge University Press, 1968).

7. Data for Table 6.1 is derived from Morrison and Coates, *Greek and Roman Oared Warships*, 289, 301, 316, 345; Casson, *Ships and Seamanship*, 54–56; Michael Pitassi, *Roman Warships* (Woodbridge, UK: Boydell, 2011), 100; Frederic Chapin Lane, *Venetian Ships and Shipbuilders of the Renaissance* (Baltimore: Johns Hopkins Press, 1934), 236; Angus Konstam, *Lepanto 1571: The Greatest Naval Battle of the Renaissance* (Westport, CT: 2005), 18–20; John H. Pryor and Elizabeth M. Jeffreys, *The Age of the Dromon: The Byzantine Navy, ca. 500–1204* (Leiden: Brill, 2006), 291–95; Horace H. Underwood, "Korean Boats and Ships," *Transactions of the Korea Branch of the Royal Asiatic Society* 23 (1934): 77–78; Zae-Geun Kim, "An Outline of Korean Shipbuilding History," *Korea Journal* 29.10 (1989): 9; and C. Nepean Longridge, *The Anatomy of Nelson's*

Ships (Hemel Hempstead, UK: Model & Allied Publications, 1974), facing pages 36 and 52.

8. Generally following John R. Hale, *Lords of the Sea: The Epic Story of the Athenian Navy and the Birth of Democracy* (New York: Penguin, 2010), 22–25. The placement of the hypozomata is debated. Here I am following Hale, who based this conclusion on a bronze votive ship model lamp found on the Acropolis, visible in plate 27b in Morrison and Williams, *Greek Oared Ships* (personal correspondence).

9. Morrison and Coates, *Athenian Trireme*, 103–6, 262–65; Morrison and Coates, *Greek and Roman Oared Warships*, 279, 345. Upper limit: Morrison and Coates, *Greek and Roman Oared Warships*, 323. John F. Guilmartin, Jr., *Gunpowder and Galleys: Changing Technology and Mediterranean Warfare at Sea in the 16th Century*, rev. ed. (Annapolis, MD: Naval Institute Press, 2003), 209–13; for a list of reasons why the later galleys would be slower, see Morrison and Coates, *Greek and Roman Oared Warships*, 279. The *Olympias* construction is described most accessibly in Morrison and Coates, *Athenian Trireme*, with further technical follow-up and revision in Morrison and Coates. *Greek and Roman Oared Warships*. For the extremity of the design, see the latter, p. 281.

10. Pryor and Jeffreys, *Age of the Dromon*, 145–46, points out that the Greek ram was not designed to "hole" a vessel; its flat-nosed, three-finned shape appears designed to crack and spring the edge-joined hull planking in a way impossible to repair immediately. See the discussion of raking in Morrison and Coates, *Greek and Roman Oared Warships*, 368–69.

11. The story is told in Herodotus; the discussion here follows the reconstruction in Hale, *Lords of the Sea*, 43–52.

12. William L. Rodgers, *Greek and Roman Naval Warfare* (Annapolis, MD: Naval Institute Press, 1964), 80, 113–15, provides some reasonable calculations on the fleet size. This account combines Hale's emphasis on maneuver (*Lords of the Sea*, 59–73) with a more traditional vision of the importance of boarding, as found in Rodgers, *Greek and Roman Naval Warfare*, 85–94. Cf. Morrison and Williams, *Greek Oared Ships*, 314–15.

13. See discussion in Hale, *Lords of the Sea*, 354–55; Casson, *Ships and Seamanship*, 323.

14. Louis Rawlings, *The Ancient Greeks at War* (Manchester, UK: Manchester University Press, 2007), 114.

15. Guilmartin, *Gunpowder and Galleys*, 78,112–13; Morrison and Coates, *Greek and Roman Oared Warships*, 326–27; Thucydides 6.42–6.44 in *The Landmark Thucydides*, ed. Robert B. Strassler (New York: Free Press, 1996); cf. Casson, *Ships and Seamanship*, 90.

16. Oded Tammuz, "Mare Clausum? Sailing Seasons in the Mediterranean in Early Antiquity," *Mediterranean Historical Review* 20.2 (2005): 145–62, esp. 155.

17. Arrian 1.20.1 in *Arrian: Anabasis of Alexander, Books I–IV*, trans. P. A. Brunt (Cambridge, MA: Loeb Classical Library, 1976) (quote).

18. This analysis derives from the logic associated with galley logistics, but the amphibious analogy and the role of bases owes much to Guilmartin's analysis in *Gunpowder and Galleys*, 78 and chapters 2 and 3.

19. Casson, *Ships and Seamanship*, 97–103; Morrison and Coates, *Greek and Roman Oared Warships*, 1–3; Morrison and Coates claim that the four may have been smaller and simpler than the three. *Greek and Roman Oared Warships*, 2–3, 29, 345. William M. Murray refutes this fairly clearly. *The Age of Titans: The Rise and Fall of the Great Hellenistic Navies* (Oxford: Oxford University Press, 2012), 51–54.

20. Diodorus 19.62.8 in *Diodorus of Sicily Vol. 9*, trans. C.H. Oldfather (Cambridge, MA: Loeb Classical Library, 1947); Casson,

Ships and Seamanship, 104; Chester G. Starr, *The Influence of Sea Power on Ancient History* (Oxford: Oxford University Press, 1989), 52; *Greek and Roman Oared Warships*, 16; Murray, *Age of Titans*, 162–70.

21. Casson, *Ships and Seamanship*, 107–16; Morrison and Coates, *Greek and Roman Oared Warships*, 269, 274; Murray, *Age of Titans*, 171–85.

22. Polybius 1.20.7, in *The Rise of the Roman Empire*, trans. Ian Scott-Kilvert (New York: Penguin, 1979); Christa Steinby, *The Roman Republican Navy: From the Sixth Century to 167 B.C.* (Helsinki: Societas Scientiarum Fennica, 2007), esp. 29–77.

23. I follow Morrison and Coates, *Greek and Roman Oared Warships*, 43–44, 270–71; contra Casson, *Ships and Seamanship*, 105, and Starr, *Influence of Seapower*, 57. Cf. J. F. Lazenby, *The First Punic War: A Military History* (Stanford, CA: Stanford University Press, 1996), 162; Steinby, *Roman Republican Navy*, 87–105; Pitassi, *Roman Warships*, 41–48. Eleven rams have recently been recovered from the sea bottom near the site of the Battle of the Aegates Islands in the First Punic War. Analysis of the rams is ongoing, but they are uniformly *much* smaller than expected for a five. Six have Latin inscriptions, indicating they were made for the Roman navy. It may be that the Roman fleet did not at all resemble Polybius's description. William Murray, "The Ship Class of the Egadi 1–10 Rams," unpublished conference paper, Archaeological Institute of America conference, Chicago, January, 2014; see also http://rpmnautical.org/egadi1ram.html.

24. Chester G. Starr, *The Roman Imperial Navy, 31 B.C –A.D. 324*, 3rd ed. (Chicago: Ares, 1941), 1–8, 193–97; Casson, *Ships and Seamanship*, 141.

25. Pryor and Jeffreys, *Age of the Dromon*, 1–6, 123–61, 143–44 (quote); Pitassi, *Roman Warships*, 40.

26. Pryor and Jeffreys, *Age of the Dromon*, 617–31; Alex Roland, "Secrecy, Technology, and War: Greek Fire and the Defense of Byzantium, 678–1204," *Technology and Culture* 33.4 (1992): 655–79; John Haldon, "'Greek Fire' Revisited: Recent and Current Research," in *Byzantine Style, Religion and Civilization*, ed. Elizabeth M. Jeffreys (Cambridge, UK: Cambridge University Press, 2006), 290–325.

27. Pryor and Jeffreys, *Age of the Dromon*, 630.

28. Frederic C. Lane, *Venice: A Maritime Republic* (Baltimore: Johns Hopkins University Press, 1973), 24, 28–29; Lillian Ray Martin, *Art and Archaeology of Venetian Ships and Boats* (College Station: Texas A&M University Press, 2001), 173; Lane, *Venice*, 27; Frederic C. Lane, "Venetian Merchant Galleys, 1300–1334: Private and Communal Operation," *Speculum* 38.2 (1963): 202n110.

29. Lane, *Venetian Ships and Shipbuilders*, 13–27, 236.

30. John F. Guilmartin, Jr., *Galleons and Galleys* (London: Cassell, 2002), 114–15; John F. Guilmartin, Jr., "The Earliest Shipboard Gunpowder Ordnance: An Analysis of Its Technical Parameters and Tactical Capabilities," *Journal of Military History* 71 (2007): 649–69; Guilmartin, *Gunpowder and Galleys*, 10, 50–52; Louis Sicking, "Naval Warfare in Europe, c. 1330–c. 1680," in *European Warfare, 1350–1750*, ed. Frank Tallett and D. J. B. Trim (Cambridge, UK: Cambridge University Press, 2010), 243.

31. Guilmartin, *Gunpowder and Galleys*, 73–78, 84–85, 116, 124–31; Lane, *Venetian Ships and Shipbuilders*, 31–32.

32. This paragraph closely follows the analysis in Guilmartin, *Gunpowder and Galleys*, 36–38, 66–67, 69, 90–91, 121–22.

33. Horace H. Underwood, "Korean Boats and Ships," *Transactions of the Korea Branch of the Royal Asiatic Society* 23 (1934): 1–99, esp. 71–84; Zae-Geun Kim, "An Outline of Korean Shipbuilding History," *Korea Journal* 29.10 (1989): 4–17; Samuel Hawley, *The Imjin War* (Seoul: Royal Asiatic Society,

Korea Branch, 2005), 104–5, 121–22; Kenneth M. Swope, *A Dragon's Head and a Serpent's Tail: Ming China and the First Great East Asian War, 1592–1598* (Norman: University of Oklahoma Press, 2009), 77; Kenneth M. Swope, "Crouching Tigers, Secret Weapons: Military Technology Employed during the Sino-Japanese-Korean War, 1592–1598," *Journal of Military History* 69 (2005): 25–27; Stephen Turnbull, *Samurai Invasion: Japan's Korean War, 1592–98* (London: Cassell, 2002), 88–90. See A. R. Collins's website on British cannonball sizes, http://www.arc.id.au/Cannonballs.html, accessed December 5, 2014, for weight of cannonballs of various sizes. Korean ship-borne cannon were substantially smaller than contemporary European versions, probably not exceeding the equivalent of a European nine-pounder.

34. Rawlings, *Ancient Greeks at War*, 109–14; compare Vincent Gabrielsen, "The Impact of Armed Forces on Government and Politics in Archaic and Classical Greek Poleis: A Response to Hans van Wees," in *Army and Power in the Ancient World*, eds. Angelos Chaniotis and Pierre Ducrey (Stuttgart: Franz Steiner Verlag, 2002), 91.

7

Gunpowder in Europe and in the Ottoman Empire

1300–1650 CE

Europe and the Ottoman Empire, 1300–1683 • The Technology of Gunpowder and Gunpowder Weapons • Siege Cannon to 1650 • The Artillery Fortress, 1450 to 1650 • Infantry and Firearms, 1450–1650 • Conclusion: A Military Revolution?

MUCH HAS BEEN CLAIMED for the significance of gunpowder in the course of military and even human history. There is little doubt that it has been made to carry too much historical weight. There is equally little doubt, however, about its importance in a variety of ways. At a very basic level gunpowder introduced a new form of energy onto the battlefield. Where virtually all earlier weaponry had relied upon muscle power (human or animal) or stored muscle power in simple machines, the chemical energy of gunpowder operates independently of human or animal strength or training. By overcoming the limits inherent in older weapons' dependence on strength and sometimes a lifetime's skill, gunpowder eventually enabled (although it did not require) a massive expansibility in army size. Anyone could light a fuse or pull a trigger. Simultaneously, it opened a trajectory of technological progression in a way that muscle-powered weapons simply could not: a bow or a sword could only be modified or improved so much. That trajectory in the long run would tip the military balance of power away from nomads and in favor of sedentary, state-based civilizations; only they could reliably produce and maintain gunpowder and gunpowder weapons.

The word "trajectory," however, is key. There was no single "best" trajectory for using gunpowder. Societies reacted to it according to their culture, their geography, their perception of utility or of threat, and much more. Furthermore, gunpowder did not just "appear," nor did it immediately overturn the political or tactical balance of power. Gunpowder weapons underwent substantial evolutionary change, and their existence instigated other changes in related fields. The innovations covered in this chapter are not just those directly related to gunpowder itself, but also its effects on forts, ships (in the next chapter), discipline, army size, violence, and perhaps even on the state. We cannot make sense of these changes in a vacuum, so this chapter will follow the development of early gunpowder weapons in both western Europe and the Ottoman Empire. Both societies were early and enthusiastic adopters of gunpowder weapons, and their comparative experience illuminates some of the key historical questions posed by their introduction.

Those questions are many. Gunpowder has been tied to the rise of the West to world dominance. It has been cited as a dominant factor in the creation of various other "gunpowder empires." And some have argued that adapting to its implications played a major role in the creation of the modern bureaucratic state. Dealing with complex problems on this scale will be difficult in one or two short chapters. This chapter provides a comparative analysis of two different cultures operating in relatively similar and deeply interconnected environments, and will eventually assess whether gunpowder created revolutionary changes in them. The following chapter will explore the origins of gunpowder in China, and then examine what happened when European and Ottoman improvements to that original invention were reexported east, west, and south.

EUROPE AND THE OTTOMAN EMPIRE, 1300–1683

To begin to analyze the specifics of a single innovation, however, requires setting a broader political stage. The Europeans and Ottomans both learned to use gunpowder while engaged in centuries of struggle with each other.

Europe 1300–1453

Western Europe in 1300 had enjoyed a relatively long period of prosperity and security from outside invasions. The Mongols had threatened, but their power and reach had receded. The Moors still ruled southern Spain but were increasingly on the defensive. The crusader states in the Near East were gone, but there was as yet no threat of a counter crusade from the east. The rising European population had produced a rebirth of commerce, an increase in wealth, and what is sometimes called the medieval origins of the modern state in France, England, and Spain. Those states, however, regularly warred with each other, with the less centralized political entities around them, and with their own still semiautonomous landed nobility. Like much of the world, Europe remained a fragmented political arena of intense military competition.

In the fourteenth century much of this picture changed. Devastating famines, probably linked to the cooling climate, were followed in 1348–49 by the Black Death. Europe's population plummeted by as much as one-third. Almost simultaneously the on-again, off-again conflict between France and England known as the Hundred Years War began its long procession of devastation and destruction. France eventually secured its position, ousting the English by 1453 from virtually all of their ancient claims to what is now modern France. Perhaps more threatening, however, Mediterranean and southeastern Europe again faced a rising power from the Islamic world.

The Ottoman Empire, 1300–1479

Turkic-speaking steppe horsemen from central Asia swept into Anatolia in the eleventh century and established the Seljuk dynasty, ruling over much of the peninsula but also locked in a struggle with the fading Byzantine Empire. The Mongol conquest in the thirteenth century altered the political landscape, but reinforced the steppe ethic and left the Turkish clans in place. The fragmented political situation at the beginning of the fourteenth century saw one such clan, the *Osmanoğlu* (Ottomans), rise to prominence. These were not nomads fresh from the steppe. Long resident in Anatolia, they were accustomed to the bureaucratic processes associated with sedentary states, and as their political control expanded, they retained and extended those capacities. In 1324 they established a capital in Bursa, a threat to Constantinople across the straits. Sometime in the 1360s they captured Adrianople, making it their capital as they established themselves in Europe. In 1387 they captured Thessaloniki from the Byzantines (but had to give it back in 1402, then recapturing it from the Venetians in 1430). In 1389 they destroyed the Serbian kingdom, and then in 1396 at Nicopolis they routed the European crusaders seeking to halt their advance. Finally, after several failed attempts, the Ottomans captured Constantinople in 1453, ending its thousand-year history as the center of the Byzantine empire. They then forced the Venetians to terms in 1479. With the Balkans in hand, the stage was set for a Turkish invasion into central Europe and even Italy.

Europe and the Ottomans, 1450–1683

Fear of the Turkish threat pervaded Europe. But at the same time the continent was on the brink of momentous changes, some of them quiet ones whose impact would only slowly become clear. Sometime in the 1440s Johannes Gutenberg invented a movable-type press. European navigators in the late 1400s combined old and new technologies to master oceanic navigation, most famously in Christopher Columbus's 1492 voyage to the New World. Also in 1492 the recently united Spanish states of Castile and Aragon completed their ouster of the Moors from Granada. In the 1490s Europeans inserted themselves for the first time into the global network of trade centered in the Indian Ocean. In 1517 the veneer of cultural uniformity imposed by Latin Christianity on most of Europe cracked when Martin Luther nailed his propositions to a church door. A major consequence of the resulting religious divide was an intensification of conflict in Europe that would not end until

1648—marked most infamously by the Thirty Years War, which concluded that year. By then the Europeans had also established themselves as colonial powers around the world, by one estimate controlling some 35 percent of the world's surface.[1]

The Ottomans, however, were equally, if not more, powerful within Europe during this period. Outside Europe they had expanded to the east, conquering Egypt from the Mamluks in 1517, extending their control over much of North Africa, and capturing Baghdad and Basra in the 1530s and 1540s. The sixteenth century also saw the Ottomans establish control over all of southeastern Europe (see Map 7.1). They besieged Vienna in 1529 and would do so again in 1683, although from that time the high tide of their power clearly began to recede.

To make sense of the role that gunpowder played (or did not) in these developments, we need to do two things: (1) explain the basics of gunpowder and firearms as a technology, and (2) compare in parallel the implementation of that technology in both Christian and Ottoman Europe over this period. This side-by-side comparison reveals that Westerners had no monopoly on the effective adoption of technology, but it will also show key differences in *how* gunpowder technology was adopted. Those distinct patterns reflected calculations based on the threat environment, differences in the capacities of the competing states, and variations in culture that were reflected in, among other things, the mobilization of infantry.

One final note: in some ways it makes little sense to compare the Ottomans to "Europe." Doing so is like comparing Spain to "Europe." The Ottoman Empire was one political entity with its own history. So was France, England, Spain, Burgundy, the Kingdom of Sicily, and all the other independent political entities in the competitive cockpit of Europe and the Mediterranean. I nonetheless persist in the comparison, because historians have often treated western Europe as a collective, and because of the claims that cultural differences between the Islamic Ottoman Turks and western European Christians were the major factors determining their respective adoption of gunpowder technology. We will see how well those claims hold up.

THE TECHNOLOGY OF GUNPOWDER AND GUNPOWDER WEAPONS

The Chemistry

Gunpowder is an explosive compound of charcoal, sulfur, and potassium nitrate (commonly known as saltpeter). Making it requires crushing each of the ingredients into a fine powder and then thoroughly mixing them in a suitable ratio. The process was first invented in China, probably evolving from a long use of saltpeter on its own as an incendiary. The first written formula from China dates to around 1040 CE. Early formulas were likely experimental alchemical modifications of pure saltpeter to produce a more effective

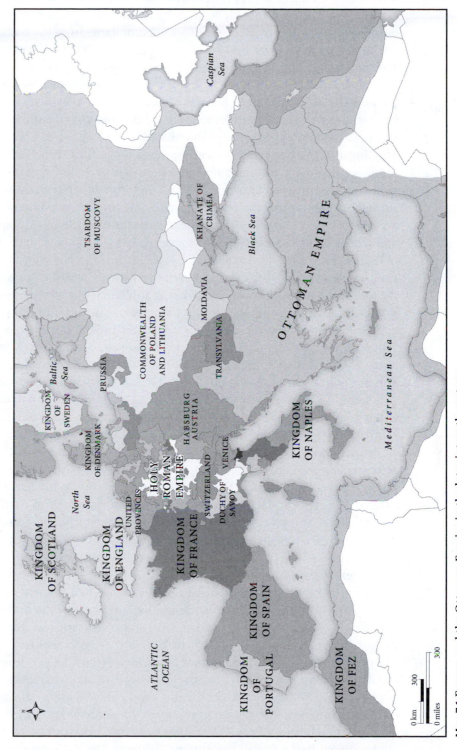

Map 7.1 Europe and the Ottoman Empire in the late sixteenth century.

KINGDOM OF SCOTLAND

KINGDOM OF ENGLAND

ATLANTIC OCEAN

North Sea

UNITED PROVINCES

KINGDOM OF DENMARK

KINGDOM OF SWEDEN

Baltic Sea

PRUSSIA

COMMONWEALTH OF POLAND AND LITHUANIA

TSARDOM OF MUSCOVY

Caspian Sea

KHANATE OF CRIMEA

Black Sea

MOLDAVIA

HOLY ROMAN EMPIRE

HABSBURG AUSTRIA

TRANSYLVANIA

SWITZERLAND

VENICE

DUCHY OF SAVOY

KINGDOM OF FRANCE

KINGDOM OF NAPLES

OTTOMAN EMPIRE

Mediterranean Sea

KINGDOM OF PORTUGAL

KINGDOM OF SPAIN

KINGDOM OF FEZ

N

0 km   300

0 miles   300

219

incendiary. Continued experimentation in China maximized gunpowder's explosive qualities. It quickly acquired military value, first as a grenade or bomb, then as a "fire lance" throwing a burst of flame from the end of a tube, later as an arrow thrower, and finally as a sphere-throwing cannon or firearm. The earliest cannon in China dates from around 1128, the earliest firearm from at least 1288. We will examine early gunpowder-weapon development in China in the next chapter, but it is important here to establish those weapons' origins in China and then to say a word about the transmission of this technology to Europe and the Middle East.[2]

Gunpowder's exact path to Europe remains unclear. It is likely that the Mongols played a role in transmitting it from east to west, just as they demonstrably moved other technologies around, sometimes deliberately, sometimes simply by opening up trade routes stretching across Eurasia. One scholar has argued for a very early origin with, or at least transmission by, Arabic alchemical scholars; the Moors in Spain were using cannon no later than the 1320s or 1330s. This route makes geographic sense, but there is confusion in the sources involving words that may have referred to "Greek fire" or some other incendiary technology now perhaps being applied to gunpowder. The general scholarly opinion is that the formula and its use in tubes to fire projectiles somehow arrived in Europe, perhaps via Italian traders operating in the Black Sea, without making much of an initial stop in the Middle East. The earliest clear reference to the formula in Europe comes from 1267, and guns are reliably described in European sources in Italy and England (as well as among the Moors in Granada) in the 1320s and 1330s. The Ottomans were close behind, probably learning the formula from Europeans in the Balkans, and clearly using guns by the 1380s (see below).[3]

In the modern "ideal" formulation, gunpowder consists of 75 percent saltpeter, 15 percent charcoal, and 10 percent sulfur. This simple statement, however, obscures a host of critical issues in its discovery and use. First, consider the process of dangerous experimentation necessary to arrive at this combination. Many variations were tried, in different places, in relative secrecy and over a long period of time. Most variations with more than 50 percent saltpeter will explode, but at different speeds (although not visible to the eye, all explosions have different "speeds"). In this respect, a key discovery in Europe was "corning," in which the powder was wetted, shaped into loaves, dried, and then crumbled, at first randomly and later (in the mid-sixteenth century) more systematically into uniform grains. This process, probably originally designed to protect the finished powder from moisture—a problem exaggerated in Europe by the nature of locally available saltpeter—also greatly increases its explosive effect. The source of the individual materials presents another issue. In Europe sulfur and charcoal were easy to obtain. Saltpeter, however, the largest component of gunpowder, was not widely available in Europe (outside of Spain) as it was in China and in India. Both of those places had naturally occurring saltpeter fields in mudflats, where lightning strikes or fires may have first suggested using it as an incendiary. Saltpeter occurs in nature as a byproduct of organic decomposition, and is particularly associated with the decomposition of human and animal waste. Lacking natural accumulations, Europeans began to create them artificially, instituting saltpeter plantations by 1380, and eventually collecting it as a kind of tax from waste-rich urban environments. Additional steps are required to purify the saltpeter, but the point here is that a complicated process was involved; it varied depending on local sources; and until the basics were fully worked out, it was expensive.[4]

The Tube and Ignition

Figuring out how to make an explosion was one thing; containing and directing that explosion to fire a lethal projectile was another. A tube is the obvious shape for pointing the force in one direction. A longer tube gives the expanding gases more time to accelerate the projectile, but the longer the tube, the stronger it needs to be, especially at the explosion's point of origin at the tube's seat (breech). This immediately poses two problems: how to create a tube that is closed at one end, and how to ignite the powder. To solve the first problem, many of the very first guns were cast; that is, molten metal was poured into a mold designed with one closed end. European bellfounders working in bronze had long experience with that basic shape, and they served as early cannon makers (indeed, the earliest European depictions of a cannon strongly resemble bells—as they did in China; see chapter 8). In Europe, however, bronze was expensive and the technology of casting iron during the thirteenth to sixteenth centuries was relatively primitive, with frequently brittle results. Therefore, many early European iron guns were wrought; that is, they were hammered and welded into shape, initially from a long plate folded into a tube. Larger guns, however, were built up like barrels, with iron staves side by side, and iron hoops sweated onto the tube to hold them together. The end was then closed with a separate "breech block" designed to close the tube and hold the powder charge.

As for ignition, the solution was relatively simple: a small hole drilled into the breech, the touchhole, was filled with powder and then ignited by a lit fuse (or "match"). For cannons it would be centuries before this basic design changed. For hand guns, however, the need to use two hands to hold and point the barrel led to the development of "locks": mechanisms that allowed the firer to ignite the charge while holding the barrel (encased in a "stock"). Locks followed their own path of technological development, from simple z-shaped serpentine triggers to matchlocks, wheel locks, and flintlocks.

Roughly speaking, we can divide the impact of gunpowder and gunpowder weapons during their first three hundred years (1300–1650) into four categories: (1) cannon, especially siege cannon in the early phases, (2) corresponding changes in fortification, (3) firearms as used by infantry (truly effective use by cavalry remained limited until the nineteenth century), and (4) cannon aboard ship. To be sure, this limited list leaves aside a lot of experimentation, some of it important, not least the use of wheel-lock pistols by lightly armored cavalrymen. But, examined in a long-term perspective, this categorization makes sense—at least until 1650, when field artillery became important.

SIEGE CANNON TO 1650

Context is key. Late medieval Europe had experienced a proliferation of local castles, built primarily of earth and timber in the eleventh century, becoming stone and increasingly complex in the twelfth and thirteenth centuries. Those castles simultaneously reflected and contributed to the decentralization of political authority. Castles controlled territory by providing security against surprise and protection for a smaller force from a larger one. If the larger force ignored the castle and its garrison, they would then have that garrison in their rear. As a result, much of medieval warfare revolved around the siege, and battles were often fought in that context of laying or trying to raise a siege.[5]

This emphasis on siege warfare meant that as cannon became available, they were quickly folded into the repertoire of siege weapons (most notably the counterweight trebuchet, which had moved into Europe from the Middle East by the early thirteenth century). The first surviving representations of guns in Europe are from 1326. There is evidence of their use in sieges already from 1331 and 1333, and they became increasingly common thereafter. Early experimentation with smaller cannon, carried on wagons, and deployed primarily for their surprise effects against personnel in battle (often called *ribauldequin*) generally faded. Effective field artillery would await three more centuries of development and is a separate story. Through the mid-fifteenth century Europeans concentrated on enlarging cannon for sieges, sometimes to an enormous scale. This effort was partly made possible by the dramatic drop in the price of gunpowder that occurred after the introduction of saltpeter plantations in Europe in the 1380s. Cannon appeared that fired round stone shot (much like the prepared stones often used by trebuchets) regularly weighing from two hundred to six hundred pounds. The spread of this technology is neatly represented by two of most famous early guns of this type: the Pumhart von Steyr, built in Austria around 1420 (which fired a 1,500-pound stone), and the Mons Meg, built in Burgundy in the mid-fifteenth century and then sent to Scotland, which fired a ball of some 549 pounds (see Figure 7.1).[6]

In a real sense the first siege cannons merely sought to duplicate the capability of catapults. The very first guns actually fired spears, in much the way that certain kinds of catapults had done. Similarly, in the fourteenth and early fifteenth century Europeans mentally placed guns into the same category as the trebuchet: although they could do great damage to the fortress

Figure 7.1 The Pumhart von Steyr, ca. 1420. Built in Austria of wrought iron using the hoop-and-stave technique; this bombard weighs ca. eight tons and fired 800 millimeter diameter stone balls.

walls, their primary function was often to shoot *over* the walls, destroying the interior. Henry V's battery of Harfleur in 1415 was described as playing "at tenys [tennis] with them that were in the toune" such that "really fine buildings almost as far as the middle of the town, were either totally demolished or threatened with inevitable collapse." In one sense this merely reflected the guns' relative inaccuracy: the interior of a town represented a larger target compared to repeatedly hitting the same spot on a wall. One early gunner who hit three targets in a row within one day in 1437 was advised to go on a pilgrimage to cleanse his soul—such accuracy could only have represented a deal with the devil. It was also the case, however, that the efficacy of the trebuchet after 1200 had led to thicker walls in thirteenth- and fourteenth-century castle design, and the first cannons did not have significantly more destructive power than late trebuchets.[7]

The 1415 siege of Harfleur may have occurred during a key transition, however, because it appears that in addition to playing at tennis, Henry's guns were essential in eventually breaching the wall. Clifford Rogers has shown that earlier guns lacked the capacity to destroy medieval walls; the success of sieges still depended on starving out the defenders over long periods of time. The direct battery of the walls only began to be effective in the 1420s and 1440s. Changes in cannon design were key. The use of the hoop-and-stave method of construction allowed gunmakers to build longer barrels; the ratio of the barrel's length to the diameter of the ball expanded from 1:1 or 1.5:1 to 3:1 or more, rapidly expanding after this initial period of experimentation to 14:1 or 30:1 by the sixteenth century. With more time for expanding gases to work, the ball's velocity increased, quadrupling the force of its impact for every doubling of the velocity of the ball. The introduction of corned powder in this period also increased the power of cannon (leading gunners to reduce the saltpeter in the formula until the strength of gun barrels "caught up" to the enhanced power of corned powder).[8]

These developments rendered the high vertical walls and hollow towers of medieval castles vulnerable, especially since medieval castles were not capable of mounting cannon to return fire. Cannon design continue to progress, in a dizzying variety of sizes and types. By the 1530s a consensus of sorts had emerged, settling on the "single-piece casting of bronze guns . . . firing an iron cannonball with a charge of corned gunpowder amounting to one-half the shot's weight." This new offensive capability contributed to the French defeat of the English ending the Hundred Years War (1453), the Spanish reconquest of Spain (1492), and even, if only slightly, to the Ottoman capture of Constantinople (1453).[9]

The early Ottoman use of siege cannon strongly paralleled developments in western Europe, but there were some key differences. Compared to its European opponents in the fifteenth through the sixteenth centuries, the Ottoman state was much more centralized and bureaucratically sophisticated. Its rapid expansion incorporated impressive demographic, agricultural, commercial, and mineral resources. Like other contemporary states, its wealth was turned into military power, but the Ottomans were better at managing that transformation than most of their contemporaries. As the empire expanded, grants of land, *timars*, were awarded to key servants of the sultan, usually for military service. As a condition of holding the grant, which was theoretically temporary (the land reverted to the sultan when the timariot died), the timariot served as a cavalryman and brought his retainers with him. The empire's vast territory supported a large number of timariots, perhaps as many as fifty thousand in 1525. The sultan also regularly called on steppe-dwelling Tatar and Turcoman allies from north of the Black Sea who fought in the usual steppe-horse-archer fashion. In addition to these forces who served on call, and most unlike the Europeans at the time, the Ottoman state maintained a standing army, called the *kapıkulu*, which most famously included the *yeni çeri*, or new army—"janissaries" to the Europeans—as well as some companies of cavalry stationed at the capital, several technical corps of gunners, gun-carriage makers, armorers, bombardiers, and miners and sappers. Lastly, the Ottomans maintained a separate artillery corps.[10]

There is some debate about how and when the Ottomans first obtained artillery. They were fighting Europeans in the Balkans from the middle of the fourteenth century, and that area, like most of Europe, was littered with medieval-style castles designed to keep out infantry and resist catapults. The

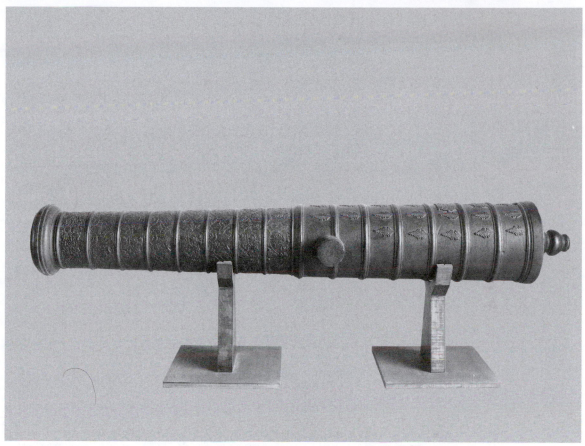

Figure 7.2 Ottoman siege cannon, bronze, cast 1581. 2.87 meters long, weighing 1,991 kg.

leading scholar on the development of Ottoman artillery suggests that they picked up cannon in Hungary and the Balkans as early as the 1380s, and then rapidly became masters of the technology. They had an effective siege train by the late fourteenth century, field artillery by the 1440s, and the standing artillery corps by the early fifteenth century as well. In 1514 the Ottomans may have had as many as 150 cannon at the battle of Çaldiran against the Safavids of Iran, and in 1526 fielded perhaps 170 cannon against the Hungarians (who apparently possessed eighty-five). And, as already mentioned, Ottoman cannon played a role, if not necessarily the decisive one, in the final conquest of Constantinople in 1453.[11]

These numbers are impressive, but some historians have claimed that the Ottomans failed to keep up with Western developments—perhaps because of some Islamic cultural conservatism—that their metallurgy was poor, or that they relied heavily on foreigners for expertise, or that they focused excessively on building giant bombards that quickly became obsolete. Gábor Ágoston and Rhoads Murphey have attacked all these assumptions, and it

Figure 7.3 French siege cannon, bronze, cast ca. 1521–30. 3.67 meters long, weighing 2,533 kg, and firing 144 mm balls.

now seems clear that the earliest that the Ottomans might have been falling behind the West was in the late seventeenth century, and some would argue for later in the eighteenth century. Supposed Ottoman cultural conservatism is the easiest to dispense with—at least on this subject. As the Ottomans encountered European and Byzantine fortresses and cannon, and even ships, they rapidly adopted them and folded them into their own military system. Furthermore, their superior logistical and financial capability in this period gave them an advantage in the number of guns they could deploy, at least until the seventeenth century. One reason was that the Ottomans, unlike Europeans, had relatively easy access to copper. They quickly shifted to making primarily bronze cannon, which were lighter and safer than early European cast-iron guns and, given their control of copper sources, were not as expensive as European bronze guns. Good-quality European cast-iron guns emerged first in England in 1543, and spread slowly thereafter; although heavier and bulkier than bronze, they cost one-third as much. The Ottomans did continue to build some giant bombards for a decade or two after the Europeans had moved away from them, and the Ottomans also tended to "retire" those large guns to fortresses, where they were displayed as symbols of power, to be observed and ridiculed by Europeans much later. Ágoston's careful inventory, however, has shown that the full scope of Ottoman

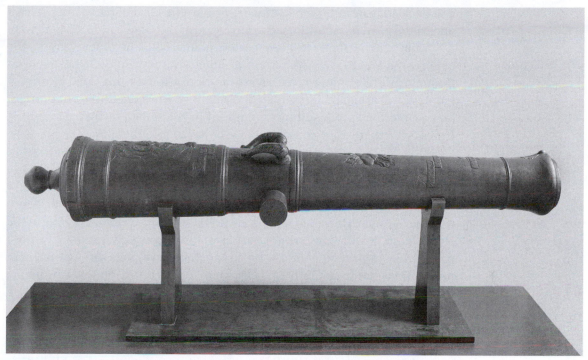

Figure 7.4 French field artillery cannon, bronze, cast 1756. A four pounder in the "Swedish style," 1.62 meters long, weighing 324 kg and firing 84 mm balls.

artillery production closely resembled that of European states. They produced a range of weapons from small to large (to gigantic), built for different purposes; from small guns firing one-ounce balls to one-pound balls, to larger types firing 68–163-pound balls. If the Ottomans did have a weakness, it was perhaps over-diversification in types of guns, leading to poor standardization and a corresponding difficulty in supplying ammunition.[12]

In some ways the accusation that the Ottomans relied heavily on foreign experts has more merit, but it is too simplistic. It seems undeniable that the Ottomans learned how to make cannon, and possibly gunpowder, from their experience fighting Europeans. But gunmaking and gunnery at that time were craft traditions. The techniques of casting bronze, working iron, milling gunpowder, and even the ballistics of gunnery were learned through experimentation and then passed on through personal observation and instruction. Techniques considered valuable spread rapidly, and were generally beyond the control of any political authority. The Ottomans' reputation for religious tolerance and their openness to advancing foreign-born subjects to high places within the empire, not to mention the empire's wealth, made them attractive customers for craftsmen—men who unfortunately usually remain anonymous and whose paths are difficult to track. The most famous example was the gun founder "Master Orban," certainly Christian, probably Hungarian, who had been working without pay for the Byzantine emperor, and decided instead to provide his services to the Ottomans, casting at least one of the great bombards used against Constantinople in 1453. There were no doubt many others, but as Ágoston points out, once they were in the empire, their skills were passed on to other Ottoman subjects, and indeed from as early as the mid-fifteenth century the Ottomans included a corps of gunners and armorers in their central standing army as professional troops. Meanwhile the European powers engaged in the same practice of taking in whichever experts they could persuade or pay to join them.[13]

In the longer term, however, the proliferation of printed instruction manuals in Europe, especially on gunnery, if not on gun founding, may have outpaced that of the Ottomans, whose Islamic traditions declined to accept the printing press until the eighteenth century. It may not be a coincidence that the Ottomans began to lose pace with European developments late in the seventeenth century, just as the military literature vastly expanded into a pan-European printed genre. A broad-ranging survey of Ottoman military publications has found only one Ottoman-authored text on firearms before the eighteenth century, a century during which the Ottomans began more actively copying European texts. Indeed, of 3,182 books on military art and science prepared between 1299 and 1923, most were translations of European works, and only seventy date from before the eighteenth century. The potential influence of this different approach to printing and publishing is even more marked in the design and construction of fortifications.[14]

THE ARTILLERY FORTRESS, 1450 TO 1650

The development of effective siege artillery accelerated at the end of the fifteenth century. Some of the key changes were simple: the lengthening of the barrel (described above), which greatly increased impact force, meant that effective siege artillery no longer needed to be monstrous; guns were increasingly standardized by size of ball; they were cast with trunnions to make changing the angle of fire a simple process; and they were mounted on two-wheeled carriages. In 1494, the French king Charles VIII invaded Italy with a mobile artillery siege train featuring all of these changes. His army progressed down and back up the length of Italy, taking cities seemingly at will. One deeply impressed Italian wrote that the new French artillery moved so quickly that it

> almost kept Pace with the Army. They were planted against the Walls of a Town with such speed, the Space between the Shots was so little, and the Balls flew so quick, and were impelled with such Force, that as much Execution was done in a few Hours, as formerly, in Italy, in the like Number of Days.[15]

Charles's artillery *was* remarkably effective, though perhaps not as decisive as it seemed at the time. What really mattered in the longer term, however, was the response of the Italian cities.[16]

(a)   (b)

Figure 7.5 *a* & *b* **The "Cow Tower" artillery tower in Norwich, England, ca. 1398.** An early tower design for artillery use. 7.5b shows the interior loop holes for all around artillery fire.

Charles's victims were among the best prepared in Europe to invent a system to counter his artillery. The Italian cities were centers of trade, flush with cash. They were ready to hire whoever could propose a reasonable solution to the new problem of artillery, and ready to pay to build what turned out to be an expensive new style of fortification, the angled-bastion artillery fortress, whose style is often referred to as the *trace italienne*, in homage to its origins in Italy.

The problem was clear. Against a medieval army, a castle was designed with a high wall supplemented by a ditch or moat to keep out men equipped with siege ladders and siege towers. Although a medieval castle might have very thick walls, especially at the base, their primary design feature was height. The advent of effective siege cannon changed the equation: the walls themselves became vulnerable, and keeping the attacker at a distance now mandated some form of equivalent return fire. Both requirements meant a redesign of fortifications: walls had to get thicker (and proportionally lower), and platforms had to be built to support cannon within the fort, positioned to maximize their fire while protecting them from the attacker's fire. There were a number of possible paths to follow to solve this problem, especially since the designer usually had to accommodate earlier walls. Initial improvisations included piling up earth mounds behind existing walls, or building low, earth-walled extensions in front of existing walls to serve as cannon platforms. Another early experiment was the "artillery tower," a round, thickly walled tower with cannon pointing in all directions, and emphasizing thick curved walls designed to deflect cannon balls (see Figures 7.5 and 7.6).

Figure 7.6 A sixteenth-century coastal artillery tower, Camber, England. Commissioned by Henry VIII in 1542.

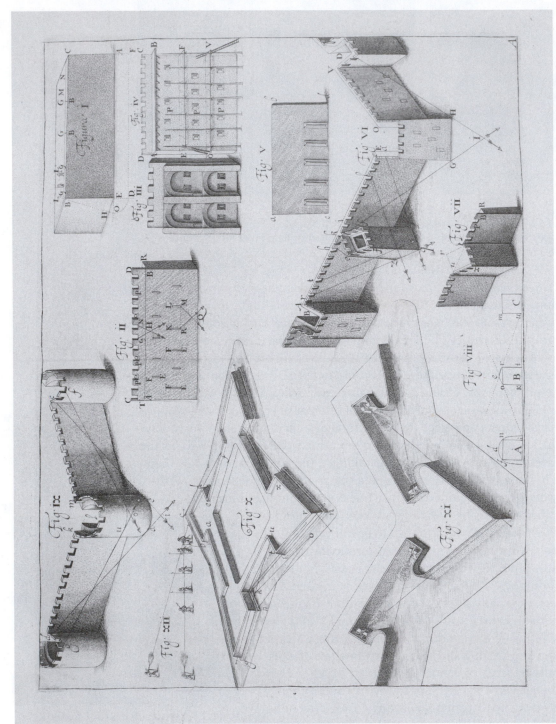

Figure 7.7 The progression in fortification styles. This 1647 manual on military fortification shows the geometry of crossing fire from different systems of walls and bastions, comparing older systems to the *trace italienne.* Start on the lower right, and progress counterclockwise. Note how the later system eliminates dead space at the foot of the wall and adds cannon in a recessed space behind the bastion for defense against a final assault on the wall.

Early sixteenth-century Italian architects, however, rapidly converged on a geometrically compelling system of linked angled bastions, usually low to the ground, with a moat, and protected by a sloped glacis. The bastions provided wide platforms for cannon; they provided for crossing fire to eliminate "dead space" at the foot of the walls; the glacis deflected shot; the moat slowed the assault of infantry; and and at least some cannon could be preserved in the recessed angles of the bastion for fire against the final infantry assault on the wall (see Figure 7.7). Creating a full circumference of such bastions that accommodated local topography was a complex exercise in surveying and geometry that was not mastered all at once, but this basic system spread throughout western Europe between 1520 and 1700. It proliferated rapidly in Italy, France, and the Low Countries, and on the Hungarian frontier, coming later to Germany (mostly after 1600) and even more slowly to England, Ireland, and northeastern Europe (see Figure 7.8).[17]

The process of innovation in this instance is a fascinating blend of culture and calculation. A real problem demanded practical solutions, at a cost that presumably discouraged frivolous suggestions. The Italian architects pulled out their quills and paper and literally began calculating. But, as historian Thomas Arnold has suggested, the form of their solution arose from Renaissance Europe's fascination with geometry. It was to them as statistics is to us—an avenue to truth and understanding, famously exemplified by Leonardo da Vinci's famous "Vitruvian Man." Once started on this particular trajectory of ever more precise geometric solutions, suggestions and improvements proliferated

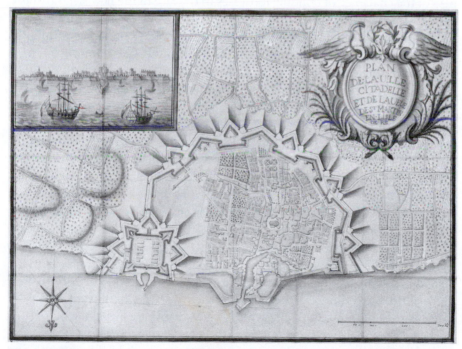

Figure 7.8 Plan of the town and citadel of Saint-Martin-de-Re, France, ca. 1650. An example of a European city fully-encompassed by the *trace italienne* style fortification system.

wildly, spreading easily through the medium of European market-oriented print culture.[18]

Beyond the clear popularity of the bastioned artillery fortress, historian Geoffrey Parker has argued that it was profoundly important in two respects. First, its cost and proliferation within Europe strained the capacity of states, slowed the ending of wars, and demanded more centralized and bureaucratized systems capable of paying for and besieging such fortresses. In a related effect, the *trace italienne* demanded larger and larger armies to garrison or besiege them, which in turn further stressed state capacity. Second, the perfected artillery fortress, Parker argues, provided a kind of ultimate security to European outposts overseas, at least when combined with European naval dominance. One way to test this argument, at least partially, is to examine the record of the Ottomans, who were certainly positioned to adopt this technique. Did they adopt it? And if so, did it change their way of war or provide them with greater imperial security?[19]

Ottoman artillery development, and even the Ottoman use of infantry armed with hand guns (see below), is fairly well understood. Ottoman developments in fortification techniques, however, are a good deal less clear. The usual assessment, including judgments by contemporary Europeans, has been that the Ottomans ignored, or at best only poorly understood, the *trace italienne*, at least until 1650, although they proved expert at besieging such fortresses.

This view needs some revision. The Ottomans demonstrated an early awareness of the challenge of building fortresses in the face of the new siege artillery. Long Ottoman experience with medieval-style fortresses can be seen in the Anadoluhisarı (Castle of Anatolia), built on the Asian side of the Bosphorus straits around 1390, characterized by high medieval walls around a central keep. Interestingly, some fifty years later they added a long, low wall designed to shelter a battery of cannon at water level, oriented to cover the straits. The Ottomans repeated that innovation at a new fortress just across the straits, Rumelihisarı, built in 1452 as part of the campaign against Constantinople. Over the next decade, the Ottomans also built a pair of forts to dominate the Dardanelles strait, Kale-i Sultaniye on the Asian side and Kilitbahir (see Figure 7.9) on the European side. Both strongly resemble the artillery towers that were just beginning to enter European fortifications at that time, and both also repeated the low-lying "water battery" (later modifications have removed most of it in Figure 7.9). These changes, reflecting what Simon Pepper has called a "lively spirit of experimentation" in Ottoman fortress design, continued into the early sixteenth century, most strikingly at the Castle of the Morea (built ca. 1500). That fort, designed to close the straits at the entrance to the Gulf of Corinth, near modern Patras, combined aspects of the angled bastion with the artillery tower at its heart, while retaining some severely conservative medieval qualities.[20]

This period of experimentation appears to have stopped or slowed, however. There is very little evidence that Ottoman fortresses built in the sixteenth and seventeenth centuries adopted the *trace italienne* technique or further refined

Figure 7.9 Ottoman fortress of Kilitbahir, ca. 1460. Built at the entrance to the Dardanelles. The round tower in the left foreground is a later form of artillery tower added in the mid-sixteenth century. A long low wall sheltering a "water battery" of artillery firing out over the straits has been destroyed. It ran along what is now a parking lot.

their own. This is a difficult generalization to prove, in part because there are no surviving Ottoman records of fortress design in this period, nor are there official plans of their forts from the time of their building. Furthermore, there was no equivalent of the European tradition of the printed manual on fort design. Even the late seventeenth-century forts built at the entrance to the Dardanelles at Seddülbahir and Kumkale represent only minor departures from other Ottoman forts on the Dardanelles built two centuries earlier. To be fair, there were many circumstances in which Ottoman planners may have deemed it unnecessary, or not worth the cost, to build new-style forts. Fortifications at Kelepha, Passava, or Zarnata in Greece and Elbasan in Albania, as well as along the pilgrims' route to Mecca, and in Yemen and in other places where the Ottomans seemingly dismissed the threat of major siege trains, all hearkened back to simpler medieval designs, while remaining quite adequate to their purpose. As a general rule the Ottomans appear to have been uninterested in proliferating fortresses; they destroyed some that they captured while preserving key ones. Some scholars have suggested that the expansionist ideology of the Ottomans throughout this period mitigated against permanent frontier fortifications, although they were happy to protect key heartland locations that could be threatened by naval forces. Perhaps most interestingly, although the Habsburgs on the Danubian frontier quickly imported Italian architects in the mid-sixteenth century to update their fortresses, and although those fortresses impressed the Ottomans, when the Ottomans managed to capture many of them they showed little interest in matching them. They instead relied on a few of those captured forts, while innovating a new tradition using ancient construction techniques, building a system of road-linked, cheap, earth-and-timber *palanka* forts. These were designed to defend against small raiding parties or to slow the advance of larger armies, including the advances of Western armies, but not to hold out against a serious siege. It is difficult to place this limited evidence into a single interpretive framework. It seems, however, that the Ottomans made only a limited investment in the artillery fortress, without that having significantly undermined their frontier security. Before making any final conclusions, we must examine the third major arena of gunpowder-related change: infantry.[21]

INFANTRY AND FIREARMS, 1450–1650

As discussed briefly in chapter 5, the basic problem facing medieval infantrymen was how to sustain armed social cohesion sufficient to overcome the physical and mental challenge posed by a charging horseman. Medieval commanders needed infantry for the pervasive sieges and to garrison the walls of castles, but in much of western Europe and among steppe peoples, troops raised solely to serve as infantry were so socially devalued that no real effort was put into making them cohesive in the face of cavalry. For that to happen required either an organically cohesive social group (that otherwise lacked horses) or a strong state willing to invest social resources in equipping and preparing infantrymen. Both types of exceptions existed at various times and places in medieval Europe, generally in those areas with less investment in the heavy horseman, and growing increasingly common and more important in the fourteenth century. We have already seen how English armies combined the raw potential of the longbow with the social investment in years, if not a lifetime, of training. Also important were some urban militias, especially in Italy and the Low Countries. Their organic communal cohesion won them important battlefield victories against horsemen, notably at several battles in Flanders between 1302 and 1304, and again later in the century. Highland and mountain communities also produced high-quality infantry. Kelly DeVries's study of fourteenth-century infantry victories, however, notes that in almost every case successful infantry forces not only chose their ground but had time to prepare it by digging ditches and pits to disrupt the cavalry charge. They then remained in a concentrated line on the defensive, in several cases constructing wagon laagers as a way to protect their flanks. The most effective infantry force of all, the system that produced the longest lasting effects and proved least dependent on extensive prebattle preparation, was the pike phalanx of the Swiss.[22]

Living in relatively egalitarian and autonomous "cantons," the Swiss had long relied on the mountains and their relative poverty to keep larger neighbors at bay. Dragged into conflict first by the Habsburg emperors in the early fourteenth century and then by the Duke of Burgundy in the mid-fifteenth century, the now-confederated Swiss cantons demonstrated that they had evolved a uniquely effective infantry. Organized in large squares of four thousand to eight thousand men each, soldiers fought alongside their neighbors. Armed with pikes and halberds, they marched in step and could move rapidly onto the attack. The square was surprisingly agile, and its members could quickly shift to defend themselves against flank attacks. When a force of cavalry charged and was pulled up short by the wall of pikes, the halberdiers emerged from within the square and used their seven-foot combination of ax blade and hook to drag men from their saddles and even to cut down their horses. The unprecedented success of the Swiss, and especially their apparent offensive capability, encouraged others first to hire them as mercenaries and then to copy the mechanics of their system. As we will see, however, copying the mechanics of a system that originally derived its cohesion from the organic communalism of its members required something new.[23]

Meanwhile firearms that could be handled by individuals were beginning to become available. Most of the earliest forms in Europe were designed to fit naturally into the role considered appropriate for nonnoble men on foot: defending walls. They first proliferated in the independent cities of Germany. These were communities inherently open to anything that would aid in preserving their relative autonomy, which in the end depended on defending their walls. Many of these early firearms, available from the early fifteenth century, were called "hook" guns, simple metal tubes with a hook near the muzzle so that they could be rested on the wall with the hook catching the recoil. From this early stage it made sense that their first use in the field would resemble their use from behind walls. The earliest version appeared during the Hussite Wars, a sectarian peasant rebellion fought in Bohemia from 1419 to as late as 1434, in which, again, a group of mostly nonnobles, without the infrastructure for cavalry, invented a way for infantry to be effective. Their primary solution was the *Wagenburg*: literally circling wagons into a kind of field fortification. They won several notable victories, and the idea spread through the region and beyond. Hook guns and their successors were obvious additions to this basic formula (see Figure 7.10a and b). From this stage, as is already hinted in Figure 7.10b, it was easy to imagine a pike square in the field as a kind of "wall." Adding men with guns to it was a relatively simple mental leap, and combining "pike and shot" into a single formation solved the weaknesses of each alone.[24]

The weaknesses of early firearms are obvious, but it is important to look more closely here at their development, because their real significance emerges as the Europeans invented ways to overcome those weaknesses. Using a hand gun required a good deal less skill than a bow; the earliest ones were simpler to make than crossbows; and they generally had greater armor-penetrating power than either. Their main weaknesses were the slow reloading process and a

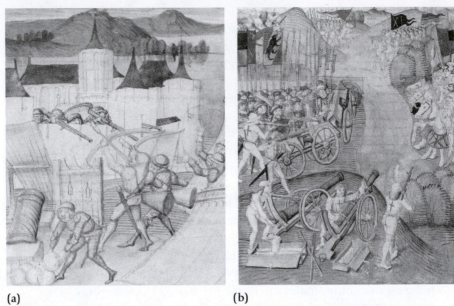

(a)   (b)

Figure 7.10 *a* & *b* Early use of firearms, from behind walls and portable walls. These two images from the Bern Chronicle, ca. 1480, show infantry using hook guns from behind a castle wall in 7.10a and then from behind a wagon laager in 7.10b.

serious lack of accuracy beyond about fifty meters. Hook guns required one hand to hold the "handle" and another to lower a lighted match to the touchhole. European smiths searched for a solution to that problem, and German gunsmiths invented the matchlock arquebus (in which squeezing a lever lowered a length of lighted match to the touchhole) in the mid-fifteenth century. From this initial effort a number of different evolutionary tracks produced a bewildering variety of types, complicated by the different languages used to describe them. Generally differentiated by their weight, their length, and the weight of ball, there were arquebuses, hackbutts, calivers, muskets, "drunken" muskets, and more. Design evolution was driven at first by a competition with armor; the heavier Spanish musket succeeded (and overlapped with) the arquebus by the mid-sixteenth century because men, especially horsemen, were demanding thicker armor. As body armor was gradually abandoned in the mid- to late-seventeenth century (especially by infantry), muskets again got lighter and smaller (the twenty-pound Spanish musket required a rest to shoot it).

None of this technological improvement solved the problem of slow reloading. Manipulating two different kinds of gunpowder (one for the charge, and one for priming the touchhole) and loading and ramming the ball into the muzzle, all while maintaining a grip on a weapon weighing from ten to twenty pounds, sometimes on a rest, and always with a lighted match (lit on both ends, just in case), required time and some degree of skill. A musketeer might get off one shot per minute. Given their relatively short range and the lack of accuracy inherent to a round ball shot from a smooth tube (the rough equivalent of a

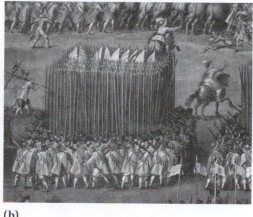

(a)   (b)

Figure 7.11 *a & b* **An arquebusier with matchlock, and a formation of pike and shot, early seventeenth century.** 7.11a shows a matchlock arquebusier from Jacques de Gheyn's famous manual of arms published in 1607. 7.11b is a detail from Pieter Snayer's mid-seventeenth-century painting of the Battle of White Mountain, here showing a pike square surrounded by a "sleeve" of "shot."

knuckleball pitch in terms of its aerodynamic unpredictability), a formation of men equipped with such weapons alone on the battlefield might get off one volley before being run down by charging cavalry.[25]

This danger led to combining musketeers into formations with pikemen. European armies experimented with various formations and ratios, generally increasing the number of musketeers over the sixteenth century as their rate of fire improved with training and technological refinement. The varying assortments of armor and weaponry required generals of the period to solve complex tactical problems, making sure that the right kind of soldier was in the appropriate place at the appropriate time. They were manipulating early field artillery, at least two kinds of cavalry, and usually three different kinds of infantry. It might be thought of as a kind of rock, paper, scissors game but with six options instead of three.

Reformers sought to simplify this problem. One way to do so was to increase the firepower of a formation of musketeers so that they could protect themselves. Several suggestions emerged in the 1570s and 1580s to produce continuous volley fire, but nothing much was attempted in practice until

1594. In a letter to his cousin, the Dutch general Maurice of Nassau, William Lodewijk suggested the "countermarch" system, in which a deep formation of musketeers (say eight to ten men) would produce continuous fire. The leading rank would fire, and then turn and march to the rear of the formation to begin the reloading process. Each rank would fire in turn, and by the time the original rank returned to the front, they would have reloaded. Alternatively, the first ranker could stand still and the man behind him would march to the front, advancing the formation slowly as it fired.

Central to making the idea work was a new understanding of training and discipline, explicitly built on ancient Roman texts—and so not new at all, but rediscovered. Intrigued, Maurice advocated the technique, although it was not used in battle until at least 1600 at Nieuwpoort against the Spanish. That rediscovery profoundly changed European military culture. Although the countermarch and the associated view of training and discipline in part proceeded from gunpowder, it was not an inevitable result. The countermarch was calculated, but it also emerged from and engaged with a broader cultural current of thought related to obedience and discipline in battle, and it interacted further with specific cultural prejudices about the men recruited as infantry. The result, uniform collective synchronized discipline, demands detailed consideration in its own right.[26]

Collective Synchronized Discipline

As discussed in chapter 4, the Romans had created a system of training designed not only to enhance the individual skills of their recruits but also to coordinate their tactical movements in a synchronized way. Vegetius, writing in the late fourth or early fifth century CE and lamenting a decline in Roman infantry, sang the praises of this then-bygone system. He praised both the individual toughness it developed and also its regularity. He called for commanders who would train soldiers "diligently," noting that they would find victory through drill-at-arms, and would acquire military expertise only through "constant exercises" and by practice moving into and out of precisely regulated linear formations.[27]

Vegetius became the most commonly read of the ancient military authors. His text passed down through many translated editions during the Middle Ages and even into the present.[28] Over the long course of the medieval period, however, his emphasis on regularity and drill had been transmuted into an emphasis on individual skill—an emphasis more in accord with the medieval vision of the role of the knightly horseman. Several fourteenth-century military advice books, some based more or less loosely on Vegetius himself, clearly emphasized individual skill and individualistic virtues as a knight's primary requirement. Christine de Pizan's widely circulated 1410 manuscript, for example, *The Books of Deeds of Arms and of Chivalry*, much of which follows Vegetius section by section, converted one of his most famous admonitions, that a good general must "train soldiers diligently," into "[He] must be adept with arms . . . [and he] should fight with competence.[29] One scholar summed up this medieval advice literature by describing its "utterly tireless, almost obsessional emphasis placed on personal prowess as the key chivalric trait."[30]

The medieval martial literature also emphasized obedience, and there is no question that medieval leaders demanded it. Certainly their battlefield formations eschewed chaotic individualism, but to a curious extent the emphasis on obedience in the advice literature was pitched to restrain excessive individual boldness—it was not on drill or formation. It is true that many medieval narrative accounts refer to closely packed, linear, and seemingly articulated ranks of infantry and cavalry (although the evidence for this among cavalry seems to decline in the late fourteenth and into the fifteenth century). Many of those same accounts, however, could be interpreted merely as an army staying together, rather than as depictions of men fighting in mutual support—something very hard to do from horseback in any circumstance.

This ethic of obedience and an awareness of the cohesive effects of tight formations provided an element of continuity upon which the new pike square began to build. That formation succeeded only through coordinated action, however, and its interplay of pikemen and halberdiers already suggests *synchronized* movement (much like the Han Chinese infantry formations described in chapter 4). Simple obedience by men in closely packed ranks is not the same thing as synchronized movement imposed through discipline, training, and drill. Although the Swiss pike formation's success derived from its organic communalism and some basic drill, and later from the steadiness of veterans, new men recruited into such a system required more thorough training. Some early experimenters even combined pikemen with archers, requiring a different kind of disciplined synchronization.[31]

The pike square's success led to a renewed interest in drill, now increasingly understood to be synchronized, edging closer to Vegetius' original meaning. Matthew Sutcliffe, for example, writing in 1593, saw the synchronization of parts as key: without "array & order" he wrote, "armes have no use." "As well can an armie march or fight being out of array," he continued, "as a body doe the functions of the body, having the partes out of frame," and success required "instruction and exercise." It was in this context of a classics-inspired professional military literature that William Lodewijk wrote the very next year to Maurice of Nassau describing the countermarch.[32]

The musketeers' countermarch required a new level of synchronization. It was more than a soldier shifting from the front to the back of a formation, or moving in and out of a square of pikemen: the countermarch was also about reloading. Every individual motion was to be conducted collectively to produce safe and simultaneous volleys of fire. The pike and the countermarch provided the tactical framework for a new vision of discipline, but a crucial further aspect of the shift in Europe was the wide social gap between the leadership and the lower-order men recruited as pikemen or musketeers. Elite leaders presumed that such men could be effective only if tightly controlled and directed by the "naturally" martial elite—who increasingly served as officers rather than warriors. Gunpowder did not *require* synchronization of effort. Rather, a cultural prejudice about those who would wield it suggested that disciplined synchronization was the only way to make it effective. In addition, shot had to be combined with pikes for their mutual protection, further increasing the need for synchronicity and incidentally imposing greater discipline on the pikemen as well (slowing the aggressive charge originally pioneered by the Swiss). Army components now had to march, fire, and maneuver in sync with other component parts. It was thus the emergence of a technology within a particular vision of social hierarchy and then filtered through a rediscovered Roman model that defined how an army should act. On this new imagined battlefield, firmly laid out, if not yet fully implemented, by the end of the sixteenth century, individualism had no place, aside from elite commanders' continued occasional quixotic challenges to single combat.[33]

The importance of this shift cannot be overstated. In essence, the sixteenth century saw the demand for skilled, but hopefully obedient, individuals working together replaced by a demand for units of soldiers shaped by synchronized collective discipline under the control of a martial elite. The difference between the two is subtle but significant, especially in its long-term implications for European military culture. Individual skill at arms was not disregarded, and it retained its chivalric appeal for the elite, but in a way that was both calculated and cultural, such skill was subordinated to group movement. We will see that this shift also had an impact on capacity, but first let us consider the Ottoman case.

Ottoman Janissaries, Volley Fire, and the Ironic Indiscipline of Slaves

The cultural and ecological origins of the Ottoman state privileged the horseman. Despite becoming a sedentary Anatolian and European power as early as the mid-fourteenth century, the Ottomans maintained the primacy of the mounted archer, although now in more varied forms. Like their European counterparts, however, they needed infantrymen for a variety of purposes, most importantly for laying sieges. True, nomads could and regularly would dismount to fight on foot, as did European knights, but it mattered to them that they rode to war, and their weapons were designed for fighting from horseback. In those circumstances, how does one recruit pure infantry? Islamic tradition provided a viable solution in the slave soldier. Islamic law allowed the enslavement of non-Muslims, and long tradition within the Islamic world endowed household slaves with a level of prestige and privilege consonant with the social status of their master. Furthermore, rulers used slaves to form a service aristocracy in order to distance and elevate their sovereign power from their free subjects. Unlike a landed, bloodline-based aristocracy, slave servitors owed their whole position and status to their master. The same principle could be extended to military service. The early Ottoman sultans claimed a percentage of the captives taken in war and incorporated them into their household as slaves. Converted to Islam (which did not technically free them) and trained as soldiers, these men gained the prestige associated with being in the personal household of the imperial ruler. From the late fourteenth through the late fifteenth century, this force of infantry, the janissaries, remained relatively small, and fought with spears and bows in a more or less traditional fashion, although they were considered particularly elite and effective. The Ottomans thus became among the first powers in several centuries on the European continent to develop an elite, salaried, and standing force of infantry. As the Ottoman Empire expanded, so did the janissary corps—slowly at first—recruiting new members through the *devşirme*, the collection and impressment into imperial service of Christian children from within the empire.

The Ottomans thus found themselves in possession of an ideal force to equip with firearms. Although the Ottomans were using siege cannon (discussed above) probably by the 1380s, it was during the 1440s that they fought against Hungarian leader János Hunyadi, who was using the *Wagenburg* tactics that he had copied from the Hussites. Recognizing its effectiveness, the Ottomans adapted a version of it, calling it the *tabur cengi*, or "camp battle." It was likely in Ottoman use by 1473, and is clearly attested from the 1560s, in later incarnations taking the form not of circled wagons but of cannon linked together by lengths of chain. Janissaries had begun using firearms in the mid-fifteenth century, and by the mid-sixteenth century the majority of janissaries were armed that way, now often lined up in ranks behind the linked cannons. The Ottoman army used its large force of cavalry on the wings to try to force the enemy into the immobile, fire-power-heavy center. For most of the sixteenth century their European foes often credited Ottoman firepower for their success, but the Europeans were in the midst of increasing their own firepower, and when the Long War of 1593–1603 broke out, the Ottomans were surprised to find themselves outgunned, both by firearms and by field artillery. The pressures of that war then led the Ottomans to institute two major reforms, one in tactics, and one in recruitment.[34]

Tactically, there is good evidence that the Ottomans invented a form of volley fire, and that they did so long before Maurice of Nassau. A potential version of drilled volley fire may have been in use as early as the 1526 Battle of Mohács (see Figure 7.12). The Ottomans were not trying to protect themselves from the threat of a cavalry charge; their chained cannon did that. Over time, however, concerned about their volume of fire, they created a

Figure 7.12 Ottoman janissaries at the Battle of Mohacs, 1526. The janissaries are lined up behind chained field artillery pieces that provide protection from charging cavalry. They appear to be conducting an early form of volley fire.

more advanced drill to increase it. The first textual description from 1605 is unequivocal in its description of drilled, synchronized volley fire:

> The Janissary regiments stood in three ranks, each musketeer with matches ready [to fire], and they lined up the big cannons chained in front of the Janissaries. Then after the first rank of the Janissaries fires their muskets, the second rank fires, too. Afterwards, the rank that fired first bends double and begins to reload their muskets. And as the third rank fires, the second rank in front [of them] bends and prepares their muskets. Then the first rank again stands up and fires their muskets.[35]

In addition, there is visual evidence of janissaries performing what appears to be the same drill during the Long War, as early as 1597, after William Lodewijk's letter describing the countermarch, but well before any European army had actually tried it in the field.

The other reform was to enlarge the janissary corps, with serious long-term consequences. Emphasizing firepower required more musketeers, and the timariot cavalry, like all noblemen whose martial role was defined by the horse, were unlikely material for footmen. In one instance in 1548, they resisted attempts to issue them pistols, as they believed the firearms were dirty and made them look ridiculous. Furthermore, from a broader perspective, the horse archer was still a critical resource, especially on the Ottomans' eastern and steppe frontiers. The Ottomans did raise some other types of infantry, but the janissaries were the primary and most privileged users of firearms. The corps jumped from an average of seven thousand to ten thousand throughout the sixteenth century to forty-five thousand to fifty thousand in the seventeenth—all of them salaried by the state. This drastic increase in the corps naturally changed the way they were recruited. The reliance on captives and the *devşirme* faded, replaced by men actively seeking the privilege and salary associated with membership, often even the sons of janissaries, although that was nominally against the rules. Although the janissaries served in garrisons throughout the empire, many of them resided in the capital, and in time their continued status as privileged armed slaves of the sultan made them, like the

Roman Praetorian Guard, arbiters of succession. In addition to this disruptive political role, they also became militarily conservative, and their political power allowed them to enforce their preferences. Although they may have been among the first to adopt volley fire, and they had clearly developed a form of drill to practice it, their social privilege left them resistant to the full military culture of uniform, collective, synchronized discipline, which in Europe depended on the social differentiation between an elite officer corps and commoner recruits. To be clear, this narrative of change within the janissary corps and their use of firearms does not encompass or explain the whole history of Ottoman military power and its decline. Quite a number of other forms of infantry existed, and other developments, especially in the late seventeenth and the eighteenth century, undermined the capacity of the Ottoman state—primarily the decentralization of armed force and taxation authority to provincial governors.[36]

Nevertheless, note how telling this story comparatively deemphasizes both the technology and even the specific technique of volley fire. What really seems to matter is the imposition of discipline in a specific way allowed by sociocultural norms. Eventually that type of imposed discipline became the norm in Europe, in time shedding the connotations of servility or lower-class status, and it continued to yield powerful battlefield results. Long after the simple mechanism of volley fire had been technologically superseded, European collective, synchronized discipline remained at the core of building a biddable mass of infantry.

The Seventeenth Century and the Crucible of War

Part of the argument here has been that the pressures of the Long War between the Ottomans and the Habsburgs on the Hungarian frontier drove tactical and institutional reform in the Ottoman army. Prolonged and intensive conflict often plays that role. The Long War has gained increasing scholarly attention as a crucible of change in southeastern Europe. Some scholars have argued that it saw the Austrians pull ahead of the Ottomans in battlefield capability, based on the pike-and-shot model, which proved impervious to the charge of the Ottoman cavalry. Others argue that the Ottoman threat pushed forward European transformations. This argument is not about tactics but about capacity. The late sixteenth-century centralized Ottoman state outstripped its contemporary opponents with its capacity to raise, supply, and move large armies. Those capabilities forced similar adaptations by the Habsburgs, and possibly by the Romanovs in Russia, in what sociologists call "institutional isomorphism," in which organizations competing side by side grow to resemble each other.[37]

A similar process has long been associated with the European Thirty Years War (1618–48). That conflict, centered in Germany but embroiling virtually every European power and infamous for its devastation and destruction, accelerated changes in European tactical systems. Most notably, King Gustavus Adolphus of Sweden improved on and spread Maurice's volley-fire tactics, while also creating a more mobile form of field artillery. Pike and shot continued to dominate, but the increasing role of volley fire emphasized the shot. The tactical evolution toward infantry firepower finally culminated with the invention of the bayonet in the late seventeenth century, first issued to troops by the French army in 1671. The bayonet, first in a "plug" form inserted into the muzzle, and later socketed to fit around the muzzle, allowed a musketeer to be his own pikeman. This greatly simplified the general's tactical dilemma, returning the battlefield to the three-part rock-paper-scissors game of infantry, cavalry, and artillery.

One interpretation of the eventual Ottoman decline relative to western Europe has focused on their failure to keep up with the changes spurred by the Thirty Years War. For much of the first half of the seventeenth century the Ottomans remained at relative peace and lacked the pressure to innovate, although they were certainly masters of the current technology. That theory is difficult to sustain, however. From 1645 the Ottomans embarked on decades of almost continuous war against Venice in Crete and against the Habsburgs in Hungary and the Balkans, right up to the final failed siege of Vienna in 1683. Furthermore, we should not consider the Ottomans as a proxy for "the East" while considering "the West" as a unified whole. Ottoman decline was no more dramatic than Portuguese or Spanish decline. Finally, it is now generally held that Ottoman relative decline began only in the 1680s, caused primarily by their deteriorating logistical capability in the face of wars on numerous fronts—many of those wars generated by changing patterns of alliances among European powers. Other, more recent scholarship acknowledges that the Ottomans fell behind by the eighteenth century, but that they recognized the problem, actively tracked developments in Europe, and followed up with reforms that kept them nearly current.[38]

CONCLUSION: A MILITARY REVOLUTION?

The question of relative Ottoman decline (or not) compared to the powers of western Europe brings us to the question of whether changes during this period related to gunpowder (or not) constituted a "military revolution." This idea and the debate over it has been one of the most prolific and productive fields in military history in recent decades—almost nothing written about the period between 1300 and 1900 can ignore the concept. Without reviewing the idea's whole long development, the basic concept has three parts: (1) sometime between 1400 and 1700 a revolutionary change occurred in the European military system related to the use of gunpowder, the demands of which (2) pushed forward processes of state centralization and modernization, especially in fiscal terms, and in combination those two developments (3) enabled the global expansion of European hegemony. Notice that each of these changes could separately be called "revolutionary." The first alone could be revolutionary within a strictly military sphere, even if it was not responsible for the other two.[39]

The most influential formulation of this thesis is the one advanced by Geoffrey Parker. He argues that the revolution in the European military system occurred in three stages: (1) siege cannon overcame the medieval castle between 1450 and 1500, leading to (2) the Italian invention of the bastioned artillery fortress from 1520 onwards, followed by (3) the rise in the significance and size of infantry forces in response to the demands of sieges and especially after the invention of volley fire in 1594. Critically, Parker also relates these three developments to European dominance at sea and their initial expansion around the globe. The connections among gunpowder, sea power, and colonialism will be discussed in the next chapter, but for now, based on the evidence in this chapter, we can ask if Europe had achieved a significant advantage over their Ottoman neighbors by 1700. We can also begin to assess whether these military changes in turn led to European state centralization. With regard to state development, Parker's argument, much refined by others, is that the expense of artillery parks and especially of bastioned fortifications favored strong centralized states. These progressively developed their fiscal capability and then enlarged their forces through hiring mercenaries, and later (as we will see in chapter 9) developed national professional armies.

Two important challenges have emerged to this idea. One is that neither the artillery parks nor the fortifications systems drastically changed the costs of war. Azar Gat has compiled evidence showing that fortifications continued to constitute relatively small percentages of state expenditure, often only 5–10 percent, and reaching 17 percent only during the radical program of fortification conducted in late seventeenth-century France by Sébastien Le Prestre de Vauban. Similarly, artillery costs in European states hovered around only 4–8 percent of overall military expenditure. Gat goes on to argue that it was not the cost of these systems that undermined smaller states or autonomous nobles, but rather that stronger national-territorial states came first—their development preceded rather than resulted from changes in warfare. They simply overwhelmed their smaller opponents based on their larger capacity. What really determined costs in the late medieval and early modern era were wages and logistics. In that sense, one might argue that the increase in the size of armies might demand more of a state's capacity—whether connected to forts or not. To that Gat argues that the increase in army size is an illusion when compared to the concurrent rise in European population. His survey of European state armies shows that although they did grow, most remained at 1–2 percent of the population over any sustained period—only radical social reconfigurations or wartime mobilizations might briefly produce greater numbers. Gat's statistics are not definitive, nor are they sufficiently developed for the whole period from 1400 to 1700, but they undermine the thesis that gunpowder and its follow-on effects led to an increase in army size.[40]

On yet another hand, however, introducing chemical energy onto the battlefield did allow a vast expansion in the pool of potential recruits, at least insofar as most Europeans imagined recruiting. For the preceding several centuries martial skill had been perceived to depend on a lifetime's training, as a knight, or perhaps as a longbowman. This expectation of skill limited the pool of recruits. It is true that a cohesive block of pikemen or a corps of cross-bowmen required less individual skill than a knight on horseback, and they had proven their effectiveness on the battlefield prior to the significant development of handguns. It was the chemical energy of the handgun, however, that truly opened the doors to recruiting just about anyone, who now could, with a relatively minimal amount of training, kill the most skilled opponent from a distance. This shift *enabled* growth in army size, even if it did not *require* it. In fact, the logistical limits on the size of a single field army remained (without regard to the population from which it was drawn): only so many men could be in one place at one time and still feed themselves. Chemical energy was replacing muscle power on the battlefield, but muscle power (human or animal) still moved their supplies (unless there was convenient water transportation nearby), and the carriers of those supplies consumed them even as they carried them, limiting the range of action and the size of the force they could supply. When army sizes did rise and logistics faltered or failed, unfed soldiers turned on the countryside, escalating the devastation and destruction of war.[41]

Where does this all leave us? Turning to our comparative case, it seems clear that the Ottoman state did not centralize because of gunpowder or its effects; they rose to power initially on the backs of the highly effective steppe archer/cavalryman combined with effective leadership. They continued expanding because of the existing strength of their state and of their bureaucratic capacity. They also proved technologically flexible, keen to incorporate new ideas and systems, a process aided by a mode of conquest that welcomed peoples of all kinds (called "renegades" by their Christian enemies). As suggested earlier, the Ottomans' power may even have encouraged centralization by the Habsburgs and Romanov Russia. Relative Ottoman decline did not begin until the late seventeenth century at the earliest, marked more by a decline in state capacity than by any lack of technological capability (although there may be value in exploring further the role of European print culture in the rapid dissemination and improvement of ideas). In one historian's view, the Ottoman Empire "evolved into a decentralized, limited monarchy whose history between 1617 and 1730 witnessed seven dethronements out of ten reigns, and where the central government's control over resources and the means of organized violence was limited by local power brokers and thus considerably diminished compared not just to its rivals but also to its own 16th-century self."[42]

By the beginning of the eighteenth century, key European states were centralizing power to a greater degree than their immediate neighbors, but the Ottoman example shows that we cannot simply explain that process by the introduction of gunpowder, artillery parks, fortifications, or even the growth of infantry armies using volley fire. The Ottomans did all of those things, but they nevertheless experienced a loss of centralized state capacity by the late seventeenth century. European logistical and fiscal bureaucracies, meanwhile, became more sophisticated, and their military techniques were further refined (if not revolutionized) in the crucible of the Thirty Years War. The most critical military refinement was not technological but social: collective synchronized drill, shaped initially by the social prejudices of the elite, but eventually accepted as a cultural value in its own right.

TIMELINE

1320s	First cannon in Europe
1380	First "hand cannons" in Europe; Ottomans using cannon
1420s	Artillery becoming effective at destroying castle walls
1440s	Janissaries begin using firearms
1453	Ottomans capture Constantinople
1460	Matchlock arquebus spreading in Europe
1520	*Trace italienne*–style fortification becoming common in Italy
1590s	Janissaries using volley fire
1594	William Lodewijk proposes the countermarch volley-fire system
1618–1648	Thirty Years War

Technology did matter. Firearms would become more sophisticated, and they played a more direct role in enabling colonial and imperial expansion against those who lacked them, or who had not invested in their development. But, as of 1650 (at least), the Ottomans were just as technologically sophisticated as the Europeans. We must turn to the next chapter to explore what role cannons, forts, and firearms played outside Europe, as well as the role of the ships that carried them.

Further Reading

Ágoston, Gábor. *Guns for the Sultan: Military Power and the Weapons Industry in the Ottoman Empire.* Cambridge, UK: Cambridge University Press, 2005.

Black, Jeremy. *A Military Revolution? Military Change and European Society, 1550–1800.* Basingstoke, UK: Macmillan, 1991.

Chase, Kenneth Warren. *Firearms: A Global History to 1700.* Cambridge, UK: Cambridge University Press, 2003.

Cipolla, Carlo M. *Guns, Sails and Empires: Technological Innovation and the Early Phases of European Expansion, 1400–1700.* New York: Pantheon, 1966.

Hall, Bert S. *Weapons and Warfare in Renaissance Europe: Gunpowder, Technology, and Tactics.* Baltimore, MD: Johns Hopkins University Press, 1997.

McNeill, William H. *The Pursuit of Power: Technology, Armed Force, and Society since*

A.D. 1000. Chicago: University of Chicago Press, 1982.

Murphey, Rhoads. *Ottoman Warfare, 1500–1700.* New Brunswick, NJ: Rutgers University Press, 1999.

Parker, Geoffrey. *The Military Revolution: Military Innovation and the Rise of the West, 1500–1800.* 2nd ed. Cambridge, UK: Cambridge University Press, 1996.

Rogers, Clifford, ed. *The Military Revolution Debate: Readings on the Transformation of Early Modern Europe.* Boulder, CO: Westview, 1995.

Tallett, Frank, and D. J. B. Trim, eds. *European Warfare, 1350–1750.* Cambridge, UK: Cambridge University Press, 2010.

Notes

1. Geoffrey Parker, *The Military Revolution: Military Innovation and the Rise of the West, 1500–1800*, 2nd ed. (Cambridge, UK: Cambridge University Press, 1996), 5.

2. Bert S. Hall, *Weapons and Warfare in Renaissance Europe: Gunpowder, Technology, and Tactics* (Baltimore: Johns Hopkins University Press, 1997), 41–42; Kenneth Warren Chase, *Firearms: A Global History to 1700* (Cambridge, UK: Cambridge University Press, 2003), 31–32.

3. Iqtidar Alam Khan, "Coming of Gunpowder to the Islamic World and North India: Spotlight on the Role of the Mongols," *Journal of Asian History* 30 (1996): 41–45; Thomas T. Allsen, "The Circulation of Military Technology in the Mongolian Empire," in *Warfare in Inner Asian History, 500–1800*, ed. Nicola Di Cosmo (Leiden: Brill, 2002), 272–84; A. Y. al-Hassan, ed., *Science and Technology in Islam*, Part 2, *Technology and Applied Sciences* (Paris: UNESCO Publishing, 2001), 107–34, esp. 130, has Arab use of cannon against Mongols in 1260, and very early in Spain (1248, and the 1320s and 1330s, the latter better supported). See also Gábor Ágoston, *Guns for the Sultan: Military Power and the Weapons Industry in the Ottoman Empire* (Cambridge, UK: Cambridge University Press, 2005), 15; Chase, *Firearms*, 58–59; Hall, *Weapons*, 42.

4. Hall, *Weapons*, 43, 74–75; André Guillerme, *The Age of Water: The Urban Environment in the North of France, A.D. 300–1800* (College Station: Texas A&M University Press, 1988), 138–40.

5. Castle function and proliferation: Philippe Contamine, *War in the Middle Ages* (Oxford: Basil Blackwell, 1984), 46, 109; John France, *Western Warfare in the Age of the Crusades, 1000–1300* (Ithaca, NY: Cornell University Press, 1999), 77–90; Robert Bartlett, *The Making of Europe: Conquest, Colonization and Cultural Change, 950–1350* (Princeton, NJ: Princeton University Press, 1993), 69.

6. This section mostly follows Clifford Rogers, "The Military Revolutions of the Hundred Years War," in *The Military Revolution Debate: Readings on the Transformation of Early Modern Europe*, ed. Clifford Rogers (Boulder, CO: Westview, 1995), 64–73. I am grateful for his repeated consultation on this subject. Also: Peter Purton, *A History of the Late Medieval Siege, 1200–1500* (Woodbridge, UK: Boydell, 2010), 401–6; Hall, *Weapons*, 44–47, 58–60, 65–66; Carlo M. Cipolla, *Guns, Sails and Empires: Technological Innovation and the Early Phases of European Expansion, 1400–1700* (New York: Pantheon, 1966), 27.

7. Rogers, "Military Revolutions," 65 (quote), 66, 69; also Hall, *Weapons*, 57. Trebuchets could sometimes breach walls, and had led to thicker medieval fortifications. They could also damage wall furnishings and reduce their effectiveness. See

Clifford J. Rogers, *Soldiers' Lives through History: The Middle Ages* (Westport, CT: Greenwood , 2007), 121–23, 150–51n46 and 54.

8. Hall, *Weapons*, 63–65, 79–80, 92; Rogers, "Military Revolutions," 66–69; cf. Kelly DeVries, "The Impact of Gunpowder Weaponry on Siege Warfare in the Hundred Years' War," in *Guns and Men in Medieval Europe, 1200–1500* (Burlington, VT: Ashgate, 2002), 227–44. A chart in Thomas Arnold, *The Renaissance at War* (London: Cassell, 2001), 38, shows mid-sixteenth-century barrel-length ratios.

9. Hall, *Weapons*, 66, 94 (quote), 123, 130–31; Rogers, "Military Revolutions"; Parker, *Military Revolution*, 8; Jeremy Black, *War in the World: A Comparative History, 1450–1600* (New York: Palgrave Macmillan, 2011), 30, 37.

10. Rhoads Murphey, "Ottoman Expansion, 1451–1556, I. Consolidation of Regional Power, 1451–1503," in *Early Modern Military History, 1450–1815*, ed. Geoff Mortimer (New York: Palgrave, 2004), 44, 78; Rhoads Murphey, *Ottoman Warfare, 1500–1700* (New Brunswick, NJ: Rutgers University Press, 1999); Colin Imber, *The Ottoman Empire, 1300–1650: The Structure of Power* (New York: Palgrave, 2003), 257; Gábor Ágoston, "Empires and Warfare in East-Central Europe, 1550–1750: The Ottoman-Habsburg Rivalry and Military Transformation," in *European Warfare, 1350–1750*, ed. Frank Tallett and D. J. B. Trim (Cambridge, UK: Cambridge University Press, 2010): 114–15.

11. Ágoston, "Empires and Warfare," 116–17; Ágoston, *Guns for the Sultan*, 1, 17–18, 20–21, 28–29; Gábor Ágoston, "Firearms and Military Adaptation: The Ottomans and the European Military Revolution," *Journal of World History* 25 (2014): 110–11; Colin Imber, "Ibrahim Peçevi on War: A Note on the 'European Military Revolution,'" in *Frontiers of Ottoman Studies: State, Province, and the West*, ed. Colin Imber,

Keiko Kiyotaki, and Rhoads Murphey (London: I. B. Tauris, 2005), 2:8–9. Kelly DeVries argues that their role may have been overplayed. "Gunpowder Weapons at the Siege of Constantinople, 1453," in *Guns and Men*, 343–62. Simon Pepper agrees that other factors such as mining and especially Ottoman numbers were most important. Simon Pepper, "Ottoman Military Architecture in the Early Gunpowder Era: A Reassessment," in *City Walls: The Urban Enceinte in Global Perspective*, ed. James D. Tracy (Cambridge, UK: Cambridge University Press, 2000), 293–94.

12. This paragraph based primarily on Ágoston, *Guns for the Sultan*, 8–10, 196–98, and Murphey, *Ottoman Warfare*, 106–11. For iron cannon, see John Frances Guilmartin, *Gunpowder and Galleys: Changing Technology and Mediterranean Warfare at Sea in the 16th Century*, rev. ed. (Annapolis, MD: Naval Institute Press, 2003), 182–83. Cast-iron cannon were invented first in England in 1543 and became widely available in northern Europe in 1580s, in the Mediterranean a bit later. Because of their weight, they were mostly used at sea or in coastal fortifications.

13. Since it was cast from bronze and not built up in iron, we technically should not call it a bombard, but our sources from the period did use that word (in addition to others). Orban's was cast in Adrianople over a three-month period. The barrel may have been between twenty and twenty-six feet long and it fired a round stone ball weighing between 1,200 and 1,800 pounds, much to the amazement of the city's defenders. Marios Philippides and Walter K. Hanak, *The Siege and the Fall of Constantinople in 1453: Historiography, Topography, and Military Studies* (Burlington, VT: Ashgate, 2011), 413–28. Ágoston, *Guns for the Sultan*, 42–48, 192–93 (also chapters 4–6 on the dependency theory in general).

14. Black, *War in the World*, 111–13, 216; Jeremy Black, *War in the Eighteenth-Century World* (New York: Palgrave Macmillan, 2013), 69. For compendia of European military publications see Max Jähns, *Geschichte der Kriegswissenschaften: Vornehmlich in Deutschland*, 2 vols. (Munich: Oldenbourg, 1889); J. D. Cockle, *A Bibliography of English Military Books Up to 1642 and of Contemporary Foreign Books* (London: Simpkin, Marshall, Hamilton, Kent, 1900). Systematic comparison to the recent bibliography of Ottoman military works is needed. Ekmeleddin Ihsanoğlu et al., eds., *Osmanlı askerlik literatürü tarihi = History of Military Art and Science Literature during the Ottoman Period*, 2 vols. (Istanbul: IRCICA, 2004), xiii–xix; Gábor Ágoston, "The Ottoman Empire and the Technological Dialogue between Europe and Asia: The Case of Military Technology and Know-How in the Gunpowder Age," in *Science Between Europe and Asia: Historical Studies on the Transmission, Adoption and Adaptation of Knowledge*, ed. Feza Günergun and Dhruv Raina (New York: Springer, 2011), 27–39.

15. Francesco Gucciardini, *The History of Italy*, trans. Austin Parke Goddard (London: Z. Stuart, 1758), 1:147–49.

16. David Potter, *Renaissance France at War: Armies, Culture and Society, c. 1480–1560* (Woodbridge, UK: Boydell, 2008), 153–54.

17. DeVries, "Impact of Gunpowder Weaponry," 233–44.

18. Arnold, *Renaissance at War*, 57; Thomas F. Arnold, "The Geometry of Power: War in the Age of Early Modern Military Revolution, 1500–1800," paper presented at the Society for Military History Conference, April 8, 1994. Jeremy Black also discusses the interplay of mathematics, geometry, and European military thinking in Jeremy Black, *Beyond the Military Revolution: War in the Seventeenth-Century World* (New York: Palgrave Macmillan, 2011), 189–194.

19. Parker, *Military Revolution*; Geoffrey Parker, "The Artillery Fortress as an Engine of Overseas Expansion, 1480–1750," in *Success Is Never Final: Empire, War, and Faith in Early Modern Europe* (New York: Basic Books, 2002), 192–221.

20. Pepper, "Ottoman Military Architecture," 301–4 (quote 301); David Nicolle, *Ottoman Fortifications, 1300–1710* (Oxford: Osprey, 2010), 51. Details on the fort at Patras in Kevin Andrews, *Castles of the Morea*, rev. ed. (Princeton, NJ: American School of Classical Studies at Athens, 2006), 130–34 and plate 30.

21. There is a brief overview in Black, *War in the World*, 174–75. One possible exception is New Navarino, built in 1573, which incorporates a number of features meant to accommodate artillery that do not appear to follow Italian designs. See Andrews, *Castles*, 49–57 and plates 7, 8, 11–13. There may be other examples, but this is not a well-studied field. In general the Ottomans often seem to have relied on whatever fortifications they found, altering them slightly but rarely building wholly new systems. Nor did they establish new urban communities needing a new fort. See Andrew Wheatcroft, *The Enemy at the Gate: Habsburgs, Ottomans and the Battle for Europe* (New York: Basic Books, 2008), 57, 61; Burcu Özgüven, "Palanka Forts and Construction Activity in the Late Ottoman Balkans," in *The Frontiers of the Ottoman World*, ed. A. C. S. Peacock (Oxford: British Academy, 2009), 176n15; Amir Pašić, *Islamic Architecture in Bosnia and Hercegovina*, trans. Midhat Ridjanović (Istanbul: Org of the Islamic Conference, 1994), 13–39; Mark L. Stein, *Guarding the Frontier: Ottoman Border Forts and Garrisons in Europe* (London: Tauris Academic Studies, 2007), 48; Lucienne Thys-Şenocak, *Ottoman Women Builders: The Architectural Patronage of Hadice Turhan Sultan* (Burlington, VT: Ashgate, 2007), 107–80, esp. 172–75; Slobodan Ćurčić, *Architecture in the Balkans: From Diocletian to Süleyman the Magnificent* (New Haven, CT: Yale University Press,

2010), 766–775, discusses several of these forts; for Zarnata (built in the 1670s) see Andrews, *Castles*, 16–20. I have personally surveyed and drawn Kelepha and Passava. For the pilgrim forts: Andrew Petersen, "The Ottoman Conquest of Arabia and the Syrian Hajj Route," in *The Frontiers of the Ottoman World*, ed. A. C. S. Peacock (Oxford: British Academy, 2009), 81–94. For arrival of Italian architects: Ágoston, "Empires and Warfare," 118–19; Ágoston, *Guns for the Sultan*, 194–95; Murphey, *Otto-man Warfare*, 111. For Ottoman impres-sions of Habsburg fortress at Uyvar: Murphey, *Ottoman Warfare*, 113. For palankas: Nicolle, *Ottoman Fortifications*, 21; Burcu Özgüven, "The Palanka: A Char-acteristic Building Type of the Ottoman Fortification Network in Hungary," *Elec-tronic Journal of Oriental Studies* 4 (2001): 1–12.

22. Stephen Morillo, "Guns and Government: A Comparative Study of Europe and Japan," *Journal of World History* 6 (1995): 75–106, esp. 79–81; Kelly DeVries, *Infantry Warfare in the Early Fourteenth Century: Discipline, Tactics, and Technology* (Woodbridge, UK: Boydell, 1996).

23. Albert Lynn Winkler, "The Swiss and War: The Impact of Society on the Swiss Mili-tary in the Fourteenth and Fifteenth Centuries," (PhD diss., Brigham Young University, 1982), 24, 54, 70, 137–40, 144, 169–70, 177; Azar Gat, *War in Human Civi-lization* (Oxford: Oxford University Press, 2006), 292, 458; Arnold, *Renaissance at War*, 84; Dennis E. Showalter, "Caste, Skill, and Training: The Evolution of Cohesion in European Armies from the Middle Ages to the Sixteenth Century," *Journal of Mili-tary History* 57 (1993): 425–26; Black, *War in the World*, 38–39. David Parrott points out that as the Swiss squares turned from cantonal defense to mercenary service abroad, the cohesion and effectiveness of the square depended less on organic com-munal cohesion and more on the veterans' experience and their sense of belonging to the regiment, no longer feeling welcome or appreciated in their home villages. David Parrott, *The Business of War: Military Enter-prise and Military Revolution in Early Modern Europe* (Cambridge, UK: Cambridge Uni-versity Press, 2012), 49–50.

24. Hall, *Weapons*, 100, 108–12; Kelly DeVries and Robert Douglas Smith, *Medieval Mili-tary Technology*, 2nd ed. (Toronto: Univer-sity of Toronto Press, 2012), 145–46.

25. Hall, *Weapons*, 95, 212; Alan Williams, *The Knight and the Blast Furnace: A History of the Metallurgy of Armour in the Middle Ages and the Early Modern Period* (Leiden: Brill, 2003), 916. Brian Todd Carey, *War-fare in the Medieval World* (Barnsley, UK: Pen & Sword, 2006), 203 summarizes de-tails on muskets, arquebuses, and other varieties.

26. Parker, *Military Revolution*, 17–23, 161; Geoffrey Parker, "The Limits to Revolu-tions in Military Affairs: Maurice of Nassau, the Battle of Nieuwpoort (1600), and the Legacy," *Journal of Military History* 71 (2007): 338–39; Olaf van Nimwegen, *The Dutch Army and the Military Revolutions, 1588–1688*, trans. Andrew May (Wood-bridge, UK: Boydell, 2010), 84–112, 289–91.

27. I develop this idea in greater detail in Wayne E. Lee, *Barbarians and Brothers: Anglo-American Warfare, 1500–1865* (New York: Oxford University Press, 2011), 85–89; Vegetius I.1, I.26, preface to III, *Epitome of Military Science*, trans. N. P. Milner (Liverpool, UK: Liverpool Univer-sity Press, 1993); Latin text from Flavius Vegetius Renatus, *Epitoma rei militaris*, ed. Carl Lang (Stuttgart, West Germany: Teubner, 1967).

28. Maurice H. Keen, ed., *Medieval Warfare: A History* (New York: Oxford University Press, 1999), 19.

29. Christine de Pizan, *The Book of Deeds of Arms and of Chivalry*, trans. Sumner Willard and Charity Cannon Willard (University

Park: Pennsylvania State University Press, 1999), 26–27.

30. Allmand's analysis of Vegetius's reception by medieval writers generally supports what I argue here. Christopher Allmand, *The De Re Militari of Vegetius: The Reception, Transmission and Legacy of a Roman Text in the Middle Ages* (Cambridge, UK: Cambridge University Press, 2011), especially 24, 284–86, 338–40. Richard W Kaeuper, *Chivalry and Violence in Medieval Europe* (Oxford: Oxford University Press, 1999), 135 (quote).

31. J. F. Verbruggen, *The Art of Warfare in Western Europe During the Middle Ages*, 2nd ed. (Woodbridge, UK: Boydell, 1997), 83–100; Hugh D. H. Soar, *Secrets of the English War Bow* (Yardley, PA: Westholme, 2010), 193–94.

32. Matthew Sutcliffe, *The Practice, Proceedings, and Lawes of Armes* (London: Christopher Barker, 1593), B4r, 85 (quote); Harald Kleinschmidt, "Using the Gun: Manual Drill and the Proliferation of Portable Firearms," *Journal of Military History* 63 (1999): 601-30.

33. This paragraph and the next are taken from Lee, *Barbarians and Brothers*, 86; Peter H. Wilson, *The Thirty Years War: Europe's Tragedy* (Cambridge, MA: Belknap Press of Harvard University Press, 2009), 139–41; and William H. McNeill *The Pursuit of Power: Technology, Armed Force, and Society since A.D. 1000* (Chicago: University of Chicago Press, 1982), 125–39. For the complexity of the fully developed pike and shot synchronization, see Clifford J. Rogers, "Tactics and the Face of Battle," in *European Warfare, 1350–1750*, ed. Frank Tallett and D. J. B. Trim (Cambridge, UK: Cambridge University Press, 2010), 203–35; Arnold, *Renaissance at War*, 97–100.

34. Ágoston, *Guns for the Sultan*, 16–19, 23–26; Chase, *Firearms*, 86, 229; Brian Davies, "Guliai-gorod, Wagenburg, and Tabor Tactics in 16th-17th Century Muscovy and Eastern Europe," in *Warfare in Eastern Europe, 1500–1800*, ed. Brian J. Davies (Leiden: Brill, 2012), 99–102; Ágoston, "Firearms and Military Adaptation," 91–98.

35. Quoted and discussed in Günhan Börekci, "A Contribution to the Military Revolution Debate: The Janissaries Use of Volley Fire during the Long Ottoman-Habsburg War of 1593–1606 and the Problem of Origins," *Acta Orientalia Academiae Scientiarum Hungarica* 59 (2006): 407–38, quote 416.

36. Halil Inalcık, "The Socio-Political Effects of the Diffusion of Fire-Arms in the Middle East," in *War, Technology, and Society in the Middle East*, ed. V. J. Parry and M. E. Yapp (London: Oxford University Press, 1975), 198–99; Ágoston, *Guns for the Sultan*, 26, 192; Murphey, *Ottoman Warfare*, 46–48; Imber, *The Ottoman Empire*, 140–42.

37. Imber, "Ibrahim Peçevi on War"; Caroline Finkel, *The Administration of Warfare: Ottoman Campaigns in Hungary, 1593–1606* (Vienna: Verband der Wissenschaftlichen Gesellschaften Österreichs, 1988); Ágoston, *Guns for the Sultan*, 194–95; Ágoston, "Empires and Warfare."

38. Ágoston, *Guns for the Sultan*, 201–2, for diplomatic reconfiguration; H. Inalcık, "Military and Fiscal Transformation in the Ottoman Empire, 1600–1700," *Archivum Ottomanicum* 1 (1980): 283–337; Ágoston, "Ottoman Empire and the Technological Dialogue"; Kahraman Şakul, "General Observations on the Ottoman Military Industry, 1774–1839: Problems of Organization and Standardization," in Günergun and Raina, *Science between Europe and Asia*, 41–56; Kahraman Şaku l, "The Evolution of Ottoman Military Logistical Systems in the Later Eighteenth Century: The Rise of a New Class of Military Entrepreneur," in *War, Entrepreneurs, and the State in Europe and the Mediterranean, 1300–1800*, ed. Jeff Fynn-Paul (Leiden: Brill, 2014), 307–28.

39. The literature on the military revolution is extensive. As introductions these three works are indispensable: Jeremy Black, *A Military Revolution? Military Change and European Society. 1550–1800* (Basingstoke, UK: Macmillan, 1991); Parker, *Military Revolution*; Rogers, *Military Revolution Debate*.

40. Azar Gat, *War in Human Civilization* (Oxford: Oxford University Press, 2006), 466–71, 474–76 (and the sources cited there). See also Morillo, "Guns and Government."

41. G. Perjés, "Army Provisioning, Logistics and Strategy in the Second Half of the 17th Century," *Acta Historica Academiae Scientiarum Hungaricae* 16 (1970). 1–51; Chase, *Firearms*, 16–19.

42. Gábor Ágoston, "Military Transformation in the Ottoman Empire and Russia, 1500–1800," *Kritika*12.2 (2011): 283 (quote) and passim. Ágoston, "Empires and Warfare."

8

Adapting to Gunpowder (or not): On the Open Seas, Africa, North America, and Asia

Maritime Power • The Gun-Slave Cycle in Africa? • Amerindians and Gunpowder • Gunpowder and the Steppe: China from Ming to Manchu • Conclusion: The Military Revolution Problem

THERE IS A GROWING trend among historians to downplay the decisiveness of gunpowder weapons in European hands, at least in the era between about 1500 and 1800. It is true, however, that gunpowder created some new and unavoidable realities. The introduction of chemical energy and an associated technology for its exploitation created two key possibilities over the long term. First, it changed the potential demographics of recruitment, since it enabled relatively untrained individuals to employ weapons to lethal effect on the battlefield. Second, harnessing chemical energy created the *possibility* of continued technological improvement far beyond the potential offered by muscle-powered weaponry. That trajectory of improvement was slow and halting at times, but it would eventually provide the tools to end the persistent threat of the steppe archer. More importantly, each succeeding step in the trajectory depended on the knowledge and infrastructure acquired in the preceding steps.[1]

However, and this is an important caveat, neither of those long-term developments was clear to peoples or individuals at the time—in 1400, or 1500, or 1600. Contests for power in those centuries turned on many factors other than the possession (or lack) of gunpowder weapons. A fully textured story reveals a great deal of contingency, and most certainly does not suggest an irresistible tide of European expansion.

Yet there was European expansion. And in many cases the arrival of Europeans and their weapons forced others to adapt to or adopt them. This chapter will tell some of those stories. It will first examine the oceanic mechanisms through which the Europeans were able to expand at all, with a brief look at their Ottoman competitors. It will then examine the Amerindian and West

African responses to the arrival of firearms. We will then conclude by exploring the paradoxical issue of China's development of gunpowder—paradoxical because despite their invention of it, and despite having a significant lead on certain technical aspects of its use, they did not realize its potential as quickly as the Europeans or Ottomans later did.

There is no one narrative in this chapter. These are case studies, and selected ones at that, each one examining how a society innovated, or coped with an innovation, in military affairs. In each case we will again find ourselves exploring the extent to which military innovations shaped, or were shaped by, the societies involved. Could changes in military technology produce a revolutionary effect in a society?

MARITIME POWER

This chapter begins by examining how gunpowder's potential was adapted for use at sea, in this case the open ocean, and it does so primarily through the example of Portugal. This provides a case study of the relationship between *sets* or *systems* of innovations. There was a good deal more to projecting oceanic power than merely putting cannon aboard a ship. Europeans were not the only ones with the capability to do so, but for various and sometimes surprising reasons, they most aggressively pursued that option, which in the end enabled their expansion around the world. Describing this spread also creates the context for much of the rest of the chapter, in which the Europeans, as invaders, introduced gunpowder weapons to other parts of the world, or, in the case of China, introduced new applications of this indigenous technology. Unlocking the oceans and enabling this early modern European expansion depended on three keys, all occurring in the fifteenth and sixteenth centuries: advances in navigation, in ship design, and the mounting of cannon in those ships.

The first key was the ability to reliably navigate a ship out of the sight of land. As discussed in chapter 6, this problem constituted a fundamental limit on galleys for most of their history, and contributed to their tendency to hug coasts and to beach each evening. The navigational problems are many: How does one know which direction one is traveling? How does one know where one is at any given moment? How does one record that information in a useful way that allows for a repeat voyage, especially by a different captain, relying only on description and not memory? The first challenge, knowing the direction of travel, was solved by the introduction of the compass from China in the early twelfth century—although they remained rare aboard ship until improvements were made in the fifteenth century. Fifteenth-century Portuguese mariners combined that basic instrument with a tradition of precise records called "rutters," in which they described "routes, compass bearings, distances and the topography of coastlines, all based on empirical evidence."[2] This kind of recordkeeping allied itself to a burgeoning (if still primitive) science of cartography to allow a mariner to plot a course and follow it while out of sight of land. Storms or even just multiple days on the open sea, however, could easily disrupt a plotted course, and some method was needed to determine one's position by observation of one's surroundings, without relying on the record of the voyage. Arab mathematicians had determined how to use the North Star's distance above the horizon to calculate latitude (one's position north or south on an imaginary grid imposed on the world). By the 1480s Portuguese sailors had switched to using the angle of the sun at noon for the same purpose, using a standard set of tables prepared in Hebrew in the 1470s and translated and revised at the initiative of the Portuguese king. The technique rapidly spread around Europe and became the basis for oceanic navigation. Accurately determining one's longitude while at sea, however, remained a nearly insuperable problem until the mid-eighteenth century.

Oceanic travel also required a vessel built to withstand the stresses of the open ocean and capacious enough to carry supplies for long voyages. Medieval northern European shipbuilding techniques provided some of the necessary foundations. Short-haul merchant vessels sailing in the North Atlantic were designed to carry a substantial cargo and built to withstand the heavy weather endemic to the region. Making them defensible in a fight was merely a matter of adding "castles" fore and aft to serve as fighting platforms for archers or crossbowmen. In time, these single-masted, square-rigged vessels grew into three-masted ships combining the older northern European square sail with the triangular lateen sails common to Portuguese fishing vessels, and probably ultimately derived from Arab trading vessels in the Indian Ocean. The square sails of the former provided expansible power (it was easy to stack sails on a mast) and were excellent for sailing downwind (or "running before the wind"), while the latter were much better for sailing as close to "against the wind" as possible, or "close-hauled." In combination they produced a highly flexible system. The most notable ship type to first combine these rigging systems was the Portuguese *caravela redonda* (see Figure 8.1).[3]

The third key was the cannon, or more precisely a new method for placing cannon aboard ship. There was more than one way to imagine the ship-gun combination, and the changes were evolutionary rather than sudden. The first century of guns aboard ship in Europe (roughly 1450–1550) saw two almost entirely separate systems: heavy Atlantic sailing vessels mounting large numbers of small anti-personnel guns high up on the vessel, and the Mediterranean galley with a very few large bronze guns mounted in the centerline on the bow and capable of destroying walls or enemy ships. Two inventions focused further development on the heavy sailing vessels. One was the ability to cast cheap iron cannons (rather than building them up

Figure 8.1 A caravel. A modern drawing of a fifteenth-century caravel combining square and lateen sails.

from wrought iron or casting them in expensive bronze), a technique developed in England in the 1540s and spreading thereafter to the Netherlands, Sweden, and then Spain by the seventeenth century. The other was the gun port.[4]

The hinged gun port's origins are obscure, but it seems to have evolved from the fifteenth-century cargo-loading door (seen in Figure 8.2) and was clearly in evidence as a gun port by 1501, with the earliest full broadside-gunned ship using gunports launched in 1511. Seemingly the simplest of ideas, it nevertheless had revolutionary results. Guns could be moved from the main deck to lower in the ship, allowing the guns themselves to be much heavier, capable of damaging or sinking an opposing ship rather than just killing crewmen. Once below decks, and mounted all along the sides of the ship (the broadside), the major limitation on the number of guns was cost. Not long after the gun port was invented, the English developed a reliable process for casting iron cannon, vastly cheapening the outfitting of a ship with numerous heavy cannon.[5]

Putting more and heavier guns aboard ship, however, created other technical challenges. To quote one naval historian: "The lowest gun deck had to be at a sufficient height above the waterline, the internal structure of the hull had to be strong enough to carry heavy loads high in the ship, and weight had to be distributed carefully in order to make the ship stiff and stable under sail. The hull also had to be built strongly enough to resist enemy gunfire."[6] Early attempts to solve these technical problems combined poorly with the temptation to pour in ever more guns and sometimes resulted in very large, unwieldy ships. The pendulum had to swing back to something more stable and maneuverable, and that happened by the late sixteenth century. In the simplest terms: the castles were reduced in height; guns were standardized with a strong focus on ship-killing cannon rather than smaller antipersonnel weapons; and the ship acquired a narrower profile (ratio of length to breadth) and a lower center of gravity. Taken together, these changes allowed for an increase in the weight of the armament of the ship relative to its displacement, rising from 1 or 2 percent of the ship's displacement around 1500 to 7 or 8 percent on the warships of the later seventeenth century.[7]

Eventually, this halting, uncertain, unpredictable, and variable evolutionary process culminated in the ship of the line: the specialty warship that dominated the oceans and seas of the late seventeenth-century world and whose dominance would continue with relatively few changes

Figure 8.2 Fifteenth-century carrack with loading port. Model of a Flemish carrack, ca. 1468. Note the loading port, forerunner of gun ports. The high fore and aft castles served as a platform for infantry and small cannon.

until the second quarter of the nineteenth century. As suggested in chapter 6, however, this process of development was not as straightforward and linear as it has sometimes seemed. The introduction of gunpowder actually first enhanced the galley's dominance in the sixteenth century, producing a relative *decline* in the military importance of sailing ships in the Mediterranean, at least for as long as guns remained expensive.

Crucially, until about 1650, even after adding gun ports and cheaper iron cannon, sailing warships and merchants ships remained almost indistinguishable. The difference was in the loading. More men, ammunition, and guns made it a ship on a war mission; more cargo (but still some guns) and it was on a trading mission. In short, from about 1550 to 1650 European oceangoing vessels were dual-purpose merchant/warships that, in one analyst's summation, "literally captured the world market for both commercial cargo-carrying and violence at sea."[8]

After 1650, however, the trend toward ship-killing capability gradually meant that any ship that hoped to compete had to be designed and manned for that more extreme purpose—it takes a very large crew to man the guns of a ship of the line while still being able to sail the ship. Purpose-built warships using classic broadside line-ahead tactics came to dominate European waters only from the middle of the seventeenth century. Once it was in place, however, managing such a large-scale and complex technological system contributed to a new kind of bureaucratic military professionalism as well as bureaucratic state formation—subjects that must await the next chapter.

For now it remains to point out one other crucial development essential to European naval power: the printing press, invented in the 1440s. The press had many consequences, but consider it simply from the point of view of the new genre of the atlas, which in some ways replaced the old Portuguese rutters. Abraham Ortelius produced a Latin edition of his *Theatrum Orbis Terrarum* in 1570, providing seventy maps of various parts of the world, followed up by no fewer than twenty-eight editions in Dutch, German, French, and Spanish before 1598. Cheap reproduction and distribution of information about the oceanic world and the techniques used to master it greatly facilitated the diffusion of capability as well an iterative process of improvement, as authors sought to outdo one another in showing their expertise.[9]

Portugal in the Indian Ocean, to 1550

The Portuguese pioneered oceanic navigation and they rapidly converted their technical success into a project of empire building. We can follow their path, and their competition with the Ottomans, to show both the effects of European maritime power and the nature of the most immediate competition (the Ottomans), and provide the background for the arrival of gunpowder in Africa and the shifting usage of gunpowder in China and Japan. Pursuing the sources of African gold and ultimately access to the Indian

Ocean trade network, the Portuguese combined private and state sponsorship to improve navigation, including promoting the translation and creation of tables of latitude. Individual mariners pushed down the coast of Africa, making their way successively past Cape Bojador (the "bulge of Africa") in 1434, and then further down the coast, until Bartolomeu Dias rounded the Cape of Good Hope in 1488. In the process he discovered the westerly winds of the South Atlantic that could speed a fleet around the cape. Vasco de Gama followed up on this success to push into the Indian Ocean, and in East Africa he used a local pilot to guide him (using the monsoon winds) to India, landing in Calicut in 1498. Once they understood this wind system, the Portuguese began regularly sending fleets around Africa, establishing themselves in various locations through South, Southeast, and even East Asia, reaching China by 1513 and Japan by 1542 (see Map 8.1 and Figure 8.3).

The primary mechanism behind this success was the cannon-equipped Atlantic sailing vessel, most commonly represented by the caravel and the *nau* (or carrack). The Portuguese quickly discovered two key realities: they had little to offer in trade, but vessels designed for the relatively benign monsoon winds of the Indian Ocean were extremely vulnerable to Portuguese cannon fire. Populous powerful empires ashore in East Africa and India and around the Arabian Sea were not susceptible to Portuguese control, but when those same powers tried to move goods by sea they found Portuguese ships impossible to resist—at least at first. The Portuguese rapidly established the *cartaz* system, requiring trading vessels to carry a pass indicating they had paid customs duties in a Portuguese-controlled port or else they would be taken as a prize. Intending to control and redirect the entire spice trade away from the Red Sea emporia and into or through Portugal, King Manuel of Portugal was explicit in his instructions to Francisco de Almeida, who sailed to India in 1505, that he should install himself at the mouth of the Red Sea, "because from there we could see to it that no spices might pass to the land of the sultan of Egypt, and all those in India would lose the false notion that they could trade any more, save through us."[10]

This story is often told as if from this point forward there was a clear trajectory of European dominance in the Indian Ocean, if not by Portugal then by their European rivals and successors the Dutch and then the English. In this telling the successful force embodied in European ships and cannon cut off the Middle Eastern powers from their former control of the spice trade and established a virtual monopoly carrying spices to Europe via the Cape.

In fact, the story is good deal more complicated. First, this Portuguese "empire" essentially controlled only assorted fortified ports and (mostly) the sea routes between them. They made no attempt to control the territorial hinterland; they often did not even control the urban space outside their fortified port citadel. It is true that they rapidly established a monopoly over the East Indian trade, but their success brought a strong reaction from other regional powers. On land it quickly became clear that most Portuguese trading

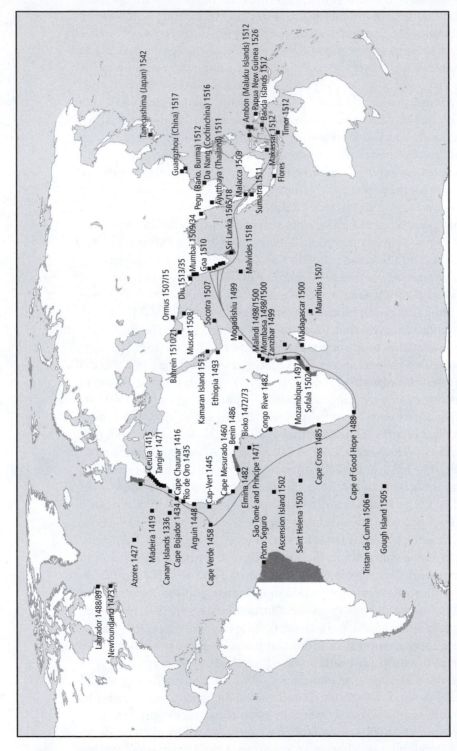

Map 8.1 Portuguese voyages, trading posts, and stations, 1415–1542.

posts would continue to exist only at the sufferance of the local rulers. In time, Portuguese dominance at sea was also contested, primarily by the Ottomans.

The Ottoman Challenge in the Indian Ocean

While the Portuguese were unlocking the puzzle of oceanic navigation, the Ottomans were rising to power in the Mediterranean. Their capture of Constantinople in 1453 sealed their transformation into a major power and also signaled their arrival as a maritime competitor. Their cultural traditions and their largely continental empire emphasized terrestrial ambitions, but competing for power and territory in the eastern Mediterranean meant having a navy. The Ottomans quickly became a major naval power, maintaining that status well into the seventeenth century, alternately competing and cooperating with their primary naval enemy, Venice. As the Portuguese moved into the Indian Ocean, they too clashed with the Ottomans. Just as the Portuguese were arriving in India, the Ottomans successfully conquered the Mamluk state in Egypt (1517), and shortly thereafter they wrested Iraq from the Safavids. This put them in control of both the Red Sea and the Persian Gulf—the traditional routes for trade from the Indian Ocean into the Mediterranean. It also cemented their position as the protectors of the holy cities of Islam and thus of the pilgrimage routes by sea to Mecca. The Ottomans thus became economically and ideologically opposed to Portuguese efforts to control the seas between India and Egypt.

Figure 8.3 A Portuguese fleet from 1507. This 1565 illustration shows the Portuguese armada sent to the Indian Ocean in 1507; this selection shows *naus* or "carracks."

This naval contest lasted for most of the sixteenth century, with the Ottomans campaigning to oust the Portuguese from their bases in India and East Africa and the Portuguese trying to establish control over the entrances to the Red Sea and the Persian Gulf. Neither power made much progress. In the long run, the Portuguese remained and the Ottoman naval presence in the Indian Ocean diminished, while local Asian and African merchants grew increasingly capable of evading Portuguese trade controls. By the end of the century much of the trade had slipped from Portuguese hands. Giancarlo Casale has argued that this period constituted a parallel and analogous Ottoman "age of exploration," in which the Ottomans invested in and sought maritime power much as the Christian European states did, although they confined their interest to the Indian Ocean and Southeast Asia. Ottoman ambitions even included sending an expedition to Aceh in what is now Indonesia. This maritime expansion, however, was not sustained, and was probably doomed from the start. The Ottoman fleet was primarily composed of galleys, perfectly serviceable in the relatively calm Mediterranean and even the Indian Ocean, and probably superior fighting ships in coastal or confined waters. If caught in open waters, however, they were no match for the heavier Portuguese ships. The Ottomans also lacked a native merchant marine, and always struggled to man their war fleets, depending heavily on levies of peasants from the Balkans to serve as oarsmen. Perhaps most crucially, support from the sultan in Istanbul proved erratic at best. Ottoman interests did not lie in the sea and their rulers were not interested in the sort of state-backed private enterprise voyages of discovery, conquest, and empire building that the Portuguese and other European powers embarked on.[11]

Diu

These generalizations may make more sense when brought to life through a fully fledged example. No single case can be representative, but the events between 1500 and 1550 at Diu, a major port on the west coast of the Indian subcontinent, convey a sense of how ships, cannon, and fortification styles converged to buttress European power. They also suggest the limits and tenuousness of that power. At the beginning of the sixteenth century, Diu, within the territory of the Sultanate of Gujarat, was a key stop on many of the trade routes crisscrossing the region.[12]

After their first voyage to India in 1497–99, the Portuguese annually (from 1500 to 1511 at least) sent fairly large fleets back into the region and beyond. These consisted of, for example, fleets of thirteen ships in 1500, twenty in 1502, and twenty-two in 1505. As the Portuguese *cartaz* system diverted trade away from the old Red Sea route via Egypt, the Mamluk sultan there sought Ottoman and Venetian help to oust the Portuguese and restore the old trade routes. In 1507 a Mamluk fleet of a dozen ships and 1,500–2,000 men arrived at Diu and allied with the Gujarati sultan there. Their combined fleet then sailed to Chaul, another coastal trading port, where they found and destroyed a small Portuguese fleet. Seeking revenge, in February 1509, a reinforced Portuguese fleet then based in Cochin sailed into Diu's harbor and attacked the Mamluk fleet, despite it being anchored under the guns of Diu's fortifications. In hard fighting the Portuguese captured eight large ships (four Egyptian round ships, two galleys, and two Gujarati ships) and sank four large round vessels (two Egyptian and two Gujarati) and many smaller galleys. In several instances the Portuguese reportedly sank major warships with a single volley, and they lost none of their own ships. Diu surrendered. In an effort to make a lasting impression, the Portuguese commander killed their prisoners, some by tying them to the mouths of cannon that were then fired.

Although Diu lay open to him, the Portuguese viceroy preferred to rely on sea power, writing to the king of Portugal, "So long as you are powerful at sea, India will be yours and if you do [not] possess this power, little will avail you a fortress on shore."[13] Later viceroys, however, hoped for a fort and base at Diu. They returned in 1513, 1520–21, and 1531 to try to retake it, but were repulsed each time. Portuguese power was rising, but it was not all-encompassing, and now the Ottomans, having destroyed the Mamluk power in Egypt, turned their attention to the Indian Ocean. Back-and-forth raiding became common. Then in 1535 the Gujarati sultan Bahadur Shah of Cambay opened Diu to the Portuguese, hoping they would help him against the rising Mughal Empire in northern India. His successor tried to reverse course, and he asked the Ottomans for help in taking back the fort the Portuguese were then building at Diu.

Aware of the threat, the Portuguese rushed the construction, creating what was essentially a medieval-style fortress, relying on vertical walls and retaining at least one tall tower. It also, however, incorporated some of the transitional elements of early sixteenth-century fortress design (described in more detail in chapter 7). The finished fort had twelve-foot-thick masonry-faced walls and three major artillery bastions, including a waterline artillery battery. Another redoubt, built across the channel from the main fort and projecting out into the navigation channel, had twenty-six-foot-thick walls. This transitional style, built to mount artillery but not yet fully designed to resist it (although with increasingly thick walls) was characteristic of many of the forts built by the Portuguese around the Atlantic and Indian Oceans between 1450 and 1540 or so.[14]

A major Ottoman fleet of fifty to eighty ships and carrying 6,500 soldiers (including janissaries) arrived in early September 1538, joining perhaps nineteen thousand Gujaratis. Although the Gujaratis had become disenchanted with their Portuguese "allies," the Ottomans had also recently violated a truce at Aden, and the Gujaratis were wary of exchanging one overweening outsider for another. Despite the fact that the Portuguese defenders numbered only eight hundred, backed by six hundred slaves, they declined to surrender. When asked, they replied with a priceless piece of bravado: "Here are Portuguese used to killing many Moors, who have for a captain António da Silveira, who has a pair of balls stronger than the balls of your basilisks [cannon]."[15] Portuguese slurs about Ottoman cannon notwithstanding, their attackers had brought a first-class siege train. During the two-month siege it first destroyed the redoubt across the navigation channel. By October 4 the Ottoman-Gujarati force had established six batteries of guns (throwing balls from 60–100 pounds) 60–150 yards from the wall. The bombardment was reducing the main fort to rubble; one bastion was quickly breached, and fighting continued at the breach for much of the month, while the Portuguese built successive counter walls to seal the breach. Then, unexpectedly, at the beginning of November, the Ottomans sailed away, having heard rumors of a relief force, thus further alienating their Gujarati hosts and allies.[16]

The Portuguese rebuilt the fort, incorporating some improvements, but still not yet in the full *trace italienne* style. The next and last major effort to wrest Diu from the Portuguese came in 1546, this time not by the Ottomans but by the Gujaratis alone. The siege lasted almost seven months, and was begun in April, when the monsoon made it more difficult for Portuguese reinforcements to be brought in from further south. The Gujarati commander brought a very large army, supplemented by laborers for filling the fort's ditch. He also brought a substantial artillery train, including five veteran Ottoman siege engineers. The Portuguese had only two hundred defenders initially, although some five separate fleets trickled in with reinforcements despite the monsoon.

Fortunately for the Portuguese, despite the great size of the enemy artillery train, the Gujarati cannon proved inferior, sometimes even defective, possibly due to troubles with the local foundry. There may also have been a shortage of gunnery experts. The Gujaratis did successfully undermine and explode one of the bastions, but the other mines were defeated or failed to explode. Despite their gunnery problems, the long bombardment reduced much of the outer wall to rubble. The Gujaratis even gained the wall, forcing the Portuguese defenders back into the houses, from where they continued to fight. On November 10, a final relief force arrived, bringing the Portuguese governor and 1,500 men. The Portuguese created a diversion, pretending to land the relief force outside the city walls in a direct attack on the Gujarati camp. As the Gujaratis repositioned to await the expected landing, the relief force, who had already landed undetected within the fort, charged out, scattering the besiegers still in their trenches and spreading panic through the now misdeployed Gujarati army. The Portuguese captured some thirty-three Gujarati guns, including a massive 14.5-foot-long 66-pounder. Immediately after the siege the fort was rebuilt in a fully modernized *trace italienne* style by the architect Francisco Pires, "introducing into the Portuguese defense system overseas, for the first time, military fortifications typical of the European Renaissance."[17] The fort remained in Portuguese hands until 1961, although it would be a mistake to attribute that longevity to the fortifications alone.[18]

European guns and ships were key to Portuguese success in India—specifically guns *in* ships. Indian or Ottoman artillery on land was generally as capable as whatever the Europeans had. Improved fortress design helped, but was hardly decisive. But equally important was the highly fragmented political environment of India, as well as the sustained and continuous support provided by the Portuguese state to the private-enterprise projects of its subjects there. In contrast, Ottoman state support withered. Meanwhile, the Mughal Empire that would eventually unite most of India was less interested in maritime endeavors and tolerated the Portuguese trading forts. The Ming

Chinese, who had explored the region prior to the Portuguese arrival with cannon-equipped fleets of staggering size, had withdrawn from the sea. Ultimately the Portuguese would succumb to the Dutch and the English, but their initial success suggests the role of European seagoing capabilities in projecting power. That projection also carried gunpowder weapons to Africa and the New World, where it had very different effects.[19]

THE GUN-SLAVE CYCLE IN AFRICA?

Almost literally in the center of this emerging swirl of European naval activity were the peoples, kingdoms, and states of West Africa. Although West Africa had long been connected to the Mediterranean and to Europe by trans-Saharan caravans delivering gold, slaves, and other exotic goods, the desert had nevertheless constituted a serious obstacle. The arrival of European ships rapidly and fatefully rearranged the position of West Africa in world trade. Along with other cargo, those ships brought gunpowder weapons with them, and here we will limit our investigation to the spread and impact of this innovation within West African societies. We cannot explain the entirety of African military systems, but we can ask specific questions about whether and how the arrival of a single complex of innovations changed warfare and even African social organizations. But first we must outline when and with what technologies the Europeans arrived, and into what African conditions.

Here too the Portuguese were leaders. As they made their way around the bulge of Africa in the middle of the fifteenth century, they established contacts in a number of different ports proceeding down the coast. Their most important long-term relationships proved to be in the Angola/Kongo region, where, uniquely, they converted many people in the region to Christianity and set up a large-scale colony in the 1580s. Initially interested in gold, as the new world colonies developed tropical products for export, primarily sugar, the Portuguese began to draw on Africa for slave labor. Other European powers followed. Each sought trade relationships with local rulers, setting up trading ports or forts, but none established an equivalent to the Portuguese colony in Angola. Not all regions of Atlantic Africa were affected by European arrival at the same time. In the Slave Coast region, for example, in the area that would later become the Kingdom of Dahomey, the Portuguese first established contact in the 1470s, but no transatlantic slave trading occurred in that region until after 1553. It remained a minor Portuguese source of slaves until the 1630s, when the Portuguese were displaced by the Dutch.[20]

Even then the slave trade in that region continued on a relatively small scale until after 1650, when the "plantation revolution" in the New World gained steam and more European states became players in that revolution. The English and French began trading on the Slave Coast in the 1660s. Looking specifically again at the Dahomey region (using trade out of the ports of

Allada and Whydah as indicators), in 1670 there were probably three thousand slaves being purchased each year, where by 1688 that had grown to twenty thousand, a plateau sustained through the early eighteenth century.[21]

As voluminous as the Atlantic slave trade became, it did so as part of a complex relationship between European traders and African rulers. Europeans in West Africa dealt primarily with *states*, not tribes or simple societies (although tribes did exist). Some of the states could be quite small, but they were nevertheless hierarchical, stratified societies, which, among other things, were often at war with each other. But, before turning to the specifics of warfare, we must look more carefully at the tremendous ecological and indeed political variation within the false unity of what is often called "Atlantic Africa."

To greatly simplify, West Africa around 1500 divided into two broad ecological zones, with the second of the two zones divided into two types of political organization (see Map 8.2a). In the north, there are successively wetter bands of semiarid savanna and grasslands moving south from the edges of the Sahara toward the forested coast. Here were generally large hierarchical states, with strong interests in the trans-Sahara trade (for slaves and other goods) and, crucially for our narrative, possessed of cavalry forces. The coastal forest zones of West Africa, although otherwise of great ecological variety, had in common a disease environment hostile to horses—especially "sleeping sickness," spread by the tsetse fly. Politically, most of that region was comparatively decentralized, made up of smaller competing kingdoms, so small that scholars have called them "small socio-cultural units organized on the basis of lineages, clans, and villages."[22] Key exceptions were the expanding kingdom of Benin (controlling much of the western end of the Niger delta), and the larger states in the Angola region, especially Kongo, Ndongo, and Loango (see Map 8.2b).[23]

West African Warfare: Functions and Tactics

Although the savanna region in the north, sometimes collectively referred to as the Sahel, had a long history of territorial empires, much of the rest of West Africa competed over the control of labor, not land. This represented a fundamental difference between African and European or Asian societies: African polities "did not recognize land as private property." The control of labor was the real source of revenue, and "ownership of slaves in Africa was virtually equivalent to owning land in western European or China."[24] Some specific locations could be important, especially the ports that became outlets for the Atlantic slave trade, but in general populations were relatively mobile, and the strategy and tactics of warfare were designed at least in part to secure the labor of the defeated army and perhaps even the defeated population as a whole. Most states had a core of professional soldiery, men trained and

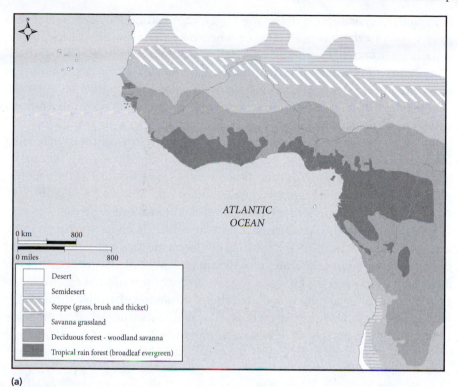

(a)

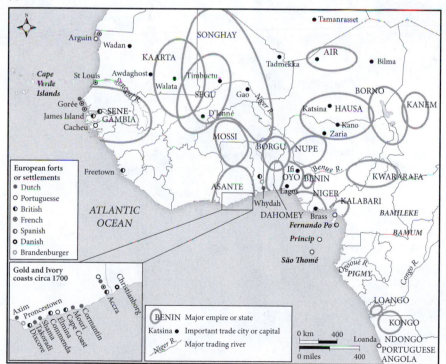

(b)

Map 8.2 *a* & *b* West African climatic zones, states, and European outposts, late eighteenth century. Map 8.2b shows modern political boundaries as reference.

disciplined beyond the skills of the larger, more ad-hoc peasant levies that were joined to the professional core when on campaign. Except for the savanna region in the north, although Africa militaries were trained and disciplined into a high state of skilled obedience, the lack of cavalry meant that most were never forced to create systems or weapons designed to resist the charge of a horseman. There were neither pikes nor the need for disciplined volley fire. Especially when fighting in the forest, battles were usually opened by an extended exchange of missile fire by troops in loose formations, using javelins and especially bows. This exchange of missile fire would eventually lead one side to charge with their heavier troops, arranged in a compact formation and armed with swords, lances, clubs, and shields (see Figure 8.4). These men were usually drawn from the professional core.

Until the 1680s the Europeans made relatively little impact on this system, meaning that neither did they militarily dominate the coast nor did their gunpowder weapons penetrate into African military practice. In terms of relative military power, the Europeans neither sought nor needed extensive territorial control. Slave traders acquired their human merchandise through the willing cooperation of local rulers and local traders. Indeed, it is probable that a heavy percentage of slaves were procured during the wars between

Figure 8.4 African man with weapons, ca. 1641. Probably from the Kongo region, here pictured fighting in Brazil.

African states, which then found a ready market for excess prisoners on the coast. Furthermore, African communities enjoyed a very significant demographic advantage compared to the arriving European fleets or even their small fortified posts. The smallish African states of the Gold Coast in the mid-seventeenth century regularly fielded armies in the thousands, ranging from four thousand to as many as twenty-five thousand. Meanwhile, local diseases generally worked very much against the Europeans. European forces that penetrated into the interior (and these attempts were rare) often melted away. For example, approximately 60 percent of the Portuguese soldiers who served in Angola from 1575 to 1590 died of disease. Even the exceptional Portuguese colony at Angola found itself usually fighting at a rough parity with its local opponents, surviving in part through adeptly keeping one African state or another on its side. Even at a tactical level there is good evidence of African military capability. In 1625 some two thousand Dutch who attacked Elmina were repulsed by some nine hundred local Elmina militiamen. The Portuguese factor at Whydah in 1727 complained that he had no way to resist the demands of the king of Dahomey when his armies showed up on the coast outside Whydah that year. In this regard, it is useful to note that although Whydah was a fortified European post, those fortifications could not provide any sort of ultimate security when isolated from the countryside.[25]

These limits on European power persisted well beyond 1680, but from that period firearms began to appear as a major factor within African military systems. Matchlocks apparently had not appealed to African rulers, but from the 1680s flintlocks began to appear in greater numbers, and they proved more attractive. One hypothesis is that matchlocks worked poorly for the purposes of African slave raiders—their burning matches gave away their positions during night or dawn raids. Sudden dawn volleys of flintlocks outside a target village, however, created panic. When loaded with small shot rather than ball they were likely to wound rather than kill, and thus provide prisoners for the trade.[26]

Flintlocks became a major trade item along the west coast, from Senegambia southward, primarily in trade for slaves. As they became more common, their price fell "dramatically in proportion as slave prices increased. Two guns were being exchanged [in Senegambia] for one male slave in 1682, but by 1718 24–32 guns were being exchanged for one male slave."[27] These price ratios produced a stunningly high rate of gun importation: Joseph Inikori has estimated that between 283,000 and 394,000 guns were imported into West Africa *per year* between 1750 and 1807.[28]

This massive influx of flintlocks immediately raises two related questions. First, did they change African ways of warring? And second, did their introduction have some effect on African state formation (as has been suggested for Europe)? For the first question there is some disagreement, but most scholars downplay any transformative role for firearms as such. Ray

Kea's detailed study of the Gold Coast region sees a major transformation, but ties it to seventeenth-century changes in mobilization rather than in technology. Where battles had previously turned on the shock action of a relatively small, elite, noble, and professional infantry (after an initial exchange of missiles), in the later part of the century he finds a growing emphasis on firepower, driven by a vast increase in conscription that brought more and more untrained men into the army, men who were most useful as archers fighting from a distance. Although this transformation seems to have been happening at exactly the period that flintlocks were rising to prominence, and indeed muskets soon replaced bows, Kea argues that a social and political transformation led to conscription and thus to tactical changes that *preceded* the significant role of firearms. In other regions the impact varied. In the cavalry zone of Senegambia guns proliferated but apparently influenced tactics not at all; they simply replaced the traditional bows. In the forest zones in and around modern Benin, however, guns did not simply replace the bows and javelins of the earlier era. They seem to have contributed to the complete disappearance of the shock combat phase of battle. This decline in shock combat was widely, if not universally, shared. With it, in all those areas except where the forest abutted the cavalry-intensive savanna, infantrymen armed with flintlocks adopted looser and looser formations (in contrast to the trend in Europe through at least the mid-eighteenth century).[29] This issue of tactical change is important to the question of changes in African state systems. Even if we accept that firearms had a restricted impact on tactics, did they nevertheless enhance the *effectiveness* of those armies that possessed them? Did they give coastal states, which had better access to European guns, an advantage over interior ones? This argument that guns enabled some states to more effectively raid for slaves, which they then traded for more guns, a so-called "gun-slave" cycle, actually originated in the eighteenth century. The Dutch director general at Elmina wrote in 1730:

> The great quantity of guns and powder which the Europeans have brought have caused terrible wars between the Kings and Princes and Caboceers of these lands, who made their prisoners of war slaves; these slaves were immediately bought up by Europeans at steadily increasing prices, which in its turn, animates again and again these people to renew their hostilities, and their hope of big and easy profits makes them forget all labour, using all sorts of pretexts to attack each other or reviving old disputes.[30]

The issues here are complex and varied regionally and over time. Our best course is to examine one region to see how the argument holds up: in this case the broad region defined by the "Coasts," the Gold, Ivory, and Slave Coasts, and especially Benin and Dahomey. On one hand, W. A. Richards finds a "high correlation between the increase in gun imports and the increase in the slave trade in the eighteenth century" in this region. He pushes the case beyond mere correlation, arguing that those states with guns became the most successful slave exporters. Robin Law, looking more specifically at Dahomey, complicates this story. He argues that the Fon people, originally a loose association living in the interior, coalesced into a state around 1625 in response to a surge in conflict and slave raiding generated by the expanding slave trade. In this analysis, state formation served as a security system against raiders. The situation worsened later in the century as the separate coastal communities of Allada and Whydah hired flintlock-equipped mercenaries from the Gold Coast to aid their slave raids into the interior, seemingly to include the new Dahomean state among their victims. This in turn pushed Dahomey into expansive wars of aggression, and they captured Allada and Whydah in 1724 and 1727, respectively. Dahomey then became a slave-trading state, using and managing the trade to deflect its effects away from its own population.[31]

For Dahomey, the Oyo Empire, and the Asante state, and possibly others, the slave trade generated a security dilemma within a region of many smaller competing states that encouraged centralization and territorial integration. "Security dilemma" is a technical term from international relations theory referring to situations like that faced by the Fon people. A rising threat forces a political actor to invest in military power, but that investment in turn appears as a threat to its neighbors, who increase their own investment, and so on in a spiraling escalation. In this case, the security dilemma fostered greater political centralization, a struggle for access to firearms, and even state formation. Walter Hawthorne found similar reactions among peripheral non-state peoples in Guinea-Bissau, who, although they might not have formed states, did become participants in the slave trade to avoid becoming its victims, thereby gaining access to guns and iron. John Thornton, although acknowledging the possibility of a gun-slave cycle on the Gold Coast, is reluctant to generalize it, largely because in his survey of African armies throughout the Atlantic region he finds a large number—especially south of the Slave Coast—that did not depend on firearms, and not a few who in fact rejected them as "coward's weapons." He further points out that the combination of a large number of African states and the many competing European traders made it impossible for an African state to monopolize or even dominate the gun trade. Dahomey's success rising up against Allada suggests this capability. Even with Thornton's cautions, however, it seems reasonable to posit that although guns did not *cause* either the security dilemma, or state formation, they were perceived as a tool to be turned to as a potential solution to the disruptions and even militarization caused by the slave trade. In other words, in the African context, what mattered most was not the technology of the gun itself but the political environment. The importance of political environment as context for the arrival of gunpowder was also characteristic of events in the New World.[32]

AMERINDIANS AND GUNPOWDER

The seemingly extraordinary Spanish success in subduing the Aztecs of Mexico (1519–21) and the Incas of Peru (1532–72) and their subsequent control over the apparently inexhaustible silver mines of the New World has often been used as evidence for the emergence of a dominant European military capability, primarily based on gunpowder weapons. How otherwise to explain how fewer than six hundred Spaniards in Mexico and 169 in Peru could conquer such vast, powerful, imperial, bureaucratic, urbanized, and centralized states? In fact, however, as much recent scholarship has shown, quite a number of other factors also contributed. First, the Spaniards unwittingly brought with them diseases heretofore unknown in the hemisphere, and therefore highly dangerous—not only to the many thousands who died but also thereby to the integrity of the Amerindian states' capacity to mobilize their human resources. Second, the imperial success of the Aztecs and the Incas meant that they ruled over recently conquered peoples, some of them eager to adopt new allies in an effort to throw off the devil they knew. Thousands of Tlaxcalans and other local Amerindians fought beside the Spanish in Mexico, presumably believing that they could control or contain the small number of newcomers. Third, the Spanish benefited from the initial advantages that accrue to an unexpected invader from a distant shore. They possessed a unity of purpose and a do-or-die desperation that contrasted to local political fragmentation, local individuals' ability to flee home, and even a kind of uncertainty-inducing "contact shock"—something the Spanish often took advantage of to seize key native leaders as hostages. Spanish steel, armor, and close-formation tactics did sometimes make a difference, and in certain crucial moments horses and the few Spanish arquebusiers proved central to generating shock and dismay among Amerindians. More importantly, however, and intertwined with all these issues, was that both the Aztecan and the Incan polities were hierarchical, stratified, monarchical states, a political system recognizable to the Spanish, which they were able first to decapitate and then to manipulate through co-opting the remaining elite into a new system of rule with the Spanish at the top.[33]

For that reason especially, the Mexican and Peruvian conquests, spectacular and world-altering though they were, proved exceptional. They did not provide a model for the conquest of the New World because most of the New World was not organized into states, and most of the Amerindian population had more time to adapt to contact shock. Disease continued to play a major role, but it was no doubt less severe on average than it had been for the densely packed urban populations of Tenochtitlan and Cuzco. Taking a longer view of Amerindian resistance, one finds that European military systems did not confer immediate decisive advantage, although they did produce change. Having dismissed the Aztecs and Incas as models, what was the more usual Amerindian response to gunpowder? And what did it mean to their lifestyle and their way of war?

Pre-Contact North America

North America was home to a tremendous variety of peoples and sociopolit-ical formations prior to European contact, but the region now comprising the Atlantic coast of the United States and Canada possessed a rough homogene-ity of lifestyle and of warfare that, with caution, we can refer to under the rubric of "Eastern Woodland." The Mississippian cultures of the Midwest and Southeast, although more centralized and urbanized, were already in the process of decentralizing when the Spanish arrived in the mid-sixteenth cen-tury, and by the time of sustained contact in the seventeenth century they much resembled their Eastern Woodland cousins. In general Eastern Wood-land polities consisted of small to medium-sized towns (from a few hundred to a thousand or more) arranged in related clusters that often acted together, especially in mutual defense. For most, subsistence depended on farming nearby fields, abandoned every few years and replaced by new clearings cut from the forest. During the winter, hunting or seasonal migration and dis-persal provided a key supplement to stored agricultural produce (depending on the regional climate and cultural practice). Hunting needs and seasonal movement meant that Amerindian peoples claimed territory on a much broader scale than was at first apparent to European observers. It also meant that stored food surplus in winter or early spring was limited, and that their societies could ill afford the men, who hunted, to be called to war in succes-sive years. Different peoples evolved a range of forms of political authority, but decisions for war and the process of recruiting participants for offensive operations depended heavily on building consensus.[34]

The motivations for war varied, but included competition for territory (or at least access to territory), imposition of tribute, punishment of diplo-matic infractions, and a cultural investment in blood revenge as a way of maintaining the group's reputation for strength. Blood-revenge requirements particularly motivated individuals, and recruiting a war party often centered on pointing out the need for revenge. The demands of blood revenge then significantly shaped tactics. A key objective for satisfying blood revenge was to take a prisoner; a scalp served as a poor second best. Women, children, and occasionally adult male prisoners were likely to be adopted into the attackers' society. Most adult male prisoners, however, would be tortured and killed as an outlet for individual and communal grief and as the culminating act of revenge. This need to take prisoners, combined with the demographic fragil-ity of a small-scale society afraid of taking serious casualties, meant that at-tackers preferred to surprise and cut off isolated small parties or even an entire enemy town if it could be caught unawares. Successful surprise could lead to heavy casualties among the defenders. In this "cutting-off way of war," open battles occurred when surprise failed, and served primarily to save face and assert strength, leading to relatively few casualties. Such battles were rarely decisive or even bloody; successful ambushes or surprise attacks, however, could be both. Tactically, the attackers would overwhelm initial resistance with arrows and then rush in with clubs to dispatch or capture the remainder. Amerindians palisaded some of their towns to prevent this kind of surprise, but some were on occasion successfully stormed, and some even besieged, depending on the ability of neighboring related towns to respond to the attackers.

After Contact: A Native American Military Revolution?

The arrival of Europeans upset this basic system in several ways, but there was also strong continuity in motives, methods, and tactics. The extent of change versus continuity remains in dispute, but contact had certain clear consequences. Even early seventeenth-century firearms were more lethal than bows *in their effects on individuals*. A wound from a bullet was much more likely to kill the victim than one from an arrow. Bullets smashed bone and were more likely to lead to infection. Guns did not increase the firepower of a group of warriors, but they made individual warriors more vulnerable, and in a demographically small-scale society the implications of greater lethality were serious. Furthermore, once flintlocks were introduced (eliminating the deer-frightening sulfurous match of the matchlocks), they proved useful weapons for hunting as well. Amerindians thereafter rapidly adopted firearms as useful in both hunting and war. As they did so, and as they dealt with firearm-equipped Europeans, they found their old woven-stick armor to be of little use, and face-saving open battles to be too dangerous (see Figures 8.5a and b). The ambush gained greater prominence and the open battle faded. Furthermore, especially as European artillery became available, the old-fashioned simple palisade forts proved not just untenable, but to be potential traps. Gunpowder weapons thus reinforced extant preferences for surprise and ambush.

If gunpowder had limited tactical implications, what about its strategic and social effects? Recall that part of the argument for a European military revolution is that technological changes in warfare generated changes in the nature of the state. In the first century of sustained contact it is possible that some Amerindian peoples, equipped with steel axes and gunpowder weapons, parlayed that access into a military superiority over their traditional enemies. The Iroquois Confederacy of upstate New York devastated and dispersed the Hurons in the 1640s, and went on in succeeding decades to establish a commanding presence over a wide region stretching from New York down much of the Ohio River drainage. In South Carolina successive peoples used their proximity to the settlers at Charlestown to raid and capture neighbors farther west to sell as slaves to the English. In the longer run, however, close contact with European settlers meant demographic decline and nearly constant pressure on land. The Iroquois, for example, may have been spurred to frequent war in part to gain captives for adoption in a

(a) (b)

Figure 8.5 *a & b* **Changes in Native American warfare.**
8.5a is a contemporary drawing of a seventeenth-century
Huron warrior, fully armored and with a bow and club. 8.5b,
also a contemporary drawing, shows an eighteenth-century
Iroquois warrior, now lacking armor, and with a musket and
tomahawk.

futile effort to stem the steady decline in their population. A more successful strategy than the taking of individual captives proved to be confederation and amalgamation. The Iroquois, the Catawbas of the Carolinas, the
Shawnees of the Ohio valley, the Creeks of Georgia, and many other peoples
found that formally confederating together or absorbing other threatened
populations provided a measure of security through numbers. By the
middle of the eighteenth century these confederated peoples had emerged
as key power brokers in the European imperial contest to control North
America.[35]

Unfortunately, Amerindian power became dependent on access to gunpowder and weapons and avoiding being besieged or trapped by European
forces equipped with cannon. Amerindians became masters of imperial diplomacy and playing one power off against another to preserve their access to
those key resources. In that process, although they retained most aspects of
their traditional social structure, their fundamental security calculus
changed. A European expeditionary force represented a profound threat to a
nucleated Amerindian village and usually could not be defeated in open
battle. Threatened populations had to flee into the forests, swamps, or mountains while their warriors attacked the logistical supports of a European
expeditionary force or raided frontier settlements to raise the political cost of
continued war. Successive years of societies fleeing their fields or sending
their men on long raids undermined basic subsistence. In essence, where
Europeans typically drew their fighting manpower from the surplus

population, and could afford to return to campaign year after year, Amerindian societies could not sustain extended operations in consecutive years. On the other hand, when Europeans operated beyond regions of white settlement and had to take supplies with them, they found themselves dependent on Amerindian allies as pathfinders, scouts, and logisticians. This usefulness is one reason why Amerindians were for so long able to maintain their role as power brokers.

GUNPOWDER AND THE STEPPE: CHINA FROM MING TO MANCHU

Why start this chapter with maritime issues and then follow up with the very different experiences with gunpowder in Africa and the New World when, after all, gunpowder, firearms, and cannon were all first invented in China? There are several reasons behind this choice. Most readers will know more about European history, so beginning with it provides an easier introduction and orientation to the relationships among technology, society, and warfare. In addition, many readers will expect China to be backward in firearms development, an assumption whose truth entirely depends on *when* one looks, and *for what purpose* firearms were used at that time. Finally, Chinese gunpowder-weapons development through about 1650 can be divided roughly into two phases: their indigenous invention and development in China through about 1500, and then a second phase stimulated by the arrival of Ottoman and Portuguese technology near the beginning of the sixteenth century. Telling the story of the latter phase is simpler after having dealt with developments in Europe and the Ottoman Empire.[36]

China had centuries more experience with gunpowder than did Europe, and there is strong evidence for a long evolutionary process involving much experimentation. Chinese sources refer to purifying saltpeter from as far back as 492 CE. There are some early, inefficient incendiary mixtures that could be called gunpowder from as early as 808 CE. The first written formula used in a military context comes from 1040, although it had clearly been in limited military use well before that. Gunpowder was first employed as an incendiary bomb or grenade—so-called thunderclap bombs were in use in 1126–27. Most telling is an inspection report of northern frontier defenses in 1257 complaining that two garrisons did not have the "several hundred thousand iron bombshells" they were supposed to have.[37]

Grenades and bombs continued in common use for centuries, both thrown and launched by catapult, but the Chinese also began developing handheld firearms and cannon. The earliest handheld firearms were much like the hook or stick guns (sometimes called hand cannons) invented later in Europe (discussed in chapter 7): both were simple tubes, ignited manually. In the Chinese case the "gun" was mounted at the end of a long wooden pole. The example shown in Figure 8.6 is a version in use not later than 1288, at

Figure 8.6 Early Chinese hand cannon, 1351 CE. This design (with the barrel to the left, the powder chamber in the central bulge, and a socket to mount on a pole to the right,) remained fairly standard from as early as 1288 to at least the 1440s, and possibly as late as the 1520s. It was fired by applying a lit match to the touchhole in the powder chamber.

least forty years prior to European cannon, and a full one hundred years earlier than any truly hand-carried firearm in Europe. Of critical interest here in terms of technological development is how this weapon clearly evolved from an even older tradition of a "fire lance." A fire lance looked very similar but spouted flame rather than a bullet, was made of bamboo or paper, and was often attached to a traditional spear—remaining useful even after being fired. The evidence for fire lances extends back to the tenth century, and they were in common use by 1132. Peter Lorge argues that by the early thirteenth century assorted bits of shrapnel were being added to the fire lance to produce a shotgun effect in addition to the blast of flame (which had as often been directed at equipment as at people). From this arrangement evolved the "fire tube," a metal barrel mounted on the end of a pole, still perhaps a projector of flame more than pellets, but clearly moving toward the true gun. Again not unlike European hook guns, these were first designed for use from behind walls or from siege towers. For the most part all these early Chinese gunpowder weapons emerged in the context of siege and naval warfare and only later moved onto the battlefield.[38]

The Chinese also led in the development of cannon (generally meaning a gun so large that it could not be held or carried as an individual weapon—the one in Figure 8.8a is being held by a spiritual being). The cannon shown in Figure 8.8a, from 1128 or some two hundred years earlier than their appearance in Europe, looks remarkably like the first European depiction shown in Figure 8.8b. Furthermore, Chinese metallurgy was generally superior to European; the Chinese could cast iron cannon as early as the thirteenth century, something that could not be done reliably in Europe until the sixteenth century.[39]

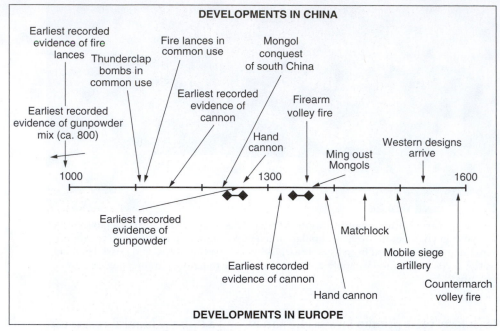

Figure 8.7 The relative chronology of gunpowder weapon development in China and Europe.

The slow pace of evolutionary development of powder, cannon, and hand weapons is important. There was much interaction between each of the three categories: weaker powder made fewer demands on the tube containing the explosion (hence the firing tubes made of paper or bamboo at early stages). Development was not linear; it was reciprocal, unpredictable, and dangerous, especially as continued experimentation with the powder created different effects: incendiary, explosive, short-duration flame spouting, and finally propellant. During this long period of experimentation, and well into the eighteenth century, the utility of firearms in China, as in Europe, was limited by the painfully slow reload time. One early solution in China was to have hand-gunners work in teams of five, with one or two to shoot and the others to reload—a drill that easily fit into long-standing Chinese traditions of drilled infantry in combined arms formations (as discussed in chapter 4). Even so, handguns remained awkward for use against cavalry in the open field, especially the steppe horse archer, and in China the utility of weapons against the steppe horseman was often a key consideration.

As for cannon, the development of heavy siege weapons was less useful in China because of the millennia-old tradition of rammed-earth forts (as described in chapter 2). Those broad and deep ramparts replicated some of the key characteristics of the artillery-resistant *trace italienne* forts invented in Italy in the early sixteenth century. Cannon could breach rammed-earth walls eventually, but this was not a common use, and there was certainly no

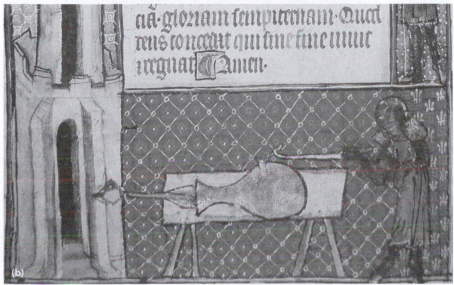

Figure 8.8 *a & b* **The first cannon, China and Europe.** 8.8a is the earliest representation of a barreled cannon, dated from 1128 (here held as firearm by a demon). 8.8b shows the remarkably similar earliest European image, from 1326.

immediate sense of their greater utility for that purpose as there had been in Europe.

Despite these key limitations, Chinese armies thoroughly integrated gunpowder in both thought and practice, attested by the astounding number of grenades expected to be in a typical frontier garrison as early as 1288. This integration returns us to the question raised at the beginning of this chapter: Since China not only invented but also heavily *invested* in gunpowder technology, at least initially, why did Chinese innovation in firearms stagnate? Or did it?[40]

Much of the answer lies in the political history of China during the first centuries of the use of gunpowder. Several dynastic transitions occurred during the long introduction of gunpowder weapons, and the peoples of the steppe played a key role. Our so-far purely technological narrative needs to be integrated into a wider story of empires' rise and fall. At the beginning of the thirteenth century, when gunpowder as incendiary and bomb was common in China, and when fire lances were just beginning to be reimagined as handguns, "China" was divided into three competing imperial entities. In the west was the Xi Xia empire; the north was ruled by the Jurchen people from the Manchurian steppe, who had invaded and now ruled it as the Jin dynasty; and the southern agricultural heartland was ruled by the Song dynasty (see Map 5.3). In the first years of the thirteenth century Chinggis Khan led the united Mongol tribes into the Xi Xia and Jin territories, eventually conquering both. The Jin submitted in 1214, rebelled, then were brought to heel by 1234. During this early period the Mongols were at first frustrated by Chinese walled cities. Chinggis Khan solved that problem through the discipline he had imposed on the tribesmen—he could now hold them committed to lengthy sieges—but also through the use of expert manpower acquired from sedentary societies farther west. With North China conquered, the Mongols then exploited its very substantial reservoirs of manpower and expertise to attack the Song. That struggle lasted some twenty years (1259–79), but here too the Mongols, now ruled by Kublai Khan, eventually succeeded, creating the Yuan dynasty ruling a united China from 1271 to 1368. The dynasty was established, however, even as the rest of the Mongol Empire began to fragment, and Yuan rule in China was troubled. With Yuan China riven by internal dissension, and battered by a series of droughts and associated famines, beginning in 1351 the Red Turban rebellion further weakened the dynasty. It finally proved incapable of dealing with the emergent southern warlord Zhu Yuanzhang, who fought his way into control of southern China and then ousted the Yuan entirely from the north as well, founding the Ming dynasty as its first emperor in 1368.

Both of these periods of warfare in south China, the conquest by the Mongols (1259–79) and their later ousting (1351–68), involved long periods of warfare in the sedentary, riverine, and heavily fortified regions south of the Yellow River, in which the capabilities of steppe cavalry were much less important. Indeed, riverine navies of massive ships carrying cannon and handgunners designed to fire over riverside fortification walls played a key role in both sets of conflicts. Although the use of siege cannon to breach the wide earthen walls of Chinese fortifications remained rare, gunpowder weapons were a natural supplement to the wide repertoire of weapons in use, and their use was so frequent as to be hardly worth discussing in the sources.[41]

The newly established Ming dynasty, having used firearms to oust the Mongols from China, retained them, and fully incorporated both handguns and cannon into their army, even creating centralized training divisions to educate soldiers in their use. There is some evidence that the Ming used three-rank volley fire against the elephants of the Maw Shan people in southwestern Yunnan in 1388. This may have been a singular instance, but firearms in general became the norm and ranked volley fire became common in Ming forces over the next several centuries. Furthermore, the Ming accorded firearms some credit for their successes. As one Ming military treatise noted, "Our first emperor Taizu (Zhu Yuanzhang), because of his remarkable military accomplishments, gained control of the whole Middle Kingdom. He possessed every sort of fire-weapon in existence from past to present, and kept them in his armouries."[42] A later Ming statesman was more explicit: "Ever since the appearance of these [firearms] weapons, China has been able to defeat the barbarians in the four directions."[43] The first Ming emperor's army ranged in size from 1.2 million to 1.8 million men, and about 10 percent were armed with handguns. The main manufactories were under orders to produce three thousand of one type of cannon, three thousand handguns, and ninety thousand arrowheads every three years (in addition to some other types of firearms and cannon). By 1450 some 50 percent of the units on the frontier were equipped with cannon. Much like the Han dynasty formations described in chapter 4, a Ming infantry company blended soldiers carrying different weapons, using the advantages of each according to circumstance (see Figure 8.9). One early Ming organization divided a company into forty men with spears, thirty with bows, twenty with swords, and ten with firearms. Within this kind of infantry formation, synchronized drill had long existed, as well as volley fire with crossbows. There was no need for the Chinese to "discover" the countermarch (see Figure 8.10).[44]

Despite this massive investment, or perhaps because of it, technological development slowed, especially in handguns, even as their use expanded. The hand cannon being produced in 1436 was nearly identical to the very first models made in the late thirteenth century, but now produced in great numbers. The serial number on one weapon indicates that there were at least one hundred thousand of that model produced in that one year, and as early as the 1370s the Ming army had 150,000 firearm-equipped *units*. The only real change in the weapons itself, however, was a general increase in the ratio of length of the weapon to its muzzle bore. That ratio grew from a highly variable range from 8:1 to 21:1 in the early fourteenth century to a more nearly standard 21:1 to 25:1 at the beginning of the fifteenth century.

This slow rate of innovation, however, needs to be put in context. The needs of the Ming army dictated priorities and levels of investment. Once they had reunified China, their primary enemy

Figure 8.9 A Ming combined-arms infantry formation. This Manchu/Qing dynasty image of the Battle of Sarhu (1618) shows a Ming infantry formation.

Figure 8.10 Ming infantry conducting volley fire. From a ca. 1639 manuscript. Although this is from a relatively late date, it is clear that this form of volley fire drill had long existed in China, first with crossbows and then with early firearms.

was again their old steppe-based foe, whose strength came from speed, maneuverability, and rapid firepower. After some early successes pursuing the Mongols out onto the steppe, later efforts either foundered logistically or were defeated badly, especially at the battle of Tumu in 1449. Thereafter the Ming reverted to the strategic defensive, strengthened the frontier fortifications and built new ones, and eventually formed what we now think of as the Great Wall at roughly the boundary between the steppe and productive agricultural land. Even the wall was sometimes not enough, however. The Mongols laid siege to Beijing in 1550 and proceeded to raid China every year from 1550 to 1566. The Ming shift to the defensive also applied to their early wars in Southeast Asia, which were scaled back after the middle of the fifteenth century.[45]

In this operational context of a strategic defensive, heavily reliant on permanent garrisons in frontier fortifications manned by an increasingly hereditary military class (although gradually replaced by mercenaries after 1500), the Ming found limited value in early firearms. Their slow reload did not immediately recommend them, and the conservatism inherent in large hereditary militaries, in which it was expensive to reequip the whole force with new weapons, and which tended to be culturally conservative about change, militated against innovation in weapons design, if not in tactics.

This is not to say the Ming were uninterested in military innovation or war in general. They possessed a very large army; they fought an average of at least one foreign war per year from 1368 to 1643; and when confronted with new weapons from the outside they readily incorporated them. There is, for example, some evidence that Ming weapons makers were stimulated by their Annamese neighbors to the south tinkering with what had originally been Ming weapons. More famously, the Ming considered the Ottoman and Portuguese weapons that arrived in the early sixteenth century to be superior to their own, and quickly added those designs, along with European gun experts, to the Chinese arsenal. Those weapons stimulated new ways of incorporating gunpowder weapons into the Ming army, but there was also a process of selection and of redesign to suit Chinese circumstances. Unlike populations in Africa and the New World, the Chinese were more than masters of the basic metallurgy and they possessed craft traditions generally superior to those of the Europeans. When confronted with new European and Ottoman firearm technology, the Chinese initially improved on them. For example, they quickly devised a solution to the problem of opening the pan on a matchlock prior to firing, which exposed the priming powder to wind and rain. Chinese technicians added a second arm to the trigger that uncovered the pan as the match was lowered. Much of this technical effort was devoted to increasing the rate of fire. For example, Chinese artisans invented a kind of magazine-fed repeater as well as a wide variety of multiple-barreled handguns, although they were still fired like hand cannon, lacking a trigger mechanism (or "lock").[46]

Perhaps the most apropos example was the Chinese response to the Portuguese breech-loading swivel gun. This was a kind of small cannon, primarily designed to fire a spread of shot against personnel, usually aboard ship. In Europe it was built up from staves of wrought iron and held together with iron hoops (as described in chapter 7). A separate iron breech block shaped like a beer mug was loaded and then wedged into the breech. Although the weaknesses of its wrought iron construction meant that it was already on the way out in Europe, its rapid-fire potential immediately recommended it to the Chinese, who had long since mastered casting complex objects in iron. So the Chinese not only made a cast iron version but equipped it with as many as nine breech blocks to allow for fairly rapid fire. These so-called *folangji* guns (Chinese derived from "Frankish") were also perfectly suited for mounting on the walls of fortification (see Figure 8.11). One Chinese source suggests that some 5,800 *folangji* were manufactured between 1523 and 1564, along with over thirty thousand other firearms of various types. The Chinese were so impressed with the basic concept that they experimented with it in miniature in handguns, as well as scaling it up for much larger guns cast in both iron and bronze.[47]

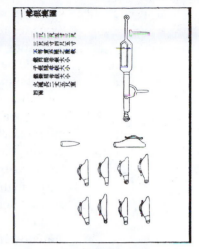

Figure 8.11 A Chinese version of a Portuguese breech-loading cannon. This Chinese drawing from 1568 shows their adaptation of the small breech-loading cannon design; here the illustrator is suggesting building each cannon with nine interchangeable, preloadable breeches for rapid fire.

These sixteenth-century responses to European weapons, combined with their own traditions, provided the Ming with a powerful combined-arms force, joining cavalry, infantry armed with a variety of weapons—notably including arquebusiers—and a substantial train of artillery. They used that army in support of Korea to resist and defeat the highly skilled veteran Japanese army, itself equipped with equivalent firearms technology, during the Japanese invasions of the 1590s (for the naval aspects of that war see chapter 6).[48]

Nevertheless, even this renewed period of innovation in response to the Portuguese and Ottoman stimulus occurred within a specific context. The Ming continued to be concerned primarily with defending their existing borders and maintaining internal security. For the latter their army was more than adequate. For the former the real threat was not the occasional Western trading ship, nor even the invading Japanese of the 1590s, who soon turned inward, not threatening China again until the 1890s. The real threat to the survival of the dynasty remained the steppe peoples to the north. The logistical challenge of the steppe limited offensive possibilities, and the much preferred solution was the old diplomatic game of keeping the various steppe tribes at odds with each other. When diplomacy failed and a real threat emerged, the Ming prepared their defenses based on the Great Wall. Those defenses did use cannon, not for bringing down walls, but rather to defend them against unarmored, fast-moving targets. They prioritized lighter, faster-reloading guns, and formations that could protect themselves from swirling horse archers. In this context, infantry armed with various weapons, including firearms, and supplemented by light, rapid-firing cannon that often spewed pellets rather than large balls, simply made the most sense.

One specific manifestation of both the continuity in the steppe challenge and the attempt to experiment with Western-improved weapons was the wagon brigade. Chinese infantry had long used portable rolling shields, often carried as part of a wagon, to help protect infantry against cavalry charges. Qi Jiguang, a successful Chinese general writing in 1571, perhaps inspired by the possibilities of the improved firearms and breech-loading cannon, made some proposals that reveal the thinking and methods common to the later Ming army. His proposed army would have reorganized infantry and cavalry brigades (each with various types of firearms in various roles), but most interesting was the wagon brigade. Each wagon was attended by two ten-man squads. The first, with six gunners, stayed and fought with and on the wagon, which mounted two swivel guns. The second squad, half armed with muskets and half with contact weapons, fought on and around the wagon, and likely, per descriptions in other sources, lifted off the wagon's side panels and deployed them side by side as a kind of shield, operating in some ways like the *tabur cengi* of the Ottomans and others (described in chapter 7). Some men fired while others repeatedly reloaded and passed weapons forward to the shooters positioned directly behind the portable walls. In total a wagon brigade had 145 wagons, 3,109 men, 8 large cannon, 256 swivel guns, and 512 muskets. As Kenneth Chase argues, this was a force designed not to chase down Mongols but to be able to resist them if caught in the open.[49]

Events proved Ming fears and military priorities to be accurate. Although the dynasty was destroyed by a peasant rebellion, the rebels were in turn swept aside by the Manchus, a largely steppe-style army (although also equipped with gunpowder weapons) that invaded and conquered China, establishing the Qing dynasty that lasted until 1911. The Manchu success and their own cultural origins as steppe archers reenergized the vision of the horse archer as a decisive component of an Asian army, and long limited their investment in gunpowder-weapons development, although they continued to use them on a large scale.

The Manchu replacement of the Ming dynasty resulted from a complex series of factors, primarily social and political. In no way was Ming technological stagnation or innocence of gunpowder weapons a major factor. The hereditary military had succumbed over the generations to various kinds of internal rot. Training standards had varied; "dead pays" (soldiers who only existed on the books but whose pay their commanders claimed and kept) proliferated; at times as many as three-quarters of the army's men were set to growing crops on the frontier to feed the other quarter; reliance on mercenaries, especially Mongols, expanded. Bursts of reforms, often in response to new threats and led by active commanders or emperors, did occur, and there is little doubt about the size and sophistication of the Ming army even at its lowest ebb. Indeed, a single description of a uniform Ming army, or even an "early" versus a "late" one, is almost impossible. It varied too much over time.[50]

The point of this section, however, has not been to explain the Ming defeat, but rather to examine the separate question of why firearms technology, having begun in China, was much more rapidly improved in Christian and Muslim Europe. As with any complex question there would seem to be multiple overlapping causes. Kenneth Chase has identified the primary reason as the Ming's calculated assessment that the greatest threat to dynastic survival was an army of steppe horsemen. Against that foe, especially out on the steppe, firearms of the period could be useful but were unlikely to be decisive. For internal war, also a key consideration during the Ming era, early cannon were not nearly as useful as they proved to be in Europe, simply because of the thick earthen-wall systems of most Chinese fortifications. Furthermore, China at that time lacked a semiautonomous feudal martial nobility protected by private fortifications. Cannons rearranged (at least somewhat) the viability of private fortifications in Europe; there was no parallel social system to rearrange in China. There was thus no incentive to develop heavy siege artillery designed to fire a single projectile at high velocity. Much more effort was invested in cannon (and rocketry) for antipersonnel purposes, for which the technological demands in gun founding and powder mix were not as demanding. The other possible application that could drive cannon development was aboard ship, where their weight and bulk was of less consequence. There too the Chinese had an initial interest during the Ming period, but after 1433, for political reasons, the Ming withdrew from the open oceans.

Ulrich Theobald has identified other related issues that may also have slowed or retarded weapons development. The state maintained an uneven monopoly on the use and production of weapons, prohibiting even the nobility from owning handheld firearms and thereby eliminating the possibility of private, market-based innovation—which in Europe, for example, may have been the source for rifling technology, originally pursued and perfected for noble huntsmen. Chase argues that after 1500 this issue of government restriction disappeared, but he agrees that there was still no private market for nonmilitary use. Theobald also points out that there was no technique of technical illustration in China, which is one reason why assessing period weapon design remains difficult. In a related vein, the Chinese produced, especially after 1500, a vast variety of hand weapons that militated against standardization and mass production. Finally, he argues along with other scholars that the international political scene in East Asia was less anarchic than in Europe. There were simply fewer competing states, and therefore less competitive pressure.[51]

CONCLUSION: THE MILITARY REVOLUTION PROBLEM

This chapter has raced through many examples in a short space, and it would be difficult to reach a single general conclusion about the impact of, or adaptation to, gunpowder weapons. But perhaps that is the real point: there was no single pattern, and much depended on context. Indeed, other examples could have been mentioned: the Safavids of Persia, the Mughals entering and eventually conquering much of India, and especially the Japanese. Each of these societies responded to gunpowder in ways differing from those tracked here and in chapter 7. The Japanese are a particularly illuminating case, because their exposure to firearms (although not gunpowder) came quite late, in the 1540s. Gunpowder weapons then became part of an ongoing process of political consolidation, and may have accelerated the political unification of the main Japanese islands. Once unified, and after failing in their attempted invasions of Korea, Japan's rulers deliberately turned inward, cutting themselves off from the outside world. There was almost no internal war or foreign invasion until the middle of the nineteenth century. In that environment military technological innovation came to a virtual halt. The gun remained a key component of warrior culture, alongside the bow and the sword, but it also remained exactly the same. We will return to the case of Japan in the next chapter.[52]

What do all of these examples say about the nature and reality of a "European Military Revolution"? Recall that the phrase has three separate meanings or components, successively more sweeping in their implications. Its simplest meaning implies a radical change in military practice, in this case referring to the European development of siege artillery, the consequent creation of the bastioned artillery fortress (the *trace italienne*), the use of drilled volley fire by infantry, and the combination of the heavy sailing ship with ship-killing cannon. There is little question that these things happened, although many scholars have argued that they happened in a more evolutionary than revolutionary way, occurring stage by stage over such a long period of time that the term revolution is inappropriate. The second meaning of the phrase is that these changes led to a growth in the size and expense of armies and navies in Europe, which in turn forced a bureaucratization and centralization of the state. And the third meaning is that these things in combination enabled the expansion of Europe at the expense of much of the rest of the world, although it acknowledges the powerful resistance of China and Japan (among other Asian powers) until the Industrial Revolution.[53]

It is relatively easy to do away with the notion that the technology by itself generated these changes. Context mattered. For example, there is no evidence that gunpowder substantially changed anything at all in China. Such changes as did occur in the Chinese way of fighting were evolutionary and slow. Nor did China power its expansion through the exploitation of gunpowder weapons. Gunpowder weapons did not dramatically alter Chinese military might relative to their neighbors: they were most relevant to fighting *within* China before the nineteenth century, especially on its rivers. Cannon deployed at sea were critical in the fight against Japan, but China had fundamentally abandoned offensive maritime expansion, and so that possibility never materialized. The arrival of gunpowder weapons in Africa and North America did affect those societies and their ways of war, but the nature of the effects varied widely, and often tended merely to accentuate existing tendencies.

What about European expansion from 1400 to 1800? Did European power in Africa, the Americas, or South Asia depend on the development of gunpowder technology? The answers are mixed. It seems clear that European *arrival* in those places was enabled by changes in maritime technology, and the cannon aboard those ships helped secure them there, but they did not enable the projection of power inland. Other factors were more important. In Africa, for example, the size of the African population and the disease environment seriously limited the potential for European empire building at all. Even the dramatic Spanish successes in Mexico and Peru were relatively exceptional and depended as much, if not more, on local political conditions and the disease susceptibility of the Amerindians as on technology. Those dramatic successes did not recur in the more politically decentralized and diffuse demographic environment of North America. Portuguese victory in India depended on hard fighting, a divided political environment, and cannon-equipped ships. European developments in gunpowder weaponry by 1500, as manifested among the Portuguese, were crucial to their gaining access to the richest trading network in the world. Without them Portugal would have failed. With them they had the opportunity to succeed, but gunpowder weapons and bastioned fortresses were hardly a guarantee.

On the other hand, political and military conditions in Europe encouraged continued investment in firearms technology. Over time that investment realized the potential of firearms by encouraging craft innovation and the building of technical infrastructure, generation by generation, until the improvements became decisive. Printing and the mobility of craft experts within an otherwise highly competitive European state system also contributed to the spread and improvement of technology. That process dramatically accelerated when merged with the new technical capabilities made possible by industrialization, as will be discussed in

TIMELINE

ca. 1000	First military use of gunpowder in China
1368	End of Mongol Yuan dynasty; beginning of Ming
1449	Mongols defeat Ming army on the steppe at Tumu; Ming revert to defensive orientation
1498	Portuguese reach India
1520s	Spanish conquest of Mexico; European and Ottoman firearms reach China
1625	Dahomean state forms under pressure of slave trade
1644	End of the Ming dynasty
1650	Emergence of ship of the line, a purpose-built warship

chapter 10. As this chapter begins to show, however, it was Europe's maritime power projection that made the difference; its "mastery of the seas (aided by naval gun power) . . . proved to be the decisive factor in its development, creating the first global trading system and precipitating the rise of capitalism in Europe."[54] That latter change, capitalism, truly rearranged the dynamics of power, as the ability to produce goods, including firearms, cannons, ironclad ships, and more, became the very measure of power. Neither European market capitalism nor industrialization was a consequence of gunpowder weapons as such. But there is little doubt that gunpowder, especially combined into the sailing ship, helped secure the profits of trade to European powers. Trade in turn urged along industrial production, the techniques of which, when applied to weaponry, empowered real European worldwide military dominance.[55]

Further Reading

Black, Jeremy. *A Military Revolution? Military Change and European Society, 1550–1800.* Basingstoke, UK: Macmillan, 1991.

Black, Jeremy, ed. *War in the Early Modern World.* London: Westview, 1999.

Black, Jeremy. *War in the World: A Comparative History, 1450–1600.* London: Palgrave Macmillan, 2011.

Chase, Kenneth Warren. *Firearms: A Global History to 1700.* Cambridge, UK: Cambridge University Press, 2003.

Cipolla, Carlo M. *Guns, Sails, and Empires: Technological Innovation and the Early Phases of European Expansion, 1400–1700.* New York: Pantheon, 1966.

Disney, A. R. *A History of Portugal and the Portuguese Empire.* 2 vols. Cambridge, UK: Cambridge University Press, 2009.

Lee, Wayne E. "The Native American Military Revolution: Firearms, Forts, and Polities." In *Empires and Indigenes: Intercultural Alliance, Imperial Expansion, and Warfare in the Early Modern World,* edited by Wayne E. Lee, 49–80. New York: New York University Press, 2011.

Lorge, Peter A. *The Asian Military Revolution: From Gunpowder to the Bomb.* Cambridge, UK: Cambridge University Press, 2008.

McNeill, William H. *The Pursuit of Power: Technology, Armed Force and Society since A.D. 1000.* Chicago: University of Chicago Press, 1982.

Mortimer, Geoff, ed. *Early Modern Military History, 1450–1815.* Basingstoke, UK: Palgrave Macmillan, 2004.

Parker, Geoffrey. *The Military Revolution: Military Innovation and the Rise of the West, 1500–1800.* 2nd ed. Cambridge, UK: Cambridge University Press, 1988, 1996.

Thornton, John K. *Warfare in Atlantic Africa, 1500–1800.* London: Routledge, 1999.

Notes

1. Kenneth Warren Chase, *Firearms: A Global History to 1700* (Cambridge, UK: Cambridge University Press, 2003), 70.

2. A. R. Disney, *A History of Portugal and the Portuguese Empire* (Cambridge, UK: Cambridge University Press, 2009), 2:40 (quote).

3. This section on navigation and ship evolution is based primarily on V. J. Parry, *The Age of Reconnaissance* (Berkeley: University of California Press, 1981), 53–113; Disney, *History of Portugal*, 2:39–42;

4. John Frances Guilmartin, *Gunpowder and Galleys: Changing Technology and Mediterranean Warfare at Sea in the 16th Century*, rev. ed. (Annapolis, MD: Naval Institute Press, 2003), 40; Carlo M. Cipolla, *Guns, Sails, and Empires: Technological Innovation and the Early Phases of European Expansion, 1400–1700* (New York: Pantheon, 1966), 30, 81. Louis Sicking points out that the earliest evidence for guns aboard ship dates from 1337, increasing thereafter and common by 1450. Louis Sicking, "Naval Warfare in Europe, c. 1330–c. 1680," in *European Warfare, 1350–1750*, ed. Frank Tallett and D. J. B. Trim (Cambridge, UK: Cambridge University Press, 2010), 240.

5. Cipolla, *Guns, Sails*, 81–82; Geoffrey Parker, *The Military Revolution: Military Innovation and the Rise of the West, 1500–1800*, 2nd ed. (Cambridge, UK: Cambridge University Press, 1988, 1996), 90, 160; Ruth R. Brown, "'A Jewel of Great Value': English Iron Gunfounding and Its Rivals, 1550–1650," in *Ships and Guns: The Sea Ordnance in Venice and in Europe between the 15th and the 17th Centuries*, ed. Carlo Beltrame and Renato Giannie Ridella (Oxford: Oxbow, 2011), 98–105.

6. Jan Glete, "Naval Power, 1450–1650: The Formative Age," in *Early Modern Military History, 1450–1815*, ed. Geoff Mortimer (Basingstoke, UK: Palgrave MacMillan, 2004), 86 (quote).

7. Cipolla, *Guns, Sails*, 83; Glete, "Naval Power," 87; John Francis Guilmartin, Jr., "The Earliest Shipboard Gunpowder Ordnance: An Analysis of Its Technical Parameters and Tactical Capabilities," *Journal of Military History* 71 (2007): 649–69.

8. Jan Glete, *Navies and Nations: Warships, Navies and State Building in Europe and America, 1500–1860* (Stockholm: Almqvist & Wiksell, 1993), 1:170 (quote); Glete, "Naval Power," 87.

9. Svat Soucek, "About the Ottoman Age of Exploration," *Archivum Ottomanicum* 27 (2010): 318; Jeremy Black, *War in the World: A Comparative History, 1450–1600* (New York: Palgrave Macmillan, 2011), 216.

10. Parker, *Military Revolution*, 104–5; Black, *War in the World*, 144, 146; Ricardo Bonalume Neto, "Lightning Rod of Portuguese India," *MHQ*, 14.3 (2002): 70 (quote).

11. Giancarlo Casale, *The Ottoman Age of Exploration* (Oxford: Oxford University Press, 2010); Soucek, "About the Ottoman Age"; Jeremy Black, *Beyond the Military Revolution: War in the Seventeenth-Century World* (New York: Palgrave Macmillan, 2011), 156, 158; Colin Imber, "The Navy of Süleyman the Magnificent," in *Studies in Ottoman History and Law*, ed. Colin Imber, (Istanbul: Isis, 1996), 1–69.

12. The following paragraphs on Diu are based on: Roger Lee de Jesus, "The Second Siege of Diu (1546) and Portuguese Warfare in India in the Sixteenth Century," paper delivered at the Society for Military History Conference, New Orleans, LA, March 2013 (cited with permission); Neto, "Lightning Rod," 68–77; M. N. Pearson, *Merchants and Rulers in Gujarat* (Berkeley: University of California Press, 1976), 10–12, 69–82; M. L. Dames, "The Portuguese and the Turks in the Indian Ocean in the Sixteenth Century," *Journal of the Royal Asiatic Society* 1 (January 1921): 1–28; Bailey W. Diffie

and George. D. Winius, *Foundations of the Portuguese Empire, 1415–1580* (Minneapolis: University of Minnesota Press, 1977), 240–41, 287–89, 294.

13. Malyn Newitt, *A History of Portuguese Overseas Expansion, 1400–1668* (New York: Routledge, 2005), 78 (quote).

14. Oscar F. Hefting, "High versus Low: Portuguese and Dutch Fortification Traditions Meet in Colonial Brazil (1500–1654)," in *First Forts: Essays on the Archaeology of Protocolonial Fortifications*, ed. Eric Klingelhofer (Leiden: Brill, 2010), 189–208.

15. Neto, "Lightning Rod," 75 (quote).

16. R. S. Whiteway, *The Rise of Portuguese Power in India, 1497–1550* (Westminster, UK: Archibald Constable, 1899), 262–64.

17. Anthony Disney, "Portuguese Expansion, 1400–1800: Encounters, Negotiations, and Interactions," in *Portuguese Oceanic Expansion, 1400–1800*, ed. Francisco Bethencourt and Diogo Ramada Curto (Cambridge, UK: Cambridge University Press, 2007), 291 (quote); Roger Lee de Jesus, "As despesas da reconstrução da fortaleza de Diu em 1546–1547," *Revista de História da Sociedade e da Cultura* 12 (2012): 217–43.

18. Whiteway, *Rise of Portuguese Power*, 311.

19. Richard M. Eaton and Philip B. Wagoner, "Warfare on the Deccan Plateau, 1450–1600: A Military Revolution in Early Modern India?" *Journal of World History* 25.1 (2014): 12–17; Black, *Beyond the Military Revolution*, 107, 115.

20. Joseph E. Inikori, "The Struggle against the Transatlantic Slave Trade: The Role of the State," in *Fighting the Slave Trade: West African Strategies*, ed. Sylviane Diouf (Athens, OH: Ohio University Press, 2003), 177.

21. Robin Law, "Dahomey and the Slave Trade: Reflections on the Historiography of the Rise of Dahomey," *Journal of African History* 27.2 (1986): 237–67 (esp. 239–41); John Thornton, *Africa and Africans in the Making of the Atlantic World, 1400–1800*, 2nd ed. (New York: Cambridge University Press, 1998), 31–32.

22. Inikori, "Struggle," 1179 (quote).

23. John Thornton, "Warfare, Slave Trading and European Influence: Atlantic Africa, 1450–1800," in *War in the Early Modern World*, ed. Jeremy Black (London: Westview, 1999), 130–32; Inikori, "Struggle," 176–81.

24. John K. Thornton, *Warfare in Atlantic Africa, 1500–1800* (London: Routledge, 1999), 16 (quote).

25. Ray A. Kea, *Settlements, Trade, and Polities in the Seventeenth-Century Gold Coast* (Baltimore: Johns Hopkins University Press, 1982), 133, 138–41; Black, *War in the World*, 176; Alfred W. Crosby, *Ecological Imperialism: The Biological Expansion of Europe, 900–1900* (Cambridge, UK: Cambridge University Press, 1986), 138–39; John K. Thornton, "Firearms, Diplomacy, and Conquest in Angola: Cooperation and Alliance in West Central Africa, 1491–1671," in *Empires and Indigenes: Intercultural Alliance, Imperial Expansion, and Warfare in the Early Modern World*, ed. Wayne E. Lee (New York: New York University Press, 2011), 167–92; John K. Thornton, *Cultural History of the Atlantic World, 1250–1820* (Cambridge, UK: Cambridge University Press, 2012), 64.

26. H. A. Gemery and J. S. Hogendorn, "Technological Change, Slavery and the Slave Trade," in *The Imperial Impact: Studies in the Economic History of Africa and India*, ed. Clive Dewey and A. G. Hopkins (London: Athlone, 1978), 247–51.

27. W. A. Richards, "The Import of Firearms into West Africa in the Eighteenth Century," *The Journal of African History* 21.1 (1980): 43–59 (quote 50).

28. Joseph E. Inikori, "The Import of Firearms into West Africa 1750–1807: A Quantitative Analysis," *Journal of African History* 18.3 (1977): 339–68. The specifics of Inikori's numbers have been challenged or supplemented, but the general scale is accepted.

29. Kea, *Settlements*, 148–58; Thornton, "Warfare, Slave Trading," 137.

30. Richards, "Import," 46 (quote).

31. Richards, "Import," 57; Law, "Dahomey and the Slave Trade."

32. Inikori, "Struggle," 185–89; Walter Hawthorne, "Strategies of the Decentralized: Defending Communities from Slave Raiders in Coastal Guinea-Bissau, 1450–1815," in Diouf, *Fighting the Slave Trade*, 152–69; Thornton, *Cultural History*, 68–69; Law, "Dahomey and the Slave Trade," 257; Thornton, *Africa and Africans*, 113–25.

33. Wayne E. Lee, "Projecting Power in the Early Modern World: The Spanish Model?" in Lee, *Empires and Indigenes*, 1–18.

34. Much of this section is based on Wayne E. Lee, "The Native American Military Revolution: Firearms, Forts, and Polities," in Lee, *Empires and Indigenes*, 49–80.

35. Alan Gallay, *The Indian Slave Trade: The Rise of the English Empire in the American South, 1670–1717* (New Haven, CT: Yale University Press, 2002); Daniel K. Richter, "War and Culture: The Iroquois Experience," *William and Mary Quarterly*, 3rd ser., 40 (1983): 528–59.

36. What follows is heavily dependent on the work of Peter Lorge, Kenneth Swope, Kenneth Chase, and Tonio Andrade (who generously supplied me with several forthcoming works, cited below) as well as the synthetic efforts of Jeremy Black. Joseph Needham's work remains essential, but is now being substantially supplemented by more recent archaeological and textual research. Specific ideas and more specialist literature are cited where appropriate.

37. Chase, *Firearms*, 31; Peter Allan Lorge, *The Asian Military Revolution: From Gunpowder to the Bomb* (Cambridge, UK: Cambridge University Press, 2008) 32–33, 40–41.

38. Chase, *Firearms*, 31–32, 58–61; Lorge, *Asian Military Revolution*, 34–38, 69; Joseph Needham, *Science and Civilisation in China*, vol. 5, *Chemistry and Chemical Technology*, pt. 7, *Military Technology, the Gunpowder Epic* (Cambridge, UK: Cambridge University Press, 1986), 222–26, provides evidence for the much earlier use.

39. Chase, *Firearms*, 32.

40. Lorge, *Asian Military Revolution*, 29, 70; Tonio Andrade, "Late Medieval Divergences: Comparative Perspectives on Early Gunpowder Warfare in Europe and China," *Journal of Medieval Military History* 13 (2015, in press).

41. Lorge, *Asian Military Revolution*, 72–73; Chase, *Firearms*, 33–34.

42. Laichen Sun, "Military Technology Transfers from Ming China and the Emergence of Northern Mainland Southeast Asia (c. 1390–1527)," *Journal of Southeast Asian Studies* 34.3 (2003), 498 (quote).

43. Sun, "Military Technology Transfers," 499 (quote).

44. Chase, *Firearms*, 36; ; Tonio Andrade, "The Arquebus Volley Technique in China, c. 1560: Evidence from the Writings of Qi Jiguang," *Journal of Chinese Military History* 4.2 (2015, in press); Tonio Andrade, *The Gunpowder Age: China, Military Innovation, and the Rise of the West, 900–1900* (Princeton: Princeton University Press, forthcoming 2015); Andrade, "Late Medieval Divergences"; Kenneth Swope, "Bringing in the Big Guns: On the Use of Artillery in the Ming-Manchu War," in *Chinese and Indian Warfare: From the Classical Age to 1870*, ed. Peter A. Lorge and Kaushik Roy (London: Routledge, 2015), 134–45 (thanks to Ken Swope for sharing an early version of this piece with me); Liew Foon Ming, *The Treatises on Military Affairs of the Ming Dynastic History, 1368–1644* (Hamburg: Gesellschaft für Natur- und Völkerlande Ostasiens, 1998), 1:50–52, 102–3, 166; Sun, "Military Technology Transfers," 500; Laichen Sun, "Ming-Southeast Asian Overland Interactions, 1368–1644" (PhD diss., University of Michigan, 2000), 31–32. More on Ming army size in Liew Foon Ming, *Treatises on Military Affairs*, 1:73–76. Note that Liew cites an early Ming census indicating a total population of 60,540,000, supporting 3,100,000 soldiers, i.e., a 5 percent mobilization rate, dramatically exceeding Gat's hypothetical

maximum (discussed in chapter 7). Note, however, that by the mid-sixteenth century the army was down to 845,800 men, at a time when the total population had surely risen. This high initial rate may also only have been possible because of their dual role as soldier-farmers.

45. Chase, *Firearms*, 39; Andrade, "Great Divergence"; data on barrels derived from chart in Needham, *Gunpowder Epic*, 290–92. This data is not precise, because Needham does not provide the barrel length, only the length of the entire weapon, including the socket for the pole. Black, *War in the World*, 83, 86.

46. Kenneth M. Swope, *A Dragon's Head and a Serpent's Tail: Ming China and the First Great East Asian War, 1592–1598* (Norman: University of Oklahoma Press, 2009), 15–16; Liew Foon Ming, *Treatises on Military Affairs*, 102–3; Chase, *Firearms*, 145.

47. Chase, *Firearms*, 143–45, 147; Swope, "Bringing in the Big Guns," citing Cheng Dong, "Mingdai houqi youming huopao gaishu," *Wenwu* 4 (1993): 79, 81.

48. Kenneth M. Swope, "Crouching Tigers, Secret Weapons: Military Technology Employed During the Sino-Japanese-Korean War, 1592–1598," *Journal of Military History* 69.1 (2005): 11–43; Swope, *Dragon's Head*.

49. Needham, *Gunpowder Epic*, 414–21; Chase, *Firearms*, 162–66.

50. Liew Foon Ming, *Treatises on Military Affairs*, 1:128, 133, 156n153; Swope, *Dragon's Head*, 19–21.

51. Needham, *Gunpowder Epic*, 390; Christopher Cullen, "Reflections on the Transmission and Transformation of Technologies: Agriculture, Printing and Gunpowder between East and West," in *Science between Europe and Asia: Historical Studies on the Transmission, Adoption and Adaptation of Knowledge*, ed. Feza Günergun and Dhruv Raina (New York: Springer, 2011), 20; Chase, *Firearms*, 49–52, 153–54; Ulrich Theobald, "Muskets and Cannons in the Late Ming (1368–1644) and Early Qing (1644–1912) Periods," paper delivered at the Society for Military History annual conference, New Orleans, March 15–17, 2013.

52. Stephen Morillo, "Guns and Government: A Comparative Study of Europe and Japan," *Journal of World History* 6 (1995): 75–106; Chase, *Firearms*, 172–96; Needham, *Gunpowder Epic*, 466–72.

53. Steven Gunn, "War and the Emergence of the State: Western Europe, 1350–1600," in Tallett and Trim, *European Warfare*, 50–73; Parker, *Military Revolution*.

54. Azar Gat, *War in Human Civilization* (Oxford: Oxford University Press, 2006), 505 (quote);

55. Black, *War in the World*, 207; Chase, *Firearms*, 70; Black, *Beyond the Military Revolution*, 189–94; David Cressy, *Saltpeter: The Mother of Gunpowder* (Oxford: Oxford University Press, 2013), William H. McNeill *The Pursuit of Power: Technology, Armed Force and Society since A.D. 1000* (Chicago: University of Chicago Press, 1982), 79–116, 176–77.

9

Institutionalization, Bureaucratization, and Professionalization: China, Japan, and Europe

1650–1815

Qing (Manchu) China • Private Enterprise War in Europe to 1650 • Institutionalization, Bureaucratization, and Professionalization in Europe, 1650–1789 • Japan's Variant Path, 1500–1868 • The Levée en Masse and Mass Conscript Armies

A CRITICAL INNOVATION in the development of modern states has been the centralization of control over military force through the combined processes of institutionalization, bureaucratization, and professionalization. States around the world traditionally mobilized, equipped, supplied, and directed armed force through networks of elites tied to a ruler through either loyalty or a coincidence of interests. There were exceptions. For example, there have been forces mobilized by an ideologically forged unity of purpose that transcended social divisions—a notable example being the initial Arab conquests of the seventh century. Something altogether different, however, emerged in China, Japan, and Europe (among other places) in the sixteenth through the eighteenth centuries. Instead of producing and directing force through networked relationships, those states began to substitute processes, bureaucracies, and institutions controlled by an impersonal state and functioning as the extension of a single directing will. There is a huge caveat here: the impersonal unitary state does not exist, and really never has. The role of local or regional leaders, elite or otherwise, hereditary, elected, or appointed, can never be discounted. Power has always been achieved and maintained through a process of negotiation among various players. Even present-day states are sometimes described by political scientists as holding power through the maintenance of a "winning coalition," the identity and size of which depend on the history of that particular state. Even autocrats and tyrants depend on well-placed supporters. As for the early modern states considered here, historians have increasingly reexamined what adjectives like "absolute" mean. They have found, for example, that the so-called absolutist rule of Louis XIV of France depended heavily on the co-optation of aristocrats and urban elites, that the Qing dynasty's bureaucracy was significantly undermanned, and that the Tokugawa Shogunate kept its 250 years of peace as much through accommodation and cultural unity as through armed force or bureaucratic sophistication.[1]

Nevertheless, Louis XIV and other kings or political elites shared a desire to harness their armed forces to a single will, and they sought ever-more effective mechanisms for tapping the financial resources of the state to support those forces. In Europe, the French Revolution dramatically accelerated this ongoing pursuit of greater state capacity and gave it a fresh twist. The Revolution swept away the old negotiated relationships of elites to monarch and produced a new form of mass conscript army. Those armies remained rooted in the institutional forms and appearances of the preceding professionalizing age, but their greatly increased size demanded yet further expansion of state bureaucracy and capacity. This expansion of state capacity represents much of what we now think of as "modernity" in the West, at least insofar as the nature of the state is concerned. This chapter thus focuses on changes in western Europe, but it also provides comparative examples. We begin with China's process of centralization and then examine the decentralized, nonbureaucratic system in Europe prior to the late seventeenth century. In each case we analyze these processes through the four primary tasks of manning/recruitment, equipping, campaign logistics, and responsiveness to central strategic direction.

A ruler's desire to exercise central control was hardly new to this time period. Indeed, considering state centralization as an innovation of this period reveals some of the drawbacks of this book's focus on innovations, especially when examining nontechnological developments. For the most part, technologies were invented only once, while ideas and institutional systems can emerge, flourish, die, and then recur much later. The bureaucratic, centralized state management of military force has such a history. To mention only the ancient empires dealt with earlier in this book, the Assyrians, Romans, and Qin/Han Chinese each implemented versions of institutionalized and bureaucratized systems for manning, equipping, supplying, and directing their armed forces. The surviving documentation of the Roman imperial military administration attests to the intricacies of its management and to the many links connecting peripheries to the center. To be absolutely clear, this is *not* to suggest that the Roman Empire was an impersonal state, in which a unitary will directed mobilization and deployment without regard for intermediate elites. But on the spectrum extending from such a hypothetical unitary centralized state down to the consensus-based authority of tribal chiefs, however, the Romans and the Han had moved the dial markedly toward centralization. One side effect of centralization, however, was the demilitarization of the local: local elites no longer had their own armed retainers; local towns and cities no longer built their own fortifications. Therefore, when the center's financial mechanisms began to break down, as happened in the later Roman Empire, the imperial army proved unable to defend the provinces. One ancient author even argued that it was the cost of maintaining the army that had undermined the entire imperial taxation system.[2] Local elites found themselves having to remilitarize their populace or make deals with the invaders. A thousand years later, Europeans of the seventeenth and eighteenth centuries found themselves again aspiring to Roman-like systems of bureaucratic centralization—in a very different context and for different historical reasons. The Romans were hardly the only ones, however, to use centralized bureaucracies to manage their military forces. Indeed, the Chinese have often been described as precocious in the invention of a civil bureaucracy, from the Qin right down to the present. The Manchu/Qing adaptation of this ancient bureaucracy provides a contemporary counterpoint to European developments.

QING (MANCHU) CHINA

"Legalist" ideology in China, emphasizing autocratic, bureaucratic, and centralized rule, dates back to the Qin dynasty (221–206 BCE) and even before. Although the ideology was initially discredited after the fall of that dynasty, subsequent dynasties, once established, relied on its precepts to foster their own control, allowing them to raise taxes and mobilize the population to an unusual degree compared to other contemporary states. The primary mechanism for this form of rule was a state bureaucracy run by professional, trained civil servants, who as a class, and even as individuals, often survived dynastic transitions and reliably served their new masters. In doing so they provided a remarkable continuity of bureaucratically mobilized state capacity.[3]

This continuity across dynasties persisted even when the new ruler arrived from outside the cultural core of Han China. As discussed in the previous chapter, the Ming dynasty, weakened and finally destroyed by internal rebellion, was replaced by the invading Manchus, who established the Qing dynasty in 1636 (although remnant Ming forces remained in the field until the 1660s). The Manchus were a tribal steppe people, horse archers like their Mongol counterparts discussed in chapter 5, who had incorporated gunpowder weapons into their arsenal, and had long experience raiding the Chinese frontier. In the early seventeenth century, as the Ming fragmented and spiraled toward collapse, China was open to a vigorous conqueror, and the Manchus stepped decisively into that role.

The first stage of the Manchu expansion proceeded much like that of Chinggis Khan: a powerful charismatic leader, Nurhachi (1559–1626) and then his son Hong Taiji (r. 1626–43), rode to victory based on the military capabilities of the steppe horsemen. The army, originally organized into eight "banners" of Manchus, incorporated new peoples as they successfully expanded their conquests, first four and eventually eight new Mongol banners, and then eight Chinese banners. The latter were filled with men from the northern Chinese frontier, and it was they who managed the firearms and artillery used to conquer the heartland of China. So far this represents the kind of "centralization" achieved by many first- or second-generation conquering tribal peoples, in which all loyalties were personal, virtually all men were warriors, and the rewards of victory welded their loyalties to the center for as long as success followed success. Armies like these were highly centralized but were hardly bureaucratic, and they proved difficult to sustain in succeeding generations.

The Manchus, however, adapted well to their new Chinese environment—now established as the Qing dynasty. Even before their full conquest of China, the Manchu rulers incorporated a Chinese civil official into each banner to manage administrative concerns. Confronted in 1673 with a rebellion by formerly allied Chinese generals (the so-called Rebellion of the Three Feudatories), the Qing demonstrated their mastery of China's civil administrative systems by raising huge armies from the Han Chinese population, reportedly as many as nine hundred thousand, despite the fact that much of the core of Han China was then controlled by the rebels. After nine years of war the Qing suppressed the rebellion, reformed the army, and then campaigned far to the west and north, adding immense territories to China, for the most part permanently (see Map 9.1). Historian Peter Perdue argues that the Qing success in mobilizing Chinese resources depended not just on their use of the civil bureaucracy but also on their successful bargain with the Chinese landed elite, in which they reduced the tax burden on them and strengthened their control over the peasantry. In return for this, the landed elite supported the continuance and expansion of the old bureaucratic systems of taxation. Once internal peace was reestablished, the imperial treasury recovered sufficiently to finance the ensuing Qing expansion.[4]

The instrument for this expansion was the reformed Manchu/Qing army, now divided into two components: the Eight Banners and the Green Standard Army. Each had a different system for manning, equipping, supplying, and directing. The banners preserved the best qualities of a professional standing army, while the Green Standard Army allowed the state to tap the immense resources of the Chinese population when necessary. During the initial conquest of China, the Manchu army had simply expanded the banner system to include conquered peoples (primarily Mongols and Han Chinese). Over time, however, especially after suppressing the Rebellion of the Three Feudatories, the dynasty phased out the Chinese banners, retained some Mongol banners for cavalry, and returned the banner army to being an ethnically Manchu force.

The banners garrisoned the capital and other key locations around China, especially near the frontier with Manchuria (and thus also near the capital in Beijing), and they lived in garrison compounds deliberately isolated from the

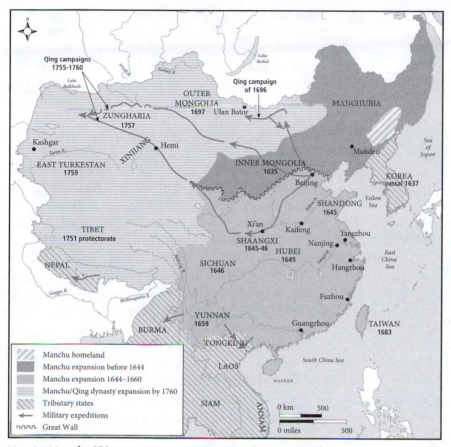

Map 9.1 Manchu/Qing conquests, 1600–1760. The Manchus first conquered much of Mongolia, and then subdued Ming China by 1660. Established as the Qing dynasty, they embarked on further expansion, eventually eliminating the threat from the steppe.

surrounding population. Banner membership was hereditary, but as it grew too large members could be reclassified as civilians. The size of the banner army varied, but its total of 250,000 men in 1757 represents a reasonable average. The emperor controlled all promotions and officer appointments. Once the dynasty was in firm control of China, the bannermen received a set salary—often at least partially in the form of a grain allowance—replacing the traditional tribal system of directly sharing the fruits of conquest. Each garrison had its own training field, and training was continuous, with an increasing emphasis on firearm-equipped infantry. Most of the cavalry came from the Mongol banners, who continued to fight in the traditional steppe manner.

Like European soldiers of this period, the bannermen's lives were increasingly centralized and institutionalized. They lived apart from the population in forts (barracks); they trained and drilled in dedicated areas; their

Figure 9.1 A Manchu bannerman officer, mid-eighteenth century. Wufu, a Qing military officer from the reign of Qianlong (1735–96).

equipment was provided by the state (although sometimes through an additional allowance for having equipment made), and they wore uniforms whose color reflected their banner affiliation. The reasons behind these developments, however, differed from those in Europe. The overall goal of securing the dynasty through the centralized control of armed force was the same, but in this case institutionalization (barracks, uniforms, state pay, and so on) was pursued in a different cultural context. The Manchus were ethnic outsiders using native Chinese bureaucratic systems and traditions to rule over a vast Han Chinese population (as well as many other ethnicities). Maintaining the loyalty of their core armed force was paramount to dynastic survival, but China had a centuries-long history of provincial administrators asserting independent power based on the loyalty of regionally stationed troops. Excluding the Han Chinese from the banners (they were virtually gone by 1779), visually and physically separating the bannermen from their surrounding communities, and providing them with key economic and legal privileges reinforced their status as a distinctive, ethnic class—obedient and responsive to the emperor alone.[5]

The huge task of expanding and defending the empire, however, demanded more men than could be provided by ethnic Manchus. The Green Standard Army filled that gap with some six hundred thousand men (in the mid-eighteenth century; the number varied) recruited from the Han Chinese population. It too, however, was structured by fears related to internal security. The command system was deliberately complicated to frustrate using it against the dynasty, and the men were distributed in small posts all around the empire. The largest peacetime unit was only five thousand men. Unlike in the banners, service in the Green Standard Army was not hereditary, although members' family networks often provided new recruits, who typically served for a lifetime.

Both armies were managed by the board of war, an arm of the civil bureaucracy, acting as it had in previous dynasties in administering pay, equipment, rations, and training. Campaign administration and logistics were the province of the Grand Council, established in the 1720s, although Manchu emperors often took the field with their army. The council created messenger relay stations to alert civilian officials along march routes to prepare for army movements, and established imperial depots for weapons and food on those routes. Paying for the army and for this expanding logistical infrastructure demanded harnessing China's immense potential wealth, something that in turn demanded a thoroughly professional and integrated governmental bureaucracy capable of tapping the increasingly market-oriented wealth of the Chinese economy. In the mid-sixteenth century the Ming had converted the centuries-old corvée labor requirement into a cash tax, greatly increasing governmental income and flexibility. Showing yet another advantage of the continuity in the Chinese civil bureaucracy, the Qing continued and improved that system. Among other changes, the Qing were able to shift the longstanding tax on peasants from a collective one imposed on village units into an individual tax that could follow the increasing number of peasants who migrated to the cities.[6]

This bureaucratic infrastructure was far from perfect. Qing emperors rejected the old Ming method of maintaining soldiers through agricultural military colonies, but they also explicitly worried about previous failures to provide for the army, especially given their promises of an openhanded reward and salary system designed to keep the soldiers loyal to the center. The administrative process, however, sometimes failed them. As in European armies, and with imperial acquiescence, officers profited from the salaries of "dead pays" (in Chinese *chi konge*: eating the stipends of vacant posts). Common soldiers in both the banners and the Green Standard Army were paid at least partly with food rations rather than cash. Higher-level military officials were supposed to spend part of their own salaries repairing the soldiers' weapons and equipment, and even to pay the bonuses for valor and proficiency. The ideal of centralized state supply notwithstanding, common soldiers in fact had to spend some of their own salaries to repair and purchase some weapons and armor. And, as in all armies, there were constant complaints that the soldiers were not maintaining their equipment or training to standard.[7]

Even during the period of its greatest successes in the mid-eighteenth century, the Qing central bureaucracy was not always up to the task on its own. In one sense, that is hardly surprising. By one calculation, the Qing dynasty's bureaucracy was not overly large relative to the population involved. Eighteenth-century France could muster one administrator for every three thousand people, while the Qing provided only one magistrate for three hundred thousand people. As Qing ambitions and conquests expanded westward, eventually reaching some three thousand miles from Beijing, they found the civil bureaucracy could not meet the challenge, and they instead turned to merchants to provide food on contract. Still, on any sort of comparative scale, their eighteenth-century success was remarkable, perhaps best demonstrated by the logistical systems that underpinned their massive campaigns of conquest in the west and north.[8]

The campaigns in the far west, sustained by a combination of state bureaucracy and commercial contractors, proved enormously capable. In the Jinchuan campaign of 1747–49 the state mobilized two hundred thousand military laborers in support of seventy thousand troops. In the second

Jinchuan campaign of 1771 to 1776, the field army increased to 129,500 and the laborers to 462,000. These laborers moved military materials across the region's many mountains; they built camps, food depots, roads, and bridges; carried casualties; repaired weapons; shoveled snow; and even guarded the food depots. Eventually the army adopted a guideline that every hundred soldiers should be assigned fifty to eighty laborers.[9]

This massive logistical infrastructure allowed a sedentary Chinese state for the first time to launch campaigns of conquest deep into the steppe. It is true that the Qing differed from their Ming, Han, or other dynastic predecessors in being originally a steppe people themselves. They understood steppe politics and played that game very well. But, as rulers of a sedentary people interested in taking and *holding* steppe territory, it was "equally fundamental," in Peter Perdue's analysis, that the Qing had solved "the logistical problem of steppe warfare. Ever since the days of the Scythians, the most effective nomadic military tactic when faced by vastly superior armies from settled empires was to withdraw further into the steppe. If the settled army pursued, it eventually outran its supply lines, making it vulnerable to devastating ambushes. If it turned back, the nomads simply recouped their losses."[10] The Qing now not only directed the operations of multiple converging columns to limit their steppe opponents' tactical options, but they also sustained those expeditions across time and space to an astonishing degree.

The Qing were motivated to these extremities by the late seventeenth-century rise of the Zunghar Mongol confederation, which itself was threatening to become another imperial power. The Zunghars had conquered Mongolia, much of modern western China, and even parts of Tibet and Kazakhstan. The Qing could not ignore this threat. In 1695 the Kangxi emperor (r. 1662–1722) led the first major counter effort in the form of three armies converging in the northern steppe of Outer Mongolia on a ninety-nine day roundtrip journey of three thousand kilometers. Although Kangxi virtually exhausted his supplies, he destroyed a Zunghar army. This three-month campaign represented what seems to have been the standard upper limit for Chinese armies campaigning in the steppe, and thereby highlights the much longer campaigns to follow in the mid-eighteenth century.[11]

Bouncing back from a major defeat in 1731, the Qing mounted three expeditions against the Zunghar Mongols from 1755 to 1759, sustaining field armies of around fifty thousand men on campaigns for *one to two years*. The individual operations saw separate armies march in converging columns far into the steppe, cross the Gobi desert, and eventually penetrate deep into what is now Xinjiang. The 1755 campaign involved two converging columns of twenty-five thousand men each on campaign from March to October 1755, an eight-month span that far exceeded the older ninety-day maximum. The second campaign overlapped with that first one in pursuit of a rebelling ally, while the third, pushing even further west against former Zunghar allies in East Turkestan, lasted nearly two years (1757–59). These astonishing logistical accomplishments depended on the preparation over the 1750s of two chains of magazines, with supplies moved over thousands of miles. As one illustration of the scale of the enterprise, the provincial governor along the western route accumulated six months of supplies for 20,000 men, amounting to 32,840 bushels of grain, 1,462 tons of noodles, 488 tons of bread, and thirteen tons of mutton. Additionally, he moved 40,000 oxen and 20,000 head of sheep into position to provide 195 tons of dried meat, plus an additional 30,000 sheep in pasture.[12]

The Qing mastery of logistics was matched by their success at cornering Mongol troop concentrations and destroying them with matchlock- and cannon-equipped infantry forces operating in conjunction with their own and allied steppe-style cavalry. After decades of warfare and a final program of massacre and ethnic eradication, by the 1760s the Qing had ended the longstanding Chinese fear of the steppe invader. Qing power in the nineteenth century declined due to internal dissension and also relative to European technological advances. There is little doubt, however, that the Qing combination of guns and an extraordinary state-centered logistical organization brought the final end of the steppe horsemen's ability to threaten or even destroy the sedentary world.[13]

PRIVATE ENTERPRISE WAR IN EUROPE TO 1650

Where the Manchu conquerors were able to take advantage of the long-established Chinese civil bureaucracy as a key component of their effort at state centralization, western European rulers since the end of the Roman Empire had depended on marshaling the resources of regional elites, tapping their own personal resources, ideologically positioning themselves as legitimate overlords, and nurturing emergent bureaucratic capacities. For the most part "ruling" meant dominating a network of lesser rulers. To reprise the phrase introduced in chapter 1, a king was simply a lord among lords, usually with more resources than most and a distinctive ideological claim to legitimacy. In part to buttress their personal power against those competing lesser lords, many western European rulers from the fifteenth to the seventeenth century came to rely habitually on mercenaries and contractors on land and sea as key components of their military force. In this evolutionary process rulers sought to replace unreliable networks of allegiance with seemingly more reliable contractual relationships. Let us pause for a moment and ask, however: *With whom* would a ruler choose to enter into a contract with? In fact, they often buttressed the apparent reliability of a contract by choosing those lords they should have been able to rely upon in any case: their own powerful subjects or nominal subjects. After all, a feudal indenture requiring the military service of a lord and his men was only a shade of gray away from a similar "mercenary" arrangement by contract. Sixteenth-century aristocrats were less autonomous than the old feudal lord in his castle, but what really changed in the late sixteenth century were the frequency, scale, and international quality of such contracts. Rather than the traditional hiring of mercenaries under a direct state contract, rulers began to draw their "elite subjects into active financial partnership in the state's activities," to include serving as "military enterprisers"—large-scale mercenary contractors, but ones with an ideological investment in the state, unlike the traditional international and stereotypically rootless mercenary. Much of this system then persisted into the more state-centralized systems of the eighteenth century, only gradually giving way to more institutionalized forms. Explaining the eventual emergence of state bureaucratic militaries requires beginning with their earlier mercenary and enterpriser forms, both on land and at sea.[14]

On Land

For land forces, hiring mercenaries as individuals or in large companies to supplement a "native" army raised through elite networks had long been an economical way of temporarily increasing one's troops. Doing so, however, required cash, and so the first truly extensive use of mercenaries in late medieval Europe occurred in the wealthy trading cities of northern Italy. This mercenary market attracted companies of men from around Europe, and the practice of hiring international mercenaries received a major stimulus after the startling victories of the Swiss in the fifteenth century. As discussed in chapter 7, the Swiss pike square proved relatively easy to copy. Soon similar formations of infantry raised primarily in the German lands of the Holy Roman Empire and known as landsknechts joined the Swiss in selling their services to rulers throughout western and central Europe (see Figure 9.2). This phenomenon, combined with the rise of a powerful Ottoman threat on land and sea in the first half of the sixteenth century, generated a dramatic increase in the size of European military establishments (measured as the sum of land forces, fleets, and fortifications). As European wars became more frequent, lasting longer and separated by shorter periods of peace, contractual arrangements grew more complex and more permanent. Gradually a profession of mercenary contractors emerged, in which the skills of the individual soldiers mattered less than the organizational and financial capacity of the contractor to raise units whose services he could sell. No longer merely supplemental, or add-on specific-skill units deployed for discrete purposes, such as mercenary crossbowmen, the units raised by contractors began to form the bulk of armies in the later

Figure 9.2 A Landsknecht loading a matchlock arquebus, ca. 1535.

sixteenth century. The French royal army in 1558, for example, was 70 percent German and Swiss. As late as the mid-seventeenth-century Thirty Years War, as France frantically built up its army to fight Spain as well, at least one-third of the force were foreign mercenaries.[15]

The processes of manning, equipping, and—in some aspects—supplying became the responsibility of the contractor. Whether it was a captain raising a company or a colonel raising a regiment, they accomplished that task in return for the ruler paying the initial costs of manning and equipping. Of key importance was the relationship between pay and supply. The contractor collected the men's pay from his employer, and, having been paid, they were expected to purchase their own food at camp markets, both in garrison and on campaign. Naturally, pay delivered in this way often made its way into the contractor's pocket, and mercenary soldiers became notorious for meeting their logistical needs by pillaging the local populace.

Partly as a result, the men in these units developed a strong corporate identity as a kind of marching community that lacked a "national," ethnic, or even religious loyalty. This sense of community included a self-identification as professionals, men whose trade they thought merited them respect and status in society. To a certain degree that respect was forthcoming. On the other hand, there was a substantial popular revulsion at their apparent rootlessness and their sometimes violent assertion of status. One contemporary described landsknechts as "a new order of soulless people [who] have no respect for honor or justice [and practice] whoring, adultery, rape, gluttony, drunkenness . . . stealing, robbing, and murder," who live "entirely in the power of the devil, who pulls them about wherever he wants."[16]

The system of hiring landsknecht regiments or similar mercenary units on short-term contracts made less sense as the wars of the later sixteenth century became longer and longer, notably the Dutch revolt against the Spanish (1566–1648), the Long War of Austria and the Ottomans (1593–1606), the French Wars of Religion (1562–98), and finally the Thirty Years War (1618–48), which engulfed Germany. Cash-strapped rulers, unable to front the initial unit costs as they had in the traditional system, increasingly turned to "military enterprisers," men who "met all the costs of raising and operating units against the offer of lump-sum reimbursements, usually made well into the campaign. The military contractor thus became a creditor rather than an employee, was militarily and politically far less subordinate to higher authorities, and developed his own priorities surrounding the preservation and deployment of his troops."[17]

Historians have long decried military enterprising as a failed formula that wreaked devastation with little positive result, but David Parrott now argues that from the point of view of the ruler, the system worked. The enterprisers successfully raised troops and allowed the state to continue to wage war for years. Indeed, Parrott argues that the enterpriser system tapped the wealth of elites otherwise untouchable by the state, not just that of the colonel-proprietors of regiments, but a host of other creditors and subcontractors, all of whom invested in the hope of profits. "Without [this system]," Parrott writes, "the Thirty Years' War would have ended far earlier because of the incapacity of the revenue-raising mechanisms of the belligerent states."[18] Furthermore, the cultural significance of martial activity for elites and would-be elites motivated them to seek such service and also tied them to their ruler; it was only from service to their own monarch that they could derive honor. "War remained the primary theatre of social and cultural esteem, and military enterprise harnessed much of the enthusiasm of the actors to play large and impressive roles."[19]

It remains the case, however, that this system experienced many breakdowns in central control, often seen first in failures to pay the men. European states did not yet have adequate structures for collecting revenue and then disbursing it to the troops. In one egregious example, the Swiss mercenaries fighting for France from 1639 to 1648 were never paid. Recognizing the problem, the Dutch somewhat precociously engineered a financial backup system aimed at preventing catastrophic failures to pay the troops, but the violence of unpaid soldiers became a motif in the art and literature of early modern European society. The closest thing to a system that emerged was that of "contributions." Rulers authorized their contracted or national troops to collect funds or goods in kind from within their operating area. The right to collect contributions served as a primary lure for major military enterprisers: they fronted their own funds or went into debt to raise the army, then repaid themselves and provided ongoing pay to the soldiers from contributions. But of course collecting contributions required more troops; more troops required more contributions; and so on. At first contributions could generate enormous profits for the military enterpriser, but that was partly because the amounts demanded could be arbitrary and enormous. Frequently, however, such demands were concentrated within strategic frontier regions, and they were soon exhausted. By the end of the Thirty Years War some states were starting to systematize contributions, pulling funds via local officials from regions where the troops were *not* located and then delivering them to the army.[20]

At Sea

Maintaining a navy presented an even steeper challenge to state capacity than land operations—as discussed in chapter 6, purpose-built warships were expensive propositions. At sea, however, the new possibilities for profit created by the European entry into the global trade network after 1500 attracted investment by both rulers and private "adventurers." Indeed, a key part of early modern European power projection emerged from the coalescing interests of rulers and merchant-adventurers. Central to this story was the combination of private and public investment with oceanic sailing technology. Sea "adventurers" did operate in the sixteenth-century Mediterranean, but there the dominant fleets were composed of purpose-built, state-run galley warships. In contrast, most of the ships plying the oceans in that century and much of the seventeenth were privately owned, and merchants were left on their own to protect their hard-won trading routes and stations. Reluctant, and even unable, to assume the role of protecting national trade on a global scale, European rulers were, however, eager to invest in and support those efforts in return for a lion's share of the income. The famous story of Christopher Columbus seeking support from various European rulers and eventually persuading Ferdinand and Isabella, newly victorious rulers of a united Spain, is emblematic of this emerging system.

Columbus had secured a good deal of private capital, and Ferdinand and Isabella would provide more, but rulers were not run-of-the-mill investors. They provided the cultural and legal legitimacy required for a merchant-adventurer to lay a claim for governorship—whether of a territory or a trading monopoly. Legally, all the profits belonged to the state; Columbus, for example, was merely given rights to a percentage. The same legal fiction prevailed with the conquistadors in subsequent generations in the Spanish New World: everything they claimed legally belonged to the crown, for which they were granted rights to land or labor or a percentage. In hard power terms the crown had only limited ability to enforce its rule; it depended on those willing to invest in the ships and the men in the hopes of a profitable return. For those adventurers to *enjoy* that profit, however, and to *display* the honor thus accrued required at least minimal adherence to the legal conventions of the state sponsor. Culture mattered: to use a modern idiom, the ruler wielded soft power over his elites, because he or she was the arbiter of their martial ambition. Homage was due, but with homage much could be won.

Over time, as states profited from oceanic trade, they increasingly invested in protecting it, or, almost as often, found themselves entangled in the follies of their merchant-adventurers, who might generate conflicts with those of another European state, or who might get themselves into an embarrassing defeat that could not be allowed to go unanswered. In some ways this was how Russia extended its dominion across Siberia, with private enterprise leading the way and then dragging the state in behind it.[21]

In addition to acting as investors and providing cultural and legal legitimacy, rulers insisted on being able to hire or conscript privately built ships to serve the state's naval needs in times of crisis—especially in home waters or around key overseas ports. Given the nature of ships during this period, it was a relatively simple matter to conjure a "war" fleet from an assortment of merchant ships. The ships might be impressed or contracted for pay; they were likely given more men than usual for combat purposes; and some might be partly modified for better wartime service. Generally, a state would lead such a fleet with a few true state-built warships, of which Henry VIII's *Mary Rose* was an outstanding example (see Figure 9.3). In general, however, in terms of structure and armament, a sixteenth-century "merchant" ship differed little from a warship. War fleets at sea, therefore, much like armies of the time, were manned and equipped through a composite of direct state investment and private enterprise. In the case of ships, an investor did not invest capital in the ship directly for the purpose of "war" in the way that a colonel-proprietor did on land, but the ship could serve that purpose regardless.

Figure 9.3 The *Mary Rose*. Launched at state order and expense in 1511, and enlarged in 1536 (this drawing is from 1546). One of several ships built by Henry VII and Henry VIII that formed the core of an English state navy.

In sum, "private venture protected much of the long-distance trade, it supplied large naval organizations with long-term or short-term chartered tonnage, [and] it ran the bulk of the trade, plunder and colonization business."[22]

In addition to these composite private-public fleets, privateering constituted another more direct sort of private enterprise war at sea. Individual ships or small fleets with the imprimatur of a ruler's legitimacy could profit by plundering the state's enemies. Such individuals might easily turn "pirate" when wars technically ended and their legitimacy as an independent actor on behalf of the state dried up. The overlaps here were significant—merchants could simultaneously be privateers, rapidly turn pirate, and then turn back again. To repeat, this was the case largely because merchant ships and ships of war, at least until the later seventeenth century, were physically almost identical, and purely state-built fleets were as yet too small to police the situation. These multiple identities had serious implications for centralized state direction of naval activity.

The infamous John Hawkins is instructive in this regard. An English adventurer in the 1560s, Hawkins became notorious for raiding Portuguese slavers off the African coast, taking their cargo and then selling the slaves in the Spanish colonies. At the time England and Spain were not at war, although tensions were high. Queen Elizabeth valued his efforts as undermining Spanish power, but they also brought repeated Spanish protests. Eventually, they helped smooth the path to war in 1585, by which time Hawkins had become a major figure in the English government. His last voyage in 1567–69 can stand in for his active career. He outfitted six ships in England, even as the Spanish protested continuously about his likely intentions. He raided slaves from Portuguese factors in West Africa and then sailed to the Caribbean. There he sailed from port to port, forcing local Spanish settlers to buy his cargo of slaves (something forbidden by Spanish law), freely bombarding the more reluctant until they agreed to trade. Driven into the main Spanish port at Veracruz by a hurricane, he was allowed to make repairs, but the very next day the Spanish fleet coincidentally arrived. After some attempt to contain tensions, fighting broke out and three Spanish ships along with three of the five remaining English ships were destroyed. Although Hawkins's last venture had ended in disaster, efforts like these continued in ensuing years. However much they enriched the English treasury and depleted the Spanish one, it would be a stretch to describe them as responsive to any kind of central strategic direction.[23]

Neither armies nor navies in this period were comprised solely of mercenaries or private ships. We have mentioned the *Mary Rose* as an example of the beginnings of a state navy. Rulers continued to rely on both contingents raised directly from their own resources, as well as ones raised via more traditional methods through elite networks. The shift to mercenaries and then to military enterprisers was an improvisational response to the lack of state capacity. Rulers floundered their way toward whatever system could raise and equip the troops they needed. By the end of the Thirty Years War, however, a reaction set in against the seeming loss of strategic control. There were times when it seemed to contemporaries that military enterprisers fought for their own purposes and profit. The greatest enterpriser of all, Albrecht von Wallenstein, was in the end assassinated in 1634 by agents of the Holy Roman emperor, who believed he had begun fighting for his own interests. The wastage and destruction associated with the Thirty Years War also encouraged a search for less damaging methods of supplying an army. What slowly emerged, based on evolutionary improvisational processes but also on deliberate calculations, were institutional and bureaucratic systems that increasingly centralized state control. Even as late as 1650 the seas seemed to be dominated as ever by relatively small frigate-type ships among whom armed merchantmen could readily take their place. That too would change in the following century, in a way even more dramatic than the changes on land.[24]

INSTITUTIONALIZATION, BUREAUCRATIZATION, AND PROFESSIONALIZATION IN EUROPE, 1650–1789

Historians tend to categorize and simplify. Choosing a date like 1650 imposes an artificial divide on what was really an evolutionary process. Similarly, historian John Lynn has created categories for armies: one category, the "contract army" applies to the earlier period just discussed, and another, the "state commission army," applies to the armies of the period in this section. There was, of course, no sharp break between the two periods. Processes from the sixteenth century persisted at times into the eighteenth. Some men became soldiers in the eighteenth century for the same reasons men had in the sixteenth, and so on. Examined from a wide perspective, however, it seems clear that a number of western European states increasingly centralized authority, especially over their armed forces, during the 1650–1789 period and beyond. In this case the broader phenomenon of "centralization" was accomplished through the linked processes of creating more complex and permanent military and fiscal institutions, through bureaucratizing authority and management, and by creating standing forces led by officers who increasingly saw themselves as professionals.[25]

Armies: Sweden and France

In some views the model for developing a state with greater centralized control over military force emerged in the Kingdom of Sweden. There, ambitious rulers in a stable dynasty ruling a relatively small state over several generations enhanced their military power by reaching deep into the countryside through taxation and conscription. Their achievement was rooted in a long period of reform negotiated among the Swedish kings, the elite, and the peasantry, perhaps beginning as early as the reign of Gustav Vasa (r. 1523–60). Gustav made a new form of local bailiff who acted directly on behalf of the king, bypassing the usual elite networks and creating a remarkably short administrative path between an individual peasant and his king. The bailiffs also generated detailed land and population registers, providing an unprecedented (for sixteenth-century Europe) amount of information directly to the king. As a result, Sweden was able to build an unusual level of military capacity relative to its size, including the largest state sailing-ship fleet in Europe by the 1560s. By no means was this a perfect centralized bureaucracy. Swedish kings continued to depend heavily on negotiating with their own elites, but these reforms, and others, allowed for the creation of a national army through conscription. From the 1600s, all men from eighteen to forty years of age were registered with the state, and the parish was expected to provide, equip, and feed one conscript for every ten men in the parish. Crucially, and unusually—because of the way it deprived them of labor—the Swedish elite not only supported this form of conscription in the estates (a kind of parliament), but also allowed them to serve long periods overseas. Far from a temporary militia, this form of conscription allowed for long-term service. Peter Wilson cautions us not to think of this as some deliberate form of modernization, however. It was the recourse of a cash-poor state, imposing a "blood tax" on its peasantry, rather than raising cash to hire professionals. Nevertheless, this conscripted national army, in the hands of King Gustavus Adolphus (r. 1611–32) and trained according to new systems of discipline, made a deep impression on the rest of Europe and catapulted Sweden to near-great-power status when he first defeated Denmark and then intervened in 1631 in the Thirty Years War.[26]

The Swedish model was important, and its reformed tactics and even its model of conscription excited the imagination of European observers, but it also had severe limits. Once Sweden was thoroughly enmeshed in the Thirty Years War in Germany, the pressure to expand its forces quickly led it to rely on the more usual military enterpriser system. It paid those enterprisers via the contribution system, to the point that hired regiments grew to outnumber the native Swedish component of the army. The Swedish population base was simply too small to sustain the kind of forces that Gustavus and his successors needed to decisively affect the massive conflict in Germany.[27]

Real change in European systems of manning, equipping, supplying, and directing began only after that war lurched toward a conclusion in 1648. The Swedes and the Dutch had begun to point the way, but the most prominent reforms occurred in France during the long reign of Louis XIV (r. 1643–1715). In one sense change was to be expected: peace brought the armies home, and rulers were unlikely to allow military enterprisers to continue to pay their armies through contributions collected from domestic sources. There was also a cultural reaction against the independence of the enterprisers and a "desire to create armies that were seen as more directly subject to the ruler's sovereign will."[28] Like many other forms of institutional innovation, however, this change was evolutionary. The aristocracy of France was hardly left out of the loop by an impersonal bureaucracy, nor did they lose their powerful cultural inclination toward military service and martial honor (although other routes to advancement and honor were opening up in this period). Instead, Louis XIV financed his growing standing national army in part by selling regimental commands to the nobility, the enormous price of which helped fund the army as a whole. Note that this was a society in which the nobility were legally exempt from normal taxation. The sale of offices was one way to tap elite wealth without technically taxing them. Similarly, other offices that developed around the national army related to supply, fortress construction, and so on were also sold. In one sense Louis simply took the old system of elite cooperation with the monarch and tightened its connections. Nobles demanded the right to serve—there were more applicants for office than there were units—and although the possibility of profit through the collection of dead pays existed, many nobles went into debt maintaining their units. The state thus continued to build its capacity on the cultural inclinations of its nobles to seek martial honor, newly channeled into more calculatedly bureaucratic forms. On these foundations France's peacetime army grew from 10,000 at the beginning of the seventeenth century, to 72,000 in the 1660s to 150,000 after 1697. Wartime strength before 1660 usually peaked at 80,000, but in Louis's reign, even as early as 1693, the French army rose to the astonishing heights of 362,000.[29]

This continued role of the aristocracy as investors in the military, if no longer exactly as military enterprisers, was paralleled, however, by change—primarily in the creation of new state agents designed to assert more central control. Alongside the many legacy offices still filled by buying and selling official appointments, the French state began to appoint *commissaires*, agents assigned specific tasks and whose appointments could be revoked at will (unlike purchased offices). Their functions at times overlapped in awkward and conflicting ways with the older type of official, but they represented a real intrusion of direct royal administration. The most famous type of these *commissaires* was the *intendants*, appointed to perform various supervisory roles over recruitment, housing, and especially supply services. Their efforts greatly curbed the corruption in the logistical contracting services, and they even acted as the ears and mouthpiece of the king in command councils heretofore dominated by aristocratic generals. Over Louis XIV's long reign this insertion of royal agents changed the nature of officership from something heavily (if not entirely) entrepreneurial to something resembling what we now call "service," in which officer-nobles self-identified as a separate class of "king's officer" and increasingly developed a professional interest in learning and transmitting best practices.[30]

There were other changes, however. Even as the state asserted a more direct role in strategic direction, logistics, and recruiting, it also began to create a new environment for the army, designed to enhance central control over both the officers and the minds and lives of the soldiers themselves. The state began to provide arms and ammunition, which previously had been charged against soldiers' wages. Uniforms became standard, issued by the state and colored to show national and regimental affiliation. Troops moving within France were now more often supplied by prestocked depots than by recourse to living off the land. Even when they were outside France on expeditionary campaigns, more thoroughgoing efforts were made to provide supplies centrally or, at a minimum, to centralize the collection of contributions. From the 1710s, troops not on campaign increasingly lived in new barracks, relieving the countryside of the burden of housing them, while improving sanitation and hygiene and also increasing their commander's control over them (see Figure 9.4).[32]

This issue of control was a central calculation within the process. The emergence of synchronized collective discipline in tactical movements in the seventeenth

Figure 9.4 The Collins barracks. Built in Dublin in 1702 to house British troops in Ireland.

Figure 9.5 The Battle of Fontenoy, 1745. Painted in the 1750s, this image emphasizes the uniformity and linearity of eighteenth-century armies.

century (discussed in chapter 7) and a general revulsion against the violent plundering of that era, encouraged a broadening of the concept of discipline to a more holistic control over the soldier's life. This represented a profound cultural reassertion of aristocratic control over martial affairs. The landsknechts and their ilk had threatened and even displaced the old medieval aristocratic monopoly on martial honor. The highly disciplined standing armies that emerged in the eighteenth century again reserved honor for officers alone, reducing the soldiers to a uniformed anonymity in stark contrast to the truculent, bombastic, and wildly colorful independent mercenaries of the sixteenth and seventeenth centuries (see Figure 9.5).[33]

France led the way in all these changes, but its innovations were quickly copied, if not in the specifics of bureaucratic administration, then in the desired outcomes. The Dutch Republic, for example, more or less simultaneously made similar reforms. After 1672, in one historian's estimation, "At an astonishing speed the Republic's land forces were . . . transformed from an army of mercenaries into a standing army of professional soldiers" based on a "greatly intensified government involvement with its troops" that changed the administration of pay and lessened the difference between paper and effective strengths. The government also paid wages more regularly, provided a new uniform every two years, and relied on new depots of stored bread (magazines) to keep fixed the price of bread for the soldiers.[34]

The Dutch example also usefully shows that these centralizing reforms were not dependent on some notion of absolutist monarchy as pursued by Louis XIV of France. The centralization of army administration, and its processes of manning, supplying, equipping, and strategic direction, was an innovation not of monarchy nor of absolutism, but of a particular notion of rule through bureaucracy that allowed a single will to penetrate down to individual members of the state, and especially to individual soldiers. That form of administration, as opposed to the more diffuse interests and complex power bases of either a mercenary or a military enterpriser system, allowed for the freer imposition of reforms including more comprehensive discipline. And as we will see at the end of this chapter, the greatest impetus for centralizing reform came not from a powerful king but from a democratic revolution.[35]

Navies

The origins of changes in war at sea were partly technological. From the mid-seventeenth century and more or less continuing through to the present day ships increasingly specialized into either warships or merchant ships. Violent competition at sea had forced ever-more specialized designs, not only resulting in ships built solely for fighting but also changing the cost basis of naval warfare and the expectation of the skills necessary to sail and fight. Innovations in the ships were closely intertwined with changes in tactics. The sixteenth-century oceanic fleets, primarily Spanish and Portuguese, operated in ways parallel to contemporary galley fleets in the Mediterranean (as discussed in chapter 6)—projecting power ashore and supporting landings and sieges. By the end of the sixteenth century, however, both the English and the Dutch were moving toward a form of naval combat based on gunnery and sailing ability in open waters. This trend accelerated rapidly after 1650 as the English, quickly copied by others, formally instituted "line ahead" tactics in their 1652–54 war against the Dutch (although it had been used as a tactic earlier, perhaps even as early as 1502). Lining up a fleet of ships in succession, bow to stern, allowed each sailing ship to use its broadside guns, maximizing both firepower and the admiral's control of the fleet (see Figure 9.6). The advantage may seem obvious, but it was no mean feat to maneuver an entire fleet so as to consistently maintain a single line ahead. Once the benefits became clear, navies built increasingly heavier ships, using standardized designs, and carrying more and more guns. These heavier ships, now designated "ships of the line," drove converted merchant ships from fighting in the line of battle. The enormous cost of building, manning, equipping, and maintaining these vessels and the complexity of managing them at sea and in battle encouraged professionalization and state-built infrastructure, not only to

Figure 9.6 The Battle of Negapatam, 1782. French and English fleets in line-ahead formation, exchanging broadsides (painted in 1786).

manage port and dockyard facilities but also to secure the necessary raw materials of shipbuilding from around the Atlantic Ocean and the Baltic Sea.[36]

One form of institution building was the creation of a corps of professional sea officers who advanced through formal systems of admission and promotion. Common sailors were recruited or pressed from the maritime population and were not typically maintained in naval service during peacetime. Professionalism was as yet reserved for the officer corps (unlike the standing armies developing on land at the same time). In wartime the cadre of officers would provide the skeleton to be fleshed out by drafts of sailors.[37]

The number of sailors required could be substantial, and although their ranks may never have swelled to the size of the major armies on the continent, the need to provide preserved food and stores in advance of their departure fostered administrative development. A British seventy-four-gun ship of the line carried a complement of around 590 men. Their rations for five months added up to approximately 41 tons of biscuit, 83,000 gallons of beer, 35 tons of pork or beef, 3000 gallons of pease porridge, 4400 gallons of oatmeal, 2 tons of butter, and 4 tons of cheese. All of this had to be baked, dried, salted, or otherwise prepared and then barreled. In 1760 alone the British Navy Board arranged the purchase of 11 million pounds of beef, 4.7 million pounds of biscuits, over 3.6 million pounds of pork and flour, 2.5 million pounds of cheese, and over a million pounds of butter.[38]

The ships themselves, easily the most complex man-made objects in the world at the time, also demanded a centralized infrastructure for their building and maintenance. To build one seventy-four-gun ship required two thousand oak trees (cured for one year), one hundred tons of wrought iron, thirty tons of copper nails and bolts, and of course the metal for its guns. In the 1780s the British navy floated about 150 ships of the line and innumerable smaller ships. The demand for guns to outfit all these ships was staggering: in 1805 Admiral Lord Nelson's fleet at Trafalgar had 2,232 guns of twelve to sixty-eight pounds compared to Napoleon's 366 guns at Waterloo in 1815, each of only six to twelve pounds.

To administer and support this enterprise the British government over the course of the eighteenth century built or expanded ports and dockyards in England and around the world. Plymouth was reorganized between 1721 and 1722; Portsmouth was expanded at the same time, and dockyards were developed in Minorca, Gibraltar, Jamaica, and Antigua (see Figure 9.7). To manage these facilities (and the associated provisioning processes) administrative bodies were either created or greatly expanded, including the Admiralty, the Navy Board, and the Victualling Board, cultivating and capturing institutional memory and expertise.[39]

Unlike Continental European powers, whose budgets were driven by armies, Britain's biggest financial challenge was its navy. As Britain worked to enhance its revenue, it too came to rely on bureaucratization. Beginning during the English Civil War—ironically a conflict fought partly to resist the king's centralization of power—the rebelling Parliament, desperate for funds, invented new financial mechanisms that greatly increased the tax burden on the population. Parliament truly came into its own as a fundraising

Figure 9.7 The royal dockyard in Chatham, ca. 1785. Aerial view of one of six royal dockyards in England, showing the scale of the enterprise.

powerhouse, however, after the Glorious Revolution of 1688. Having forced out James II and replaced him with William and Mary, Parliament had arrogated much greater power to itself, but then proved willing to raise taxes that even its members would have to pay. Parliament created the Bank of England and the Sinking Fund, the latter a mechanism to borrow money against the security of future tax income. This solution rapidly proved its worth as Britain embarked on more than a century of almost continuous war from 1688 to 1815, interrupted more by truces than lasting peace. For Britain these were primarily naval wars, because it was naval power that protected its increasingly commercial and global economy. Britain could rapidly raise money in the lending market, but it also had to increase its taxing efficiency in order to repay those loans. To do so, Britain created a new professional bureaucracy of excise men and then continually reformed it, generating an ever more reliable stream of revenue. Ironically, the subjects of Britain, ruled by a king and a representative parliament, paid substantially more taxes per capita than their absolutist-monarch-ruled French opponents. These processes established solid government credit over the course of the eighteenth century, creating a level of confidence and a pool of investors willing to buy government debt. Over the period from 1689 to 1815 the British national debt grew from under 5 to over 10 percent of the gross national product. Investor confidence, however, also increased over that time, allowing interest on government loans to drop from 9 percent to under 5 percent. Britain was thereby able to sustain an unheard-of level of both debt and per capita government expenditure.[40]

Ending this section on the subject of taxation highlights how finances underlay virtually all the developments discussed thus far, from Qing taxation to Habsburg reliance on military enterprisers who were willing to gamble on future military success, to French reforms that extracted aristocratic wealth by exploiting their desire for martial service, and finally to the British invention of deficit-financing their fleets to protect a global trade, the excise taxing of which would pay back the loans. In all these cases, the revenue from more efficient taxation systems was plowed back into increased military capacity. Taxation and its efficiency also factored into the unification of Japan. There, however, the consequences for the military capacity of the state differed markedly in the long term.

JAPAN'S VARIANT PATH, 1500–1868

As mentioned very briefly at the end of the last chapter, historians have often used Japan from the 1570s through the 1850s as an example of how the adoption of gunpowder can lead to different historical trajectories. Japan can also be considered from the perspective of state centralization. On one hand, in the short term, the centralization of governmental power through administrative reforms in manning, equipping, supplying, and directing armies *did* produce greater state capacity, and indeed led to the unification of Japan under a single, long-lasting government. On the other hand, in the longer term that centralization resulted in technological stagnation and isolationism rather than expansionism. State centralization on its own, like firearms on their own, was no determinant of a state's future.

From the end of the fifteenth century centrifugal political forces had divided the Japanese islands into more than one hundred petty states, each ruled by a politically autonomous lord, or daimyo. The shogun, one-time de facto ruler of Japan had been reduced to one lord among the rest, with the emperor a mere figurehead. In the absence of a central government, the daimyo competed violently with each other. In fact, the period (1467 to 1600) is referred to as the Sengoku era: the age of the country at war. The daimyo of this era built their power bases on new forms of political and military organization. The wars of the earlier age had been characterized by undisciplined bands of elite mounted warriors (the *bushi* class) raiding, destroying, and plundering for individual honor and immediate short-term reward, but not to take, hold, and administer new territories. The daimyo began their rise to power by welding groups of these men to themselves, initially through grants of land. Over time, however, they increasingly brought the bushi into contractual arrangements, paying them in rice (fundamentally a de facto currency) and maintaining them as a standing force based at the daimyo's castle. Simultaneously, the daimyo sought to exploit—that is, to tax—those territories more efficiently, by reforming tax collection, estate administration (especially through land-and-people surveys), and judicial processes. Efficiently managed estates promised greater rewards when conquered and absorbed, than when treated as objects of plunder. Furthermore, rather than distributing those new territories as grants to retainers, the daimyo usually administered them directly, using the produce to hire more men to pursue further territorial goals. Much like the mercenary systems of contemporary Europe, mobilizing forces through cash or rice payments rather than relying on kinship or other networks made it easier for a daimyo to translate military success into further force expansion. This represented a key transition, although it was evolutionary rather than revolutionary in nature.[41]

Enhanced administrative capability and larger, more permanent military forces wrought a change in the very nature of the daimyo armies. As one victorious daimyo absorbed another's power base, the armies enlarged, and many of the bushi class, originally highly trained light horsemen armed with bow and sword, became officers in command of *ashigaru* troops drawn from the peasant class. Here, especially, the use of cash made the difference. The peasants were neither militia nor conscripts; they were recruited with pay and then trained and disciplined under a strong central authority (the daimyo) to fight as infantry in a standing army. As in Europe, this constituted a shift from the "lifetime of training" model of raising small armies of brilliantly skilled individual warriors to raising larger armies equipped and

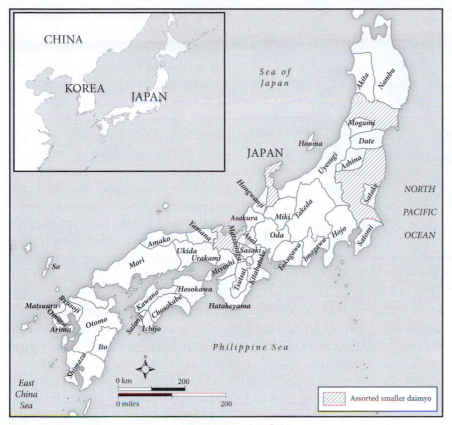

Map 9.2 Sixteenth-century Japan, showing major daimyo.

trained to fight in sync with different arms, multiplying their individual efficacy through unity of action. In Japan this initially meant formations of pike- and bowmen, and later, after the introduction of the matchlock by the Portuguese in 1543, formations of men with pikes combined now not only with archers but with blocks of gunners. This mutual reliance arose for the same reason that it had in Europe: the slow reload speed of matchlocks. In Japan, however, the long and widespread dominance of archery meant that *both* archers and pikemen continued to be deployed in a synchronized way to protect the musketeers.

Working now within a political economy that readily converted conquest into further military power, the stage was set for one daimyo's success to create a snowball effect, as conquering some allowed him to simply force the submission of others. By the 1570s this process had reduced the hundreds of daimyo to roughly twenty. At that point one daimyo, Oda Nobunaga, was well on his way to unifying Japan. Some historians have attributed at least part of his success to his investment in firearms. This argument usually explains his great victory at Nagashino in 1575 as a result of his invention of volley fire

Figure 9.8 Matchlock-equipped Japanese infantry. Here seen training with a mechanism designed to hold the barrels level, from an 1855 manuscript.

by musketeers who used rapidly erected fences to protect themselves from the traditional bushi cavalry. This standard narrative of Nagashino is now questioned, including his alleged use of volley fire at this early date. But more important is Stephen Morillo's argument that Nobunaga, and the other successful daimyo, had long based their armies on the expanded recruitment pool provided by hired peasants, without regard to the arrival of matchlocks. Matchlocks only slightly modified their already synchronized infantry tactics of pikemen and archers.[42]

The daimyo of the 1570s, though fewer, now held much larger territories. Further consolidation through outright conquest would be difficult. Unification came, but it followed a complex path. Nobunaga was killed in an ambush in 1582, and Toyotomi Hideyoshi, one of Nobunaga's leading officers and a self-made former farmer, continued his work. Hideyoshi eventually subdued or co-opted the remaining daimyo into his circle, not through outright conquest but by overawing the remaining competitors and deftly maneuvering to acquire the title of imperial regent. To legitimize and cement his rule, Hideyoshi then invaded Korea in the 1590s (as discussed in chapter 6). The invasion eventually failed, but it succeeded in redirecting the now massive military potential of Japan against outsiders. Hideyoshi died in Japan while his army was being defeated in Korea. A struggle over the succession was won by yet another clan leader, Tokugawa Ieyasu, who built on the foundation left by Nobunaga and Hideyoshi.[43]

By 1615 Ieyasu had accomplished the final unification of Japan. He and his heirs then dismantled the many competing armies and the recruitment systems created during the Sengoku era. Ieyasu's heirs established the Tokugawa Shogunate, ruling alongside a figurehead emperor until 1868. In one sense the shogunate's program of demilitarization was its greatest act of centralization. The remnant daimyo who had been forced into confederation with Ieyasu were required to reside every other year in Edo, where they spent their funds and remained under the shogun's eye. The shogun restricted the number of their private retainers, and also restricted the ownership of weapons to an increasingly closed samurai class. The great daimyo could retain land and bear weapons, but the smaller landholders were required either to forfeit their land and become dependent retainers or surrender their weapons. The armies of peasants disappeared, and the peasants themselves were now forbidden to own weapons, a process begun as early as 1588 under Hideyoshi. Hideyoshi also initiated another great act of state centralization: he conducted a major census of land and people, beginning in 1584, that listed and then tied the peasant class to the land and greatly increased the state's capacity to tax. In essence Hideyoshi had removed the middleman: local military lords surrendered their land and became stipendiary officials of the state, with their stipends paid by the taxes that went straight into the state's coffers. The now landless lords received the cultural satisfaction of remaining armed. Following the establishment of the Tokugawa Shogunate, except for two brief rebellions, there were no battles in Japan, and after 1639 Japan virtually closed itself off from Europeans, with only the Dutch allowed to maintain a sharply limited trade. Japanese trade and diplomacy continued, especially with their Asian neighbors, but, hoping to prevent the reemergence of any daimyo challengers, the state carefully controlled the entry of foreigners and the exit of its own subjects. As for firearms, Japanese warriors never stopped using them, and indeed marksmanship was folded into the elaborate ritualized cult of the warrior that persisted until 1868. But in the absence of internal conflict or external invasion, they had no real need to improve these weapons.[44]

In one sense Japan's centralization of power was so complete that developing further military capacity was simply not necessary. Now in control of the whole Japanese archipelago, the new state maintained a near monopoly of force—although the remaining daimyo were allowed to keep retainers in limited numbers. Somewhat protected by geography, having eschewed expansionism, and now consolidating foreign trade into the state's hands, the Tokugawa Shogunate achieved the pinnacle of power by its strictest definition: commanding obedience without the actual use of force. It did not do so entirely through authoritarian military power; the peace also rested on shared cultural assumptions among the elite about the nature and function of government. Among other things, Ieyasu and his successors *did not* claim the imperial throne. They ruled in the emperor's name, thus preserving a unified cultural sphere within which the other daimyo could continue to rule their own domains. Or, in one historian's analysis, in the long term, the strength of the shogunate "lay not in its capacity to fight but in its capacity to prevent a fight from starting."[45] Viewed in a comparative light, however, no equivalent consolidation of power occurred in Europe, or even within a single European state. However much European monarchs of the seventeenth and eighteenth century tried to arrogate power to themselves, theirs remained founded on negotiations among themselves and a variety of other sources of power and legitimacy within the state, primarily the aristocratic landowning elite, but also the church and the growing economic strength of the merchant elite. Ironically, it was the French Revolution, often perceived or at least remembered as a great upheaval *against* centralized control, that opened new doors for centralized state control over the population. In doing so, it thereby armed and energized one of the most successful attempts in history to impose a single central rule over Continental Europe—Napoleon's.[46]

THE *LEVÉE EN MASSE* AND MASS CONSCRIPT ARMIES

The French Revolution has long been considered a turning point in European history. Among its many consequences was the rise of mass conscript armies as part of a new assertion of the central power of the state. In this new paradigm, all subjects and indeed all resources of the state were arrogated to its control for the purposes of war. For such a dramatic redefinition of the subject-ruler relationship to occur required more than improvisational thinking, bureaucratic innovation, or kingly pressure. It necessitated a wholesale shifting of the foundations of the state. At times, the shift was based on pure violence. Members of the aristocratic class who had been truculent negotiating partners even for Louis XIV were now simply killed or driven out. Factions continued to struggle within France over control of the regime, but whichever faction was ascendant found itself holding untrammeled state power. One reason for this ascendancy of the state was immediate and political. The revolution had many enemies, domestic and foreign, and the revolutionaries chose to protect their experiment by force. The rhetoric of self-defense provided a compelling legitimacy to the exercise of power. Another reason was ideological. The logic of the revolution demanded a new conception of history in which progress had a trajectory that demanded the nation's full commitment to achieve it, even if that commitment included a form of war that tapped the full resources of the nation and unleashed new extremes of violence. The final reason was the elaboration of a professional bureaucracy to control and administer the vastly enlarged army. The great irony, of course, is that a revolution often thought of as democratic and liberating in fact allowed those at the center of power to assert ever-more control over the state's subjects, even if they were now to be called citizens.[47]

This is not the place to describe the intricate details of the French Revolution, but a quick summary is in order. In 1789 Louis XVI found himself in the grip of a revenue crisis created by war debt, compounded by a social crisis precipitated by famine. His attempt to resolve the revenue crisis by calling the Estates General for the first time since 1614 unleashed pent-up political energy, which initially resulted in the creation of a constitutional monarchy. Then, when Louis sought international support to roll back the revolution, its leaders arrested, tried, and executed him. The other monarchs of Europe feared the spread of such ideas, and France found itself at war with much of Europe (the War of the First Coalition, 1792–97).

Militarily, the first moves of the war were a disaster for France, partly because revolutionary politics had gutted the old, largely aristocratic officer corps. The revolutionary government embarked on a series of tactical and technical reforms, many of which had been discussed in previous decades but were now implemented for the first time. The most important was the emergency conscription of all citizens, known to history as the *levée en masse*. The armies of 1791 and 1792, primarily composed of volunteers stiffened by the remains of the old army, proved just sufficient to defend the frontiers. But as enemies gathered again in 1793, the National Convention issued a decree for all citizens to rise in defense of the state:

- From this moment until that in which our enemies shall have been driven from the territory of the Republic, all Frenchmen are permanently requisitioned for service in the armies.
- The young men shall fight; the married men shall forge weapons and transport supplies; the women will make tents and clothes and will serve in the hospitals; the children will make up old linen into lint [for bandages]; the old men will have themselves carried into the public squares to rouse the courage of fighting men, to preach the unity of the Republic and hatred of Kings.
- The public buildings shall be turned into barracks, the public squares into munitions factories, the earthen floors shall be treated with lye to extract saltpetre.
- All firearms of suitable calibre shall be turned over to the troops. . . .
- All saddle horses shall be seized for the cavalry; all draft horses not employed in cultivation will draw the artillery and supply-wagons.[48]

The first *levée* provided a vast accession of human resources to the French state. By the summer of 1794 the revolutionary army had at least 750,000 men on the books, a commitment of men unprecedented in Europe, representing a vast cross section of French society. These men remained the core of the revolutionary armies until 1798, when the principle of universal obligation was converted into annual conscription of age classes by ballot. During the same period, even as various factions replaced one another in ruling the French state, a new form of rationalized bureaucratic army administration emerged that concentrated power in the hands of the state leadership. None of these changes was linear, planned, or part of a conscious process of modernization. Nevertheless, they destroyed the nobility as a privileged class and shifted the basis of sovereignty from the person of the monarch to an abstract "nation," based on constitutionalism and a "purely legal-rational authority." These changes created room for the development of a rationalized, hierarchical, and empowered bureaucracy that greatly enhanced the power of the state over its citizens.[49] The *levée* and the conscription system, combined with the new bureaucracy of army administration, finally eliminated the last vestiges of the military enterpriser system.

Equipped with legions of conscripts from the most populous country in Europe, and having invested in technological, tactical, and organizational reforms, France then came under the political control of a man with the ambition, charisma, and military skills to convert a republic into an empire. In the course of Napoleon's wars of conquest, he presented state after state with an existential conundrum. The size and power of his armies, the speed and brilliance of his operations, and the breadth of his ambition threatened to extinguish the old political order. In response to that emergency other states found the need and the will to tap their population and enhance state power in new ways. All the major (and many minor) Continental powers adopted some form of conscription—Britain used it only for the navy—either on their own initiative or as required to do so by a conquering Napoleon. Sometimes they merely modified or expanded old forms of the militia, but the need to match France's vast numbers was clear. Furthermore, especially in the later years of the wars with France, as Austria, Russia, and Prussia summoned up their last reserves to finally defeat Napoleon, state elites also motivated their population by cultivating a new sense of patriotism, a love of the nation. After the final defeat of Napoleon in 1815, the victorious powers tried to resurrect the prewar political configuration, and smaller professional armies dominated briefly, but the genie had been let out of the bottle. The later nineteenth and twentieth centuries were dominated by mass conscript armies, still tinged with the rituals, uniforms, and drill of the eighteenth century, officered by professionals from that same tradition, but now managed by modern state bureaucracies, and filled by citizens alight with the fires of nationalism.[50]

CONCLUSION

This chapter has almost entirely dodged the question of whether the growth in the centralized power of European states resulted from changes in weaponry or tactics. The military revolution thesis, as discussed in chapter 7, claims among other things, that the elaboration of state power, especially in its bureaucracy and taxing capacity, followed from the new demands of war created by new technologies of war. Similar claims have been made for non-European powers, notably the Ottomans, the Safavids of Persia, and the Mughals, for whom it is claimed that artillery led those dynasties to build more centralized and bureaucratic states.[51] These claims for gunpowder-induced centralization have been widely disputed, if not entirely dismissed. What we can say, based on this and the previous chapter, is that new gunpowder weapons had no such effect in Ming (or Qing) China, where they were easily absorbed into the existing military system without major social or political ramifications. Such also seems to be the case for Japan, following Morillo's argument that the trend toward increasing administrative capacity preceded the arrival of Portuguese matchlocks.

For Europe, Parrot's description of a strong continuity in the use of military enterprisers, whether the seventeenth-century version that saw aristocrats providing whole armies on contract or the eighteenth-century version in which the martial inclinations of aristocrats led them to put their wealth toward raising regiments incorporated into a national army, would also seem to downplay the role of either changing technology or tactics. What was changing, though slowly, was the relationship of the aristocrat to the state, and the driving factor there were changes not in military technology but in the political arrangement of power.

It is also important to acknowledge that such rearrangements of power were not necessarily consciously understood as part of a program of modernization through centralization. The reforms that occurred in Europe before 1789 were reshufflings of the old consensus between the monarch and the nobility. The reshuffling did tend to focus more and more on the state center, but the nobility and other social elites remained necessary to the raising and sustaining of military force. State centralization was not perfect, nor even necessarily the most "efficient" solution to building state capacity, nor was it adopted uniformly across Europe in a constantly accelerating linear process. There were many fits and starts.[52]

Nevertheless, conscious or not, however much dependent on elite cooperation, and however imperfect, state institutionalization and bureaucratization of the military on land and sea did increase in Europe after 1700, and it did so in a way that enhanced centralized control. Institutional permanence, and with it long, continuous service, fostered professionalization—especially in the navies. In addition to its other effects, military professionalization in Europe, for cultural reasons related to social snobbery about the capabilities of common soldiers, a fascination with geometry, and a vigorous print culture (among other things), produced armies that were made to appear uniform, that resembled each other, and that preferred a tactical system on the open field that relied on synchronized movement producing volley fire. This system, typified in the "musket/bayonet, horse, and cannon" system of the eighteenth century, was only just beginning to become operationally superior to the armies of other Old World empires in India, China, Persia, Turkey, and Japan when the French Revolution provided a dramatic new twist. The revolution swept away the old carefully negotiated state-elite consensus and thus greatly enhanced the potential capacity of European states by providing the ideological basis and the existential requirement for conscription, and thus much larger armies. As it happened, however, that particular capacity was primarily used only

TIMELINE

1467–1600	The Sengoku era in Japan: the age of the country at war
1543	Arrival of Portuguese and their muskets in Japan.
1618–1648	Thirty Years War in Germany; peak of the military enterpriser system
1639	The beginning of Japanese isolation from Europe
1643–1715	Reign of Louis XIV (French centralization of armed force)
1688	Establishment of Parliamentary supremacy in Britain
1735–1795	Reign of the Qianlong emperor
1760	Last Qing campaign against the Zunghars
1789	The French Revolution
1793	*Levée en masse* in France

within Europe until the twentieth-century world wars. What enabled European expansion in Africa and Asia (and into continental North America) were first the sailing ship armed with cannon, as described in the previous chapter, and then improved financial efficiency tethered to an increasingly commercialized global trading economy (exploited most effectively by Britain), and finally the even more dramatic changes in production and in the very nature of energy unleashed by the Industrial Revolution, described in the next chapter.[53]

In contrast, although both China and Japan greatly centralized power within the state, harnessed the wealth of their populations to a substantial degree, and initially invested heavily in the new gunpowder technologies introduced from Europe, both also turned away from the sea. Furthermore, centralization was neither inevitable nor unstoppable. China's Qing dynasty, for example, relied on a centralized bureaucracy to manage military needs, but it also prided itself on governing with a light administrative footprint. The limited capacity of the central government proved incapable of confronting emerging challenges in the nineteenth century, including increasing localism, rebellions, and new European technological capabilities. Qing China and Tokugawa Japan remained extremely powerful states throughout this period, but, lacking global trading's acceleration of commercialization and financial sophistication, neither was prepared to invest in emerging industrial capability.[54]

Further Reading

Black, Jeremy. *Beyond the Military Revolution: War in the Seventeenth-Century World*. New York: Palgrave Macmillan, 2011.

Black, Jeremy. *War in the Eighteenth-Century World*. New York: Palgrave Macmillan, 2013.

Blaufarb, Rafe. *The French Army, 1750–1820: Careers, Talent, Merit*. Manchester, UK: Manchester University Press, 2002.

Brown, Howard G. *War, Revolution, and the Bureaucratic State: Politics and Army Administration in France, 1791–1799*. Oxford: Clarendon, 1995.

Chickering, Roger, and Stig Förster, eds. *War in an Age of Revolution, 1775–1815*. Cambridge, UK: Cambridge University Press, 2010.

Conlan, Thomas D. *Weapons and Fighting Techniques of the Samurai Warrior, 1200–1877 AD*. London: Amber, 2008.

Di Cosmo, Nicola, ed. *Military Culture in Imperial China*. Cambridge, MA: Harvard University Press, 2009.

Elliott, Mark C. *The Manchu Way: The Eight Banners and Ethnic Identity in Late Imperial China*. Stanford, CA: Stanford University Press, 2001.

Glete, Jan. *War and the State in Early Modern Europe: Spain, the Dutch Republic and Sweden as Fiscal-Military States, 1500–1660*. London: Routledge, 2002.

Kaiser, David. *Politics and War: European Conflict from Philip II to Hitler*. Cambridge, MA: Harvard University Press, 1990.

Lynn, John A. *Giant of the Grand Siècle: The French Army, 1610–1715*. Cambridge, UK: Cambridge University Press, 1997.

Morillo, Stephen. "Guns and Government: A Comparative Study of Europe and Japan." *Journal of World History* 6.1 (1995): 75–106.

Mortimer, Geoff, ed. *Early Modern Military History, 1450–1815*. Basingstoke, UK: Palgrave Macmillan, 2004.

Parrott, David. *The Business of War: Military Enterprise and Military Revolution in Early Modern Europe*. Cambridge, UK: Cambridge University Press, 2012.

Perdue, Peter C. *China Marches West: The Qing Conquest of Central Eurasia*. Cambridge, MA: Harvard University Press, 2005.

Rodger, N. A. M. *The Command of the Ocean: A Naval History of Britain, 1649–1815*. New York: W. W. Norton, 2004.

Tallett, Frank, and D. J. B. Trim, eds. *European Warfare, 1350–1750*. Cambridge, UK: Cambridge University Press, 2010.

van Nimwegen, Olaf. *The Dutch Army and the Military Revolutions, 1588–1688*. Translated by Andrew May. Woodbridge, UK: Boydell, 2010.

Waley-Cohen, Joanna. *The Culture of War in China: Empire and the Military under the Qing Dynasty*. London: I. B. Tauris, 2006.

Wilson, Peter H. *The Thirty Years War: Europe's Tragedy*. Cambridge, MA: Belknap Press of Harvard University Press, 2009.

Notes

1. Bruce Bueno de Mesquita, Alastair Smith, Randolph M. Siverson, and James D. Morrow, *The Logic of Political Survival* (Cambridge, MA: MIT Press, 2003); William Beik, "The Absolutism of Louis XIV as Social Collaboration," *Past and Present* 188 (2005): 195–224. Qing and Tokugawa examples are discussed further below.

2. E. A. Thompson, ed. and trans., *A Roman Reformer and Inventor: Being a New Text of the Treatise* De Rebus Bellicis (Oxford: Clarendon, 1952), 112 (V.1).

3. Edward L. Dreyer, "Continuity and Change," in *A Military History of China*, ed. David A. Graff and Robin Higham, rev. ed. (Lexington: University Press of Kentucky, 2012), 23.

4. Paul Lococo, Jr., "The Qing Empire," in Graff and Higham, *A Military History of China*, 115–33; Peter C. Perdue, "Military Mobilization in Seventeenth and Eighteenth-Century China, Russia, and Mongolia," *Modern Asian Studies* 30.4 (1996): 757–93, esp. 770–73; William T. Rowe, *China's Last Empire: The Great Qing* (Cambridge, MA: Belknap Press of Harvard University Press, 2009), 28–29.

5. Mark C. Elliott, *The Manchu Way: The Eight Banners and Ethnic Identity in Late Imperial China* (Stanford, CA: Stanford University Press, 2001), 177–79, 191, esp. 350–51.

6. Yingcong Dai, "The Qing State, Merchants, and the Military Labor Force in the Jinchuan Campaigns," *Late Imperial China* 22.2 (2001): 35–36; Perdue, "Military Mobilization," 772–73.

7. Yingcong Dai, "Military Finance of the High Qing Period: An Overview," in *Military Culture in Imperial China*, ed. Nicola Di Cosmo (Cambridge, MA: Harvard University Press, 2009), 297–302.

8. Dai, "Qing State," 45.

9. Dai, "Qing State."

10. Perdue, "Military Mobilization," 776 (quote).

11. Peter C. Perdue, "Fate and Fortune in Central Eurasian Warfare: Three Qing Emperors and Their Mongol Rivals," in *Warfare in Inner Asian History: 500–1800*, ed. Nicola Di Cosmo (Leiden: Brill, 2002), 375–76.

12. Perdue, "Military Mobilization," with an expanded analysis in Peter C. Perdue, *China Marches West: The Qing Conquest of Central Eurasia* (Cambridge, MA: Harvard University Press, 2005), esp. 272–89.

13. Lococo, "Qing Empire," 128–29.

14. David Parrott, *The Business of War: Military Enterprise and Military Revolution in Early Modern Europe* (Cambridge, UK: Cambridge University Press, 2012), esp. 71–78 (quote 77); David Parrott, "From Military Enterprise to Standing Armies: War, State, and Society in Western Europe, 1600–1700," in *European Warfare, 1350–1750*, ed. Frank Tallett and D. J. B. Trim (Cambridge, UK: Cambridge University Press, 2010), esp. 78.

15. Parrott, *Business of War*, esp. 76–77; Parrott, "From Military Enterprise to Standing Armies," 80. French numbers in 1635 from Colin Jones, "The Military Revolution and the Professionalisation of the French Army under the Ancien Régime," in *The Military Revolution Debate: Readings on the Transformation of Early Modern Europe*, ed. Clifford Rogers (Boulder, CO: Westview, 1995), 150.

16. Olaf Van Nimwegen, "The Transformation of Army Organisation in Early-Modern Western Europe, c. 1500–1789," in Tallett and Trim, *European Warfare, 1350–1750*, 167; Parrott, *Business of War*, 59–67; John A. Lynn, *Women, Armies, and Warfare in Early Modern Europe* (Cambridge, UK: Cambridge University Press, 2008); Joel F. Harrington, *The Faithful Executioner: Life and Death, Honor and Shame in the Turbulent Sixteenth Century* (New York: Farrar, Straus & Giroux, 2013), 8–9 (quote).

17. Parrott, "From Military Enterprise to Standing Armies," 74–75, 80–81 (quote on 75).

18. Parrott, "From Military Enterprise to Standing Armies," 83 (quote).

19. Parrott, *Business of War*, 259 (quote).

20. Van Nimwegen, "Transformation of Army Organisation," 170.

21. Jeremy Black, *War in the World: A Comparative History, 1450–1600* (New York: Palgrave Macmillan, 2011), 180.

22. Louis Sicking, "Naval Warfare in Europe, c. 1330–c. 1680," in Tallett and Trim, *European Warfare, 1350–1750*, 239; Parrott, *Business of War*, 37; Jan Glete, *Navies and Nations: Warships, Navies and State Building in Europe and America, 1500–1860* (Stockholm: Almqvist & Wiksell, 1993), 1:161 (quote).

23. Kris E. Lane, *Pillaging the Empire: Piracy in the Americas, 1500–1750* (Armonk, NY: M. E. Sharpe, 1998), 34–40.

24. Van Nimwegen, "Transformation of Army Organisation," 161–62. But compare Parrott, "Military Enterprise," 77, and Glete, *Navies and Nations*, 167.

25. John A. Lynn, "The Evolution of Army Style in the Modern West, 800–2000," *International History Review* 18.3 (1996): 505–45.

26. Geoffrey Parker, *The Military Revolution: Military Innovation and the Rise of the West, 1500–1800*, 2nd ed. (Cambridge, UK: Cambridge University Press, 1996), 52–53; E. Thomson, "Beyond the Military State: Sweden's Great Power Period in Recent Historiography," *History Compass* 9 (2011): 269–83; Parrott, *Business of War*, 99, 126–29; Peter H. Wilson, *The Thirty Years War: Europe's Tragedy* (Cambridge, MA: Belknap Press of Harvard University Press, 2009), 185–87; Jan Glete, *War and the State in Early Modern Europe: Spain, the Dutch Republic and Sweden as Fiscal-Military States, 1500–1660* (London: Routledge, 2002), 177–78, 189–212.

27. Parrott, *Business of War*, 125–34, 183–84.

28. Parrott, "From Military Enterprise to Standing Armies," 88–95, 89 (quote).

29. Jones, "Military Revolution and the Professionalisation of the French Army," 155–57; John A. Lynn, "Recalculating French Army Growth during the *Grand Siècle*, 1610–1715," in Rogers, *Military Revolution Debate*, 125. The figures used here are based on Lynn's update of his calculations in "Revisiting the Great Fact of War and Bourbon Absolutism: The Growth of the French Army during the *Grand siècle*" in *Guerra y sociedad*

en la monarquía hispánica (2 vols): Política, estrategia y cultura en la Europa moderna (1500–1700), Enrique García Hernán and Davide Maffi, eds. (Madrid: Consejo Superior de Investigaciones Científicas 2006), 1: 49–74; John A. Lynn's correspondence with author, February 22, 2015.

30. Jones, "Military Revolution and the Professionalisation of the French Army," 157–58; also Gábor Ágoston, "Empires and Warfare in East-Central Europe, 1550–1750: The Ottoman-Habsburg Rivalry and Military Transformation," in Tallett and Trim, *European Warfare, 1350–1750*, 132–33; Ira D. Gruber, *Books and the British Army in the Age of the American Revolution* (Chapel Hill: University of North Carolina Press, 2010).

31. John A. Lynn, *Giant of the Grand Siècle: The French Army, 1610–1715* (Cambridge: Cambridge University Press, 1997), xiv–xv.

32. Jones, "Military Revolution and the Professionalisation of the French Army," 159–62; John A. Lynn, "How War Fed War: The Tax of Violence and Contributions during the *Grand Siècle*," *Journal of Modern History* 65 (1993): 286–310, repeated and expanded in Lynn, *Giant*, 184–217.

33. Wayne E. Lee, *Barbarians and Brothers: Anglo-American Warfare, 1500–1865* (New York: Oxford University Press, 2011), 178–88; Jeremy Black, *Beyond the Military Revolution: War in the Seventeenth-Century World* (New York: Palgrave Macmillan, 2011), 185; John Keegan, *The Face of Battle* (New York: Viking, 1976), 176.

34. Olaf van Nimwegen, *The Dutch Army and the Military Revolutions, 1588–1688* (Woodbridge, UK: Boydell, 2010), 518–19.

35. Black, *Beyond the Military Revolution*, 185.

36. Black, *War in the World*, 166–7; Glete, *Navies and Nations*, 175–76 (many more details 180–206); Black, *Beyond the Military Revolution*, 160–61.

37. Glete, *Navies and Nations*, 173–74.

38. For daily ration see N. A. M. Rodger, *The Wooden World: An Anatomy of the Georgian Navy* (New York: W. W. Norton, 1986), 83; for 1760 purchases: Philip Harling, *The Modern British State: An Historical Introduction* (Cambridge, UK: Polity, 2001), 42.

39. Richard Harding, "Sea Power: The Struggle for Dominance, 1650–1815," in *Early Modern Military History, 1450–1815*, ed. Geoff Mortimer (Basingstoke, UK: Palgrave Macmillan, 2004), 184; N. A. M. Rodger, *The Command of the Ocean: A Naval History of Britain, 1649–1815* (New York: W. W. Norton, 2004), 579.

40. Scott Wheeler, *The Making of a World Power: War and the Military Revolution in Seventeenth-Century England* (Stroud, UK: Sutton, 1999); John Brewer, *The Sinews of Power: War, Money and the English State, 1688–1783* (New York: Alfred A. Knopf, 1989); Harling, *Modern British State*, 42–43.

41. Much of this section follows the basic argument in Stephen Morillo, "Guns and Government: A Comparative Study of Europe and Japan," *Journal of World History* 6 (1995): 75–106. This combines the usual separate periodization of the Sengoku from 1467–1568 and the Azuchi-Momoyama periods (the rise of Nobunaga and Hideyoshi) from 1568 to 1600. The succeeding Tokugawa, or Edo, period is usually taken to begin in 1600 and last till 1868. Karl F. Friday, *Samurai, Warfare & the State in Early Medieval Japan* (New York: Routledge, 2004), 165–68.

42. Nagashino discussed by Parker, *Military Revolution*, 140; disputed in T. Conlan, *Weapons and Fighting Techniques of the Samurai Warrior, 1200–1877* (London: Amber, 2008), 165–76. Morillo, "Guns and Government."

43. Morillo, "Guns and Government"; John Whitney Hall, ed., *The Cambridge History of Japan*, vol. 4, *Early Modern Japan* (Cambridge, UK: Cambridge University Press, 1988), 45–53, 78–80.

44. Conlan, *Weapons and Fighting Techniques*, 8–11; Black, *War in the World*, 121; Hall, *Cambridge History of Japan*, 7; Ronald P. Toby, *State and Diplomacy in Early Modern Japan: Asia in the Development of the Tokugawa Bakufu* (Princeton, NJ: Princeton

University Press, 1984); Michael S. Laver, *The Sakoku Edicts and the Politics of the Tokugawa Hegemony* (Amherst, NY: Cambria, 2011), 2–5, 115; William E. Deal, *Handbook to Life in Medieval and Early Modern Japan* (New York: Oxford University Press, 2007), 149; Anne Walthall, "Do Guns Have Gender? Technology and Status in Early Modern Japan," in *Recreating Japanese Men*, ed. Sabine Frühstück and Anne Walthall (Berkeley: University of California Press, 2011), 25–47.

45. Conrad D. Totman, *Politics in the Tokugawa Bakufu, 1600–1843* (Berkeley: University of California Press, 1988), 63 (quote).

46. Hall, *Cambridge History of Japan*, 3; Totman, *Politics in the Tokugawa Bakufu*, xiv, xvi, 4, 235–37, 246–47.

47. David A. Bell, *The First Total War: Napoleon's Europe and the Birth of Warfare as We Know It* (Boston: Houghton Mifflin, 2007), esp. 77, 115, 190–91.

48. Quoted in T. C. W. Blanning, *The French Revolutionary Wars, 1787–1802* (New York: St. Martin's, 1996), 100–101.

49. Alan Forrest, *Soldiers of the French Revolution* (Durham, NC: Duke University Press, 1990), 80–84; Howard G. Brown, *War, Revolution, and the Bureaucratic State: Politics and Army Administration in France, 1791–1799* (Oxford: Clarendon, 1995), esp. 9–10, 270, 283–85.

50. Dominic Lieven, *Russia Against Napoleon* (New York: Penguin, 2009), 232–33; Ute Frevert, *A Nation in Barracks: Modern Germany, Military Conscription, and Civil Society*, trans. Andrew Boreham with Daniel Brückenhaus (Oxford: Oxford University Press, 2004), 10–22, 47, 50–51, 54–55, 59–60; Alan Forrest, Karen Hagemann, and Jane Rendall, "Introduction," in *Soldiers, Citizens and Civilians: Experiences and Perceptions of the Revolutionary and Napoleonic Wars, 1790–1820*, ed. Alan Forrest, Karen Hagemann, and Jane Rendall (New York: Palgrave Macmillan, 2009), 1–2, 3; Thomas Hippler, *Citizens, Soldiers and National Armies: Military Service in France and Germany, 1789–1830* (New York: Routledge, 2006); Bell, *First Total War*, 296–97.

51. Marshall G. S. Hodgson, *The Gunpowder Empires and Modern Times* (Chicago: University of Chicago Press, 1974); William H. McNeill, *The Age of Gunpowder Empires, 1450–1800* (Washington, DC: American Historical Association, 1989).

52. Black, *War in the World*, 196; Black, *Beyond the Military Revolution*, 171.

53. Douglas M. Peers, "Revolution, Evolution, or Devolution: The Military and the Making of Colonial India," in *Empires and Indigenes: Intercultural Alliance, Imperial Expansion, and Warfare in the Early Modern World*, ed. Wayne E. Lee (New York: New York University Press, 2011), 81–108; Black, *War in the World*, 207.

54. Rowe, *China's Last Empire*, 33, 285–86.

10

The Age of Steam
and the Industrial Empires

1815–1905

Invention and Production • Coal and Steam Navies • Scrambling for Empire •
The Rise of Japan

FOR MANY YEARS military historians have been asking what "modern" war is and what conditions produced it. In question is more than a mere adjective. The world wars seemed to represent such a profound break from everything that had come before that they required special explanation. Their catastrophic scale seemed to define a new form of human conflict, and their conclusion with two atomic explosions seemed to presage worse to come. There had been war, and now there was "modern war," a form of war apparently defined by its scale, by the societal commitment to waging it, and by the level of destruction and death that it entailed. For much of the twentieth century it seemed that modern war must be "total" war, with the full commitment of societal resources and the abandonment of many customary restraints. Having declared the existence of total war, historians immediately began searching for the developmental stages that had preceded it. Where had it come from?

Now, decades after World War II, and with the end of the Cold War reducing the threat of nuclear confrontation, it is abundantly clear that not all future war will resemble the great wars of the twentieth century. Furthermore, as any review of events immediately makes apparent, not all wars of the twentieth century were total, or even tending toward total.[1] The meaning of "modern" must be sought elsewhere, disconnected from the world wars, or the word must simply be discarded as nondescriptive. Nevertheless, the world wars command our attention, as do the conflicts that preceded them. The processes that made the world wars what they were, were closely related to the processes that escalated Western military power over much of the rest of the world during the late nineteenth and twentieth centuries. This chapter, together with the next, examines the technological and institutional development of mass industrial armies and navies that occurred across the nineteenth and early twentieth centuries. Chapters 12–14 then examine the many responses to the problems posed by mass industrial armies, responses from both inside and outside the Western world. There is little question that the experience of the world wars continues to reverberate, and the military innovations of the twentieth and twenty-first centuries, for good and ill, owe much to that experience.

Within the period covered in this and the remaining chapters, roughly 1820 to the present, two realities loom large. The first is that technological innovations have become increasingly important in war. Ideas about how to use them remain critical, and much of chapter 14 will examine ideas designed to attack apparent Western technological superiority, but, as Quincy Wright's monumental *Study of War* argued decades ago, in the modern era technology has become far more central to the nature of war. Tied to the increasing centrality of technology has been a significant acceleration in the pace of change, and a concomitant struggle by military planners to keep up with that pace, although they have often failed to master the multiplying variables. In some ways the slaughter and apparent futility of World War I is a story of an initial failure to understand the variables, followed by years spent in combat trying to master them.[2]

This chapter focuses on the first and most critical of the technological changes: the Industrial Revolution itself. The harnessing of a new mineral source of energy and the invention of machines to automate production provided a new outlet for human inventiveness in peace and in war. There are a variety of possible paths to follow in exploring the impact of industrialization on war, but here we focus on its effects at sea. Ships were the most complex preindustrial human creations, and for much of the last two centuries they remained the most complex industrial machines. They were also central to the expansion of Western power around the world, and it was the Japanese ability to adopt and adapt to European steam and steel navies that launched them into the ranks of world powers.

INVENTION AND PRODUCTION

The word "revolution" notwithstanding, the Industrial Revolution was a process, not an event. Even more critically, what made it revolutionary was that the process became recursive and self-reinforcing. Changes in one arena of activity reinforced or accelerated changes in another. The process began in eighteenth-century Britain, where a particular combination of expanding population, available investment capital, a mercantile-oriented political establishment, a shortage of firewood, and a surge in craft production created the necessary preconditions.

Interactions among five key arenas of activity combined to generate revolutionary change: mining, the development of the steam engine, the creation of machines to do work (initially in textile manufacture), changes in iron production, and the combination of several of these into new transportation systems—notably the railroad and the steamship. But in one sense the process started with coal. Long before the eighteenth century, much of England, especially the population of London, had relied on coal rather than wood for heating. The north of England was supplied with rich veins of coal relatively near the surface, and coastal shipping could cheaply transport the fuel to the booming population of London. Over time, however, deeper and deeper mine shafts required constant pumping to remove water, and animal-powered pumps faltered as the shafts went ever deeper. In 1712 Thomas Newcomen developed an engine that burned coal to produce steam inside a metal cylinder. Rapid cooling of the steam back into water generated a vacuum inside the cylinder. Atmospheric pressure (14.7 pounds per square inch at sea level) then pushed a piston down into the cylinder. The movement of the cylinder tripped a valve; the vacuum was released; the weight of the pump chain on the other end of the rocker arm controlling the piston pulled the piston back out; and the cylinder again filled with steam. From the perspective of a later era this "atmospheric steam engine" was highly inefficient in terms of its energy output per ton of coal, but Newcomen's invention was designed to pump out coal mines, so the supply of coal was no obstacle.

Newcomen's engines proliferated in the coal fields over several decades, until James Watt, who began his experiments with steam by working on a model of a Newcomen engine in 1763, developed several key improvements. By 1765 his experiments led him to add a separate condenser that essentially doubled the engine's efficiency by not having to reheat the cylinder on each stroke. In 1784 he patented the reciprocating engine (the piston was powered in both directions) that also used a crank to produce rotary motion, suitable for use in a factory. By 1800 other inventors had hit on the idea of using the pressure of the steam itself to push the piston *out* of the cylinder at pressures far greater than 14.7 psi, rather than relying on atmospheric pressure to push it *in*. This allowed for a potentially enormous expansion of power, provided that the machinery could be built to sufficient accuracy—most notably, the perfection (or tolerance) of the piston's fit within the cylinder. We will return to that story momentarily.[3]

Within this same period, inventors began looking for ways to save labor costs in the many stages involved in the making of cloth. As the machines they invented succeeded, the price of cloth dropped and the size of the market increased substantially, further spurring invention to serve that market. In essence, what they invented were "machines that do work." The idea now seems so basic to us that it is hard to recognize how revolutionary those machines were. Prior to the eighteenth century, converting energy into mechanical motion to accomplish repetitive tasks was fairly rare. Grain or olive mills were a primary example, whether powered by wind, water, or animal, but the most sophisticated early examples of such machines were mechanical clocks.

Figure 10.1 Clock from Dover Castle, England, 1550–1600.

Close examination of early manufacturing machines readily suggests that the clock may have provided some of the inspiration (see Figures 10.1 and 10.2). Clocks convert an energy input (gravity or a mainspring) into reciprocal motion (the escapement) to move complex rotary gear combinations to generate a variety of actions at predictable intervals. Both the steam engine and early textile machines relied on similar mechanisms to regulate *and automate* repetitive, rotary and/or reciprocal mechanical motion. Among world cultures, Europeans were uniquely invested in the development of precision timekeeping, and ultimately of clocks. The Chinese had an early interest in clockwork motions powered by water, but that interest faded. Historian David Landes argues that Western Christian monastic communities had a unique need to mark the day's and night's prayer times. The need to do so at night, in particular, was specific to Christian monks. Mechanical clocks emerged to solve this problem, and as their complexity and accuracy increased, so did the capacity to automate a host of mechanical motions from a single energy input, not just moving the clock hands but also ringing bells, opening doors, parading figures in and out of a clock tower, and so on.[4]

Clocks were machines that did complex work long before that idea was applied to production, but their development may have provided the key technological and ideational foundations. Richard Arkwright's 1770 "water frame" spinning machine was in part based on a design produced by a clock maker, and it is certainly no coincidence that James Watt spent much of his youth apprenticed to a clock maker. Over the course of the eighteenth century, machines doing work in the textile industry proliferated. The flying shuttle, invented in 1733, although it was not fully automated, sped up weaving and allowed for much wider looms. That increase in productivity put pressure on the supply of thread, which led James Hargreaves to invent the spinning jenny in 1764. Other machines for spinning followed in the 1760s and 1770s. And as the supply of thread increased, pressure reverted to the weaving end, leading to Edmund Cartwright's 1789 power loom—although it took some years before weaving was fully automated. The key attribute of all these machines was that, like clocks, they automated certain repetitive processes. Automation allowed multiplication: with an old-fashioned spinning wheel, the worker could manage only one spindle of thread at a time, since the process required the constant attention of both hands. Spinning machines automated work that formerly required hands, and now needed a worker merely to turn the machine and feed in raw materials. In essence, the only limit on multiplying the spindles was available power, something that first watermills and then the improving steam engines provided.

Moving water in general provided a key intermediate power source in two ways: rivers provided power for early factories, while canals provided the first form of cheaper transportation, moving inexpensive bulk goods to seaports or cities. Britain's industrial revolution was already in full swing based on the power of moving water, but, once the new techniques of production were harnessed to the steam engine, the effects multiplied even more rapidly. The power provided by steam engines dramatically increased the production of iron, by powering both bellows and hammers and allowing ever larger masses of iron to be worked into

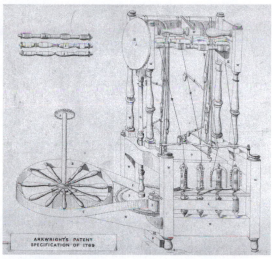

Figure 10.2 Richard Arkwright's "water frame" spinning machine, patented 1769. One of several spinning or weaving machines invented in the late eighteenth century.

shape. Large-scale, cheap iron production enabled, among many other things, the laying of track and the building of iron bridges to carry the emergent railroad system, driven by steam-powered locomotives. Those trains in turn revolutionized the accessibility of manufactured goods by dramatically lowering the cost of transporting them to market, further incentivizing inventions related to automating production. The first steam-powered locomotive was introduced in the 1780s, and the first practicable ones, much like the Newcomen engine, were used at the mines to transport coal (where there had long been a system of wooden tracks for that purpose and where coal was cheap). The results were so promising that the development of a national network in England began soon thereafter, beginning in 1830 with the Liverpool and Manchester Railway, carrying both freight and passengers (see Map 10.1).

This brief summary of changes in these four fields is intended only to hint at the large-scale processes and how they influenced and indeed accelerated each other. Many of the developments recursively facilitated each other: steam engines made of iron became cheaper and more efficient as ironworking techniques improved. As transportation costs dropped, the incentive to centralize and expand production motivated further efforts at machine automation, and so on. But it may help to dig deeper into at least one example of these sorts of reciprocal effects as a way of understanding not only how this process of innovation proceeded but also the relatively early interaction between industrial and military technology. Some disagreement remains about the extent to which weapons production stimulated industrial processes, but the consensus is that it did not to a significant degree. Nevertheless, the story of James Watt's cooperative relationship with John Wilkinson and the relationship between

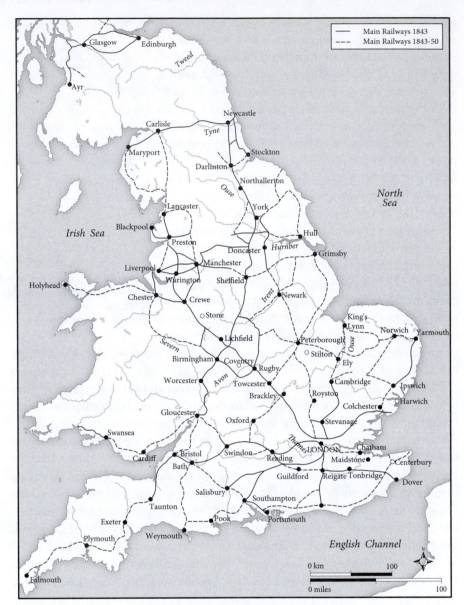

Map 10.1 The initial expansion of British rail lines, to 1850.

the improved steam engine and the boring of cannon highlights the synergy that could be achieved through intersecting industrial processes—in part because military technology involved some of the most complex and expensive products then being made—most notably cannon and ships.[5]

In the several decades after Newcomen's engine, English metalworkers made major improvements in the casting of iron (meaning pouring molten iron into prepared molds, rather than shaping it through the highly labor intensive beating of hot iron into shape—i.e., wrought iron). These changes were based partly on changing the fuel source from wood or charcoal to coke (a form of processed coal that burns cleaner and hotter), and also on other technical improvements. As a result, whereas Newcomen's original engine had been made of brass cylinders, lead pipes, a wooden beam, and a few wrought iron parts, newer versions used almost entirely cast iron components.[6]

Meanwhile, John Wilkinson, continuing in a family business, was casting iron cannon. Traditionally a cannon had been cast by pouring the metal into a mold that included a plug defining the interior of the barrel. The plug was usually wood wrapped in clay, and was burned out of the completed cannon. In the 1730s, Frenchman Jean Maritz developed a boring machine that could drill out a more precise barrel from a solid casting, allowing for a stronger, lighter, and more accurate cannon. Although there was some effort made to keep the technique secret, it quickly spread around Europe. In 1774 Wilkinson patented his own version in Great Britain. Although he had been supplying ordnance to the army for some years, the improved accuracy of his lathe-bored cannon increased his business enormously.[7]

At this point, Wilkinson's career intersected with that of James Watt. Watt's design improvements to Newcomen's engine depended on converting his insight into a working reality. Watt spent the years between 1762 and 1769 perfecting it on a full scale and submitting his design for patent protection. A key problem in his design was overcoming the lack of precision in the steam cylinders, moderately important in Newcomen's original engine, but critical in Watt's more efficient design. Watt turned to Wilkinson's boring machine to give him the necessary precision.

Watt's engine, vastly improved by Wilkinson's lathe, was then put to use improving output in the iron industry, in which the technical improvements referred to earlier had as yet barely affected total levels of production. The third Watt steam engine ever made was delivered to Wilkinson to power the bellows he used in smelting iron; it was the first steam engine used for something other than pumping. Then in 1777 Wilkinson asked Watt to supply him with an engine capable of raising a hammer of 1,680 pounds (compared to a normal blacksmith's five-pound sledgehammer). Watt delivered that first forging steam engine in 1781. Soon thereafter it was used to power the very rotary lathe that Wilkinson had invented to bore the cylinders, speeding up the boring process substantially (see Figure 10.3a and b). This sort of reciprocal effect was central to the speed and ultimate impact of the Industrial Revolution, as each set of inventions enabled, improved, or suggested another.

The interrelatedness exemplified by the inventions of John Wilkinson and James Watt was at the heart of the Industrial Revolution. Once the revolution was underway, that synergy accelerated technological change at an astonishing rate, much greater than anything seen before. But the complexity of the interdependence of its components also made it difficult to copy, especially by societies outside the cultural framework that created it. The Industrial Revolution was not a "thing" to copy; it was a process built on a constantly

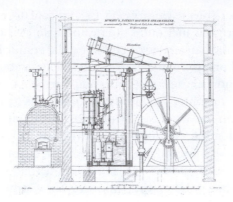 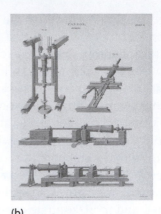

(a)   (b)

Figure 10.3 *a & b* **The Watt steam engine and variations of Wilkinson's cannon borer.** Note the clockwork-like quality of the steam engine's workings. Both are near-contemporary technical illustrations.

growing and integrated infrastructure. Those processes and capabilities did spread, however, at different paces and with different emphases depending on the other nation's resources, governmental involvement, and overall linguistic and technical familiarity with what was happening in Britain. In part this was simply a function of proximity: western European nations took direct advantage of British expertise and purchased British machinery. Industrial innovations were pursued as capitalistic enterprises in an open market. At times governments did try to keep certain secrets, but industrial espionage was already in full swing, and private manufacturers wanted wider markets. Quite often, even developments geared expressly for the military were legally available on the open market.[8]

The unfolding process of industrialization transformed societies. It changed work patterns, transportation norms, gender relations, trade networks, financing, ideas about the state's role in the economy, and more. The rest of this chapter, however, focuses on its impact on a specific kind of capacity: the capacity to invent and then build those inventions. The Industrial Revolution quite literally provided the tools to build two sorts of things previously beyond imagination. One was iron machinery made to highly precise tolerances, and the other was the ability to create and shape very large objects made of iron or steel. Wilkinson's steam hammer hints at the second category: the ability to manipulate large masses of iron. Watt's lathe hints at the other: the ability to take an invention and apply both mechanical power and precision to rapidly machine metal to exact tolerances (it is in this sense that "to machine" becomes a verb).

Both manipulating and machining, however, required a higher level of capital investment than had been needed in traditional craft production. In general, industrialization favored the scaling-up of enterprise, as high levels of initial capital investment encouraged larger-scale enterprises capable of generating significant returns. These new large enterprises employing semi-automated factory production dramatically increased output, which encouraged the search for new markets. This became critically important especially after 1850 as other European powers began to catch up after Britain's initial head start, and Britain sought to maintain its advantage. The competitive quest to expand markets to serve the newly industrially productive economies encouraged imperial land grabs.[9]

Finally, changes in transportation systems, both on land and at sea, dramatically increased speed while reducing cost, and created dependence first on coal and then on oil to sustain the system. The Industrial Revolution began the process of tipping the human economy from one based on organic energy to one based on mineral energy (see the introduction to the book). That transition had many implications for military activity, from stimulating the growth of cities (which concentrated production, populations for recruitment, and vastly increased their strategic importance), to radically altering logistical systems, to rearranging strategic geography to emphasize controlling points on the landscape as much as, or even more than, controlling expanses of organic-energy-producing territory. This meant it was more rewarding to control localized industrial zones than it was to control large swathes of agricultural land, although the latter's importance never fully disappeared. We will return to this issue in warfare on land in the next chapter, but in the nineteenth century, nowhere was this rearrangement of strategic geography more noticeable than in war at sea.

COAL AND STEAM NAVIES

Wooden, side-gunned sailing ships dominated the Napoleonic Wars, even as the first steam-powered vessels were beginning to ply the inland waterways of the United States (in 1807) and Britain (in 1811). In fact, wooden ships continued to be the measure of power at sea at least through the 1850s, even as the capabilities provided by industrial developments—manipulating large masses of metal and machining metal precisely and cheaply—were initiating a period of instability and unpredictability in the contemporary understanding of what sorts of ships would next dominate the seas.[10]

There are two separate but related stories here. One is the story of changes in ship construction, armor, and guns, especially on those ships designed for war on the open seas with industrialized peer competitors. The other is a story of inland power projection from the sea, involving related construction, armor, and gun issues, but deployed in the different context of war against nonindustrial powers. Most of the technological development (especially in guns and armor, if not in steam engines) was urged along by the mutual fears of the industrial powers—primarily Britain and France, and later Germany—whose specific innovations were then copied or purchased by other industrializing powers (the United States, Russia, Italy, Austria, Spain, and eventually

Japan) in their attempts to stay relevant at sea. Within that arena, for almost all of this period, Britain retained a significant advantage in both numbers and capability, even when other states might build individually superior ships. But in the other context, that of industrialized powers against nonindustrial ones, there was almost no comparison. Even the relatively weak industrial forces of the United States or Spain conferred enormous advantages against a nonindustrial power.

These two separate stories are combined here into three overlapping stages of development. The first stage was marked primarily by the changes implicit in ships being powered independently of the wind. That development was not immediate, especially in ships used for military purposes. The use of steam engines at sea remained highly problematic for military forces through 1830—they were severely underpowered for moving a vessel loaded down with cannon—and Britain, the world's leading naval power, rightly resisted early adoption of steam warships. Their slow speed and relatively small size (due to the low power of early steam engines) and the vulnerability of the paddle wheel restricted most early steam warships to harbor defense, tugs, and the like. The commercial market, however, labored on, improving the efficiency of the engine itself. It came into common use in the 1820s and 1830s for short-distance packets (boats on scheduled routes). A further key impulse for improvement emerged from the desire to speed communication between Britain and its colony in India, while also taking advantage of the potential for shallow-draft designs that could safely steam upriver. Sailing ships of the line grew larger in this period, wielded enormous broadsides, and continued to define blue water naval power. Even at this early stage, however, steam's capacity to deliver firepower inland, up rivers, ignoring the wind and more capable than sailing ships of navigating the shallows, had decisive effects in the projection of Western power, especially in Africa and Asia. This reality was radically demonstrated by the steam-powered gunboat *Nemesis*, which played a key role in the First Opium War between China and Britain from 1839 to 1842 (see Figure 10.4).[11]

Despite rising British industrial production, there was no particular demand in China for British goods. Chinese production capacities and quality were more than enough to satisfy domestic needs and desires. Chinese tea, on the other hand, was in great demand in Britain, while the only British trade good that found a strong market in China was opium produced in India. The tea-opium exchange greatly enriched a number of British merchants, who then petitioned the British government to use coercive force whenever the Chinese government tried to restrict the flow of opium. Until the 1830s, however, China's military strength, continental size, and complex harbor and river systems had rendered it invulnerable to British military pressure. The steam-powered gunboat tipped the balance in favor of the British.[12]

In a testament to the importance of commercial stimuli to technological development, the *Nemesis* did not emerge from the Royal Navy but from the

Figure 10.4 The East India Company's steamer *Nemesis*. Here shown destroying Chinese war junks in January 1841, from a mid-nineteenth-century publication.

British East India Company's efforts to secure its communications with Britain and to operate forcefully in Asian waters. The company built a series of private, armed gunboats, culminating in the launch of the *Nemesis* in 1839. It was iron-hulled and steam-powered, and the company immediately dispatched her in secret to China. In the process it became the first iron ship to round the Cape of Good Hope. It displaced 660 tons, was 184 feet long and 29 feet wide, and drew only six feet of water when fully loaded. For armament it carried two pivot-mounted thirty-two-pound guns, five brass six-pounders, six smaller cannons, and a rocket launcher. The *Nemesis* reached Macao on November 25, 1840, where the war had been going on for five months. Traditional British ships of the line, navigating the complex harbor, sometimes towed by smaller steamships, blasted the coastal fortifications, allowing troops to land. The obsolete Chinese navy was quickly defeated, and the British fleet ascended the river to Canton (now known as Guangzhou). As the river narrowed and the channels became shallower and more elaborate, the *Nemesis*'s maneuverability and shallow draft proved her worth, and it continued to destroy riverine warships and riverside forts (see Map 10.2a and b). The expedition's commander noted that the *Nemesis* destroyed "five forts, one battery, two military stations, and nine war junks, in which were one hundred and

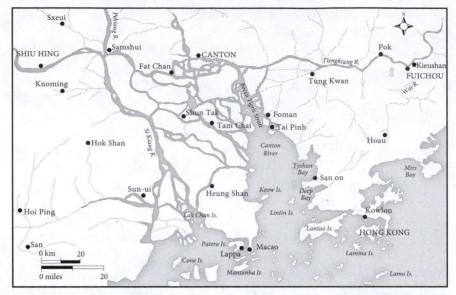

(a)

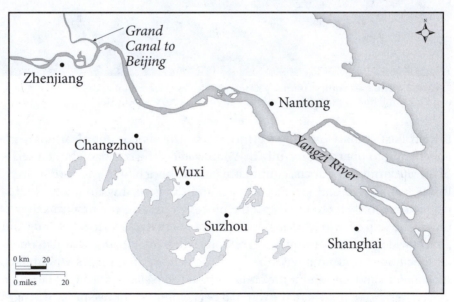

(b)

Map 10.2 *a & b* **The river and harbor systems leading to Canton and to the Grand Canal at Zhenjiang during the Opium War.** Both maps convey the complexity of islands and channels overcome by steam navigation and rendering key Chinese cities and the crucial Grand Canal vulnerable to British artillery fire and troops.

fifteen guns." Despite the capture of several key cities, China continued to resist until 1842, when another British flotilla, reinforced by additional steamships from India, sailed up the Yangzi River, brushed aside the massive Chinese blocking fleet, and moved to cut off the junction with the Grand Canal supplying the capital at Beijing. China quickly sued for peace.[13]

The steam-powered gunboat, delivering artillery deep inland—something it also did in Africa and in South and Southeast Asia—in some ways represented a major increase in relative European power. Whereas previously, European military power had not exceeded or even matched that of the great Asian empires except at sea, now some of that seaborne capability moved inland. Furthermore, once territory was occupied, European colonizers used steam-powered railroads and telegraphs to maintain their power in continental interiors (see chapter 11). For the rest of the century, no Asian or African power could really match these capabilities. But European naval developments did not stop there. European powers that shared in the technological capacity unlocked by industrialization continued to compete with each other, and these interlocking and self-reinforcing processes led to ever-increasing rates of change.

The Second Stage

The pace of change and the resulting uncertainty about what technological paths to pursue characterized the second stage of development (roughly 1830–1870). In some ways this uncertainty was coupled with institutional resistance to change exercised by naval officers committed to the ships they knew and the wind-based strategic geography they understood. Indeed, as the career of the *Nemesis* demonstrated, this first decisive use of steam-powered gunboats occurred only because of the enterprising nature of the profit-oriented East India Company. At the same time, it is not exactly true to say that the British Royal Navy dug in its heels and opposed iron and coal ships. Industrializing Britain possessed the wealth and the industrial capacity to lead in most technical arenas, and the Royal Navy maintained an active interest in emergent possibilities. Replacing an entire fleet, however, was a supremely expensive proposition, and there was a good deal of uncertainty over what combination of iron, steam, wood, and sail would prove most effective in a military context. There was little question, for example, that paddle-wheel steamers were highly vulnerable to cannon fire, and the paddle further limited the size of the broadside (notwithstanding experiments that put the paddle in the middle of the ship). The emergence of exploding-shell guns at roughly the same time, however, seemed to render even the largest wooden sailing ships vulnerable. Experimentation proceeded apace in both the commercial and military sectors, with competing state navies offering innovations that others then felt compelled to match. The story is complex, but a few key moments can be identified.

The steam engine itself underwent a more or less continuous process of refinement and improvement, with each change tending to increase its power and efficiency. The key to its long-run military importance, however, was the screw propeller, which removed the vulnerable paddle wheels, freed up the entire broadside of the ship for carrying guns, and allowed the entire steam apparatus to be placed below the waterline (save the funnel exhausts). Early versions of the propeller (from the late 1830s to the 1850s) could not yet match the speed of paddle-wheel ships, but were retrofitted to sailing ships of the line as an auxiliary power source. In that role the technology was perfected until it could replace sails entirely decades later. The development of the screw propeller provides another example of how inventors, the institutional navy, and commercial ventures could interact. The first seagoing screw-driven vessel, the *Archimedes*, was launched in 1838, designed to be shown off to the Royal Navy, by Francis Pettit Smith, a private inventor. The navy, although not fully persuaded, did begin to imagine steam-powered screws as auxiliary power for sailing ships of war. Smith, meanwhile, turned to a merchant shipbuilder who enthusiastically adopted the design, and even redesigned his massive iron steamship (the *Great Britain*), then on the stocks, to incorporate the screw as the prime mover, with sails relegated to auxiliary power. The navy did not make a similar transition for another twenty years.[14]

Even as steam power and the screw propeller infiltrated into wooden sailing ships as an auxiliary power source, those ships continued to serve as the primary element of sea power through the 1850s. That status was finally undermined by the parallel and contemporaneous developments in guns firing explosive shells. In 1823 French gun designer Henri Paixhans introduced exploding shells for flat-trajectory cannons (shells had long been used in mortars). Prior to the shell gun, a massive ship of the line was really vulnerable only to another such ship. Now, however, even a few rounds of exploding shells could devastate a wooden ship, in large part by setting it on fire. This had the initial effect of empowering smaller and cheaper ships carrying fewer cannon, creating an asymmetric potential much like that later posed by torpedoes. The first versions remained unreliable because building a fuse that would explode at the right moment in the shell's trajectory toward a moving target in a body of water was tricky. Gradual improvements, however, proved their worth, and French naval planners were persuaded that shell guns had played a decisive role in the Russian defeat of the Ottomans at the Battle of Sinop in 1853.

In response, first the French and then the British, already experimenting with iron-hull construction (recall that the *Nemesis* and some other nonoceanic vessels had been built of iron), applied that technology within the traditional ship design of the broadside-firing, sail- and screw-driven steamships, in which the steam engine remained an auxiliary power source. The French *Gloire* and the HMS *Warrior* represented these departures. The *Gloire*, begun in 1857 and launched in 1859, was wood-hulled but then armored with iron.

The HMS *Warrior*, launched in 1860 in response to news of the *Gloire*'s construction, was the first armored oceangoing warship built from iron from the ground up (the *Nemesis*, and others like it, though built of iron, was not armored and could only be called "oceangoing" under a very liberal sense of that term). With the *Warrior* the British navy also committed itself to reversing the role of sail and steam—sails were now the auxiliary power. It is worth emphasizing too, that the capacity to manufacture armor was emerging as a result of ongoing changes in the industrial production of iron. Early armor achieved its thickness from riveting or bolting together relatively thin sheets of wrought iron boiler plate ("laminated armor"). It was only in the 1850s that wrought iron plate in a four-inch thickness became available; by the 1860s British mills could produce armor plate twelve inches thick, even as American ironclads of that period typically only had two inches of laminated armor.[15]

Despite their technical inferiority to both French and British counterparts, American ironclads became famous because they were actually used in action. Until the Crimean War of the mid-1850s there had been almost no significant naval conflict since 1815, and even that war saw relatively little naval activity. In contrast, the American Civil War included a prolonged naval conflict, primarily pitting the Union Navy against the Confederacy's blockade runners. The duration of the conflict and its spur to improvisation and invention provided further evidence for the necessity of armor and the potential power of shell guns. Public reaction in Britain to the seeming invulnerability of the Confederate ironclad CSS *Virginia* pressured the Admiralty to move more quickly to an all-iron fleet. The USS *Monitor*, with its low freeboard and rotating turret, also suggested the possibility of entirely new designs for ships—lower to the waterline, mounting fewer, heavier, shell-firing guns in rotating turrets. These new possibilities further complicated the choices that navies had to make. Which combination would work?[16]

This uncertainty about the military application of changing technology persisted after the American Civil War, as Europe entered another mostly peaceful period, at least at sea. The extent of this uncertainty is suggested by the general reaction to the Battle of Lissa in 1866, in which ships of the Austrian fleet successfully rammed several Italian ships, sinking one and damaging others. In the absence of other significant fleet actions for the next couple of decades, many capital warships thenceforth were designed to include a ram. Cultural conservatism also influenced some navies, notably the American one, for many years. They resisted change even as its pace accelerated, as measured by the proliferation of ship designs using different combinations of propulsion, guns, and armor. The stability of the basic design inherent to the sailing ship from 1650 to 1830 was gone. Britain meanwhile continued to lead the way, rising to whatever specific technical challenge France might offer, in part because of Britain's underlying financial and industrial lead, and in part because British leaders and the British public felt that their security depended on it. Britain's general lead in naval power also allowed it to respond to challenging innovations in calculated ways. No one new ship could challenge British hegemony, and so they could wait for emergent technologies to mature before adopting them.[17]

The Third Stage

The third stage, lasting from roughly 1870–1905, but strongly overlapping with the previous one, in many ways persisted as an age of uncertainty. Now much of the technological development (the ram fad notwithstanding) centered on the competition between guns and armor (steam engines continued to improve, with oil-fired engines replacing coal at the very end of this period, and speed remained a key criteria, but for simplicity's sake we focus on guns versus armor). All the industrial powers with navies had now committed themselves to ships made of iron (and steel from the mid- to late 1870s) and powered by steam (sails on larger ships of war were abandoned from about 1880), and began a race to build ever faster, more heavily armored ships, carrying bigger and bigger guns and now firing explosive shells. Technical failures abounded, but the basic dialectical progression of shell gun versus armor (along with the power plant to drive the heavier ships) persisted, and also rapidly escalated the cost per ship. As historian Antulio Echevarria points out, a good deal of this late nineteenth-century arms race among the Western industrial powers (soon to be joined by Japan) was qualitative rather than quantitative, as the pace of technological change accelerated, and as other Western nations shortened Britain's engineering and industrial lead.[18]

Table 10.1 charts the progression in gun size versus armor thickness in a general way; the seeming inconsistencies actually reflect technological

Ship	Launch date	Main gun bore size	Breech- or muzzle-loading	Max eff. range (yards)	No. and caliber of main guns	Shell weight (lbs)	Armor belt/ turret/deck (inches)
Warrior	1860	7"	Both	3,500	26–68 lb & 10–110 lb	68 & 110	4.5/–/–
Prince Albert	1864	9"	Muzzle-loading		4–9"	250	4/10.5/–
Monarch	1869	12"	Muzzle-loading		4–12"	600	7/10/–
Inflexible	1876	16"	Muzzle-loading	8,000	4–16"	1700	24/17/3
Colossus	1882	12"	Breech-loading	8,000	4–12"	714	18/16/3
Trafalgar	1887	13.5"	Breech-loading	12,000	4–13.5"	1250	20/18/3
Majestic	1894	12"	Breech-loading	10,000	4–12"	850	9/14/3
Dreadnought	1906	12"	Breech-loading	20,400	10–12"	850	11/12/3

Table 10.1: **The development of shell guns and armor in British capital ships**. The chart over-simplifies some complex issues. Not all twelve-inch guns, for example, are the same. The *Dreadnought's* Mk X guns were a significant improvement over the *Majestic's* Mk VIII.

change. For example, in 1890 nickel-steel armor was invented, followed in 1894 by the German Krupp firm adding chromium and manganese to nickel steel and combining the alloy with a new face-hardening forging technique. Although developed in Germany, the armor was sold around the world as "Krupp-cemented" armor, and it soon became standard on major warships. This change allowed armor to become thinner and lighter than its iron predecessor while being more effective. As reflected in the table, armor initially thinned thereafter, but the upward trend in thickness within the new type of steel simply resumed. In the same decade, guns rapidly grew, firing faster and at longer ranges, and now using smokeless powder that greatly increased muzzle velocity (more in chapter 11), while new fuses and armor-piercing exploding shells were developed to deal with the new armor. Each of these changes (and others, such as quick-firing smaller-caliber guns) affected the appearance of upward progression shown in Table 10.1, but the basic technological back-and-forth between offense and defense persisted.[19]

The physical configuration of the ships carrying these guns and bearing that armor also varied as shipbuilders experimented with design. The so-called predreadnought era of the 1880s and 1890s did see some standardization, with a typical capital ship displacing 12,000–14,000 tons, bearing four

Figure 10.5 The pre-dreadnought HMS *Majestic* leaving Portsmouth, 1906. Note the guns of varying sizes; main guns are in revolving deck turrets, one visible here forward of the bridge.

twelve-inch main guns and twelve to fourteen six-inch secondary guns (later versions of the smaller guns were quick-firing), moving at speeds up to eighteen knots and protected by nine inches (or more) of steel-alloy armor. Ironically, these ships got their first combat tests in the hands of Asian powers, in the Sino-Japanese War (1894–95) and the Russo-Japanese War (1904–5). Both wars were closely observed by the European naval powers and the role of long-range gunnery in the latter war particularly motivated or accelerated the last major round of changes in capital ship design: the British all-big-gun HMS *Dreadnought* of 1905, capable of new rates of speed and armed with more large guns of a single uniform caliber and substantially greater effective range. At the time, the *Dreadnought* seemed to represent a revolutionary new standard of naval power. One either had a competitive fleet of dreadnought battleships or one did not.[20]

The focus on the dreadnought class battleship as the new measure of power fit neatly with the theory about the role of naval power in determining state power that circulated widely during this time. American naval officer Alfred Thayer Mahan's *The Influence of Sea Power on History*, first published in 1890, became an instant favorite among many naval thinkers in the United States, Great Britain, Germany, Japan, and elsewhere. It purported to be a history of how Great Britain's navy had not only preserved that nation during the wars of the seventeenth and eighteenth centuries (Mahan later expanded that history to include the Napoleonic Wars), but had in fact expanded Great Britain's power and wealth. Embedded in his history, however, and made explicit in his later writings, was a theory that "command of the sea," and all of its associated advantages, would fall to the power that could defeat its opponent in a decisive clash of fleets. The only ships that really mattered in such a clash would be the capital ships concentrated together for that one battle.

This widely propagated theory encouraged the focus on the *Dreadnought*, and it further stimulated other rising powers (primarily Japan, Germany, and the U.S.) to invest heavily in capital ships so as not to be deprived of the rewards flowing from command of the sea. Mahanian "Navalism" also argued that the rewards and requirements of sea power demanded colonial bases. Not only would colonies provide mercantile wealth; in the new strategic geography of coal-fired, wind-independent ships, they would provide places to renew coal supplies. This joint military and economic "need" for worldwide colonies helped spur the European competitive race for empire from the 1870s through the First World War. Mahan's theories had a number of weaknesses, but perhaps the most critical one was that he wrote at exactly the wrong time. Technology was about to deal a serious blow to his conclusions, especially as cheap torpedoes and submarines began to render expensive capital ships highly vulnerable, and even more so as airplanes developed sufficiently for use at sea.[21]

The one naval power that did not fully embrace the Mahanian view of sea power and how to achieve it was France. There had long been a naval strategy based on attacking an enemy's commerce via a combination of privateers and small units of commerce raiders. This so-called *guerre de course* had been pursued by a variety of powers in earlier centuries, including Britain. France, however, returned to it repeatedly in the face of British naval supremacy. In the late nineteenth century, France codified the strategy as the *jeune école* (new school). Privateering had essentially been outlawed by international agreement, but the concept of commerce raiding by dispersed fleets of small ships was energized by the recurring hope that some new technological shift would render the great fleets of capital ships vulnerable. Furthermore, facing budget reductions after their defeat by Prussia in 1871 and the growing cost of new capital ships, French *jeune école* thinkers hoped the new technology would come cheaply in a rapidly built fleet of smaller ships. Among other innovations, this French strategic tendency helped produce Paixhans's shell guns, and also led to innovations in torpedoes, torpedo boats, and then in the ships designed to stop them, the torpedo boat destroyers. Eventually submarines would most effectively carry the banner of the *jeune école*.[22]

This narrative of naval technological change over the course of the nineteenth century necessarily obscures and simplifies many complex institutional and technical issues. It only touches on doctrinal development and, to give one example of a topic still undiscussed, has largely ignored intense design debates over speed versus armor—a debate that raged even hotter after 1906. From a global perspective, however, these issues are almost beside the point. At issue in this chapter is not the specifics of technological change, but rather the ability to build and manage such steel monsters (and their guns) at all, and then the mechanisms by which that ability spread. In our current age of "national security" and export controls on high technology, some may find it surprising that for virtually all of the nineteenth century very many industrial innovations, even specifically military ones, spread via commercial exchange, and not just imitation. This was not necessarily true at the level of ship design, but it certainly was so in terms of the machinery and the industrial capacity to build the components. France in the 1850s, for example, while in a naval arms race with Britain, was buying key machinery from a company in Glasgow, which was also supplying Russia and Turkey. And it was Robert Whitehead, a British engineer working for the Austrian navy, who developed a self-propelled torpedo. The Austrians could not afford to buy exclusive rights, and so Whitehead sold his design, and many later refinements, to navies around the world. Modern submarines proliferated in world navies after 1890 in part through the efforts of the private Electric Boat Company, based in the United States. And in the late nineteenth century and right up to 1914, Britain and the United States were building warships with the latest refinements for sale to Japan, Turkey, Brazil, Argentina, and Chile.[23]

Industrial production, especially naval industrial production, also began to rearrange the role of the state in producing military technology. After reviewing all the technological changes in this chapter, one might be forgiven for thinking that technological change simply progressed on its own, as each inventor aspired to make something better. In fact, the *desire* for military technological advantage was an old one that, as always, was driven or limited by an assortment of contingent political realities. What the industrial revolution had done was *enable* a much faster rate of change. That rate of change in and of itself acquired political characteristics as politicians and the public scrambled to understand and act on its implications.

William McNeill and others have identified the last twenty years of the nineteenth century and the decade before World War I as a period of crucial change in how new military technology emerged. McNeill argues that up until that point most technology emerged from the efforts of fertile minds motivated by a commercially competitive international marketplace. Good ideas competed with each other, and the better ones were purchased. Toward the end of the nineteenth century, however, that process was slowly supplanted by state-commanded technology. In a command economy, the state's agents specified performance criteria to national suppliers, and then became the sole purchasers of that technology. Command economies can accelerate invention because they provide a guaranteed market (having specified the invention they seek). But since there is a sole purchaser, the system tends to encourage inherently inefficient monopolies. The process also quickly becomes political, as military planners and industrialists connive at persuading legislatures to fund the ships and guns that both want built—something now referred to as the "military-industrial complex."[24]

Naval technology played a key role in these developments. Britain's wood and sail supremacy was ebbing in the face of steam and iron ships and increased competition, but their network of bases around the world, their commanding initial lead, and a period of European peace at sea after the Crimean War had preserved at least the illusion of continuing maritime dominance. Then in 1884 a journalist in Britain alerted the public to the French fleet's supposed equivalency with Britain's. The ensuing public outcry motivated the government to initiate massive new spending programs. As Germany and then other nations joined in the competition at sea, cranking up ever more expensive fleet-building programs, Britain's naval enthusiasts and shipbuilders found it increasingly easy to turn a nationalistic and maritime-security-conscious public into allies against a budget-conscious government. The navy got what it wanted.[25]

SCRAMBLING FOR EMPIRE

The race for naval power—now defined by steam and steel and joined by Germany, Japan, and the United States—was tightly connected to the European (and later Japanese) scramble for empire, most notably in Asia and Africa. Industrialization, within then-dominant economic theories, not only encouraged nations to pursue colonies in the belief that they needed new markets and new sources for raw materials, it also provided the tools to make those conquests possible. For example, Jules Ferry, the prime minister of France in 1883, explained the connection between industrialization and imperialism, by citing the "need for export markets" to absorb the goods of France's industrial population, as well as the fact that "a warship cannot carry more than fourteen days' worth of coal. . . . Thence the necessity of having on the oceans provision stations, shelters, ports for defense and revictualling."[26]

Justifying the desire for empire was one thing; the ability to seize it was another. Before the late nineteenth century, European militaries had enjoyed serious technological advantages only in the New World and in Australasia. Africans had suffered from a less severe technological gap, and that gap was easily offset by the challenging geography and the many diseases endemic south of the Sahara. Against Asian opponents, however, European advantages narrowed substantially, except at sea. Industrialization provided the capacity for what Daniel Headrick has called the *means* of empire in four basic ways, three of which are discussed in this chapter. The first was the elaboration of Western (industrial) naval superiority to a level difficult for late- or nonindustrializing nations to match. The second was the way that steam power, either via steam-powered gunboats or via railroads, rearranged strategic geography, allowing for the easier delivery of firepower and the necessary logistics deeper inland—both as cannon mounted in the ship itself and as cargo delivered for land forces' use. The third derived from late nineteenth-century medical advances that outlined a germ theory of disease and established key disease-prevention measures, especially the use of quinine against malaria from the 1840s. The fourth was the multiplication of infantry firepower, a factor dealt with in the next chapter, along with a fifth factor not considered by Headrick, namely, African allies and African manpower.[27]

In some ways the Opium War marked the beginning of this process. It demonstrated the use of war to gain access to markets; it showcased the world-spanning capacity of the British to deploy force; and the steam-powered *Nemesis* and its counterparts delivered critical firepower to the interior. These latter two issues highlight the change in strategic geography created by steam power. Ships at sea were no longer bound by wind patterns, and that freedom extended much deeper inland than previously. Although not available in China in the 1840s, railroads greatly facilitated later European imperial conquest and control in Africa—often financed by the commercial need to carry products to port, but also well suited to delivering firearm-equipped infantry. But railroads, steam power, and industrialization in general also reoriented strategic geography in other ways. They made different kinds of places more important to control. They emphasized nodes related to mineral energy: coal mines, steam-powered factories, railroad terminals and junctions, and port facilities and coaling stations. In this "punctuated" strategic landscape, all those *points* acquired a much greater importance than any particular points had in an organic economy, in which territorial *area* or expanse had mattered more.[28]

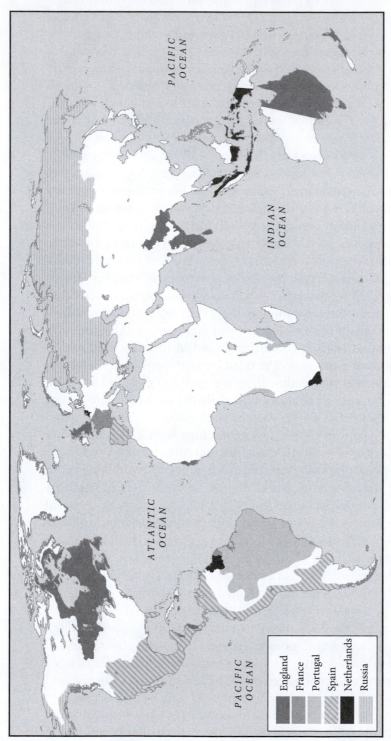

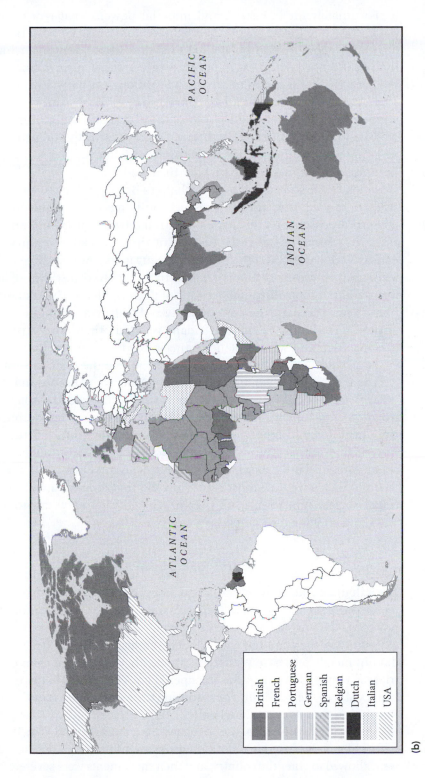

(b)

Map 10.3 _a_ & _b_ The expansion of European territorial empires. (_a_) shows European outposts and colonial territory ca. 1815. (_b_) shows the rapid expansion in territorial control by ca. 1914. Modern political boundaries are shown in (_b_) for reference.

Legend:
- British
- French
- Portuguese
- German
- Spanish
- Belgian
- Dutch
- Italian
- USA

PACIFIC OCEAN

INDIAN OCEAN

ATLANTIC OCEAN

Fortunately for industrial and imperial powers, that reorientation initially worked to their benefit when fighting nonindustrial powers. Heavy industrial firepower could be applied to secure select locations, which could then be defended with near impunity, while in some areas railroads progressively carried military influence inland (although usually still in a punctuated manner, defined by railroad lines and junctions). And for a variety of nationalistic, economic, and power political reasons, beginning in the late 1870s and progressing rapidly through World War I, the industrial powers, meaning much of Europe, the United States, and Japan, began a competitive "scramble for empire" (compare Map 10.3a and b).

Much of the scramble was to catch up to Britain, which already had massively expanded its worldwide presence, building on key eighteenth-century territorial possessions in Canada, Australia, the West Indies, and India to assert its claims in the early decades of the nineteenth century to South Africa, various Mediterranean islands, Singapore, Aden, Hong Kong, and Sierra Leone. Most of these claims initially involved just a port or coastal fort—without controlling much or any of the hinterland. The later nineteenth century saw British possessions multiply and many became more expansively territorial, including Egypt, the Sudan, assorted other large territorial colonies in Africa, and several island chains in the Pacific.[29]

From the 1880s other European powers joined the rush, most notably in Africa (and to a lesser extent in continental Asia, where European influence—other than in India—was somewhat more indirect, wielded through the control of key points). By 1900 the only independent regions remaining in Africa were Ethiopia and Liberia. The United States piled on after the Spanish-American War, occupying Cuba, Puerto Rico, the Philippines, and some other Pacific islands, as did Japan in Korea, Manchuria, and Taiwan. It is Japan to which we now must turn. How did that long-isolated, highly traditional society transform itself over roughly thirty-five years from 1870 to 1905 into an industrial, imperial world power?

THE RISE OF JAPAN

The calculated steps by which Japan rose from self-imposed isolation and technological backwardness to possessing a fleet of steel-armored, steam-powered, shell-firing battleships that vanquished Russia in 1905 provides a case study in the complexity of adopting industrial capability. The Japanese did not merely purchase Western weapons; they developed their own industrial capacity, and then became an imperial power and rival to the West. Japan's history shows the possibility of absorbing the complex fruits of the Industrial Revolution through calculated policy.

Since early in the rule of the Tokugawa Shogunate (founded in 1600), Japan had deliberately closed itself off to European influence. Only a few outsiders were allowed to enter the country, and their movements were severely restricted.

The end of this isolation and the beginning of radical change in Japan is usually dated to the arrival in July 1853 of US commodore Matthew Perry in Tokyo Bay with a squadron of four warships, including two steam-powered frigates, one armed with new Paixhans shell guns. Although internal pressures had been building within Japan to open its doors, Perry's arrival forced the issue. He demanded that the Japanese open trading relations, and other Western powers rapidly followed suit in pressing for access. Once the reality of Japan's weakness was forcibly laid bare, change followed rapidly, although not without resistance and internal factionalism. Ironically, the shogun proved less interested in military modernization than some key daimyo lords.[30]

Civil war followed in the 1860s, and with it a scramble to buy modern weapons (rifles, artillery, Gatling guns, and so on) and to rearm the peasants who had nominally been forbidden to bear arms for some two hundred years. Violence against European foreigners brought European retaliation and a decline in the power of an increasingly defenseless shogun. In January 1868 the teenage Meiji emperor abolished the shogunate, and the emperor, supported by key daimyos, defeated the shogun that same month. This "Meiji Restoration" made the emperor a real head of state again and laid the groundwork for Japanese nationalists to initiate a program of modernization and military reform. The Japanese army initially took most of its advice from the French, supplanted by German advisers after 1871, but here, as elsewhere in this chapter, our primary concern is with industrial capacity and naval power. While it would be possible to tell a story of Japanese industrialization and its consequent rise to power through an analysis of the army, the navies of the late nineteenth century represented the most complex products of industrialization. From virtually nothing, Japan catapulted itself into having the third largest navy in the world by 1920. That achievement was a deliberate, calculated response to security fears, and it came at some cost to the traditional culture of Japan. In short, Japan industrialized for military, not commercial purposes.[31]

To be sure, Japanese industrialization was rooted in some shifts that took place before 1853, including an expanding intellectual community and a rise in commercial activity, but there is little question that the shock of 1853 was the primary motivator. As a consequence, unlike in Europe, the industrializing process relied heavily on government encouragement and even direct intervention. Economic historians have debated the extent of government intervention and how much such intervention was responsible for the industrial facilities built in Japan in this period, but there is good evidence that the arsenals, state shipyards, and factories served as "highly effective centers for the absorption and dissemination of Western technologies and skills." As a minimum, Japan's "strong army" policy and the wars with China in 1894 and Russia in 1905 "provided, at crucial junctures, the demand necessary for assuring the survival and for aiding the growth of often financially and technologically struggling private firms in the shipbuilding, machinery, and machine-tool industries."[32]

Japanese industrialization began as imitation through purchase, and was shaped heavily by imported technology, although in the long run such direct importation had only a limited effect on total output. In the first few years after Perry, but prior to the Meiji Restoration, some reemergent daimyos had begun, with European advice, to construct Western-style ships, including steamships. Even so, industrial capacity did not spring up overnight. By 1884 only seventy-two of some 1,981 nongovernment factories were powered by steam. Flooded by European products, and with exports drying up, the Japanese economy suffered through the transition; much of its hard-won gold and silver reserve flowed out of the country. The government enacted a severe financial retrenchment in the 1880s, at some cost to the Japanese population, but it successfully boosted home industrial production. Between 1885 and 1920 the gross national product (GNP) had nearly tripled, with manufacturing growth at 580 percent.[33]

The heavy-industry part of this growth—steel, shipbuilding, and engineering—was closely tied to the government's desire for a modern navy. After Perry's arrival, and after seeking both Dutch and French advice, Japan built a naval yard and a few ships, primarily sailing ships and some with steam auxiliary. After the restoration in 1868, the desire for a more modern navy persisted, but the need to reestablish the sovereignty of the state favored first creating an army and a coastal defense system. Despite this delay, however, within twelve years the state had built four major arsenals and three shipyards. Each had the ability to repair modern small arms, cannon, and basic machinery, and, with the input of foreign advisors, began to produce their own modern weaponry in the early 1880s.[34]

The timing of Japan's naval modernization was perhaps fortuitous with respect to ongoing changes in European navies, because the innovations that radically transformed European navies took place in the 1870s through the 1890s (as discussed above), and Japan was able to observe and copy them. Japan also lacked the burden of an extant but aging and increasingly obsolescent wooden sailing fleet. Japan switched completely to iron steamships in the middle of the 1880s, and in that same decade began its own limited program of construction in state-run naval yards. Making this switch depended on industrial capacity, so to sustain that program the state built a five-ton blast furnace and imported three twelve-ton steam hammers, a twelve-ton crane, and skilled labor from England. Meanwhile, Japanese technicians were sent abroad to France and Germany to acquire key skills, and their knowledge helped the arsenal at Tsukiji succeed in making modern steel in the early 1880s. By 1884 the arsenal was producing many of the steel components of modern munitions.[35]

In addition to state arsenals and shipyards, private-firm construction accelerated at the end of the century, but Japan remained heavily dependent on purchasing ships, mostly from Britain, whose models Japan generally copied in its own shipbuilding. There were exceptions, and the Japanese often provided their design criteria to contracted European yards—they did not simply purchase used or even preset European-designed ships. In the 1880s Japan flirted with the ideas of France's *jeune école* approach and as a result began a program of purchasing torpedo boats and cruisers.[36]

Purchase of ships and key industrial machinery, domestic construction, and sending workers abroad for training all complemented each other, and the overall program began to bear fruit in the mid-1890s on the eve of the Sino-Japanese war (1894–95). At that point the Japanese navy could claim that, "in designing and supervising the construction of warships, virtually no assistance from foreigners was required."[37] The Japanese navy then possessed "a small but growing number of light, fast warships, essentially unarmored, but powerfully armed, some of which were rated the best of their type in any navy in the world," although they still lacked the major capital ships that defined a European battle fleet in the Mahanian mode. For the time being, Japan's leadership considered that last step to be too expensive.[38]

Hand in hand with growing naval power came a renewal of Japan's imperial ambitions. As discussed in chapter 6, Japan had invaded Korea centuries earlier, only to be finally defeated by Chinese intervention. After that, Japan had kept to itself until the Meiji Restoration in 1868; Japan was raiding Taiwan by 1871, and in 1879 it annexed the Ryukyu Islands. Factions within Japan immediately began calling for Japanese imperial expansion into Korea. Japan forced Korea to open trade relations and then continued to pressure its government, finally using the assassination of a pro-Japanese Korean rebel as the pretext for war with China over who would dominate Korea. As in the sixteenth-century wars, naval power was again key. Japan's navy during the war with China consisted of four older capital ships, one armored cruiser, seven protected cruisers, twelve unprotected cruisers, seven gunboats, and twenty-six torpedo boats (most purchased from abroad). The Chinese fleet, also purchased abroad, was nominally more powerful, but the Japanese ships were newer, faster, and armed with newer, quick-firing guns. On both land and sea, Japan enjoyed a nearly continuous string of successes in the nine-month war. From the Japanese point of view, however, their victory was rendered hollow by Germany, France, and Russia interfering in the peace negotiations to dash Japanese hopes of seizing the Liaotung Peninsula. Worse, almost immediately Russia took advantage of the moment to commence its own moves into Manchuria.[39]

The war put Japan on course to a confrontation with Russia, but it also stimulated Japanese industrial capacity and sparked a more ambitious naval program, through both purchase and domestic production. The public in Japan and key nationalistic factions reacted in a hostile manner to the Western intervention in the peace with China. The Japanese diet (parliament) almost doubled the size of the army, while the Imperial Navy's expansion program called for 104 new ships (primarily from Great Britain and the United States), including four battleships and eleven armored cruisers, to be completed between 1896 and 1905. This ambitious plan was later modified to a goal of six battleships and six armored cruisers by 1905—the so-called six-six fleet program. Although revenge was the primary motivation for the building program, it also fit neatly into the tenets of Mahan's theory of sea power, translated into Japanese in 1896, which encouraged colonial expansion and the possession of a blue-water, capital-ship navy.[40]

Naval production proceeded apace. By 1895 Japanese arsenals were producing their own smokeless powder for their quick-firing guns; by the next year the newly opened Kure shipyard had "two blast furnaces, 248 pieces of large machinery, and a twenty-ton steam hammer used in producing steel, plus a full line of ordnance ranging from shells and torpedoes to large guns and warships." Foreign purchase of warships, however, primarily from Britain, remained central to the navy. Ninety percent of the postwar expansion plan would be foreign-built, especially as Japan was now seeking full-sized capital ships.[41] Nevertheless, by the turn of the century Japanese shipyards were producing engines and guns comparable to those found on Western capital ships. They had built five new protected cruisers in Japanese yards, using Japanese designs and materials (and imported British guns). Some sixty-three torpedo boats, using European designs and materials, were assembled in Japan, some of which improved on Western designs. And where Japan had been purchasing torpedoes from Germany in the 1880s and in the 1890s, they began making their own in 1897.[42]

All this naval expansion was directed toward the looming confrontation with Russia over Manchuria. Although opinions in Japan remained divided over the right course of action, Japanese leaders agreed on the threat posed by Russia's version of European imperialism. The Russian moves were generated by frustration with other powers' intervening against Russian expansion westward at the expense of the Ottomans. Japan strengthened its international position by signing a treaty of amity with Great Britain in 1902. In 1903 six months of negotiations with Russia designed to secure Japan's freedom of action in Korea failed, largely because Russia did not believe Japan would risk war, and so negotiated neither seriously nor promptly, making it appear that they were stalling for time to build up their forces and fortifications in Manchuria. To Russia's surprise, and therefore prior to Russia's concentrating land or naval forces in the region, Japan declared war in February 1904.[43]

The Japanese launched a surprise attack on the Russian Pacific fleet based in Manchuria at Port Arthur, and under cover of that attack landed ground forces in Korea, occupying that country by the end of April 1904 and preparing to move into Russian-occupied Manchuria. The Japanese Third Army, with Port Arthur as its objective, landed on June 6. As Japanese planners were well aware, the Trans-Siberian railway was as yet incomplete, and Russian reinforcements were slow to arrive. The land war quickly devolved into a slog dominated by trenches, wire, and machine guns, presaging the battles of World War I.

Map 10.4 The Russo-Japanese War theater, 1904–5.

The damaged Russian fleet initially took shelter in Port Arthur, but was then forced out to sea by land operations around the port. On August 10, in the Battle of the Yellow Sea, despite some operational blunders, the Japanese fleet under Admiral Togo Heihachiro seriously damaged the Russian flagship, killed the Russian admiral, and scattered the remaining ships, mostly to locations where they were later destroyed or to harbors to await the arrival of reinforcements from Russia's Baltic fleet. That fleet, lacking bases en route to recoal its ships, and diplomatically isolated by British support for Japan, struggled to reach the Pacific. Although they were accompanied by German-flagged colliers, the Russian admiral insisted that his warships carry 50 percent more coal than their bunker capacity between recoalings. Coal was stacked everywhere aboard the ships, including the mess decks. Meanwhile, the Russian army besieged in Port Arthur surrendered on January 2, 1905.[44]

Aware that Port Arthur had fallen, the Russian Baltic fleet hoped to punch through the straits between Japan and Korea to the Russian port further north at Vladivostok, there to unite with the remaining Russian Pacific fleet and recover from the long voyage. The Japanese fleet, having refitted in Japan after the Yellow Sea engagement, and having adjusted their gunnery tactics as a result of lessons from that battle, prepared to meet the Russians. Although the Japanese ships were marginally smaller than those of the Russian Baltic fleet, they were faster and generally newer, and their crews fresh and confident. They annihilated the Russians in the Tsushima Strait between Japan and Korea on May 27 and 28, 1905. Only three Russian ships out of some thirty-eight made it to Vladivostok. Japan not only became the first non-Western power to win a war against a major industrial Western state, but they did so at sea, that most industrial of theaters. Japan also became a full-fledged member of the imperialist club: it annexed Korea in 1910.[45]

Ironically, given Japan's late arrival as an industrial power, the Russo-Japanese naval fight in the Yellow Sea was the first great fleet action between steel battleships in world history. The many interested foreign observers drew a variety of sometimes contradictory lessons from the battle there and at Tsushima. At a strategic level, many interpreted the war as validating Mahan's dictum to concentrate the fleet for a decisive battle. Both battles had been decisive, giving Japan local command of the sea and the ability to sustain their troops ashore in Manchuria. Tactically, the lessons were less clear, but some at least saw an argument for a new emphasis on long-range gunnery, beyond the reach of torpedoes or the smaller quick-firing guns. Future construction would thus follow the "all-big-gun" model, with new range-finding and gun-control systems, introduced in 1906 by Britain's HMS *Dreadnought*. Both the strategic and tactical lessons would seem less relevant within a very few years, however, as submarines and airplanes began to play a role in war at sea.

The innovation at issue here, however, is not gun design or tactics. It is industrial capacity, of which a steel and steam navy was merely the most sophisticated and complex expression. By most measures, Japan had succeeded in adopting that innovation, despite arriving late to the game, and despite enormous financial obstacles and a lack of natural resources (see Figure 10.6). Culturally, Japan rapidly adapted European military practice to its own. The Japanese readily sought European advice about managing complex industrial systems, something visually marked by their adoption of European uniforms. Their adaptations went beyond aesthetics, however. Saneyuki Akiyama, the operations officer of the Japanese combined fleet at Tsushima, for example, had studied in the United States as a lieutenant, becoming something of a protégé of Mahan, and had accompanied the American fleet outside Santiago de Cuba during the Spanish-American War. On the other hand, although the Meiji government had eliminated the samurai class and

Figure 10.6. Japanese battle cruiser *Kurama*. Launched in 1911 from Japan's navy yard at Yokosuka. Represents the fulfillment of Japan's ambitions to develop military-industrial capacity.

broadened the base of military service by conscription—two measures that initially met with violent resistance—they also managed to turn older cultural notions of samurai values into a new culture of obedience and loyalty to the emperor.[46]

In considering Japan's successful adoption of industrialized war, however, we should acknowledge that in this case, capacity divides into two intimately connected issues: industrial infrastructure and finance. To gain the infrastructure required to build, maintain, and supply a modern navy, Japan had rapidly built a mix of private and state-sponsored facilities, shrewdly accepting advisers from various countries and sending their own technicians to Europe for training. Both the infrastructure and Japan's direct purchase of large capital ships during this period required substantial financing. To that end, the Japanese government rearranged its taxation system to support industrialization. Then, during the Russo-Japanese war, it ran a highly successful domestic war-bonds program. It successfully secured capital loans from European and American lenders, something that other late-industrializing European powers also did in their attempts to catch up in industrial military capability. With loans secured, the Chinese and Russian wars and their associated programs of naval and armaments production provided key stimuli to private industrial development, which now seemed to have a guaranteed client in the Japanese military. Private iron and steel firms (vis-à-vis government operations) produced only 10 percent of Japanese output before the Russo-Japanese War, but by 1913 that had jumped to 25 percent. In contrast, Russia initially had great difficulty securing loans abroad. Finally, Japanese calculations of Russian logistical weakness proved accurate. Japan had absorbed the new strategic geography of industrial warfare at land and at sea and they developed new tactics, rapidly assimilating the lessons of the first naval engagements in Port Arthur and the Yellow Sea to make improvements that made the difference at Tsushima.[47]

Japanese industrialization through World War II fell short in many ways. Japan's battle fleet in World War I was still primarily purchased from abroad (although Japan had begun producing armored cruisers and even the semi-dreadnought *Satsuma* during the Russo-Japanese War). The continued sense that the country was lagging behind technologically led to a renewed government-driven effort in the 1930s. One analyst points out that the developing electrical sector, in particular, remained dependent on foreign imports: from 1922 to 1929 some 80 percent of steam generators were imported, and 20 percent remained foreign-made in the mid-1930s. Some economic historians have even asked if Japan might have industrialized *more* quickly without the artificial governmental emphasis on those heavy industries linked to military technologies, but that counterfactual scenario lies beyond our power to explore here.[48]

CONCLUSION

Industrialization transformed warfare in a host of ways. It changed strategic geography by emphasizing the control of discrete points on the landscape rather than expansive territorial spaces. Ironically, however, industrialization also provided the new transportation and communications systems that made such territorial control more accessible, while transforming the projection of power across the oceans. Industrialization initiated a period of constant invention motivated by a complex and shifting combination of private profit and guaranteed state funding that we are still in today. Perhaps the most durable legacy of this period is the perceived importance of technology, and specifically *of having the latest technology*, as a measure of military power. This has meant a truly dramatic increase in the significance of financial capacity. In Azar Gat's calculation, the "*share* of wartime military spending out of the total GNP tripled from some 15 per cent for the leader (Britain) in the eighteenth century . . . to around 50 per cent in the twentieth century."[49] And that growth in military spending as a share of GNP occurred within the truly fantastic explosion in the overall size of the GNP itself created by industrialization.

In one sense this emphasis on spending should not surprise us. We have already noted the key role of failing Roman finances in the late Empire, or the substantial advantage that Ottoman state treasuries lent their military forces during the sixteenth century. The availability of disposable capital has always mattered in war, even when expressed in terms of food as pay (as it was, for example, in sixteenth-century China and Japan). But for most of human history states used capital to raise manpower. The lack of capital had never undermined the steppe nomads' military effectiveness, nor had it prevented the Swiss pike phalanx from emerging from the mountains and reshaping the European battlefield for decades. Capital's added significance in an industrialized world comes from the need to devote an ever larger share of it to military technology vis-à-vis manpower. Since the nineteenth century, as Gat writes, states sought to "arm the available (and ultimately finite) manpower with more, costlier, and more *advanced* military hardware."[50] To be sure, medieval and early modern military leaders also wanted the best or most recent hardware, but industrialization has changed the *pace* of technological change, and thus even further emphasized societal financial capacity.

There have been exceptions in the modern world, and chapter 14 explores the emergence of techniques developed specifically to work around the supposed necessity of modern military technology. But the significance of financial capacity for providing the latest technology persists. The demand for capital sufficient to sustain or initiate industrialization in some ways proved the greatest obstacle for those societies seeking to copy what had happened in the West. The Ottomans, the Russians, Egypt, China, and Japan all sought to imitate western European military techniques, but the most important aspect of those techniques by the middle of the nineteenth century was their industrial weaponry. The strain of reorienting their societies toward industrial production and of restructuring taxation systems to support either direct purchase or industrialization, themselves produced internal resistance. Japan succeeded relatively rapidly, as did Russia, although Japan's path veered into nationalistic militarization, and Russia's eventually generated political revolution. China and the Ottomans failed, at least initially. Their resurgence as industrially equipped powers would take another century. The next chapter explores the implications of all of these changes for war on land, taking industrialization more or less as a given, noting again the shifting strategic geography generated by railroads, but focusing on industrialization's effects on firepower, and therefore on the need to protect exposed troops. Men moving against industrialized firepower would have to seek shelter in trenches.[51]

TIMELINE

1712	Newcomen steam engine
1764	Spinning Jenny
1829	The *Rocket* steam locomotive wins trials to power the Liverpool and Manchester railway
1859/1860	*Gloire* launched; HMS *Warrior* launched
1866	Ram used in naval battle
1868	Meiji Restoration in Japan
1894–95	Sino-Japanese War
1894	Krupp-cemented armor
1904	Battle of the Yellow Sea in the Russo-Japanese War: first battle between steel navies

Further Reading

Black, Jeremy, ed. *War in the Modern World since 1815*. New York: Routledge, 2003.

Bönker, Dirk. *Militarism in a Global Age: Naval Ambitions in Germany and the United States before World War I*. Ithaca, NY: Cornell University Press, 2012.

Chickering, Roger, Dennis Showalter, and Hans Van de Ven, eds. *The Cambridge History of War*. Vol. 4, *War and the Modern World*. Cambridge, UK: Cambridge University Press, 2012.

Glete, Jan. *Navies and Nations: Warships, Navies and State Building in Europe and America, 1500–1860*. 2 vols. Stockholm: Almqvist & Wiksell, 1993.

Evans, David C., and Mark R. Peattie. *Kaigun: Strategy, Tactics, and Technology in the Imperial Japanese Navy, 1887–1941*. Annapolis, MD: Naval Institute Press, 1997. Reprint, 2012.

Headrick, Daniel R. *The Tools of Empire: Technology and European Imperialism in the Nineteenth Century*. New York: Oxford University Press, 1981.

Kennedy, Paul M. *The Rise and Fall of British Naval Mastery*. London: Macmillan, 1983.

Lambert, Andrew, ed. *Steam, Steel and Shellfire: The Steam Warship, 1815–1905*. London: Conway Maritime Press, 1992.

McNeill, William H. *The Pursuit of Power: Technology, Armed Force and Society Since A.D. 1000*. Chicago: University of Chicago Press, 1982.

Ralston, David B. *Importing the European Army: The Introduction of European Military Techniques and Institutions into the Extra-European World, 1600–1914*. Chicago: University of Chicago Press, 1990.

Westwood, J. N. *Russia against Japan, 1904–05*. Albany: State University of New York Press, 1986.

Notes

1. Despite the book's title, this is a primary point of Jeremy Black, *The Age of Total War, 1860–1945* (Lanham, MD: Rowman & Littlefield, 2006).

2. Quincy Wright, *A Study of War* (Chicago: University of Chicago Press, 1942).

3. William Rosen, *The Most Powerful Idea in the World: A Story of Steam, Industry, and Invention* (Chicago: University Of Chicago Press, 2012), 103–14, 185–88.

4. David S. Landes, *Revolution in Time: Clocks and the Making of the Modern World*, rev. ed. (Cambridge, MA: Belknap Press of Harvard University Press, 2000), 1–142, esp. 58.

5. Clive Trebilcock, "'Spin-Off' in British Economic History: Armaments and Industry, 1760–1914," *The Economic History Review* New Series, 22.3 (1969): 474–90.

6. Much of the following discussion of Watt and Wilkinson is based on Thomas Southcliffe Ashton, *Iron and Steel in the Industrial Revolution* (Manchester, UK: Manchester University Press, 1924), 41–72.

7. William H. McNeill, *The Pursuit of Power: Technology, Armed Force, and Society Since A.D. 1000* (Chicago: University of Chicago Press, 1982), 167.

8. McNeill, *Pursuit of Power*, especially, 224, 240–41, 255; Paul M. Kennedy, *The Rise and Fall of British Naval Mastery* (London: Macmillan, 1983), 191.

9. Peter N. Stearns, *Interpreting the Industrial Revolution* (Washington, DC: American Historical Association, 1991), 29, 31, 36; Kennedy, *British Naval Mastery*, 191.

10. Daniel R. Headrick, *The Tools of Empire: Technology and European Imperialism in the Nineteenth Century* (New York: Oxford University Press, 1981), 18.

11. Andrew Lambert, ed. *Steam, Steel and Shellfire: The Steam Warship, 1815–1905* (London: Conway Maritime Press, 1992), 14–20; Headrick, *Tools of Empire*, 19–37.

12. Headrick, *Tools of Empire*, 45ff.

13. Headrick, *Tools of Empire*, 34–36, 47–54 (quote 50).

14. *Archimedes* story in Lambert, *Steam, Steel and Shellfire*, 32–33; Jan Glete, *Navies and Nations: Warships, Navies and State Building in Europe and America, 1500–1860* (Stockholm: Almqvist & Wiksell International, 1993), 2:444–45.

15. Lambert, *Steam, Steel and Shellfire*, 52, 73.

16. Jesse A. Heitz, "British Reaction to American Civil War Ironclads," *Vulcan* 1 (2013): 56–69; Howard J. Fuller, *Clad in Iron: The American Civil War and the Challenge of British Naval Power* (Westport, CT: Praeger, 2008), 128–58.

17. Lambert, *Steam, Steel and Shellfire*, 58; Alex Roland, W. Jeffrey Bolster, and Alexander Keyssar, eds., *The Way of the Ship: America's Maritime History Reenvisioned, 1600–2000* (Hoboken, NJ: John Wiley, 2008), 189–93.

18. Antulio J. Echevarria II, "The Arms Race: Qualitative and Quantitative Aspects," in *The Cambridge History of War*, vol. 4, *War and the Modern World*, ed. Roger Chickering, Dennis Showalter, and Hans Van de Ven (Cambridge, UK: Cambridge University Press, 2012), 163–180.

19. Holger H. Herwig, *"Luxury" Fleet: The Imperial German Navy 1888–1918* (London: George Allen & Unwin, 1980), 25; David C. Evans and Mark R. Peattie, *Kaigun: Strategy, Tactics, and Technology in the Imperial Japanese Navy, 1887–1941* (1997; repr., Annapolis, MD: Naval Institute Press, 2012), 53–54. The data in Table 10.1 is primarily from Lambert, *Steam, Steel and Shellfire*, 94, 168–69, 111.

20. Lambert, *Steam, Steel and Shellfire*, 8.

21. Kennedy, *British Naval Mastery*, 214–15; Rolf Hobson, *Imperialism at Sea: Naval Strategic Thought, the Ideology of Sea Power, and the Tirpitz Plan, 1875–1914* (Leiden: Brill, 2002), 154–77; Dirk Bönker, *Militarism in a Global Age: Naval Ambitions in Germany and the United States before World War I* (Ithaca, NY: Cornell University Press, 2012), 39–41, 253–59.

22. Arne Røksund, *The Jeune École: The Strategy of the Weak* (Leiden: Brill, 2007); Theodore Ropp, *The Development of a Modern Navy: French Naval Policy, 1871–1904* (Annapolis, MD: Naval Institute Press, 1987), 19–22, 155–80.

23. See the US State Department website "Overview of U.S. Export Control System," http://www.state.gov/strategictrade/overview/, accessed March 11, 2014; Lambert, *Steam, Steel and Shellfire*, 12; Katherine C. Epstein, *Torpedo: Inventing the Military-Industrial Complex in the United States and Great Britain* (Cambridge, MA: Harvard University Press, 2013), 3–5; Robert K. Massie, *Castles of Steel: Britain, Germany, and the Winning of the Great War at Sea* (New York: Ballantine, 2003), 21–22, 122–23.

24. McNeill, *Pursuit of Power*, 292–94; Epstein, *Torpedo*.

25. Kennedy, *British Naval Mastery*, 209.

26. Jules Ferry, speech of July 28, 1883, in *The Human Record*, vol. 2, *Since 1500*, 4th ed., ed. Alfred J. Andrea and James H. Overfield (Boston: Houghton Mifflin, 2001), 295–98 (quote); Hobson, *Imperialism at Sea*, 79–83, 303–4.

27. Headrick, *Tools of Empire*.

28. Azar Gat, *War in Human Civilization* (Oxford: Oxford University Press, 2006), 545; John Landers, *The Field and the Forge: Population, Production, and Power in the Pre-Industrial West* (New York: Oxford University Press, 2003).

29. Kennedy, *British Naval Mastery*, 181–82, 213.

30. Much of this paragraph follows the summary in John P. Dunn, "The Non-Western World Responds to Imperialism,

1850–1914," in Chickering, Showalter, and Van de Ven, *The Cambridge History of War*, 4:94–118 (esp. here 101–14).

31. Dunn, "Non-Western World," 106–7 (more on this is in chapter 11); Evans and Peattie, *Kaigun*, xx.

32. Kozo Yamamura, "Success Illgotten? The Role of Meiji Militarism in Japan's Technological Progress," *Journal of Economic History* 37.1 (1977): 113–35 (quote 113). See also the comments by Richard Rice in the same issue in "Success Illgotten, Comment," 136–38, and E. Sydney Crawcour, "Industrialization and Technological Change, 1885–1920," in *The Economic Emergence of Modern Japan*, ed. Kozo Yamamura (Cambridge, UK: Cambridge University Press, 1997), 93.

33. Edward S. Miller, "Japan's Other Victory: Overseas Financing of the War," in *The Russo-Japanese War in Global Perspective: World War Zero*, ed. John W. Steinberg, et al. (Leiden: Brill, 2005), 466; This paragraph is derived substantially from E. Sydney Crawcour, "Economic Change in the Nineteenth Century," in *The Economic Emergence of Modern Japan*, ed. Yamamura, 1–49; and Crawcour, "Industrialization," in *ibid.*, 50–115. (esp. pp. 42, 45, 51).

34. Evans and Peattie, *Kaigun*. 5–8; Yamamura, "Success Illgotten," 114ff.

35. Evans and Peattie, *Kaigun*, 10, 14; Yamamura, "Success Illgotten," 114–16, 118, 123.

36. Evans and Peattie, *Kaigun*, 12, 14, 16–17.

37. Yamamura, "Success Illgotten," 118 (quote).

38. Evans and Peattie, *Kaigun*, 19 (quote).

39. Dunn, "Non-Western," 107; Stewart Lone, *Japan's First Modern War: Army and Society in the Conflict with China, 1894–95* (New York: St. Martin's, 1994), 1–5; Yoji Koda, "The Russo-Japanese War: Primary Causes of Japanese Success," *Naval War College Review* 58.2 (2005): 11–44 (here 16); Evans and Peattie, *Kaigun*, 50.

40. Koda, "Causes of Japanese Success," 16, 20; Evans and Peattie, *Kaigun*, 24.

41. Evans and Peattie, *Kaigun*, 59–60 (quote).

42. Yamamura, "Success Illgotten," 120–21, (quote 121); twenty-six of the torpedo boats were later canceled and replaced with a smaller number of destroyers built in Britain. Evans and Peattie, *Kaigun* 38, 62–63.

43. Koda, "Causes of Japanese Success," 11–44.

44. Koda, "Causes of Japanese Success," 44n13; J. N. Westwood, *Russia against Japan, 1904–05* (Albany: State University of New York Press, 1986), 142.

45. Koda, "Causes of Japanese Success," 34–36; Evans and Peattie, *Kaigun*, 115–29

46. Koda, "Causes of Japanese Success," 44n12; Lone, *Japan's First Modern War*, 8–9; Edward Drea, "The Imperial Japanese Army (1868–1945): Origins, Evolution, Legacy," in *War in the Modern World Since 1815*, ed. Jeremy Black (New York: Routledge, 2003), 98–99; David B. Ralston, *Importing the European Army: The Introduction of European Military Techniques and Institutions into the Extra-European World, 1600–1914* (Chicago: University of Chicago Press, 1990), 160–67.

47. Ralston, *Importing the European Army*, 165; Crawcour, "Economic Change," 47 for the financial reforms of the 1880s; Lone, *Japan's First Modern War*, 89–92 for war bonds; Christopher M. Clark, *Sleepwalkers: How Europe Went to War in 1914* (London: Allen Lane, 2012), 29; Crawcour, "Industrialization and Technological Change," 95; Boris Ananich, "Russian Military Expenditures in the Russo-Japanese War, 1904–5," and Edward S. Miller "Japan's Other Victory: Overseas Financing of the War," both in Steinberg et al., *The Russo-Japanese War in Global Perspective: World War Zero* (Leiden: Brill, 2005), 449–64, 465–84.

48. Rice, "Success Illgotten, Comment," 137.

49. Gat, *War in Human Civilization*, 525 (quote, emphasis in original).

50. Gat, *War in Human Civilization*, 515–30, 529 (quote).

51. Ralston, *Importing the European Army*, passim, esp. 173–80.

11

Men against Fire

1861–1917

The American Civil War: A False Dawn of "Modern War"? • Prussian Reforms, a General Staff, and German Unification • Firepower • Firepower and the Scramble for Empire: Dahomey and Ethiopia • World War I

INDUSTRIALIZATION AFFECTED WAR within and outside Europe in markedly different ways. Within Europe, the nature and scale of war changed, but traditional rivalries remained. Simultaneously intoxicated and alarmed by the rapid evolution of armaments that industrialization brought, European states raced to outdo each other. Innovations proliferated across a spectrum of military activities, but the military power of the major states remained roughly equivalent. In contrast, those innovations greatly enhanced the relative power of European states (and the United States) compared to the nonindustrialized world. Chapter 10 examined the naval dimension of that rearrangement. This chapter looks at land warfare. Unable to survey all the inventions of the era, it focuses on key changes related to the increase of firepower, especially infantry firepower, and the responses to that increase, culminating in the infamous trenches of the western front in World War I.

This focus on firepower continues our examination of the consequences of industrialization. The innovation in question is not modern rifles, machine guns, or artillery, but a new source of productive power and a new means of production that allowed for far more sophisticated and precise manufacture of iron and steel objects. Discoveries in chemistry were also central to the story of firepower, but the real capacity detailed in this chapter is one of human inventiveness unleashed on newly malleable metal.

In addition to examining firepower and responses to it within the United States and Europe, this chapter also explores its significance to Western imperialism. We will follow two African colonial adventures in detail: the French in Dahomey (now Benin) and the Italians in Ethiopia. Those examples will show the difficulty nonindustrialized states had in keeping pace with Western capabilities. They will also reveal the key role of Western logistical capacity and communications, another by-product of industrialization, in making Europe the ruler of the much of the world by 1900. Finally, in parallel to the story of firepower, a key development in this period was the creation of professional general staffs, based on the Prussian model. That innovation would have enormous consequences for the nature of civil-military relations in general and on the outbreak of World War I in particular.

THE AMERICAN CIVIL WAR: A FALSE DAWN OF "MODERN WAR"?

Historians have often portrayed the American Civil War as the beginning of a new industrial age of modern war. Both sides raised mass national armies through conscription; railroads proved key to logistics and therefore to strategy; the telegraph revolutionized communication among civilian and military leaders; ironclads announced a new era of steam and steel ships; and key changes in the volume and accuracy of infantry firepower produced a more lethal battlefield. The latter produced, by the end of the conflict, trench warfare and a strategic stalemate broken only by grinding attrition and devastation.

This traditional understanding of firepower's role in the Civil War begins with a relatively simple invention. Before the 1850s infantry firepower came almost exclusively from muzzle-loading, smoothbore muskets firing a round lead ball. That technology had remained relatively stable for several hundred years, changing only in the ignition system, the matchlock giving way to the flintlock in the eighteenth century. When fired, the round ball rattled down the length of a smoothbore barrel and then knuckleballed through the air without spinning and with a notoriously imprecise trajectory. Their accuracy was negligible—almost random beyond a hundred meters. The multistep loading process was relatively simple; most soldiers could fire three rounds a minute. Spiral-grooved, or "rifled," barrels had existed since perhaps the 1500s, but their great cost had restricted their use mostly to wealthy hunters. The rifling gripped the ball as it traveled down the barrel and imparted a spin to it, greatly improving its accuracy. The rifle achieved military renown in the hands of German *Jäger* (hunter) units of light infantry in the eighteenth century and during the American Revolution (American craftsmen had elaborated a particularly accurate version of the rifle). As military weapons, however, rifles' value was limited by their much slower reload speed— ramming the bullet down the muzzle took several additional steps—as well as the greater expense to make them.[1]

In the late eighteenth and early nineteenth centuries a variety of attempts were made to overcome both the cost and reload speed associated with rifled barrels. American inventor John Hall, for example, invented a new breech-loading rifle that bypassed the slow ramming of a ball down the barrel. Political challenges and technical difficulties hindered official adoption, even by the US Army, which at that time was quite small. Larger armies found it even more challenging to embrace similar changes because of the expense of re-equipping the whole force. Then in 1847 French army officer Claude-Étienne

Minié invented a cheap and simple way to combine the accuracy of a rifled barrel with the reload speed of a musket while avoiding technical problems associated with loading at the breech. His conoidal bullet fit loosely in the barrel, allowing it to be rapidly rammed down the muzzle, but it had a hollow base with an iron plug. When fired, the base of the bullet expanded to grip the rifling and gain spin, therefore achieving greater range and accuracy (later versions dispensed with the plug). So-called rifled muskets (technically an oxymoron) designed to fire the new "Minié ball" could shoot accurately to five hundred meters and more, and were even equipped with long-range sights.[2]

This new technology proliferated quickly, partly because of emergent industrial production technologies that allowed for more rapid production of standardized rifle barrels. Rifled muskets saw extensive use in the Crimean War (1853–56) and became the standard weapons of both the Union and Confederate armies in the American Civil War. In addition to the new rifling, percussion-cap locks replaced flintlocks in igniting the powder charge, with the great advantage of being both waterproof and faster to load. Armed with American-made Springfields, French Miniés, or British Enfields, outfitted with percussion-locks and firing Minié balls, both sides fielded large masses of men capable of firing rapidly and accurately at much longer ranges than before. Infantry tactics, however, continued to emphasize shoulder-to-shoulder formations, in line or column. On the defense, the new rifles provided devastating firepower when directed against attacking formations using such Napoleonic tactics. The result was tactical stalemate. Soon soldiers, of their own accord, began scratching out firing pits or throwing up improvised breastworks. By 1864, the Union Army's approach to Richmond offered a preview of the trench fighting of World War I.[3]

At least, this is the story as it has long been told as part of the larger narrative of the Civil War as the beginning of "modern" war. There were indeed many aspects of the fighting in the American Civil War that did highlight industrial changes, and they may have pointed toward a future of war involving mass conscript armies supplied with industrial-era arms and equipment. Perhaps the most notable among these was the role of the railroad in moving troops over long distances and in sustaining operations of large armies within a confined theater that otherwise would have been stripped bare of food. The existence and placement of railroads therefore shaped operations. Battle after battle was fought to control key rail junctions (or their riverine equivalents on the Ohio and Mississippi Rivers).

The view of a firepower-generated battlefield stalemate, however, has been thrust aside. Careful analysis of Civil War combat has shown that the capabilities of the rifled muskets, especially in terms of accurate, long-range fire, were rarely decisive. Despite their real accuracy at ranges out to five hundred meters or more, in practice the parabolic trajectory of the bullet, the lack of open fields in heavily forested North America, the smoke produced by black powder, the lack of training in using long-range sights, the continued need to stand and load at the muzzle, and a conservative tactical preference for preserving fire for short-range volleys meant that long-range aimed fire was rarely used until late in the war, and then primarily by snipers and skirmishers. The primary exchanges of small-arms fire by Civil War infantry continued to be conducted at ranges around one hundred meters, where admittedly the newer rifles were significantly more lethal than older muskets, but not on a revolutionary scale (see Figure 11.1). Furthermore, most battlefield artillery remained muzzle-loading guns firing a combination of solid shot, shell, and canister in line-of-sight direct fire. Like the new rifled muskets, new rifled artillery had greater range, but its impact was limited for many of the same reasons as for the rifled muskets (smoke, forests, and so on). The 1850s had seen the invention of reliable shells designed to explode in the air and scatter shrapnel (named for an early version designed by Briton Henry Shrapnel), which produced a new capability in dealing with massed infantry. Still, artillery seemed to play the same role on the battlefield that it had in the Napoleonic Wars.[4]

As for the trenches, historian Earl Hess, following up his work on the limited impact of the rifled musket, observed that field fortifications emerged less because of new levels of firepower and more from situations in which armies remained in continuous contact. Attacks that failed did not necessarily lead to a retreat and separation. This was especially true as General Ulysses S. Grant actively sought to maintain contact during the campaigns around Richmond and Petersburg in 1864. Under those circumstances soldiers threw up breastworks or even dug trenches as they remained under enemy

Figure 11.1 The Battle of Raymond, May 12, 1863. During the Vicksburg campaign, in a drawing in *Harper's Weekly*. Many contemporary depictions focus on the climactic charge. This drawing is more representative of most combat: the exchange of musket fire at about 100–150 yards.

observation. Of critical importance, the field fortifications of the Civil War were almost exclusively breastworks, built *above ground*, rather than true trenches (siege works did use true trenches, as they always had). The former were easier to build but they they were inadequate against ever more powerful rifles and cannon, as would become clear over the next fifty years.[5]

Modern commentators, enamored of the old vision of the American Civil War as a harbinger of true modern war, long lamented what they saw as contemporary European observers ignoring its apparent lessons about the impact of increased firepower and how it produced trenches, stalemate, and long wars. But European observers may have been more observant than many realized. Furthermore, the Europeans had contrasting examples of rapid and decisive wars to draw upon, most notably the Wars of German Unification in 1864, 1866, and 1870–71.

PRUSSIAN REFORMS, A GENERAL STAFF, AND GERMAN UNIFICATION

An explanation of what happened in Prussia must first start with the shattering impact of the Napoleonic Wars at the beginning of the century. As discussed in chapter 9, the French Revolution's *levée en masse* and France's subsequent program of conscription produced vastly enlarged armies. Simply moving such large forces required new forms of management and planning. Maps in military history texts (including this one) can be, and usually are, deceptive. Armies typically do not move in a single coherent arrow down a single route—especially once they number more than ten to fifteen thousand men. Armies move in a series of roughly parallel columns, using different local roads to end each day in roughly the same vicinity, unless geographical features, like a mountain pass, truly provides only a single option. Campaign armies in postmedieval Europe rarely numbered more than twenty to thirty thousand men until the eighteenth century, when a few armies swelled to more than sixty thousand. That doubling reflected improvements in European agriculture that increased yields per acre, making it possible to support larger forces on the countryside. This increase prompted a change in thinking about how to move armies. In one calculation, a single force of thirty thousand men and its baggage would stretch over fifty kilometers of road.[6]

Some wartime armies in the eighteenth century were enormous, especially those of Louis XIV, but logistical constraints and the need to garrison the many fortifications often restricted campaign armies in a single theater to the 60,000 to 80,000 range. French military writers in the late eighteenth century were already addressing this problem by proposing to divide an army into self-contained "divisions," each of which would contain all of the components necessary for independent operation (its own infantry, cavalry, artillery, scouts, and so on). Divisions could move independently on more widely separated routes, impose less of a burden on the countryside, and still act in mutual support. The renewed growth in army size wrought by the French Revolution, and especially the tendency for those armies to be concentrated into a single operational area, demanded scaling up the division concept into corps (made up of several divisions), partly to distribute the army across many more roads, but also to spread its logistical needs over an even wider area. Such armies often forsook a baggage train and fed themselves entirely off the countryside. Under this system a single campaign army of several corps might begin its march along a front a hundred miles wide or more, all acting under a single set of orders, and although moving independently nevertheless operating as a single army able to converge on a single battlefield (see Map 11.1).[7]

Planning such a campaign presented significant challenges. Rates of march had to be calculated with respect to the varying topography that different corps would encounter on their separate routes, not to mention the different total distances to be covered. Napoleon, however, managed this problem in his famously capacious mind. Historian David Chandler recounts one example of Napoleon's ability in this regard:

> In September 1805, the Emperor and his staff came across a unit . . . that had become separated from its parent formation during the long approach-march from the Channel coast to the Rhine. Its commander had mislaid his orders and did not know where to find his division. While his staff officers busied themselves poring over maps and thumbing through countless notebooks and duplicate orders, Napoleon there and then, without reference to any book or any assistant, informed the astounded officer of the present location of his parent formation and where it would be on the next three nights, throwing in for good measure a detailed résumé of its strength and the military record of the divisional commander. At that time there were no less than seven *corps d' armée*, or 200,000 men, on the move; no more need be said.[8]

The *levée en masse* and Napoleon's personal skill at managing these newly enlarged armies had two key effects. First, most of his opponents (except Britain) felt compelled to adopt some form of conscription in order to compete with, if not match, French army size. After Napoleon's final defeat, most states returned to smaller professional armies, seeking to contain the potential political dynamite of a mass conscripted army. Prussia was something of an exception. Prussia again returned control and officership in the army to the aristocracy, but Prussia remained a relatively small state with respect to the other great powers. Sustaining its claim to that status necessitated retaining a form of national conscription in which roughly one-third of each year's age class did military service for three years and then passed into the reserves. This system, progressively modified, would be a key aspect of the eventual Wars of German Unification. Just as significant was the second effect of Napoleon's victories, also centered in Prussia. After Napoleon defeated Prussia

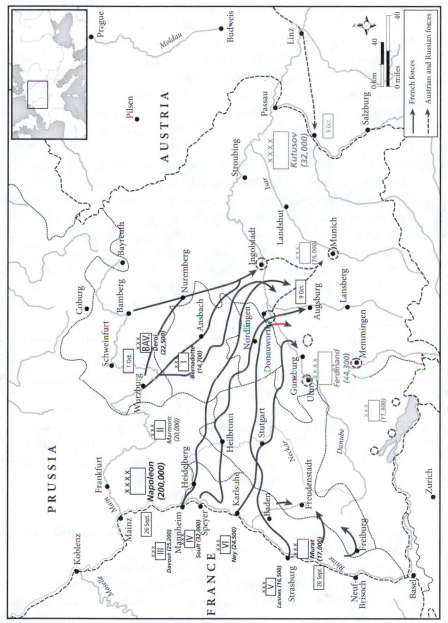

Map 11.1 Napoleon's 1805 campaign against Austria. At the opening of the campaign Napoleon's forces (some 210,000 men) were dispersed in independent corps across nearly two hundred miles. His plan had them marching along independent converging routes to meet simultaneously in the rear of the Austrian main army at Ulm.

in 1806–7, a generation of reform-minded officers of the Prussian army began to contemplate how to manage these new challenges.

The shock of defeat provided the catalyst, and the impetus for reform spread across a generation of Prussian officers anxious to redeem their army and create the capacity to defeat Napoleon. Among the reformers, August Neidhardt von Gneisenau and Gerhard von Scharnhorst can be singled out. In the longer term, their ideas came to be represented by the writings of a younger man, Carl von Clausewitz, trained by both and famous as the author of On War (Vom Kriege), published posthumously by his wife in 1832. Clausewitz began his analysis of war from the Enlightenment-era premise that war, like the natural world and, indeed, like other human activity, was subject to natural "laws" that could be discerned through rational analysis. With understanding would come greater control. Although Clausewitz began with reason, he was also struck by the example of the French Revolution's appeal to the passion of the masses. This concern with the role of passion was further leavened by the practical, hard-headed insistence of his mentors and his own experience fighting in the Napoleonic Wars. Both led him to rise above pure reason to acknowledge the unpredictable, found both in the emotions of the public and in the very nature of war itself. In the words of historian Lawrence Freedman, Clausewitz "understood that rational policy could impose itself on war, but it was always competing with the blind natural forces of 'violence, hatred, and enmity,' as well as probability and chance."[9] His theories on the nature of war continue to shape military thought to this day.

Of more immediate institutional significance, however, was the reformers' creation of first a war college (Kriegsakademie) and then a planning general staff and a general staff with troops, both subsumed under a single chief of staff. This seemingly simple sentence conceals a host of critical changes that took some decades to mature in Prussia, and then proliferated around the Western world and beyond. Officer training academies existed around Europe during the eighteenth century, but they focused on technical fields like artillery and engineering, and they tended to be cadet schools suited for junior officers. Commanders in the field relied on an ad hoc collection of senior officers to provide advice based on their experience. The Prussian reforms emphasized training officers for more senior positions and encouraged them to consider war at the strategic level. Furthermore, the reformers managed to make success in the Kriegsakademie and appointment to the staff a mark of success, of elite status. The staff thus attracted the best officers and trained them in a uniform approach to managing an army. Furthermore, the permanence of the staff in peacetime meant that a professional group of officers was always at work considering the next war and the implications of emerging technology.

The two types of staff worked synergistically. Officers posted to the planning staff both created and learned a uniform "doctrine" (more on the meaning and development of doctrine is in chapter 12). Those men then returned to field units as staff officers, where they disseminated a common approach to managing and fighting the army. Eventually, this process of doctrinal dissemination and the imposition of a uniform course of study allowed the chief of staff to issue orders to field commanders in general principles, leaving the details to them, thereby avoiding the difficulty of developing and communicating detailed orders for separately moving corps. In essence the general staff helped solve the administrative problems created by much larger armies and institutionalized procedures accomplishing what Napoleon had essentially done on his own. The system also elevated the chief of staff to a position of great civil-military importance. The state would no longer be subject to the unpredictable and idiosyncratic command of a hereditary monarch. In a perhaps unfortunate development, however, the chief of staff would grow to have great influence over civil policy. In Prussia, one relatively benign example of this influence can be found in railroad development.[10]

Because the Prussian staff system for the most part emerged prior to industrialization in Prussia, it was fortuitously positioned to study the new weapons and the larger systemic changes presented by innovations like railroads and the telegraph. The first major deployment of soldiers by rail occurred in 1859, when the French moved half their army (130,000 men) to Italy by rail prior to the Battle of Solferino. All the major powers quickly recognized the potential value of rail-delivered logistics, but the Prussian general staff planned pro-actively. They used their influence within the state not only to promote rail construction but also to plan the placement of rail lines to expedite future mobilizations. Prussia was building railways in the 1840s at twice the rate of France and continued to press ahead in the ensuing decades, very often with military needs taking priority over commercial interests. Throughout the 1860s the Prussian army deepened its involvement in and commitment to the use of rail, until in 1872 the general staff created a "fully centralised controlling body" for railroad planning and mobilization use, which would plan the specifics of the numbers of engines, cars, load time, intervals, and more.[11]

Prussia's maintaining the nation-in-arms and its development of the general staff system played a key role in the rapid unification of Germany under Prussian auspices in the German Wars of Unification in the 1860s and 1870s. Those conflicts, in turn, profoundly influenced the ways in which militaries around the world perceived the future of war and the role of firepower, and their approach to the commencement of hostilities in 1914. But first we must look back to the 1814 Congress of Vienna, in which the powers victorious over Napoleon met to shape what they hoped would be a more balanced postwar Europe. German-speaking central Europe posed a major problem. Napoleon had forced many of the hundreds of autonomous principalities and petty states into the Confederation of the Rhine, but delegates at the congress deemed that too radical a change. They eliminated many of the tiniest states and replaced them with a hodgepodge of thirty-eight medium-sized

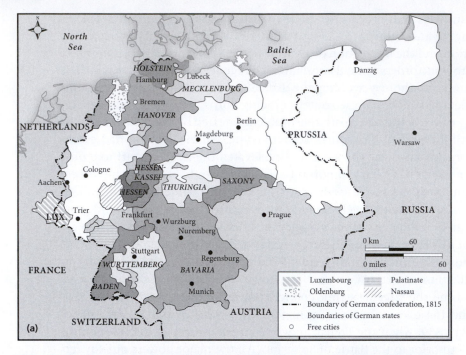

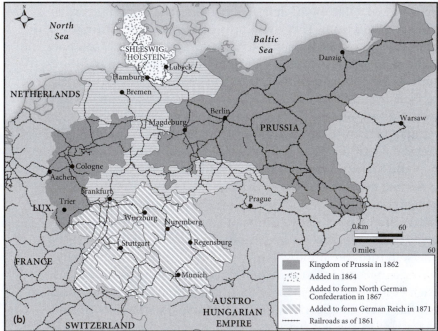

Map 11.2 *a & b* German unification. (a) shows the German states as reorganized by the Congress of Vienna in 1814–15. (b) shows the regional rail network as of 1861 as well as the progressive unification of Germany by Prussia between 1864 and 1871.

entities loosely grouped into a German Confederation, of which the two largest were Prussia and Austria. Over the next forty years Prussia gained greater influence over the confederation, and the rise of popular nationalism in mid-nineteenth-century Europe further encouraged a program of unification, carefully planned not to draw the intervention of France, Russia, or England.

Meanwhile the Prussian military, after stumbling through several crises in the 1830s through the 1850s, reached new heights of sophistication under Helmuth von Moltke, who served as Chief of the General Staff from 1857 to 1888. His long tenure was complemented by that of Otto von Bismarck, who became minister president of Prussia in 1862, and who remained in power for nearly thirty years, resigning from his post of chancellor of a united Germany in 1890. The army provided Bismarck the muscle to pursue his program of uniting the assorted German principalities into a single state. In turn Bismarck used civil power to provide the army with the money and conscripts Moltke sought.

Unification unfolded through three short, sharp wars between 1864 and 1871, each preceded by Bismarck's diplomatic maneuvers designed to avoid provoking a multipower intervention against Prussia. The military operations of each war were marked by rapid and massive mobilization of Prussian reserves, who moved to the frontier on trains and then rapidly advanced to overwhelm their opponents. The exact combination of factors varied in each war, as even within that short time span weapons technology and mobilization capacity changed. In the first war, against Denmark, Austria acted as a Prussian ally and Prussia absorbed the Schleswig-Holstein region after rapidly overrunning Danish defenses. Disputes with Austria over the spoils of that war led to the Austro-Prussian War of 1866. Although greatly aided by Austrian incompetence, Prussia's ability to mobilize quickly and coordinate converging movements of separate corps into Austrian Bohemia defeated Austria's forward forces in battle at Königgrätz. The combined troop total in that battle of some 450,000 exceeded that of all previous recorded battles. Prussian victory seemed to open a clear path to march on Vienna, but Bismarck held the reins. He instead offered Austria peace, ending the war in a mere seven weeks and establishing a North German Confederation that excluded Austria and avoided outside involvement.[12]

Unwilling to intervene in 1866, France nevertheless felt threatened by rising Prussian power, and Napoleon III had his own hopes that a war would consolidate his domestic position. Provoked by Prussian diplomatic moves, France actually declared war first in 1870. Both countries were industrial powers. French forces generally were better equipped, possessing a newer, more effective breech-loading rifle and an early form of machine gun (more on which below), but Prussia had revamped and improved its artillery corps with new steel, breech-loading, rifled artillery. The major difference between the two powers was their recruitment systems. Although Prussia's victory over Austria had alerted France to the potential size of Prussia's army, and the French military had begun their own program of conscription, their reforms were not fully in place by 1870. France had continued to rely on a smaller professional army, and its plans for a massive reserve force remained theoretical. When war came, by the seventeenth day of mobilization France had fielded only 238,188 men. Prussia mobilized more men more quickly. By the eighteenth day 1,183,000 men were in uniform and armed, and 462,000 were on the French frontier ready to advance into France. Within weeks, despite repeated French tactical success based partly on the superior French rifle, their armies had been outmaneuvered and trapped. The surrender of the French field armies led to a revolution in Paris and a mass mobilization of the population, but Paris was already under siege, and the end was merely delayed. The defeat of France freed Bismarck to absorb the remaining southern German states into a united Germany.[13]

The swift defeat of Austria and the even more startling defeat of France riveted the world's attention. What was the secret of Prussian success? What key lessons could be drawn for future conflicts? Prussia's quick, decisive victories overshadowed longer or less decisive wars in the Crimea, Italy, and America. The Prussian model seemed to be the path of the future, and the European powers, as well as America and Japan, each sought to analyze and import the Prussian system.

Most observers interpreted the German Wars of Unification as suggesting a new set of criteria for future success in war, criteria that in some ways departed from the Napoleonic model. Future operations would depend on the strategic offensive, carried out by large armies of conscripts, rapidly mobilized and moved to the front by rail, where they would fight battles dominated by a seemingly paradoxical combination of defensive firepower that would be overcome by aggressive, offensive firepower sustained by enthusiasm and high morale. Wars would be short, partly because states lacked the resources to sustain a long struggle under these intense conditions.

These last two characteristics, the emphasis on the tactical offensive and the expectation of a short war, arose because of a growing recognition of a new level of infantry firepower on the battlefield. The pace of change in infantry and artillery firepower left post-1871 planners struggling to reconcile new technologies with past wisdom.

FIREPOWER

Although the rifled muskets of the American Civil War may not have constituted a firepower revolution as previously thought, other weapons that emerged during that war enabled a continuing rise in an infantryman's rate of fire. The technology of a muzzle-loading musket had remained basically stable between roughly 1500 and 1840. The changes in the lock that provided the ignition for the powder charge were important, but did not fundamentally change the weapon's firepower; the decline in reload time was incremental and slow. Industrialization, however, unleashed new capabilities in machining and shaping metal. Individual inventers, both institutional and entrepreneurial, continued to improve firearms, but now the incremental changes came faster and faster. The British army's standard musket, the famous "Brown Bess," remained in service from 1722 to 1838, and even in 1838 they were merely retrofitted with a percussion-cap lock. In contrast, the Prussian (and then German) army between 1848 and 1912 changed its primary infantry firearm five times.[14]

Each new model represented yet another incremental change in available technology, but each was considered significant enough to warrant production of hundreds of thousands of such arms. By the 1880s the combined result of the increments had become truly revolutionary. The conoidal Minié ball made famous in the American Civil War was one such increment, but it was really a technological stopgap. The desire for the accuracy of a rifled barrel without the laborious process of forcing a bullet down the full length of that barrel had always suggested loading from the breech. But machining a breech that could be opened and then closed tightly enough to contain the explosion of a powder charge had proved a substantial obstacle. Eighteenth-century attempts at a breech-loading rifle had generally foundered on the limits of precision machining. An individual craftsman could successfully make such a weapon, but production was slow and each weapon was unique, with each piece individually worked to fit the others. Over the first half of the nineteenth century, new industrial techniques of standardizing and automating production not only enabled new breech-loading designs but also slowly enabled truly interchangeable parts manufactured by machines.[15]

Without going into all the technical details, we will note that several competing forms of breech-loading rifle emerged in the late 1840s. The Prussians were the first to field one for their entire army, the famous Dreyse needle gun used in the Prussian army from 1848 and fully deployed to great effect against the Austrians in the Austro-Prussian War in 1866. Breech-loading allowed a soldier to load and fire much more quickly, and to do so while kneeling or even lying down. The French quickly responded with their own equivalent in 1866, the Chassepot, similar in design to the needle gun but more reliable and with a longer range. American commercial firms, meanwhile, had invented repeating breechloaders, such as the Spencer and the Henry rifle. These weapons not only loaded at the breech but could be preloaded with seven to sixteen rounds, which were now metal cartridges combining powder, bullet, and primer all in one watertight package. Some military planners disliked the repeaters, fearing both the logistical challenges of supplying enough ammunition to soldiers likely to burn through their supply much faster, and also the fact that the early repeaters tended to fire a smaller round, with a smaller charge, and therefore with less range or stopping power. Single-shot breechloaders therefore dominated militaries through the end of the Franco-Prussian War. Even this shift signaled a substantial increase in firepower on the battlefield, but there were other concurrent changes.[16]

The American Civil War and the German Wars of Unification saw the first appearance of hand-cranked "machine guns" in the United States and France: the Gatling gun in the former and the mitrailleuse in the latter. Both had multiple barrels, were mounted on a heavy wheeled carriage, and relied on a hand crank for firing. The mitrailleuse (deployed in 1866) had twenty-five barrels and could fire 150 rounds per minute out to one thousand to two thousand yards (see Figure 11.2). Although available to the French army during the war in 1870, it had been adopted in great secrecy, and the army had conducted very little training with it. Officers organized the guns into batteries, placed them in the open, and generally treated them like artillery. They had little effect on the war.[17]

Artillery also underwent a substantial evolution during this period, another process enabled by new precision machining techniques, but in this case especially by new manufacturing methods that produced steel from pig iron: the Bessemer converter of 1856 and the Siemen-Martin open hearth process of 1864. Casting guns from steel, first pioneered by the Krupp firm in the 1830s and 1840s, allowed them to be both lighter and stronger, and more suited to rifling and breech-loading than iron cannon had been. Soon those guns were also being mounted on recoilless carriages that absorbed the recoil without moving the cannon's position, allowing for more rapid fire. Furthermore, as discussed in the previous chapter, artillery now fired exploding shells, creating devastating effects at much greater range.[18]

MITRAILLEUSE (FRONT VIEW).

Figure 11.2 The French mitrailleuse, deployed in 1866. A contemporary illustration of this early French hand-cranked "machine gun." Each plate held twenty-five bullets, each individually fired down its own barrel.

Timing is everything. All these changes were only just becoming available during the German Wars of Unification, and their full implications were not yet clear. There was little doubt that infantry firepower was on the rise, and indeed the breech-loading rifle had encouraged Moltke to rely on firepower in the tactical offensive in a whole new way. He now eschewed the bayonet charge and shock combat as the decisive moment of battle. On the basis of these technologies, showcased from 1859 to 1871, a consensus emerged on the future role of firepower. The consensus acknowledged the increase in firepower but planned to overcome it by maneuver. An attack stopped in one location could be shifted elsewhere, eventually overwhelming a defender.[19]

It was only after 1871, however, that infantry firepower really began to accelerate, based on an increasingly rapid accumulation of incremental deliberately sought technological changes and one entirely unexpected one: nitrocellulose, or "gun cotton." Originally discovered in 1846, gun cotton was not rendered into a form usable in a rifle as smokeless powder until 1885 in France. The new powder burned with more power than traditional saltpeter-based gunpowder, and it burned more thoroughly, generating no smoke or ash byproducts. Rifles using smokeless powder achieved much higher velocities: the first French version of smokeless powder nearly doubled a rifle's muzzle velocity. Rifles using the new powder could therefore be designed with smaller-caliber bullets and still retain their stopping power. Smaller-caliber bullets meant that a soldier could carry more, rendering the older repeater designs of the 1850s more attractive. Various forms of clip-fed internal and then external magazines emerged, typically holding eight to ten rounds, and a sliding bolt action to feed the next round into the breech. All of these changes took place in a new generation of rifles from the 1880s and early 1890s: the French Lebel of 1886, the German Mauser of 1888, the Austrian Mannlicher of 1889, the British Lee Metford of 1889, the Russian Mossine of 1891, and the Norwegian-designed American Krag-Jørgenson of 1893 (see Figure 11.3 and Table 11.1).[20]

Ascribing a country of origin to each of these weapons obscures somewhat the nature of innovation during this period. We have described the changes in rifle design as "rapidly accumulating incremental" ones. Typically, no one change was sufficiently revolutionary that an army would immediately invest in replacing its expensive stock of weapons. So where did the innovations come from? And when did the increments reach a tipping point such that an army did change to a newer model? We have already noted that between 1848 and 1912 the Prussian/German army changed its infantry rifle five times, and the Germans were hardly alone in adopting new models at such a rate. The innovations themselves typically came from private individuals or companies seeking to market their wares to national militaries capable of making large purchases. Officers in those national militaries were tightly tied to the aristocratic classes and culturally suspicious of inventors' and entrepreneurs' profit motives. On the other hand,

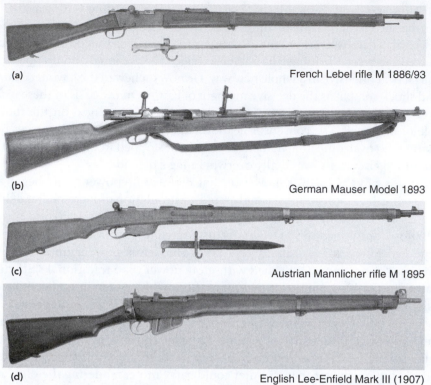

(a)   French Lebel rifle M 1886/93

(b)   German Mauser Model 1893

(c)   Austrian Mannlicher rifle M 1895

(d)   English Lee-Enfield Mark III (1907)

Figure 11.3 Late nineteenth-century smokeless powder military rifles. The similarities in outward appearance belie a host of small incremental changes between the first (the Lebel), and those available to the armies of WWI. (a) is a French Lebel M 1886/93; (b) is a German Mauser Model 1893, based on the 1889 design; (c) is an Austrian Mannlicher M 1895 and (d) is an English Lee-Enfield Mark III (1907).

the proliferation of permanent general staffs had created an influential coterie of officers dedicated to planning the next war and professionally committed to not falling behind their neighboring enemies in an environment of intense military competition. When enough changes accumulated, calculation overruled culture, and military men lobbied their civilian masters for the funds to update their forces—often helped along by the lobbying efforts of the manufacturers. The Great Powers tended to prefer products made by domestic firms, but it was not a hard and fast rule. The amount of lobbying required varied by state, but countries in Europe in this period, in part prodded by popular nationalistic fervor, lived in legitimate fear of each other. The companies involved, however, remained profit-seeking agencies, and most of their products were free of what today would be called "national security holds"; companies openly marketed their wares abroad and found purchasers in the smaller European countries, the United States, the Ottoman Empire, and beyond.

Most of the innovations discussed here were basically mechanical and, once on the market, relatively easy to copy by any firm (or national armory)

Nationality	Model name	Year introduced	Loading/action	Powder	Rate of fire	Magazine capacity	Bullet size
British	Brown Bess	1722	muzzle (smoothbore)	black	3/minute	none	18mm
Prussian	Needle gun	1841	breech, single-shot	black	10–12/min	none	15.4mm
US	Springfield	1861	muzzle (rifled)	black	3/minute	none	15mm
US	Spencer	1860	breech, lever	black	~14/min	7	13mm
French	Chassepot	1867	breech, single-shot	black	8–15/minute	none	11mm
Swiss	Vetterli	1867	breech, bolt	black	~20/min	11	10mm
German	Mauser M71/84	1871/1884	breech, bolt	black	~20/min	none/8	11mm
French	Lebel	1886	breech, bolt	smokeless	~20/min	8+2	8mm
US/Norwegian	Krag-Jørgensen	1886	breech, bolt	smokeless	~20/min	5	8mm
German	Gewehr 88 (M.88)	1888	breech, bolt	smokeless	~20/min	5	7.92mm
British	Lee Metford	1888	breech, bolt	black	~20/min	8 or 10	7.7mm

Table 11.1: **The emergence of modern rifles**. This chart obscures some additional complexities, but generally indicates the significant increase in infantry firepower brought by lever-action and bolt-action smokeless-powder rifles in the 1880s. Note that the rate of fire with a lever-action or bolt-action rifle can vary, depending on the magazine design.

with access to modern industrial infrastructure. This pattern varied depending on the initial capital investment required. The expense of naval innovation, for example, tied it far more intimately to the demands of a single state, and many of those innovations were easier to keep secret. But with firearms an individual inventor of the nineteenth century could hold in his mind a clearly formed notion of what sorts of improvements an army might want, and actively seek, under the conditions of industrialization and automated production, to provide such weapons. Most of the changes were incremental and accumulating because many minds were working on the problem in a competitive commercial-military marketplace. Still, as gun cotton demonstrated, some innovations could emerge out of the blue.[21]

A similar cumulative process produced an even more dramatic increase in the firepower of machine gun technology. Hiram Maxim, born in the United States and living in Great Britain, invented a machine gun that far surpassed the hand-cranked Gatling or the mitrailleuse. Those early weapons provided the impetus for thinking about rapid, automatic fire; Maxim was the first to successfully use the force of the recoil to eject the spent cartridge and automatically load a new one. A gunner merely had to hold the trigger down and could fire six hundred rounds a minute through a single barrel kept cool by a water jacket. Similar designs using the gases released in the firing of each round to power the weapon soon followed in other countries. Great Britain adopted the Maxim in 1889, as did Germany and Russia soon thereafter. Other industrialized nations, including Japan, followed suit with one model or another in the two decades before World War I. Incremental accumulating changes in machine guns soon produced ever lighter and more reliable guns.[22]

The implications of this rise in infantry firepower, and especially of the capabilities of machine guns, were not entirely clear. Most of Europe remained at peace until 1914, but the Boer War in South Africa (1899–1902), the Russo-Japanese War in 1904–5, and the Balkan Wars of 1912–13 showcased the new level of firepower and in turn encouraged improvements in field fortifications. Troops now had to dig deeper into the ground rather than using earth piled up in embankments, because modern muzzle velocities and artillery capabilities sliced through the old defenses. Furthermore, barbed wire, introduced to the battlefield in the 1890s, could protect entrenchments, and the entrenchments themselves were now designed to emphasize the defensive firepower provided by static, well-supplied machine guns firing in interlocking fields of fire—much like that created by the bastions of *trace italienne* fortresses of an earlier era. Field fortifications played an additional role in stiffening the resistance of relatively untrained conscripts, a truism that extended back to the poorly trained militia of the American Revolution, who could win major victories when protected by fortifications.[23]

With the benefit of post–World War I hindsight, modern commentators have criticized contemporary observers of these three turn-of-the-century conflicts for failing to recognize how improved infantry firepower had greatly enhanced the defensive, especially when employing modern field fortifications. The killing fields of the Russo-Japanese War in particular strongly foreshadowed what would happen in France and Belgium from 1915 to 1917. Contemporaries, however, correctly noted that in each of those wars the winning approach was the strategic offensive, and the military planners continued to believe in the power of the offensive through 1914.

Technologically, doctrinally, and in terms of the scale of likely mobilization, the European powers would enter World War I unprepared for the enhanced power of the defensive. They remained fixated on a doctrine of the offensive that would exaggerate the impact of improved infantry and artillery firepower. Prussian doctrine during the Wars of Unification, copied by the French prior to the Franco-Prussian War, emphasized an offensive technique that built up an overwhelming volume of fire, shattering the enemy, followed by a bayonet charge to put them to flight. The presumed lessons of the Franco-Prussian War continued to dominate thinking, despite the accelerating changes in infantry firepower after 1871. Military planners did recognize the new lethality of small-arms firepower and artillery, and were beginning to emphasize smaller formations, advancing in smaller groups, alternating fire and movement, and maintaining an open order, rather than the old shoulder-to-shoulder formations. But faith in the attack remained central, and as armies grew larger through conscription the prospects for highly trained forces managing the complexities of small unit fire and movement diminished, and some planners simply rejected the idea of a creeping, scattered force of attackers.

Instead "moral factors" were extolled. Nothing, it was averred, spurred enthusiasm like a mass of men charging with a bayonet (after a suitable firepower-based softening up of the enemy defenders). Colonel Ferdinand Foch of France, who during World War I would be the hero of the Marne and by 1917 the chief of the French General Staff, argued in the years before the war, "To charge, but to charge in numbers, therein lies safety. . . . With more guns we can reduce his to silence, and the same is true of rifles and bayonets, if we know how to make use of them all." The French focus on élan and the bayonet charge was perhaps stronger than most, and indeed the French army's tactical sophistication seems actually to have regressed between 1871 and 1894, but Foch's views were hardly unique. The "cult of the offensive" was widespread.[24]

Historian Antulio Echevarria has suggested that military theorists in Germany had fully recognized the emergent obstacle of defensive firepower and had designed techniques to overcome it, but by 1914 those theories had not yet been fully transmitted to the army.[25] Eric Brose, however, argues that debates within the German army were won by those who "emphasized the superiority of man and morale over machine and firepower" and therefore emphasized "tight infantry formations and shock attack tactics, large-unit cavalry charges featuring waves of massed horsemen, and offensive field artillery tactics that maximized mobility and valor while neglecting firepower and marksmanship."[26] Either way, the German army was unprepared for the defensive firepower on display in late 1914. By early 1915, having occupied a significant chunk of France and Belgium, the Germans gave up the offensive and dug in to hold on to their gains, setting the stage for the notorious stalemate from 1915 to 1917. Before turning to that problem, however, we need to examine the impact of modern firepower on Europe's relative power in the rest of the world.

FIREPOWER AND THE SCRAMBLE FOR EMPIRE: DAHOMEY AND ETHIOPIA

Chapter 10 examined three of the four key factors identified by Daniel Headrick as central to Europe's rapid assertion of dominance over much of the world during the last twenty to thirty years of the nineteenth century. Undeniably the most important piece of the puzzle was simply the ability to deliver European forces to Africa and Asia and then to sustain them there with reliable maritime supply, buttressed by steam-powered ships carrying cannon. Without that capability, little else would have happened. The fourth factor cited by Headrick and other historians is industrialized firepower. It has long been an article of faith that European imperial conquests of the late nineteenth century depended on firepower to multiply the impact of a single European soldier on the battlefield. Movies like *Zulu* or *Zulu Dawn* have popularized that notion, emphasizing the difference between Europeans armed with repeating rifles and the spear-carrying Zulu warriors. The rare European defeats were explained by dramatically superior enemy numbers. This is not an unreasonable conclusion. Certain incidents seemed to support it, such as Britain's first colonial use of the Maxim machine gun in the Matabele Wars in the mid-1890s, in which small forces mowed down thousands of charging warriors.[27]

Looking deeper, however, at the role of technology in providing enhanced firepower to European infantry, thereby enabling the second great wave of European imperialism, reveals a more complex story. Two examples, considered at some length, can provide deeper context for discussing the complexities of firepower and the role of African manpower in the European scramble for empire.

Dahomey

As discussed in chapter 8, the Kingdom of Dahomey coalesced in late seventeenth-century West Africa in response to the pressures of the slave trade (see Map 11.3). With the end of the legal slave trade in the early nineteenth century, the kingdom's economy shifted to the production and sale of palm oil, primarily exported through its port at Cotonou. In the late nineteenth century Dahomey became caught up in the European scramble for empire in Africa, and its experience reflects a common pattern. Dahomey was unique, however, in having a long tradition of an elite all-female corps of warriors, called "Amazons" by European observers. Fortunately for our understanding of this war, these women warriors were subjected to a plethora of observers' reports and modern studies.[28]

French-Dahomean relations began to fracture in the 1880s. At that time the neighboring Porto Novo kingdom, long a tributary state of Dahomey, looked to use a relationship with France to achieve independence from Dahomey. In 1889 a French emissary also demanded that Cotonou be surrendered to French control. Dahomey refused. As was often the case in these situations in Africa, a small community of French merchants were already resident in Cotonou. Their manipulations precipitated the crisis, including fraudulently claiming that Cotonou had been surrendered by treaty in 1868 and again in 1878. The French government then justified military intervention to the French domestic political audience by claiming to need to protect the merchants. The small French forces already present were built up to 360 men, of which 299 were Senegalese and Gabonese *tirailleurs*. They assumed control of Cotonou on February 21, 1890.

The use of tirailleurs hints at one of the complexities in the story of European firepower in Africa. Literally translating to "skirmishers," at this time the word was simply the French designation for locally recruited colonial troops.

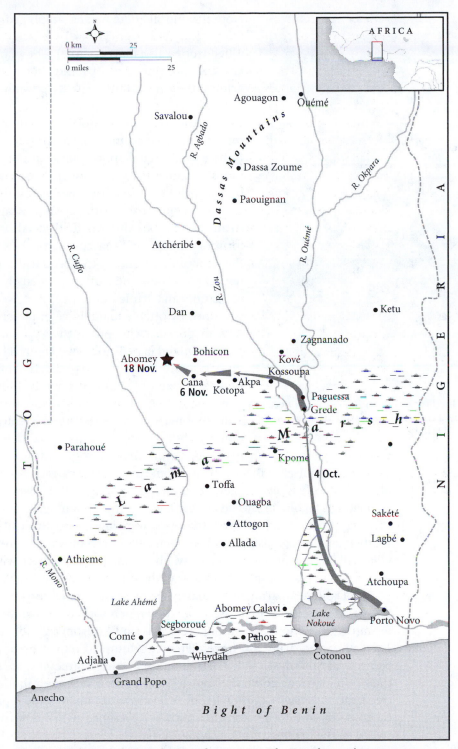

Map 11.3 Dahomey during the French conquest. The French army's movements indicated by the arrows are those from the campaign of 1892. After the capture of Abomey, Behanzin fled north to Atchéribé. A final French campaign farther into the interior was launched in 1893.

DÉBARQUEMENT D'UN BATAILLON
DE TIRAILLEURS ALGÉRIENS AU MAROC

Figure 11.4 Algerian *Tirailleurs* in French service.
Here shown in a contemporary print arriving in
Morocco in 1911, led by white officers.

Note that "local" here means simply "African," not
truly local (although, as we will see, truly local
allied troops also played a role). The practice of recruiting indigenous troops and then training and
arming them in a European style was widespread
among the European powers. Elsewhere in Africa,
such colonial troops were often called *askaris*. Such
men were recruited in a variety of ways, often not
from a single people but from a variety of ethnicities, sometimes the very ethnicities being displaced
by European wars in Africa. Being a tirailleur or an
askari not only carried the economic appeal of a
steady income but also provided social status in the
form of a traditional masculine role of soldier and
the economic resources to become the head of a
household. These men often formed the majority
of "European" armies in Africa, and were further
sustained by often equally large or larger groups of
African porters, who provided key logistical support for inland expeditions (see Figure 11.4).[29]

In response to the French occupation of Cotonou,
King Behanzin of Dahomey mobilized his army. At
that time Dahomey had a two-part force: a standing
army of some four thousand supplemented by a national militia about twice that size. The so-called
Amazons formed an elite corps within the standing
army. At the outset of the war the Dahomean army was armed primarily with
old flintlocks, and even some bows and arrows, as well as swords for close
combat. The regular army had almost no program of training, although its soldiers were regular campaigners and many were likely veterans. Unfortunately
for their venture against the French, their usual form of war was the raid on a
village or, at best, an assault on a city. They had little experience with pitched
battles, having fought in perhaps four in the fifty years before 1890.[30]

The Dahomean army immediately attacked the French force in Cotonou,
but failed in several hasty assaults. The French forces had eight-shot Lebel
repeating rifles and four cannons, as well as support from a gunboat off shore.
The Dahomean army did force a French column to retreat back into Porto
Novo, while also destroying the surrounding palm oil trees. Facing the loss of
their primary trade good, the French backed down, although the subsequent
treaty formally gave Cotonou to France in exchange for an annual payment of
twenty thousand francs and the continued presence of Dahomean administrators in the town to provide civil governance.[31]

Alarmed by these clear signs of the inadequacy of his army, Behanzin
used the peace to begin a major program of rearming. The state bought

1,700 breech-loading or repeating rifles from German merchants in the region, including 300 Peabodys (1862 breechloader), 133 Winchesters (several models from 1860s and 1870s, all repeating breechloaders), 648 Chassepots (1866 breechloader), 200 Albinis (1867 breechloader), 240 Sniders (1866 breechloader), and 200 Spencers (1860 repeating breechloader). In addition, Behanzin purchased six Krupp cannon, five French mitrailleuses, and four hundred thousand cartridges as well as shells for the cannon. Other estimates suggest that Dahomey acquired a total of some four to six thousand modern rifles. The rifles generally went to the standing army, replacing their flintlocks. The militia, however, provided their own equipment, which remained outmoded; in 1891 they seem to have been using the discarded flintlocks of the standing army. Behanzin's upgrading of the armed forces, however, does not seem to have drastically changed Dahomean tactics. The soldiers advanced, fired, and then retired to reload, creating a highly fluid and individualistic battle line.[32]

Meanwhile pro-imperialist French officials maneuvered to persuade the French parliament that renewed war would be necessary, awaiting a provocation to justify a more extensive attack on the Dahomean heartland. The excuse came on March 27, 1892, when a few Dahomean soldiers fired on a French official cruising on a gunboat up a river into Dahomean territory. The French declared war and rapidly assembled a 2,164-man force, of which 930 were African colonial troops. They moved inland on the Ouémé River by boat, accompanied by five gunboats and sustained by 2,600 porters from Porto Novo (see Map 11.3).[33]

French forces carried the eight-shot Lebel repeating rifles—the first military firearm to use the new smokeless powder. In Dahomey the Lebel became notorious for penetrating palm trees and killing soldiers hiding behind them. Interestingly, however, some French accounts suggested that it was their bayonets that made the difference; in close combat the bayonets outreached the blades of the Dahomeans, and they were used to countercharge Dahomean frontal assaults. The French also had machine guns and their famous breech-loading 75 mm cannon that would remain in service into World War II.[34]

During the ensuing month, as the French expedition marched overland to Cana, the twelve thousand men and women of the Dahomean army were almost entirely destroyed as they tried to stop them. French forces advanced in a secure square formation to prevent subunits from being isolated or cut off. Dahomean rifle fire often flew high, while subpar shells from their Krupp-made guns often did not explode. Alert French sentries prevented dawn surprises, and bayonet charges pushed the defenders out of blocking positions, despite sometimes spectacular bravery by the Dahomean defenders, and despite the Dahomeans resorting to foxholes and trenches as the French advanced closer and closer to Abomey. French soldiers' narratives of the campaign focused on the ferocity of Dahomean attacks (noting especially the Amazons), the poor marksmanship of the Dahomeans, the effectiveness of French volley fire with Lebel rifles, and the role of the bayonet charge. French cannon and machine guns had been important during the first war, when the French had been defending at Cotonou; they appear less frequently during the march on Abomey. During the march the French suffered losses of fifty-two Europeans and thirty-three tirailleurs killed, with 224 and 216 respectively wounded, compared to perhaps two thousand Dahomean dead and three thousand wounded. The Amazon corps was virtually wiped out.[35]

The French army halted at Cana on November 6. A round of negotiations ensued, but French demands proved unacceptably high. The French occupied Abomey on November 18 and Behanzin fled north. The French assumed the war was over and dispersed garrisons around the coastal region and in the central part of the country near Abomey. Behanzin, however, now in the north, regrouped an army of some two thousand and tried to lead a rump state. Eventually the French determined to stamp out this last spark of resistance. They tried to depose Behanzin by proclamation, but the Dahomeans refused to abandon their king. Eventually the French launched another campaign into the north, and Behanzin's forces slowly evaporated, until he was little more than a hunted refugee. A group of Dahomean nobles offered the southern half of the kingdom to France, and the French appointed a puppet king to rule in the north under French advisement. Behanzin was finally betrayed and arrested in January 1894.

So did firepower make a difference in Dahomey? At one level it clearly did. French forces were uniformly equipped with a more capable rifle than the Dahomeans, although Behanzin's purchase of so many somewhat older rifles indicates their availability on the world market. French artillery and on occasion their machine guns also made a difference. At the same time, however, French accounts emphasized the role played by their bayonets. They were effective in close combat, and they helped drive Dahomean defenders out of foxholes and trench works. But in another sense what mattered was method, not technology: it was not simply the Lebel rifle; it was the Lebel rifle fired in disciplined salvos against an exposed charging enemy, by men who repeatedly reformed into squares when surrounded by the more numerous Dahomeans. Ironically, what few indications there are from the Dahomeans themselves suggest that they feared French firepower, while the French, in the midst of a debate back in France about the decisive effects of a bayonet charge, focused on the role the bayonet had played in battle. What also mattered was the French commander's ability to sustain his force during their inland march, partly by using riverine communications, and partly by thorough administrative preparation, including using a substantial number of African porters. Without these methods, all the firepower in the world would have mattered little. In answering the larger question about the role of modern firepower in enabling European imperialism in Africa, Dahomey provides mixed results.

Ethiopia

Logistical challenges, albeit on a much larger scale, also bedeviled the Italian campaign in Ethiopia, this time with a much different result. In 1896 the Ethiopians defeated the Italians at Adowa (or Adwa) and maintained their independence. Although exceptional, the reasons for Ethiopia's success further emphasize the mix of key variables that empowered European conquest elsewhere, and the equivocal role of firepower in that process.

Like other European powers, Italy was swept up in the scramble for empire in Africa, less driven than most by the need for markets, and more by the cultural pressures of political ambition and the desire to stand alongside the great powers of Europe. As Ottoman control over the ports and trade routes of the Red Sea and East Africa weakened, the European powers maneuvered to find advantage. Italy turned its attention to the port of Massawa on the Red Sea. Encouraged by the British, who desired only that the rival French not get it, and despite Ethiopian claims to the port, and even despite earlier Ethiopian-British treaties, Italy occupied Massawa in February 1885. Italy then used that toehold to expand its imperial influence. Two years later, five thousand mostly traditionally armed Ethiopians, aided only by some old muzzleloaders, successfully destroyed a column of some five hundred Italians marching to reinforce an Italian outpost. The defeat, however, only rallied Italian enthusiasm for imperial expansion.[36]

Meanwhile, in a classic imperialist tactic of divide and conquer, Italy courted Sahle Maryam, a regional ruler in Ethiopia, as a rival to the current Ethiopian king, Yohannes. As part of that courtship, the Italians supplied Maryam with 4,700 Remington breech-loading repeaters and 220,000 cartridges. When Yohannes died in 1889, Maryam made himself King Menelik II of Ethiopia and signed a treaty of amity with Italy. The treaty seemed to solidify his hold on power. Buried in a vague translation, however, it also contained an Italian claim to a protectorate that Menelik neither recognized nor accepted.[37]

At that time, Italy was consolidating its control around Massawa, having declared it and its immediate hinterland to be the colony of Eritrea. As part of their consolidation, the Italians followed the lead of other European powers in creating battalions of askaris. In the spring of 1895, Italian forces, now heavily buttressed by askari troops, defeated what they saw as a regional rebellion in Eritrea. Blaming Menelik for the rebellion, the Italians moved forces into Ethiopia proper, seemingly intending to stay.[38]

Menelik responded by mobilizing an enormous army to oppose his former benefactors. His methods of mobilization were ancient, based on a semifeudal militia system, but the effect in this case was to generate a very large national army. Remarkably, Menelik had successfully folded potential and former rivals into his court—including even Yohannes's son. The Italians, not unreasonably, kept waiting for this coalition to fall apart, but by mid-December 1895 Menelik had some one hundred thousand men on the move, and early victories cemented his command of the army. He had a four-to-one numerical advantage over Italian forces in Ethiopia and Eritrea, and his men were well armed with modern rifles and ten French-built Hotchkiss quick-firing artillery pieces, in addition to two mountain guns captured from the Italians in the first battle of the campaign.[39]

Menelik's weaponry reflected the many ways that modern or nearly modern firearms arrived in Africa in tremendous numbers. Imperial competition and hopes for profit led to some sixteen million firearms being imported into Africa during the nineteenth century. Although Menelik lacked the capacity for local production, he acquired large numbers of guns by other means, both as gifts and through purchase abroad. In 1894 Maryam had waged an internal consolidation war against the Welayta, during which his forces had some fifteen thousand French Gras rifles, an 1874 model (which presented jamming problems for his troops), as well as some Vetterlis (probably the 1879 model, another breech-loading repeater). He also had the nearly five thousand Remington breech-loading repeaters gifted to him by the Italians, and there is other evidence of arms traders at work in Ethiopia during the 1880s and 1890s. The French, irritated by Britain's backing of Italy, sent as many as a hundred thousand rifles and two million tons of ammunition to Menelik through the governor of French Somaliland. Many, if not most, of Menelik's soldiers in 1895–96 therefore had breechloaders, if not repeaters. The Italian army at that time was equipped with a new generation of magazine-fed repeaters, but their askaris had older single-shot breechloaders inferior to those of Menelik's men, but deemed sufficient by the Italians for the use of their colonial allies.[40]

The battles that followed hinged not only on the Ethiopians' possession of modern rifles and artillery, but also on the cohesion and size of Menelik's army and Italian miscalculations. In the first battle, Menelik's vanguard of almost forty thousand men hit an Italian outpost of two thousand men at Amba Alage. Virtually none of the garrison were European: 1,300 were askaris, and the rest were men recruited from local chiefs. The garrison's cannon decimated the closely packed attackers, but the Ethiopians still quickly overran the fort. They then assaulted and besieged a second outpost of one thousand carefully fortified men at Mekele. The Ethiopians' Hotchkiss guns proved too light to breach the walls, but the attackers eventually forced a surrender by cutting off the Italians' water supply.[41]

Menelik continued his march north toward the main Italian army, dug in at Adigrat, within Ethiopia proper (see Map 11.4). The Italians had some seventeen thousand men—roughly half Italian and half askari or local troops. Menelik maneuvered to threaten Eritrea and thus forced the Italian commander to come out and meet him. The Italians were well beyond the small rail line they had built within Eritrea, and their supplies now came slowly overland on mule and horseback. After a long stalemate with both armies facing each other but unwilling to attack, Menelik again moved, and the Italians pursued. The Battle of Adowa opened precipitously as one of the three Italian

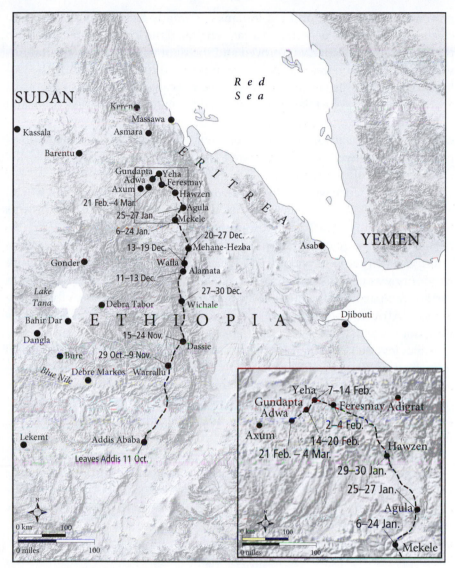

Map 11.4 The Adowa campaign, Ethiopia 1895. The map shows the Ethiopian army's advance against Italian forces moving south from Eritrea. Based on Jonas, *Battle of Adwa*, 114.

columns advanced too far too fast in the dark, and its vanguard was caught unsupported and quickly destroyed by attacking Ethiopians. The remainder of that column, some 4,076 men (only one hundred of whom were white Italians) and four artillery pieces, then came under attack. The Italian response was confused, and Menelik detected and attacked a gap between the first column and one moving up to reinforce it.

Far from being raw recruits, the veteran Ethiopians used concealment and disciplined fire and movement to advance on the Italian positions. Although they took heavy casualties from the defenders' artillery, their superior numbers were decisive, and the Italians apparently lacked any form of machine gun. Menelik's penetrating attack encircled the Italian center, and with the left column effectively destroyed and the right wing isolated, the Italians sounded a general retreat. Menelik's men pursued relentlessly while the isolated right wing was entirely destroyed. Few escaped, and 1,900 Europeans and 1,500 askaris were taken prisoner, in addition to the nearly five thousand Europeans and two thousand askaris killed. A similar number of Ethiopians died on the battlefield, and many of their ten thousand wounded subsequently died as well. Feeling betrayed by their fellow African askaris, the Ethiopians cut off their right hands and left feet as punishment.[42]

The Italians failed where other European powers had succeeded. Or, we can just as accurately say, Menelik succeeded where so many other African powers had failed. Many of the variables present in the Italo-Ethiopian War also characterized many other European-African conflicts in the late nineteenth century. Firearms were widely available to both sides (although European weaponry was perhaps slightly more modern); European logistics strained to sustain campaigns in the interior; European armies remained heavily dependent on African troops trained in a European manner; and machine guns were not yet widely available. The Italians may have managed some of these variables less well than their European counterparts elsewhere, but the critical difference was that Menelik was more successful than nearly any African equivalent at rallying a full national resistance. He overcame the internal divisiveness that plagued most African societies faced with invasion. Just as in premodern imperial adventures, the invader usually had the advantage of political unity, at least in the campaign area; the defender had to cope with whatever internal fractiousness had already been in place before the invasion.

Within all these dynamics firepower could make a significant difference, usually on those occasions when the technological gap was relatively wide and when European logistics had been carefully secured. It is also fair to say that as technology continued to change, and especially as machine guns became more widely available within European forces, the firepower differential proved crucial to the European *maintenance* of power within Africa, even if it had not been central to the initial conquest. Among other differences, in the postconquest policing environment there was no longer a central figure like Menelik or Behanzin available to finance the purchasing of modern weapons; "rebels" against colonial rule generally struggled to acquire such weapons, and small police forces, equipped with machine guns, could overcome even very large numbers of rebels. The Germans, for example, used a small number of machine guns to successfully suppress rebellions in German Southwest Africa and Tanganyika in 1904–7.[43]

Firepower may not have been decisive in the race for empire, but that race, both in Africa and in the rest of the world, heightened the international tensions that eventually led to the catastrophe of World War I. In that war, infantry firepower mattered very much indeed.

WORLD WAR I

The outbreak of World War I is a complex story, often told, which fortunately does not need detailed retelling here. In June 1914 a Serbian assassin shot the heir to the throne of Austria-Hungary. In doing so, he unwittingly activated a series of interlocking alliances and fears that rapidly drew into war nearly the whole of Europe as well as European territorial colonies around the world. Grand political dynamics notwithstanding, much of how the war itself played out can be connected to our concern here with infantry firepower. In 1914 every major European power continued to believe that the increase in defensive firepower was best overcome by a spirited offensive. After all, victory required attacking the enemy. Just as crucially, the powers shared a belief that when war broke out it would be ended by the rapid movement of a mass army marching from their railheads (a railroad terminus) on the frontier into the enemy's country. After the Prussian successes of 1871, their general staff system had been widely copied, sometimes idiosyncratically, but nonetheless each power now had a permanent staff of military planners weighing the probabilities and planning for the next war.[44]

In 1914 the German plan for war (the Schlieffen Plan, named for the German chief of staff who had devised it) against a presumed Franco-Russian alliance involved a massive swinging wheel into northern France through Belgium, seeking to envelop Paris through rapid marching, and then surrounding and destroying the French army, knocking France out of the war in time to deal with the slower-mobilizing Russians (see Map 11.5). For their

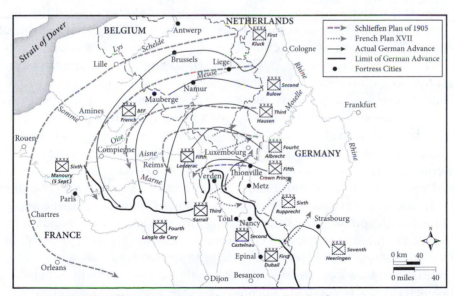

Map 11.5 The Schlieffen Plan compared to the actual path of German armies in the fall of 1914. The map also shows French Plan XVII. The German First Army's swing south to avoid the Netherlands was a late alteration to the plan.

part, the French planned to push directly into the heart of Germany via the Duchy of Luxembourg and along the French-German border—a plan designated Plan XVII. Each of these plans was far more than merely proposed arrows on the map. They included detailed mobilization schedules and arrangements for trains to arrive in the right place to get newly called-up reservists to the right spot on the frontier as quickly as possible. Altering these plans to conform to political circumstance proved nearly impossible. When mobilization was declared by the respective powers, their military machines lurched forward almost of their own accord.

This is not to lay sole responsibility for the war at the feet of military planners. Many political and ideological dynamics pushed the nations toward war. Nevertheless, the shared strategic culture that emphasized rapid mobilization for an offensive war played a crucial role in the war's outbreak. What the planners *believed* would happen shaped their response to the threat of war and the advice they gave their political masters. There were few moments more dramatic and tragic than when Kaiser Wilhelm of Germany briefly grasped at the straw of possible French neutrality during the crisis in July, before the start of fighting. Diplomatic hints from Great Britain suggested that France might be willing to opt out of its alliance with Russia. When the kaiser suggested as much to his Chief of the General Staff, Helmuth von Moltke (the nephew of the Moltke discussed earlier in this chapter), Moltke nearly collapsed with anxiety. He protested repeatedly that he had only one plan for war with Russia, and not only did that plan attack France first, but it was already in motion. The kaiser insisted that there must be alternatives, and their argument left Moltke "almost hysterical." Moltke feared that the kaiser still hoped for peace, and in the end, when Moltke insisted that his complex mobilization plan could not be changed, Wilhelm rebuked him, saying, "Your illustrious uncle would not have given me such an answer. If I order it, it must be possible." Moltke backed down in despair, only to be reprieved when further British telegrams dashed the hopes of French neutrality.[45] The war would open as Moltke, and Schlieffen before him, had planned.

In part Moltke's desperation reflected a growing awareness among military planners that a short war, although preferable, was no longer inevitable. Indeed, a long grinding war of nations, a *Volkskrieg*, had become one of Germany's strategic fears. Fearing that outcome, German planners grasped at the straw of a desperate push into France to ensure a quick decision. Moltke understood how new mass conscript armies raised from nationalistic populations could prolong the war. Knowing the size of Russia's population, Moltke predicted that even if he defeated France quickly, Germany would face "a *Volkskrieg* that will not be settled by the means of one decisive battle . . . rather it will be a long, difficult struggle with a nation that will not give in before the entire strength of its people is broken."[46]

At first, however, the German offensive ground forward and seemed to validate prewar hopes. The attack pushed through Belgium and reached the nearly undefended French border only two days behind schedule. Meanwhile the French offensives, correctly anticipated by the German staff, had been stopped. German violation of Belgian neutrality had brought the British into the war, but German planners still hoped to end the conflict before the small British professional army could make much of an impact. Indeed, the German First Army on the right wing initially sliced through the arriving British. The French retreated to defend Paris, and the Germans failed to outpace them there. German soldiers were now many long footslogging miles from their supplies gathering at railheads in Belgium. At that point the German First Army commander decided to swing east of Paris to avoid it and encircle the French army. French reserves arriving in Paris by rail, however, moved out from the city and in the ensuing Battle of the Marne stopped the German advance (see Map 11.5). The Germans repositioned along the Aisne River, and each side then began a "race to the sea" (Map 11.6), seeking an open flank to the north. By November, having reached the sea, both sides were digging in along a five-hundred-mile front that extended from Switzerland to the English Channel.

The defensive potential of modern firepower, especially machine guns employed in improved field fortifications as developed over the previous thirty years, created the unexpected stalemate that defines the popular image of trench warfare in World War I. That image—of mud-spattered soldiers suffering through endless months of living in trenches, vulnerable to artillery, and periodically sent "over the top" by distant generals in futile charges against their equally entrenched and suffering enemy, only to be mown down by machine gun fire while entangled in barbed wire or drowning in one of the millions of flooded shell holes that pockmarked no man's land—is both all too accurate and far too simplistic. The tactical stalemate was real: overcoming defensive firepower proved far more difficult than had been anticipated. But the efforts to overcome it were sincere, sophisticated, changing, and all too often frustrated.

At the center of the problem was the vast increase in infantry firepower, supplemented by the relatively recent advent of the true machine gun. Masses of men moving in the open could now be destroyed by a small number of stationary men operating machine guns. Even armed with repeating breech-loading rifles, men moving on the attack struggled to generate enough firepower to match that of the emplaced machine gun, or even to keep its gunners' heads down. In some ways the German army's rapid advance in the fall of 1914 was only possible because of French and British prewar reluctance to expand machine gun deployment. Machine guns of the era were heavy and did not lend themselves to then-current offensive-minded thinking. Furthermore, logisticians continued to fear their potential rate of ammunition consumption.

This reluctance—one key civilian even referred to it as "fanatical hostility"—persisted among some generals, especially British ones, well into the war. As late as July 1915, when pressed by the munitions office about exactly how many machine guns needed to be ordered, Field Marshal Lord Herbert Kitchener, the secretary of state for war, replied that "the proportion

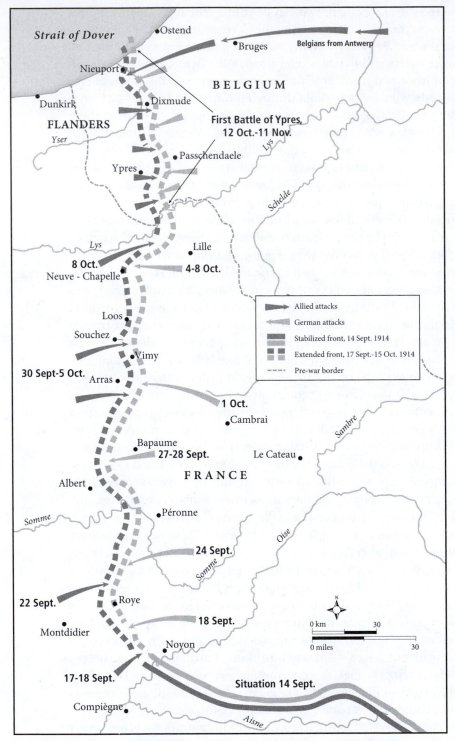

Map 11.6 The "Race to the Sea" from September 14 to November 11, 1914.

was to be two machine-guns per battalion as a minimum, four as a max-imum, and anything above four was a luxury." When the British minister of munitions (and future prime minister) David Lloyd George was presented with that estimate he ordered his staff to "take Kitchener's maximum (four per battalion); square it, multiply that result by two; and when you are in sight of that, double it again for good luck." That ad hoc math suggested thirty two guns per battalion with thirty-two more in production as replacements; and by the end of the war that number had become the War Office's official planning figure. Concerned nonetheless that he might have gone too far in overruling Kitchener, George reported his conscience cleared some weeks later when he saw a photo of "dead Highlanders lying in swathes in front of a single German machine-gun on the battlefield of Loos."[47]

The German army was only somewhat less conservative in its approach to machine guns. At the start of the war each German infantry regiment (of three battalions) had a machine gun company of six guns, and thus corresponded to Kitchener's two guns per battalion. But Germany had far more total machine guns available in 1914, and more rapidly expanded their use. Between 1914 and 1916 Germany increased the number of machine guns in the regimental machine gun company from six to twelve (thus four per battalion), and then in the fall of 1916 they shifted to one company of machine guns per battalion, initially with four guns per company, then six, then eight, then ten, and finally twelve. All of this was in addition to the infantry companies acquiring their own light machine guns in fall 1916. France in 1914 followed the same basic model of two machine guns per battalion, steadily increasing the number thereafter, although not to the extent that the German army did.[48]

The immediately obvious solution to defensive firepower was what had long been used in such circumstances: artillery. In the first few months of the war, while the armies were still maneuvering in the open, artillery was often pushed far forward with the infantry on both the offense and the defense, much as it had been in the Napoleonic era. Those guns' crews, however, proved vulnerable to the increased range and volume of infantry firepower. Guns were rapidly shifted to the rear to fire indirectly, from behind cover or from a much greater distance. A lack of reliable communication from forward observer to artillery battery, however, limited accuracy, especially when used to support offensives whose real target was no longer *massed* infantry but scattered ma-chine gun positions. As the trench lines settled into place in late 1914, there was insufficient artillery available to overcome dug-in defenders. As produc-tion got rolling in 1915 and 1916, more guns were brought to bear on enemy positions, in an effort to destroy or suppress defenses, as well to cut the barbed wire now commonly used in front of entrenchments. Long preliminary bom-bardments were then followed by infantry assault across no man's land.[49]

Those charges did not always fail, but their occasional successes prompted defensive adaptation. Trenches were elaborated and provided with deep dug-outs for protection from artillery (see Figure 11.5). Machine guns were placed

Figure 11.5 Trench warfare, World War I. British troops in crude, roughly dug trenches await the signal to attack in the Third Battle of Ypres, October 30, 1917.

with interlocking fields of fire, while the trench lines themselves were thickened. The attacker confronted not a single trench but a row of successive trenches extending from one thousand meters to five thousand meters in depth (see Figure 11.6). The attacker in turn increased the length and scale of the bombardment. The British offensive at the Somme in 1916, for example, began with 1,437 artillery pieces firing 1.5 million shells over a week. In 1917, the British preliminary bombardment at Passchendaele lasted over sixteen days and involved the firing of 3.5 million shells. Artillery thus became the largest killer of the war: in the German army 58.3 percent of casualties were from artillery and 41.7 percent from small arms. Since all that artillery was firing indirectly from long range and could not be guided by the infantry about to attack, success depended on careful preplanning and timing. The artillery would cease at a predetermined time, and the infantry immediately attacked, in the so-called race for the parapets, attempting to cross no man's land before the enemy defenders could emerge from their dugouts and set up their machine guns. Barbed wire, shell holes, mud, and the burden of their equipment slowed the attackers, and they often lost the race. In response artillerymen devised techniques of "walking the

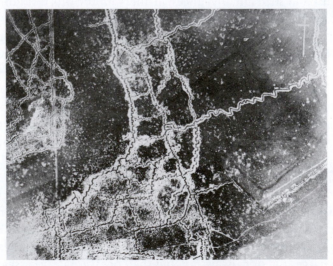

Figure 11.6 Aerial photo of British (left) and German (right) trenches, July 22, 1917. Trenches between Loos and Hulluck, separated by "no man's land."

fire," continuing the bombardment directly in front of their attacking troops, lifting and moving the fire farther and farther on predetermined schedules. In response, defenders deepened their lines yet again, often only weakly holding the first lines of trenches and keeping reserves in trenches farther to the rear, alerted and deployed in response to long preliminary bombardments and prepared to counterattack. Even if successful, the exhausted attackers often had no means of communicating with their commanders to the rear, and were unable to call for reinforcements or even for artillery fire to defend their newly won position.[50]

Each new attempt to break the tactical stalemate by the attacker was met by fresh defensive innovations, all of which were rooted in the defensive firepower of men deployed in increasingly creative ways. The German army was entrenched on French and Belgian soil, putting the onus on the French and British to attack, but the Germans also participated in the quest to break the stalemate. They were the first, for example, to use poison gas on an offensive. This too failed to affect the deadlock. For their part, the British and French experimented with artillery fire control, and the British eventually introduced the first tanks, all in an effort to find a winning combination for restoring offensive warfare.

This is by no means a complete tactical narrative of the ground war, but we must acknowledge how the stalemate created by firepower affected much else beyond the trenches of the western front. As the combatants began to grasp the magnitude of the problem, they turned to mobilizing their populations for a long struggle. An anonymous British officer writing in a popular periodical in February 1915 warned his audience that the struggle was no longer one of armies, but one of nations and of national will: "This is a war of attrition," he wrote, "attrition in the trenches, in the home, in the markets, in the workshops, in the counting-houses and stock exchanges." It was to be a "trial of endurance" that demanded the mobilization of the home front to support the coming "months and months" of thinning down the enemy ranks.[51] A century's development of nationalistic ideology had created a population that was, if not always enthusiastic, at least willing to support such a war. Even huge victories seemed to produce little decision as yet more of the enemy populace could be recruited and sent to the front to replace their losses. Furthermore, the nations of Europe committed ever-increasing percentages of their national resources to the war. Weeks of preparatory bombardment required months of factory production of artillery shells. Expanded munitions production drew women into the work force to replace the millions of men now at the front. Colonial troops from Africa and India were shipped into the trenches of France. New alliances with distant allies were brokered (primarily in the Balkans, but eventually with the United States) seeking to tip the resource balance one way or another. The sense of grinding attrition was perhaps best captured by the German strategy in 1916, in which the German Chief of Staff Erich von Falkenhayn argued that decisive victory on the battlefield had become elusive, but that an attack launched at a key French city and sustained for weeks or months would force ever greater French commitment to defend it, eventually bleeding the French lifeless and leading to the moral collapse of their army. The French did defend against the German attack at Verdun for eleven months, with intense commitment, and both sides suffered enormously, but almost equally, and without decision.

The war on the western front ground on. Diversions and secondary theaters in Turkey, the Balkans, Africa, and beyond made little difference to the stalemate in the west. The Germans sought to starve Britain through submarine attacks on merchant shipping, including "unrestricted submarine warfare" against neutral shipping. Britain depended on imports for much of its food, and German planners believed that Britain could be starved into defeat. Attacks on American shipping, however, brought protests, and Germany temporarily backed down. Then in 1917, convinced that Britain was on the brink of collapse, and desperate to break the stalemate, Germany again began unrestricted submarine attacks, a decision that brought the United States into the war on the Allied side, with the promise of millions of men for the front and vastly increased industrial production.

The war on the eastern front differed, but produced its own frustrations. The surprising early German victory at Tannenberg in 1914 saved Germany from a Russian invasion, but did not knock Russia out of the war. On its heels against Germany, Russia found success against Austria-Hungary, which survived only through massive German reinforcement. This stalemate often lacked trenches but was no less real. The vast territory allowed a greater freedom of movement, but also demanded better logistical services to convert a battlefield victory into a territorially decisive campaign. More sophisticated German staff work and better-trained troops regularly defeated the Russian army. Finally the Russian state, riven by internal division and unable to sustain the lengthening war, collapsed in February 1917 into an assortment of competing political parties—eventually dominated by the Bolsheviks, who took power in October. The Russian army continued to fight for some months, but ever more weakly, until a German advance in March 1918 finally led the new Bolshevik government to sign a separate peace.

TIMELINE

1814	First establishment of Prussian general staff
1815	Final defeat of Napoleon;
1847	Minié ball invented; allows for "rifled muskets"
1848	"Needle gun" breech-loading rifle introduced to Prussian army
1860	Spencer repeating rifle invented in America
1861–65	American Civil War
1864–71	German Wars of Unification
1864	Battle of Königgrätz has historic high of some 450,000 combined troops in a single battle
1886	First smokeless powder rifle (French Lebel)
1889	Maxim machine gun purchased by British army
1892–93	French conquest of Dahomey
1896	Ethiopians defeat Italians in Battle of Adowa
1914–18	World War I

CONCLUSION

The Russian collapse allowed the Germans to shift their forces to the west in one last effort to break open the war before American forces began to flood into France. This chapter ends in 1917, on the cusp of those German offensives, because in them the Germans sought and found a new way to use infantry firepower to enable movement, not just to create stalemate. Simultaneously, the French and British also had matured new systems for offensive warfare, which they put into action after the German offensives failed that summer. These seeds of a new form of maneuver warfare depended partly on new tactical techniques, combined with an increasingly sophisticated synchronization of effort. The Allies' attacks also leaned on the arrival of yet another technology: the tank. That quest to solve the problem of men against fire and to restore maneuver and decision to the battlefield is our next story.

Further Reading

Black, Jeremy, ed. *War in the Modern World since 1815*. New York: Routledge, 2003.

Chickering, Roger, Dennis Showalter, and Hans Van de Ven, eds. *The Cambridge History of War*. Vol. 4, *War and the Modern World*. Cambridge, UK: Cambridge University Press, 2012.

Gat, Azar. *A History of Military Thought: From the Enlightenment to the Cold War*. Oxford: Oxford University Press, 2001.

Headrick, Daniel R. *The Tools of Empire: Technology and European Imperialism in the Nineteenth Century*. New York: Oxford University Press, 1981.

McNeill, William H. *The Pursuit of Power: Technology, Armed Force and Society since A.D. 1000*. Chicago: University of Chicago Press, 1982.

Neiberg, Michael S. *Fighting the Great War: A Global History*. Cambridge, MA: Harvard University Press, 2005.

Philpott, William. *War of Attrition: Fighting the First World War*. New York: Overlook, 2014.

Strachan, Hew. *European Armies and the Conduct of War*. London: Routledge, 1983.

Strachan, Hew. *The First World War*. New York: Penguin, 2003.

Vandervort, Bruce. *Wars of Imperial Conquest in Africa, 1830–1914*. Bloomington: Indiana University Press, 1998.

Wawro, Geoffrey. *The Austro-Prussian War: Austria's War with Prussia and Italy in 1866*. Cambridge, UK: Cambridge University Press, 1996.

Wawro, Geoffrey. *The Franco-Prussian War: The German Conquest of France in 1870–1871*. Cambridge, UK: Cambridge University Press, 2003.

Notes

1. Alexander Rose, *American Rifle: A Biography* (New York: Delta Trade, 2009), 14–16.
2. Rose, *American Rifle*, 69–98.
3. Joseph T. Glatthaar summarizes this old understanding in "Battlefield Tactics," in *Writing the Civil War: The Quest to Understand*, ed. James M. McPherson and William J. Cooper, Jr. (Columbia: University of South Carolina Press, 1998), 63–69.

4. Earl J. Hess, *The Rifle Musket in Civil War Combat: Reality and Myth* (Lawrence: University Press of Kansas, 2008); Paddy Griffith, *Forward into Battle: Fighting Tactics from Waterloo to the Near Future*, 2nd ed. (Novato, CA: Presidio, 1990).

5. Earl Hess, *Field Armies and Fortifications in the Civil War: The Eastern Campaign, 1861–1864* (Chapel Hill: University of North Carolina Press, 2005); Nicholas Murray, *The Rocky Road to the Great War: The Evolution of Trench Warfare to 1914* (Washington DC: Potomac, 2013), 242.

6. Geoffrey Wawro, *The Austro-Prussian War: Austria's War with Prussia and Italy in 1866.* (Cambridge, UK: Cambridge University Press, 1996), 18.

7. Hew Strachan, *European Armies and the Conduct of War* (London: Routledge, 1983), 34–35.

8. David G. Chandler, *The Campaigns of Napoleon* (New York: Macmillan, 1966), xxxvi.

9. Strachan, *European Armies*, 90–95; Lawrence Freedman, *Strategy: A History* (New York: Oxford University Press), 94 (quote).

10. Strachan, *European Armies*, 98–99.

11. Wawro, *Austro-Prussian War*, 11; Strachan, *European Armies*, 122–23.

12. Wawro, *Austro-Prussian War*, 5, 8.

13. Michael Howard, *The Franco-Prussian War* (New York: Routledge, 1988), 40, 78, 60.

14. The Dreyse needle gun from 1848; Mauser M.71 from 1871; internal magazine Mauser M.71/84 in 1884; then the smokeless powder, magazine-fed Gewehr M.88, followed by the famous Mauser 1898.

15. Often claimed to have been achieved by Eli Whitney in the late eighteenth century, true interchangeability actually came later, primarily through the efforts to produce breech-loading rifles in the Springfield, Massachusetts federal armory. Rose, *American Rifle*, 69–91, 102–7.

16. Rose, *American Rifle*, 122–31.

17. Howard, *Franco-Prussian War*, 36.

18. Strachan, *European Armies*, 117–19.

19. Wawro, *Austro-Prussian War*, 23.

20. Daniel R. Headrick, *The Tools of Empire: Technology and European Imperialism in the Nineteenth Century* (New York: Oxford University Press, 1981), 99; Rose, *American Rifle*, 231–37. The Lebel lacked the detachable magazine, but it was the first smokeless-powder small-caliber rifle, and it initiated this rapid period of imitation, in which the detachable box magazine became standard. The Lee-Metford of 1888 still used black powder; it was updated as the Lee-Enfield beginning in 1895. Different sources will give slightly different dates for each of these weapons, depending on whether they refer to date of invention, service adoption, or widespread use. The use of the year in the model number and identifier was not yet standard.

21. William H. McNeill, *The Pursuit of Power: Technology, Armed Force and Society Since A.D. 1000* (Chicago: University of Chicago Press, 1982), esp. 262–306; Rose, *American Rifle*.

22. Strachan, *European Armies*, 113–14.

23. Murray, *Rocky Road to the Great War*, esp. 225–27.

24. Strachan, *European Armies*, 115–17; Michael Howard, "Men against Fire: The Doctrine of the Offensive in 1914," in *Makers of Modern Strategy*, ed. Peter Paret (Princeton, NJ: Princeton University Press, 1986), 510–26 (quote p. 514); Murray, *Rocky Road to the Great War*, 211–218.

25. Antulio J. Echevarria II, *After Clausewitz: German Military Thinkers before the Great War* (Lawrence: University Press of Kansas, 2000), 218.

26. Eric Dorn Brose, *The Kaiser's Army: The Politics of Military Technology in Germany during the Machine Age, 1870–1918* (Oxford: Oxford University Press, 2001), 4.

27. Bruce Vandervort, *Wars of Imperial Conquest in Africa, 1830–1914* (Bloomington: Indiana University Press, 1998), 28–55; Douglas Porch, *Wars of Empire* (London: Cassell, 2006), 119–30; John Ellis, *The Social History of the Machine Gun* (Baltimore:

Johns Hopkins University Press, 1975), 79–107; Headrick, *Tools of Empire*, 115–24.

28. David Ross, "Dahomey," in *West African Resistance: The Military Response to Colonial Occupation*, ed. Michael Crowder (New York: Africana, 1971), 144–69; Robert B. Edgerton, *Warrior Women: The Amazons of Dahomey and the Nature of War* (Boulder, CO: Westview, 2000), 104–20; Stanley B. Alpern, *Amazons of Black Sparta: The Women Warriors of Dahomey* (New York: New York University Press, 1998), 191–207; Douglas Porch, *The French Foreign Legion* (New York: HarperCollins, 1991), 245–67.

29. Richard J. Reid, *Warfare in African History* (Cambridge, UK: Cambridge University Press, 2012), 148–52; Michelle Moyd, *Violent Intermediaries: African Soldiers, Conquest, and Everyday Colonialism in German East Africa* (Athens, OH: Ohio University Press, 2014); Vandervort, *Wars of Imperial Conquest*, 42–44; Anthony Clayton, *France, Soldiers and Africa* (London: Brassey's Defence Publishers, 1988), 78–79.

30. Ross, "Dahomey," passim, esp. 153–54.

31. Alpern, *Amazons*, 193–96.

32. Ross, "Dahomey," 158, 168n14; Porch, *French Foreign Legion*, 255; Alpern, *Amazons*, 63, 197.

33. Alpern, *Amazons*, 198–99.

34. Edgerton, *Warrior Women*, 105; Porch, *French Foreign Legion*, 257–58, 260, 262.

35. Trench detail from Alpern, *Amazons*, 202–3, 206.

36. Raymond Jonas, *The Battle of Adwa: African Victory in the Age of Empire* (Cambridge, MA: Belknap Press of Harvard University Press, 2011), 4, 34–42, 150.

37. Jonas, *Battle of Adwa*, 69–73, 90–91.

38. Jonas, *Battle of Adwa*, 102–5.

39. Jonas, *Battle of Adwa*, 139.

40. Porch, *Wars of Empire*, 121; Jonas, *Battle of Adwa*, 56, 52; Vandervort, *Wars of Imperial Conquest*, 160.

41. Jonas, *Battle of Adwa*, 122–29, 138–41.

42. Jonas, *Battle of Adwa*, 149, 200–201, 212–15, 233; Vandervort, *Wars of Imperial Conquest*, 163.

43. Bruce Vandervort, "War and Imperial Expansion," in *The Cambridge History of War*, vol. 4, *War and the Modern World*, ed. Roger Chickering, Dennis Showalter, and Hans Van de Ven (Cambridge, UK: Cambridge University Press, 2012), 78.

44. There are many histories of World War I. The following is primarily based on Hew Strachan, *The First World War* (New York: Penguin, 2003); Michael S. Neiberg, *Fighting the Great War: A Global History* (Cambridge, MA: Harvard University Press, 2005); William Philpott, *War of Attrition: Fighting the First World War* (New York: Overlook, 2014).

45. Christopher Clark, *The Sleepwalkers: How Europe Went to War in 1914* (New York: HarperCollins, 2013), 531–33 (quotes).

46. Quoted in Philpott, *War of Attrition*, 43.

47. David Lloyd George, *War Memoirs of David Lloyd George*, 2 vols. (London: Odhams, 1938), 1:359–60, 362 (quotes).

48. Frank Buchholz, Janet Robinson, and Joe Robinson, *The Great War Dawning: Germany and Its Army at the Start of World War I* (Vienna: Verlag Militaria, 2013), 141–42; John Ellis and Michael Cox, *The World War I Databook* (London: Aurum, 2001), 231–32, 239.

49. Philpott, *War of Attrition*, 143, 146; Sanders Marble, *British Artillery on the Western Front in the First World War: 'The infantry cannot do with a gun less'* (Burlington, VT: Ashgate, 2013), 43–53.

50. The details of trench systems differed by country and over time. See Tony Ashworth, *Trench Warfare, 1914–1918: The Live and Let Live System* (New York: Holmes & Meier, 1980), 4–7; Geoffrey Parker, ed., *Cambridge Illustrated History of Warfare* (Cambridge, UK: Cambridge University Press, 1995), 286, 279; Robert Weldon Whalen, *Bitter Wounds: German Victims of the Great War, 1914–1939* (Ithaca, NY: Cornell University Press, 1984), 42.

51. Philpott, *War of Attrition*, 96 (quote), 132, 136.

12

Wars of Maneuver

1918–2003

Doctrine • Avoiding Deadlock: Methodical Battle, Blitzkrieg, and Deep Battle •
The German Model? • The Arab-Israeli Wars • AirLand Battle

ALTHOUGH PROSECUTED on a huge scale, with seemingly intractable and highly destructive consequences, World War I remained the province of the old troika of infantry, artillery, and a now much diminished horse cavalry. Contrary to the usual image of thickheaded generals sending their troops forward blindly and without regard for casualties, the fighting on the western front from 1914 to 1917 saw nearly constant attempts to devise ways out of the firepower-induced deadlock. By the end of 1916 infantry tactics had shifted dramatically, but none of the adjustments brought decisive results. By 1918, however, the accumulation of changes combined with some key innovations seemed to promise an end to the long, bloody stalemate. Some of those innovations were technological and some were organizational. All of them were grist for the mill as the world's postwar armies tried to absorb the lessons and meaning of World War I. During the ensuing two decades assorted states reached different conclusions about the future of war, and they designed different approaches according to their interpretations and their resources. For the industrialized nations, it is probably fair to break down their strategies into three categories—categories that emerged during World War I and then persisted and morphed over the course of the century in response to technological changes and ensuing wars. In brief, those categories were to try to: (1) win through resources, patience, and carefully calibrated offensive combinations of infantry and artillery; (2) win through restoring speed and decisiveness to the battlefield–in short, through maneuver; or (3) win from the air. This chapter and the one following treat these categories separately in a somewhat artificial manner. This chapter deals with the first two categories, focusing on the quest for maneuver and operational decisiveness on the battlefield. That quest resulted most famously in the so-called German blitzkrieg of World War II, but also in various related forms in the Soviet, Israeli, and

American armies (among others) through 2003. Note that the innovation here is not "tanks," but the network of linked ideas closely associated with the availability of motorization and armoring of both transport and firepower to overcome the apparent limits of the traditional troika of foot- and wagon-borne infantry, artillery, and cavalry.

Chapter 13 will address the third category, namely, how some strategists repeatedly tried to imagine a new path to victory waged solely or primarily from the air. Techniques, technologies, and theories of air power changed, but they shared the hope for a less destructive, more decisive form of war, with the glaring exception of a nuclear form of war *so destructive* that it was best not to be waged at all. Both sets of developments emerged primarily in the industrialized West. Chapter 14 will therefore turn to how non-Western powers and peoples innovated in response.

DOCTRINE

Before turning to the specifics of maneuver, however, the twentieth century, and especially the years after World War I, can be seen as the period in which the modern form of "doctrine" came into being, with significant consequences for the future of warfare. Stretching back into the sixteenth century, European soldiers had produced and consumed a genre of military "manuals," essentially books written for profit and then sold to military men interested in ideas about how war was changing and anxious to keep up with the latest developments. Over the years some of these books, for example Humphrey Bland's 1727 *Treatise of Military Discipline*, would become semicanonical for a decade or two. In Bland's case, his manual established a more or less uniform set of instructions for the British army, detailing how units should build camps, conduct drills, and discipline their troops (see Figure 12.1).

The Prussians led the way in this field, issuing several standard drill books from the 1740s, while the French published army-wide standard regulations in 1753 and 1754. Part of the professionalization process in eighteenth-century European armies revolved around the production and consumption of these books, and they functioned as more or less official mechanisms of national standardization (see chapter 9). The nineteenth-century creation of general staffs on the Prussian model (see chapter 11) further contributed to this process of standardization and professionalization, crucially adding a nearly constant process of planning for the next presumed war. The old manuals had tended to focus on the responsibilities of relatively small units and the duties of their officers; they were essentially tactical and administrative. War planning, on the other hand, encompassed every movement of an entire national force, and even the alignment of state infrastructure (such as railroads), against a specific projected enemy. The earliest doctrinal publications tended to be merely officially sanctioned versions of the old manuals. They were first published in Prussia in 1870, and then in various editions by the

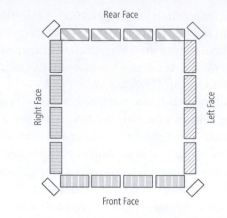

The Front of the Battalion

Figure 12.1 An illustration from Humphrey Bland's *Treatise of Military Discipline* (1746 edition), showing how to form a square (redrawn for clarity).

other Western powers over the following decades. Unlike war plans, doctrine is generic—it describes general circumstances and "standard" reactions. Military doctrine is intended to generate uniformity across an army, both in officers' understanding and interpretation of their environment and also in the creation of a shared language, contributing to clarity in the writing and reception of orders.

Today, doctrine continues to fulfill this function of providing guidance and a common template for employing the instruments of force, whatever those might be, but the many new technologies introduced during World War I and since have changed the relationship between doctrine and procurement. For example, a generic set of instructions for the employment of infantry as late as 1870 could easily be modified in response to changing conditions without requiring a vast new program of weapons production. The rapidly shifting capabilities of aircraft and motorization, however, meant that peacetime militaries began constantly adjusting their calculations of how they would fight the next war. Doctrinal writing became essentially an *imaginative exercise.* Planners now asked questions such as "Given the capabilities of a particular vehicle, how many should a unit have?" Or, turning that question on its head, "Given what I would like to see happen on the battlefield, what vehicle capabilities do I want, or can I reasonably expect to have, within the next five years?" These were not simple problems, and they were aggravated by the long lead times involved in developing new arms and equipment, but institutional militaries felt (and still feel) compelled to solve them. Their solutions then had major ramifications for what kinds of equipment were produced. That equipment, in turn, represented a difficult-to-ignore capital investment. In other words, existing equipment acted as an anchor on doctrinal development even while published doctrine shaped and validated the design of future equipment. This interaction of doctrine and technological development underlies much of the rest of this chapter and the next.[1]

Before turning to specifics, however, we must review three key terms that underpin almost all modern doctrine: tactics, operations, and strategy. Unfortunately, there are almost as many definitions as there are people trying to define them, and most readers (and authors) think they intuitively know the difference. But we should at least attempt some clarification, because much of twentieth-century doctrinal development is embedded in the differences between these three levels of war. In essence, as already hinted in the discussion of eighteenth-century manuals, "tactics" involves the actions and movements of troops within the range of the enemy's weapons, which, for most of the history of war, also meant within their range of vision. Although this definition is complicated by the development of long-range weapons, tactics in World War I basically revolved around the problem of crossing no man's land: how to integrate artillery fires with infantry movement; how to get from a friendly trench to an enemy one; and, once there, where to place weapons to defend against counterattack. "Operations" (or campaigns) are regional movements of troops, usually conducted while not under fire or observation, and designed to produce a tactical advantage in the resulting battle. Crucially, the term also refers to movements intended to convert tactical success into large-scale results that correspond to the strategic goal of the fighting. "Strategy" refers to the deployment of resources and forces on a national scale and the identification of key objectives (territorial or otherwise) that operations are then designed to achieve. The emergence of the modern concept of doctrine in part reflected the growing need to standardize the army's actions at the operational level of war. Armies were now much larger both spatially and in terms of personnel, and they operated in separate large formations, necessitating a standard set of practices and expectations (as discussed in chapters 9 and 11). Eighteenth-century manuals were almost exclusively tactical—they standardized how officers commanded troops in the face of the enemy. Modern doctrine, although it also continues to address tactical issues, at least attempts to define shared best practices at the operational level (if not always at the strategic level).

AVOIDING DEADLOCK: METHODICAL BATTLE, BLITZKRIEG, AND DEEP BATTLE

As discussed in chapter 11, in the face of modern, entrenched firepower, offensive tactical success—taking enemy trenches—was difficult, but not rare. The defender, however, retained the operational freedom to reinforce the area under attack. The attacker was exhausted and lacked the ability to bring in reinforcements to exploit their initial success. The result was a strategy of attrition until one side could no longer muster reinforcements at all. In many ways, this seeming inability to convert tactical success into operational results in World War I defined doctrinal debate for the next seventy years. Doctrinal development after the war was more than a problem of calculation, however; it was also a cultural phenomenon reflecting a generation battered and exhausted by war. Though likely apocryphal, the story of a German staff officer at the conclusion of the Versailles treaty negotiations saying to his French counterpart "We'll see you in twenty years" reflected a real fear that war would come again all too soon. For much of the European public that fear was intolerable, and their anxieties found expression in such things as the League of Nations; the Washington Naval Treaty of 1922; the Kellogg-Briand pact of 1928, in which some fifty-four nations renounced the use of aggressive war; and a substantial outpouring of cultural denunciations of war and arms manufacturers. The antipathy to war was at least partly shared in Germany initially but soon was replaced there by a desire to overturn the verdict of 1918, which had held Germany responsible for the First World War. Regardless, no one wanted another lethal deadlock. This cultural pressure interacted with institutional militaries' calculations about the future of war and was greatly shaped by each government's sense of its financial and industrial capacity to produce new doctrines and new equipment. Within the confines of this chapter we can consider the choices of only a few nations. The contrasting but interrelated doctrines of France, Germany, and the Soviet Union reveal a great deal about the different possibilities available within what was basically an identical technological capacity—all three powers possessed basically the same level of technological knowledge, even if their productive capacity differed and changed over time.

Interwar France and Methodical Battle

In France the problem of balancing the competing pressures of culture, calculation, and capacity proved particularly acute. As exhausted as it was, France was nevertheless one of the victors of World War I. The final "Hundred Days" campaign of late summer and fall 1918 had rolled back the German armies and seemingly validated the most matured form of French and British combined-arms methods. Their evolved tactics now relied on carefully controlled but less predictable artillery preparation, followed by equally carefully orchestrated infantry advances coordinated with continuing and shifting artillery fire, supported by a new and growing array of tanks and aircraft. The new tactics were undeniably effective, but they were predicated on centralized control, broad frontal advances, and progressively destroying the defender's armed forces while simultaneously outproducing the enemy in artillery shells, tanks, and aircraft. France's ultimate victory had a variety of implications for how it approached the problem of the next war.

Figure 12.2 French Renault FT-17 tank, World War I.

One implication was simply material. At the end of World War I France found itself in possession of nearly 3,500 FT-17 tanks (see Figure 12.2). By almost any standard that tank was obsolete by the end of 1918. It weighed a mere 6.5 tons, was operated by a two-man crew, could travel at only 4.8 mph over a maximum 25–30 mile range, and was usually armed with a 7.92 mm machine gun—a weapon not much different from those used by the infantry in the trenches. Despite their obsolescence, those thousands of tanks repre-sented a material limitation: the French could not afford to just dump them, and in fact they remained the most common model in the French army into the 1930s. Stating this fact is not to repeat the old myth that the French army in 1940 was saddled with fewer and inferior tanks to the Germans. It instead suggests the role that this existing stock played in shaping the French *under-standing* of armored capability. For many French military planners, the FT-17 dominated the imagination of what tanks could do, and therefore of what their role in combat should be.

Despite that imaginative hurdle, there were officers in the French army who pushed discussion about the potential of new models and the different combinations of characteristics those new models should possess. Various commissions during the 1920s and 1930s were set up to investigate the technological and doctrinal possibilities of tanks. The other effect of the success of tanks in World War I, however, was French faith in the methods they believed had won the war in 1918, a doctrine that the French came to call "methodical battle." In essence it expected that artillery would destroy enemy defenses, which infantry would then occupy. In the absence of widely available wireless communication with which to communicate to the artillery batteries, this process required centrally controlled, preplanned, and carefully coordinated artillery shelling in conjunction with infantry movements. Within that scheme of thinking tanks functioned as *aids* to infantry movement. They would accompany the infantry forces, at the rate of walking infantrymen, and ease the occupation of already blasted enemy defenses. The underlying assumptions behind this doctrine were that the massive mobilization of relatively untrained conscripts required centralized control and oversight; the war would be both long and dominated by the defensive; and France would eventually win through superior industrial mobilization that would produce the wealth of material required for methodical battle.[2]

To be clear, this vision *included* tanks, and indeed allotted them a key role, but internal debates created an environment in which tanks were produced without coordination with doctrine. French tank advocates continued to champion the deployment of tanks in independent operations. Indeed, somewhat ironically, institutional fractures within the army allowed for development of so-called breakthrough tanks, but the infantry's dominance over doctrine found no place for those vehicles' capabilities. Dominated by the mental model of the FT-17 and its ilk, the French infantry wanted lots of tanks, and they insisted on light ones. Their understanding of infantry movements from 1918 suggested that getting conscripts to move forward without tanks would be difficult. Since the doctrine envisaged broad linear advances, they demanded tanks spread all along the line to stiffen the infantrymen's morale. The demand for numbers meant that the tanks needed to be produced cheaply. Cheapness demanded they be relatively light (armor was expensive, as was a heavier engine for a heavier vehicle), and their presumed role of accompanying walking infantry downplayed the value of speed.

One result was the Renault R35, produced in various experimental models, in full production by 1936, and eventually becoming the most common tank in French service by 1940. Interestingly, the R35 was comparatively both light *and* slow: at 10.6 tons it traveled at 12.5 mph, with a range of 81 miles, and it was generally armed with a 37 mm gun. Contrast the British Cruiser MkII (A10), designed in 1934, weighing 14.3 tons and capable of 16 mph, or the Soviet BT-5, designed in 1933, at 11.5 tons but capable of speeds up to 45 mph and with a 45 mm gun. Furthermore, given the projected role for tanks in "methodical battle," French models were not designed for flexible command structures. Many lacked wireless radios, and those with them were designed to communicate up the command hierarchy, responding to the centralized control envisioned in the doctrine, not with each other or with their accompanying infantry.[3]

The French army did not lack advocates for tanks in a different role. Most famously Charles de Gaulle pressed for a motorized and armored force in his *Vers l'armée de métier* (toward a professional army; translated into English as *The Army of the Future*) in 1934 and in other writings produced in response to the German invasion of Poland in 1939. His and others' advocacy had some impact, producing the Char B1 tank, with more armor and heavier guns (it had two), as well as independent armored units. The army as a whole, however, still lacked a vision of how to employ such units, and they therefore proved incapable of influencing events once the German offensive of 1940 gained momentum.

German Shock Troops of World War I and the "Blitzkrieg" of World War II

Meanwhile Germany shared the same basic cultural and military problem—the fear of deadlock—but confronted a very different set of postwar circumstances. It wanted to overturn the Treaty of Versailles and reclaim territories lost in the war—a goal requiring offensive warfare—and it lacked the burden of an existing inventory. The treaty had limited the German army to one hundred thousand men, and had deprived it of tanks, aircraft, and heavy artillery.

A crucial element in Germany's postwar doctrinal development was the perception that the infiltration tactics adopted for the spring offensive of 1918 suggested a way to avoid the feared deadlock. The word they used was not "blitzkrieg," a term invented later and by others, but *Bewegungskrieg* or "war of movement." That term suggested their goal. One source of the deadlock in World War I was the lack of connection between the role of "concentration" at the operational level and at the tactical level. For example, generals examining a large-scale map could identify salients, or bulges in the enemy lines, and propose an operational concentration of forces to attack the "shoulders" of such salients. In their minds, by doing so they were in fact *massing* force at a key *point*. Tactically, however, at the point of the attack, literally at the tip of the arrow drawn on the map, the movement forward was still conducted as a mass attack by relatively undifferentiated infantry moving evenly across a wide front. Even when successful, after their assault those forces had lost their initial local advantage of mass, and they lacked the ability to continue deeper into the enemy lines until friendly reinforcements arrived and their artillery had been repositioned to support the next attack. Put in other terms, there was prebattle operational maneuver to position forces for the battle, but there was as yet no capability to resume operational maneuver if tactical success was achieved.[4]

It was at the tactical level that the Germans made significant changes in preparation for their offensives in the spring of 1918. These changes came from several directions, consisting of different component parts suggested by individuals and by the soldiers themselves, until they achieved coherence enough to be acknowledged as a single, superior method to be encouraged by the higher command and to form the core of the 1918 offensive. One source of change was the deliberate reorganization of German defensive tactics on the western front beginning in late 1916. The new system emphasized smaller units operating more independently in forward strongpoints, designed to allow an allied offensive to exhaust itself before reaching the main defense lines, followed by aggressive counterattacks by reserve troops held far enough away to avoid the preliminary artillery bombardment. This tactical shift emerged from suggestions provided from junior officers on the front, collated and analyzed by two German staff officers, who then received firm backing from the high command. Every aspect of this new defensive system—organization, tactics, and equipment—emphasized local initiative and decision-making, as well as fragmented, nonlinear movement centered on key weapons.

Simultaneously, old notions of elite *Sturm-bataillons* had supported the existence of separate specially trained units tasked with specific attack missions. One of those, commanded by Captain Willy Rohr, achieved local fame in the German Fifth Army, which directed him in late 1915 and early 1916 to begin training other units in his techniques. In August 1916 Rohr's techniques and his training efforts received official approval from the new chief of the German General Staff, Paul von Hindenburg, and his deputy, First Quartermaster General Erich Ludendorff.

The German army remained on the strategic defensive through the allied offensives in the spring of 1917. By late summer, however, their defensive tactics combined with the now spreading availability of troops trained in Rohr's *Stoßtrupp*, or shock troop, tactics, led to significant successes at Riga in Russia in September 1917 and in the Caporetto offensives in Italy in October to November of 1917. To be sure, both the Italians and the Russians were exhausted opponents, but these stunning successes suggested the potential of the new tactics to provide the kind of breakthrough capability that had been missing through much of World War I.

Shock troop tactics depended on infiltration and independent command at the local level. *Stoßtrupp* assault units advanced as small independent units, organized around key heavy weapons, especially a lighter machine gun, but also including recently introduced flamethrowers and their own light mortars. Moving in squad-sized groups or columns, avoiding conventional linear formations, the units bypassed enemy strong points and used local terrain to move deeply into and *through* enemy positions. Furthermore, the local attacking commander retained the authority to control his continued forward movement, and he assumed control over follow-on forces moving into his area, even if he was outranked. This local flexibility contrasted with the centralized Allied command system, which rapidly collapsed as the infiltrating Germans cut off units from their headquarters. There were other tactical components to the German 1918 offensives, some shared with the Allies, including careful infantry-artillery coordination and changes to the usual process of preliminary bombardment emphasizing greater precision and responsiveness. But what was unique here was a vision of operational success based on decentralized command and control (*Auftragstaktik*, or "mission tactics") in which commanders defined the mission but allowed their subordinates the autonomy to determine the precise methods, and that entailed initial surprise, deeply penetrating columns massed on narrow fronts, and the disruption of enemy rear-area communications.[5]

These tactics were the centerpiece of German plans for a massive offensive toward Paris in the spring of 1918. The Germans needed to move swiftly, before the Americans arrived in large numbers. Fortunately for Germany, it reached an armistice with the Russian revolutionary government in December 1917, confirmed by the Treaty of Brest-Litovsk on March 3, 1918, which allowed it to move troops from the eastern front to the western. This would be Germany's last blow against the Allies, and it was a heavy one. The offensive kicked off on March 21, 1918, and within a few weeks it threatened Paris to an extent not seen since August 1914. The confusion created by German infiltration led some Allied commanders to order unnecessary retreats. Several British commanding officers ordered retreats as they lost contact with units, who were in fact still successfully defending their bypassed positions. Parts of the British lines fell back thirty-eight kilometers in four days (see Map 12.1).

Foreshadowing problems with German doctrine in World War II, however, the offensive lacked strategic vision. General Ludendorff had announced that his only intention was to "punch a hole into [the allied line]. For the rest, we shall see."[6] Historians since have pointed out that the German innovations were almost entirely tactical and lacked vision at the operational-level, which could have converted tactical success into strategic results. Partly as a result, the offensive soon lost its momentum and petered out, largely due to the inherent limitations of infantry carrying their own supplies across a blasted landscape, as well as the exhaustion of the German army more generally. Gains were soon rolled back by swelling Allied numbers, improved tactics, and the Allies' increasing dominance in tanks and aircraft in the summer and fall of 1918. Despite the strategic failure of the offensive, the specific tactics suggested a path for future developments. Of particular importance to German doctrinal adaptation after the war was the role of infiltration and independent operational maneuver after a tactical breakthrough.[7]

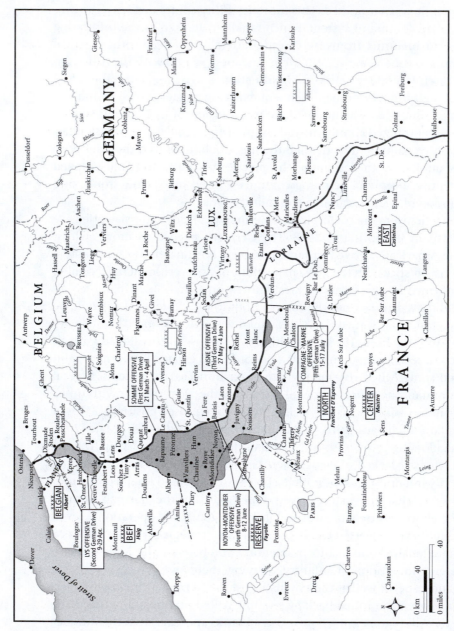

Map 12.1 German offensives on the Western Front, spring 1918.

After World War I, the limitations imposed by the Treaty of Versailles provided an ironic advantage to the Germans, who were not burdened by surviving stocks of equipment. Perhaps even more important, the much reduced German military actively encouraged a culture of studying what had happened in World War I. There was, after all, no substantial army to train or maintain. In addition to their own 1918 tactical innovations, German thinking was influenced by the works of British military writers J. F. C. Fuller and B. H. Liddell Hart, whose early works on the potential of tank warfare were read widely around the world. (We should observe that some early writings in the 1910s and 1920s postulated a future of purely tank armies; that idea, although initially influential, was quickly discarded or ignored by the armies considered in detail here in favor of some form of combined arms.) The Germans also experimented cheaply, using mock-up vehicles, or even secretly relying on Soviet facilities and equipment. Admittedly, this was an "advantage" perceived only in hindsight. Moreover, not everyone in the German military agreed on the exact implications of their experiments, and German industrial infrastructure raced futilely to match what the military wanted in 1939 and 1940. Nevertheless, German offensive doctrine, unit organization, and training proved more flexible and successful than that of their initial opponents, and this seems in retrospect to have provided a model that echoed through the rest of the century.[8]

The fundamental limitation on the infiltration tactics of 1918 had been the inability of infantry to move quickly enough once a breakthrough had been achieved. Worse, supplies and reinforcements moving by foot or wagon could neither catch up to nor keep up with the leading elements. The clear technological answer after the war lay in motorization and mechanization—not just tanks but armored transport and/or trucks for the supporting artillery, infantry, and more. Furthermore, given the limits of industrial production (capacity), the Germans determined to concentrate such assets in specific units rather than distributing them throughout the army. Thus were born panzer (tank) divisions, then corps, then even panzer armies. Since the basic concept was to strike hard at narrow points, combining tactical air support with the traditional artillery bombardment and then penetrating deeply, it made sense to concentrate firepower and mobility in those leading assault troops who could both overwhelm and/or bypass initial resistance, move rapidly into the enemy rear areas, disrupt enemy command and control, carry their own sustaining resources, and then isolate those bypassed enemy units, leaving them to confront the more slowly advancing German infantry.

In essence, however, this solution remained a *tactical* one that only loosely defined operational goals. It proposed methods for breaking through an enemy defensive line. The same elements that made the breakthrough would then maneuver at an operational level in what was essentially improvisational pursuit, now rendered more effective by the organizational concentration of mechanized forces. A separate and older German strategic culture of

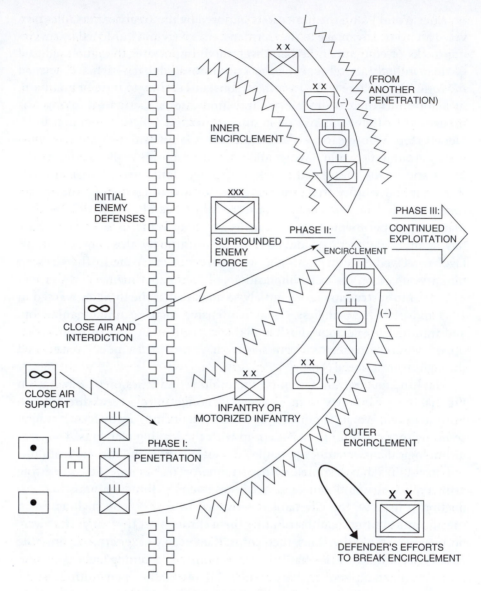

Figure 12.3 A "Kesselschlacht." In this representation a Panzer division leads each attacking column, followed by an infantry division providing security from enemy attack against the flanks of the penetration. Ideally the follow-on infantry would also be motorized as part of a Panzer corps.

pursuing encirclement more or less naturally suggested itself as the goal for those penetrating columns. In its ideal formulation, two widely separated penetrating columns would meet and enclose large chunks of enemy forces, creating a *Kesselschlacht*—a "cauldron battle" (see Figure 12.3).[9]

As some critics have pointed out, this so-called blitzkrieg was not a full-fledged *operational* doctrine. Michael Geyer goes so far as to call it "the opposite of a doctrine. Blitzkrieg operations consisted of an avalanche of actions that were sorted out less by design than by success." This may take things too far. It *was* a tactical doctrine for breakthrough, if not for operational maneuver, and it was employed by an army that encouraged improvisation and aggressive maneuver, and that had a long tradition of seeking climactic battles of encirclement. Furthermore, successful penetration had the result, intended or not, of disrupting enemy command, control, and logistics—which is an operational result, not merely a tactical one, nor simply attrition of enemy forces. That disruption further exaggerated the benefits of German reliance on improvisation; the more the Allies' ability to respond was undermined, the more German improvisation could take advantage. Ultimately, command paralysis set in. A later generation of doctrinal writers would call this "getting inside the enemy's decision cycle" (see below, and also chapter 13). Thus calculated doctrine and strategic culture combined in the German army to create a pattern of behavior that looked more carefully planned than it really was.[10]

Germany's late 1930s rush to crank up its armaments production generated tanks that were in many ways ill-suited to the tactical ideal of fire and movement that was central to the emerging German doctrine. The Panzerkampfwagen (PZKW) Mark I had only a machine gun. The PZKW Mark II did have a 20 mm cannon, but very thin armor. During the 1940 invasion of France, these remained the two most common German tanks, but they were concentrated in the panzer divisions. Crucially, they were equipped with wireless radio capability, suiting them to the decentralized execution and flexibility demanded by German doctrine. In contrast, French tanks often had radios only for the command tanks and relied on hand signals or flags to maneuver small units.

In 1940 the Allies necessarily adopted a linear defense spread along the entire French-German and French-Belgian frontier, relying on the famous Maginot Line fortifications on the French-German border to free up reserves for a mobile defense against the expected German attack through northern and central Belgium. The Germans attacked all along the Belgian and Netherlands frontier, but sent a high percentage of their armored forces into the geographically rougher but more weakly defended Ardennes forest in southern Belgium (see Map 12.2). Roughly twenty-eight German tank battalions concentrated in seven divisions attacked along a seventy-kilometer front, while the French distributed their thirty-six tank battalions more or less evenly along the entire frontier in support of infantry armies. As the attack penetrated into Allied rear areas, the French and British command structure quickly dissolved in chaos. An effective, coordinated defense became impossible. Britain's forces in France retreated to the coast and evacuated from Dunkirk; German forces then turned south toward Paris and France capitulated within six weeks of the initial invasion.

In essence, both France and Germany gambled on the nature of war in an uncertain future. Technological capability was literally changing as they

Map 12.2 German invasion of Belgium, the Netherlands, and France, spring 1940. This map shows only the initial invasion from May 10 to June 4. German armies then turned south and captured Paris on June 14.

wrote about it, but the Germans gambled with a system that encouraged low-level improvisation, so they reacted more quickly and more appropriately in actual wartime conditions. German planning sought to disrupt the enemy through penetration and exploitation, in the belief that, once disrupted, the enemy force was relatively easily annihilated. With the enemy's armed forces destroyed, in accord with Clausewitz's theories, the state would be forced to capitulate. It was a far from perfect system, and German doctrine had a tendency to overvalue tactics, rely on operational improvisation, and undervalue logistics. The German veterans of victories in Poland, Norway, France, and Yugoslavia, however, would take that system into Russia and there repeat, at least initially, their astonishing success—a success partly explainable by what had happened within the Soviet army.[11]

Soviet Deep Battle

One of the many ironies of the German invasion of the Soviet Union was that German thinking about maneuver warfare was a less sophisticated version of Soviet "deep battle" doctrine, created during the previous generation. Similar technological capabilities, similar firepower-based challenges, and even some shared training experiences produced similar basic understandings of the role of armored and combined-arms penetration and exploitation, but Soviet deep battle was operationally more complex and more ambitious. Unfortunately for the Soviet army, Joseph Stalin had sacrificed that advantage on the altar of internal politics and his own paranoia.

Deep-battle doctrine reflected both the politics and the geography of Russia and the creation of the Soviet Union. Politically speaking, much as defeat in World War I had left Germany with a postwar clean slate in terms of material investments, political revolution in Russia had eliminated the traditionalist elements of the tsarist army. Again, this was an "advantage" that took some time to realize—untrained and inexperienced political appointees in the Red Army fell into a number of disasters during the Russian Civil War (1917–1922). Ultimately, however, the Bolsheviks prevailed and began to rebuild the army, with the explicit intent to make it an army of the proletariat and to export the revolution. Revolution had provided an open intellectual arena, as well as an offensive orientation designed to take the revolution on the road. Geography and history, however, also shaped the nature of the doctrine that emerged.

Much of the territory of the Russian Empire—by 1922 the Soviet Union—sprawled across the central Eurasian steppe, stretching into Mongolia and beyond to the Pacific Ocean. This vast expanse of territory had been conquered through a centuries-long conflict with nomadic steppe peoples, marked in particular by the Mongol conquest and domination of the Russian principalities in the thirteenth century. Eventually, Muscovy emerged from Mongol rule as the dominant regional power, progressively folding other Russian principalities into its empire, even more slowly expanding against settled European enemies to the west, and against the potent, but usually divided, nomadic horse archers of the steppe to the east. In the process the early modern Russian military became a kind of house divided: some forces were designed and organized around developing Western technology and techniques, and others were designed to cope with the mobility and logistical challenges associated with the steppe.[12]

This division did not always make for an army respected by its Western neighbors. For some Russian officers, however, the experience of steppe fighting, and the nomads' long tradition of vast, self-sustained, sweeping movements designed to encircle and harass slower-moving sedentary armies, opened their minds to the possibility of combining this ancient steppe system with the newly available technology of motorization and mechanization. Lieutenant General Mikhail I. Ivanin turned his long experience on the steppe into a study of the nomadic way of war, first published in 1846 and revised in 1875, after which it circulated widely as a textbook at the Russian General Staff Academy (officially the Nicholas General Staff Academy). Arguably, in that role it influenced key figures who would lead the early Soviet army, especially Marshal Mikhail Tukhachevsky. It is difficult to prove any direct linkages between this long experience on the steppe and specific doctrinal developments in the 1920s and 1930s, but as historian Bruce Menning has suggested, "Over . . . three centuries the idea of using mobility and mass to hit deeply and decisively has remained a surprising constant in Russian military thought—if not always in practice." Menning specifically documents a long history from the eighteenth century of Russian armies using large independent forces of cavalry to strike deep in the enemy's rear and sow confusion.[13]

In addition to this steppe-fighting background, the Soviets in the 1920s, like the Germans, were clearly influenced by early British writing about tank warfare (who were also explicitly influenced by the Mongol example, using a somewhat inaccurate history). The Soviet version quickly took its own direction, however, emphasizing true strategic depth as well as a commitment to armor and infantry as a combined-arms effort—after all, the revolutionary experience mandated the proletariat's central role in the army. Tukhachevsky and his circle of officers in the 1920s and early 1930s developed a cutting-edge combination of infantry, mechanized infantry, artillery, cavalry, and aviation forces designed first to create the necessary breakthrough in a mass-oriented, centrally controlled manner much like that practiced by the Western allies in 1918, but then followed by a deep penetration with as yet uncommitted "mobile groups" designed to create havoc in the enemy rear area.

In the simplest comparative terms, in the German *Bewegungskrieg*, armored formations with supporting mechanized infantry led the attack, both creating the breakthrough and then conducting the penetration and exploitation, followed by separate formations of foot infantry that cleaned up the surrounded enemy still in the "kettle." Soviet deep battle led with conventional infantry attacks, supported by infantry support tanks and massive artillery fires on a narrow front, usually launched after a successful deception to create surprise. Once the breakthrough was achieved, a second echelon of fresh troops, typically armored and mechanized, penetrated and exploited to a much greater depth—less concerned with creating a kettle than with maneuvering throughout the enemy's depth, disrupting their control and supply systems.[14]

In its details, the Soviet writers seemed to combine a close study of World War I, especially the German infiltration tactics of 1918, with revolutionary politics and their own experience of steppe warfare. One Soviet army writer, Georgii S. Isserson, writing in 1932, explained that the difficulties of World War I "turned on the enormous defensive strength of a positional front, the absence of political stimuli in soldiers for overcoming this, superiority of defensive over offensive means, the necessity for concentrating enormous means of suppression, complexity in organizing and conducting offensive actions, etc.; that is, in a military-technical sense they were localized completely in the realm of *tactics*." He then critiqued the German offensives of March 1918, arguing they were sent "not in the direction which promised an operational result, but in the direction where the front could be, tactically speaking, more easily crushed." In other words, the German *Stoßtrupp* attacks were designed to achieve attrition, not operational maneuver. Laying out a program for Soviet reforms, he argued that they must conduct "a deep offensive which breaks through and fractures the combat front to its entire operational depth, and, finally, [delivers] swift, annihilating blows for the purpose of decisively and completely routing the enemy. Under these conditions, the mission of our operational art is *to substantiate and form a theory of a deep annihilating operation*."[15]

What Isserson, Tukhachevsky, and other Soviet writers produced they called "deep battle" or "deep operation" (*glubokaya operatsiya*). Arguably, this doctrine was formulated and in place prior to the full articulation of the German version, and there is a good chance that Soviet thinking reached the Germans during their military cooperation in the 1930s. Another vector was M. J. Kurtzinski's 1935 German-language presentation of Soviet writers, published in Germany as *Taktik schneller Verbände: Russische Ansichten über die Verwendung motorisierter und mechanisierter Einheiten* (tactics of rapid formations: Russian views on the use of motorized and mechanized units). In 1937 Heinz Guderian, a leading proponent of armored warfare in Germany, quoted a Soviet writer, via Kurtzinski's translation, arguing that "a decisive success is attainable only through the simultaneous destruction of the main enemy deployment to its entire depth, in both tactical and operational dimensions. This demands the action of strong, fast-moving forces which possess great striking power and mobility."[16]

As with other contemporary powers, Soviet doctrine often exceeded the state's industrial capacity to uniformly equip their army as desired. The Soviets nevertheless were on a path to creating a formidable army based on the firepower and mobility of large, independent motorized and armored forces, imbued with a doctrine of aggressiveness, exploitation, and attack designed to penetrate the full depth of an enemy defense—not dozens of kilometers but hundreds. Furthermore, the early development of deep battle doctrine—by some measures it was a firm concept as early as 1928—allowed for the production of materiel and the creation of an army organization designed to support it. Doctrine helped drive weapon design and production.[17]

Such a doctrine also required extensive training and a deep and wide communications network. Massive formations of vehicles needed to communicate with each other and with higher headquarters; maneuvering them required experience and training. Here politics intervened. In the summer of 1937, in the last of a series of purges of real and imagined political opponents, Stalin moved against the army leadership. The government imprisoned or executed some 40 percent of the officer corps, including Tukhachevsky and his supporters. Discredited by association, his work on deep battle faded, at least until the Germans seemed to prove the validity of the concept in 1939 and 1940. By then it was too late to rebuild what had been dismantled in time to resist the German invasion in the summer of 1941.

Fortunately, many of Tukhachevsky's ideas, and even his organizational innovations, survived in the Soviet army stationed in Siberia under General Georgy Zhukov. He demonstrated the efficacy of Soviet training in deep battle against the Japanese at Khalkhin Gol in August 1939. Massing 469 light tanks, 426 other armored vehicles, 679 guns and mortars, and over five hundred aircraft, all supplied in the middle of a vast barren wilderness by thousands of trucks, he deceived and then encircled the Japanese army, entirely destroying it. Although not reliant on the breakthrough imagined in deep battle, the armored concentration, sweeping operational movement, and logistical support over long distances were all hallmarks of Tukhachevsky's training programs.[18]

This was not, however, the Soviet army that faced the German onslaught in 1941. Zhukov's army in Siberia had been isolated from the purges by distance. The main army in the west was simultaneously undermined by the purges, in the throes of reorganization, and unnecessarily surprised by the German attack. In those circumstances the German *Bewegungskrieg*, despite its vastly underdeveloped logistical infrastructure and the continued shortage of both tanks and motorized infantry, ran rampant through the Red Army. The Germans repeatedly encircled and captured vast numbers of Soviet defenders. Multiple *Kesselschlachts* captured 250,000 soldiers west of Minsk, 500,000 at Kiev, 650,000 at Bryansk and Vyazma, and so on. Finally, in December the advance ground to a halt practically within sight of Moscow as the temperature plummeted, extraordinary Soviet efforts produced streams of weapons from factories relocated east of the Urals, and Zhukov's Siberian divisions arrived on the scene (see Map 12.3).

German power was hardly exhausted. They launched new offensives in the summer of 1942 and again in 1943, but the Soviets had been given time to recover. American and British aid began to arrive via the Lend-Lease program, providing hundreds of thousands of trucks to buttress the already well-developed Soviet logistical systems. Not unlike the progress of German tactical development from 1916 to 1918, the Soviets first revamped their defensive tactics to emphasize independent strongpoints and local counterattacks rather

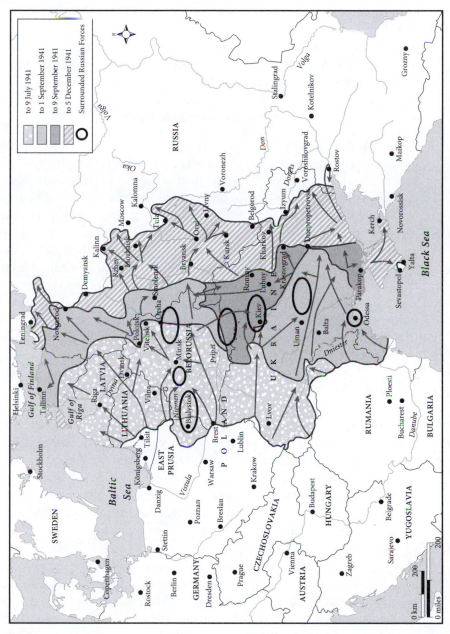

Map 12.3 German invasion of the Soviet Union, through December 1941. Note multiple kesselschlacht-style encirclements.

Legend:
- to 9 July 1941
- to 1 September 1941
- to 9 September 1941
- to 5 December 1941
- Surrounded Russian Forces

than linear defenses and then relearned, partly through Zhukov—now a rising star in the army—Tukhachevsky's deep-battle doctrine. In the course of fighting, the Soviet Army also actively refined the doctrine, moving from a two-echelon attack to three (see Figure 12.4). The first two echelons would create the breakthrough *and* establish a clear corridor for the third mobile echelon to launch through. By the end of the war, the Soviet army was conducting highly sophisticated operational maneuvers on a huge scale, based on the multiple echelon attack. After the failed German attack at Kursk in July 1943, the Soviets went on the offensive and never let up.[19]

THE GERMAN MODEL?

In the first decades after World War II the idea that it was the Germans who had mastered maneuver warfare and who had been overwhelmed only by the vast material resources of the Allies (including the Soviets' endless population and considerable industrial production) became enshrined as an article of faith among historians and Western military planners. Soviet doctrinal sophistication seemed improbable in light of their massive initial defeats, and German generals' memoirs were careful to blame their failures on the irrationality of Hitler and the impossibility of withstanding Allied industrial capacity and the supposedly mindless frontal assaults of the Soviets.

That view contains multiple truths, but almost as many falsehoods. Allied industrial production unquestionably played an important role in the defeat of Germany. German forces surely were tactically proficient, and their leaders were often masters of improvisational operational maneuver. It was equally true, however, that both the Soviets and the Western powers gained substantial expertise at *Bewegungskrieg*, and, partly because of industrial capacity, they proved more adept than the Germans at managing the necessary logistics. Although specific institutional histories can explain these different national approaches to logistics, it is also valid simply to say that the long Russian and then Soviet experience of warfare in the vast steppe frontier gave them a great appreciation for managing supplies, while the necessity for the United States to project power beyond the oceans naturally encouraged the development of a large logistical "tail." Having industrial capacity and an appreciation for logistics does not, however, rule out fighting capacity. The Soviet offensive into Germany (and southeastern Europe) and the Western allies' amphibious invasion and then liberation of France, for example, required the assembling of men and materiel on an enormous scale, but it also required substantial skill in operational maneuver. The more historians have studied the Soviet, American, and British campaigns of 1943–1945, the more they have recognized the tremendous increase in Allied skill at the war of maneuver.

Even so, as the euphoria associated with the end of World War II turned into an uneasy and increasingly bipolar US and Soviet confrontation, the necessity and value of maneuver warfare appeared to wane. Nuclear weapons dominated the Cold War. They seemed to suggest that any future war would

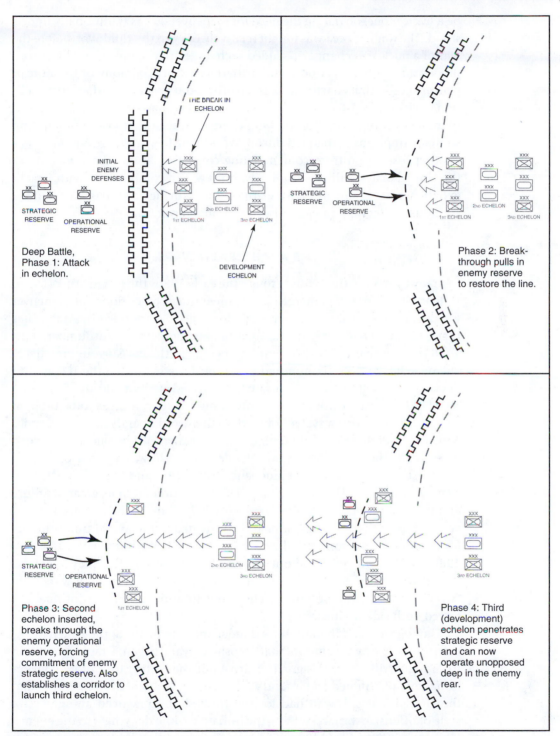

Figure 12.4 Soviet Deep Battle. This series of drawings represent the fully evolved version of Soviet Deep Battle, more or less as practiced from 1943 onwards, with three separate echelons. This basic doctrine was revived in the Cold War Soviet Army with new terminology. The "development echelon" became the "Operational Maneuver Group."

be a nuclear one, obviating the need for maneuver war as traditionally understood. The war in Korea was fought relatively early in the Cold War, before the fear of a nuclear exchange precluded such large-scale, conventional confrontations among the great powers. Furthermore, the geography of the Korean peninsula—both its narrowness and its ruggedness—militated against traditional visions of "maneuver." General Douglas MacArthur's flanking amphibious landing at Inchon in 1950 came closest to that vision, replicating similar campaigns he had led during World War II. The war in Vietnam was another distraction from contemplating conventional maneuver warfare in the United States military. Ironically, however, in combination with Israel's experience (especially in 1973), Vietnam later provided a kind of backhanded stimulus to renewed American interest in maneuver war.

THE ARAB-ISRAELI WARS

In many eyes, from the 1950s through the early 1980s the Israeli army (Israeli Defense Force, or IDF) emerged as the preeminent practitioner of maneuver warfare. In one sense, the Israelis had no choice. Surrounded by Arab states that had vowed to destroy the new nation, and desperately outnumbered (in 1948 there were roughly thirty million people in the five surrounding likely enemy states to only six hundred thousand Jews in Israel), the IDF had to devise and execute a form of warfare that avoided attrition, deadlock, or anything like a war that would eventually allow greater resources to be brought to bear. They needed a system of warfare that would paralyze their enemies with speed. Rather than fight their enemies' soldiers one by one, they needed to persuade them quickly, and wholesale, that flight was a better option. In their first two major wars after independence, in 1956 and 1967, they achieved exactly those aims. Then in 1973 the IDF experienced both its greatest failure and its greatest success. Israel's experience helped make the case for maneuver warfare in the modern world, and it provided a crucial and timely model for the American reconceptualization of maneuver war in the late 1970s and 1980s. It is worth pointing out, however, that the Israeli achievement occurred within the shadow of the Cold War. In some ways these wars were "won" because the superpowers chose not to allow them to continue and forced both sides to the table.[20]

Having won and then preserved independence in 1948, the Israeli army, led from 1953 by its chief of staff Moshe Dayan, began a rapid transition from a guerrilla force designed to drive out the British to a more conventional mix of armored and infantry forces, using equipment from France and the United States. Dayan had long advocated and practiced an aggressive style of offensive warfare, seizing the initiative while denying it to the enemy. He later recounted a 1948 visit to New York in which he met an American tank company commander from World War II, who described to him a particularly risky and aggressive version of some of the Americans' offensive tactics during that war. Impressed, Dayan became committed to expanding the role of armor in the IDF. According to historian Robert Citino, Dayan developed an early list of basic principles, emphasizing surprise, moving straight to the attack, constant motion, leading from the front, using large forces on narrow frontages to overwhelm resistance, keeping up a "constant barrage of firepower as much to frighten and scatter the opponent as to kill him," and then using infantry to occupy ground taken by the armor.[21] In many ways this was an intensification of the German system of infiltration and later of blitzkrieg: overwhelm the enemy's ability to respond with rapid attacks on communication and command capability. This was all the more important in Israeli thinking since they did not want to engage in annihilating the enemy force, which might lead to high Israeli casualties, nor did the political situation suggest that they fight to take and keep significant amounts of Arab territory. Instead, in 1956 the Israelis planned to force the surrender or flight of the Egyptian army in the Sinai Peninsula by striking deep into its rear, bypassing its main defenses, and cutting them off. The Israeli offensive was remarkably, if sometimes almost accidentally, effective. Five thousand Egyptian soldiers were captured by the Israelis, while the IDF had only 172 killed and 700 wounded.

Their success encouraged the IDF to focus even more on the rapid movement of armored forces, in conjunction with airpower, and to aggressively further *decentralize* their command structure. The most potent successes in 1956 had seemingly come when local commanders had acted on their own initiative, responding to changing conditions, and their aggressiveness in doing so had broken open the enemy's defenses. The 1967 war seemed to confirm all those lessons. Believing that an Egyptian and Syrian attack was imminent, the Israelis launched a preemptive strike in June 1967. They successfully destroyed both enemy air forces on the ground, and the ensuing Israeli armored offensive sliced through Egyptian defenses (their way eased by unchallenged Israeli air support), raced toward the passes back to Egypt, closed them, and then annihilated the confused and retreating Egyptian army in just six days of fighting.

In some ways, however, the Israelis were seduced by their own success. The apparent power of the pure armor-and-air combination led the IDF to devalue the role of infantry and artillery. The one-two punch had been enough in 1956 and in 1967. When Egypt and Syria launched their own surprise war during the concurrent Yom Kippur/Ramadan holiday in October 1973, the Israelis mounted a successful defense in part because of their *tactical* superiority, not because of any ability to maneuver at the operational level. Their initial counterattacks proved disastrous in the face of improved Egyptian planning. In the end, however, Israeli armor and aggressive independent action turned the tide. The details are worth a closer look.[22]

The Egyptian plan was designed to surprise the relatively few Israeli defenders stationed directly on the banks of the Suez Canal, cross it, and advance methodically only six to nine miles, thereby remaining under the umbrella of newly deployed surface-to-air missile defenses (SAMs) positioned on the west bank of the canal. This would force the Israelis to counterattack prepared defenses without secure air support. Meanwhile the Syrians would attack with overwhelming numbers toward the Golan Heights in the north. In its initial stages the plan worked perfectly for the Egyptians, if not for the Syrians (see Maps 12.4 and 12.5).

A relatively tiny Israeli armored force, dug in on the Golan Heights, and brilliantly using a series of pre-prepared hull-down tank fighting positions, devastated the waves of advancing Soviet-supplied Syrian armor. Their success here was hardly "maneuver war"; it was simply gunnery superiority. Better-trained Israeli tankers in prepared positions outgunned a more or less linear advance. Even so, the Israeli forces in the southern sector on the heights were ground down to virtually nothing and pushed off the high ground. Their extraordinary delaying action, however, bought time for the arrival of Israeli reinforcements. They restored the line on the heights and then launched an attack more suited to their traditional way of war, seizing the operational initiative and counterattacking so successfully that the road to Damascus seemed open—if the international political situation had allowed such a radical move.

Meanwhile in the Sinai, initial Israeli counterattacks suffered from their purity. The overlapping umbrella of Egyptian air defenses held off the Israeli air force, and the Israeli tanks charged unsupported by infantry or artillery into the teeth of a prepared Egyptian defense. The Egyptians had dug in with a new generation of antitank guided missiles (ATGMs) supplied by the Soviets that could match or exceed the ranges of the tanks while presenting a much smaller target. Egyptian general Saad el-Shazly remarked in his diary that the sole Israeli tactic seemed to be the "cavalry charge," which his defenders easily "stopped with heavy [Israeli] losses."[23] This was not maneuver at all. It sought the initiative; it was aggressive; and it rested on a belief that the enemy could be overwhelmed by firepower, but it did not account for the increasingly overlapping radii of different weapons systems operating in depth. The Egyptian SAM screen and the ATGMs (in combination with more traditional tanks and artillery fire) demanded that an attacker increase the simultaneity of effects at different ranges. The Israelis needed to attack the enemy all along their depth, as well as their front. Fortunately for the Israelis, the Syrian failure on the Golan Heights led the Syrians to solicit an Egyptian advance, and when the Egyptians moved forward they exposed themselves to Israeli counterattacks (the ATGMs were positional weapons, and at that time could not be used on the move). This second round of Israeli counterattacks eventually succeeded in crossing the Suez to the west and rolling up the Egyptian rear (thus attacking the enemy in depth, as well as

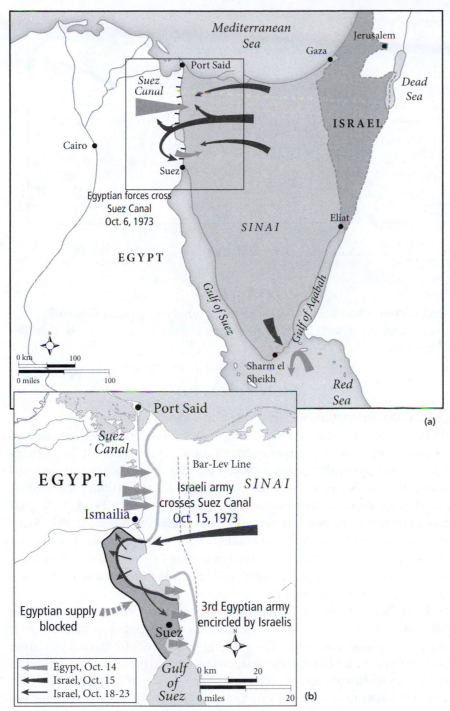

Map 12.4 *a & b* The Yom Kippur War, 1973, Sinai front.

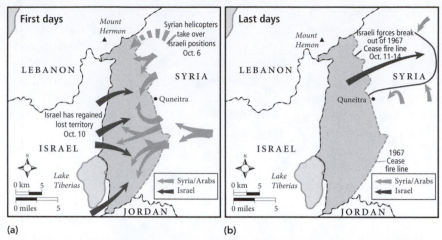

Map 12.5 *a & b* The Yom Kippur War, 1973, Golan Heights front.

breadth), but it had been a near-run thing. Analysts around the world—not least among them the United States—would take lessons from both sides' experiences.

AIRLAND BATTLE

The Israeli experience, especially in 1973, had a profound impact on US Army thinking, all the more so given the coincidental timing of the US withdrawal of ground forces from Vietnam in March of that year. The war in Vietnam proved a profoundly dispiriting experience for American officers. Defeat and the deep divide between the American public and the military left a bitter taste. Perhaps even worse, those feelings merged with the tail end of the draft years and the first years of the new All-Volunteer army to leave the US Army (and much of the US military) a veritable wreck. Discipline was poor—drug use was up; officers feared to walk the barracks at night—and they had lost a war. The road back to a professional and effective army was long and hard and involved reforms on a number of fronts.

Arguably one of the most important reforms was a conscious refocusing of the Army's mission on the conventional challenge posed by the Soviet army in the plains of Europe. The ongoing nuclear confrontation promised only mutual destruction if those weapons were used (see chapter 13), and so the real Soviet threat seemed to be that they might use overwhelming conventional forces to invade western Europe without the need to use nuclear weapons. Confronted by the clear numerical superiority of Soviet and Warsaw Pact forces, US Army planners imagined the problem as one not unlike that faced by the Israelis on the Golan Heights: how to destroy a multiechelon armored advance with inferior numbers, and, even more importantly, how to fight and win the *first battle* in a future that seemed to promise wars of great rapidity, fought with weapons capable of wiping out both sides within hours if not minutes. Ironically, given the role of industrial production in World War II, the United States now found itself on the wrong end of a war of numbers. In consequence, American war planners deliberately turned to the systems and thinking of both the Germans and the Israelis. By doing so they invented, or reinvented, a whole new way of ground warfare for themselves.

That new way did not emerge all at once. In the wake of Vietnam, stung by defeat and apparent institutional devolution, the US Army turned inward and sought to revitalize the virtues of traditional military culture. The Army's leadership rejected the liberal hedonism it perceived in America's wider culture, but it also acknowledged the corrosive effects of its own bureaucratic systems, systems that simultaneously emphasized ticket punching and expected zero defects. Those were the very systems that, especially under the pressure of war, had undermined the ideals of service and integrity. Part of revitalizing a traditional military culture was refocusing on a clear and manageable mission: the conventional confrontation in Europe. The challenge was the lack of American capacity in the face of distant operations against Soviet numerical preponderance. After World War II, rather than relying on large conventional forces, American planners had economized by counting on the nuclear deterrent. American society in the 1970s was not prepared to restore conventional capacity by returning to the scale of mobilization seen in World War II. Indeed, it had just ended the draft entirely. American officers would need to come up with an alternative, a calculation, a military plan or system designed to solve the numbers problem.

The first attempt, shepherded into being by General William E. DePuy, the first commander of the Army's new Training and Doctrine Command (TRADOC), founded in 1973, was something called "Active Defense." In many ways DePuy's system reflected a traditional American way of ground warfare, and its roots lay in his own thinking and experience preceding the Yom Kippur War of 1973. He emphasized the power of the strategic defensive and relatively static firepower to reduce the enemy through attrition. In one sense, when DePuy and his subordinates intensively analyzed the Yom Kippur War, they saw the first half of the Golan Heights battle as validating his then-emerging model: superior Israeli gunnery, fighting from a well-constructed static defense, had devastated waves of Syrian tanks. For DePuy, who was responding at that time primarily to his sense of the Army's decline in professionalism and preparedness, the keys were simply to have a tactically well-trained and technologically up-to-date force, tightly integrated with tactical air support, which could rely on the power of the defensive.[24]

Critics both civilian and military quickly emerged. Much of their criticism was based on their understanding of German maneuver warfare in

World War II. As one critic complained (without perhaps understanding the limits of German thinking): "German operational art in World War II emphasized maneuver, whereas US operational art, with some notable exceptions, tended to emphasize the application of firepower to achieve the attrition of the enemy forces."[25] The debate was sometimes simplified into one supposedly between "attritionists" and "maneuverists," with the latter emphasizing those aspects of German operational doctrine that pushed for rapid action and disruption of the enemy's ability to react—to get inside the enemy's "decision cycle."

The formalized theory of attacking the decision cycle emerged in the United States in the 1970s, but it took some time to emerge in official doctrine. The general idea of disrupting the enemy's ability to respond was an old one, but it acquired new salience during World War I as the distance between fighting front and headquarters lengthened, initially filled only by easily cut telephone wire. German infiltration tactics were designed to take advantage of that vulnerability, but, as discussed previously, at the strategic and operational levels those tactics were still being used within the overall paradigm of attrition. Interwar British armor theorists B. H. Liddell Hart and J. F. C. Fuller, their German readers, and especially Soviet deep battle proponents were moving toward something different, in which penetration at the operational level (not just the tactical level) enabled more than attrition. Such movement would attack a modern army's complex command and communication systems. During the 1970s, US Air Force colonel John Boyd, based partly on his critical study of German tactics in 1918 but also on a wide reading of military history, began circulating a briefing called "Patterns of Conflict," in which he outlined his theory of the "OODA loop." In it he argued that every decision-maker goes through a series of steps in (1) observing the environment, (2) orienting mentally or interpreting that observation, then (3) deciding on a course of action, and finally (4) acting. In combat, Boyd argued, whether air-to-air tactical combat or operational-level ground warfare, one should seek to "get inside the loop" of the enemy. If one's forces can act in such a way to change the environment before the enemy has finished orienting and deciding, then the enemy's decision is based on already outdated information. Each time one achieves that effect, it becomes easier to repeat as the enemy's disorientation slows their OODA cycle further, until paralysis or panic sets in.

Boyd criticized the Army's 1976 Active Defense doctrine as ignoring this dynamic, continuing instead within the attrition paradigm. As James Burton summarized Boyd's argument, Active Defense advocated "maneuver in order to shoot at the enemy. Boyd preached the opposite—shoot in order to create opportunities to maneuver—and maneuver in order to create chaos, panic, and collapse and get behind the enemy to capture his forces." Boyd persisted in pushing his theory in all the services, and his ideas repeatedly worked their way up the chain of command.[26]

At the same time that Boyd and other American reformers were looking backward to German techniques from the world wars, they also were actively assessing technological changes in relationship to Soviet multiechelon attack doctrine. Soviet deep-battle doctrine had evolved further since the war, retaining its overall emphasis on creating a rupture with its first attack echelon, which would force NATO to commit its operational reserve. That reserve would be defeated and penetrated in turn by the second echelon, pulling NATO's strategic reserve into the fight. The third Soviet echelon could defeat the strategic reserve and embark on true strategic deep penetration. The multiecheloned depth of a Soviet attack seemed to undermine the impact of using maneuver to destroy the first or even the second echelon. The depth of a Soviet attack also seemed to lessen the probability of any conventional maneuver getting deep enough into the Soviet rear areas to disrupt their command and control.

Attempts to think through this problem occurred within the context of the military's efforts to redefine and restimulate its intellectual culture. DePuy's Active Defense may have been short lived, but his broader effort as TRADOC commander to enhance the quality of *thought* in the service, through schools, professional journals, and the advocacy of intellectual achievement as a career stepping stone (an effort generally matched by the other services) paid long-term dividends. From that intellectual ferment, led in the late 1970s by the new TRADOC commander, General Donn A. Starry, emerged the AirLand Battle doctrine, encapsulated in the new field manual, *FM 100-5*, published in 1982 (revised in 1986). That doctrine emphasized a combination of maneuver with different types of fires, conducted at a tempo designed to overwhelm an enemy's ability to react. Furthermore, it demanded using multiple weapons platforms and angles of approach—artillery, tactical missiles, tactical air support, flanking maneuvers by ground forces, and perhaps even airmobile or airborne infantry landings deep in the enemy rear—to engage the Soviet attacking forces throughout their full depth. These "deep strike" attacks would hit every echelon *simultaneously*. The effect would be disruption and annihilation at the same time (see Figure 12.5). The key words in the new manual, whose meanings should be clear from this discussion, were initiative, agility, depth, and synchronization.

Boyd's emphasis on the decision cycle and explicit reference to German and Israeli practices were embedded throughout the final published version of AirLand Battle (the 1986 edition of *FM 100-5 Operations*). In that manual, US forces were supposed to seize and hold the initiative, "so that by the time the enemy reacts to one action, another has already taken place, disrupting his plans and leading to late, uncoordinated, and piecemeal enemy responses. It is this process of successive concentration against locally weaker or unprepared enemy forces which enables smaller forces to disorient, fragment, and eventually defeat much larger opposing enemy formations."[27] In this formulation, the first half of the Golan Heights battle was less impressive than the

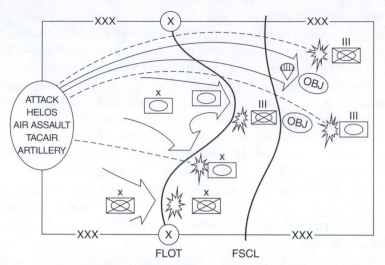

Figure 12.5 AirLand Battle and the Deep Attack. This diagram shows one phase in a Deep Attack. The key here is the use of air power and new long-range artillery and tactical missiles to attack the second and third Soviet echelons while the first is engaged in close combat at the FLOT (forward line of troops).

second half, in which the Israelis mounted an unexpected flanking counter-attack—a maneuver that a later TRADOC commander cited as his inspiration for critiquing Active Defense doctrine. An even better example was the second half of the 1973 Sinai battle, in which local commanders pushed for and executed a sweeping maneuver across the Suez Canal and into Egypt, thoroughly disrupting Egyptian command and control and essentially ending the war. Achieving this kind of operational speed, the "maneuverists" argued, required adopting less centralized command structures. They specifically cited German *Auftragstaktik*.[28]

This new doctrine spoke to the culture of the Army officer corps. Its aggressiveness and vigor resonated with their desire to *act*, to engage an enemy on one's own terms—an experience frequently lacking in Vietnam (the war in Vietnam is discussed in greater detail in the next two chapters). The doctrine's focus on maneuver also served as a deliberate means of turning away from and forgetting the experience in Vietnam. Coincidentally, the doctrine was published in 1982, just as the challenge of the Soviet Union seemed to take on a new urgency. The détente of the 1970s gave way to a chillier period of the Cold War when the Soviets invaded Afghanistan in 1979, an event that helped bring Ronald Reagan and a new rhetoric of confrontation to the presidency in 1981. Although President Jimmy Carter had begun to crank up the engines of American weapons procurement in the late 1970s, it was Reagan's expansion that truly provided the capacity for the Army to build the tools they imagined necessary for AirLand Battle, tools that, ironically, had been first proposed in DePuy's 1973 call for qualitative superiority. These were the "big five": the M-1 Abrams tank, the M-2 Bradley infantry fighting vehicle, the UH-60 Blackhawk utility helicopter, the AH-64 Apache attack helicopter, and the Patriot antiaircraft defense system. All moved from experimental stages into active units in the early 1980s, as did some other key artillery systems with deep-strike capabilities. Furthermore, although the "big five" were conceived before the publication of AirLand Battle in 1982, the ongoing revision of their design criteria deliberately reflected the new doctrine. As in the Soviet army of the 1930s, doctrine was creating procurement criteria. This American surge of Army procurement after 1981 reflected not just a political shift but also a cultural one, visibly manifested in the continued electoral support for Reagan's program. Americans slowly resumed their trust of the military as an institution, and in its new form as a volunteer force and viable career alternative in tough economic times, it attracted and retained better educated soldiers.[29]

The American army then enjoyed almost ten years of peace to refine and disseminate its new doctrine through its system of military schools, perhaps most notably the School for Advanced Military Studies, founded in 1983 by the principal author of *FM 100-5*, Brigadier General Huba Wass de Czege, who regularly invited John Boyd to brief the students. The Army also used that time to integrate its new weapons systems with AirLand Battle in an advanced training area in the California desert, until it was called on to oust the Iraqi army from Kuwait in 1990–1991. In some tellings, the American military's performance in that war validated all these developments, both doctrinally and technologically. A massive Iraqi army, repeatedly touted in the media as the "fourth largest army in the world" and presumably hardened after eight years of war with Iran, was routed and largely destroyed in four days of ground combat.

But was it a battle of maneuver? More to the point, was it a battle that hinged on the independent initiative of small-unit commanders? One critic thinks not:

> Operation Desert Storm was strictly controlled from the top down. There was no room for initiative, or even for significant maneuver options, below corps level. Commanders at all levels were instructed where and when to move and were not permitted to find their own way to the objectives. In essence, the coalition armies simply lined up and swept forward, careful to maintain contact with the friendly forces on their flanks. Like rigidly disciplined Macedonian phalanxes, divisions and brigades had to march and stay dressed to the flanks.[30]

In contrast, others have pointed to incidents such as the Battle of 73 Easting, at the outset of which a single American troop of armored cavalry (a company-size mix of tanks and infantry fighting vehicles) seized the initiative upon making contact with enemy, attacked through and beyond its preplanned halt point, and destroyed several companies of Iraqi armor and mechanized infantry in under thirty minutes of fighting. Still others have pointed to the more recent American invasion of Iraq in 2003, the conventional stage of which followed a very different format from the vast orchestrated wheel of 1991. The plan in 2003 called for rapid penetration and exploitation along narrow frontages following and crisscrossing the Tigris and Euphrates Rivers, ultimately aimed at Baghdad. Ground commanders repeatedly altered plans and initiated operational maneuvers designed to exploit emergent weaknesses. Notable among them was the Third Infantry Division's decision to sweep through Baghdad in a "thunder run," testing the assessment that Iraqi defenses around the city had utterly collapsed.[31]

Of course, neither the Gulf War of 1991 nor the opening battles of the Iraq War in 2003 can be explained merely through the maneuvering of ground forces. Telling that more complicated story requires integrating the simultaneous histories of airpower, precision technology, and theories of a "revolution in military affairs."

TIMELINE

1918	Operation Michael: The German spring offensive on the western front using new infiltration tactics
1920–22	British authors J. F. C. Fuller and B. H. Liddell Hart begin writing and lecturing about future of tank warfare
1928	Deep-battle doctrine solidifying in the Soviet Army
1930s	German and Soviet military exchanges
1937	Stalin purges the Soviet Army officer corps; deep battle disavowed
1939	Battle of Khalkhin Gol; Soviet General Georgy Zhukov defeats the Japanese using deep-battle techniques
1939–41	Period of German offensive success: Poland, Norway, Belgium/France, opening campaigns into the USSR
1943–45	The return of Soviet deep-battle operations
1973	Israeli recovery from initial near disaster in the 1973 Yom Kippur War
1982	First publication of US AirLand Battle doctrine in *FM 100-5* (revised 1986)

CONCLUSION

Western states' competition with each other in combining mass conscript armies with industrial weapons and logistics produced a fearsome deadlock in World War I. Fearing a repeat of that deadlock, those same nations then refined their ideas about warfare—first tactically and then operationally—and combined them with emergent technologies to restore maneuver to the battlefield. There was nothing inherent to the technology that restored maneuver. As proof, one need only point to the Iran-Iraq War, fought from 1980 to 1988 with both Western and Soviet-supplied weapons. In that war neither side proved capable of sustaining maneuver warfare, to the point that they often deployed their tanks in fixed positions. The eight-year deadlock proved enormously costly to both countries and resolved virtually nothing. The Western powers, however, invested both intellectually and technologically in maneuver warfare.[32] In time, that investment, especially in combination with the simultaneous investment in airpower discussed in chapter 13, rendered Western forces, and especially the American military at the end of the twentieth century, vastly superior to the conventional forces of virtually any conceivable opponent. At the same time, however, that superiority did not go unnoticed, and alternative forms of challenge emerged.

Further Reading

Bellamy, Christopher. *The Evolution of Modern Land Warfare: Theory and Practice.* London: Routledge, 1990.

Boff, Jonathan. "Combined Arms during the Hundred Days Campaign, August–November 1918." *War in History* 17.4 (2010): 459–78.

Bronfeld, Saul. "Fighting Outnumbered: The Impact of the Yom Kippur War on the U.S. Army." *Journal of Military History* 71.2 (April 2007): 465–98.

Citino, Robert M. *Blitzkrieg to Desert Storm: The Evolution of Operational Warfare.* Lawrence: University Press of Kansas, 2004.

Citino, Robert M. *The German Way of War: From the Thirty Years' War to the Third Reich.* Lawrence: University Press of Kansas, 2005.

Doughty, Robert A. *The Seeds of Disaster: The Development of French Army Doctrine, 1919–1939.* Hamden, CT: Archon, 1985.

Habeck, Mary R. *Storm of Steel: The Development of Armor Doctrine in Germany and the Soviet Union, 1919–1939.* Ithaca, NY: Cornell University Press, 2003.

Herzog, Chaim. *The Arab-Israeli Wars: War and Peace in the Middle East from the War of Independence through Lebanon.* Rev. ed. New York: Vintage, 1984.

House, Jonathan M. *Combined Arms Warfare in the Twentieth Century.* Lawrence: University Press of Kansas, 2001.

Kiesling, Eugenia C. *Arming against Hitler: France and the Limits of Military Planning.* Lawrence: University Press of Kansas, 1996.

Naveh, Shimon. *In Pursuit of Military Excellence: The Evolution of Operational Theory.* London: Frank Cass, 1997.

Showalter, Dennis. *Hitler's Panzers.* New York: Berkley Caliber, 2009.

Notes

1. Although I do not necessarily follow his definitions precisely, a key discussion of doctrine is Barry R. Posen, *The Sources of Military Doctrine: France, Britain, and Germany Between the World Wars* (Ithaca, NY: Cornell University Press, 1984).
2. Eugenia C. Kiesling, *Arming against Hitler: France and the Limits of Military Planning* (Lawrence: University Press of Kansas, 1996), 183, 171.
3. Kiesling, *Arming against Hitler*, 142.
4. For a history of "blitzkrieg" as a term, see Shimon Naveh, *In Pursuit of Military Excellence: the Evolution of Operational Theory* (London: Frank Cass, 1997), 106–7.
5. This discussion of German infiltration tactical development is from Bruce I.

Gudmundsson, *Stormtroop Tactics: Innovation in the German Army, 1914–1918* (New York: Praeger, 1989), and Timothy T. Lupfer, *The Dynamics of Doctrine: The Changes in German Tactical Doctrine During the First World War*, Leavenworth Papers 4 (Fort Leavenworth, KS: Combat Studies Institute, 1981).

6. Quoted in Michael S. Neiberg, *Fighting the Great War: A Global History* (Cambridge, MA: Harvard University Press, 2009), 317.

7. David T. Zabecki, *The German 1918 Offensives: A Case Study in the Operational Level of War* (London: Routledge, 2006); Nick Lloyd, *The Hundred Days: The Campaign that Ended World War I* (New York: Basic Books, 2014).

8. Mary R. Habeck, *Storm of Steel: The Development of Armor Doctrine in Germany and the Soviet Union, 1919–1939* (Ithaca, NY: Cornell University Press, 2003), xi; Azar Gat, "British Influence and the Evolution of the Panzer Arm: Myth or Reality?," *War in History* 4 (1997): 150–73, 316–38; R. L. DiNardo, "German Armor Doctrine: Correcting the Myths," *War in History* 3 (1996): 384–97.

9. Robert M. Citino, *The German Way of War: From the Thirty Years' War to the Third Reich* (Lawrence: University Press of Kansas, 2005), 253–56.

10. Michael Geyer, "German Strategy in the Age of Machine Warfare, 1914–1945," in *Makers of Modern Strategy*, ed. Peter Paret (Princeton, NJ: Princeton University Press, 1986), 527–97, 585 (quote); Citino, *German Way of War*; Naveh, *In Pursuit*, 106–9.

11. On Clausewitz: Lawrence Freedman, *Strategy: A History* (New York: Oxford University Press), 93.

12. John L. H. Keep, *Soldiers of the Tsar: Army and Society in Russia, 1462–1874* (Oxford: Clarendon, 1985); Thomas Esper, "Military Self-Sufficiency and Weapons Technology in Muscovite Russia," *Slavic Review* 28.2 (1969): 185–208.

13. Chris Bellamy, "Heirs of Genghis Khan: The Influence of the Tartar-Mongols on the Imperial Russian and Soviet Armies," *Journal of the Royal United Services Institute* 128 (1983): 52–60. Christopher Bellamy, *The Evolution of Modern Land Warfare: Theory and Practice* (London: Routledge, 1990); Bruce W. Menning, "The Deep Strike in Russian and Soviet Military History," *Journal of Soviet Military Studies* 1.1 (1988): 9–28, 10 (quote).

14. Naveh, *In Pursuit*, 224–25; C. J. Dick, "The Operational Employment of Soviet Armour in the Great Patriotic War," in *Armoured Warfare*, ed. J. P. Harris and F. H. Toase (New York: St. Martin's, 1990), 88–123, esp. 110–17; Patrick Porter, *Military Orientalism: Eastern War through Western Eyes* (New York: Columbia University Press, 2009), 113–40.

15. Harold S. Orenstein, trans., *The Evolution of Soviet Operational Art, 1927–1991: The Documentary Basis* (London: Frank Cass), 1: 48–49 (quote), 54 (quote).

16. Heinz Guderian, *Achtung-Panzer: The Development of Armoured Forces, Their Tactics and Operational Potential*, trans. Christopher Duffy (London: Arms & Armour, 1995), 152; Naveh, *In Pursuit*, 110, esp. n26; Habeck argues that the separate doctrines were achieved simultaneously and independently. The Soviet version emphasized more mass and central control, as well as greater depth. Habeck, *Storm of Steel*, esp. 294. Habeck's analysis is central to this section.

17. Naveh, *In Pursuit*, 179–80.

18. Jonathan M. House, *Combined Arms Warfare in the Twentieth Century* (Lawrence: University Press of Kansas, 2001), 95.

19. Dick, "Operational Employment"; Richard Simpkin, *Deep Battle: The Brainchild of Marshal Tukhachevskii* (London: Brassey's Defence Publishers, 1987), 39–65. Figure 12.4 is partly based on drawings and advice provided to the author by

Robert Citino, modified by the discussion in Simpkin, *Deep Battle*.

20. Robert M. Citino, *Blitzkrieg to Desert Storm: The Evolution of Operational Warfare* (Lawrence: University Press of Kansas, 2004), 155.

21. Citino, *Blitzkrieg to Desert Storm*, 158 (quote).

22. Williamson Murray, "Conventional War, 1945–2000," in *The Cambridge History of War*, vol. 4, *War and the Modern World*, ed. Roger Chickering, Dennis Showalter, and Hans Van de Ven (Cambridge: Cambridge University Press, 2012), 493–514, esp. 506–9.

23. Quoted in Citino, *Blitzkrieg to Desert Storm*, 179.

24. Richard Lock-Pullan, "'An Inward Looking Time': The United States Army, 1973–1976," *Journal of Military History* 67 (2003): 483–511; Citino, *Blitzkrieg to Desert Storm*, 254–57.

25. George A. Higgins, "German and U.S. Operational Art: A Contrast in Maneuver," *Military Review* 65.10 (1985): 22–29 (quote 23).

26. James G. Burton, *The Pentagon Wars: Reformers Challenge the Old Guard* (Annapolis, MD: Naval Institute Press, 1993), 41–55 (quote 54); Grant T. Hammond, *The Mind of War: John Boyd and American Security* (Washington, DC: Smithsonian Institution Press, 2001), 136–54.

27. US Army, *FM 100-5 Operations* (Washington, DC: Department of the Army, 1986), 16 (quote).

28. Saul Bronfeld, "Fighting Outnumbered: The Impact of the Yom Kippur War on the U.S. Army," *Journal of Military History* 71.2 (April 2007): 465–98; Eitan Shamir, "The Long and Winding Road: The US Army Managerial Approach to Command and the Adoption of Mission Command (*Auftragstaktik*)," *Journal of Strategic Studies* 33.5 (2010): 645–72.

29. On the "big five": Frank N. Schubert and Theresa L. Kraus, eds., *The Whirlwind War: The United States Army in Operations Desert Shield and Desert Storm* (Washington DC: US Army Center of Military History, 1995), 29–34.

30. Robert R. Leonhard, *The Art of Maneuver: Maneuver Warfare Theory and AirLand Battle* (Novato, CA: Presidio, 1991), 269; Richard M. Swain, *Lucky War: Third Army in Desert Storm* (Fort Leavenworth, KS: US Army Command and General Staff College, 1997).

31. Stephen D. Biddle, "Victory Misunderstood: What the Gulf War Tells Us about the Future of Conflict," *International Security* 21.2 (1996): 139–79; Williamson Murray and Robert H. Scales, Jr., *The Iraq War: A Military History* (Cambridge, MA: Belknap Press of Harvard University Press, 2003); Gregory Fontenot, E. J. Degen, and David Tohn, *On Point: The United States Army in Operation Iraqi Freedom* (Fort Leavenworth, KS: Combat Studies Institute Press, 2004).

32. Stephen D. Biddle, *Military Power: Explaining Victory and Defeat in Modern Battle* (Princeton, NJ: Princeton University Press, 2004), argues for the creation of a modern system of offensive tactics dependent on "cover, concealment, dispersion, small-unit independent maneuver, suppression, and combined arms integration," the complexity of which requires a substantial investment in training. His observations, although acute, are almost entirely tactical. The additional complexities of operational maneuver actually strengthen his argument (quote 35).

13

The Lure of Strategic Air Power, the Nuclear Paradox, and the Revolution in Military Affairs?

1915–2003

Strategic Bombing, 1915 to July 1945 • Nuclear Weapons as Air Power • The Nuclear Shadow and Limited War in Korea and Vietnam • The Return of Strategic Air Power and the Revolution in Military Affairs?

THIS CHAPTER, like the last one, traces the history of an idea over a century of war, in this case an idea even more tightly linked to technology. The title of this chapter is intentionally specific. The story here is not one of air power in general, but rather of that particular subset of ideas associated with winning a war entirely or primarily through bombing targets beyond the battlefield, usually within an enemy's territory—so-called strategic bombing. For much of the twentieth century, air power proponents focused heavily on strategic bombing's war-winning potential. That hope shaped strategy, procurement, and eventually even the development of nuclear weapons. The term "strategic bombing" can have a variety of meanings, but, like the theories and hopes for maneuver war discussed in the previous chapter, the concept was born from the frustrations of World War I. In the case of strategic bombing, however, the idea of defeating one's enemy from the air with less expenditure of blood and treasure than fighting on the ground, repeatedly recurred as evolving technology begat seemingly fresh solutions. This set of ideas combined with an investment in bombing technologies has been almost entirely a Western phenomenon and, for much of its history, one dominated by British and American thinking, joined by the Soviet Union during the nuclear era. In part this exclusivity was because those states were concerned more than most with *distant* power projection, and in part it was a matter of industrial capacity. Some other states that possessed the capability, however, such as Japan, for a variety of reasons never invested heavily in the doctrine or the equipment to conduct strategic bombing (although Japan did conduct a significant "terror bombing" campaign against Chinese cities in the late 1930s).[1]

The pursuit of military victory through the air, born in World War I and pursued at great cost and with mixed results in World War II, then took a strange turn with the development of nuclear weapons. Nuclear weapons represented the acme of the idea, but at such an extreme that they disabled themselves, a paradoxical situation that some more prescient thinkers recognized almost immediately. Strategy theorist and historian Bernard Brodie, writing in 1946, mere months after the atomic bombing of Hiroshima and Nagasaki, argued, "Thus far the chief purpose of our military establishment has been to win wars. From now on its chief purpose must be to avert them. It can have almost no other useful purpose."[2] When the Cold War nuclear confrontation finally ended in 1991, strategic air power with conventional weapons experienced a kind of rebirth, transformed by new precision technologies and networking capabilities. The combination of these new capabilities from the air with the armor, firepower, and maneuver doctrines explored in the previous chapter represented an extraordinary challenge to the rest of the world. How nonindustrial developing nations invented paths and methods of resistance in response to Western dominance is the subject of the next chapter.

STRATEGIC BOMBING, 1915 TO JULY 1945

Among the many responses to the bloody stalemate of World War I was the quest to find a way around, through, or in this case *over* it. The war came only a few years after the invention of powered flight, and the technology was fresh. Under the pressures of war it matured rapidly, and as it did some began to hope for a way to break the stalemate of trench warfare and to avoid future deadlocks by attacking from the air. In the earliest stages airplanes were seen only as adjuncts to the battle on the ground, primarily as a mechanism for observation. The value of such observer planes led to efforts to shoot them down with "pursuit" planes. Other pursuit planes were then used to protect the observation planes, and so on. We are concerned here, however, with something beyond this tactical use of air power.

In the 1830s Clausewitz (discussed in chapter 11) had suggested that the ultimate aim of combat was to force the enemy to submit to one's will. Writing in the aftermath of the Napoleonic Wars, he concluded that the usual way to achieve that was to destroy the enemy's armed forces, after which the leaders of the state would have no choice but to submit. Air power, in the form of bombing, offered up the hope of avoiding the hard shell of the enemy's military might, instead attacking the more vulnerable heartland: a "strategic" use of air power that would lead to submission. This hope saturated British and American thinking about air power after World War I. Post–World War I theorizing, however, was based on the limited experience of bombing in that conflict.[3]

The first serious attempt at strategic bombing in World War I relied not on planes but on airships. The Germans launched Zeppelin raids on Great Britain beginning in January 1915 (see Figure 13.1). The Zeppelins eventually

Figure 13.1 German armored Zeppelin. Starting out on bombing raid over England, Sept. 1915.

dropped some six thousand bombs totaling about fifty thousand pounds of explosives, killing some 556 people. German planners hoped to induce panic in the British population, becoming the first in a line of planners who believed in the fragility of the relationship between the ruling class and the working classes—a relationship that could be attacked directly from the air. Kaiser Wilhelm of Germany initially sought to limit the raids to clearly military targets. Technical problems interfered, as they would again and again in the next hundred years, and those restraints slowly eroded. The population of London became the primary target. One pattern that emerged from these attacks, and would be repeated in later wars, was that the bombings produced more civilian anger and calls for reprisal than they did panic. In another hint of things to come, although the Zeppelins at first seemed unstoppable, British defenses quickly adapted, and by late 1916 the airships had been rendered ineffective. The challenge-and-response dynamic worked here as it had in many other arenas of combat. In the air, however, the dynamic seemed to work even faster. Capabilities and corresponding countermeasures evolved very rapidly.[4]

During World War I, Germany, France, Britain, and Italy all developed fixed-wing bombers designed to fly from bases close to the front, cross the trench lines, and then bomb industrial and economic targets. These early efforts produced another pattern that would be seen again: when British efforts at bombing German steel factories seemed to have little effect on German aircraft production, military planners claimed instead that there had been significant "moral effects." The Germans went the furthest in developing such bombers, producing the Gotha and the "Giant", both designed to attack Britain directly. They carried fewer bombs than a Zeppelin, but their speed and maneuverability reduced their vulnerability. The raids began in May 1917 and turned to London in June of that year. They too seemed initially unstoppable, but again, instead of panic, they produced anger and calls for reprisal.[5]

By the end of the war, pushed by such calls for reprisals, Britain had developed an Independent Force (IF) of bombers—meaning in this case that their missions would be determined independently of the tactical requirements at the front lines. Hugh Trenchard, whose ideas would greatly shape postwar British bombing doctrine, took command in June 1918. In a 1917 memo, Trenchard had imagined that such a force would directly attack the enemy's "production, transport and organization," forcing them to commit resources to their defense, and would also "produce discontent and alarm among the industrial population."[6]

Key to the existence of the IF was its *strategic* role, autonomous from events on the front lines. Modern doctrinal terms encompass three basic types of targeting for bombers: "strategic core," referring to some target in the enemy heartland that is central to their war effort; "strategic military," generally referring to interdiction bombing to prevent military assets or logistics from reaching the battlefield; and "close air support," referring to air attacks on enemy military assets already in contact with friendly ground forces. Within each of these broad categories there was and remains debate over what effects one should seek and how one should achieve them. Trenchard here revealed a bifurcated view of the "strategic core": industry *and* civilian morale. He was not alone in this regard; the tension between these two visions persisted for decades. Very often planners could claim to be attacking both at the same time, but the emphasis mattered. As for Trenchard, over time he leaned more and more heavily on the morale effect—sometimes to the frustration of his superiors.[7]

British experiences deeply informed the American view of air power. After entering the war in 1917, liaison officers from the United States arrived in Britain, rapidly adopting the position that night bombing attacks on German morale and materiel would "put an end to the war far more quickly than sending one or two million men to line the trenches."[8] Early American production priorities, set by those less enthused with bombing, instead focused on observation and pursuit planes. By 1918, however, American interest in bombardment as a war-winning strategy was on the upswing.[9]

Whether emphasizing attacking enemy morale, production, or the bonds between the political leadership and the population, these visions shared a hope to shorten the war, and perhaps to win it unaided by ground forces. Advocates of air power hoped to end the increasingly unbearable bloodshed through the air. And that vision of rapidity and decisiveness took hard hold in popular

Figure 13.2 *Lens Being Bombed.* Otto Dix's 1924 etching from his cycle of work titled Der Krieg, representing the fears of a new kind of war from the air.

and military culture after the war. No doubt this war-winning vision for air power eventually would have occurred in the absence of World War I, but the war presented an immediate and visceral problem—the stalemate and carnage of the trenches—and encouraged a perhaps too hopeful vision for the future of bombing. It bears restating that these visionaries hoped for a *less* painful future, one without the kind of suffering produced by World War I, but ironically, they sought to achieve that goal through massive destruction and even by terrorizing the civilian population.

Hopeful visions of air power notwithstanding, the postwar years saw a flowering of fears about its future. Surely modern industrial populations, concentrated in cities, were intensely vulnerable. Their physical vulnerability only accentuated the presumed shallowness of their loyalty to the state in an era during which labor mounted a near constant challenge to the state support of capital—visibly attested by the parliamentary success of a new British Labor party on one end of the spectrum and the Bolshevik Revolution in Russia on the other end. A whole genre of novels, art, and futurist work emerged to predict the destruction of cities from the air, especially with gas bombs (see Figure 13.2).[10]

Of those futurists, the most widely distributed and discussed was Giulio Douhet, an Italian air enthusiast and officer whose obstreperous insistence that the Italians should commit more resources to bombers had finally gotten him court martialed and imprisoned in 1916. Restored to service in 1918, he published *The Command of the Air* in 1921. His direct influence on any given postwar air force is difficult to assess, in part because the ideas he articulated were a kind of common currency; his work simply systematized them. Douhet argued that the airplane's "complete freedom of action and direction" meant that "nothing man can do on the surface of the earth [could] interfere with a plane in flight, moving freely in the third dimension." Invulnerable squadrons of bombers would return the offensive to war, flying over the defensive stalemate below them and erasing the distinction between soldier and civilian. The latter would be subjected to the combined effects of explosive, incendiary, and poison-gas bombs, which would target the "peacetime industrial and commercial establishment; important buildings, private and public; transportation arteries and centers; and certain designated areas of civilian population." In the end, he said, "How could a country go on living and working under this constant threat, oppressed by the nightmare of imminent destruction and death?"[11] Influenced by British theorists working on the same ideas, without citing Douhet or even necessarily knowing his work directly,

British prime minister Stanley Baldwin famously agreed with this assessment, when in 1932 he declared to the House of Commons that "no power on earth can protect the man in the street from being bombed. Whatever people may tell him, the bomber will always get through."[12]

Inspired by these potentialities, a number of European states, the United States, and Japan committed to building bomber forces. Some used them in colonial campaigns in Africa and the Middle East in the 1920s and 1930s, most notably Italy, which used gas and conventional bombs in Ethiopia in 1935. Other than Britain and America, however, most Western powers had lost interest in strategic bombing by the late 1930s. Italy and France focused on the air arm for close air support of ground operations. Germany and the Soviet Union both explored Douhet-like theories with great initial enthusiasm in the 1930s, but later deemphasized them, if not fully abandoning them, in favor of producing aircraft for the ground support role. Some of these doubts arose from discouraging reports of the efficacy of bombing during the Spanish Civil War (1936–39).[13]

Other than Britain and the United States, Germany came the closest to developing a strategic bombing capability during World War II. Germany's development of an air force had been limited by the Treaty of Versailles until Adolf Hitler abrogated the treaty in 1933. Hitler officially announced the existence of the Luftwaffe in 1935. Germany developed a large bomber force, following up on its World War I experience by exploring theories of strategic bombing against an enemy's industrial base and morale, but they never fully implemented such a program, nor did they achieve much success designing long-range bombers. They did conduct terror bombings in Warsaw in 1939, and threatened them elsewhere that year and in 1940. Their eventual efforts against Britain in 1940 were either unsystematic or focused on the more immediate goal of air superiority over the Channel to cover an amphibious landing in the British Isles. During the war against the Soviet Union, there was almost no attempt to bomb Soviet industrial facilities, which were moved out of range east of the Ural Mountains during the 1941 invasion.[14]

The Spanish Civil War also had produced the most famous cultural representation of fears of what bombing meant for the civilian population with Picasso's *Guernica*. Despite Douhet's and others' claims that bombing would shorten wars and ease their pain, strong ethical doubts remained about indiscriminately bombing civilians. Those doubts profoundly influenced the Anglo-American bombing campaigns of World War II, even if in the end such doubts were progressively undermined by the practical problems of destroying distant targets.

Britain and America followed different but related paths in their approach to strategic bombing in the years between the wars. In both countries, especially the United States, the quest for institutional independence and validation of an independent air force played a key role. In Britain, many of Douhet's ideas, such as that the bomber would always get through and the decisiveness of morale bombing, were already present during World War I and were buttressed by inflated postwar official surveys of the bombing. Hugh Trenchard famously claimed in a 1919 postwar official report, utterly without evidence, that "the moral effect of bombing stands undoubtedly to the material effect in a proportion of 20 to 1."[15]

After briefly being sidelined, Trenchard was recalled to peacetime service as Chief of the Air Staff, functionally the head of the newly unified and independent Royal Air Force (RAF). He remained in that position until 1930. In that role, as Tami Davis Biddle has shown, he elevated some of his exploratory ideas of 1917 and 1918 into a dogma that failed to take account of changing conditions, even as the RAF successfully developed its own defenses against bombers, most importantly including radar. Trenchard's dogma rested on the belief that offensive tactics would force the enemy to reallocate resources for air defense, and that the morale effect would dominate over the material one. Against critics who might accuse him of indiscriminately attacking civilians, he resorted to the "quick war" argument: "Air action will be far less indiscriminate and far less brutal and will obtain its end with far less casualties than either naval blockade, a naval bombardment, or sieges, or when military formations are hurled against the enemy's strongest points."[16] Trenchard was not the only voice in the Royal Air Force, and he had always expressed interest in bombing enemy industrial capacity, but his shift of emphasis toward morale bombing continued to hold sway during Britain's World War II bombing campaign.[17]

American air planners, meanwhile, crafted their own vision of strategic bombing, deeply influenced by the British experience in World War I, but also reflecting differences in American culture and calculation. The basic idea, suggested already in World War I and then dramatically reinforced by the Great Depression, rested on the fragility of the modern industrial economy and therefore of an industrially equipped military. The morale of the work force was not the issue, but rather the interdependence of the various components of modern industrial production (the very interdependence that had helped the industrial revolution accelerate the pace of change, as discussed in chapter 10). The US Army Air Service (as it was called before 1926) did not immediately leap to this strategy. During and immediately after the war, the service continued to emphasize observation planes. Beginning as early as the appointment of Major General Mason Patrick as chief of the Air Service in 1921, however, American airmen, influenced by the British and prodded by domestic air power advocates like Brigadier General William "Billy" Mitchell, began pushing harder for an independent role for the Air Service. Patrick's plan for the Air Service specified that "bombardment aviation especially will act with ground troops only in very rare instances."[18]

In crucial and mutually reinforcing ways, this desire for an independent *role* derived from and motivated the push for an independent *institution*. Institutional independence demanded an autonomous offensive role, not merely one that was auxiliary to the mission of the ground forces. The technology of the airplane in and of itself did not determine its role. Conservative traditionalist generals did not reject the airplane; they wholeheartedly embraced, for example, its observation role in World War I. That role fit within existing paradigms. Traditionalists were unwilling, however, to invest capacity in ideas that had not been put to the test. To gain that investment air power enthusiasts had to claim an offensive capability, even a war-winning capability, to justify a fully independent institution, which in turn could then lay claim to resources. The semantics in the United States of an "air service" versus an "air force" were significant (the Army Air Service became the Army Air Corps in 1926 and the Army Air Forces in 1942).[19]

Even once the air arm was institutionalized, however, there was more than one potential theory for its use. In one logic, for example, one builds an air force much like a navy, designed primarily to first defeat its opposite and thus establish air superiority over the battlefield (parallel to the Mahanian command of the sea discussed in chapter 10, in which ship design focused on defeating peer enemy ships first). American air planners, however, pursued a strategic theory positing the war-winning capability of a "true" air force. By 1928 they were already downplaying the air superiority mission, and instead developing a doctrine that prioritized centrally controlled bombardment of strategic targets beyond the reach of ground forces. Two of these three doctrinal components (central control and bombing) were designed to sustain or suggest the independence of the Air Force from the Army. The other, the "distant targets," depended on an elaboration of the strategic theory that had first emerged during World War I.[20]

That theory, which came to be known in America as that of the "industrial fabric" or "industrial web," posited that crippling or destroying certain key components of an industrial economy would bring down the rest. This focus was encouraged by ethical concerns about indiscriminate targeting of civilian populations. To carry out their goal, American planners stressed not only that they would target specific industrial facilities but that they would hit them with extraordinary accuracy. Biddle suggests that the powerful role of "Taylorism," the progressive tradition of scientific corporate management in America, contributed to this emphasis, encouraging a kind of systems analysis of an enemy economy.[21]

Furthermore, American strategic culture had long sought to minimize expenditure in its national defense, relying on the Atlantic Ocean as a buffer against other modern powers. Within that paradigm, air power enthusiasts like Billy Mitchell argued that bombers were the best and cheapest defense—far cheaper than battleships. Not everyone in uniform agreed, and Mitchell's eventual insubordination, like that of Giulio Douhet, got him court-martialed. But Mitchell's ideas helped lead American planners to seek bombers capable of both long-range and accurate bombing—accurate enough to hit a ship at sea, and long-range enough for the target to be *far out* at sea.[22]

Figure 13.3 A B-17 "Flying Fortress." A bomber from the Eighth U.S. Air Force during the bombing raid on Nuremburg, Germany.

Those capabilities, especially accuracy, were then touted in media campaigns to the American public, persuading them that American fliers could put a bomb in a pickle barrel, although the existence of the new and highly classified Norden bombsight (deployed from the early 1930s) was kept secret for some years. The Americans also modified Douhet's belief in the invulnerability of the bomber. Simply operating in three-dimensional space was likely insufficient defense, but a force of heavily armed bombers flying in a formation designed to emphasize defensive firepower, they argued, would be invulnerable. The result was the B-17 "Flying Fortress" bomber, first introduced in 1938 and soon to become the emblem of the American bombing campaign in Europe, alongside the B-24 and later, in the Pacific, the B-29.[23]

As the US Army's air arm joined the war in 1941 they held on to these assumptions and plans despite British experiences earlier in the war. The British, already predisposed to emphasize morale over physical effects, and motivated to retaliate after indiscriminate German bomb attacks in 1940, rapidly discovered the difficulties in either hitting industrial targets or overcoming German defenses. A 1941 British inquiry into industrial bombing determined that only 30 percent of the bombers (much less the bombs) arrived within five miles of the targets, and the percentage was even lower in the industrial Ruhr. British tactics soon devolved into area bombing at night, increasingly using incendiary bombs. Such generally indiscriminate methods began in October 1940 and were the norm by February 1942.[24]

By earlier agreement between President Franklin Roosevelt and British prime minister Winston Churchill, when the United States entered the war in December 1941, Germany was prioritized as the more serious threat. Germany was also, however, difficult to come to grips with immediately, except through the air. American air planners' faith in the war-winning potential of a precision, daytime bombing campaign against Germany's industrial web had taken shape even before American entry. Plans drawn up in the summer of 1941 laid out three major tasks for the Army Air Forces:

a. Destroy the industrial war making capacity of Germany.
b. Restrict Axis air operations.
c. Permit and support a final invasion of Germany.[25]

This priority list, sustained for the next three years, reflected an honest belief that bombing could win wars, but it also served the institutional desire to keep the US campaign separate from the British and to advocate for establishing the US Army Air Forces (USAAF) as its own service separate from the Army. Once deployed to England, the US Eighth Air Force began bombing even as it somewhat tardily initiated a systems analysis of the German economy. Early bombing raids were almost practice runs, with planners as yet unsure which strand of the industrial web most needed pulling. In 1943 analysts identified six key systems (submarine construction yards, aircraft industry, ball bearings, oil, synthetic rubber, military transport vehicles) scattered across seventy-six target areas, that once destroyed would "gravely impair and might paralyze the western Axis war effort." They also identified German fighters as an "intermediate objective" to be attacked simultaneously.[26]

In 1943, as the Allied Combined Bomber Offensive (CBO) was getting underway, the British Bomber Command, under Air Marshal Sir Arthur Harris, resisted this kind of specificity. Harris preferred to bomb cities as an attack on the population itself. In making that recommendation he did not mince words: Bomber Command should seek, he said, "the destruction of German cities, the killing of German workers, and the disruption of civilised community life throughout Germany."[27] The Americans followed their own path, focusing first on U-Boat pens and Luftwaffe factories. The former proved difficult to damage, and the Germans rapidly built a deep belt of air defenses to protect the latter. American hopes for the invulnerability of formations of heavily armed bombers were quickly shattered, as were their hopes for the vulnerability of the German economy. Despite the bombing, German fighter production soared, and German antiaircraft fire forced the bombers higher and higher. Cloud cover consistently interfered with targeting, and the Norden bombsight, even as it was continually improved, proved less accurate than expected. All these issues collided spectacularly in the raids on Schweinfurt and Regensburg in August and October 1943. The ball bearing plants there had been identified as a key "bottleneck" industry, but in two raids American bomber losses were extreme; in the second some 198 of 291 planes were shot down or damaged. Worse, the Schweinfurt plants continued to operate.[28]

American tactics changed during the winter of 1943/1944 when effective long-range fighters came online to escort the bombers to their targets. The creation of those fighters represents its own fascinating story, but even with their arrival the overall *strategy* of the bombing campaign remained the same: to target specific German industrial capabilities. The presence of the escort fighters, however, began to change the results, and the failure of precision also led to changes in the *tactics* of bombing. In terms of results, the escorts began to seriously damage the Luftwaffe. In theory this was the desired outcome: under the "Pointblank directive," the strategic mission for the CBO since August 1943 had been to degrade the capacity of the Luftwaffe. But the initial strategy had been to attack aircraft production by attacking related factories. With the introduction of long-range escort fighters, however, German fighter pilots began to lose the fight in the sky when they rose to meet the incoming bombers.

In the spring of 1944, American bombers shifted to hitting transportation networks in France and Germany, especially "marshaling yards," the great train depots that sprawled across the heart of European cities. Intending to isolate the Normandy beaches from German reinforcements, the tactics of hitting such area targets in the center of cities began to resemble area bombing. The Americans also increased the proportion of incendiaries in their bomb loads and found themselves increasingly relying on less precise radar targeting through the clouds. As just one example of the problems with accuracy, the USAAF and RAF attacked the synthetic oil plant in Leuna, Germany, a combined twenty-three times from May to November 1944. Of twenty American attacks, five were conducted visually, three combined visual and radar targeting, and the remaining twelve were executed with radar only. The radar attacks dropped only 5 percent of their bombs within the 1.2-square-mile target area. In all the attacks, 84 percent of the Allies' bombs dropped outside the factory area. In effect, if not in intention or in rhetoric, by 1944 the American air force was conducting area bombing, with the side effect of destroying the Luftwaffe with their fighter escorts.[29]

All these trends continued through 1944 and into 1945, with increasing effects as allied bomber production accelerated and ground advances opened up more bases from which to launch attacks. American air planners' commitment to destroying Germany's industrial web never wavered, even as in practice the tactics had come to resemble area bombing. American Chief of the Army Air Forces General Henry "Hap" Arnold held to this theory through the end of the war, arguing in November 1945 that the United States' "Strategic Theory" of air war envisioned air power that would "so deplete specific industrial and economic resources, and on occasion the will to resist, as to make continued resistance by the enemy impossible."[30] During the war he resisted the diversion of bombing assets to support army operations or even for the interdiction campaign against the rail lines leading from Germany into France preparatory to the D-Day invasions.[31]

In the end, the vast commitment of resources to the bombing campaign had three effects. First, it devastated the German air force. Second, the attack on industry prompted a wholesale restructuring of German production that initially saw it actually increase dramatically through the summer of 1944. From that point, however, German production faltered, and then declined steeply, in particular as spring and summer raids targeted German oil refineries in Ploiești, Romania, and in the German heartland. Third, and simultaneously, area bombing intensified as well, including deliberate "morale" attacks such as the nearly complete destruction of Dresden in a combined British and American effort in February 1945 (see Figure 13.4). In the face of the Allied demand for unconditional surrender, however, German armies fought on. For that political objective, victory from the air proved elusive.[32]

Figure 13.4 Dresden after the firebombing in February 1945.

In Japan, meanwhile, the strategic bombing campaign followed a similar but much more rapid and horrific trajectory. American planners were long aware of the special vulnerability of Japanese cities, where homes were built primarily of wood and paper. US Army Chief of Staff General George Marshall suggested even before Pearl Harbor, "If war with the Japanese does come, we'll fight mercilessly. Flying fortresses will be dispatched immediately to set the paper cities of Japan on fire. There won't be any hesitation about bombing civilians—it will be all out."[33] Nevertheless, air planners began their work with the same industrial targeting plans. As they had for Germany, the planning staff in 1943 identified seven target types spread across fifty-seven key targets. One of those targets, however, absent from the list for Germany, was simply "urban industrial areas." Planners hoped that such attacks would result in the euphemistic "dislocation of labor by casualty." As General Arnold's deputy later phrased it more simply: "It made a lot of sense to kill skilled workers by burning whole areas."[34] These were not the morale attacks of old; this was an attempt to cut Japanese industrial production by attacks on the workers themselves. In any event, serious bombing had to await both the new long-range B-29 bomber and the island-hopping campaign to free up bases in the Marianas Islands within reach of Japan, as early efforts to bomb Japan from bases in China were generally unsuccessful.

Operations from the Marianas began in November 1944, and pilots soon discovered that weather and other conditions over Japan made for even less precise results than had been achieved in Europe. The switch to deliberate, full-scale area incendiary attacks came relatively quickly, especially after the appointment of Curtis LeMay as the commander of all bombing efforts over Japan in early 1945. From March to July 1945, LeMay orchestrated incendiary attacks on sixty-six Japanese cities, with terrifying success. Most notoriously, the raid on Tokyo in March generated a firestorm that boiled the water in the city's canals and killed as many as one hundred thousand people, more than would die from the atomic bomb at Hiroshima (see Figure 13.5).

Pausing for a moment to think about calculation, culture, and capacity in the American firebombing of Japanese cities reveals the important ways in which those categories of analysis overlap. American calculations assessed the impact that incendiary destruction via area bombing would have on the industrial laboring population of Japan. Those specific calculations fit within the broader paradigm of their strategic culture, which emphasized direct air attacks on the enemy's economic capacity. Arguably, American racist attitudes about the Japanese (a racism reciprocated by the Japanese) eased that calculation. Historian Tom Searle has argued that "neither LeMay nor the USAAF abandoned precision bombing in favor of area bombing. Instead, they supplemented an unspectacular precision bombing campaign with a stunningly successful urban incendiary campaign."[35] Racism did not *cause* that calculation; that calculation was made according to their vision of the role of air power, regardless of the race of the enemy. But the concerns

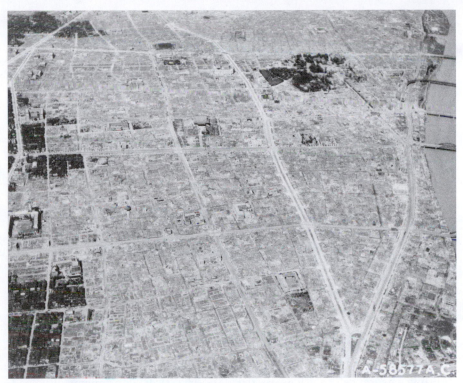

Figure 13.5 Tokyo after the firebombing of March 1945.

Americans had raised about the morality of attacks on civilians in Europe barely surfaced in the Pacific campaigns, and the widening gap between the still persistent rhetoric of attacking industry and the reality of indiscriminately killing civilians could be sustained only on the backs of cultural assumptions about the enemy in question.[36]

Despite this level of destruction, the Japanese fought on, as had the Germans until their country was fully occupied. In Japan the decisive blow may or may not have been the two atomic bombs dropped in early August 1945. Many historians have argued that the simultaneous Soviet invasion of Manchuria was at least as important, or the US submarine campaign that by 1945 had almost completely cut Japan off from fuel and other key military resources. In many eyes the theory of a war-winning strategy through bombing alone had been discredited. The quest to avoid stalemate and attrition had produced "yet another instrument of attrition, another method by which industrial societies could beat each other down."[37]

Still, the power and efficacy of air power more broadly was undeniable, and that reality, combined with the stunning effects of the atomic bombs, bore institutional fruit. The US Air Force gained its long-sought institutional independence in 1947. In air leaders' eyes, not only had the bombing campaign against Japan led to its surrender without the necessity of a ground invasion, and not only had the atomic bomb simply been a natural extension of strategic bombing doctrine, but its successful drop very near the designated aim point demonstrated that even atomic bombing was precision work, and not "wanton, indiscriminate bombing."[38] Those leaders of a now separate institution carried their strategic and institutional culture forward, including their belief in the war-winning capacity of strategic bombing, a belief suddenly, strikingly, and at least seemingly validated by atomic weapons. In historian Kenneth Werrell's words, in the ensuing decades "the Air Force narrowly saw its mission as strategic [usually nuclear] bombardment at the expense of all else. . . . In fairness, this choice . . . was instrumental in waging and winning the Cold War. However, it came at a cost. As we shall see, technology developed for the strategic operation fared badly during the limited wars that America fought."[39]

NUCLEAR WEAPONS AS AIR POWER

Development of the atomic bomb in the United States began in the late 1930s, spurred in part by fears that the Nazi Germany might be pursuing such a weapon. From 1942 the United States committed enormous resources to overcoming the numerous technical problems that such a weapon presented, in a crash program codenamed the Manhattan Project. In a remarkable demonstration of wartime economic capacity, the United States simultaneously pursued multiple theoretical solutions to the various technical problems involved, hoping that in each case at least one solution would work. In the end they all worked, and the United States produced two different bomb types, both of which tapped the energy released by the fission, or splitting, of atoms.

Without going into all the physics, it is important to understand the basic nature of an "atomic" fission bomb versus the later "thermonuclear" fusion bombs developed in the early 1950s. A fission-based explosion occurs when sufficient fissionable material (uranium-235 or plutonium-239) is briefly forced together to form a "critical mass." The mass is then bombarded with free neutrons by a neutron initiator; as those neutrons collide with the large nuclei of the U-235 or P-239 atoms they break them apart. This fissioning releases enormous amounts of energy and also more neutrons, which then hit more nuclei, and so on, in a "chain reaction." Critically, however, the very act of exploding disperses the fissile material, destroying the critical mass and ending the fission reaction. There is, therefore, a sharp upper limit to the explosive power of a fission bomb.

Manhattan Project scientists built both P-239- and U-235-based bombs, using two different techniques to achieve critical mass. The first was tested at the White Sands site in New Mexico in July 1945, after Germany had surrendered. Harry S Truman, president of the United States from the death of Roosevelt in April 1945, was informed first of the weapons' existence and then of the successful test, and he agreed to use them against Japan. His motives and the morality of that decision remain the subject of intense debate, but there is little doubt from the planning staff's point of view that using them was simply an extension of what they were already doing to Japanese cities. The second bomb was dropped on Hiroshima on August 6 and the third on Nagasaki on August 9; a fourth would have been available about a week later. Air Force leaders were quick to claim that the success of atomic weapons merely validated their vision of strategic bombing as the primary focus for air power—these new bombs were not unique; they simply demonstrated what they had been arguing all along.[40]

In the immediate aftermath of the Japanese surrender and the end of World War II, the United States found itself in the enviable position of being physically unscarred by the war, with a rapidly expanding economic base, and in possession of a nuclear monopoly. Even as the confrontation with the Soviet Union began to devolve into the Cold War, and despite concern over the size of the Soviet Union's conventional army, American possession of airbases ringing the Soviet Union seemed to give the United States a dominant position (although the United States by 1948 had perhaps as few as fifty atomic bombs, plans were for four hundred by the beginning of 1951). The Soviet Union, however, had infiltrated the Manhattan Project, which allowed it to explode its own test bomb in August 1949, far earlier than anyone had predicted.[41]

Events then unfolded rapidly. A mere week after US intelligence sources publicly revealed that the Soviets had tested a fission bomb, Mao Zedong declared victory in the Chinese Communist Party's war for control of mainland China. Meanwhile, Soviet premier Joseph Stalin had committed to vastly increasing Soviet conventional forces: they would swell from 2.8 million in 1948 to 5 million by 1953. American scientists chose this moment to reveal to Truman the possibility of a "super," or thermonuclear, bomb, and he authorized its development in January 1950. Later that year he approved National Security Council memo 68, committing American foreign policy to "containing" communism to its current borders. In yet another "meanwhile," in January 1950 Kim Il-Sung, the communist ruler of North Korea, sought and received approval from Stalin to launch an invasion of American-supported South Korea, which he did on June 25 that year.[42]

All of these crises, and others in Greece, Turkey, and elsewhere, created the conditions for the Cold War nuclear and conventional arms race that continued until 1991. Understanding the nuclear confrontation and the strategies that emerged within it requires a basic understanding of the size of a thermonuclear explosion. The physics here is extremely complex, but initiating a fusion reaction requires an enormous amount of energy input. Indeed, a fusion bomb is detonated by the explosion of a fission bomb, and the fusion explosion actually generates additional fission-based explosions as well. The nature of a fission explosion limited its magnitude: the Hiroshima bomb, for example, released twenty kilotons of energy (the measurement refers to the equivalent of twenty thousand tons of TNT). There is no theoretical upper limit to the power of a fusion bomb. Some Manhattan Project veterans even feared that a sufficiently large fusion explosion could ignite the atmosphere, engulfing the entire world. A typical fusion warhead might range from five megatons to eighteen megatons—representing five to eighteen *million* tons of TNT. Several tests have greatly exceeded those amounts, sometimes to the surprise and dismay of the testers.

Once given the green light, American scientists tested the first hydrogen bomb in 1952. Once again infiltrators helped the Soviet Union, just a year later, to catch up to the Americans. As powerful a memory as the vision of the destruction of Hiroshima and Nagasaki was and remains, those atomic explosions paled beside the potential power of a thermonuclear blast. What made it even more frightening was its relative cheapness. The United States would have needed many thousands of fission bombs (and associated delivery systems) to utterly destroy the Soviet Union, but it required only hundreds of fusion bombs. The largest fusion bomb ever tested, the Tsar Bomba, detonated by the Soviet Union in 1961, released over fifty megatons of energy, more energy than the sum total of all the conventional bombs dropped in World War II (it was initially designed to release one hundred megatons, but it was modified for safety reasons to contain the reaction).[43]

Through the end of the 1950s, however, the actual US-Soviet confrontation remained mostly theoretical and was dominated by the United States. The Soviet Union did not yet have delivery systems to threaten North America, although the United States was committed to defending a vulnerable Europe. American political leaders deemed the massive Soviet conventional arsenal too expensive to match, and US dominance in the nuclear arena meant that it was unnecessary to do so. American planners therefore leaned again on the old vision of a cheap war-winning strategy through air power, now nuclear.

Initially, the Air Force continued to emphasize the supposed precision targeting of enemy industrial resources. Military plans through the early 1950s focused on bombing Soviet industrial capabilities, generally concentrated in cities. An early version of the plan, for example, identified petroleum resources scattered among seventeen different cities. One US Air Force target researcher in 1951 asserted, in what can only be called a monument to self-delusion, that American nuclear bombing plans would not be "area attacks" like those conducted by the British in World War II, but instead would be "precision attacks with an area weapon."[44] Furthermore, planners throughout the early 1950s argued that any war with the Soviets would have to be won immediately, using nuclear weapons, in the doctrine of "massive retaliation."[45]

Massive retaliation focused budgetary attention on the Air Force, and specifically its Strategic Air Command (SAC). Founded in 1946, SAC served as the command headquarters for all the Air Force's nuclear assets, initially just the bombers, but eventually including the land-based nuclear missile force as well. The Air Force encouraged fears of Soviet capability, playing up a supposed (although mythical) "bomber gap" from 1954, and successfully lobbying for increased American bomber production. In a circular reinforcing process, the desire to rely on cheaper nuclear weapons channeled resources in that direction, and the channeling of resources into nuclear capability in turn reified their importance to military planners and some political leaders, who then relied on them as the solution to most problems. American crisis diplomacy in the late 1940s and 1950s reflected this thinking. Although some evidence is still not available, the United States threatened, considered threatening, or actively planned to use nuclear weapons during several crises, including in Iran in 1946 (possibly threatened), the 1948 Berlin airlift (considered), Korea in 1953 (threatened), Vietnam during the Dien Bien Phu siege in 1954 (considered), the Quemoy-Matsu crisis in 1954 (suggested by the Joint Chiefs), and the 1958 Quemoy-Matsu confrontation (planned for by the military, but President Eisenhower then told them to avoid their use), and the use of nuclear weapons was seriously considered by President Kennedy during the Berlin Crisis in 1961.[46]

This situation seemed to change in 1957 when the Soviet Union launched *Sputnik 1* into orbit. Delivering a satellite into space also demonstrated the ability to deliver a warhead around the world, and by 1959 both the Soviet Union and the United States had deployed fusion warheads mounted in the nose of intercontinental ballistic missiles (ICBMs) (see Figure 13.6).

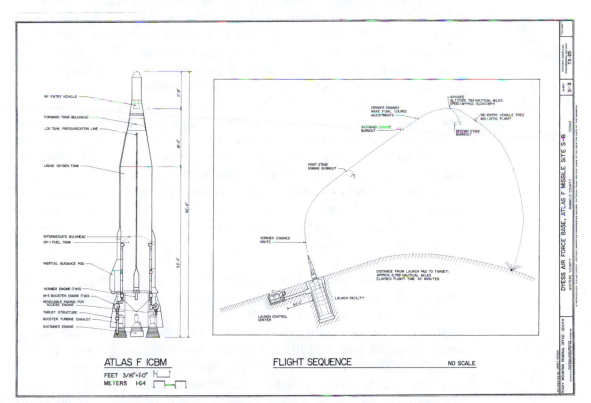

Figure 13.6 Atlas F ICBM flight sequence. Technical drawing of an Atlas nuclear missile, based at Dyess Air Force Base. The Atlas was the first operational U.S. ICBM, brought online in 1959.

Both nations also developed submarine-launched ballistic missiles (SLBMs) by 1960, although those did not have intercontinental range. These technological developments stoked fears among American military planners and the public. Americans now found themselves at an enormous conventional disadvantage, and the public *believed* themselves at a disadvantage in missile development as well. John F. Kennedy ran his presidential election campaign on this supposed "missile gap" and the need to get tougher. As it turned out, there was no missile gap. Kennedy had already learned during his 1960 election campaign that the Americans were still in a dominant strategic position in terms of nuclear weapons.

Reality, however, was not perception. Neither side knew enough about the other's capabilities to be certain of their strategy. Should they plan for deterrence, retaliation, or preemptive strike? Both felt a political need to continue to talk tough, to maintain the credibility of their threats, and to build or deploy fresh capabilities. This lack of knowledge and a dependence on massive retaliation helped produce the infamous confrontation over the Soviet deployment of nuclear missiles in Cuba, where a communist revolution led by Fidel Castro had triumphed in January 1959.[47]

The resulting Cuban Missile Crisis profoundly frightened both sides and began a process of transforming the Cold War. Ironically, and even paradoxically, however, that transformation depended on continuing the nuclear arms race and formalizing a doctrine designed to make them useful without using them. Bernard Brodie, quoted at the beginning of this chapter, had recognized in 1946 that atomic weapons represented something fundamentally different from previous weapons. Their only utility was deterrence. Thermonuclear weapons only made this insight more compelling. President Eisenhower had already begun to realize the need to focus on deterrence rather than any eventual usage. Several times he had found himself dissuading his military planners from relying on nuclear strikes to solve regional crises. Then in late 1962, Secretary of Defense Robert McNamara began to formalize this emerging consensus as "assured destruction." The term was first used in 1964, later to be prefixed with "mutual." Mutual assured destruction (MAD) would remain the guiding doctrine for US nuclear strategy for the remainder of the Cold War.[48]

In essence MAD required that nuclear forces be designed to survive a surprise first strike and be capable of launching a retaliatory strike of such magnitude that the attacker would suffer unacceptable losses. The prima facie logic is unassailable, but it produced a host of paradoxical consequences. It encouraged the arms race to an arguably absurd degree; far more nuclear weapons would be produced in order to guarantee that enough would survive a first strike to provide a second, retaliatory strike. The resulting increase in numbers was staggering, with the combined arsenal of nuclear warheads reaching some seventy thousand. MAD also guided the types of weapons produced, with both the United States and the Soviet Union pursuing the so-called triad force structure of nuclear delivery systems based in missile silos scattered around the continent, in bombers, and launched from submarines. The Soviets had less bombing capacity, and dominated a larger continental landmass on which missile silos could be spread, and so their version was sometimes called a modified, or continental, triad.

The stability of MAD also required "credibility"; each side had to convince the other that they would in fact launch a retaliatory strike, even if doing so would basically destroy much of the world. Capabilities were developed and diplomacy was conducted to sustain the credibility of the second strike, and under the 1972 Anti-Ballistic Missile treaty, both sides forswore building anything except minimal missile defenses. MAD gained further stability as both powers developed more and more sophisticated distant early warning systems and especially satellite surveillance. Each allowed for some confidence in knowing that a strike had been launched and providing time to order a counter strike. Satellite intelligence also allowed each side to detect mobilization procedures and to more confidently assess the other's nuclear forces, and thus to know the potential size of the force that would have to be destroyed to prevent a second strike.[49]

Other factors, especially the issue of precision, however, undermined the stability of MAD. From the 1950s the Air Force had long been uncomfortable with a strategy of deterrence based on pure "countervalue" targeting. Some terminology is necessary here. "Countervalue" refers to targeting the industrial capability or the population of the enemy state. "Counter-force" strategies target the enemy's military arsenal, in this case meaning their nuclear weapons. Massive retaliation under Eisenhower assumed countervalue targeting, in part based on American superiority in delivery systems during the 1950s, and in part as a doctrinal continuation from World War II. As Soviet capabilities increased, especially with the introduction of ICBMs in 1961, planners began to examine counter-force strategies. To the delight of Air Force planners, Defense Secretary McNamara pushed the idea through the middle of 1962. In one sense, the early nuclear-age reliance on countervalue targeting had been the only choice, since neither bombers nor early nuclear missiles had guidance precise enough to directly target a single missile silo, and enemy submarines were essentially invulnerable. In the late 1960s, however, the US investment in precision began to bear fruit (see Table 13.1).[50]

That investment in precision came *despite* McNamara's calculated reversion to a strategy of deterrence, and *despite* the fact that it undermined the stability of MAD. Although countless hours of calculation were invested in the value of, and means to achieve, nuclear precision, the quest for it is better explained in terms of military and organizational culture. On one hand, the services had never been comfortable with MAD's "balance of terror." Terror bombing did not appearl to US planners in the 1960s or 1970s any more than it had in the 1920s. They consistently sought capabilities for precision strikes that could disable their opponent, either by striking industry or by attacking

Year	Weapon	Type	CEP (meters)	Nationality
1943	B-17 with Norden sight	Aerial bomb	330	US
1958	SS-N-4	SLBM	3,704	USSR
1959	Atlas D	ICBM	3,334	US
1960	Polaris A1	SLBM	3,704	US
1961	SS-6	ICBM	3,704	USSR
1962	Minuteman I	ICBM	2,037	US
1962	Titan I	ICBM	1,204	US
1962	SS-7	ICBM	2,778	USSR
1964	Polaris A3	SLBM	926	US
1966	Minuteman II	ICBM	482	US
1966	SS-9	ICBM	926	USSR
1970	Minuteman III	ICBM	389	US
1971	Poseidon C3	SLBM	463	US
1973	SS-N-6 mod 2	SLBM	1,852	USSR
1975	SS-17 mod 1	ICBM	444	USSR
1979	Minuteman III (improved)	ICBM	259	US
1979	Trident C4	SLBM	463	US
1983	Tomahawk (TLAM-N)	SLCM	80	US
1986	Peacekeeper	ICBM	111	US
1990	Trident DS	SLBM	111	US
1998	JDAM (GPS-guided)	Aerial bomb	5	US

Table 13.1: **The progression of accuracy in nuclear delivery.** Only selected missiles/bombs are shown and a World War II "dumb" bomb and a current-day GPS-guided bomb are given for comparison. CEP (circular error probable) refers to the radius of a circle around the target in which 50 percent of the warheads aimed at that target will land. ICBMs are silo-launched intercontinental ballistic missiles; SLBMs are submarine-launched ballistic missiles (generally shorter range); SLCMs are submarine-launched cruise missiles. There are other, even more accurate cruise missiles in the current US inventory, but they are not listed here.

Soviet first-strike capabilities directly. In addition, inter-service rivalry and budget strife led the Navy and the Air Force to compete in presenting to Congress ever more precise weapons development programs. In the early 1970s, for example, the US Navy began to push for a strategic nuclear-capable cruise missile (SLCM), launchable from a submarine, and operating with a wholly new and more precise guidance system than that used by ballistic missiles. The Air Force, although it had explored cruise missile technology in earlier decades, had so far resisted cruise missile development, partly in the fear that it might supplant bombers. Now challenged, the Air Force quickly took up its own separate cruise missile program.[51]

The irony was that even as McNamara returned the nation to a strategy of deterrence, technological capacity and institutional culture were making available precision weapons capable of counter-force targeting. The Soviet Union, not unreasonably, interpreted the arrival of such weapons as a deliberate, calculated strategy to build a first-strike counter-force capability. Soviet fears led to their own massive nuclear buildup in the 1970s. That buildup in turn allowed presidential candidate Ronald Reagan to claim an emerging (although mythical) "window of vulnerability." Reagan's election, his anti-Soviet rhetoric, his push for intermediate-range ballistic-missile (IRBM) deployment in Europe (which would reduce warning time after a launch to a mere fifteen to thirty minutes), and his pursuit of a space-based missile defense system (the Strategic Defense Initiative—often called "Star Wars" in the press) dramatically undermined Soviet confidence in MAD. By the early 1980s the Soviets began to fear an American first strike, and some accounts suggest that the 1983 NATO Able Archer exercise almost prompted a Soviet nuclear attack. When both sides realized how narrowly they had escaped a nuclear misunderstanding, it helped prompt President Reagan and Mikhail Gorbachev of the Soviet Union to begin serious nuclear reduction talks in the mid-1980s.[52]

By the last years of the Cold War the two-sided nuclear buildup arguably had reached an absurd level (see Table 13.2). It was certainly partly responsible for undermining the economic stability of the Soviet Union. But, setting aside the still-debated role of the arms race in the breakup of the Soviet Union, the Soviet collapse also helped reveal how far the arms race had begun to exceed rational limits within the United States. As early as 1970, American admiral Stansfield Turner, newly assigned to command a carrier task group in the

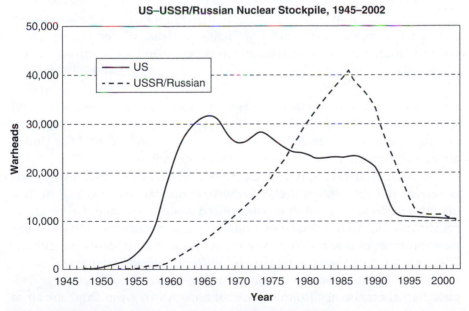

Table 13.2: **US and Soviet/Russian warhead stockpiles, 1945–2002.**

Mediterranean, was stunned to discover that one of his aircraft's targets in the event of a nuclear exchange was a tiny railroad bridge in Bulgaria. He could only conclude that the United States had more nuclear weapons than it really needed. A year later, during a briefing on US nuclear targeting, he learned that the United States in 1972 had about twenty-seven thousand nuclear warheads, including a large number of short range "tactical" warheads (down from 32,500 in 1967). Given those numbers, and his previous encounter with the targeted Bulgarian bridge, Turner was taken aback at the intent of the briefing: to prepare the audience of senior military officials to push for additional long-range systems for targeting industrial and economic targets in the Soviet Union.[53]

What the briefers were describing to Turner was the "Single Integrated Operational Plan," or SIOP—essentially a list of targets for American nuclear weapons, managed by the Strategic Air Command. By 1991, as the Soviet Union was falling apart from the inside, the SIOP had become massively overdeveloped. It was by then a nearly impenetrable listing of some 12,500 targets to be hit (some repeatedly) by over ten thousand nuclear warheads, more or less automatically upon the initiation of a nuclear exchange (the United States had decommissioned many tactical warheads, but had built many more long-range ones, and by 1991 it had some twenty-one thousand nuclear warheads). When General George Lee Butler took command of SAC that year, after overcoming the resistance of his staff, he began examining each of those targets one by one. That review horrified him. There were too many warheads and not enough significant targets. Butler later said, "With the possible exception of the Soviet nuclear war plan, this was the single most absurd and irresponsible document I had ever reviewed in my life."[54] The SIOP was so secret, and the planners so compartmentalized, that it had effectively escaped rational control. Butler initiated a massive reduction in targets, took the bombers off constant alert, and advocated a reformed "living" SIOP that would undergo constant review with a rationalized "stable nucleus" of key targets. These changes would then allow a substantial reduction in the American nuclear arsenal. Butler also immediately canceled a then-planned $40 billion nuclear modernization. In 2005, the United States retained over 10,500 nuclear warheads. The 2002 Nuclear Posture Review suggested drawing down to around two thousand warheads, and the 2010 Nuclear Posture Review suggested an eventual drawdown to around 1,150 warheads. In March of 2014 the United States had approximately 1,550 operational warheads.[55]

Butler's and Turner's epiphanies, surprising them despite their many years of service and their intimate familiarity with nuclear weapons and nuclear planning, reflected the power of internalized assumptions and the internally consistent logic that had driven the arms race forward. For them, those insights were moments of breaking out from the confines of an institutional culture. Historian Michael Sherry used the phrase "technological fanaticism" to describe how American bombing planners in World War II could progress with great logical consistency from a theory of how to win a war from the air to strategically undirected wholesale destruction with no immediate vision of how that destruction would end the war, but with an unwavering commitment to continuing it. That "fanaticism" persisted into the Cold War, attaching itself to nuclear weapons. A belief in the efficacy of destroying industry to end war more quickly and reduce suffering had proceeded of its own logic, prodded by institutional protectionism, to the point where the extinction of human life on earth had become a real possibility. In General Butler's retrospective view:

> We believed that superior technology brought strategic advantage, that greater numbers meant stronger security, and that the ends of containment justified whatever means were necessary to achieve them. . . . [Those beliefs] spawned successive generations of new and more destructive devices and delivery systems. They gave rise to mammoth bureaucracies with gargantuan appetites and global agendas. They incited primal emotions, stirred zealotry and demagoguery, and set in motion forces of ungovernable scope and power.[56]

Butler's critique is deeply informed, but in some analysts' eyes the existence of nuclear weapons averted World War III and led to the end of great-power war in general. In this view, although the potential for apocalypse had been real, it had never been likely. As for the *idea* of strategic bombing, depending on one's perspective, under MAD strategic air power had either disabled itself or wildly succeeded. Fostering strategic airpower (in the expanded sense that includes both strategic bombers and missiles) had been the centerpiece of national military production. The strategy behind that production, however, was to build forces to prevent their use and to force the other side not to use theirs.

In the end, neither side did use them. Apocalypse was avoided, but its looming shadow had other strategic effects during the Cold War. Even prior to formalized MAD, the existence of nuclear weapons created a fear of escalation that limited many wars, and may even continue to do so. And although nuclear weapons at one level seemed to justify old theories about the ultimate superiority of air power, in limited wars nonnuclear strategic bombing proved less decisive than its proponents hoped.

THE NUCLEAR SHADOW AND LIMITED WAR IN KOREA AND VIETNAM

A standard theory within the discipline of political science to explain the actions of states describes them as actors within an anarchic system of sovereign states. In the absence of enforceable international rules, self-interest dominates state decision-making. International relations therefore produce more or less constant competition, often violent. Within individual violent conflicts self-interest continues to operate. As Clausewitz noted, a state will increase its commitment of resources to the conflict in accordance with the perceived importance of the outcome. The greater the importance, the greater the commitment, and the higher likelihood of *escalation*. Nuclear weapons presented the possibility of a catastrophe at the end of such escalation. Some scholars have suggested that the existence of nuclear weapons is a primary explanation for the lack of massive conventional wars between great powers and the overall decline in deaths from war since World War II—a prediction made by Bernard Brodie in 1946. That claim remains debatable, but their role in limiting war during the Cold War is much clearer. For that era the usual anarchic multi-state system was dominated by two superpowers. The bipolarity of the confrontation meant that many wars (although not all) carried implications for the superpowers, who, fearing escalation, intervened or sought to manage those conflicts so as to avoid a nuclear showdown. In the resulting limited wars, the US Air Force, primarily designed and programmed to bomb industrial targets as a means of winning a war, struggled to find a clear role.[57]

Korea

During the Korean War (1950–53), for example, the US Air Force entered the war with a set of problems. Although the American public had been persuaded of air power's potential by the bombing campaigns of World War II, the destruction had also produced a backlash of international public opinion that was particularly relevant in the emerging propaganda competition of the Cold War. Both superpowers, seeking to cultivate clients and allies around the world, painted each other as the real threat to world peace. Furthermore, industrial targeting would not work against North Korea. Supplied by China and the Soviet Union, it had little industrial infrastructure worth destroying other than ports and transportation nodes. American political leaders rejected calls for strategic attacks on North Korea's industrial sources in China or the Soviet Union in fear of escalating the war enormously, potentially putting western Europe at risk of a Soviet nuclear attack.

These limits did not obviate other forms of strategic bombing: civilian morale again became a target. The United States attacked North Korean cities after China intervened in the war, and beginning in the spring of 1952 the US initiated an "air pressure" campaign to try to force an armistice. That campaign included planning language echoing the early part of the century: "Whenever possible, attacks will be scheduled against targets of military significance so situated that their destruction will have a deleterious effect upon the morale of the civilian population."[58] Eventually the air planning staff advocated destroying North Korean dams, and thus the irrigation system required for North Korea's rice crop. Nervous about appearing to produce famine deliberately, American airmen claimed that targeting the dams was part of an "interdiction effort," since their destruction would flood key rail lines and bridges. Those attacks of course, also flooded the rice fields and emptied the reservoirs usually used for irrigation.[59]

To be sure, close air support for US and allied ground troops, provided by Air Force, Navy, and Marine Corps attack aircraft, was indispensable to success on the ground, but strategic air power remained effectively neutralized—except insofar as its existence in the form of a nuclear threat continuously bounded the conflict. The United States never took the use of nuclear weapons off the table, and assorted stalemates during the war repeatedly brought up that possibility. Finally, in 1953 the United States actively threatened their use, a gambit that seems to have played a key role in finally achieving a ceasefire.[60]

Vietnam

The US war in Vietnam from 1965 to 1973 presents an even more complex example of the difficulty of using strategic bombing in a limited war in the nuclear age. US bombing of industrial targets in North Vietnam not only failed to end the war in the South, but it may have been actually counterproductive. The story begins with the Viet Minh communist insurgency's final destruction of French colonial rule in Vietnam in 1954. The Geneva Accords negotiated that year partitioned the country into a communist north and a noncommunist south. Unlike in Korea, however, the new North Vietnamese government did not launch a massive conventional invasion. Instead, it supported a guerrilla war in the south, infiltrating its own regular forces into that part of the country. The program of infiltration expanded dramatically in 1964 and 1965. Since 1954 the United States had gradually stepped up its support for the South until the expansion of North Vietnam's direct involvement and the teetering of the South Vietnamese government eventually brought deeper American commitment. Direct intervention was then justified by a North Vietnamese attack on American destroyers in the Gulf of Tonkin in 1964.

The initial American response was to turn to air power, specifically to bombing strategic industrial and air-defense targets in the North, with the intent of gradually pressuring the regime to cease supporting the war in the South. The "Rolling Thunder" bombing campaign against North Vietnam lasted three years, from March 1965 to November 1968, dropping 643,000 tons of ordnance on that country. (Over the course of the war from 1965 to 1973, the United States dropped some eight million tons of bombs on North Vietnam, Laos, Cambodia, and South Vietnam, of which only 10 percent was dropped on the North. In contrast, the allies in World War II dropped two million tons of bombs in Europe.)[61]

The Rolling Thunder campaign had a variety of problems. Air Force advocates, then and now, argued that political limitations prevented them from waging an all-out bombing campaign on North Vietnamese industrial targets. But those "political limits" were real and of great significance: the US president's number one priority was to avoid intervention by either China or the Soviet Union and the consequent potential for nuclear escalation. American political leaders settled on a policy of "graduated military pressure," increasing over time, hoping that it would bring the North Vietnamese to heel while avoiding international expansion of the conflict.[62]

Furthermore, even if there had been no political limit on the bombing campaign, there were very few industrial facilities in North Vietnam to bomb. In language reminiscent of World War II planning documents, American military planners, seeking points of pressure, developed plans to attack "POL [petroleum, oil, and lubricants] storage, selected airfields, barracks/training areas, bridges, railroad yards, port facilities, communications, and industries." They further recommended that this be done in a "sharp, sudden blow" that would "paralyze the enemy's capability to move his equipment around and supply people in the South."[63] These recommendations led to intense debates among military and civilian leaders in the United States over political effects and the issue of civilian casualties, but few recognized at the time that North Vietnam's support for a guerrilla war in the South was not heavily dependent on either industry or modern transportation infrastructure. The decision to gradually escalate attacks was predicated on the belief that bombing some targets successfully would demonstrate that other more important targets were vulnerable, and the North would relent in fear of future attacks.

The intellectual and operational links between this industrial targeting and the use of air power in World War II were direct. The Air Force Chief of Staff during the 1964 bombing planning was General Curtis LeMay, famed for his success against Japan in 1945. His planners identified eighty-two fixed sites and twelve lines of communication as the key components of North Vietnam's modern infrastructure. Destroying those targets, which LeMay argued could be accomplished in just sixteen days, would utterly disrupt North Vietnam's economy and war effort without ever requiring a direct attack on the civilian population. Political considerations extended the time frame from LeMay's sixteen-day plan to the graduated-pressure option. Key civilian population centers such as Hanoi and Haiphong, for example, were initially placed off limits (remaining so until June 1966), as were sites dangerously close to the Chinese border. Political considerations also affected planning by emphasizing the strategic *interdiction* aspects of the campaign, since disrupting the North's ability to supply the war in the South seemed to be the central strategic problem. Both objectives, industrial targeting and strategic interdiction, however, contained within them the seeds of their own failure.

With respect to the first objective—destroying the North's industrial capacity—even had there been no political limitations, it is unclear what the difference would have been. By the end of Rolling Thunder in 1968 virtually all of North Vietnam's industrial infrastructure had been destroyed, including oil storage, power generation, and rail transportation. The war continued nonetheless, in part because neither the Vietnamese economy nor the fighting in the south depended on those assets. The civilian population was accustomed to life with little or no centralized electrical grid, and much of the infrastructure, including the trains, ran not on oil but on coal or wood. Furthermore, imports from the Soviet Union and China continued and even expanded. North Vietnam's gross national product actually increased by 6 percent during the bombing campaign of 1965, and continued to go up thereafter.[64]

As for the interdiction campaign, although 90 percent of Rolling Thunder's total bomb tonnage hit transportation targets, it had little impact on Communist activities in the South. According to prisoners' interviews, both the southern guerrillas and members of the North Vietnamese army (People's Army of Vietnam or PAVN) operating in the South fought on average in fewer than three engagements in twenty-six months. They chose their times of engagement. Lacking geographical chokepoints or specific resource requirements, that kind of war effort simply did not need much materiel. A CIA analysis in December 1965 suggested that North Vietnam's entire war effort in the South needed only a daily average of twelve tons of external supplies.[65]

Moreover, some scholars both during and after the war argued that Rolling Thunder actually worked against US political goals and advanced those of North Vietnam (although admittedly at great cost in civilian lives). North Vietnamese politicians deliberately played up the collateral damage to rally their own population, to sow seeds of disapproval within the US domestic audience, and to win further support from China and Russia (see Figure 13.7). American political restraints on the bombing combined poorly with the unavoidable civilian casualties, as limited as they were in many ways. An American analyst as early as 1966 suggested that "the U.S. campaign may have presented the [North Vietnamese] regime with a near-ideal mix of intended restraint and accidental gore."[66] Historian Mark Clodfelter goes further, arguing that American political and military leaders were blinded by their air power convictions; that belief in the efficacy of reaching over and beyond the front lines to attack the industrial and moral heart of the enemy kept them from understanding the true nature of the war they were fighting. Instead of understanding the real problem, military leaders turned automatically to their preferred solution. And, as in World War II, despite their strong initial preferences to avoid indiscriminate attacks on civilians, it proved a slippery slope from ineffective attacks on production and transportation networks to attacks on civilian "morale," although none of those attacks ever approached the indiscriminate quality of the firebombings of World War II.[67]

The use of strategic air power in Vietnam shifted several times after 1968 as conditions changed, but it is important to note that far more tons of ordnance were

Figure 13.7 A North Vietnamese propaganda poster. It reads: "Is this Nixon's military target?" Although from a later period than Rolling Thunder, it is representative of the bombing campaign's propaganda consequences.

Figure 13.8 Bicycles on the Ho Chi Minh trail. Bicycles carried much of the load on the trail, representing a highly dispersed target for interdiction bombing, as well as one easily capable of bypassing bombed-out bridges or fords (see Figure 13.9).

dropped in tactical or interdiction missions in the South from 1965 to 1968 than in the strategic missions in the North. One shift after 1968 was to focus the interdiction campaign on the Ho Chi Minh trail rather than on transportation networks inside North Vietnam. The logistical backbone of the North's war in South Vietnam infiltrated that country via low-tech routes through Laos and Cambodia, with much of the supplies carried along the trail on backs and bicycles (although trucks also mattered; see Figures 13.8 and 13.9). Unfortunately for US forces, however, even the largest estimates of the southern war's logistical requirements simply did not amount to much. Interdiction bombing could never be thorough enough to stop a guerrilla campaign. Furthermore, the Vietnamese constantly repaired and improved the trail. Despite almost nonstop interdiction bombing, totaling some 1.3 million sorties, by 1973 a truck could drive the full length of the trail and remain concealed under the natural and carefully augmented jungle canopy except at river crossings. Ironically, the plane the Vietnamese feared the most was not a bomber at all but the AC-130E, a cargo aircraft with cannon and machineguns mounted on its side.[68]

Later bombing campaigns were more effective, but the conditions of and goals for their use differed. In 1972, after American ground forces had been almost entirely withdrawn, North Vietnam launched its regular army, including tanks, on a conventional invasion of the South. Under those circumstances, the American "Linebacker" bombing campaign (May 10 to October 22, 1972) proved highly effective. The North Vietnamese army suffered severely, and with Chinese and Soviet support waning North Vietnam agreed to peace talks. When the talks stalled, President Nixon authorized Linebacker II (December 18–29, 1972), an intense bombing campaign against assorted strategic targets in the North—many of them rebuilt after the bombing halt of 1968 and others now vulnerable due to the change in international political arrangements (some formerly restricted areas were now opened to bombing). Over just a few days American aircraft dropped some twenty thousand tons of bombs while simultaneously mining the port at Haiphong. North Vietnam agreed to a peace treaty, but the effect of bombing on their decision remains debated. It is certainly clear that the treaty provided political cover for the final US withdrawal of ground forces from Vietnam, something well known to the North Vietnamese leadership. They may simply have accepted the treaty knowing the United States was pulling out, rather than having been forced to accept it by Linebacker II.[69]

Figure 13.9 Bombed-out bridge on the Ho Chi Minh trail, Laos.
Note the continued use of the ford, also bombed.

Notwithstanding the difficulties of getting the desired political results from the bombing campaigns, the tremendous burst of military spending associated with Vietnam combined in unexpectedly fruitful ways with the specific frustrations of that war. The interdiction missions and the increasing desire to bomb strategic targets with less collateral damage helped spur the development of precision-guided munitions (PGMs), or "smart bombs." The Linebacker missions included the first significant use of camera-guided ("electro-optical") and laser-guided bombs, precision weapons that were credited with some of the increased interdiction effectiveness of that campaign. Furthermore, the interdiction effort along the Ho Chi Minh trail, movement along which was mostly invisible from the air, led the Americans to deploy a vast array of ground sensors, whose signals were then linked to an intelligence collection center that in turn dispatched bombing missions. After American withdrawal from Vietnam, the evolutionary development of precision munitions and networked intelligence-collection technologies continued apace, in part because of the Americans' willingness to spend capacity on maintaining a qualitative lead over their Soviet counterpart. American air forces, however, did not again experience significant combat until the Gulf War of 1991, when their newly unveiled capabilities suggested to some that there had been a "revolution in military affairs." Ironically, it was theorists in the Soviet Union who first began to fear that the United States was on the verge of achieving a significant leap forward in conventional force capability based on this linking of precision munitions and intelligence collection, something the Soviets called a "Military-Technical Revolution." The Americans, however, pursued a variety of technological possibilities more or less willy-nilly, without an overarching theory, but driven by interservice rivalry and the apparently boundless pursuit of qualitative advantage, while reflecting a long and accelerating American cultural investment in substituting firepower for manpower. The Americans first suspected the potential of their own capabilities by reading Soviet reports on the topic in the late 1980s. The events of 1991 then seemed to crystallize the revolutionary leap, while also leading to a renewed faith in a revised form of strategic bombing. Precision-guided munitions seemed to offer a way to restore decisiveness to strategic bombing without the all-or-nothing quality of a nuclear exchange.[70]

THE RETURN OF STRATEGIC AIR POWER AND THE REVOLUTION IN MILITARY AFFAIRS?

The Soviet Union's economy eventually collapsed and the state dissolved in 1991, at least partly because of the economic strain of the arms race. The sudden disappearance of the nuclear confrontation appeared to shift dramatically the dynamics of international politics. Where superpower interventions had been limited by fear of the other's response (or by fear of the propaganda consequences on the ideological struggle for clients), President George H. W. Bush in 1991 could declare a "new world order," in which the former opponents could now cooperate in shaping a more peaceful world. In this case President Bush was referring specifically to reversing the Iraqi invasion of Kuwait in August 1990.

The ensuing Gulf War (January 17–February 28, 1991) opened with a month of bombing preparatory to a short and overpowering land campaign into Iraq and Kuwait by coalition forces. Planning for the air campaign reflected a revived and revised view of strategic air power. Colonel John A. Warden III presented a plan for the preparatory bombing based on an elaboration and restatement of the industrial web theory called the "five-ring model" of a modern state (see Figure 13.10). In this model, each ring represented a different class of targets, decreasing in importance as one moves away from the bullseye. Warden's theory suggested that early and heavy attacks on the central rings would disrupt the regime (later writers would refer to this as "strategic paralysis"). It is essential to point out that this theory was designed to produce temporary paralysis to enable strategic defeat. It was not an effort to utterly destroy the enemy's economy, as it had been for both World War II planners and Cold War nuclear planners. This was a new vision for the role of air power, although still in a strategic war-winning mode.[71]

Warden's initial Instant Thunder plan called for two phases of air attack. In the first, relatively traditional phase, coalition fliers and missiles would attack enemy aircraft and air defenses to free up the skies for coalition

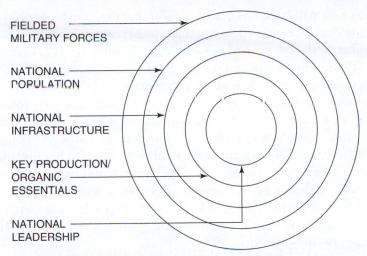

FIELDED
MILITARY FORCES

NATIONAL
POPULATION

NATIONAL
INFRASTRUCTURE

KEY PRODUCTION/
ORGANIC
ESSENTIALS

NATIONAL
LEADERSHIP

Figure 13.10 John Warden's "Five-Ring" model of the modern nation-state. Warden's model provided the conceptual foundation for the initial planning of the Desert Storm air campaign.

bombers. Those bombers, in the second phase, would use precision munitions to strike at strategic targets, including traditional "industrial" facilities, especially oil production, but now focusing more sharply on key communications and political targets. Their destruction, Warden argued, would render the Iraqi state incapable of directing its armed forces, and the paralyzed Iraqi army would not need to be targeted at all. In the end, however, Warden's superiors revised his plan to lengthen the bombing and included a very substantial attack on Iraqi armed forces. The actual five-week air campaign, especially as briefed each day to the international press corps, seemed to demonstrate a radically new effectiveness for air power, including much ballyhooed videos of precision-guided munitions flying into ventilation shafts or hitting single armored vehicles.[72]

The riveting gun camera evidence left little doubt that a new level of precision had been achieved, and later details from attacks on Iraqi oil facilities supported that impression. Some 540 bombing sorties, the vast majority conducted over a single fifteen-day stretch, reduced Iraqi oil production at twenty-eight facilities by 90 percent. This accuracy contrasts sharply with the oil-targeting campaign in World War II, during which sixty-nine German refineries were hit by fifty thousand sorties dropping 185,541 tons of bombs, but only cut production by 60 percent. On the other hand, much of the Gulf War air campaign was not directed at strategic targets, nor did it use precision munitions. In fact, only 11 percent of the strike sorties were conducted against strategic targets. Of the 222,479 bombs or missiles dropped (excluding cruise missiles), 209,625, or 94 percent, were unguided "general purpose bombs," and 21 percent of those were dropped from high altitude by aging B-52 bombers, originally built for the nuclear mission. Despite Warden's emphasis on achieving state paralysis, it is not at all clear that the Iraqi leadership experienced it, or that attacks on strategic targets (other than Iraqi air defenses) had much effect on the outcome of the war.[73]

Even the accuracy of the tactical bombing campaign against Iraqi forces in the field raised questions, at least with respect to cost and benefits. According to a postwar Defense Intelligence Agency (DIA) estimate, in forty-four days of bombing, air strikes destroyed 1,680 tanks, armored personnel carriers, and artillery pieces. Coalition ground and air forces, in the four days of the ground war, destroyed 4,817 (74 percent of the total destroyed). To be sure, there was a clear synchronicity of effect: weeks of coalition bombing had demoralized Iraqi forces, even leading many crews to abandon their exposed vehicles. And Iraqi prisoners regularly cited the B-52 strikes as particularly terrifying, an opinion shared by Vietnamese soldiers and guerrillas who had experienced B-52 strikes twenty-five years before.[74]

Further analysis after the war, and especially the failure of the strategic component of the campaign to bring down the regime or obviate the need for a ground war, revived discussion of what air forces should primarily target. Everyone agreed about attacking enemy air defenses first and achieving command of the air, but what should come after that? Within the three broad categories of targeting—strategic core, strategic military/interdiction, and close air support—there is debate over the effects one should seek and how one should achieve them. Strategic interdiction and even close-air-support campaigns can be designed to attack military units and vehicles, or they can be targeted at troop morale or at roads and rail networks. Each requires different air tactics and even different equipment. We have already seen the essential division in late World War I and during World War II over whether the strategic core was the industrial web or civilian morale, or both at once.

The question of what constituted the strategic core (Warden's inner rings) took on renewed importance in the wake of the Gulf War. Discussions of the presumed Revolution in Military Affairs (RMA), although much broader than air power, centered on paralyzing the enemy's political and military command capability, a goal that played well into the US military's preference for high-tempo war. Chapter 12 discussed how maneuver war theory in its modern version sought to get inside the decision cycle of its opponents—to be able to react to changing events more rapidly than the enemy. Precision munitions, targeted in such a way that they *lengthened* the enemy's decision cycle by taking out command and communication, was combined with a networked ability to deliver information that *shortened* the US decision cycle. Taken together, these technologies suggested to some a radically new capacity to dominate the battlefield.

The air campaign in Kosovo in 1999 furthered the debate. From some perspectives it appeared that the United States had forced the Serbian government to cease its ground operations within Kosovo entirely through a seventy-eight day bombing campaign. Had victory solely through the air finally been achieved? As in 1991, a closer look suggests reality was more complicated. The first problem was that the strategic goal presented a serious mismatch with the initial results. The US policy goal was to force the Serbian government and army to cease ethnic-cleansing operations against the majority ethnic Albanian population in Kosovo. The bombing campaign, under NATO command but dominated by American forces, lacked a clear connection between this policy goal and its conduct of operations. Bombing actually accelerated ethnic cleansing, because its initiation freed the Serbians from needing to show restraint without disrupting or slowing down the movements of Serbian forces doing the killing and burning. Serbian forces inside Kosovo actually tripled in size during the bombing.[75]

The second problem emerged from NATO's shifting and uncertain notion of what to bomb. The preference remained for strategic core targets, but was that industry? State communications? Civilian morale and/or support for the regime? Early strikes, beyond the usual opening attacks on air defense systems, focused on hitting Serbia and Serbian president Slobodan Milošević, but in the end NATO aircraft attacked all these targets, including factories, television stations and broadcast towers, party headquarters, ministry buildings, the electrical grid, bridges, and more. Most embarrassingly, misled by outdated maps, NATO planes hit the Chinese embassy in Belgrade. It was never clear, however, how the destruction of any of those targets would slow the atrocities occurring daily in Kosovo.[76]

There were also strenuous efforts to bomb Serbian forces in Kosovo, but the natural focus was on armored vehicles and artillery pieces, and a host of problems intervened. Sophisticated Serbian air defenses forced high-altitude release of laser-guided bombs. In Europe, however, bad weather or cloud cover was common (cloud cover exceeded 50 percent almost three-quarters of the time). Clouds obscured the camera used to direct the laser—and thus the bomb—onto the target. Meanwhile the Serbians built a host of decoy vehicles and successfully camouflaged the real ones. One postwar estimate, countering a more optimistic wartime briefing by the US Joint Chiefs of Staff, suggested that NATO had dropped twenty-three thousand weapons in seventy-eight days of bombing (of which 29 percent were precision-guided munitions), but knocked out only fifty-two Serbian combat systems (fourteen tanks, eighteen armored personnel carriers, and twenty artillery pieces).[77]

The debate over exactly why the Serbian president finally agreed to terms remains unresolved. He never revealed what the critical point was in his own mind. Advocates for and against strategic bombing continue to debate whether the success of the Kosovo Liberation Army on the ground in the last days of the bombing, or the growing likelihood of NATO ground forces, or the withdrawal of Russian support, or simply the bombing alone finally forced his hand. One thing, however, was clear: US use of precision-guided munitions was increasing. A far larger percentage of the munitions dropped in 1999 were precision versus those dropped in 1991, although the limitations of laser guidance in cloudy skies and from high altitude were also now clear. It was *not* obvious, however, whether attacking the Serbian decision cycle, or even Serbian command and control over their armed forces, had mattered at all.

Nevertheless, air power theorists had been reworking some of Colonel Warden's ideas from 1991 and had produced an updated version, something they called "shock and awe," first published in 1996. The term has been subject to much misuse and misunderstanding since its first widespread appearance in the media in 2003. The idea demanded not overwhelming and stupefying force so much as an especially rapid and especially precise bombing of key political and communications assets, occurring with such rapidity and simultaneity that the armed forces of the state would be paralyzed from perceptual overload. In short, their decision cycle would simply freeze up. The theory was not that different than Warden's, but it even more strongly emphasized US information dominance and precision delivery capabilities, including new Global Positioning System (GPS)-guided bombs, as well as other increasingly accurate delivery systems (see Figure 13.11).[78]

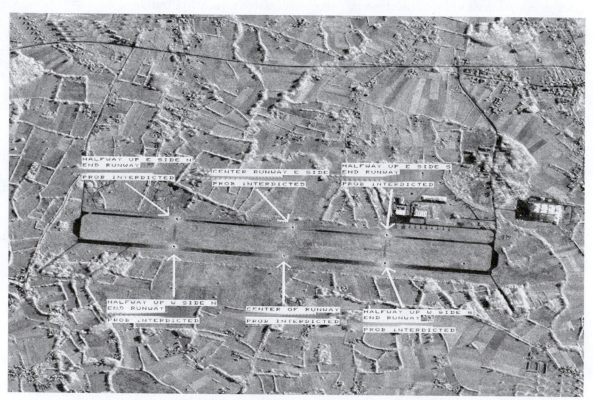

Figure 13.11 The Accuracy of GPS-guided bombs, 1999. This Serbian airfield was hit in 1999 by a single U.S. B-2 bomber. It dropped six GPS-guided JDAM bombs, precisely hitting each intersection on the airfield. This photo documents the precision capable against targets with fixed GPS coordinates as well as the small number of bombs needed to render the field non-operational.

Some of those new capabilities were showcased during the American ousting of the Taliban government from Afghanistan in 2001, but there the regime's resources were so primitive that strategic core bombing was almost nonexistent. The overwhelming majority of air power use in Afghanistan was some form of close air support, vastly improved by precision munitions and networked target-information relay. One measure of the change in capability is provided by a seemingly simple statistic. During the 1991 Gulf War only 20 percent of aircraft sorties were "redirected after launch," meaning that 80 percent were provided their target prior to leaving their bases. For stationary, strategic core targets that represents little problem, but close air support or even some forms of interdiction missions might find their targets had long since moved on. The problem was establishing communications systems that relayed real-time target location information to the incoming pilot. In Afghanistan in 2001 US forces could bounce target information from one platform to another to another, literally around the world, on networked information systems. A drone-mounted video camera, capable of determining a target's GPS coordinates, could relay that information to B-52s flying thousands of feet up, which could then drop GPS-guided bombs with phenomenal accuracy onto those coordinates without ever seeing the target. In 2001 some 43 percent of sorties were redirected after launch, and in Iraq in 2003 that figure jumped to 80 percent. Interestingly, it was in 2003 that a "shock and awe" campaign was actually attempted. Unlike Afghanistan, Iraq *was* a highly centralized and technically advanced state, and the opening days of bombing sought to paralyze the state and its army. Aspects of the campaign worked, but the Iraqi army continued to move, and by the second week of the initial invasion campaign two-thirds of the strike missions had shifted to troop targets. That shift accounts for the high percentage of sorties redirected after launch.[79]

CONCLUSION

Even in 2003 it was unclear whether the dreams of the air power enthusiasts of 1917 had come to fruition. During the Cold War, nuclear weaponry seemed to promise almost "frictionless war." Clausewitz's purely hypothetical notion of endless escalation as each side sought to dominate the other seemed to have been

TIMELINE

1918	End of World War I
1921	Publication of Douhet's *Command of the Air*
1938	First B-17 bomber
1945	Atomic bombs dropped on Hiroshima and Nagasaki; end of World War II
1950–1953	Korean War
1952	First fusion bomb test, United States
1957	*Sputnik*
1962	Cuban Missile Crisis
1965–1968	Rolling Thunder bombing campaign in Vietnam
1983	Able Archer nuclear scare
1991	Collapse of the Soviet Union; Desert Storm air campaign
1999	Kosovo air campaign
2001	Campaign against the Taliban regime in Afghanistan
2003	US invasion of Iraq

brought to life with consequences that threatened the entire planet. Fortunately that level of destructiveness was so extreme that in one sense nuclear weapons disabled themselves—for the most part nuclear strategy sought to deter, not defeat. Meanwhile, continued American pursuit of victory through strategic air power, fitting in neatly with a long-established American strategic culture that preferred to spend firepower over manpower, had produced new capabilities. By the turn of the twenty-first century strategic bombing could be done with great precision and rapidity. Although Air Force leaders are no longer fixated on strategic core bombing, technological advances instead have produced a new temptation to fight wars from a distance, using standoff precision bombs and missiles. Even so, one must still identify a target worth hitting. The Taliban in Afghanistan and the insurgents in Iraq quickly learned how to avoid becoming targets.[80] Effective air power requires three components: identifying a target, relaying that target information, and then effectively hitting that target. The latter two components have been very efficiently mastered in recent decades. Identifying the target, however, remains a challenge, whether that target is some form of "strategic core" or a dispersed group of armed insurgents hiding among the population—a tactic now increasingly common among those seeking to avoid the overwhelming firepower dominance of Western nations. The innovation of modern guerrilla and terrorist insurgency, originally created to avoid that firepower, and the Western response of counterinsurgency, are the subjects of the next and final chapter.

Further Reading

Adamsky, Dima. *The Culture of Military Innovation: The Impact of Cultural Factors on the Revolution in Military Affairs in Russia, the US, and Israel.* Stanford, CA: Stanford University Press, 2010.

Biddle, Tami Davis. *Rhetoric and Reality in Air Warfare: The Evolution of British and American Ideas about Strategic Bombing, 1914–1945.* Princeton, NJ: Princeton University Press, 2002.

Budiansky, Stephen. *Air Power: The Men, Machines, and Ideas that Revolutionized War, from Kitty Hawk to Gulf War II.* New York: Viking, 2004.

Clodfelter, Mark. *The Limits of Air Power: The American Bombing of North Vietnam.* New York: Free Press, 1989.

Crane, Conrad C. *Bombs, Cities, and Civilians: American Airpower Strategy in World War II.* Lawrence: University Press of Kansas, 1993.

Freedman, Lawrence. *The Evolution of Nuclear Strategy.* 3rd ed. New York: Palgrave Macmillan, 2003.

Gaddis, John Lewis. *The Cold War: A New History.* New York: Penguin, 2005.

Gat, Azar. *A History of Military Thought: From the Enlightenment to the Cold War.* Oxford: Oxford University Press, 2001.

Overy, R. J. *The Air War, 1939–1945.* Chelsea, MI: Scarborough House, 1991.

Sherry, Michael S. *The Rise of American Air Power: The Creation of Armageddon.* New Haven, CT: Yale University Press, 1987.

Werrell, Kenneth P. *Chasing the Silver Bullet: U.S. Air Force Weapons Development from Vietnam to Desert Storm.* Washington, DC: Smithsonian Books, 2003.

Notes

1. There were bomber advocates in Japan, but they did not develop a full-blown concept of strategic bombing as a separate war-fighting strategy; it remained an auxiliary to land and naval forces. Japan did resort to long-range terror bombing in China in an effort to bring down the Chinese Nationalist government. Mark R. Peattie, *Sunburst: The Rise of Japanese Naval Air Power, 1909–1941* (Annapolis, Md.: Naval Institute Press, 2001), 85–7, 103, 115–22.

2. Bernard Brodie, ed., *The Absolute Weapon* (New York: Harcourt, Brace, 1946), 76 (quote).

3. The sections that follow through 1945 are heavily dependent on Tami Davis Biddle, *Rhetoric and Reality in Air Warfare: The Evolution of British and American Ideas about Strategic Bombing, 1914–1945* (Princeton, NJ: Princeton University Press, 2002). Specific page references are given where appropriate.

4. Biddle, *Rhetoric*, 20–23; John H. Morrow, Jr., "States and Strategic Airpower: Continuity and Change, 1906–1939," in *The Influence of Airpower upon History*, ed. Robin Higham and Mark Parillo (Lexington: University Press of Kentucky, 2013), 37–60, here 42. On the fragility of the working class's relationship to the state, see Geoffrey Best, "The Militarization of European Society, 1870–1914," in *The Militarization of the Western World*, ed. John R. Gillis (New Brunswick, NJ: Rutgers University Press, 1989), 14.

5. Biddle, *Rhetoric*, 26, 29–35, 74.

6. Quoted in Biddle, *Rhetoric*, 37.

7. Biddle, *Rhetoric*, 40, 45; I. B. Holley, Jr. *Ideas and Weapons: Exploitation of the Aerial Weapon by the United States during World War I* (Washington, DC: Office of Air Force History, 1983), 138–39.

8. Quoted in Holley, *Ideas and Weapons*, 135.

9. Holley, *Ideas and Weapons*, 139.

10. I. F. Clarke, *Voices Prophesying War, 1763–1984* (London: Oxford University Press, 1966), 30–163.

11. Giulio Douhet, *The Command of the Air*, trans. Dino Ferrari (New York: Coward-McCann, 1942; repr., Office of Air Force History, 1983), vii–viii, quotes on 9–10, 16, 20, 22.

12. Thomas Hippler, *Bombing the People: Giulio Douhet and the Foundations of Air-Power Strategy, 1884–1939* (Cambridge: Cambridge University Press, 2013); Morrow, "States and Strategic Airpower," 37 (quote).

13. Morrow, "States and Strategic Airpower," 48–56; David E. Omissi, *Air Power and Colonial Control: The Royal Air Force, 1919–1939* (Manchester, UK: Manchester University Press, 1990); David R. Jones, "The Emperor and the Despot: Statesmen, Patronage, and the Strategic Bomber in Imperial and Soviet Russia, 1909–1959," in Higham and Parillo, *Influence of Airpower*, 115–43, esp. 124–35.

14. Kenneth P. Werrell, *Death From the Heavens: A History of Strategic Bombing* (Annapolis, MD: Naval Institute Press, 2009), 46–57; R. J. Overy, *The Air War 1939–1945* (Chelsea, MI: Scarborough House, 1980) 119–20; Stephen Budiansky, *Air Power: The Men, Machines, and Ideas that Revolutionized War, from Kitty Hawk to Gulf War II* (New York: Viking, 2004), 221–34. As discussed in chapter 12 with respect to tanks, the lack of a stockpile of obsolete aircraft in many respects aided the modernization of the Luftwaffe.

15. Biddle, *Rhetoric*, 60–62; Budiansky, *Air Power*, 131 (quote).

16. Trenchard (1928) quoted in Beatrice Heuser, *The Evolution of Strategy: Thinking War from Antiquity to the Present* (Cambridge, UK: Cambridge University Press, 2010), 331.

17. Biddle, *Rhetoric*, 69–127.

18. Holley, *Ideas and Weapons*, 158–59, 168–70, 173; David E. Johnson, *Fast Tanks and Heavy Bombers: Innovation in the U.S. Army, 1917–1945* (Ithaca, NY: Cornell University Press, 1998), 85 (quote).

19. Johnson, *Fast Tanks*, 58–59, and 81–91.

20. Johnson, *Fast Tanks*, 91, 93, 156.

21. Biddle, *Rhetoric*, 163; Johnson, *Fast Tanks*, 162.

22. Johnson, *Fast Tanks*, 83, 88, 163.

23. Biddle, *Rhetoric*, 161–67.

24. Overy, *Air War*, 110; Biddle, *Rhetoric*, 189, 195–97, 217.

25. Quoted in Johnson, *Fast Tanks*, 169–70; Budiansky, *Air Power*, 287.

26. Biddle, *Rhetoric*, 209; Charles Webster and Noble Frankland, *The Strategic Air Offensive against Germany, 1939–1945*, vol. 5, *Annexes and Appendices* (London: HMSO, 1961), 273–83 (quotes). The number of systems and targets changed several times, partly as allied forces brought more targets within range. See Overy, *Air War*, 74, 111.

27. Quoted in Biddle, *Rhetoric*, 220.

28. Biddle, *Rhetoric*, 224.

29. Werrell, *Death From the Heavens*, 120–21; compare the changing wartime bombing accuracy in Budiansky, *Air Power*, 328; Thomas R. Searle, "'It Made a Lot of Sense to Kill Skilled Workers': The Firebombing of Tokyo in March 1945," *Journal of Military History* 66 (2002): 103–34, 108–9; Biddle, *Rhetoric*, 253–54, 245.

30. Quoted in Heuser, *Evolution of Strategy*, 334–35.

31. Biddle, *Rhetoric*, 233; Budiansky, *Air Power*, 288.

32. Budiansky, *Air Power*, 328–29; Biddle, *Rhetoric*, 229, 232, 236–37, 243, 239, 254–55.

33. Quoted in John W. Dower, *Cultures of War* (New York: W. W. Norton, 2010), 168.

34. Searle, "It Made a Lot of Sense," 117–18 ("made sense" quote); Biddle, *Rhetoric*, 264 ("dislocation" quote).

35. Searle, "It Made a Lot of Sense," 128 (quote); the strongest statement for the role of racism in the American war in the Pacific is John W. Dower's *War without Mercy: Race and Power in the Pacific War* (New York: Pantheon, 1986).

36. Biddle discusses the rhetoric/reality divergence, and the contemporary concerns about indiscriminate bombing, in *Rhetoric*, 255–60, 268–69; Conrad C. Crane, *Bombs, Cities, and Civilians: American Airpower Strategy in World War II* (Lawrence: University Press of Kansas, 1993).

37. Lawrence Freedman, *The Evolution of Nuclear Strategy*, 3rd ed. (New York: Palgrave Macmillan, 2003), 21 (quote).

38. Budiansky, *Air Power*, 340–41.

39. Kenneth P. Werrell, *Chasing the Silver Bullet: U.S. Air Force Weapons Development from Vietnam to Desert Storm* (Washington, DC: Smithsonian Books, 2003), 7 (quote).

40. Telephone conversation transcript, General Hull and Colonel Seaman [*sic*], 1325, 13 Aug 45, available as document no. 72 in William Burr, ed., *The Atomic Bomb and the End of World War II: A Collection of Primary Sources*, National Security Archive Electronic Briefing Book no. 162, http://www2.gwu.edu/~nsarchiv/NSAEBB/NSAEBB162/, accessed August 5, 2014; Budiansky, *Air Power*, 340–41.

41. David Alan Rosenberg, "American Atomic Strategy and the Hydrogen Bomb Decision," *Journal of American History* 66.1 (1979): 68, 71; Mark Clodfelter, *The Limits of Air Power: The American Bombing of North Vietnam* (New York: Free Press, 1989), 12.

42. This paragraph is based on Joseph Smith, *The Cold War*, 2nd ed. (Oxford: Blackwell, 1998), 33, 36; John Lewis Gaddis, *The Cold War: A New History* (New York: Penguin, 2005), 35–41.

43. "*Big Ivan*, The Tsar Bomba ('King of Bombs')," at http://nuclearweaponarchive.org/Russia/TsarBomba.html, accessed December 2, 2014.

44. Quoted in Conrad C. Crane, *American Airpower Strategy in Korea, 1950–1953* (Lawrence: University Press of Kansas, 2000), 11.

45. Rosenberg, "American Atomic Strategy," 64, 68, 70–73.

46. Douglas P. Lackey, *Moral Principles and Nuclear Weapons* (Totowa, NJ: Rowman & Allanheld, 1984), 44–49, discusses several of these episodes; also Smith, *Cold War*, 61; Francis J. Gavin, "What We Talk about When We Talk about Nuclear Weapons: A Review Essay," H-Diplo/ISSF Forum no. 2 (2014), 11, available online at http://issforum.org/ISSF/PDF/ISSF-Forum-2.pdf, accessed July 10, 2014; Bernard C. Nalty, "The Air Force Role in Five Crises, 1958–1965: Lebanon, Taiwan, Congo, Cuba, Dominican Republic," United States Air Force Historical Division Liaison Office, June 1968, available online at http://www2.gwu.edu/~nsarchiv/nukevault/ebb249/doc10.pdf, accessed July 21, 2014; Fred Kaplan, "JFK's First Strike Plan," *Atlantic Monthly*, October 2001, 81–86, available online at http://www.theatlantic.com/past/docs/issues/2001/10/kaplan.htm, accessed July 21, 2014; Rosenberg, "American Atomic Strategy," 69; Edward Kaplan, *To Kill Nations: American Strategy in the Air-Atomic Age and the Rise of Mutually Assured Destruction* (Ithaca, NY: Cornell University Press, 2015).

47. C. Dale Walton, "Weapons Technology in the Two Nuclear Ages," in *The Cambridge History of War*, vol. 4, *War and the Modern World*, ed. Roger Chickering, Dennis Showalter, and Hans Van de Ven (Cambridge, UK: Cambridge University Press, 2012), 472–92 (here 476, 482).

48. Freedman, *Evolution of Nuclear Strategy*, 231–33; Walton, "Weapons Technology," 482–83; Gaddis, *The Cold War*, 80–81; for a recently declassified 1961 assessment of the likely damage of a nuclear exchange, one that seems to have profoundly shaken President Kennedy, see National Security Archive, "Studies by Once Top Secret Government Entity Portrayed Terrible Costs of Nuclear War: Reports of the Net Evaluation Subcommittee," http://nsarchive.gwu.edu/nukevault/ebb480/, accessed April 13, 2015.

49. Gaddis, *The Cold War*, 81.

50. Freedman, *Evolution of Nuclear Strategy*, 222–30, esp. 230; Walton, "Weapons Technology," 483. Data for Table 13.1: all SLBM and ICBM figures from Donald MacKenzie, *Inventing Accuracy: A Historical Sociology of Nuclear Missile Guidance* (Cambridge, MA: MIT Press, 1990), table A.1 and A.2 (selected missiles only); http://missilethreat.com/missiles/tomahawk-variants/; http://www.bga-aeroweb.com/Defense/JDAM.html, both accessed December 3, 2014. World War II accuracy varied over time, since it depended on the bombardier and the navigator rather than an independent guidance system. This is a rough average from Department of the Air Force, *The United States Strategic Bombing Surveys*, *Summary Reports* (Maxwell Air Force Base, AL: Air University Press, 1983), 13.

51. Kenneth P. Werrell, *The Evolution of the Cruise Missile* (Maxwell Air Force Base, AL: Air University Press, 1985), 151, 156. The key source here is MacKenzie, *Inventing Accuracy*, passim, esp. 3–4, 384–85.

52. Peter Vincent Pry, *War Scare: Russia and America on the Nuclear Brink* (Westport, CT: Praeger, 1999), 33–44; National Security Archive, "The Able Archer Sourcebook," available online at http://www2.gwu.edu/~nsarchiv/nukevault/ablearcher/, accessed December 3, 2014; Nate Jones, "Stasi Documents Provide Details on Operation RYaN, the Soviet Plan to Predict and Preempt a Western Nuclear Strike; Show Uneasiness over Degree of 'Clear-Headedness about the Entire RYaN Complex,'" at *Unredacted* (blog), January 29, 2014, http://nsarchive.wordpress.com/2014/01/29/stasi-documents-provide-operational-details-on-operation-ryan-the-soviet-plan-to-predict-and-preempt-a-western-nuclear-strike-show-uneasiness-over-degree-of-clear-headedness-about-the-entire-ryan/#_ftnref1, accessed December 3, 2014.

53. Tom Sauer, *Nuclear Inertia: U.S. Nuclear Weapons Policy after the Cold War* (London: I. B. Tauris, 2005), 162; Stansfield Turner,

Caging the Nuclear Genie: An American Challenge for Global Security (Boulder, CO: Westview, 1997), 7–9.

54. Speech given by General George Lee Butler in Montreal, March 11, 1999 to the Canadian Network against Nuclear Weapons, available online at http://www.waging peace.org/general-lee-butler-addresses-the-canadian-network-against-nuclear-weapons/, accessed July 23, 2014 (quote).

55. Sauer, *Nuclear Inertia*, 157–58, 164; "Highlights of the Nuclear Posture Review," *Washington Post*, April 7, 2010, http://www.washingtonpost.com/wp-dyn/content/graphic/2010/04/06/GR2010040604804.html, accessed July 24, 2014.

56. Michael S. Sherry, *The Rise of American Air Power: The Creation of Armageddon* (New Haven, Conn.: Yale University Press, 1987), passim, esp. 251–255, 316; Lee Butler, "A Voice of Reason," *Bulletin of Atomic Scientists* 54.3 (May/June 1998): 58–9 (quote).

57. Kenneth N. Waltz, *Man, the State, and War* (New York: Columbia University Press, 1959); Kenneth N. Waltz, *Theory of International Politics* (New York: Random House, 1979); Brodie, *Absolute Weapon*, 74–75. Even after the Cold War, in the so-called Second Nuclear Age, nuclear weapons may continue to operate as a restraint on international war. The old system of anarchic interstate relations seems permanently altered by their existence. Walton, "Weapons Technology," 472, 487, 491. Steven Pinker, *The Better Angels of our Nature* (New York: Penguin, 2011), 268–78, explores that idea but discredits it; Pinker prefers the role of shifts in "reason" very broadly defined as well as a surge in economic interdependence, but one might argue that a rational fear of nuclear weapons played a role in the shifting attitudes toward war.

58. Quoted in Clodfelter, *Limits of Air Power*, 17.

59. Clodfelter, *Limits of Air Power*, 17–18.

60. Smith, *Cold War*, 61; this paragraph relies on Crane, *American Airpower Strategy in Korea*, esp. 6–9.

61. Clodfelter, *Limits of Air Power*, 129; Budiansky, *Air Power*, 329, 383–84.

62. Much of this paragraph is based on Clodfelter, *Limits of Air Power*, passim, summarized on 43–45. Key points on 68, 76–77; 127, 85.

63. Clodfelter, *Limits of Air Power*, 46, 47 (quotes).

64. Clodfelter, *Limits of Air Power*, 134–37; Ronald H. Spector, *After Tet: The Bloodiest Year in Vietnam* (New York: Free Press, 1993), 16.

65. Spector, *After Tet*, 90; Clodfelter, *Limits of Air Power*, 134, 93.

66. quoted in Clodfelter, *Limits of Air Power*, 138.

67. Clodfelter, *Limits of Air Power*, 118, 127.

68. Bernard C. Nalty, *The War against Trucks: Aerial Interdiction in Southern Laos, 1968–1972* (Washington, DC: Air Force History and Museums Program, 2005), 295, 297; Military History Institute of Vietnam, *Victory in Vietnam: The Official History of the People's Army of Vietnam, 1954–1975*, trans. Merle L. Pribbenow (Lawrence: University Press of Kansas, 2002), 262.

69. Werrell, *Death from the Heavens*, 219–24; Clodfelter, *Limits of Air Power*, 147–202.

70. Clodfelter, *Limits of Air Power*, 167; Werrell, *Chasing the Silver Bullet*, 152; Seymour J. Deitchman, "The 'Electronic Battlefield' in the Vietnam War," *Journal of Military History* 72 (2008): 869–87; Dima Adamsky, *The Culture of Military Innovation: The Impact of Cultural Factors on the Revolution in Military Affairs in Russia, the U.S., and Israel* (Stanford, CA: Stanford University Press, 2010), 26–31, 58–74. For American preference for firepower, see Adrian R. Lewis, *The American Culture of War: The History of U.S. Military Force from World War II to Operation Iraqi Freedom*, 2nd ed. (New York: Routledge, 2012).

71. Edward C. Mann, *Thunder and Lighting: Desert Storm and the Airpower Debates*

(Maxwell Air Force Base, AL: Air University Press, 1995), 33–47; John Buckley, "Air Power and the Modern World," in *War in the Modern World since 1815*, ed. Jeremy Black (London: Routledge, 2003), 242.

72. Mark Moyar, "The Era of American Hegemony, 1989–2005," in Chickering, Showalter, and Van de Ven, *Cambridge History of War*, 566–88, esp. 569–70; Werrell, *Death from the Heavens*, 286.

73. Thomas A. Keaney and Eliot A. Cohen, *Gulf War Air Power Survey, Summary Report* (Washington, DC: GPO, 1993), 76, 65, 72, fig. 12, p. 65, and table 3, p. 103, available online at http://www.afhso.af.mil/shared/media/document/AFD-100927-061.pdf, accessed July 30, 2014; Werrell, *Death from the Heavens*, 290.

74. There are multiple and conflicting estimates. This is based on postwar DIA figures that represent something of a compromise between other sets of numbers, as found in Department of the Air Force, *Gulf War Air Power Survey* (Washington, DC: GPO, 1993), 2:211, 213; Clodfelter, *Limits of Air Power*, 196; for the Gulf War: Stephen Peter Rosen, *War and Human Nature* (Princeton, NJ: Princeton University Press, 2005), 131; Department of Defense, *Final Report to Congress on the Conduct of the Gulf War*, April 1992, 186, available online at http://www.dod.mil/pubs/foi/operation_and_plans/Persian GulfWar/404.pdf, accessed December 2, 2014.

75. Bruce R. Nardulli, Walter L. Perry, Bruce Pirnie, John Gordon IV, and John G. McGinn, *Disjointed War: Military Operations in Kosovo, 1999* (Santa Monica, CA: RAND, 2002), 56; Dag Henriksen, "Inflexible Response: Diplomacy, Airpower, and the Kosovo Crisis, 1998–1999," *Journal of Strategic Studies* 31.6 (2008): 825–58, esp. 829.

76. Henriksen, "Inflexible Response," 826; Benjamin S. Lambeth, *NATO's Air War for Kosovo: A Strategic and Operational Assessment* (Santa Monica, CA: RAND, 2001), 20–60.

77. Nardulli et al., *Disjointed War*, 48, 51–56; Lambeth, *NATO's Air War*, 87–88, 128–38.

78. Harlan K. Ullman and James P. Wade, *Shock and Awe: Achieving Rapid Dominance* (Washington, DC: Center for Advanced Concepts and Technology, 1996).

79. US Army, *Serving a Nation at War: A Campaign Quality Army with Joint and Expeditionary Capabilities*, included with testimony to the House Armed Services Committee, available online at https://ia802607.us .archive.org/27/items/armytransformati 00unit/armytransformati00unit.pdf, accessed July 30, 2014.

80. Stephen Biddle, "Afghanistan and the Future of Warfare," *Foreign Affairs* 82.2 (March–April 2003): 31–46.

14

Bringing Down the State: Guerrillas, Insurgents, Terrorism, and Counterinsurgency

1930–2014

The Revolutionary Response to the Industrial State: Mao, Giap, and Guevara •
Terrorism and Insurgency by Terrorism • Counterinsurgency and Counter Terror

THE PRECEDING three chapters documented the military consequences of what has sometimes been called the "great divergence." For much of history, the power of European states relative to the rest of the world, especially to China, was significantly inferior or, at best, on par. Colonization and then industrialization, however, unlocked financial and technological capacities that elevated key European states and some of their former New World colonies to a dominant economic and military position in the world. The industrializing powers also continued their wars with each other, refining their techniques for use against their peer competitors, while other powers like Japan and the Ottoman Empire copied the entire process, built domestic industrial capacity, and sought to stay in the race. Still other powers, such as China, Egypt, and some smaller European states, tried instead to purchase the industrially produced weapons of the West, but continued to fall behind, at least through World War II (Japan and the Ottoman Empire also relied on purchase, but differed in investing more heavily in building their own industrial capacity).

By the mid-nineteenth century these developments empowered leading European states to build on their older colonial possessions (which accounted for some 35 percent of the world's surface) and swiftly to impose much larger empires on the world (amounting to some 84 percent of the world by 1914) and to bully if not occupy China. Those developments, however, also created the conditions in which the European states nearly destroyed one another in World War I and World War II. The world wars in turn set the stage for the bipolar superpower confrontation of the Cold War from 1949 to 1989.[1]

The asymmetry of technological and productive capacity between industrialized states and those not yet industrialized stimulated calculated, nontechnological innovation. Specifically, it fostered creative adaptations of techniques long used in wars of the weak against the strong. Industrial states in turn continued to adapt, while the products and consequences of industrialization, urbanization, and globalization created new blends of asymmetrical conflict and innovative ways of resisting industrialized states.

This chapter explores all of these phenomena, beginning with the emergence of revolutionary people's war as theorized by Mao Zedong in 1930s China. It then examines the spread and adaptation of his ideas during the Cold War and their further modification, almost beyond recognition, in post–Cold War globalized terrorism. Mao's original theory and the hybrid versions that followed presented serious challenges to the strategic culture of industrial states. Those states had long designed their militaries and their military thinking to fight each other in relatively symmetrical conflicts. Responding to this new form of war required new doctrines of counterinsurgency, and then, enabled by new technologies, even newer strategies of counter terror.

Before turning to Mao and his successors, however, one must acknowledge that so-called guerrilla warfare has deep roots. Asymmetry of power existed before industrialization, and even war between equivalent states had long included "irregular" forms of warfare that resembled those of guerrillas. Rebels against a state government, or resistance movements by occupied populations more generally, have nearly always been heavily outclassed if not outnumbered by their opponent—even when military technology was broadly available outside the bounds of formal militaries. Such "irregulars" naturally turned to hit-and-run attacks or ambushes on small isolated parties. Their tactics traditionally depended on difficult or isolated terrain into which they could disappear. Even so, such forces were usually at a sharp disadvantage, and regular troops could eventually run them to ground. On a few occasions extended guerrilla campaigns had notable effects on a state army; indeed, the word "guerrilla" owes its popularization to the damaging war the occupied populace waged against Napoleon's forces in Spain from 1809 to 1814.

State armies have traditionally regarded guerrilla forces with disdain. Almost by definition, a state-formed military had among its missions supporting the established hierarchy, and it was typically led or officered by the upper echelons of that hierarchy. Such men saw an armed and insubordinate populace as a threat. Furthermore, in part because of their sense of desperation or built-up social resentment, guerrilla forces have often seemed to wage a style of violence that departed from accepted norms. For their part, state armies recognized the strategic value of small forces conducting hit-and-run style attacks, but, prejudiced as they were against indiscriminately arming the populace, state armies have often developed special "partisan" units. Such units were designed to fight in a guerrilla style, while remaining responsive to hierarchical control. It was only in the twentieth century that the term "partisan" acquired its modern use as a synonym of guerrilla.

The line between informal, nonuniformed guerrillas and official, uniformed partisans could be very blurry. One of the first comprehensive efforts to impose a code of conduct on an army's use of violence, the so-called Lieber Code adopted by the Union Army during the American Civil War, was written initially to clarify and define the difference between the two, and the consequences for the former. The Lieber Code and many of the international conventions that followed were thus symptoms or artifacts of a longstanding principle of Western strategic culture: war should be waged by the officially established and hierarchically led armed forces of the state. Within this frame of reference, the results of war were legally binding on future behavior between states. Furthermore, war itself was believed to be decided by some form of decisive clash between those forces, in what one legal historian has called a *jus victoriae*. Civilians fighting as guerrillas violated both those norms. In an earlier era this led to a more savage form of war, as states repressed guerrillas without mercy and guerrillas responded in kind. In the modern era the savagery remains, but guerrilla movements also developed a more comprehensive strategy defining a path to ultimate victory that often had eluded guerrillas of the past.[2]

THE REVOLUTIONARY RESPONSE TO THE INDUSTRIAL STATE: MAO, GIAP, AND GUEVARA

World War I rocked but did not destroy the stability of the European empires established around the world in the late nineteenth century. In some ways the peace treaty signed at Versailles in 1919 simply presumed and perpetuated the prewar European imperial system—now including Japan. Germany's colonial possessions were distributed to the victorious powers as "mandates," to be administered on behalf of the newly established League of Nations, but often treated in fact as colonies. For many colonized peoples around the world, however, the war encouraged them to question European control. Crucial leadership cadres and movements emerged in the interwar years, many with leaders educated in the West. Equally crucially, many of those movements or leaders were inspired by the successful Communist revolution in Russia in 1917.

The cataclysm of World War II then dramatically altered the global power dynamic. Although Germany no longer had a colonial empire to lose, the war destroyed those of Japan and Italy and dramatically weakened the colonial grip of the nominal victors Britain, France, Belgium, and the Netherlands. The war empowered the other victors, the United States and the Soviet Union, but they soon turned on each other in the Cold War competition for worldwide influence. These three international dynamics—the desire for independence in many parts of the colonized world, the weakened economic power but still resilient military strength of the old colonial powers, and the superpower competition—spawned a host of asymmetric wars of decolonization or superpower proxy wars. In those conflict environments, new approaches to guerrilla war, or "people's war," took root.

Mao Zedong

China's experience provided a vital model. More specifically, from China emerged the theory of revolutionary people's war as propagated by Mao Zedong (1893–1976). Mao developed his ideas in a hybrid context of fighting both an internal revolutionary war against the Nationalist Chinese (Guomindang) government and a war against the invading industrial power of Japan. Both the Guomindang and the Chinese communist movement had emerged in the wake of the collapse of the Qing imperial dynasty in 1912 as revolutionary movements, both seeking to establish a new, modernized, and united China. The Nationalists under Chiang Kai-shek gained the advantage during the late 1920s, seemingly crushing the Red Army of the Chinese Communist Party (CCP). The CCP's battered remnants retreated to the mountains. Subsequent, poorly managed Nationalist campaigns, however, managed to inspire and enlarge the Red Army. In 1931 the Japanese army precipitated a war in Manchuria, designed to impel Japan into an expansionist war. Chiang chose to appease the Japanese, surrendering Manchuria and demilitarizing the border, to provide time to campaign once more against the CCP. He seemed close to success in 1934, forcing the Red Army into the "Long March," as it retreated far to the west and then the north. Unfortunately for Chiang, his own troops were initially unwilling to launch yet another campaign into the depths of western China, and then Japan launched a full-scale invasion in July 1937 (see Map 14.1).

The Red Army was thus reprieved. Although a shell of its former self, with much of the old leadership stripped away or discredited by defeat, the remaining hard core of survivors regrouped under the leadership of Mao Zedong, himself now a deeply experienced fighter and organizer. Contemplating how to defeat the Nationalist government, but also adapting his thought for how to deal with the Japanese invader, Mao developed a strategy for war by a weaker power against a stronger one. In the end, Mao never really deployed his forces or his theory against Japan; that war was fought by the Nationalists, and Japan was ultimately defeated by the United States. Japan's invasion, however, in distracting the Nationalists, had created vast areas in which Mao and the Red Army could reestablish themselves, and during the postwar era they again directly confronted a weary Nationalist government. In a complex series of mostly conventional campaigns, the CCP won that contest in 1949, forcing the Nationalists to flee to the island of Taiwan, while mainland China came under the united rule of the CCP.

Although Mao never enacted his theories about revolutionary war in their strictest sense, they did provide a core consistency to the Red Army's strategy,

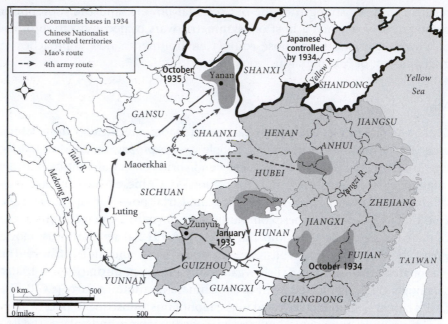

Map 14.1 The Long March, 1934. Chinese Communist forces were forced to retreat into the far west of the country by Nationalist Forces in 1934. Meanwhile Japan had occupied Manchuria, and would soon invade China.

most especially his uniting of the political and the military. His writings, collected and published in a variety of ways, also proved enormously influential. It makes sense, therefore, to consider his theory as such, rather than to narrate the specific details of his campaigns. A brief caveat first. Mao's personal role in the campaigns against the Guomindang and even the formulation of his theory has been somewhat exaggerated. Nevertheless, his role was significant, and the theory remains ascribed to him, and shall be referred to as such here.[3]

Mao faced the classic problem of the weak against the strong, but now in an industrial context. The guerrillas or partisans of earlier centuries had been weaker than state military forces, but they possessed roughly similar capabilities, man for man, as their opponents. Mao and the other twentieth-century guerrilla or revolutionary movements that followed him lacked industrial capacity to produce their own weapons, or often even the finances to buy them on a large scale. The Cold War would ease that problem, as the superpowers armed their proxies, but Mao was not yet in a position to take advantage of this. In addition, orthodox Marxist-Leninist revolutionary theory was built on the presumed discontent of an *urban* working class (the proletariat), which in China was but a small one. Mao recognized that his revolution would depend on the vast spaces and the vast population of China's *rural* hinterland. The old guerrilla techniques of small-scale raids launched from difficult terrain and retreats back to them, however, would not swell into a nationwide movement. Mao's first insight, therefore, was to precede the military with the political.

Mao's people's war was as much about political indoctrination of the army and the population as it was about military technique. The soldiers themselves would serve as the agents of revolution. They would treat the peasants as their comrades, offering them land reform, improvements in their lives, and agency in their futures, all while paying them for the soldiers' food and shelter—in marked contrast to either the Nationalist army or the Japanese invaders. Peasant support or connivance would allow Mao's forces to move freely through the countryside, fed and hidden by the peasants, into whose ranks they could quickly disappear if threatened by large numbers. Mao famously said that the guerrilla must move among the people as a fish swims in the sea. This quote is often taken simply to refer to the ability of the guerrilla to disappear into the civilian population. It did mean that, but its larger significance was that the guerrillas would remain among the population, and not simply hide in the mountains awaiting some temporary advantage. For Mao, China's population *was* the covering terrain. In this sense Mao sought to make the war about the mobilization of people, not the mobilization of industrial resources. He would fight industrial superiority with the will of a populace energized by his political program. Mao was also ruthless, however, and would terrorize or kill those who failed to cooperate.

The military challenge was to coopt and politicize the population while not being destroyed by the superior firepower of an industrially equipped enemy. Given the demographic and geographic size of China, Mao hypothesized a three-phase war during which he would conduct three different types of warfare in different combinations, depending on the phase. All were designed to *protract* the war, exhausting his opponent while simultaneously increasing his own resources at his opponent's expense. In the first phase, Mao presumed the superiority of his opponent, who would advance into the countryside, occupying great swathes of territory and creating natural salients (see Figure 14.1). During that phase (the offensive), Mao advocated avoiding conventional positional warfare (one of his three "types" of warfare), except in the defense of key bases deep inside China, typically within mountainous regions. During that phase, however, the enemy's forward movement would provide opportunities for "mobile" warfare (the second of his "types"). This was comprised of fast-moving attacks along the flanks of the enemy's movement, conducted by Red Army regular forces, supplied by those permanent bases outside enemy control. Finally, within the occupied territory, guerrilla attacks (the third type), conducted by irregular forces operating from temporary bases, would conduct sabotage, assassination, and attacks on targets of opportunity designed to unsettle the enemy and testify to the continued resistance of the Red Army as whole. Guerrilla warfare would assume an even more important role in the long second phase, that of "strategic stalemate."

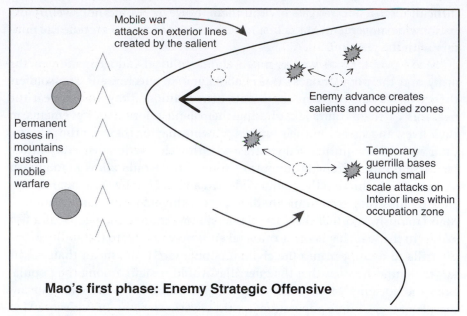

Figure 14.1 The first phase in Mao's three-phase vision of protracted war.

The enemy's advance would have stopped or slowed, and continued guerrilla operations would gradually weaken their position while capturing equipment for the Red Army and sustaining the political operations designed to keep the population engaged in the struggle and opposed to the occupier's puppet government.

Over time, the protraction of conflict would exhaust the enemy, especially a foreign invader that depended on a minimum of domestic popular support at home and at least noninterference from the international community. Protracting the war made both those conditions less likely. Crucial to making the theory work would be judging the correct moment to shift between phases, and for this Mao preached flexibility, rather than following a set schedule. The most difficult moment to assess was when to shift to the third phase, the "counteroffensive," which could only begin after the Red Army had gained sufficient strength. During the latter stages of the second phase, mobile warfare by regular forces equipped with captured enemy materiel would become more common, until finally the enemy had weakened sufficiently that the Red Army could begin conventional positional warfare, this time on the offensive, liberating and holding occupied territory and assuming sovereignty.[4]

Mao's theory would have enormous influence in the decades to come, an influence greatly, and perhaps wrongly, magnified by the ultimate victory of the CCP in China in 1949. China's circumstances were in many ways unique; two elements immediately stand out. One was Mao's ability to use China's enormous size both to set up permanent protected bases and to then trade space for time. In China, size provided the necessary sanctuary for Mao's theory to work. Second, the Guomindang government was thoroughly exhausted by the war against Japan, and the CCP's victory was more conventional than is usually remembered.

Nevertheless, Mao's paradigm of a three-phase war and his emphasis on the role of guerrilla warfare would be adopted by numerous theorists, with varying emphasis on the culminating conventional counteroffensive. Perhaps more important was his emphasis on political mobilization to sustain the *protracted* quality of the war. Indeed, that would become the most important characteristic in many revolutionary wars to follow, even when there seemed little hope of a third, conventional phase. Militarily, the guerrilla techniques he described were central to achieving protraction. These fundamental ideas were transmitted to the world in different formats and combinations between the 1930s and the 1960s. Mao's theory emerged in a formal shape first during a series of lectures in Yanan in 1938. The text of those lectures was rapidly disseminated in China. By the end of that year his ideas had been accepted by the party as a whole and distributed to all party officials and military commands. It was published in Chinese in Guilin in the spring of 1939, and an English version emerged as early as May 1939 in some five hundred copies, with a new preface by Mao. A later, more widely distributed official Chinese government translation into English appeared in 1954 as *On Protracted War*, then again in 1958 as part of a large *Selected Works* edition. From that point, titles and versions of the theory proliferated, with one highly influential English translation by Samuel Griffith appearing in 1961 as *Mao Tse-Tung on Guerrilla Warfare*. Many other editions followed.[5]

Vo Nguyen Giap

Mao's influence was particularly marked in the wars of the Vietnam (Communist) Workers' Party (VWP), first against the French, then against the newly created South Vietnam, eventually against the Americans allied with the South, and then finally against South Vietnam on its own again, until North Vietnam's ultimate victory and the unification of the country in 1975. The Vietnamese, however, in developing their own resistance to Western industrial powers (or the Western-equipped South Vietnam), lacked the geographic luxury of trading space for time as Mao's theory required—Vietnam was a much smaller country. Furthermore, in the Americans they encountered a formidable and capable foe, with huge advantages in firepower and air power. Mao's theory had to be reformulated and adapted for the Vietnamese context. The primary theorist in this case was Vo Nguyen Giap (1911–2013), but it is essential to point out that the communist war plans in Vietnam were constantly debated by various factions within the party. Giap wrote and published his theories, and was able to claim ultimate responsibility for the party's victories, but rarely did their war effort simply follow a single unified plan or theory.[6]

By the outbreak of World War II, what is now Vietnam had long been under French rule as part of "French Indochina"—a colony that also included Laos and Cambodia. As in many other European empires, however, World War I and especially World War II seemed to offer the prospect of disrupting or even throwing off colonial rule. Indigenous resistance movements organized themselves around a variety of principles, but in Vietnam the most powerful organization was that inspired by communism and led by Ho Chi Minh (1890–1969), a man deeply disappointed by the Allies' failure to follow through with their wartime promises of decolonization.

Ho's movement adopted, and adapted for Vietnam's circumstances, many of the organizing principles suggested by Mao for first mobilizing and then militarily organizing a poor agrarian peasant population. Ho was in Yanan in 1938 and Guilin in 1939, during which time he participated in Red Army cadre training—while Mao's theory was first being distributed. Ho's Viet Minh movement even set up an office in Guilin in 1941. Ho and other Vietnamese leaders were thus deeply familiar with Mao's theory, and when the new communist government in China recognized the emergent Democratic Republic of Vietnam in 1950, it provided not only material support but also military advisors, establishing the Chinese Military Assistance Group in Vietnam. In January 1951, Giap himself traveled to China for direct consultations.[7]

Over the course of the late 1940s and early 1950s, sustained guerrilla campaigns by the Viet Minh (the military arm of the VWP) eroded French will to continue the war, despite massive American aid, and Viet Minh forces even established control over much of Laos. In 1953 France launched a desperate bid to draw Vietnamese guerrillas into the open and cut the supplies to their forces in Laos by creating an intrusive but dangerously isolated base in the north at Dien Bien Phu. The French gamble gave Giap, the Viet Minh commander, an opportunity to conduct a positional campaign. Viet Minh forces laid siege to the French outpost, disrupted their aerial resupply, and ultimately overran the base, capturing almost twelve thousand French soldiers. The demoralizing defeat led to the French departure in 1954 and a treaty dividing the country into a communist north (the Democratic Republic of Vietnam—DRV) and a non-communist south (Republic of Vietnam-RVN). The latter was supported by an American foreign policy determined to stem the spread of communism. The division was supposed to be temporary, pending a plebiscite, but all sides recognized the probability of a long-term division (see Map 14.2). The DRV, led by Ho, was at first preoccupied with building a new nation in the North, but was ultimately determined to unify the country under their rule—although the party leadership was in part dragged into the war by activists for the struggle in the South. Eventually the DRV actively sponsored the National Liberation Front (NLF) guerrillas fighting in the South (pejoratively called the Viet Cong by South Vietnamese leaders and the Americans). As time went on, that support included infiltrating the South with regular troops from the People's Army of Vietnam, or PAVN.[8]

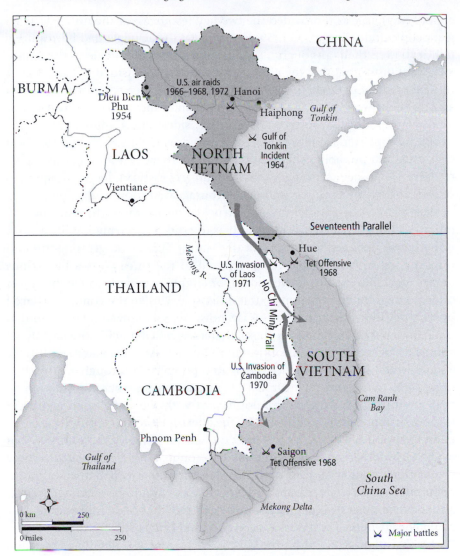

Map 14.2 Vietnam as divided in 1954. Note how the Ho Chi Minh Trail runs primarily through Laos and Cambodia. Map also indicates the location of some key campaigns.

Despite these crucial shifts in political conditions, and despite ongoing arguments within the DRV about appropriate strategy and timing, it is still possible to outline that strategy's basic principles. Perhaps even more than Mao had, the Vietnamese tightly fused the political and the military struggle, a fusion they named *dau tranh*, a phrase loosely and inadequately translated as "struggle." The unified struggle demanded a political side coequal to the military side—often described as the hammer and the anvil. Giap wrote afterward that political work in the ranks was of the "first importance"; he called it "the soul of the army."[9] In some ways the political side received greater emphasis, as it provided the two key resources for the military struggle: people and will. Before 1959, for the DRV the struggle had been purely political. Even then, although it supported the armed struggle in the South, it was not until 1963 that the military aspect truly intensified.[10]

The political struggle in turn was divided into three components: action among one's own people—essentially propaganda and motivation directed at a population already more or less on their side; action among the enemy people—propaganda and even violent action designed to sow dissension and disloyalty and possibly gain converts; and finally action among the enemy military—"message" sending, often through terroristic violence, designed to subvert the enemy's soldiers' morale, encourage desertion, and so on.[11]

Meanwhile, the parallel military struggle, meant to destroy the enemy's military through armed action, as well as to erode the enemy's political will, initially was designed along specifically Maoist lines as progressing through three stages. In his writings, Giap referred to the three phases by various names: guerrilla-mobile-conventional, or simple-complex-mobile, but most often contention-equilibrium-counteroffensive. Unlike the conditions faced by Mao in China during the first phase, however, Vietnam could not afford to trade space for time. Their first phase, therefore, relied much more heavily on guerrilla war and continued political mobilization. Many isolated small-scale attacks would serve to convince the neutral population through a "combination of selective terrorism, intimidation, persuasion, and massive agitation . . . that the future lies with the rebels and not with the established regime."[12] In time such processes would enlarge the guerrilla forces and put the government forces on the defensive, creating the second phase of "equilibrium," in which large forces could be concentrated to conduct mobile war against more conventional military targets of the regime. These attacks remained opportunistic but were on a larger scale, with guerrilla operations continuing. Eventually the rebel forces would achieve sufficient size and capability so that they could engage in the third phase, a conventional offensive.

Mao's influence on this thinking is clear, and US intelligence efforts during the American war in Vietnam collected diaries and notes from NLF leaders that suggested just how pervasive Mao's theories and Giap's writings had been in their training. Circumstances and debates with other leaders in the DRV led Giap to make some key modifications early on, and he also correlated the military strategy to a three-tiered system of mobilization and further adjusted the strategy over time, both within and between the different phases. The root of the approach in both Vietnam and China was to control the loyalties of the peasants, appealing to them in part through promises of land reform and redistribution. By capturing a village, they undermined the reach of the government—ousting, killing, or simply coopting village officials. In the words of a party planning document in Vietnam: "If the system of village and hamlet councils . . . is paralyzed, then our secure base areas will be enlarged, the government will no longer be able to recruit troops and

Figure 14.2 General Vo Nguyen Giap (*back left*) with President Ho Chi Minh (*second from right*). From a photo taken in 1950.

obtain forced labor. . . . Destruction of the government's local apparatus is the first step in bringing about the rapid collapse of the government."[13]

Residents of such villages were then to be organized into small groups of guerrillas as part of Giap's lowest tier of mobilization, the so-called popular troops. Lightly armed but replete with local knowledge, they provided the muscle for local political recruitment and intimidation, as well as acting as a training ground. Select veterans of the popular troops were recruited into the next tier—the regional troops. Regional troops also tended to use guerrilla tactics but operated on a more full-time basis, and often away from their home villages in larger concentrations. Experience in the regional troops prepared its veterans for service in the regular troops—those capable of conventional operations. During the French war experienced regional troops were carefully reserved for the eventual initiation of the conventional phase of the war. In Giap's words, written after the French war, "Tempered in combat and stimulated by victories, the guerrilla formations created condition for the growth of the regional troops. And the latter, in their turn, promoted the development of the regular forces. For nine successive years, by following this heroic path bristling with difficulties, our People's Army . . . became an army of hundreds of thousands strong, successively amalgamating into regiments and divisions."[14]

Like Mao, Giap encouraged guerrilla leaders during the French war to seek small victories, to "exhaust little by little" the enemy forces, avoiding casualties, "even at the cost of losing ground."[15] This is hardly earthshakingly original advice for a guerrilla force; such would have been standard practice for all partisan or guerrilla forces. In some ways, however, this urging, composed retrospectively after the French war, arose from several costly defeats incurred when attempts to move from the defensive guerrilla-war phase to the mobile war of the equilibrium phase proved costly and forced a readjustment.[16]

The even greater difficulty of making the shift from the second phase to the third became a centerpiece of debates within the DRV from the early 1960s. In some ways, those internal debates defined the character and chronology of American involvement in Vietnam. As historian Lien-Hang Nguyen has shown, by 1963 the rise to power of Le Duan, General Secretary of the Central Committee from 1960, altered Vietnam's use of Mao's paradigm. Le Duan advocated a "general offensive and general uprising" strategy (GO-GU) that would skip the second, equilibrium stage of Mao's strategy and combine a sudden conventional offensive with a nationwide uprising designed to spark the masses to join in overthrowing South Vietnam's government.

The VWP accepted Le Duan's plan, and the GO-GU offensive that followed in 1964 nearly succeeded, but it also resulted in direct American intervention. The introduction of American air and firepower forced the Vietnamese back to the first stage through 1966, generally avoiding main force engagements and relying more heavily on guerrilla warfare, albeit more aggressively than in the traditional Maoist version. American firepower, however, was damaging: the guerrilla forces had to become more accepting of casualties and defeat. The guerrillas' traditional willingness to surrender ground now had to be supplemented with a new willingness to absorb tremendous casualties. That they accepted this was testament to the depth and breadth of the political program. Of course, this acceptance was also made possible by the existence of North Vietnam as a separate state, funneling the Cold War–fueled support of the Soviet Union and China into the guerrilla war in the South.[17]

In 1967 Le Duan renewed his call for the GO-GU strategy, again attempting to blend a PAVN and an NLF offensive to inspire a general popular uprising. After violent political maneuvering within the DRV, Le Duan won the debate, sidelined Ho Chi Minh and Giap, and ordered what became known as the Tet Offensive for January 30, 1968. PAVN troops launched a major incursion into South Vietnam while NLF regional forces initiated their own attacks, and previously hidden guerrilla units or individual saboteurs went to work on regime targets. Militarily, the attacks were crushed, at great cost to the NLF and the North. Politically, however, the Tet Offensive fatally undermined American political will—even if that was not immediately clear inside Vietnam. American forces in Vietnam began drawing down in 1969, dropped dramatically in number in 1971, and were virtually gone by 1972. Once again Le Duan resurrected the third phase and ordered a conventional invasion of the South. American air power intervened against exposed PAVN conventional forces, and RVN forces resisted successfully. By 1975, however, the United States was unwilling even to intervene from the air, and the final invasion of that year rapidly overran RVN forces and unified the country under Communist rule.[18]

The full narrative of the wars in Vietnam and its neighbors is far more complex than can easily be summarized here, but with respect to understanding the fundamental innovation achieved by Mao, transmitted to Vietnam, adapted there, and then retransmitted elsewhere, there are several key points. First, there was no single moment of invention. Painful experience in China and many internal debates among the Chinese Communist revolutionaries produced a set of ideas about people's war that were crystallized in Mao's 1938 lecture and then diffused and published as being entirely his. Second, this vision of people's war emphasized political mobilization of a disenfranchised and frequently landless peasant population to provide the manpower and will to overcome the industrial resources of its state-based opponents. In one sense the vision returned to older "organic economy" forms of mobilization discussed in the introduction and in earlier chapters: what mattered were numbers of people, even if primitively armed, sustaining themselves from resources widely dispersed across the landscape, sometimes actually growing food for the cause, and politically severed from the usual mobilization processes of the ruling enemy state. After the war, Vietnamese general Dan Vu Hiep recalled how they sustained their forces operating in the Central Highlands of South Vietnam on cassava—each soldier cared for five hundred plants to sustain them when supplies from the North did not arrive. Furthermore, he recalled, "Every year we grew [cassava] closer to our objective. When we wanted to lay an attack on Highway 14, for example, we started very far away, but each year we planted closer and closer."[19] Mao and his imitators had thus redefined "capacity" away from its modern industrial meaning. Their wars were to be about people and will. Modern weapons and materiel would come via capture, not production (although in the Cold War era most weapons actually came from the Soviet Union or China).

Nevertheless, even within Mao's theory, the people's army would *eventually* require sufficient firepower and material to engage in conventional positional war. To get to that point the theory provided a structured vision of incremental shifts in tactics corresponding to relative changes in power (and to shifts in international opinion and support). Those tactics were designed to *protract* war and thus erode political will. In its briefest essence, Mao's theory provided a vision for eventual success despite weakness by psychologically preparing its adherents for protracted conflict, while also providing a military method to ensure protraction. And, in historian Douglas Pike's analysis, "The *fact* of protracted conflict, rather than the issue of war itself, becomes the chief destructive force at work, eroding fundamental virtues and values such as loyalty, integrity, and honor, without which a society cannot exist."[20]

The Vietnamese version, also a collaborative and evolutionary process eventually crystallized in the writing of Vo Nguyen Giap, adapted the theory to a smaller land mass and to accommodate a greater frequency of tactical defeat. These changes made Mao's original theory more flexible and gave it greater staying power. Giap's version did not depend on "many small victories"; it instead accommodated many defeats. After 1963, Le Duan's aggressive version hoped to avoid the drawn-out equilibrium phase entirely, jumping from the guerrilla phase directly to a national uprising reinforced by conventional forces. In the end, Communist success at creating the state of North Vietnam and then conquering South Vietnam depended as much on international factors and the dynamics of the Cold War as it did on any particular theory of protracted war, but the theory mattered. What is more, the theory attracted great attention from other would-be revolutionaries and anti-imperialists around the world.

Che Guevara

One such successor version of people's war was that articulated by Che Guevara (1928–67) for revolutionary conflicts in Latin America and beyond. Che was deeply influenced by Mao's original vision, while he also sought an objective larger than just local or regional liberation. His goal was the complete destruction of Western, primarily American, imperialism. His life, successes, and theories had a notable influence on subsequent movements.[21]

Born Ernesto Guevara in Argentina in 1928, Che traveled widely in Latin America, and what he saw persuaded him of the corruption of the capitalist system and its perpetuation of puppet regimes subservient to the United States. By the fall of 1954 he had joined the communist revolutionary movement of Fidel Castro (b. 1926), then training in exile in Mexico. Che's and Castro's careers are thus intimately intertwined, with Castro then already an experienced leader and Che a younger adherent soon to assume a greater role as a theorist and intellectual of revolution. Castro had already tried once and failed to initiate a revolution in Cuba, and orthodox Leninist thought suggested that the necessary conditions for communist revolution did not yet exist in Latin America; there simply was no industrial proletariat. Like Mao, therefore, Castro and Che were seeking a way to develop a revolutionary impulse in a rural peasantry, and Castro in particular was frustrated by the restraints of orthodox communist theory that told him to wait.[22]

Castro and his brother Raúl organized a small guerrilla band in Mexico, where Che joined them. There, under the tutelage of guerrilla-war veteran and theorist Alberto Bayo (1892–1967), they began to conceptualize the method that would later be called *foquismo* or focoism. Bayo had served in the Spanish army in Morocco in the 1930s fighting Islamic guerrillas. He had also interviewed veterans of Augusto César Sandino's successful guerrilla revolution in Nicaragua. Bayo's later work also showed the influence of Mao's thought, and Che clearly studied Mao directly. The result was a hybrid of traditional guerrilla war, Maoist theory, Bayo's experience and interpretation of Sandino's success, and Che's own thinking.[23]

Che proved to be a key figure in the military aspects of Castro's successful revolution in Cuba. Castro had hoped to achieve more or less conventional success with a small force of dedicated revolutionaries. Che recognized the potentially "catalytic role" of a small group in propagating a revolution: they became the focus, the *foco*, around which discontent could coalesce into a people's struggle. But Che, unlike Castro, wanted that initial group to rely on guerrilla tactics, and thereby prolong the struggle in the Maoist sense of pro-tracted war. In his manual on guerrilla war published in 1960, after the regime of Fulgencio Batista had been successfully overthrown, Che wrote that "guerrilla warfare is a phase that does not afford in itself opportunities to arrive at complete victory." It must "develop continuously until the guer-rilla army in its steady growth acquires the characteristics of a regular army."[24] Unlike Giap's long and careful political preparation prior to beginning the armed struggle, however, Che argued that "it is not necessary to wait until all conditions for making revolution exist; the insurrection can create them."[25] This was the essence of *foquismo*: using a small armed vanguard, relying on peasant protection and rough terrain, to provoke the government into a re-sponse that would undermine the regime's legitimacy. The reactions of the state would aggravate the discontents of the countryside and thereby widen the revolution.

Originally Che confined his theory to "Caribbean-type" dictatorships that were already authoritarian and whose legitimacy was suspect. In time, how-ever, Che argued that this vulnerability to revolution had a broader geopolit-ical dimension. The success in Cuba and the support of China and the Soviet Union would create conditions of resentment and discontent against capital-ist, imperialist regimes in Asia, Africa, and Latin America—what he called the "tricontinental" aspect of the struggle. In 1967, Guevara called for "repeated blows against imperialism"—for "two, three or many Vietnams" as the means to a brighter future.[26] Western and American intervention on behalf of puppet regimes would expose them as such and would foster revolutions that could coalesce around the *foco*. In the end, his methods did not often succeed. Re-gimes justified their own repressive methods based on the existence of revo-lutionary activity, and in the Cold War context they could reliably turn to the United States for counterrevolutionary aid. Many revolutionaries in Latin America, preferring a Maoist or Vietnam-like approach, rejected the potential of the *foco* to initiate a successful revolution in the absence of a more deeply laid politicization of the countryside. The communist rebels of the 1980s in Latin America, resurgent after defeats in the 1960s, turned to the Vietnamese and Nicaraguan models as much as they did to Che's.[27]

These three examples of China, Vietnam, and Cuba only scratch the sur-face of the many efforts around the world to deploy a variant of people's war to overcome the rapidly growing dominance of Western firepower and air power. The success those movements had, however, often seemed to depend on the Cold War context in which the nuclear umbrella provided by the Soviet Union prevented unrestrained intervention by Western states. As the intensity of the Cold War ebbed and flowed, and especially as the relationship between Communist China and the Soviet Union cooled, individual communist revolutions in Africa, Asia, and Latin America were more or less likely to succeed depending on the exact configurations of the great powers at the moment. When the Cold War ended, Mao's formula seemed less likely to overcome Western technological superiority. Ironically, the *foco* of Che seemed to provide a hint of another way to challenge that dominance. In some ways the fundamental thinking behind the *foco* resembles another strategy of the weak: terrorism.

TERRORISM AND INSURGENCY BY TERRORISM

Today, hardly any word is more fraught than "terrorism." Many definitions have been offered, with the most general one being simply attacking an unarmed population in order to intimidate them, or their state, into changing their attitudes or policies. Within this broad definition "terrorism" can be found throughout human history, in the hands of gangs, warlords, armies, and even states themselves. Our interest here, however, is in the smaller subset of activity in which a politically organized and disciplined organization, otherwise incapable or unwilling to engage in open armed conflict, uses spectacular and intimidating violence against unarmed populations or civilian infrastructure. Terrorism under this definition is a *strategy*, independent of the criminal connotations of the word. Attacks on the defenseless combined with propaganda operations constitute a strategy designed in response to the growing gap between the firepower available to a modern state and that of any given would-be insurgent.[28]

The shift from protracted people's wars of revolution to potentially *even more protracted* campaigns of terrorism by relatively small groups of activists reflects major changes in the international political arena, but its origins extend back into the Cold War. With the collapse of the Soviet Union in 1991, with China's retreat from sponsoring revolution abroad, and with the United States' similar retreat since 1991, revolutionaries could no longer find material and financial support from a major state. Even so-called "rogue states" like Libya and Iran, which supported terroristic insurgencies, typically could not provide the level of support or the security against outside intervention that had existed during the Cold War. In other words, North Vietnam's immunity from American invasion was a Cold War reality that no longer exists. Iran's support for Hamas in the Palestinian territory and for Hezbollah in Lebanon almost constitutes an exception, as it is significant enough for both of those organizations to engage in a combination of open armed conflict and terrorism that some analysts have labeled "hybrid war." In general, however, most insurgents relying on terrorism have done so in the absence of significant state-based support.[29]

This seeming disadvantage is offset by other aspects of the changing world environment. Urbanization has created a new kind of refuge in modern cities, especially those in the developing word which have swelled to an order of magnitude larger than what they were even in the mid-twentieth century (see Table 14.1). Policing urban spaces now presents a similar set of problems to chasing guerrillas into the jungles, deserts, or mountains, with the very significant added complication of a large, innocent, civilian population. Furthermore, military downsizing in the post–Cold War era unleashed a global unregulated arms trade on a larger scale than ever before, making formal state supply less of a necessity. Finally, the globalization of media reportage, first via television and now the Internet, has provided heretofore unimaginable and inexpensive access to a global population.[30]

Terrorism as a political tactic of the weak predated 1991. Some of its basic outlines as a strategy for political change came into focus during the 1960s and 1970s. Modern political terrorism has at its heart the intent to communicate to a variety of audiences. Lacking their own channels to reach a wide audience, early practitioners of modern terrorism designed their attacks to achieve the "propaganda of the deed." Analyst John Mackinlay singles out the Palestinian Liberation Organization (PLO) and the Irish Republican Army (IRA) as two organizations that pioneered the idea within the modern world. Where Maoist revolutionaries had sought to cultivate and mobilize a local population while persuading the state of the inevitability of defeat through a long war of attrition, the IRA and PLO began with a largely sympathetic local audience but lacked the resources and the space to engage in a traditional guerrilla conflict. In Mackinlay's terms, their insurgency was based on a "dispersed" population and therefore required distinctive techniques. In the "propaganda of the deed" they resorted to acts of spectacular violence against civilian targets, such as the PLO's taking Israeli athletes hostage during the 1972

Western Cities		
	1950 (in millions)	*2010 (in millions)*
New York	12.34	18.37
London	8.36	9.70
Paris	6.28	10.46
Moscow	5.36	11.46
Rome	1.88	2.75

Eastern Cities		
	1950 (in millions)	*2010 (in millions)*
Tokyo	11.27	36.83
Osaka	7.01	19.49
Shanghai	4.30	19.98
Cairo	2.49	16.90
Guanghzhou	1.34	9.62
Karachi	0.45	14.08
Istanbul	1.08	12.70
Baghdad	0.58	7.20

Table 14.1: **Growth in the urban population, 1950–2010.** Most cities in the table were chosen as representative of the largest cities in the world in 1950. In 1950 Guangzhou, Karachi, Istanbul and Baghdad were relatively small, but by 2010 had surged into major cities. In general, compare the relatively steady growth in Western cities to the much more rapid growth in the developing non-Western world; by 2010 a whole crop of non-Western cities have moved into the top ranks.

Figure 14.3 A masked PLO terrorist during the 1972 Munich Olympics. This photo has become virtually a symbol of the emergence of modern terrorism.

Olympics in Munich, or airline hijackings, or bombings in public spaces (especially commuter transit facilities), all of which immediately generated intense worldwide media coverage (see Figure 14.3).[31]

Media coverage meant an audience, and for the terrorist strategist there were (and are) different intended audiences for any act of spectacular violence. One is the already friendly audience of fellow travelers, for which the message is that the organization exists, is continuing to act on their behalf, and deserves their financial support—perhaps more than some other competing group. A second audience is the political leadership and the political public of the enemy state, for whom the violence signals the continuing costs of its policies. Crucially, terrorists are also *prodding* this second audience, hoping for the "overreaction." Much as Che Guevara argued that the actions of a few guerrillas would force a state to reveal its own corrupt and oppressive nature, terrorist strategy hopes to spur state reactions so violent that they undermine the legitimacy of that state or its policies. The capacity of the state to wield violence greatly exceeds that of the terrorist; the terrorist need only provoke it and then hope for recruits and support in response to the state's violence. A third audience is the international public, reached via media coverage of violence, and often especially the coverage of negotiations with hostage rescue teams and such, which provide a platform for terrorist organizations to state their grievances. This form of awareness raising carries its own risks, however, as organizations presenting their grievances via the propaganda of the deed could find themselves increasingly marginalized by that international audience; the worse the act, the more unified the international response. As a result, most terrorism campaigns of the 1970s through the 1990s were highly episodic: occasional spectacular acts meant to communicate diverse messages without provoking a global response unified in its condemnation.[32]

In this respect, the attacks on American targets by al-Qaeda on September 11, 2001, represented an important turning point both in the world response to terrorism and in the use of terrorism as a strategy for insurgency against occupiers or state regimes. Al-Qaeda differed in the first instance because it was not organized within or against a specific state in the midst of an occupation or invasion. Instead, it claimed to seek the end of American military presence in Saudi Arabia (US forces remained there in small numbers after the 1991 Gulf War), but it also claimed a larger intention to reestablish an Islamic caliphate based on the interpretation of Islam of its leader, Osama bin Laden (1957–2011). The organization also differed from traditional guerrilla groups in being a multinational, multiethnic movement, operating with only a limited territorial presence—primarily training camps located in ungoverned spaces. The organization launched several attacks before 2001, including a truck bomb in the parking garage of the World Trade Center in New York in 1993, car bombs at the US embassies in Tanzania and Kenya in 1998, and a suicide boat-bomb attack on the USS *Cole* in Yemen in 2000. None of these attacks prompted a massive reaction from the United States, nor did they dramatically change al-Qaeda's global profile. The crashing of airliners into the Pentagon and the World Trade Center, however, had enormous aftershocks. The spectacular quality of the deed was not in doubt; few acts have been more visibly shattering or more widely broadcast. But the consequences for al-Qaeda were complicated. On one hand, the attacks at least temporarily unified world opinion against "terrorism" writ large. This was more than merely symbolic unification; inherently secretive national intelligence agencies became willing to cooperate and share information (primarily with the United States, but also more generally). State governments in places like Pakistan and Uzbekistan, among others, provided basing or overflight rights on an unprecedented scale for the campaigns the United States launched in response. On the other hand, those campaigns created the "overreaction" that terrorists often seek.

Within weeks of the 9/11 attacks, the United States began a campaign in Afghanistan to unseat the ruling Taliban regime, rightly perceived to have sheltered al-Qaeda in that country. Rapidly overwhelmed by a combination of American air power and resurgent anti-Taliban militias within Afghanistan, the Taliban leadership and al-Qaeda members retreated into and over the eastern mountains into the poorly regulated areas of western Pakistan. NATO and other international forces joined American troops in occupying and rebuilding Afghanistan, but American planning effort and force deployment had already shifted to focus on Iraq—indeed, by some accounts it had done so even before the escape of the Taliban and al-Qaeda to Pakistan.

Where there had been an unprecedented level of international unanimity about the invasion of Afghanistan, many nations thought the planned invasion of Iraq lacked legitimacy. The political dynamics of what followed in Iraq are too complicated to narrate here, but the point is that a shift occurred in the use of terrorism as a strategy for insurgency. Al-Qaeda was more than a bit surprised at the extent and thoroughness of the American reaction to the 2001 attacks. Over the next ten years their leadership was seriously degraded, including ultimately the killing of bin Laden by US forces in May 2011. Unfortunately, the extent of the US overreaction was almost more than they could have hoped for when it came to the invasion and occupation of Iraq. The presence of so many American troops in Iraq from 2003 to 2011 created the opportunity for jihadists around the world to participate in a fight many had long desired, while others were newly inspired to become insurgents by what they saw as the suffering of fellow Muslims in Iraq. The core al-Qaeda group was reeling from American attacks and focused intelligence, but American wars in Islamic countries were also generating regional al-Qaeda affiliates where they had not existed before, including al-Qaeda in Iraq (AQI), in Yemen and Saudi Arabia (al-Qaeda in the Arabian Peninsula—AQAP), in North Africa (al-Qaeda in the Islamic Maghreb—AQIM), and in Somalia (al-Shabaab), as well as the al-Nusra Front in Syria and Lebanon, and numerous other affiliated or semiaffiliated groups (see Map 14.3).

In addition, the chaotic takedown of the Iraqi government in March 2003 aggravated long-suppressed religious and ethnic factionalism within that country, creating a fruitful environment in which terrorists could operate. In effect, resistance to American occupation in Iraq became a kind of "insurgency via terrorism." The organized and centrally directed guerrilla forces of a Maoist insurgency or the occasional acts of spectacular violence by the terrorists of the 1970s were replaced by hundreds of bombings or attacks *per week*. Such tactics had been used in past guerrilla wars to intimidate or remove local state officials or loyalist populations, but they had always been seen as the "political" adjunct to the larger-scale violence waged by guerrillas against the state's armed forces. Terrorist tactics against civilians now dominated the insurgency, seeking either to delegitimize the "collaborationist" Iraqi government or to intimidate or remove the opposite religious faction, with the very significant tactical addition of suicide bombing. Most terrorists of earlier periods had planned ways to survive their own attacks; the recruitment of suicide bombers, eventually to include both sexes, made such attacks much harder to prevent. Still, it is important to recognize that suicide bombing is merely a single tactic within the larger strategy of insurgency by terrorism.[33]

Saying this, however, raises the question of what this "strategy" seeks to achieve. How will the terrorist insurgent achieve his ultimate goal? This returns us to the question of communication and audience. To be fair, much of the violence in Iraq between 2004 and the American withdrawal in 2011 was internal ethnoreligious conflict; although it was enabled by the American invasion, it was not motivated directly by the American presence. A good proportion of the violence was so motivated, however, especially the violence waged by AQI. In their case it is reasonable to say that a strategy existed, insofar as their attacks were intended to speak to a variety of different audiences, much like those of the terrorist organizations of the 1960s and 1970s, but with new twists. The attackers first played to their current members, conducting and then advertising their attacks—often now via YouTube videos— to persuade the already converted that the organization was still effective (see Figure 14.4). There is some irony here. Reversing the situation explored in chapter 2, in which the chariot, an invention of the steppe, better served well-resourced states, new technologies like Internet-based social media platforms, cell phones, YouTube, and more, all developed by the industrialized West, now were being used to organize and inspire insurgencies against it.

Second, terrorist insurgents played for the support of those who might be leaning toward their cause, again with a message saying "See what we can do to our enemy." Suicide bombing as a tactic fits unusually well into this

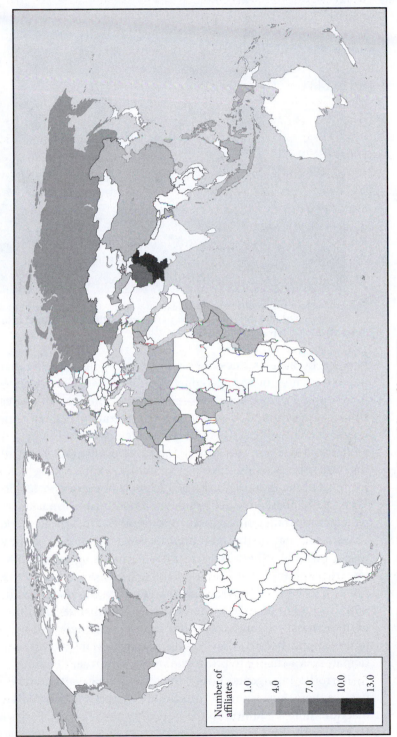

Map 14.3 Al-Qaeda affiliate organizations around the world, as of late 2014.

Figure 14.4 Insurgent video propaganda. Although blurry, militants posted many videos like this on YouTube to document their active operations against U.S. forces in Iraq in the 2000s.

strategy, because its "message" is so strong: there are individuals so committed to the cause, or so angered by their enemy's actions, that they are willing to give up their lives. Terrorist organizations thus carefully select and sponsor suicide attackers and then lionize them through "martyr" videos. This message is even more effective once their state opponent has begun using its own violence in reaction, because doing so activates traditionalist revenge-seeking. An otherwise nonideological family, experiencing collateral damage from bombing or being disturbed in their homes by state-sponsored "night raids" (often based on deliberately planted misinformation), may nurture a revenge imperative throughout that family's kinship network. One famous example is that of the grandmother suicide bomber, a sixty-four-year-old woman who blew herself up near Israeli troops in Gaza in 2006. Her daughter later explained that "her son had been killed by Israelis, that her mother's house had been destroyed, and that another grandson was in a wheelchair with an amputated leg."[34] Beyond such familial revenge motivations, and perhaps most troubling of all for any sort of theory of war, some people fought simply because they could—because a war was happening and to participate was a chance to prove one's valor or virtue.[35]

Terrorist insurgents' hopes for such revenge attacks are why the state itself is their third audience: attacks are designed to provoke state violence in reaction. But in addition to the hoped-for provocation, the persistence of attacks over the long term also sends a message about future costs. This is close cousin to Mao's "protracted war," but there is no real sense of actual military attrition here; it is purely an attrition of political will. American casualties in Iraq and Afghanistan have been comparatively tiny by almost any historical measure, although the financial cost has been staggering (about which more below). The fourth and final audience is that of international public opinion, which the terrorist strategist hopes to swing against his enemy by using spectacular tactics as a tool to gain visibility for their message.[36]

Squaring these assorted messages and achieving policy goals presents a difficult problem for the terrorist strategist. Research into international public response to such a strategy suggests that the insurgents' message of protracted costly conflict has at times succeeded. The simultaneous March 2004 Fallujah and Sadr uprisings in Iraq (one Sunni, the other Shiite), for example, convinced many Americans that success in winning hearts and minds was not forthcoming. On the other hand, the same polling research indicates that if the American public is convinced of the "rightness" of a conflict, they will remain committed to it, and it is the very tactics of terrorism that convince them of that rightness. Terrorism as a strategy thus creates its own dilemma— it must be violent, spectacular, and sustained in order to convince the movement's various audiences of its messages, but the specifics of terrorist tactics also tend to convince their opponent that the movement using those tactics must be resisted and destroyed. Whether a territorially ambitious terrorist insurgency succeeds or not will end up depending on assorted other complicating factors specific to where it is active.[37]

In some ways this terrorist dilemma is what happened in Iraq. In 2007, the American political public was persuaded (barely) that an additional effort was needed in Iraq—a short term "surge" in military force would sufficiently reestablish security so that a strong and stable Iraqi government could take over the war effort. Simultaneously, and almost coincidentally, the Sunni tribes of Anbar province became disenchanted with the insurgency's violence and instead tied their fate to the Americans. They fought AQI forces and provided newly comprehensive intelligence on local insurgents, driving AQI forces underground. Meanwhile the years-long Sunni-Shiite militia conflict had essentially been muted by de facto ethnic cleansing: neighborhoods were increasingly physically divided along religious lines. Violence in Iraq declined dramatically, and the United States completed its withdrawal in 2011 (after failing to strike an agreement that would allow a small-scale continued presence there).

AQI had not been destroyed, however. Now, in 2015, it is clear that AQI was driven underground but successfully protected its financial resources— another aspect of a globalizing economy that helps to shield terrorist organizations. When civil conflict in Syria deteriorated into a full-scale civil war in late 2011, Sunni fighters flowed into the area from the region and from around the world, some of whom were brought under AQI's umbrella. Now known as the Islamic State (IS, sometimes ISIS or ISIL), they are paid using harbored funds, now greatly enlarged by territorial control-based revenues from oil and taxation, while fighting to fulfill al-Qaeda's old dream of an Islamic caliphate.

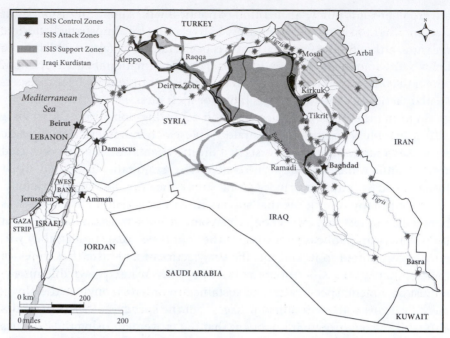

Map 14.4 Territory under IS control or threat as of late 2014. Map derived from one prepared by the Institute for the Study of War, Sept 10, 2014.

This territorial ambition has deep roots within the various al-Qaeda regional affiliates, who frequently have focused more on attacking local regimes than on engaging the United States directly; that ambition also continues to animate Taliban forces who hope to rule again in Afghanistan.[38]

In this regard a fascinating manual for insurgency prepared by 'Abd Al-'Aziz Al-Muqrin, a senior leader in AQAP in the early 2000s, killed by Saudi security forces in 2004, shows direct influence from Mao's three-stage theory. It posits an eventual jihadist conventional army, partly modeled on the successful mujahedin insurgency that effectively ousted the Soviet Union from Afghanistan in 1989. Al-Muqrin begins with the need for protraction and the necessity of managing the process of phasing up through Mao's three stages, but there are differences. He acknowledges that setbacks might force a return to earlier stages; he incorporates new components to the model; and his listing of what types of warfare should occur in each stage differs somewhat from Mao's. For example, reflecting a new globalized world and the role of communication in terrorist strategy, Al-Muqrin notes that during phase one, otherwise dominated by guerrilla warfare of small-scale hit-and-run attacks—which also differs from Mao—there would additionally need to be "spectacular operations which will create a positive media impact . . . to demonstrate the existence or power of these groups, as well as to rub the enemy's nose in the dirt, and to embolden the people to fight and to energize the youth to take up arms against the enemy."[39]

What Al-Muqrin advocated in 2003 bears a striking resemblance to the Islamic State's program in 2014 and 2015. Taking advantage of arms liberated by the Syrian civil war and their own increasingly deep pockets, the IS launched conventional attacks into Sunni and Kurdish areas of Iraq, securing more material from a surprisingly fragile Iraqi army, and capturing several major cities in Iraq as well as key oil facilities.

In general, however, ruling is a tougher task than rebelling. The Taliban, for example, who as insurgents courted the population with the promise of swift justice as a benefit of their future rule, are now finding it difficult to maintain that image in regions where they are in de facto control. Similarly, although Al-Muqrin may have copied some of Mao's military thinking, there is no sign that either he or other IS leaders have engaged in Mao's parallel political program of courting the population. Terroristic organizations, even ones battling for territory, have their own strategic culture, and their spectacular acts of violence, especially the Internet-broadcast beheadings of Western journalists, have prompted a surprisingly large coalition of Western and Sunni Arab nations to begin air operations against the IS, as well as direct Shiite Iranian support to the Iraqi army.[40] That reliance on air power reflects a trend within Western responses to guerrilla insurgencies and terrorism, the larger story of which is our next concern.

COUNTERINSURGENCY AND COUNTER TERROR

Like modern guerrilla war or insurgency, counterinsurgency (or COIN) by state forces has a long history. What is innovative in modern conditions is the development of a full-fledged and identifiable doctrine of counterinsurgency, one primarily designed to respond to Maoist-inspired insurgencies. Through the end of World War I, state responses were usually confined to violent repression. Ideologies designed to buttress the authority of the state, whether in Europe or China (less so in India), defined rebels as beyond mercy. Campaigns against rebels, therefore, were usually little concerned with winning them over, at least not until their strength had been crushed. Rebellions that swelled into true civil wars tended to be fought with conventional forces, and thus there was no need for a special form of warfare to counter them. In some exceptional circumstances a state might consider the value of "winning the hearts and minds" of the populace, especially when they were considered to be past or future subjects in need of reconciliation to state rule. The most famous example in the premodern era was the British war against the American rebels from 1775–1783, during which at least some senior British commanders actively courted the populace as the most efficient means to restore civil control over the countryside. Even then, such calculations often ran afoul of older cultural attitudes toward rebels, and some British commanders continued to rely on repression by fire and sword.[41]

French, British, and American Counterinsurgency

This older contrast between "hearts and minds" and "fire and sword" in some ways continues to encapsulate the problem in modern counterinsurgency. The imperative of pacifying the people by attacking the roots of their complaints is balanced against the security imperative to defeat the armed insurgents. Can one achieve pacification without security? Conversely, can one achieve security without pacification (since the latter denies recruits to the insurgents)? This problem of balance is exemplified by two of the classic instructional texts on counterinsurgency, both written by French army officers based on their experiences in Vietnam (1945–54) and Algeria (1954–62). The two authors, David Galula and Roger Trinquier, are often represented as being at opposite ends of a spectrum. In reality, they recommended many of the same things, but differed in emphasis on certain key points. Trinquier represents what has been called the *guerre révolutionnaire* school, which emerged in the French army in the wake of their defeat in Indochina. French army officers, Trinquier among them, embittered by defeat, closely analyzed Maoist theory, and argued against targeting guerrillas with conventional force operations. They proposed achieving security through forced population resettlement while cracking terrorist organizations through the judicious use of torture in interrogation. Trinquier cared little for the ideology or motivations of the insurgents. Galula, taking more account of what had spurred discontent and rebellion in the first place, focused on the population and its needs. But Galula was no aid worker, and like Trinquier he recommended managing the populace, keeping strict track of who was who and where they were supposed to live, using cordon-and-search operations to locate guerrillas, and then maintaining garrisons among the newly cleared population. Waged area by area, in what is sometimes called the "ink spot" strategy—a term dating to French operations in Indochina in the 1890s—these methods, according to Galula, would encourage and empower the pro-counterinsurgent minority.[42]

The point here is not to cast either Galula or Trinquier as right, wrong, or even especially innovative. Instead it is to show how the innovation of people's war, with its own theory of how to cultivate popular cooperation and then to progress from weakness to strength to victory, in turn inspired calculated thinking in how to stop such an insurgency. Beginning with Galula and Trinquier also shows that there is no unified COIN theory, except perhaps Mao's insight that what matters is the loyalty of, or at least the managed *control* of, a broad swathe of the population (among COIN theorists this has produced the phrase "population-centric warfare"). Trinquier's vision of control was harsher and more coercive than Galula's, but the similarities were real, based in the unavoidable problem of sequencing security and pacification. As it happened, French wars of counterinsurgency, especially in Algeria, were influenced more by Trinquier and the *guerre révolutionnaire* school.

Galula, a minor figure in French operations at the time, has had an outsized influence on American COIN theorists after 2004, as have American perceptions of the British experience with insurgencies.

Britain's extensive empire forced it to cope with numerous wars of decolonization, and Britain gained a reputation for being particularly competent at counterinsurgency. Their defeat of a communist insurgency in Malaya from 1948 to 1960 by cultivating the population has often been cited as a key example of how providing aid and development can isolate insurgents by denying them access to or influence within the wider population—something we might call "uplift-pacification." Indeed, British lieutenant general Sir Gerald Templer, directing operations in Malaya, introduced to the modern lexicon of counterinsurgency the phrase that victory depended on "the hearts and minds of the people." A complex set of idiosyncratic factors, however, played into British success there, especially that the insurgent group almost wholly consisted of ethnic Chinese living in Malaya. Few ethnic Malays supported the communist movement, in part because Britain had already promised an independent Malayan state. Furthermore, it is important to recognize that the British campaign included a fair amount of violence and even atrocity. A centerpiece of their strategy was to relocate hundreds of thousands of villagers into fortified camps, depriving the guerrillas of both the food the peasants produced and the ability to hide within that population. The resettlement camps in Malaya were managed relatively humanely, but historically such forced population movements have rarely been well received or violence-free, nor were they in Malaya (see Figure 14.5). The perception of supposed British aptitude for uplift-pacification has been undermined further by recent historical work. Close examination of British counterinsurgency tactics in Malaya, Kenya, Yemen, Northern Ireland, and elsewhere has revealed the extent to which British forces, driven by the nature of the fight, found themselves using violence far beyond their usual norms of conduct. One specialist simply notes that "coercion, not conciliation, was the mainstay of British policy." British efforts at uplift-pacification, he argues, were "usually under-funded and under-resourced."[43]

In contrast to the supposedly gentler and more effective British way of counterinsurgency, the American military has been roundly criticized for its conduct of the war in Vietnam. The usual, and indeed still partly accepted version of this critique, is that the United States never recognized the extent to which the war was a civil war within the Vietnamese population, and focused instead on northern subversion. Furthermore, the critique goes, US operations within South Vietnam through 1968 focused too exclusively on "search and destroy" operations, that, in combination with forced village resettlement and the designation of "free fire zones," led to civilian casualties and resentment. In essence, the United States focused too much on security, and not enough on pacification. The usual narrative is that after the Tet Offensive in 1968 and the subsequent change in American commanders from

Figure 14.5 Aerial view of a newly completed government-funded resettlement village in 1950s Malaya.

General William Westmoreland to General Creighton Abrams, US operations became more population-centric, only then showing promise of real results. American domestic political will, however, finally collapsed.

This narrative, like the standard narrative of the British in Malaya, no longer holds up well. Among other things, the differences between Westmoreland's operations and Abrams's were not that pronounced. There were also some fairly sophisticated attempts from the beginning of the war to practice village-level security through small garrisons living among the villagers, one version under the US Marines Combined Action Platoons (CAP) program, and another, beginning in May 1967, via the interagency Civil Operations and Rural Development Support (CORDS) program. It remains the case, however, that neither of these programs received the emphasis or funding that went to more conventional operations or the air campaign. Furthermore, in the face of persistent and aggressive external support from North Vietnam, village-based, population-centric counterinsurgency struggled to achieve the necessary security for pacification to take hold.[44]

Whatever COIN lessons the United States did learn during the Vietnam War were quickly forgotten. As part of the successful effort to restore efficiency and morale after eight years of draining and demoralizing war in Vietnam, the Army institutionally refocused its attention on conventional war and the potential confrontation with the Soviet Union (as discussed in chapter 12). Part of this reorientation involved a deliberate setting aside of counterinsurgency in Army training, doctrine, and education. The strategic culture of the US Army, much like the strategic culture of almost any modern state army, preferred to concentrate on fighting similar opponents. In the wake of the Cold War, however, unconventional missions between 1991 and 1999 in northern Iraq, the Balkans, Somalia, and elsewhere forced the US military to consider how to deal with a variety of situations. A proliferation of official labels and definitions reflected the military's long effort to forget the counterinsurgency mission in Vietnam, as well as ongoing institutional struggles to define emerging irregular missions: Low Intensity Conflict (LIC), Military Operations Other than War (MOOTW), asymmetric conflict, hybrid war, and eventually counterinsurgency. Each had their turn in the manuals of the 1990s and 2000s.[45]

Counterinsurgency attracted the most attention as the insurgency in Iraq seemed to spiral out of control beginning in late 2004 and 2005. At this point, we must stop and consider an intriguing convergence and confrontation of late twentieth-century innovations, with implications that are continuing to play out as this book is being written. The precision targeting systems discussed in the previous chapter (primarily launched from airborne platforms, but also including cruise missiles and some ground-launched systems) combined with networked intelligence sharing and command systems, had seemed to many to promise a "revolution in military affairs" (RMA). The United States campaign against the Taliban government in Afghanistan in 2001 leveraged those capabilities to rapidly destroy Taliban forces and regime facilities. As Stephen Biddle has pointed out, however, the role of air power in that victory has been somewhat overplayed; Taliban forces soon learned to camouflage themselves from US air power, and substantial fighting on the ground was required.[46]

The US invasion of Iraq in 2003 also leveraged new RMA-related capabilities, this time combined with a ground invasion force, to again rapidly destroy regular regime forces and facilities. When postwar stabilization failed and the hydra-headed insurgency began to escalate, however, many of those RMA-associated capabilities proved less useful. Precision targeting demanded not only rapid intelligence sharing but accurate and precise intelligence *collection*. Insurgents hiding in a sprawling urban environment like Baghdad and its environs proved difficult to target precisely. Precision delivery *was* valuable; there were times when it could provide extraordinary results on clearly and correctly identified targets in both Afghanistan and Iraq. But accident and sometimes deliberate misinformation from supposedly friendly sources also led to precise strikes on the wrong targets: weddings, civilians, and even friendly forces. The international and local political implications of that sort of collateral damage were the same as they had been in Vietnam.

They eroded political will at home and they spurred resistance and resentment locally—this despite the undeniable improvement in precision and a real decrease in the absolute numbers of civilian casualties.

With the situation in Iraq deteriorating and the RMA-related capabilities not providing quick solutions, the US military, despite its slow-to-change strategic culture, began to turn its attention to the history and theory of counterinsurgency. Once it had done so, the resources brought to bear were substantial. The US military's capacity to engage a problem once it has been identified can be overwhelming. Tapping military and academic experts, who in turn drew upon Galula's early theories, the supposed lessons of the Malayan emergency, and selected aspects of what had gone wrong in Vietnam, the Army and the Marine Corps produced a new doctrine for counterinsurgency, embodied in *FM 3–24: Counterinsurgency* (2006).

Critics immediately emerged. Some criticized the history that had been used in writing the manual: Galula had failed; Malaya had been both exceptional and more violent than described; US pacification techniques in Vietnam had been doomed to fail, regardless of resourcing or emphasis. Other critics within the Army feared that this shift of attention had gained too much momentum within the service's strategic culture and that it boded ill for the future efficacy and flexibility of the Army if confronted with other types of missions. Others claimed that the new doctrine then being operationalized in Iraq under the command of General David Petraeus was overly fixated on the Maoist model of people's war. Against a Maoist insurgency, uplift-pacification via development and governmental reform was a central part of undermining communist insurgents' usual appeal to the landless poor based on the inequities built into their lives—something that neither AQI nor the Taliban attempted to do. Furthermore, COIN doctrine admitted up front that success required a long-term commitment of force and capital. It was not at all clear the American public had that level of patience.[47]

In Iraq, as discussed earlier in this chapter, a fresh commitment of troops (the "surge") combined with the parallel reaction of the Sunni tribes and the follow-on effects of ethnic resettlement allowed the counterinsurgency campaign to reduce violence by a measurable degree. That provided necessary political cover for a US withdrawal—something Barack Obama had promised in his successful campaign for president in 2008. In Afghanistan, however, a more diffuse population, a smaller commitment of forces on the ground, and years of relative inattention due to the war in Iraq had allowed the Taliban to regain its footing. The prospect of another long counterinsurgency war there proved politically unpalatable.

In 2007 and 2008 a debate emerged in the United States about what its goal in the region should be: pacification and stabilization of an independent Afghanistan, or degradation of the terrorist networks that actually threatened the United States. Here again, the fruits of the RMA emerged to tempt American strategists. The campaign in Afghanistan, relatively small though it was,

was eating away at both the financial and military capacity of the United States. Repeated deployments to Iraq and Afghanistan were wearing out troops and equipment, and the costs of operating such a high-tech force in such a remote environment were staggering. Planning estimates in 2009 for the cost of sending more forces to Afghanistan used the figure of one billion dollars for every thousand troops. A breakdown of that figure noted that from purchase to delivery in the field a gallon of fuel cost roughly four hundred dollars. In 2012 the Pentagon reported that the cost of a single soldier in Afghanistan had risen from $600,000 to $850,000 or even $1.4 million per year, and was continuing to rise. The full cost of the wars in Iraq and Afghanistan is almost impossible to gauge, given legacy expenses in veterans' medical care, pensions, and the interest being carried on funds borrowed to pay for the war. As of the fall of 2014, however, the Congressional Budget Office estimated that "between September 2001 and June 2014, lawmakers appropriated about $1.6 trillion for operations in Iraq and Afghanistan and for other war-related activities."[48]

UAV's and "Counterterror" Standoff War

This level of expenditure and domestic war weariness put immense pressure on the newly elected President Obama to fulfill his promise to end the war in Iraq, to focus on Afghanistan and the pursuit of al-Qaeda, and to find a way to end that war as well. President Obama opted for a limited surge of troops, but also imposed a deadline for full US withdrawal. In practice the war from 2008 to 2014 became a kind of hybrid of traditional counterinsurgency—although with only limited nation-building or uplift-pacification aspects—combined with a targeted counterterror campaign to assassinate senior al-Qaeda leadership taking refuge outside the war zones, primarily in Yemen and Pakistan. Although barely officially acknowledged, media reports and eventual admissions by the White House revealed an ongoing and intensive use of unmanned aerial vehicles (UAV), commonly called drones, both to offer real-time, continuous surveillance in those areas and then to provide precision strikes.

The ability to conduct targeted assassinations with precision-guided missiles fired from GPS-guided, satellite-linked drones emerged as a by-product of the developments discussed in the previous chapter. The Air Force had long focused on marrying precision weapons to manned aircraft in their continuing quest for the combination of systems that would allow for war-winning targeting from the air. The motivations for developing UAVs differed from the quest for precision and strategic bombing, but their development was urged along and enabled by the same technologies. At first, UAVs were seen primarily as providing reconnaissance and spy capabilities without the risk of losing a pilot and with the added benefit of much cheaper operations and much longer loiter times over a target. Although the idea dated back to

Figure 14.6 An armed drone over Afghanistan. Popularly referred to as the Predator, this is in fact the MQ-9 Reaper, here armed with a Hellfire missile and a Paveway II laser-guided bomb.

World War II, serious development and real funding came in the 1960s from the National Reconnaissance Office. Both the CIA and the US Air Force flew thousands of UAV reconnaissance missions in Vietnam and probes of Chinese air defenses in the early 1970s. The end of the war, budget cuts, the inability to safely land many of the early versions, and the general culture of the pilot within the Air Force slowed progress in drone technology until the 1990s. Then, developments in computer processing and eventually satellite-based navigation and communication allowed remote, over-the-horizon piloting for the first time. Drones achieved new visibility within the military when the newly developed Predator (the first model to use piloting via satellite) was used in Bosnia and Kosovo to provide targeting intelligence. Various drone models continue to play key roles in providing long-term localized and regional surveillance, but our concern here is with their use in a counterterror role via targeted killing. First equipped with a precision Hellfire missile in 2001, the Predator was used to provide precise air support in Afghanistan and then also in Iraq after 2003. In both environments the Predator was highly successful in an operational role supporting troops on the ground as a supplemental form of close air support.[49]

The Predator and its more advanced armed version, the Reaper, have achieved greater renown and infamy, however, in the counterterror role. Unwillingness among US officials even to discuss the program makes it difficult to analyze, but the *idea* is predicated on the combination of long-term aerial surveillance with the ability to deliver a precision strike on a specific individual (or small group) with little to no collateral damage. That idea also relies on the belief that a terrorist organization depends on its leadership and is a relatively small-scale opponent vulnerable to leadership attrition. Ironically, this is not fast-moving "shock and awe" from the air. It is slow degradation, and is designed to operate under the political radar, avoiding the problems of commitment of political will experienced by traditional counterinsurgency campaigns. It also conveniently avoids taking prisoners, whose long-term detention has become a hot and seemingly irresolvable political issue. The legality of the program under international law and even under domestic US law remains in dispute, and its effectiveness at degrading al-Qaeda's ability to operate remains unclear, compared to its demonstrated effects at generating resentment and even motivating al-Qaeda or Taliban recruits in Pakistan and Yemen and beyond. The antiterror drone campaign, however, is just the most recent example of the challenge-and-response dynamic in military innovation. In this case, the culture of the United States and its reliance on standoff technology that distances its domestic population and even its uniformed personnel from actual conflict zones is pitted against a radical ideology that uses atrocity and explosive suicide as a weapon while hiding among a civilian population of which international opinion is increasingly protective (see Figure 14.7).[50]

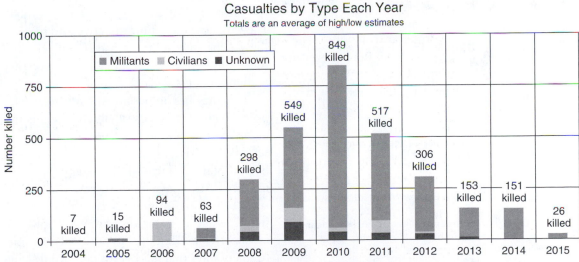

Figure 14.7 Estimates of casualties from U.S. drone attacks based on Pakistani media coverage. This data was assembled by Peter Bergen of the New American Foundation. Of note here is the strong spike as the U.S. shifted to a counterterror strategy in 2008 after the election of President Obama. International and domestic political opinion, however, has led to a reduction in drone strikes and improvements in their accuracy. *Source*: New America http://securitydata.newamerica.net/drones/pakistan-analysis.html

CONCLUSION

Woe betide the historian who dares to make predictions about the future of war. There is certainly no cause to declare its obsolescence as so many historians were tempted to do in the 1970s. Armies are even less likely to disappear, as many of them around the world continue to fulfill one of their oldest functions: maintaining internal security.[51] We can and should inquire, however, as British general Rupert Smith has done, about the continuing utility of force. Is the current conflict environment into which Western powers are likely to be drawn so complex as to obviate the value of military intervention? Smith argues that the new paradigm of "war amongst the people" is characterized by "strategic confrontation between a range of combatants, not all of which are armies, and using different types of weapons, often improvised." In this paradigm "there is no predefined sequence [of peace-crisis-war-resolution], but rather a continuous criss-crossing between confrontation and conflict." In that environment, he declares, the utility of using force is increasingly less clear.[52] Emile Simpson, in an analysis that dovetails with much of this chapter, argues that modern war—some prefer the term "postmodern" war—is no longer about destroying armed forces; it is now about audience effects. The problem, as Smith also notes, is that modern Western armed forces are the products of an industrial competition to defeat each other in symmetrical combat. They are now incredibly effective and increasingly expensive relics of a different era and may not be suited to producing the necessary audience effects.[53]

This may be too pessimistic for those who point to circumstances in which it seems imperative to intervene forcefully. To many observers, the rise of the undeniably barbaric Islamic State in Iraq and Syria suggests such a moment. And make no mistake: those industrial "relics" are immensely capable of inflicting damage. Strategic planners, however, must correlate "damage" to political outcome. In many ways that has been a perennial struggle. Early in this book we observed that for most of history battles were not won by killing as such, but rather by creating sufficient fear that the enemy fled the field. Killing some

TIMELINE

1938	Mao Zedong's lectures on guerrilla war
1949	Victory of Mao's Chinese communist revolution
1954	Viet Minh defeat of the French; Guevara arrives in Mexico
1959	Castro's revolution succeeds in Cuba
1965	US ground troops arrive in Vietnam
1975	The final defeat of South Vietnam
2001	9/11 Terrorist attacks in the United States and the campaign against the Taliban regime in Afghanistan
2003	United States invades Iraq
2005	Insurgency in Iraq against American forces begins to escalate
2011	American withdrawal from a seemingly stable Iraq
2014	Emergence of ISIS and the fracturing of Iraq

of the enemy encouraged the others to flee, but moral collapse was the real goal, and could be achieved in other ways. Similarly, strategic bombing of production capacity during World War II was an attempt to create or find a new correlation between damage and political outcome relevant to the industrial age. This is what Clausewitz had in mind when he made war a subset of politics. Future innovations in warfare, whatever they might be, must be even more cognizant of that reality.

Further Reading

Daddis, Gregory A. *Westmoreland's War: Reassessing American Strategy in Vietnam.* New York: Oxford University Press, 2014

Dosal, Paul J. *Comandante Che: Guerrilla Soldier, Commander, and Strategist, 1956–1967.* University Park: Pennsylvania State University Press, 2003

Herring, George C. *America's Longest War: The United States and Vietnam, 1950–1975.* 4th ed. Boston: McGraw-Hill, 2002.

Kilcullen, David. *The Accidental Guerrilla: Fighting Small Wars in the Midst of a Big One.* New York: Oxford University Press, 2009.

Mackinlay, John. *The Insurgent Archipelago.* New York: Columbia University Press, 2009.

Moran, Daniel. *Wars of National Liberation.* London: Cassell, 2001.

Pike, Douglas. *PAVN: People's Army of Vietnam.* Novato, CA: Presidio, 1986.

Porch, Douglas. *Counterinsurgency: Exposing the Myths of the New Way of War.* Cambridge, UK: Cambridge University Press, 2013.

Nguyen, Lien-Hang T. *Hanoi's War: An International History of the War for Peace in Vietnam.* Chapel Hill: University of North Carolina Press, 2012.

Rid, Thomas, and Thomas Keaney, eds. *Understanding Counterinsurgency: Doctrine, Operations, and Challenges.* New York: Routledge, 2010.

Notes

1. Daniel R. Headrick, *The Tools of Empire: Technology and European Imperialism in the Nineteenth Century* (New York: Oxford University Press, 1981), 3.

2. Francis Lieber and Richard Shelly Hartigan, *Lieber's Code and the Law of War* (Chicago: Precedent, 1983); John Fabian Witt, *Lincoln's Code: The Laws of War in American History* (New York: Free Press, 2013); James Q. Whitman, *The Verdict of Battle: The Law of Victory and the Making of Modern War* (Cambridge, MA: Harvard University Press, 2012).

3. Thomas Kampen, *Mao Zedong, Zhou Enlai, and the Evolution of Chinese Communist Leadership* (Copenhagen: Nordic Institute of Asian Studies, 2000), 65, 76–77, 120–21.

4. Mao Tse-Tung, *On the Protracted War*, 2nd ed. (Beijing: Foreign Languages Press, 1960). See also John Mackinlay, *The Insurgent Archipelago* (New York: Columbia University Press, 2009), 17, 22–23.

5. Pingchao Zhu, "Regional Politics: Wartime Relations between the CCP and the Guangxi Warlords, 1936–1944," *Asian Profile* 33.1 (February 2005): 1–15, esp. 6; Pingchao Zhu, *Under the Banner of Nationalism: Wartime Culture in Guilin, 1938–1944* (Lanham, MD: Lexington Books, forthcoming), chapter 1 and 2. My thanks to Pingchao Zhu for sharing parts of his manuscript with me. He also provided details from Wei Huanling, "Kangzhan shiqi Mao Zedong sixiang zai Guilin wenhua cheng de chuanbo yu shijian" [The dissemination and practice of Mao Zedong thought in the wartime culture in Guilin], in Wei Hualin, ed., *Guilin kangzhan wenhua yanjiu wenji* [Collected essays on the studies of wartime culture in Guilin], vol. 2 (Guilin, China: Guangxi shifan daxue chubanshe, 1995), 18–39, and Wan Yizhi, "New Discovery of Mao Zedong's Lost Writing Piece," in Liu Shoubao and Wei Hualin, eds., *Guilin kangzhan wenhua yanjiu wenji* [Collected essays on the studies of wartime culture in Guilin], vol. 5 (Guilin, China: Guangxi shifan daxue chubanshe,1997), 82–87. The later history of English-language publication is from Douglas Pike, *Viet Cong: The Organization and Techniques of the National Liberation Front of South Vietnam* (Cambridge, MA: MIT Press, 1968), 33.

6. Lien-Hang T. Nguyen, *Hanoi's War: An International History of the War for Peace in Vietnam* (Chapel Hill: University of North Carolina Press, 2012), 2, 17–28, outlines the deeply factionalized and complex history of the Communist war effort against the French. It was rarely if ever a monolithic movement.

7. Wen Fengyi and Qin Bing, *Guilin kangzhan wenhua chen qiwen yishi* [Interesting wartime cultural stories in Guilin] (Guilin, China: Guangxi shifan daxue chubanshe, 2013), 58; Chao Yuwen, "Lun Guilin kangzhan wenhua de guoji xing" [On the international features of Guilin's wartime culture], in Wei Huanlin, *Guilin kangzhan wenhua yanjiu wenji* [Collected essays on the studies of wartime culture in Guilin], vol. 3 (Guangxi shifan daxue chubanshe, 1995), 24–40. (details provided by Pingchao Zhu); Nguyen, *Hanoi's War*, 25–26.

8. Nguyen, *Hanoi's War*, 40–47.

9. Vo Nguyen Giap, *People's War, People's Army*, facsimile edition (New York: Praeger, 1962), 55 (quote).

10. This paragraph and the two following are based primarily on Douglas Pike's two studies, *Viet Cong*, esp. pp. 36–40, and *PAVN: People's Army of Vietnam* (Novato, CA: Presidio, 1986), 211–25.

11. Pike, *PAVN*, 231, 212; personal communication with Lien-Hang Nguyen, December 9, 2014.

12. Pike, *Viet Cong*, 38 (quote).

13. Pike, *Viet Cong*, 34–35; Jeffrey Race, *War Comes to Long An: Revolutionary Conflict in a Vietnamese Province*, rev. ed. (Berkeley: University of California Press, 2010), 42, 106 (quote).

14. George K. Tanham, *Communist Revolutionary Warfare: From the Vietminh to the Viet Cong*, rev. ed. (New York: Praeger, 1967), 45–55; Giap, *People's War, People's Army*, 52–53 (quote).

15. Giap, *People's War, People's Army*, 48 (quote)

16. Nguyen, *Hanoi's War*, 27–28.

17. Nguyen, *Hanoi's War*, 64–65, 79; Pike, *PAVN*, 221–22.

18. Nguyen, *Hanoi's War*, 88–109, 111–14, 232–34.

19. Christian G. Appy, *Patriots: The Vietnam War Remembered from All Sides* (New York: Viking, 2003), 11 (quote).

20. Pike, *PAVN*, 215 (quote).

21. Paul J. Dosal, *Comandante Che: Guerrilla Soldier, Commander, and Strategist, 1956–1967* (University Park: Pennsylvania State University Press, 2003), 314–16.

22. Che Guevara, *Guerrilla Warfare*, 3rd ed., edited by Brian Loveman and Thomas M.

Davies, Jr. (Lincoln: University of Nebraska Press, 1985), vii–viii.

23. Dosal, *Comandante Che*, 46–61.

24. Guevara, *Guerrilla Warfare*, 54–55 (quote).

25. Guevara, *Guerrilla Warfare*, 50 (quote).

26. Che Guevara, "Message to the Tricontinental," available at https://www.marxists.org/archive/guevara/1967/04/16.htm, accessed December 9, 2014 (quote).

27. Guevara, *Guerrilla Warfare*, x, 13, 14.

28. A useful discussion of the definitional problems is Alex P. Schmid, "The Definition of Terrorism," in *The Routledge Handbook of Terrorism Research*, edited by Alex P. Schmid (New York: Routledge, 2011), 39–157, esp. p. 86–87; see also Lawrence Freedman, "Terrorism as Strategy," *Government and Opposition* 42.3 (2007): 314–39.

29. Williamson Murray and Peter Mansoor, eds., *Hybrid Warfare: Fighting Complex Opponents from the Ancient World to the Present* (Cambridge, UK: Cambridge University Press, 2012).

30. Mackinlay, *Insurgent Archipelago*, 11, 27–35; David Kilcullen, *Out of the Mountains: The Coming Age of the Urban Guerrilla* (New York: Oxford University Press, 2013), esp. 16. Data for Table 14.1 is primarily derived from UN, Department of Economic and Social Affairs, Population Division, "World Urbanization Prospects, the 2014 Revision," available at http://esa.un.org/unpd/wup/CD-ROM/WUP2014_XLS_CD_FILES/WUP2014-F11a-30_Largest_Cities.xls, accessed April 4, 2015.

31. Mackinlay, *Insurgent Archipelago*, 54–58.

32. Freedman, "Terrorism as Strategy," 321–22; Peter R. Neumann and M. L. R. Smith, *The Strategy of Terrorism: How it Works, and Why it Fails* (New York: Routledge, 2008), 40; Freedman, "Terrorism as Strategy," 325.

33. One index of the number of attacks was that provided in the "Petraeus report" of 2007, in which the American commander General David Petraeus sought to persuade the US Congress that the situation was improving. Text of the report available at http://www.defense.gov/pubs/pdfs/Petraeus-Testimony20070910.pdf; data slides available at http://www.defense.gov/pubs/pdfs/Petraeus-Testimony-Slides20070910.pdf (note especially slide no. 2), both accessed October 2, 2014; Mia Bloom, *Dying to Kill: The Allure of Suicide Terror* (New York: Columbia University Press, 2005).

34. Steven Erlanger, "Grandmother Blows Self Up in Gaza Suicide Blast," *New York Times*, November 24, 2006, available at http://www.nytimes.com/2006/11/24/world/middleeast/24mideast.html?_r=0, accessed October 2, 2014 (quote).

35. David Kilcullen, *The Accidental Guerrilla: Fighting Small Wars in the Midst of a Big One* (New York: Oxford University Press, 2009), esp. 37–38.

36. John W. Dower, *Cultures of War: Pearl Harbor, Hiroshima, 9–11, Iraq* (New York: W. W. Norton, 2010), 524; R. Kim Cragin, "A Recent History of al-Qa'ida," *The Historical Journal* 57:3 (September 2014): 803–824.

37. Christopher Gelpi, Peter D. Feaver, and Jason Reifler, "Success Matters: Casualty Sensitivity and the War in Iraq," *International Security* 30.3 (2005): 7–46.

38. Howard J. Shatz, "How ISIS Funds its Reign of Terror," *The Rand Blog*, September 8, 2014, http://www.rand.org/blog/2014/09/how-isis-funds-its-reign-of-terror.html, accessed December 10, 2014.

39. 'Abd Al-'Aziz Al-Muqrin, *Al-Qa'ida's Doctrine for Insurgency: 'Abd Al-'Aziz Al-Muqrin's A Practical Course for Guerrilla War*, trans. Norman Cigar (Washington, DC: Potomac, 2009), 6–9, 93–4, quote p. 96. For other evidence of al-Qaeda's conscious use of people's war ideas, see Patrick Porter, *Military Orientalism: Eastern War through Western Eyes* (New York: Columbia University Press, 2009), 62–3.

40. Azam Ahmed, "Unruly Factions Hurt Taliban's Bid to Capture Afghan Hearts,

and Territory," *New York Times*, January 2, 2015; Ben Hubbard, "Islamic State Imposes Strict New Order in Mosul, and Deprivation is a Result," *New York Times* December 13, 2014.

41. Wayne E. Lee, *Crowds and Soldiers in Revolutionary North Carolina* (Gainesville: University Press of Florida, 2001), 197.

42. Note that Galula originally wrote both of his books in English; Trinquier wrote in French but was quickly translated into English. Peter Paret, *French Revolutionary Warfare from Indochina to Algeria: The Analysis of a Political and Military Doctrine* (New York: Praeger, 1964); Christopher Cradock and M. L. R. Smith, "'No Fixed Values': A Reinterpretation of the Influence of the Theory of *Guerre Révolutionnaire* and the Battle of Algiers, 1956–1957," *Journal of Cold War Studies* 9.4 (2007): 68–105; Roger Trinquier, *Modern Warfare: A French view of Counterinsurgency* (New York: Praeger, 1964); David Galula, *Pacification in Algeria, 1956–1958* (Santa Monica, CA: RAND, 2006); David Galula, *Counterinsurgency Warfare: Theory and Practice* (Westport, CT: Praeger Security International, 1964, repr., 2006), esp. 52–56; Frederick Quinn, *The French Overseas Empire* (Westport, CT: Praeger, 2001), 143–44; Grégor Mathias, *Galula in Algeria: Counterinsurgency Practice versus Theory*, trans. Neal Durando (Santa Barbara, CA: Praeger, 2011), esp. 7, 18–54; Etienne de Durand, "France," in *Understanding Counterinsurgency: Doctrine, Operations, and Challenges*, ed. Thomas Rid and Thomas Keaney (New York: Routledge, 2010), 11–27.

43. David French, *The British Way in Counterinsurgency, 1945–1967* (Oxford: Oxford University Press, 2011), 2, 175 (quotes); Christopher Hale, *Massacre in Malaya: Exposing Britain's My Lai* (Stroud, UK: The History Press, 2013), esp. 283–98; Douglas Porch, *Counterinsurgency: Exposing the Myths of the New Way of War* (Cambridge, UK: Cambridge University Press, 2013).

44. Gregory A. Daddis, *Westmoreland's War: Reassessing American Strategy in Vietnam* (New York: Oxford University Press, 2014); Michael Peterson, *The Combined Action Platoons: The U.S. Marines' Other War in Vietnam* (Westport, CT: Praeger, 1989); Richard A. Hunt, *Pacification: The American Struggle for Vietnam's Hearts and Minds* (Boulder, CO: Westview, 1995); John Southard, *Defend and Befriend: The U.S. Marine Corps and Combined Action Platoons in Vietnam* (Lexington: University Press of Kentucky, 2014); Gregory A. Daddis, *No Sure Victory: Measuring U.S. Army Effectiveness and Progress in the Vietnam War* (New York: Oxford University Press, 2011), 115–31. There is an excellent summary of the debates in David Fitzgerald, *Learning to Forget: US Army Counterinsurgency Doctrine and Practice from Vietnam to Iraq* (Stanford, CA: Stanford University Press, 2013), 19–38.

45. Conrad C. Crane, *Avoiding Vietnam: The U.S. Army's Response to Defeat in Southeast Asia* (Carlisle, PA: Strategic Studies Institute, 2002); Fitzgerald, *Learning to Forget*, 203–14.

46. Stephen Biddle, "Afghanistan and the Future of Warfare," *Foreign Affairs* 82.2 (2003): 31–46.

47. French, *British Way*; Porch, *Counterinsurgency*; Mathias, *Galula*; Fitzgerald, *Learning to Forget*; Gian Gentile, *Wrong Turn: America's Deadly Embrace of Counterinsurgency* (New York: New Press, 2013); Mackinlay, *Insurgent Archipelago*.

48. Roxana Tiron, "$400 per Gallon Gas to Drive Debate over Cost of War in Afghanistan," *The Hill*, October 16, 2009, http://thehill.com/homenews/adminis tration/63407–400gallon-gas-another -cost-of-war-in-afghanistan-, accessed September 30, 2014; Laura Shaughnessy, "One Soldier, One Year: $850,000 and Rising," *Security Clearance* (CNN blog), February 28, 2012, http://security.blogs .cnn.com/2012/02/28/one-soldier-one -year–850000-and-rising/, accessed

September 30, 2014; "Iraq and Afghanistan," Congressional Budget Office website, https://www.cbo.gov/topics/national-security/iraq-and-afghanistan (quote), accessed September 30,2014 (this report can no longer be found on the CBO website, but a similar conclusion was reached by the Watson Institute Study, published in March 2013, "Iraq: 10 Years after Invasion," Costs of War website, http://costsofwar.org/iraq–10-years-after-invasion, accessed December 10, 2014).

49. Thomas P. Ehrhard, *Air Force UAVs: The Secret History* (Arlington, VA: Mitchell Institute Press, 2010); Richard Whittle, *Predator: The Secret Origins of the Drone Revolution* (New York: Henry Holt, 2014).

50. United Nations, "SRCT Drone Inquiry," http://unsrct-drones.com/report/63, accessed October 3, 2014; there is a useful ongoing discussion regarding the legality of the program on the *Blog of Rights*, "Targeted Killings," https://www.aclu.org/blog/tag/targeted-killings, accessed October 3, 2014; Lloyd C. Gardner, *Killing Machine: The American Presidency in the Age of Drone Warfare* (New York: New Press, 2013).

51. Jeremy Black, "Military Organisations and Military Change in Historical Perspective," *Journal of Military History* 62 (1998): 888, 891; Jeremy Black, "Determinisms and Other Issues," *Journal of Military History* 68 (2004): 1228.

52. Rupert Smith, *The Utility of Force: The Art of War in the Modern World* (London: Allen Lane, 2005), 5, 183 (quotes).

53. Emile Simpson, *War from the Ground Up: Twenty-First-Century Combat as Politics* (New York: Columbia University Press, 2012), esp. 1–9.

Credits

Frontispiece: Gianni Dagli Orti / The Art Archive at Art Resource, NY, AA380812.

Fig. 1.1 Courtesy of John Mitani.

Fig. 1.2 Erich Lessing / Art Resource, NY, ART53334.

Fig. 1.3 Library of Congress.

Fig. 1.4 Drawing based on a photo in James Mellaart, *Çatal Hüyük: A Neolithic Town in Anatolia* (New York: McGraw-Hill, 1967), plate 46 (p. 94).

Fig. 1.5 akg-images / picture-alliance / dpa, AKG2749219.

Fig. 1.6 Drawing based on Jean Guilaine and Jean Zammit, *The Origins of War: Violence in Prehistory*, trans. Melanie Hersey (Malden, MA: Blackwell, 2005), Figure 29 (p. 109).

Fig. 1.7 © The Trustees of the British Museum / Art Resource, NY, ART464648.

Fig. 1.8 © The Trustees of the Natural History Museum, London, 058372.

Fig. 1.9a Alfredo Dagli Orti / The Art Archive at Art Resource, NY, AA325794.

Fig. 1.9b Alfredo Dagli Orti / The Art Archive at Art Resource, NY, AA325795.

Fig. 1.10a Werner Forman / Art Resource, NY, ART112995.

Fig. 1.10b Werner Forman / Art Resource, NY, ART181255.

Fig. 1.11 Gianni Dagli Orti / The Art Archive at Art Resource, NY, AA374163.

Fig. 2.2 © The Trustees of the British Museum / Art Resource, NY (detail), ART495941.

Fig. 2.3 Drawing based on David W. Anthony, *The Horse, The Wheel, and Language: How Bronze- Age Riders from the Eurasian Steppes Shaped the Modern World* (Princeton, NJ: Princeton University Press, 2007), 374.

Fig. 2.4 Drawing based on Mary Littauer and Joost H. Crouwel, *Wheeled Vehicles and Ridden Animals in the Ancient Near East* (Leiden: Brill, 1979), fig. 36.

Fig. 2.5 Scala / Art Resource, NY, ART125785.

Fig. 2.7 Drawing based on Edward H. Shaughnessy, "Historical Perspectives on the Introduction of the Chariot into China." *Harvard Journal of Asiatic Studies* 48.1 (1988): 197.

Fig. 2.8 akg-images / Osprey Publishing / Angus McBride, AKG3547915.

Fig. 2.9 Gianni Dagli Orti / The Art Archive at Art Resource, NY, AA388437.

Fig. 2.10 De Agostini Picture Library / G. Dagli Orti / Bridgeman Images, DGA593301.

Fig. 3.1 © The Trustees of the British Museum / Art Resource, NY, ART316861.

Fig. 3.2 Erich Lessing / Art Resource, NY, ART13321.

Fig. 3.3 Erich Lessing / Art Resource, NY, ART13326.

Fig. 3.4 De Agostini Picture Library / G. Nimatallah / Bridgeman Images, DGA508057.

Fig. 3.5 Werner Forman / Art Resource, NY, ART342357.

Fig. 3.6 The original artifact has long been missing. This drawing is based on Austen Henry Layard, *The Monuments of Nineveh* (London: John Murray, 1853), vol. 1, plate 69.

Fig. 3.7 bpk, Berlin / Antikensammlung, Staatliche Museen, Berlin, Germany / Johannes Laurentius / Art Resource, NY, ART190242.

Fig. 3.8 De Agostini Picture Library / Bridgeman Images, DGA418892.

Fig. 3.9a Erich Lessing / Art Resource, NY, ART322473.

Fig. 3.9b Photo by Sarah C. Murray, University of Nebraska-Lincoln, Argos_museum_panoply_41109.JPG.

Fig. 3.10 Drawing based on a photo in P. A. L. Greenhalgh, *Early Greek Warfare: Horsemen and Chariots in the Homeric and Archaic Ages* (Cambridge: Cambridge University Press, 1973), fig. 38 (p. 65).

Fig. 3.11 Drawing based on a photo in Pierre Sauzeau and Thierry Van Compernolle, eds., *Les armes dans l'Antiquité* (Montpellier, France: Presses Universitaires de la Méditerranée, 2007), figs 2 and 3 (p. 330–31).

Fig. 3.12 Drawing based on a photo in A. M. Snodgrass, *Arms and Armor of the Greeks* (Baltimore, MD: Johns Hopkins University Press, 1999), fig. 26.

Fig. 3.13 Photo courtesy of Ryan Jones, Calgary, Alberta, Canada.

Fig. 4.1 Erich Lessing / Art Resource, NY, ART101861.

Fig. 4.4 bpk, Berlin / Muenzkabinett, Staatliche Museen, Berlin, Germany / Art Resource, NY, ART494020.

Fig. 4.5 Bildagentur Geduldig / Alamy, DH2WEC.

Fig. 4.6 ©ullstein - Archiv Gerstenberg / The Image Works, EULS0694812.

Fig. 4.8a Collection of the Lowe Art Museum, University of Miami / Gift of George and Julianne Alderman / Bridgeman Images, LWE410380.

Fig. 4.8b The Real Bear / Wikimedia Commons / http://commons.wikimedia.org/wiki/File:Summer_Vacation_2007,_263,_Watchtower_In_The_Morning_Light,Dunhuang,_Gansu_Province.jpg.

Fig. 5.1 Drawing based on http://de.wikipedia.org/wiki/Datei:Carnuntum_map_Roman_city.gif.

Fig. 5.2 The Pierpont Morgan Library, New York, MS M.638 fol. 12r.

Fig. 5.3a The Pierpont Morgan Library, New York, MS M.43 fol. 9v.

Fig. 5.3b The British Library Board, MS ADD 54180, fol. 121v.

Fig. 5.3c Bibliothèque nationale de France, Département des manuscrits, Français 24364 fol. 22r, http://gallica.bnf.fr/ark:/12148/btv1b60002590.

Fig. 5.3d Bodley 264 Romance of Alexander Fol. 67v / ©Bodleian Library, Oxford University.

Fig. 5.3e © British Library Board. All Rights Reserved / Bridgeman Images, BL283297.

Fig. 5.3f Album / Art Resource, NY, orz000490.

Fig. 5.4 bpk, Berlin / Ethnologisches Museum, Staatliche Museen, Berlin, Germany/Piotr Shimkevitch / Art Resource, NY, ART495942.

Fig. 5.5 Or.Ms 20 f.124v. Edinburgh University Library.

Fig. 6.1a Drawing based on Michael Wedde, *Towards a Hermeneutics of Aegean Bronze Age Ship Imagery* (Mannheim, Germany: Bibliopolis, 2000), Figure 643.

Fig. 6.1b Drawing based on photo in Frederick H. van Doorninck, Jr., "Protogeometric Longships and the Introduction of the Ram," *The International Journal of Nautical Archaeology and Underwater Exploration* 11 (1982): fig. 2 (p. 78).

Fig. 6.1c Drawing based on a photo in Lionel Casson, *Ships and Seamanship in the Ancient World* (Princeton, NJ: Princeton University Press, 1971), figure 30.

Fig. 6.1d © The Metropolitan Museum of Art. Image source: Art Resource, NY, ART406514.

Fig. 6.1e Royal Ontario Museum, ROM2005_4032_1.

Fig. 6.1f © The Trustees of the British Museum / Art Resource, NY, ART331159.

Fig. 6.2 Photo by: Port Rowers in Olympias on the Thames, June 1993 (Rosie Randolph).jpg / © The Trireme Trust.

Fig. 6.3 Olympias under oar, Poros, July 1987 / © The Trireme Trust.

Fig. 9.8 Royal Armouries Library, Leeds, A13.369.

Fig. 10.1 ©SSPL / The Image Works, ESSP0121854.

Fig. 10.2 SSPL/Science Museum / Art Resource, NY, ART403452.

Fig. 10.3a ©Science Museum/SSPL / The Image Works, ESSP0155187.

Fig. 10.3b ©SSPL / The Image Works, ESSP0142459.

Fig. 10.4 Private Collection / Ken Welsh / Bridgeman Images, KW270883.

Fig. 10.5 © Imperial War Museums (Q 21479).

Map 10.4 Map primarily based on David C. Evans and Mark R. Peattie, *Kaigun: Strategy, Tactics, and Technology in the Imperial Japanese Navy, 1887–1941* (Annapolis, MD: Naval Institute Press, 1997. Reprint, 2012), 96.

Fig. 10.6 © Imperial War Museums (Q 22414).

Fig. 11.1 North Wind Picture Archives, EVCW3A-00192.

Map 11.1 Map primarily based on the map "Central Europe, 1805—French Strategic Envelopment, Situation, 26 September–9 October," in the map collection of the United States Military Academy, Napoleonic Wars, http://www.westpoint.edu/history/sitepages/napoleonic%20wars.aspx.

Fig. 11.2 Private Collection / © Look and Learn / Bridgeman Images, LLM959117.

Fig. 11.3a akg-images / Interfoto, AKG1365722.

Fig. 11.3b © National Maritime Museum, London / The Image Works, ENMM0507406.

Fig. 11.3c akg-images / Interfoto, akg1365764.

Fig. 11.3d akg-images / Interfoto, AKG1372879.

Map 11.3 Modified from base map in David Ross, "Dahomey," in *West African Resistance: The Military Response to Colonial Occupation*, ed. Michael Crowder (New York: Africana, 1971), 145.

Fig. 11.4 akg-images, AKGORD24253.

Map 11.4 Map based on Raymond Jonas, *The Battle of Adwa: African Victory in the Age of Empire* (Cambridge, MA: Belknap Press of Harvard University Press, 2011), 114.

Map 11.6 Map based on Richard Holmes, ed., *The World Atlas of Warfare* (New York: Viking Penguin, 1988), 142.

Fig. 11.5 Private Collection / Peter Newark Military Pictures / Bridgeman Images, PNP700934.

Fig. 11.6 © Imperial War Museums (Q 45786).

Fig. 12.2 Private Collection / Peter Newark Pictures / Bridgeman Images, PNP870190.

Maps 12.4 a & b and 12.5 a & b are based on https://chronicle.fanack.com/wp-content/uploads/sites/5/2014/10/October_war_bigmap_04_1c72b45ecc and https://chronicle.fanack.com/wp-content/uploads/sites/5/2014/10/October_war_bigmap_05_3334949295.jpg.

Fig. 13.1 Library of Congress, LC-USZ62-29811.

Fig. 13.2 *Lens wird mit Bomben belegt* (Lens is Destroyed by Bombing), plate 33 from *Der Krieg* (The War), 1924, Dix, Otto (1891-1969) / Minneapolis Institute of Arts, MN, USA / The John R. Van Derlip Fund and Gift of funds from Alfred and Ingrid Lenz Harrison and the Regis Foundation / Bridgeman Images, MNS882827. © 2015 Artists Rights Society (ARS), New York / VG Bild-Kunst, Bonn.

Fig. 13.3 Library of Congress, 3c29782u.

Fig. 13.4 Library of Congress, LC-USZ62-94454.

Fig. 13.5 Library of Congress, 3c11516u.

Fig. 13.6 Library of Congress, HAER TX-25 (sheet 3 of 3).

Table 13.2 is derived from data provided by the Natural Resources Defense Council, at http://www.nrdc.org/nuclear/nudb/dafig11.asp.

Fig. 13.7 Poster in personal collection of Christian Lentz, Durham, NC. Photograph by Wayne Lee.

Fig. 13.8 (AP Photo/Vietnam News Agency), 59010102756.

Fig. 13.9 U.S. Air Force photo.

Fig. 13.11 U.S. Air Force photo.

Fig. 14.2 ©Pictures From History/The Image Works, ECPA0024333.

Fig. 14.3 (AP Photo/Kurt Strumpf, Files), 72090512274.

Fig. 14.4 From https://www.youtube.com/watch?v=IBpMsxQlkLs&t=4m39s.

Fig. 14.5 © Imperial War Museums (K 13796).

Fig. 14.6 U.S. Air Force Photo / Lt. Col. Leslie Pratt.

Index

Page numbers followed by *f* indicate figures, *t* indicate tabular material, and *m* following a page number indicates maps.